# Playboy's
# Hugh Hefner

## EMPIRE OF SKIN

# What is Blood Moon Productions?

Biographies that Focus on the Ironies of Fame

## www.BloodMoonProductions.com

Award-Winning Entertainment About
How America Interprets Its Celebrities

# PLAYBOY'S
# HUGH HEFNER

PROMOTIONAL PHOTOS FOR *PLAYBOY AFTER DARK*

## EMPIRE OF SKIN

### DARWIN PORTER & DANFORTH PRINCE

# *Playboy's Hugh Hefner, Empire of Skin*

Darwin Porter and Danforth Prince

Copyright 2018, Blood Moon Productions, Ltd.
All Rights Reserved
www.BloodMoonProductions.com
Manufactured in the United States of America

ISBN 978-1-936003-59-4

Cover Designs by Victor Stanwick (www.FastSmartWebDesign.com) &
Danforth Prince
Distributed worldwide through National Book Network
(www.NBNBooks.com)

# PREVIOUS WORKS BY DARWIN PORTER
## PRODUCED IN COLLABORATION WITH BLOOD MOON

### BIOGRAPHIES

*Carrie Fisher & Debbie Reynolds*
*Princess Leia & Unsinkable Tammy in Hell*

**Rock Hudson Erotic Fire**

**Lana Turner,** *Hearts & Diamonds Take All*

**Donald Trump,** *The Man Who Would Be King*

**James Dean, *Tomorrow Never Comes***

**Bill and Hillary,** *So This Is That Thing Called Love*

**Peter O'Toole,** *Hellraiser, Sexual Outlaw, Irish Rebel*

**Love Triangle,** *Ronald Reagan, Jane Wyman, & Nancy Davis*

**Jacqueline Kennedy Onassis,** *A Life Beyond Her Wildest Dreams*

**Pink Triangle,** *The Feuds and Private Lives of Tennessee Williams, Gore Vidal, Truman Capote, and Famous Members of their Entourages.*

**Those Glamorous Gabors,** *Bombshells from Budapest*

**Inside Linda Lovelace's Deep Throat,** *Degradation, Porno Chic, and the Rise of Feminism*

**Elizabeth Taylor,** *There is Nothing Like a Dame*

**Marilyn at Rainbow's End,** *Sex, Lies, Murder, and the Great Cover-up*

**J. Edgar Hoover and Clyde Tolson**
*Investigating the Sexual Secrets of America's Most Famous Men and Women*

**Frank Sinatra,** *The Boudoir Singer. All the Gossip Unfit to Print*

*The Kennedys*, All the Gossip Unfit to Print

*Humphrey Bogart, The Making of a Legend* (2010) , *and*
*The Secret Life of Humphrey Bogart* (2003)

*Howard Hughes,* Hell's Angel

*Steve McQueen,* King of Cool, Tales of a Lurid Life

*Paul Newman,* The Man Behind the Baby Blues

*Merv Griffin,* A Life in the Closet

*Brando Unzipped*

*Katharine the Great,* Hepburn, Secrets of a Lifetime Revealed

*Jacko, His Rise and Fall,* The Social and Sexual History of Michael Jackson

*Damn You, Scarlett O'Hara,* The Private Lives of Vivien Leigh and Laurence
Olivier (co-authored with Roy Moseley)


FILM CRITICISM
*Blood Moon's 2005 Guide to the Glitter Awards*
*Blood Moon's 2006 Guide to Film*
*Blood Moon's 2007 Guide to Film, and*
*50 Years of Queer Cinema, 500 of the Best GLBTQ Films Ever Made*

NON-FICTION
*Hollywood Babylon, It's Back! and Hollywood Babylon Strikes Again!*

NOVELS
*Blood Moon,*
*Hollywood's Silent Closet,*
*Rhinestone Country,*
*Razzle Dazzle*
*Midnight in Savannah*

# OTHER PUBLICATIONS BY DARWIN PORTER
## NOT DIRECTLY ASSOCIATED WITH BLOOD MOON

### NOVELS

*The Delinquent Heart*
*The Taste of Steak Tartare*
*Butterflies in Heat*
*Marika* (a roman à clef based on the life of Marlene Dietrich)
*Venus* (a roman à clef based on the life of Anaïs Nin)
*Bitter Orange*
*Sister Rose*

### TRAVEL GUIDES

**Many Editions and Many Variations** of *The Frommer Guides*,
*The American Express Guides, and/or TWA Guides, et alia* to:

Andalusia, Andorra, Anguilla, Aruba, Atlanta, Austria, the Azores, The Bahamas, Barbados, the Bavarian Alps, Berlin, Bermuda, Bonaire and Curaçao, Boston, the British Virgin Islands, Budapest, Bulgaria, California, the Canary Islands, the Caribbean and its "Ports of Call," the Cayman Islands, Ceuta, the Channel Islands (UK), Charleston (SC), Corsica, Costa del Sol (Spain), Denmark, Dominica, the Dominican Republic, Edinburgh, England, Estonia, Europe, "Europe by Rail," the Faroe Islands, Finland, Florence, France, Frankfurt, the French Riviera, Geneva, Georgia (USA), Germany, Gibraltar, Glasgow, Granada (Spain), Great Britain, Greenland, Grenada (West Indies), Haiti, Hungary, Iceland, Ireland, Isle of Man, Italy, Jamaica, Key West & the Florida Keys, Las Vegas, Liechtenstein, Lisbon, London, Los Angeles, Madrid, Maine, Malta, Martinique & Guadeloupe, Massachusetts, Melilla, Morocco, Munich, New England, New Orleans, North Carolina, Norway, Paris, Poland, Portugal, Provence, Puerto Rico, Romania, Rome, Salzburg, San Diego, San Francisco, San Marino, Sardinia, Savannah, Scandinavia, Scotland, Seville, the Shetland Islands, Sicily, St. Martin & Sint Maarten, St. Vincent & the Grenadines, South Carolina, Spain, St. Kitts & Nevis, Sweden, Switzerland, the Turks & Caicos, the U.S.A., the U.S. Virgin Islands, Venice, Vienna and the Danube, Wales, and Zurich.

## BIOGRAPHIES

*From  Diaghilev to Balanchine, The Saga of Ballerina Tamara Geva*

*Lucille Lortel, The Queen of Off-Broadway*

*Greta Keller, Germany's Other Lili Marlene*

*Sophie Tucker,  The Last of the Red Hot Mamas*

*Anne Bancroft, Where Have You Gone, Mrs. Robinson?*
*(co-authored with Stanley Mills Haggart)*

*Veronica Lake, The Peek-a-Boo Girl*

*Running Wild in Babylon, Confessions of a Hollywood Press Agent*

## HISTORIES

*Thurlow Weed, Whig Kingpin*

*Chester A. Arthur, Gilded Age Coxcomb in the White House*

*Discover Old America, What's Left of It*

## CUISINE

*Food For Love, Hussar Recipes from the Austro-Hungarian Empire,*
*with collaboration from the cabaret chanteuse, Greta Keller*

## AND COMING NEXT FROM BLOOD MOON
## *Kirk Douglas: More Is Never Enough*

# To the Memory of Players Passed

## We extend special thanks

—and dedicate this biography of Hugh Hefner—
to the Playboys and Playmates who contributed to the
Sexual Revolution that altered bedtime in America, and
to those who stumbled, fell, failed, or died during the
pursuit of their hopes and dreams.

### Rest In Peace

This Bunny, who's ready for her
closeup, wants to improve literacy,
liberate America, find love,
guarantee happiness, and pay tribute
to her friends and lovers from other
times and other places.

# Contents

Throaty at the Playboy Mansion. In a murky sting operation linked to official efforts to curtail pornography and the drug trade, Bobbie Arnstein, Hef's chief assistant, commits suicide. Sex, drugs, and celebrity at the Playboy Mansion (West) become notoriously and famously interconnected. Christie Hefner becomes "Hare Apparent," chief cost cutter, and chairperson of Playboy's board of directors. Interludes with Jimmy Carter, David Bowie, porn king John C. Holmes, and a raft of Bunnies who "kiss and tell." Casino-license horrors for Playboy operations in Atlantic City and London.

# A Word About Phraseologies:

Since we at Blood Moon weren't privy to long-ago conversations as they were unfolding, we have relied on the memories of our sources for the conversational tone and phraseologies of what we've recorded within the pages of this book.

This writing technique, as it applies to modern biography, has been defined as "conversational storytelling" by *The New York Times,* which labeled it as an acceptable literary device for "engaging reading."

Some people have expressed displeasure in the fact that direct quotes and "as remembered" dialogue have become a standard—some would say "mandatory"—fixture in pop culture biographies today.

But Blood Moon is not alone in replicating "as remembered" dialogues from dead sources. Truman Capote and Norman Mailer were pioneers of direct quotes, and today, they appear in countless other memoirs, ranging from those of Eddie Fisher to those of the long-time mistress (Verita Thompson) of Humphrey Bogart.

Best wishes to all of you, with thanks for your interest in our work.

**Danforth Prince**
President and Publisher
Blood Moon Productions

# PLAYBOY'S HUGH HEFNER
# EMPIRE OF SKIN

STOCK.ADOBE.COM

"At last, a hot, well-timed, retro-vintage book about the Jackrabbit King with plenty of tail but no spin, an overview of Hefner's Bunny Tales as assembled by players outside the orbit of Playboy Enterprises. Who else but Blood Moon could have done it? Wanna know more about Hugh Hefner's *Empire of Skin?* Come play with us.... and keep reading!"

# PROLOGUE

Hugh Hefner didn't walk through the 20th Century: He romped through it until he became decrepit and the glamour and allure of his brand inevitably faded. As both a pioneer of the Eisenhower era and eventually, as an anachronism of the 21st Century, he was the sparkplug that lit the sexual revolution of the 1960s, changing America and its presuppositions about entertainment, sex, and manhood, for the rest of the 20th Century and beyond.

Hefner was the most famous—and infamous—magazine mogul in history, a cultural warrior, a visionary, an empire-builder, and a pajama-clad pipe-smoker with a pre-coital grin. Widely envied and widely emulated, he provoked rage in censors, militant feminists, and religious zealots. Some readers remember him with surges of emotion as a "swinging uncle" who helped them, during their puberty, discover earthly delights. Lauded by millions, Hefner was denounced for exploiting women and defined by others as "the father of sex addiction," "a huckster," "a lecherous low-brow feeder of our vices," "a misogynist," and, near the end of his life, "a symbol of priapic senility."

The revolution Hefner unleashed was so successful that *Playboy* itself faced the danger of becoming *passé*. "Most Americans today think the sexual revolution happened in the sixties and seventies," Hefner said. "As they recall, it lasted only a short time and gave us the Swedish Bikini Team, *Debbie Does Dallas*, unwed teenage mothers, date rape, and AIDS."

"The story I envisioned was a far grander event," he continued, "one that was inextricably connected with the history of the 20th Century. If viewed over a one-hundred-year span, the sexual revolution would be seen for what it was: A great struggle involving ideas, champions, and villains. We would chart the liberation of men and women, of language, the body, the imagination."

\*\*\*

Famously eccentric, Hef became known for quirks that included a "nonstandard" dress code, never wearing underwear, and elevating sleep-

1

wear (i.e., pajamas) to a personal trademark, regardless of the hour of the day or night.

His admirers were wide-ranging. The Rev. Jesse Jackson praised him as a strong supporter of civil rights. Larry King hailed him as a "giant of free speech and a devotee of the First Amendment." He was favorably compared to Citizen Kane, Walt Disney, and F. Scott Fitzgerald's *The Great Gatsby*. Gloria Steinem, one of the 20th Century's most ardent defenders of women, went underground, working long hours as a "cocktail Bunny" to expose him. J. Edgar Hoover, a closeted and vengeful homosexual, hounded and investigated him; and John F. Kennedy became an avid fan. During Hefner's heyday, some of the biggest male movie stars in Hollywood came to frolic with various forms of Bunnies and Playmates behind the guarded walls of the Playboy Mansion, stripping nude in the Grotto and eventually migrating to the rotating beds upstairs. Even a future U.S. President came for some visits. "Donald Trump had an appreciation of Bunny Tail," Hef said.

Always provoking either public commentary or private gossip, Hefner was indeed, something to talk about. Columnist Ross Douthat delivered a scathing denunciation, defining him as "the father of sex addiction, a pretentious huckster, a lecherous low-brow Peter Pan, a flesh peddler, a leech-like feeder of our vices with custom-tailored erotica that was misogynist, a leering predator, a wicked and destructive American, and, finally, a desperate member of Prospero's Court with a Red Death at the door."

Hef's last Viagra-fueled May-December marriage to the very beautiful Crystal Harris, sixty years his junior, was as eccentric and as idiosyncratic as the man himself. It provoked one of his most famous, bemused, and controversial quotes: "There's nothing wrong with a man marrying a girl who could be his great-granddaughter."

Before departing from his earthly paradise—the spectacular gardens surrounding his Shangri-La—this avatar of sybaritic male pleasure delivered a final word of advice: "Life is too short to be living someone else's dream."

We at Blood Moon Productions are proud to present this one-of-a-kind overview of the events surrounding the life and career of one of America's most influential trend-setters. The first post-mortem unauthorized biography of the father of America's skin trades as we know them today, it's the distillation of an era that will never come again. Happy reading to all of you, with admiration and respect for the man sometimes known as the Jackrabbit King and Bunny Master, **Hugh Hefner.**

# Chapter One

# BEFORE LAUNCHING AMERICA'S SEXUAL REVOLUTION
## "THE WORLD'S SWINGINGEST BACHELOR" IS BORN ON A WINDY AFTERNOON IN CHICAGO

# WORLD WAR II
### HEF JOINS THE ARMY, SURVIVES BOOT CAMP, DATES "VICTORY GIRLS," WATCHES MOVIES, AND DREAMS OF BECOMING A CARTOONIST & ILLUSTRATOR

At Camp Hood during World War II, Private Hugh Hefner was taught how to become a rifleman.

He quickly became a sharpshooter. "I had a real talent for firing at a target."

During his first furlough in the autumn of 1944, Hef, with Millie Williams, attended a football game at Steinmetz, their alma mater. She was now a freshman at the University of Illinois. He pledged "undying love" to her.

**A newborn named Hugh Marston Hefner** came into the world at 4PM on April 9, 1926. Born in a suburb of Chicago to parents who were natives of Nebraska, his arrival was on a particularly blustery afternoon with cold winds roaring in from Canada.

His mother was Grace Caroline Swanson (1895-1997), who was born into a prosperous family. Her father owned seven farms, the land tilled by sharecroppers. The Swanson in her name was apt, as in the 1920s, she bore a slight resemblance to the reigning screen vamp of the day, Gloria Swanson, but without any of her elaborate pretentions, costumes, and makeup.

Hef's father, Glenn Luscious Hefner (1896-1976), was quite poor, the son of sod farmers who barely made a living, but in time raised enough money to send him to college.

Glenn and Grace fell in love in grade school, their romance blossoming in high school and thriving throughout their college years. They would marry shortly after graduating.

Grace, who had wanted to become a missionary throughout the course of her childhood, was the smarter of the two, becoming the high school valedictorian. Glenn was a star athlete, the state champion in track. He also was a star player on the basketball court.

Although Hugh—nick-named "Hef" throughout the rest of his life—had na-

Although Hef was born in the suburbs of Chicago, his mother Grace and his father Glenn had Puritan roots from the bleak landscapes of Nebraska. They followed a strict religious code.

It was obviously beyond their wildest imagination that their son would become "the Father of the Sexual Revolution."

tive roots in Nebraska, he had been born in Chicago. He later defined his origins as "Midwestern, conservative, and Methodist."

His bloodline extended back to Sweden on his mother's side and to Germany and England for his father's heritage. Glenn was a direct descendant of William Bedford (1590-1657), who arrived as a pilgrim in the New World aboard the *Mayflower*. Bedford later became the second governor of the Plymouth colony.

In time, the Bedford family tree "branched" out to encompass not only Hef, but Noah Webster, Christopher (*Superman*) Reeves, and Clint Eastwood.

"My parents were strict but college educated and rather liberal, tolerant people," Hef recalled. "They never paddled a mischievous boy like myself. A tough lecture was all I got for one of my major crimes. They never raised their voices to me—or to each other."

"Grace did not believe in working on the Sabbath. She fried chicken the night before and left it in the fridge for our Sunday dinner. She didn't wash the dishes until early Monday morning."

To a large degree, Glenn was an absentee father, rising most mornings at 6AM, leaving for work before his children woke up, and returning just before midnight. At that hour, Hef was usually asleep, as was Grace, who retired at 9PM most nights with her Bible. Glenn's dinner was always waiting for him on the stove.

Many years later, Hef said, "I guess I wanted a father like the one I saw in the movies—Judge Hardy (Lewis Stone) in those Andy Hardy movies starring Mickey Rooney. The judge always gave rebellious Andy sage and loving advice."

Glenn worked as a CPA for the Advance Aluminum Corporation and managed to hold onto his job by "slaving away" seven days a week, even on Sunday, which Grace objected to. But he was so devoted, he made himself indispensable to his employers and was never laid off like millions of other Americans.

"He wasn't around when I was grow-

Sweet and cherubic, Hef was born to an emotionally distant father and mother. Each of them had an aversion to physical contact.

5

ing up, so he hardly was my male role model," Hef said. "In some cases, or so I'm told, that can turn a boy into a homosexual, hardly the case with me."

Hef's younger brother, Keith, was born in 1929, just before the Wall Street Crash that ushered in a worldwide depression. Partly because Grace and Glenn managed to hold onto their jobs throughout the 1930s, their family survived and always had food on the table. In contrast to the millions of Americans losing their homes during the Depression, Glenn moved his family into a new and larger house at 1922 North England Avenue in the community of Austin, on the west side of Chicago. "For entertainment, my mother and I gathered around the radio for most of

Huddled together Keith (left) and his older brother, Hef, turned to each other for the love and support they didn't get from their parents.

the 1930s, listening to programs and, as always, those *Fireside Chats* by FDR about the fate of the nation."

Even though it lay just beyond the city limits of downtown Chicago, Austin, when the Hefners first moved there, had the feel of a small Midwestern town. That meant July 4 picnics and parades with the marching high school band, elaborate family Thanksgiving dinners, a local movie house, Christmas carols from the "Yuletime Singers," football games in the autumn, baseball games in summer, and a corner drugstore.

In the 1930s, as Hef was growing up, and before the racial tensions of the 60s and 70s, Austin still had a community vibe and a lot of green belts and woodlands. On his bike, he set out to explore the surroundings. At times, he'd leave his bike and wander into the woods "to see what I could see. I was looking for close encounters with animals, which fascinated me. One summer afternoon, I met Peter Rabbit, a large white bunny with pink eyes and a bushy tail. I didn't move, but stood perfectly still, not wanting to frighten him. We stared at each other for a while until I think he began to suspect that I might be sizing him up for a tasty dinner. He hopped away and disappeared into the forest."

From that day on, he talked about that rabbit so much that Grace purchased a woolen blanket for him with bunny patterns on it. It became Hef's security blanket. But with the passage of time, it became worn and tattered. The bunny blanket ended up lining the box of his pet dog, Wags.

"That Peter Rabbit I saw in the forest that day stuck in my mind," Hef said. "I never knew that from that day forth, my image would forever be linked to a rabbit."

One day, while wandering in a forest, Hef had a close encounter with a white bunny.

In time, he'd designate it as the symbol of a vast empire.

\*\*\*

As a shy boy growing up, Hef inhabited a world of imagination and fantasy. He abandoned his goal of becoming a veterinarian, preferring instead a profession as a cartoonist. Ignoring homework, he did poorly in school. He spent most of his time in class drawing cartoons.

After school, he retreated to his bedroom to draw more sketches on his pad. Once, he created a comic series, making himself the epicenter of narrative about "Goo Hefner," a boy whose life was filled with nonstop adventure.

When Hef was five, the comic strip that most inspired him was Buck Rogers, a fictional soap opera character created by Philip Frances Newlan. Hef was so enthralled by the character that he followed the Buck Rogers saga in any form he could find it—in the comics, on radio, in movies, and beginning in the 1950s, on television.

For the rest of his life, Hef kept a Buck Rogers rocket ray gun hanging on the wall of his bedroom in the Playboy Mansion in Los Angeles. "Buck Rogers conditioned Americans, namely me, to the concept of space exploration, anticipating the U.S. moon landing."

Buck Rogers inspired Hef in the creation of his own intergalactic hero, "Cranet." He also devised "Metallic Man," a human robot inspired by the character of Superman. The Wild West legends of Jesse James and Billy the Kid also intrigued him, as reflected by characters he created for his cartoon strip, *Jigs and Spike*.

The hugely successful action-adventure comic strip, *Terry & the Pirates*, also had an impact on him. *[Originating in 1934, it eventually reached a peak readership of 31 million readers.]* Created by Milton Caniff, it featured the lush and exotic "Dragon Lady," leader of a band

The dashing Buster Crabbe became filmdom's first sci-fi hero, Flash Gordon. But Hef as a boy fell in love with his co-star, Jean Rogers, who became his ideal fantasy woman and remained so for the rest of his life.

of looting pirates. Interacting with her was Pat Ryan, a two-fisted journalist and pipe smoker. Hef vowed that when he grew up and was allowed to smoke, he would become a pipe smoker, shunning cigarettes. In time, the pipe—surpassed only by the bunny—became his most identifiable trademark.

By 1934, Hef fell under the spell of yet another comic book hero, *Flash Gordon*, created to compete with Buck Rogers. Flash Gordon's home turf was the planet Mongo, whose kingdoms included a jungle, a colony submerged under the sea, and a flying city.

Hef's first movie idol was Buster Crabbe, a two-time Olympic swimmer turned Hollywood matinee star. On screen, Crabbe managed to incarnate most of Hef's heroes: *Tarzan the Fearless* (1933), *Flash Gordon* (1936), and *Buck Rogers* (1939). "I was never a homosexual," Hef said. "But if I were, I'd go for Buster—dashing, very handsome, and with hair of gold."

"My sexual interest centered on his co-star, the baby-faced blonde, Jean Rogers. Her revealing costumes, with heaving breasts and exposed midriff, seemed daring to me at the time. She became the woman of my dreams, and for the rest of my life, I searched for her in the body of another woman. Some gals came close, but none ever equaled Jean's allure for me."

It has been said that Hugh Hefner was a natural-born and very gifted publisher. Before his tenth birthday, as a "literary entrepreneur," he established *The Bi-Weekly News,* a newsletter-style roundup of events in the neighborhood. He typed it on his old Royal typewriter, and peddled it door to door, selling it for one cent. "In those days, a penny could actually buy you something, like some candy."

He credited Walt Disney's Mickey Mouse, a comic series he followed avidly, with teaching him how to draw. A faithful reader of the funny papers, he also followed Chester Gould's *Dick Tracy.*

He was an avid reader of everything except his school books. As an early teenager, he waded through the works of Arthur Conan Doyle, the creator of Sherlock Holmes and his faithful companion, Dr. Watson. Inspired, Hef created his own detective adventure. His evil criminal was called "The Skull," and he was pursued by Shawhawk, Hef's version of Sherlock, with the Dr. Watson character known as Sowhat.

Years later, both his fans and his detractors wondered where Hef got the idea of hanging around wearing a bathrobe and smoking a pipe. In response, Hef said, "Sherlock Holmes at 221B Baker Street in London spent a lot of time in his living room smoking a pipe and lounging around in an expensive bathrobe."

He also became an avid follower of *The Phantom,* a comic character who wore a skull ring, leaving its imprint wherever he went. As the first of the logos he associated himself with, Hef designed his own marker, a circle divided into four sections, each with a black dot. "Of course, as I grew older, that marker was replaced by the *Playboy* bunny."

He would have preferred spending his Sundays with his cartoon characters, but Grace insisted he attend Sunday school. Whereas most of his classmates

Hef (lower right) would one day become an arbiter of men's fashion and style.

But when this family portrait was snapped during the depths of the Depression in 1932, the Hefner family—including little brother Keith and Grace—were anything but style setters.

were docile and obedient, Hef was confrontational, challenging his teachers about the "fairytales they were spreading."

He'd heard from some of the older guys at school that the story of Adam and the apple in the Garden of Eden was a symbolic allegory, a legend designed to conceal a darker meaning. A football player told him "The Bible wasn't describing an actual apple. The 'forbidden fruit' was his fucking Eve."

Hef was greatly influenced by seeing his first depiction of nudity as evoked by Adam and Eve in the Garden of Eden.

Years later, he envisioned running a male-female nude centerfold in his magazine, but decided to kill off the male.

One Sunday, after relaying that interpretation to his teacher, he was dismissed from class and sent home. He spent the rest of the day drawing cartoons of Adam and Eve romping naked in the Garden of Eden, with a snake lurking in a tree in the background.

He had never seen a nude woman before, and so he had to imagine her shape. He could hardly have imagined that beginning in a few years, he'd spend many hundreds of hours looking at, and evaluating, pictures of naked women.

He had no interest in regular studies in school and deplored classes in arithmetic and history. As his teachers tried to lecture, he drew cartoons on his school writing pads. Several letters of complaint were sent home to Grace, who chastised him, urging him to buckle down and pay attention to his lessons.

He once wrote, "Why I Waste Time," loosely formatting it as a sort of poem. "I think I get to dreaming of something I might do. And I forget my studies and what I'm supposed to do."

When the pastor of their church came over for Sunday dinner, Hef took the opportunity to challenge him on a biblical story that confused him. "I have a hard time believing some of those wild tales in the Bible. Perhaps you can solve a puzzle for me. If Adam and Eve had two sons, Cain and Abel, and they went forth to populate the world, how could two young men do that without a woman?"

Dismissing Hef's concern, the pastor seemed embarrassed: "God moves in mysterious ways."

Grace was a specimen of American Gothic womanhood. She wore horn-rimmed glasses and arranged her gray hair in a bun, and favored shoes with low heels and dresses crafted from simple cotton. Despite her Puritan roots, she had been educated and was not a right-winger. She was a peace lover, opposed to war. Preaching racial tolerance, she was not a bigot, telling Hef, "You must remember this: We are all God's children."

As regards which of his sons he particularly favored, Glenn had no favorite, seemingly indifferent to his sons. But as her sons grew older, Keith later perceived that Hef was clearly Grace's favorite: "If mother had to face *Sophie's Choice,* and a brutal Nazi officer ordered that she had to send one of her two children to the gas chamber to save the other, I'm sure mother would have pushed me into the arms of the Nazi, sending me to my death to save Hef."

Any sex education Hef got as a boy came from the sanitized *Parents' Magazine*, which Grace used as a guideline for rearing her boys.

The all-white and blondish family was her fantasy.

[*Keith was referring to* Sophie's Choice *(1982), starring Meryl Streep in an Oscar-winning performance. To save her son, she shoved her daughter into the arms of the Nazi killer, then wept bitterly at the implications of her choice.*]

Grace was bringing up her boys according to the dictates of *Parents Magazine,* a periodical launched in 1926, the year Hef was born. It featured scientific information on child development, health, safety, behavior, discipline, and sex education. Much to her horror, she knew she needed to at least provide some kind of information about sexual relations, if only to explain procreation and birth. "That way, they won't learn the facts of life from boys in the schoolyard," she told her husband, who refused to discuss sex with his sons, except for warning about the danger of masturbation, which he had read leads to insanity.

"I must have believed dear ol' dad," Hef recalled. "I didn't masturbate until I turned eighteen."

"My parents were emotionally very cold," Hef claimed. "They never kissed or hugged Keith and me, and I'd never seen them hug and kiss each other. They frowned on any kind of display of affection. They must have had some body contact at one point in their lives. How else could mother have had Keith and me? I must have suckled at my mother's breast, something I bet Glenn never did."

One night, Grace admitted, "Your father is a sex maniac, demanding it once or twice a month. I dread it when that time comes. A wife has to endure sex for the pleasure of her husband, never for herself. I want you to remember that for the rest of your life. Try not to force sex on your future wife and have it only on rare occasions, perhaps when you want to have a child of your own."

"Actually, sex was about the last thing I ever wanted to talk over with my parents," Hef said. "Some boys told me that their dads made them aware of the birds and bees—but not my dear ol' dad."

"Even when we went swimming in a public pool in summer, and dad took us, he always went inside a toilet booth and locked the door before stripping down and putting on a pair of swimming trunks. He never wanted us to see him naked. I suspected that when he had sex with mother, she was only half dressed, pulling up her dress and pulling down her bloomers."

"Later in life, I would be accused of being a sex maniac, but that was hardly the case during the first two decades of my life. I may have morphed into the world's chief advocate of hedonistic sex but didn't see semen until I was grown. It looked all gooey and white, although I knew it was needed for making babies. It took a while for me to learn that some women even swallowed it after giving a man a blow-job. Homosexual men were said to be very fond of it."

Although sex scandals would plague Hef for most of his life, the first scandal had already occurred within his own family. One very embarrassing day, word reached the Hefner household that Glenn's father, James Hefner, had been arrested, charged, and convicted of child molestation. He'd become involved with a number of nine, ten, or eleven-year-olds, fondling their unformed vaginas. Apparently, there had been no attempt at penetration. He was now in prison in Burlington, Colorado.

"Talk about liking 'em young," Hef later said. "I prefer young women myself, but I always insist they be eighteen. Of course, maybe a mature-looking fifteen or sixteen-year-old might have snuck into my bed, but I didn't know that. We always called really young gals jailbait. I'm my grandfather's son, but he 'dated' far too young. In time, I learned that some men went for sex with five or six-year-olds, although how that was done, I didn't really want to know."

***

In 1933 Grace took her sons to the Chicago World's Fair, billed at the time as a celebration of "The Century of Progress."

Hef later credited the trip with "changing my life." He and Keith squealed with delight as they took the "Sky Ride," an elevated conveyance that transported them from one end of the fair to the other, where they were reunited with their mother.

Although the malaise of the Great Depression had settled over the land, the exhibits at the World's Fair reflected the optimism of the future and made Hef feel a lot better about earning a living when he came of age. The modern architecture, the sleek new cars, the sense of

At the Chicago World's Fair of 1933, Hef saw his first depiction of a nude woman, the notorious fan dancer Sally Rand. He was fascinated and would spend the rest of his life evaluating pictures of nude women.

economic optimism, and even a cigarette-smoking robot hurled him into the world of tomorrow.

Walking through an exhibition area called "The Streets of Paris," Hef came upon a provocative poster depicting the world's most notorious fan dancer, Sally Rand. Her privates were concealed behind a large white fan. Grace pronounced it as "outrageously vulgar." Many fairgoers agreed with her, and during the course of the exhibition Rand was arrested four times by the police, who charged her each time with indecent exposure.

Grace tugged at Hef's shirt, pulling him away from the poster toward other, more respectable exhibitions. He later learned that Rand came out on stage wearing only high heels, her modesty preserved by fluttering ostrich feathers as she danced to the music of Chopin and Debussy. "She played *peek-a-boo* with her body like a winged bird as she swooped and twirled on stage," wrote one reporter.

"Sally Rand had an enormous influence on me," Hef acknowledged years later. "At the fair, I saw for the first time a poster of a performer exhibiting her body for profit. Little did I know at the time that I would become the major purveyor in the world of women flaunting their ample attributes before an eager male audience, providing visual fantasies for them to jerk off if they couldn't get the real thing."

The next day, he spent hours at the desk in his bedroom, working on a drawing of a naked woman hiding behind a fan. Without knowing it, he had stumbled onto his lifetime profession. After he finished his cartoon of the fan dancer, he pasted it up on his bedroom's wall alongside his drawing of Adam and Eve in the Garden of Eden.

\*\*\*

At the age of five, Hef was overcome with a fascination that turned him into an addict for life—that is, a movie addict. The first film he ever saw at the Montclare Theater was the 1930 *Ladies Love Brutes,* which had Mary Astor on the verge of divorcing Fredric March while stirring up a romance with George Bancroft. Grace later regretted taking her son to that movie, considering it "tasteless."

Samuel Brown, the manager of the local movie house, knew Grace as a neighbor. Whereas she came to his theater with Hef every Saturday night, she opted to leave his younger brother at home, paying a babysitter fifty cents to watch out for him. Soon, Hef began to slip away on his own, especially on Saturday afternoon, when the theater presented a double feature of adventure films and westerns, drawing a kiddie audience.

As time went by, he showed up two or three times on weekdays, too, for the regular bill of recently released romances, dramas, and comedies. Brown, who lived down the street from the Hefners, didn't like such a young boy spending time in the dark at his movie house alone, but allowed it anyway, warning an usher "to keep a lookout for the kid. He's 'queer bait' for any boy molester."

Regardless of what was on the bill, Hef regularly lost himself in the celluloid fantasies.

Years later, he reflected, "Who could resist Ginger Rogers dancing with Fred Astaire? I took my little brother to see Ginger dance—in high heels, no less—with Fred Astaire in *Top Hat* (1935). Keith developed a crush on her, and he stole a black-and-white still of her to display on the wall of his bedroom."

"I was a sucker for any movie choreographed by Busby Berkeley. He devised elaborate musical productions that involved complex geometric patterns, using a bevy of gorgeous showgirls and props as fantasy elements in kaleidoscopic on-

After watching Fred Astaire dance with Ginger Rogers in *Top Hat* (1935), Hef developed a lifelong fascination with the dancing duo, and screened their musicals over and over at the Playboy Mansion in Chicago.

"Keith fell hard for Ginger," Hef said. "I mean he really had it bad."

15

screen spectaculars. I devoured the dancing girls, deciding when I got a little older that I would date only blondes. Of course, when the 1940s arrived, I had already deviated from my goal, having gone off with non-blondes. Hedy Lamarr in 1940 taught me to appreciate brunettes, as did Rita Hayworth, who proved that a redhead could give me a youthful erection."

"Back to 1933 when I went to see *Footlight Parade*, I fell big-time for the image of Joan Blondell on the screen. The one thing I liked about sassy, wise-cracking Joan was she looked like she wouldn't leave any date with blue balls. Incidentally, her co-star was James Cagney, and, in time, I would see most of his movies."

Hef was only six years old when he saw Joan Blondell in *Blonde Crazy* (1931).

He knew after seeing that movie that he'd devote the rest of his life to pursuing blonde goddesses.

"Keith may have been hooked onto Ginger, but I became a sucker for Alice Faye, my blonde goddess. Yes, the same Alice Faye who was Archie Bunker's fantasy woman in that latter-day sitcom, *All in the Family*."

"By 1940, though, I had deserted Alice as my fantasy woman when Betty Grable on the screen entered my life. She would be my favorite pinup until Marilyn Monroe came along."

"When I was in the Army, I pasted Grable's famous cheesecake photograph onto the back of my locker door. Grable was photographed from the rear, with a come-hither look for men who liked to enter through the back door. Eventually, I found out why she'd been photographed from that angle: She was pregnant at the time."

In addition to the current films it regularly screened on weeknights, the Montclare Theater presented vintage silent films too, but only on Sundays. Hef made it a point to see them, carefully avoiding mentioning anything to Grace, as she believed that going to the movies on the Sabbath—a day devoted to prayer and Bible reading—was a sin. . "I was fascinated by the emoting of those silent screen stars, who had to use their faces, not their voices, to convey emotion."

"As a foreshadow of my future stint in the Army, I sat wide-eyed, watching John Gilbert play a young wastrel who faces the horror of war in *The Big Parade* (1925). After D.W. Griffith's *The Birth of a Nation* (1915), *The Big Parade* was the

Sexy Betty Grable became the pinup goddess of the soldiers who fought World War II.

She was voted "the girl we'd most like to meet in a trench."

second most-popular of all the silent. For at least a week or two, I wished I looked like Gilbert except for his pointy nose."

He was fascinated by *The Sheik* (1921), starring Rudolph Valentino. Hef found it intriguing that an Arab chieftain could mesmerize even a "civilized woman," casting a magnetic spell over her. It appeared that if a man were alluring enough, he could conquer any woman, "well, almost any woman."

He also sat through the famous chariot race and sea battle in MGM's *Ben-Hur* (1925), starring the gay actor Ramon Novarro. In making this trouble-plagued film, the studio had spent the then unheard of sum of four million dollars. It became a favorite of his, and three decades later, in 1959, he was eager to see the remake of that film, starring Charlton Heston in the title role, with the gay actor Stephen Boyd cast as Messala.

"Of them all, John Barrymore's *Don Juan*, made the year I was

John Barrymore was the lover on and off the screen with his leading lady, Mary Astor. "He was a great inspiration to me, Hef said. "I wanted to be a modern-day Don Juan."

born (1926), really created my role model for the future. This was the first feature-length film to utilize the Vitaphone sound-on-disc system with a synchronized musical score and sound effects but without dialogue."

"It entered film history as a classic known for having the greatest number of kisses, 127, in any movie. "John kissed his leading ladies, Mary Astor and Estelle Taylor, and in Mary's case, so I heard, did more than

Hef was so thrilled with King Kong, the emblematic tale of Beauty (Fay Wray) and the Beast, that he had it screened periodically for the rest of his life.

kiss her. He was the star and she was only a starlet, so he demanded that she visit his trailer every afternoon to service him, and she did."

It certainly wasn't just the romantic films that attracted Hef. He was enraptured watching *King Kong*, the pre-Code "Beauty and the Beast" thriller. Released in 1933 and hailed as the greatest horror movie of all time, it starred Fay Wray, Bruce Cabot, and a giant ape who lusts for Wray and at one point picks her up in his mammoth paw from his perch atop the Empire State Building.

After watching it, he began creating his own horror cartoons.

Years later, during his residency within the Playboy Mansion in Chicago, he on occasion ordered that *King Kong* be screened for his guests.

At a Hollywood party in 1988, Hef met Wray, the original "Scream Queen." She told him she was writing her memoirs, but so far, she did not have a title for it. "Call it *On the Other Hand,*" he advised her, "and be assured that all Kong fans will get it."

He had not lost his fascination with animals and made it a point to see any movie starring Johnny Weissmuller as *Tarzan.* His favorite of the Ape Man's films was the 1934 *Tarzan and His Mate,* a pre-Code adventure populated with huge snakes, man-eating lions, and stampeding elephants. He enjoyed the near nudity of Maureen O'Sullivan, who portrayed Tarzan's mate, Jane.

The film sparked dreams for Hef about becoming an explorer and hunter one day, pursuing lions or other creatures in the jungles of Africa. He pictured himself as a budding young Ernest Hemingway. "As Tarzan, I will have a chimp as my faithful sidekick."

\*\*\*

When he was in the fourth grade, seated across from Audrey Zimmermann with her long blonde curls, Hef became conscious of the sexual allure of girls. "In those days that moppet, Shirley Temple, was all the rage with her chubby cheeks and goody-goody dialogue in such films as *Curly Top* (1935). She filled me with nausea. If a nine-ear-old girl could be sexy, Audrey—and not Shirley—was most alluring. But before I could go after her, she moved with her family to Los Angeles, my future home."

Hef recalled "getting erections" watching scantily clad Johnny Weissmuller and Maureen O'Sullivan emote in *Tarzan and His Mate* (1934).

"I also dug Tarzan living in harmony with nature."

"My first kiss came from Dolly Bloomberg when I was in the eighth grade," Hef said. "All the boys thought Dolly was one hot little number. She was a brunette with a beautiful, smiling face. At a birthday party, we played kissing games, and I got a wet one planted on my lips by Dolly. I'd never been kissed before, and it sent an electric shock up my spine—and a stirring in a nether region, too."

"That night marked the beginning of my getting kissed by hundreds of girls when I grew up. Forget John Barrymore in *Don Juan* with those 127 kisses. The Great Profile came nowhere near my record. The real Don Juan was said to have seduced 1,000 women. Eventually, I would beat that record, becoming the Don Juan of the 20th Century."

"My first actual date was with Mary Turnbull when I was twelve years old and so was she. Whenever someone asked me how old I was at that time, I always said, 'going on thirteen.' I was that anxious to become a teenager, because I'd heard from boys at school that that was when puberty set in. At least some of them had started playing around. We'd heard stories that a thirteen-year-old girl at our school got pregnant and had to drop out of school. At least that was the rumor."

"On my first outing with Mary, I took her to the Montclare Theater—what else was there to do? We saw *Jesse James* (1939) with Tyrone Power and Henry Fonda."

"After the movie, we walked across the street and had a chocolate malt at the drugstore. Then we strolled home holding hands. She was my neighbor, living on New England Avenue. On the way back, she pissed me off. All she talked about was Ty Power, telling me how beautiful he was. She was president of his fan club at school. She was also a member of fan clubs devoted to Errol Flynn and Robert Taylor."

"At her doorstep, I had forgiven her and moved to kiss her, but she slapped my face."

"Not on the first date, you silly little boy," she told him.

"Back in my bedroom, when I pulled off my clothes and before putting on my pajamas, I studied my image in the mirror. I didn't like what I saw. I'd have to figure out how to get through my life without Ty Power's looks."

"I didn't see much future in Mary and me as a couple. That became obvious when she showed me this notebook on which she'd written the names of six other boys she was also dating. At the bottom of her list, I noticed the name of Hugh Hefner scribbled in."

"The short time I hung out with Mary was well spent," he said. "It led to a discovery that changed my life."

By his second year, he began to dress more fashionably, wearing a fedora like Humphrey Bogart, a scarf, and a well-tailored overcoat, always in black. He hopes his more mature look would attract high school beauties.

"Mary and I never went on a date again, but she invited me over to her home, where her basement had been turned into a playroom with a record player," Hef said. "She always invited kids from school, and we danced, listened to music, drank coke, and played ping-pong. I got pretty good at doing the jitterbug. When the party got real naughty, we played kissing games, which was all the rage back then."

A commercial artist, her father drew cartoons for *Esquire*, a magazine founded in 1933, not a good time to jumpstart a periodical in the middle of the depression. But it had risen to a circulation of 100,000, selling at fifty cents a copy.

As he flipped through the pages of the magazines, Hef was spellbound by *Esquire*'s art work. He asked her if he could borrow a thick stack of them, with his promise to return them. She reluctantly agreed but warned him that they were treasured possessions of her father, and to take care of them. That night in his bedroom, he stayed up late, slowly turning the pages of every copy of *Esquire*.

One day, Hef would go to work for *Esquire*, which featured early cheesecake rather sanitized. The magazine would inspire him to launch *Playboy*.

"It was more than a girlie magazine," Hef said. "It ran stories by two of my favorite authors, Ernest Hemingway, who had written *The Sun Also Rises,* and F. Scott Fitzgerald, who had created the character of *The Great Gatsby.* I fantasized about Fitzgerald's Gatsby, but not Ernesto's hero, Jake Barnes. He was impotent."

Special features within *Esquire* back then included alluring and sexy illustrations of "The Petty Girl." Crafted and designed by pinup artist George Petty, they were beautiful, scantily clad, and provocative. For some reason, Petty made their legs longer

This illustration for Bestform bras was crafted by George Petty in 1944.

Hef cut pictures of Petty Girls from newspapers and magazines to decorate the walls of his bedroom.

and their heads smaller than those of the real-life models who had posed for them.

Hef was so excited by the Petty Girls and the cartoons they appeared in that—with no intention of returning them to their owner—he pasted them onto the walls of his bedroom. When Grace discovered his wall art, she demanded that he remove them. Eventually, she relented and let him keep them as wall decorations. When he began to masturbate, the pinups were his inspiration for "the big blast-off."

One Petty Girl torn from the pages of *Esquire* stood out from the others, It depicted an alluring young woman in a pinkish bunny suit with floppy ears and a bushy tail. "I jacked off to that bunny every night of my life for the next few weeks, except on Sunday. All I needed was for Grace to catch me masturbating on a Sunday."

*[Years later, when Hef served in the Army during World War II, he was amused to see Petty Girls replicated on the noses of both bombers and*

*fighter planes. He became such a lifelong fan of The Petty Girl that in 1999, he was asked to write the foreward to the book* Entitled Petty: The Classic Pin-Up Art of George Petty.]

\*\*\*

In 1940, *Esquire* branched out with additional depictions of all-American cheesecake. One of the most famous was "The Vargas Girl," the fantasy creations of a Peruvian illustrator, Alberto Vargas. American males devoured his idealized illustrations of voluptuous, scantily attired women.

His first movie poster depicted the half-naked actress, Zita Johann, as a sales incentive for her new movie, *The Sin of Nora Moran* (1933). Today, his poster is a collector's item. Hef managed to get a copy to add to his wall art.

Vargas worked for *Esquire* between 1940 and 1946, crafting some 180 illustrations of American womanhood. Like George Petty, Vargas' cartoons were replicated as "nose art" for Allied bombers and fighter planes during World War II.

*[By 1959, Vargas would be working for Hef himself, publishing his pinups in* Playboy.]

\*\*\*

In September of 1939, England declared war on Nazi Germany after

The Peruvian artist, Alberto Vargas, weaned Hef from The Petty Girl and taught him the sensual pleasures of the Vargas Girl.

Certain moralists were outraged when Vargas designed the poster art for *The Sin of Nora Moran* (1933), starring Zita Johann.

23

its brutal invasion of Poland. Like many other Americans, the Hefner family didn't seem overly concerned, at least at the beginning, since Franklin Roosevelt had promised to keep the United States out of foreign wars. Their sense of non-involvement changed, of course, after the Japanese attacked Pearl Harbor.

That year (1939) turned out some of the greatest movies in Hollywood history, including Greta Garbo's *Ninotchka*, Bette Davis' *Dark Victory*, and John Steinbeck's *Of Mice and Men*.

Hef's most memorable movie experience that year involved sitting through *Gone With the Wind*. Clark Gable's depiction of Rhett Butler, the rogue, and Vivien Leigh's performance as Scarlett O'Hara, stunned him.

He was also affected by the premises of *Mr. Smith Goes to Washington*. In it, James Stewart played an idealist congressman. After seeing it, Hef decided that one day he, too, might grow up to be an idealist fighting for causes as yet unknown. At the time, government censorship and civil rights had not even occurred to him.

Also in 1939, Judy Garland starred in *The Wizard of Oz*, skipping along in her ruby-red slippers after Shirley Temple was not available. The movie appealed to Hef's sense of fantasy, and he drew his cartoon version of its major characters, including "The Wicked Witch of the West." He later discarded them as not being original enough.

*Wuthering Heights*, starring Laurence Olivier and Merle Oberon, appealed to Hef's sense of romance. He pictured himself as Heathcliff, wandering the bleak Yorkshire Moors in pursuit of a doomed love.

\*\*\*

As World War II heated up and moved more threateningly toward America's shores, Hef began to pay more attention to the news. Some older boys he talked to feared they would soon be drafted. The prevalence of war was reflected in his cartoons. In one, he depicted a gang of Nazi soldiers, intent on rape, ripping the dress off a school girl in Paris.

In another cartoon series he devised, the Nazis had conquered

New York and Washington, D.C., and were headed west into the Great American Heartland. Hef depicted bands of brave soldiers standing at the "gates" of Chicago to turn back the invaders.

As he was growing up, he'd added inches to his height—"and inches somewhere else too," he noted. After his enrollment in January of 1940 at Steinmetz, the local high school, he continued drawing and writing his short stories. As an author and illustrator, he found inspiration in H.G. Wells' *The War of the Worlds* and in Sax Rohmer's *The Insidious Dr. Fu-Manchu*. With his weekly allowance, Hef bought a subscription to *Weird Tales*, a sensationalist sci-fi monthly magazine. One issue depicted a nearly naked woman being lifted up by an evil man and tossed into the gaping mouth of a huge alligator.

He also drew cartoons of walking dead men, "invisible" hounds, demonic bats, evil horned Satans, menacing mummies, and swamp monsters. Grace was horrified at his drawings, complaining to her husband, "I fear our boy has the Devil in him."

High school Hef, horny and geeky, with a definite charm and aspirations as a cartoonist and illustrator.

In reference to his first year of high school, Hef described himself as: "a scrawny weakling, no football player— that's for sure," he said. He picked up a book about bodybuilding written by Charles Atlas, a leading fitness advocate of his day. Advertisements for Atlas' fitness regimes appeared in magazines everywhere. They showed a bullying, muscle-

Flanked by two classmates, Hef is in the center of this detail from a class photo.

bound man with a girl on a beach. He kicks sand in the eye of a skinny guy, who then states his intention of transforming himself and his confidence through weightlifting.

According to Hefner, "After two weeks of body-building, I abandoned it as a hopeless cause. I just gave up. I would never become the perfect specimen. I decided in the future to attract girls using my wit, charm, and mind. And so I did."

A normally shy boy, Hef became extroverted in high

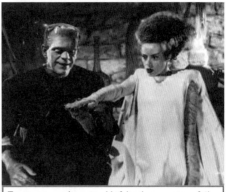

From an early age, Hef had a sense of the campy macabre.

He was fascinated by the Frankenstein legend after seeing Boris Karloff and Elsa Lanchester in *Bride of Frankenstein* (1935).

It inspired him to write his own tale of horror, The Creator of Gideon.

school, and soon became one of the fixtures of the gang he belonged to. Its members, both girls and boys, hung out together most afternoons beginning at 3PM, when they met at a local drugstore, jitterbugging to the sounds coming from the jukebox.

In Hef's sophomore year, he launched a paper, *Hour Glass,* filled with high school news and gossip. During his junior year, he wrote articles and drew cartoons for "the school rag," *Steinmetz Star.* More successful than *Hour Glass* was his launch of a newspaper marketed to grade school students, *The Pepper,* which is still published today.

As publisher, Hef solicited bylined stories from wannabe writers, and sold advertising to local merchants, sometimes designing the ads himself.

For a while in the early 1940s, when they were all the rage in high schools across the country, Hef became fascinated by horror stories, telling Grace, "I'm gonna become the next Edgar Allan Poe."

Hef was thrilled to see Boris Karloff on the screen in the Montclare Theater's revival of the 1930 version of *Frankenstein.* He also rushed to a screening of *Bride of Frankenstein* (1935). Featuring Elsa Lanchester as Frankenstein's bride. It was advertised as: "THE MONSTER DEMANDS A MATE!"

"Elsa practically turned me off women for life," Hef said.

Around this time, filled with youthful enthusiasm, he launched *Shudder* magazine, later defining it as a forerunner of *Playboy,* even though it had almost nothing to do with his later magazine. At one point, from within his basement, he made himself up as the monster Frankenstein, asking his brother Keith to snap a picture of him. "I fancied myself as 'The Mogul of Horror,'" he said.

As part of yet another youthful experiment, he organized a fraternity for aficionados of horror movies, "The Shudder Club." As its president, he created an official handshake, membership pins, logos, and a password. He even devised what he called a "decoder circle" so club members could exchange secret messages.

From his base in Chicago, he wrote letters to those masters of cinematic horror, Boris Karloff and Bela Lugosi, inviting them to join his club as honorary members. Both of them agreed.

Although *Shudder* survived for only five editions, it taught him many lessons. Years later, reviewing that time in his life when he was unsure of where or how to focus on the magazine trades, he said, "Only one roadblock stood in my way," he said. "I had no damn money."

Briefly and fleetingly, Hef decided he should try to become an actor. After some tryouts, he was awarded the starring role, that of Hector Fish, with the Green Curtain Players at Steinmetz High School. He'd also made a best friend, Jim Brophy, and both of them wrote and starred in a school play entitled *Putting Out the Steinmetz Star,* a highly exaggerated account of their work on the school paper.

During the summer of 1942, Hef began to self-identify as a director and star of movies. He wrote *Return from the Dead,* a screenplay for a black-and-white short film about a scientist who dabbles in reanimation, bringing a corpse back to life. In his tale, he cast himself as a demented scientist who learns that his lab creations are horrible monstrosities, not quite among the living but also not completely dead. His friend Jim Brophy was configured in the story as a reincarnated monster. At the time, Hef was harboring a crush on a female student, Betty Conklin, whom he cast as the female lead.

"Maybe I was just dreaming, but I thought of putting Betty on what was called 'the casting couch.' That was merely a dream, not something to act upon."

Clearly inspired by Boris Karloff's screen version of *Frankenstein*, *Return from the Dead* was shot using Hef's 16mm hand-held camera.

Hef's younger brother Keith assisted him with the film's production. Its goriest and most dramatic scene was shot in the basement of their family home. Hef was filmed with "blood" (melted Hershey's chocolate) spurting from his lips as the character he was playing entered a death spiral. At the finale, he tumbles down a stairwell before his left hand weakly rises before falling to the cement. THE END.

Hef remembered his high school years as the happiest of his life. A lot of his contentment had to do with Brophy. "He was the first real friend I ever had. We planned our days together, and each dawn brought some new adventure. We were very different personalities but drawn together like a horse and carriage. At least for a while, I also had a girlfriend, Beverly Allen. A shapely brunette, she was real cute, but our romance hardly survived the football season."

\*\*\*

"Jim was a hell of a lot smarter than I was," Hef claimed. "We called him 'The Einstein of Steinmetz.' He wanted to be a scientist and a professor of physics."

In his spare time, Brophy was a ham radio operator. He and Hef became best buddies and saw each other every day of their lives, even on weekends. Like Hef, Brophy was a movie buff. Together, they saw almost every feature at the Montclare.

One of their favorites was *Road to Singapore* (1940) with

Collaborators and cohorts, Hef (left) and Jim Brophy were best buddies,

They become known as "The Bing Crosby and Bob Hope" of Steinmetz High School.

28

Bob Hope and Bing Crosby. After seeing it, they publicly defined themselves as the Bob Hope and Bing Crosby of Steinmetz High. "All that's missing is Dorothy Lamour in a sarong," Hef said. "She became my dream gal for a while, until I returned to Betty Grable."

Brophy and Hef soon became the two most popular boys in school, especially after they organized a gang of their own and invited girls to join. According to Brophy, "only 'hep' guys and dolls in equal ratio were allowed in our elite little club, a group of swingers. Hef was our main jive talker, his favorite expression was 'Jeeps Creeps.'"

*[This was a derivation of "Jeepers Creepers," which itself was a derivation of "Jesus H. Christ," an expression viewed by some as too profane.]*

"Jim and I became the two hep cats and jive talkers of our class," Hef said. "My classmates called me 'Hep Hef.' If you weren't a member of our gang, you were dubbed a crappy bunch of squares, who just didn't get it. Only the hottest of the 'Stein studes' were allowed to join our gang."

During the final two years of high school, Hef and Brophy, as a writing and audio team operating as the Hefner-Brophy Radio Records Enterprise, worked together in a basement studio, crafting at least thirty-five recordings to play for and amuse their friends. Their plots were inspired by the scary shows then popular on the radio. Their first recording was *The Curse of the Egyptian Hand,* followed in the spring of 1942 by *Tales from the Crypt.*

*[In October of 1938, Orson Welles had terrified America with his broadcast of War of the Worlds. Listeners deserted their radios and fled in horror, fearing that there was an actual invasion from Martian. Borphy and Hef duplicated the panic broadcast.]*

In addition to their writing and recording efforts, both of them starred in plays they presented to their classmates. In one, *Pistol-Packin' Mama,* Hef played a cowboy with Brophy dressed as his girl, hairy legs and all.

Nearly all of Hef's dates included Brophy and his girlfriend, Janie Borson.

"I called our dates in the early 1940s 'rumble seat love,'" Hef said. "Me and my gal sat in the rumble seat and Jim stayed in the front seat, making out with his lady."

"The first time I really fell in love—okay, call it puppy love— was during my sophomore years. It was with a shapely brunette, Betty Conklin. She ruffled my feathers, tickled my thyroid, electrocuted my spine, and generated electric waves in my balls."

"She and I were the best jitterbuggers at school, and she was sweet sixteen and perky. She was also a drummer with a set of drums in her living room, where she presented concerts for me. Her cultural icon was America's most famous drummer at the time, Gene Krupa."

"Betty worked at a soda fountain across the street from the Montclare movie house, and I spent a lot of time perched on a stool watching her make chocolate malts. I drank a lot of them myself— with extra chocolate, of course. We danced to the music of Tommy Dorsey and Glenn Miller, and both of us believed at the time that Frank Sinatra, that skinny kid from Hoboken, sang the most romantic songs."

The dances they attended were in the school's gym. Along with their classmates, they had to take off their shoes to protect the floor. "Betty and I stood out at the sock hop."

"We even talked of marriage after we got out of college," Hef said. "But heartbreak was in store for me that autumn. Betty picked the captain of the football team as her date for the school hayride— and left me standing in the October wind."

"I mourned her passing for a long time, but that didn't stop me from dating because I was girl crazy. Along came Dorothy Novak and Edith Bioski. As I dated around, I learned that a girl's breasts come in different sizes like a man's dick."

"The upperclassmen were carrying 'rubbers' with them in case one of them got lucky that night. No one wanted to knock up a high school girl during a heavy makeout session. Personally, I wanted to remove all restrictions on high school sex. If rubbers prevented pregnancy, then why should teens be denied sexual pleasure? Sex should be about having fun when you're young."

"At long last, 1944 rolled around, the time for my graduation,"

Hef said. "I had campaigned for a jukebox to be installed in the dining room cafeteria, and that advocacy had led me to be elected Student Council President."

The shy boy who entered high school had been voted "Most Popular," "Most Likely to Succeed," "Best Orator," "Best Dancer," and "Class Humorist."

"My pictures were all over the yearbook, the *Silver Streak.*"

"For the school prom, I took Dot (Dorothy Novak), and it was the first time I ever wore a tux—rented, of course."

"The high school yearbook gave me a writeup:"

*HUGH HEFNER: Cartoonist and feature writer…other half of Hefner-Brophy combination…likes jiving with Dot, giving comic scripts with Broph, crooning, writing horror stories and songs…hopes to crash radio or movies one of these days…since coming to Steinmetz from Sayre two years ago Hef has written (with Broph), directed, and acted in two STAR plays, acted in two Green Curtain productions, appeared in some dozen B. of E. sponsored radio broadcasts, run for the Steinmetz track team…president of Student Council, D.A. of Student Court, and vice-president of Green Curtain Players and As We Like It Club…calls everybody "Slug" or "Fiendish"…pet expression is "Jeeps creeps."*

\*\*\*

During the sexual revolution of the 1960s and in reference to his high school years, Hef granted an interview to William Davidson of the popular *Saturday Evening Post,* known for its Norman Rockwell covers:

"When I was in high school, my mother Grace had tried to instill in me her puritanical outlook on sex, a horrid thing never to be mentioned. I became repressed and was emotionally upset when I'd entered high school. I was too shy to put my arm around a girl, much less hold her hand. I was a very introverted young man, going through a difficult period of adjustment."

He went on to assert that his younger brother, Keith, was more "outgoing than me. The first time as a kid when he got a hard-on, he went to Grace to find out what was happening to his little cockie."

"The answers I was getting about sex just did not make sense to me. Did an evil Satan lurk in the heart of every boy wanting to break out of his confinement to terrorize little girls? I thought not, and I set out to find my own answers to the truth. I had to admit I had a hard time getting over my repression and all the bullshit that had been imposed on me."

"I was raised behind a wall of restrictions my mother dictated. She had a strong sense of morality. Obviously, in time, I broke free of her values."

"Amazingly," he later confessed, "the 'Future King of Sex and Smut,' as my enemies called me, never got laid in high school."

***

"As a young man, I was always falling in love, one gal at a time," Hef said. "As I grew older, and my love life became more intense, my pattern changed."

"I was still true to my one love, but had other dates on the side, which meant that I was playing the field but pretending to be faithful, which I was but only in my fashion."

"To be in love with a girl is to shout to the world: 'I'm alive! I'm vital!' Romance can be bittersweet and can lead to heartbreak. But lack of romance can mean emotional devastation and loneliness."

"When I was only seventeen, in December of 1943, life became complicated for me, a 115-pound weakling who had an I.Q. of 152. My power was in my brain, not in my muscles."

"In January, I was due to enter the U.S. Army. Our men were fighting and dying in Europe and the Pacific against those killer Japs."

"Before Christmas, I was about to commit the unforgivable sin," he confessed. "Jim Brophy was still my best friend, and he was away for a few days. Quite by chance, I ran into his gal, Janie Borson, on the street. We went for a long walk at twilight time. It was a cold night, and we were bundled up. We had a long, soulful talk about our futures."

"I didn't mean for it to happen, but in the park, we looked into each other's eyes. I suddenly hugged her to me and gave her a long, lingering kiss. The French do it with tongues and everything. Instead of slapping my face, she clung to me."

"Oh, Hef, I care so much for you," she confessed. "In all those double dates when I was with Jim, my eyes were on you."

"We kissed and kissed some more," Hef said. "We had five more dates before I had to leave and before Jim came back. We vowed never to tell him. We did promise to write two or three times a week until we sorted out our feelings. It's always been commonplace for a man to fall in love with his best friend's gal."

As if falling for Borson had not complicated his life enough, Mildred

According to Hef, "Mildred ('Millie') Williams came into my life as my first serious romance. Little did I know that it would lead to marriage. When I went into the Army, she was 'the gal I left behind,' but not for long."

Williams emerged at a going-away party at the home of a friend. He'd passed her several times in the corridors at school, but had never spoken to her.

At the party, he took a more detailed look, later claiming, "She was as cute as a bedbug, her brunette coiffure in bangs, and she was dressed in the typical bobbysox garb, showing off her shapely legs as she danced. At one point, she plopped down in my lap and gave me an off-to-war kiss. I was turned on from that night forward."

"We began to date, and our relationship grew as she shared her dreams of the future with me, and I downloaded on her what I'd like to do after the Army. Before I left for the induction into the military, I dated her every night I wasn't with Janie. We grew serious with each other—there was heavy petting."

"When I dated her, she worked for the Mars Candy Company. I met her after work, and we dined together. Dine is not the right word. We ate at the drugstore, and our order was always the same:

cheeseburgers and cherry Cokes."

"I met her devoted Catholic family of four sisters. Her stern father was a blue-collar street conductor spouting the communist propaganda line and bragging on the system in Russia. A lot of guys became commies during the Depression era with all its unemployment. I listened, never vouching my real opinion."

Millie was born on March 10, 1926, the same year Hef was. "She played the violin and staged a private concert for me. Even though I still had the hots for blondes, I was not opposed to the idea of making it with a brunette."

"It was Millie who saw me off to the battlefields of World War II, although, as it turned out, I never saw battle."

"Before I said goodbye to her, we promised to write each other faithfully, which, for my part, I did. She also came through with very loving letters."

"After kissing her goodbye, I uttered my last immortal words, which I stole from a song by The Andrews Sisters."

"Don't sit under the apple tree with anyone else but me until I come marching home."

***

In the wake of Hef's death, an article in *The Washington Post* by Alex Horton was headlined: THE MILITARY CHANGED HUGH HEFNER & YEARS LATER HE CHANGED THE MILITARY.

Horton wrote, "War transcends time, and so do the urges of men who fight them. Especially when it comes to *Playboy*. Hefner forged social revolution partly because of his own time in uniform during World War II, a one-man counter-offensive against the buttoned-up social movements in post-war America. But he would also revolutionize how the country thought about the conflicts to come."

"In January of 1944, I passed the Army physical at an induction center in Chicago," Hef said. "This olive-skinned Italian American juggled my balls during a physical. It was like being assaulted by the enemy, since at the time, America was at war with Mussolini."

"Before he took hold of my balls to give them a good feel, no man—nor woman, for that matter—had tangled with my precious jewels. I'd never had a human hand on them since I learned to go to the potty by myself and also learned how to bathe myself."

"I made it through that nude encounter and spent some time at the Army's Specialized Training Reserve Program in the Chicago area. We had to watch slides of how men's genitals looked when they contracted the clap or syphilis. The slides were so graphic that it could have turned us off sex for life."

By March of 1944, he was transferred to barracks which had been erected on the campus of the University of Wisconsin at Madison. "I arrived with all the comforts of home: My comic books, cartoons, sketchpads, my books, and even hangars for my clothes. I soon realized that for the next few weeks, I would have no need for my junk. I was in Boot Camp, or 'Camp Hell,' as I called it."

"We had this drill sergeant, who years later would return to my memory when I saw how Monty Clift and Frank Sinatra were brutalized in *From Here to Eternity* (1953)," he said.

"I'd never felt so isolated, so lonely, in my life," he said. "I lived with two other guys sleeping on cots in this crowded room. One was a hairy beast from Detroit, who passed wind a lot—that's a polite way of saying he farted. The other was a tough guy from the Bronx, who resembled the future movie star, Ernest Borgnine. All they talked about was sex and football."

"I dreaded the rugged training," he said. "One afternoon, as we were crawling on the ground on a rainy day, this drill sergeant pressed his booted foot on my neck, sinking me into this deep muddy puddle. I reared up looking like *The Creature from the Black Lagoon.*"

Founded in 1848, the University of Wisconsin was one of 131 colleges and universities that nationally sponsored the V-12 College Training Program, offering cadets a path to a Navy commission.

"My roomies wanted to be officers," Hef said. "Not this kid. My hope was to not only survive Boot Camp but to come out of all this horror a free man raring to get on with my show and back to civilian life and the two women I loved. Of course, I would face the awkward decision of having to select only one of them. Gone were the days when men were allowed to have a harem, which was my secret desire."

After Boot Camp, Hef was sent to Fort Sheridan, a mobilization and training center. Known today as the Sheridan Reserve Center, it had been established during the Spanish-American War in 1886.

From Hef's bleak and sparsely furnished room in the barracks, he could gaze upon the Fort Sheridan Water Tower, a landmark that was visible from many miles away. During World War II, more than half a million men had been processed through this center into active duty. As a young soldier, the future general, George Patton, trained here. The fort stood in Lake County, Illinois, bordering High Park, Lake Forest, and Highwood.

During the late spring of 1944, Hef, along with his fellow cadets, were shipped to Fort Hood, a military post that had been erected in 1942 outside Killeen, Texas, and named after a Confederate general. Halfway between Austin and Waco, it was the largest military base in the world, encompassing 215,000 acres. Throughout World War II, one of its stated goals had involved training and testing soldiers in the use of tank destroyers.

At the camp, Hef joined some 95,000 troops preparing to go to war. *[He was not the only future celebrity who learned military tactics at Fort Hood. Other notables included baseball great, Jackie Robinson, and later, the King of Rock 'n Roll, Elvis Presley.]*

Hef had never fired a gun until one morning his drill instructor placed an M1 Garrand in his hands, a .30 caliber semi-automatic rifle in standard use during World War II. General Patton had called it "the greatest battle implement ever devised."

To Hef's surprise, within days, he had learned to shoot faster than he ever expected—in fact, he ended up winning a sharpshooter badge for this newly acquired skill. "I became the male equivalent of Annie Oakley. No bird flying over Texas was safe from me with my rifle."

"We were also taught how to throw grenades in the wilds of the Texas desert. We were being trained to hurl them at Nazis manning machine guns. We were told, in the words of my sergeant, 'to get ready to blow the dingleberry-clinging asses off those Nazi bastards killing our men on the battlefield.'"

At Fort Hood, "stranded in the middle of nowhere" (his words), he went through a bleak period of loneliness and frustration. He even composed a song, "I'd Make a Hell of a Good Civilian (That's Exactly What I'd Like to Be)".

He continued writing notes and drawing cartoons for his autobiography. *School Daze* was no longer an appropriate title, so he changed the name of his saga to *G.I. Doze, Volume 8.* His schoolboy alter ego, Goo Heffer *(sic)*, became G.I. Goo, whom he identified as "jerk."

Nights were spent watching movies at the canteen. In those days, studios rushed films to G.I. camps before they were released to the general public. In 1944, his two favorites starred Betty Grable in *Four Jills in a Jeep* and *Pin Up Girl.*

"Betty Grable remained my favorite wartime star, but I also got off on the seductive charm of Rita Hayworth and Linda Darnell."

"As a soldier, I certainly couldn't boast of my distinguished military record, like that future movie star, Audie Murphy, who became the most decorated American soldier of World War II. To tell the truth, when my superior officers learned I could type, I became a typist for their letters and communications. In those days, most men in the Army didn't know how to type, feeling that typing was something for girls training to become a secretary to some male boss. I call my being assigned to the typewriter a 'dandy break.' It sure as hell beat peeling potatoes in KP or an even more odious task, cleaning the stinking latrines where two hundred guys went to take a crap."

Sometimes at the typewriter, he wrote love letters to Millie Williams and Janie Borson, who was still involved with his best buddy, Jim Brophy. "He still hadn't found out about Janie and me."

When not otherwise occupied, he continued to draw his cartoons, this time depicting life in the military. "The guys really appreciated my cartoons, even the officers."

"In every Army camp in which I was stationed, I drew cartoons for the local camp newsletters," Hef said. "I got such a great response to them that I submitted my best ones to the national army newspapers *Yank* and *Stars & Stripes*. Both publications rejected them, calling them 'too amateurish.'"

He admitted that his "trials and tribulations" were slightly fictionalized for greater reader interest. He also claimed that some of the sexual exploits of his roommates were highly exaggerated, too.

One of his "roomies," for obvious reasons, was nicknamed "Long John." He'd saved up his meager pay for weeks for a special visit to a whorehouse positioned just outside the perimeter of Fort Hood.

After Long John had gotten a Saturday night pass, he visited the bordello. He later told Hef, "I bought all eight girls for a one-hour session. I had them all jaybird naked and lying on their backs on the carpet. I fucked every one of them, going down to the last of the line, a Mexican gal who looked no more than twelve. I spurted my baby-making juice into this little *puta,* as they called them south of the border."

Three weeks later, Long John invited Hef to go with him to the bordello. Hef turned him down. "I just wasn't interested in that kind of sex," Hef said. "As a soldier, I dreamed of more romantic encounters."

"Okay, suit yourself," Long John said. "I hope I don't wake up one night and find you going down on me. I suspect you're queer."

"You're safe," Hef assured the braggart.

***

After Fort Hood, Hef continued with his anti-tank maneuvers when he was transferred to Camp Gruber in the neighboring state of Oklahoma. Located near Braggs, Oklahoma in the Cookson Hills, 14 miles southeast of Muskogee, it was only two years old. In addition to field maneuvers, he learned to pilot a small plane.

"While at Camp Gruber, my 'maties' and I feared that any day we might be shipped to the battlefields of France. In June of that year, the Allied armies under Eisenhower had landed on the beaches of Normandy. The western push had begun to cross the Rhine into Germany. But Hitler had found our weakest link on the western front and sent his men into the Battle of the Bulge, creating a massacre on both sides."

"When I got a pass, I wandered into the neighboring town where I met this cute little bobbysoxer, a junior in high school named Lori," Hef said. "I invited her to the local movie house with me. It was showing Veronica Lake in *Hold That Blonde* (1945), a movie that had not yet gone into general release. To my surprise, she invited her girlfriend, a gal called Ethel, to go with us."

"We sat way up in the balcony and didn't get to see much of the film. Lori gave me deep kisses, and they were followed by even deeper kisses from Ethel. They let me feel their breasts. Those jugs of Ethel were much bigger than Lori's. The gals even unbuttoned my shirt and felt my chest, but their hands didn't wander below the belt, where they would have found something hard as steel."

At long last, in October of 1944, Hef got a furlough and headed back aboard an overcrowded train to Chicago. At home in Austin, he had a long-overdue "hook up" (his words) with Jim Brophy, still his best pal. Apparently, he never learned of Hef's involvement with Janie Borson. Any possible romantic entanglements between these two friends were avoided since Jim had moved on to another love, Muriel, who became the first Mrs. Jim Brophy.

"Janie went on to another lover at UCLA, and I devoted all my attention on my furlough to Millie, then enrolled at the University of Illinois."

He dated Millie—"no sex, but a lot a heavy petting." She came back to Austin to join him, and he was seen escorting her to a football game at Steinmetz, their former high school.

After his furlough, Hef was transported to Camp Chaffee (now the Fort Chaffee Maneuver Training Center), where in addition to typing, Hef received additional training in anti-tank maneuvers. Everything there was new, having been founded in 1941, the year America entered the war. Chaffee stood on the western border of Arkansas near the city of Fort Smith.

During the war, it sheltered a prisoner of war camp, populated by Nazi soldiers captured on the battlefields of Europe. The fort also provided housing for war refugees. As such, Hef got an up-close and personal look at some of the victims of "Hitler's War."

In the years to come, some of his fellow soldiers developed cancer and died because of the release into the air of fumes from burning asbestos during several fires at the base.

*[Following his induction into the Army in 1958, Elvis Presley endured "the most famous haircut in American history" at Fort Chaffee. The shearing was widely photographed, his picture appearing on frontpages across America.]*

"The war was still raging, but it looked like victory was ours, at least in Europe," he said. "There was a lot of talk that even if Hitler surrendered, the war against the Japs might rage until 1948."

After Chaffee, Hef was transferred once again, this time to Fort George C. Meade, named after a Civil War general. It stood on Maryland's Route 175, along the Baltimore-Washington Parkway near the Baltimore/Washington Airport. Dating from 1918 during World War I, it was also a prisoner of war camp, housing Nazi soldiers.

Since both the port of Baltimore and the capital at Washington were within an easy commute of the base, Hef, on furlough, got to visit both cities several times. "There was more sex going on in all the history of those cities, or at least that was my impression."

All of his fellow soldiers told him that "the gals are really putting out," Hundreds of single girls had flocked to Washington to work in wartime offices. "Many of them were easy lays," Hef said. "perhaps viewing it as their patriotic duty to let our servicemen screw them. They were known as 'Victory Girls,' although my buddies in the Army referred to them as 'Chippies.'"

"It wasn't exactly romantic sex," Hef claimed. "Just soldiers and their lays of the moment getting some momentary relief from the pressure of those horrible times we had to endure, with people getting massacred all over the world."

He recalled visiting a seedy tavern at the port of Baltimore. "I was with some guys drinking and listening to the top tunes on the jukebox when word was passed around that there was a gal with big tits in the men's room servicing one and all. The bitch had them lined up at the door for quickie blow-jobs. I joined the roster, with about eight other soldiers in front of me. The gal looked no more than eighteen, but she was a real sword swallower, taking on all comers. (Yes, that's the right word.)"

When he had to spend a lonely weekend at Fort Meade, he devoured copies of *Yank*, even though that periodical had rejected his cartoons. He was intrigued with a particular feature, called the "Pinup Girl of the Month." During the next decade, he was perhaps inspired by this feature when he regularly designated a "Playmate of the Month" in *Playboy*.

As a boy, Hef had followed the cartoons of Milton Caniff in *Terry and the Pirates*. Now, *Yank* was running cartoons of "Miss Lace," a sexy heroine who often appeared in a low-cut gown. As publisher of *Playboy*, he would later run Caniff's "sexy outtakes," as he called them.

This cover of *Yank* magazine became an inspiration in Hef's future when he launched *Playboy's* Playmate of the Month.

The editors at Yank selected Esther Williams as their Pinup Girl of the Month.

She went on to become MGM's "Daughter of Neptune" in numerous flicks.

After VE Day, with the German surrender, America shipped its warriors to deliver the death blow to Imperial Japan. To prepare for what was thought to be necessary—that is, an invasion of the Japanese islands—Hef was sent west to Oregon. Established in 1942, Camp Adair, a training facility north of Corvallis, was home to 40,000 soldiers and personnel, making it for a time the second-largest city in Oregon.

"When I was given time off, I roamed the countryside, a haven for fish and wildlife. Beautiful scenery, but not too many girls on the hoof."

During his stay, wounded sailors and Marines were shipped here for recovery and rehabilitation after battling the Japanese in the Pacific. As a volunteer, Hef worked with nurses in the wards, tending to the wounded.

He was still writing to Millie Williams but claimed, "I wasn't all that serious after all these months of separation. My heart was straying as I thought of other girls. I guess I had plenty of time to think about her at war's end. For all I knew, she was dating the captain of the football team."

After Oregon, Hef was shipped east again, this time to Fort Pickett in Virginia, near the town of Blackstone. "Another fort named for a Confederate general," he said. "I thought rebel generals were supposed to be traitors, battling the U.S. government."

Late in the summer of 1945, after Harry S Truman authorized the dropping of atomic bombs on Hiroshima and Nagasaki, Japan finally surrendered. "But my fellow Army buddies thought we'd still be shipped overseas as an occupation Army," he noted in his memoir. "This marks the beginning of the Atomic Age. Where does Goo go from here?" [He was referring to his cartoon character.]

He was dreaming of going home to Millie, writing her eighty letters between March and the end of August. "I dream of being with you," he wrote. "Of course, being a fella in love, I guess I think of some slightly different things than you do at times. A lot on the physical side."

"As a soldier I dated many gals," he confessed. "All their names became a blur: Betty Sue, Daisy, Stella, Mary, Rebecca, Jane, Dolly, and at least three Lindas. I never remembered their last names. Once, when I dated a Jewish girl, one of my roommates called me a 'kike lover.'"

"I grew up in a world of tolerance, mostly created by my mother. But with my Army buddies, I saw racial prejudice up close, finding it repugnant. There was a natural prejudice against the Japs because of the war, but some men used the most vicious comments for what they called 'niggers.'"

"I was hoping to get my discharge just weeks after the war," he said. "But in January of 1946, I was made a corporal, and my superior officer suggested I might consider a post-war career in the military. Not for me, buddy. I wanted to bolt. All over America, Johnny was marching home, often to find the girl he left behind married to some other guy. 'Dear John' letters were being sent to soldiers still abroad."

"Finally, in May of 1946, as the fields of Illinois were bursting into bloom, I took the train back to Chicago, filled with recently discharged soldiers. Our military duty was at an end, but I thought of all the poor boys who were buried under some foreign soil."

*[David Allyn, author of* Make Love, Not War, *wrote: "Hefner's two years in the Army constituted an important touchstone in what would eventually become* Playboy. *For real military discipline to exist, race, class, and other social distinctions cannot matter. The postwar migration of gay men to cities like San Francisco and New York contributed to more cosmopolitan world views among some veterans. Hefner, for example, developed more tolerant progressive views on homosexuality. His social attitudes, as later reflected in* Playboy, *were influenced by his time in the service, where he was exposed to men and women from a vast range of backgrounds."*

"The war in Vietnam was labeled Playboy *magazine's war," wrote Ward Just of* The Washington Post. *"In the war zone,* Playboy *was a rallying point and a communal touchstone when it arrived among powdered drink mix. Soldiers as a group leafed through its issues, and also read articles of the unraveling support of the war among citizens back home.*

"Stacks of faded and tattered copies of Playboy *crowded the bunks of soldiers in Vietnam and in sweltering tents in Kuwait during Desert Storm," wrote Alex Horton. "They were slid into Care Packages with a wink."*

"We prevailed," Hef said, "in spite of anti-porn lobbyists pressuring the Pentagon to keep* Playboy *away from the troops. What in hell were they expecting? That these guys reading* Playboy *would grab and rape their buddies?"*

*In time, however, readership declined among military men as the world went digital during the wars in Afghanistan and Iraq. Soldiers were offered salacious videos and photos for free.]*

IN WAR AND PEACE
FAME TAKES MANY FORMS

In Chu Lai, Vietnam, site of a U.S. military base from 1965 to 1971, a local beer joint and bordello billed itself as a Playboy Club, replete with logo and playmates.

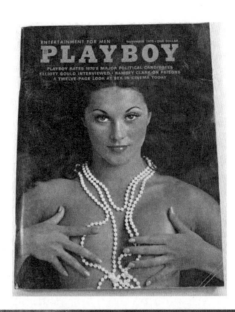

The lower photo shows the hole blown into the side of a U.S. HUEY helicopter shot down over the Mekong Delta during the ravages of the Vietnam war. The Playboy Logo, a prominent, proud, and defiant "morale-builder" during the darkest days of the fighting, remained unharmed.

Soldiers in the field asserted that the magazine helped boost their confidence, too. Displayed "on top" is the cover of *Playboy's* November 1970 edition.

Interpreted as a distraction from the gritty reality of war abroad and social unrest at home, it was released a few months after the expansion of U.S. military activities into Cambodia.

# Chapter Two

# ORGIASTIC & AVAILABLE

### AS AN ARMY VET & SWINGER IN POSTWAR CHICAGO

# HEF RUNS WILD

### ORGANIZING ORGIES & MAKING STAG FILMS
#### AFTER LEARNING THAT HIS BRIDE HAS BEEN UNFAITHFUL

#### IN HIS SEARCH FOR A JOB AS A CARTOONIST & ILLUSTRATOR, HEF IS REPEATEDLY REJECTED OR TRIVIALIZED

### THE FIRST EDITION OF *PLAYBOY* LAUNCHES IN DECEMBER 1953 WITH A

# NUDE MARILYN MONROE

### AS ITS CENTERFOLD

Although alert to the boost that her appearance on the cover of *Playboy* might have shot into her career (and the boost her likeness on its cover gave to the first edition of *Playboy*), Marilyn never really forgave Hef for the fact that she received no real reimbursement for his use of her likeness on the magazine's inaugural edition.

"On my first week back home in Chicago, I experienced what I called 'the ex-G.I. Blues,'" Hef said. "So did millions of other guys."

Consumed with confusion and doubts about his future, he asked himself many questions: Should he pursue a career in cartooning? Would he be able to think for himself after two years of having the Army do his thinking for him? Would he be able to make a living since millions of returning soldiers faced unemployment lines?

Although World War II had ended, 1946 found a world in turmoil, filled with the devastation of much of Europe and trouble spots around the globe. In the wake of the death of F.D.R. in 1945, President Harry S Truman now occupied the White House. At a speech in Fulton, Missouri, Sir Winston Churchill proclaimed that an Iron Curtain had encircled Eastern Europe. The U.S. granted the Philippines its independence. After many delays, Howard Hughes finally made a full release in 1946 of his controversial film *The Outlaw*, which Hef attended three times, mainly to take in the ample breasts of Jane Russell. That same year, Yogi Bari made his Major League baseball debut.

The first meeting of the United Nations was held at Long Island. Gas sold for fifteen cents a gallon, and the average cost of a new home was $5,000. On the French Riviera, the bikini made its debut that July. Around the same time, in America, Tupperware was introduced and the

In 1946, with his term of duty in the U.S. Army behind him, Hef had to find a new gig. His first question was, "How can I fit into this new age of post-war consumerism?"

(top photo) Service personnel returning from the war found a raft of consumer goods, temptingly presented with subliminal sexual overtones, awaiting their ability to pay for them.

(lower photo): According to this publicity picture from Air Canada, flight attendants could rejoice because of the addition of nylon stockings to their uniforms. Severely rationed during the war, the sheer, transparent fabric added to the subliminal sexual content of postwar consumerism.

first film festival was held at Cannes. The Cold War was launched, as tensions between the Soviet Union and the United States burst out. Also in 1946, U.S. military troops seized control of the U.S.'s railroads as 250,000 workers went on strike. Some 30 million Chinese were dying from starvation. By 1946, the War Crime trials at Nuremburg were in full swing, as the losers had to pay for their crimes against humanity in the recent war. Dean Martin made his singing debut. At a football game, Hef watched the "Fighting Illini" sweep to victory in the Big Name Championship. Reports surfaced that an unidentified spacecraft had crashed in the desert near Roswell, New Mexico, and the government was suppressing news of its discovery and information about the dead bodies of the space aliens found on board.

To perfect his skill as an artist, Hef enrolled in the Art Institute of Chicago, one of the best in America. Founded in 1879, the academy was one of the oldest and largest in the nation.

During his first summer as a civilian, he began dating Mildred Williams again, now calling her Millie. On some weekends, she packed a picnic lunch for them, which they enjoyed at Indiana Dunes at the Southern tip of Lake Michigan. He also invited her to go to the school dance but learned that she did not have a formal gown. With money he'd saved, he bought one for her. On the night of the dance, he showed up on her doorstep wearing a bow tie like Frank Sinatra did and presented her with a kiss and a corsage. After the dance, both of them drove to a secluded area where they indulged in heavy petting but no sexual intercourse. She told him she wanted to finish her courses at the University of Illinois and was afraid of getting pregnant.

To earn money, he tried to sell post-war vacuum cleaners door to door but found only five buyers. One woman told him, "A broom was good enough for my mother, and it's good enough for me."

That autumn, he, too, enrolled at the University of Illinois, where he majored in psychology. "I didn't want to be a shrink, but I did want to know

In postwar America, everyone had heard or could relay a joke about door-to-door salesmen and either their exploits as rakes or their dismal failures at their "art of the deal."

As one of the stages on his road to fame, even Hef tried his hand at door-to-door sales, emulating the dapper and congenial gent in the photo above, but with markedly less successful results.

what made men tick. Perhaps so that I could understand myself." As minors, he chose subjects more directly in tune with his goals—creative writing and art.

His classes in writing were held at the home of a noted screenwriter, Samson Raphaelson, who had written the script for *The Jazz Singer,* which had been released as the first talkie in 1927, and which had starred Al Jolson. He had also written the filmscript for *Suspicion* (1941) for Alfred Hitchcock, starring Joan Fontaine and Cary Grant. It won a Best Actress Oscar for her.

At the University campus, he roomed at the Granada Club, an independent boarding house run by a den mother who had lost her husband during the war. "She was like a surrogate mother to us," Hef said. His roommate was Bob Preuss, who said that Hef was the most popular boy in the dorm. "He always had a gang of fun-loving guys following him around."

He drew cartoons for the campus newspaper, *The Daily Illini,* often working with Gene Shalit, who would go on to become a famous TV film critic.

Hef edited the school's humor magazine, calling it *Shaft* and selling it for twenty cents a copy. In each issue, he ran a picture of the "Coed of the Month," fully clothed, perhaps a harbinger of the nude centerfold in *Playboy.* His cartoons made him a sort of campus celebrity. One series noted that with all the young men enrolled under the G.I. Bill, "There were five guys to every gal." He had a solution: Divide each woman into five parts. He found a flaw in that system, however: "There was bound to be a fight over which part of the female anatomy a guy got." He also said that if a man couldn't find a girl to date, he should know that, chemically speaking

At the University of Illinois, Hef drew cartoons and became the editor of *Shaft*, the campus humor magazine.

He selected a coed, Carol ("Candy") Cannon, as *Shaft's* "Coed of the Month." She remained, of course, fully dressed throughout her photo shoot, but she planted an idea in his head:

One day, when he was editor of his own magazine, maybe he'd run a Playmate of the Month...and a nude one at that!

(i.e., for their chemical content, at least), they are worth only ninety cents.

As a hobby, he took up flying lessons, which he'd first attempted during his stint in the Army, piloting a small plane over the skies of Oklahoma. In Illinois, he managed to get a pilot's license and performed aerial stunts in his Stearman Trainer, a biplane. From below, his schoolmates watched as he performed pins, loops, stalls, and Immelmanns [*maneuvers in which an airplane reverses its direction and increases its altitude based on the execution of a half loop followed by a half roll.*]

On a date with Millie, she presented him with three "cheesecake shots" of herself clad in swimwear. She assured him that the photos had been snapped by a girlfriend of hers, but he was not so sure. "I pinned them to the wall of my bedroom."

"As for Millie herself, I was confused about where our relationship was headed. Perhaps on the road to nowhere, like so many college romances. I soon learned that she had not been waiting for me while I was in the Army. She'd dated a number of young men at the University of Illinois."

"The first time I saw her when I got back, I noticed she was wearing some guy's fraternity pin. I was thinking about asking her to go steady, but she resisted at first, preferring to play the field, I guess. But I finally talked her into it. During my time at the university, we dated all the time. I called it two and a half years of foreplay. That's how long I needed to graduate, since I took summer classes. Other than heavy petting, we still hadn't done the dirty deed. She was still afraid of getting pregnant before graduation. A few times, we almost went all the way, and she seemed willing, but I pulled back at the last minute. I was twenty-two years old when I got my first piece of ass. I went to her bed as a virgin. I had wanted to save myself for her."

"In this book on sex I'd read, I learned that a young man reaches his sexual peak at nineteen. That meant I'd missed out on three years of fun, perhaps a lot more. I knew some guys who told me they had started screwing around when they turned fourteen."

"From my Army training, I knew about rubbers. We were taught to put one on before putting it in. I was exploding with sexual energy and could hold back no more. I was getting god damn tired of being a virgin."

The big event—i.e., the loss of his virginity—occurred at the seedy Hotel Walford in the neighboring town of Donford, where a little room cost $12 a night.

"We stripped nude in front of each other, marking the occasion of my putting the better part of myself into the innards of another human being. I admit that's not the most romantic way of describing our encounter. I'd waited for years for this coming-of-age ritual, but it was soon over and rather mechanical. A real disappointment. I feared I'd failed as a lover, as she didn't seem to enjoy it too much. I didn't understand why people got so hysterical about sex. It didn't appear to me to be such a big deal. In spite of that, we still talked about getting married as soon as we graduated."

***

Almost daily, Hef obsessed about his future career, still dreaming of breaking into publishing on some level, preferably as a cartoonist. "A cartoonist must have strong ideas to put across, and I want to make some statement about sex, although I fear my views are too progressive for the average American's taste and morals. I also thought I might write short stories, as I had done as a boy, and even a novel about a young man coming of age and giving in to his sexual desires like a male nympho."

It was at this time that he, like thousands of others, rushed to the bookstore to purchase a copy of the first edition, published in 1948, of Alfred C. Kinsey's *Sexual Behavior in the Human Male*. A zoologist at Indiana University, Kinsey ignited waves of shock and outrage with his findings. Information revealed in the 12,000 interviews he conducted with sexually active men addressed subjects formerly viewed as taboo and challenged conventional beliefs about sexuality.

Hef devoured page after page of the massive volume, which sent his mind spinning, wondering how he could incorporate his findings in his own work and cartoons. He was still at the university when Kinsey pub-

"No book had greater influence on me than *Sexual Behavior in the Human Male* by Alfred Kinsey," Hef said.

"There was a lot to be learned from the doctor—first, women were just as sexually active as men, and men, though they will deny it, have a tinge of homosexuality in them—maybe more than a tinge."

lished his book, and Hef wrote about it in *Shaft* magazine. "If American laws were rigidly enforced, ninety-five percent of all men and boys would be jailed as sex offenders....Our moral pretenses, our hypocrisy, on matters of sex have led to incalculable frustrations, delinquency, and unhappiness."

Privately using "locker room talk," with his fellow dormitory roommates, he shocked some of them with his frank talk about sex. "In spite of their outward sexual pretensions, American men under the sheets, especially in the dark, do *everything*. Forgive my potty mouth, but they are sucking cock, fucking their buddies up the ass, eating pussy, nibbling on nipples, sucking toes, rimming 'rosebuds,' and doing it not just the old-fashioned way, but in every acrobatic position."

Kinsey wasn't much for pinning labels on men, viewing them as neither hetero or homo, more bisexual than anyone had known. He suggested that almost every man, except the most Neanderthal, had both impulses in him, although some concealed it better than others.

The doctor claimed that nearly 46% of all males experienced attraction to other men and that at least 37% acted on that impulse during the course of their lives. When Kinsey later published his report on women, Hef learned that half of all married men committed adultery, and that one out of every four women had sex with a man not her husband.

He later admitted that the Kinsey report made him wonder about his own sexuality. "Was I a secret queer? After all, I was crazy about Fred Astaire. I put on cologne. I typed. But Ernest Hemingway also typed and was a symbol of the macho male. Of course, he typed standing up at an elevated table so he wouldn't get a fat butt."

"Later, from the mouth of Gertrude Stein and others, I learned that Papa Hemingway may have harbored a secret desire for his fellow novelist, F. Scott Fitzgerald. At least he once asked Fitzgerald to go with him to a urinal in Paris so he could check out his dick."

"And yes, in the open showers in the Army barracks, I spent quite some time checking out the cocks of my fellow soldiers. I assume that all men do that, if for no other reason than finding how you size up with the competition. Perhaps that is a perfectly natural thing to do."

"Based on what I read in Kinsey, I blamed the repressive society I grew up in, a lot of the Victorian repression coming from my mother, who had learned it growing up on the plains of Nebraska. A lot of my male friends claimed I had sex on the brain, talking about it all the time. In fact, I thought about sex every thirty seconds. It seemed I was not alone in doing that. Regardless of what I did in the future, I wanted to go into some form of publishing to liberate the American male."

***

*"In the early 1950s, I not only married my college sweetheart, but initially accepted the routine embraced by almost all of my generation. You got a job, you got married, got a place of your own and started raising a family. It was a time to put aside the dreams of childhood. It was a time to grow up. To begin living, in effect, the life my Puritan parents lived. Although my own Puritan roots ran deep, I hated it!"*

—Hugh Hefner

Millie Williams graduated from the University of Illinois in June of 1948 and was soon granted a position as a schoolteacher in Southern Illinois. Every weekend, Hef took a train from Chicago to be with her.

Because of the time he'd spent in the Army, he did not graduate until February of 1949. She told him she wanted to be a June bride, and they planned their future together. During Christmas of 1948, he'd already given her a small engagement ring, all that he could afford.

He had more than marriage on his mind after graduation. Facing no prospects, he set about trying to find a job. No newspaper in Chicago wanted a cartoonist.

When the weather turned warm, Hef and Millie spent a week at Devil's Lake in Wisconsin, boating, fishing, swimming, and making love. He called it "a time of sexual intimacy and shared innocence when both of us were getting ready to face the realities of life."

"This guy snapped a picture of Millie and me in our bathing suits," he said. "I looked like a 115-pound weakling in my trunks, a failure in one of those Charles Atlas bodybuilding ads. I nicknamed myself 'Slim Slimmerville.' Glenn Bishop was a popular

Despite his dozens of later assessments of himself as a rebel and iconoclast who didn't believe in marriage, Hef on his first trip up the aisle had all the accoutrements of the conservative bourgeoisie of the 50s, That included matrons and maidens of honor, bridesmaids, white tulle, wedding veils, and corsages.

In the center are newlyweds Millie and Hef.

model at the time, appearing only partially clothed, mostly in swimwear. He was the pinup boy of 1950s homosexuals. He had the kind of body I envied, a real swimmer's build without being overly muscled. But I was too lazy to spend all day in a gym."

In April of 1949, two months before his marriage, he got a job with the Chicago Carton Company, and was placed in charge of hiring and firing at $45 a week. He disliked the work, principally because of its employment policies. His bosses warned him, "No Jews, no niggers." He held onto the post for five months before he exploded in anger at one of his bosses and stormed out of the plant.

He had nothing lined up as a replacement. He applied to several companies for work but was turned down by each of them. In his spare time, he sent his cartoons to the major Chicago newspapers, but each of them rejected his work.

Although he had no means of support, Hef nonetheless married Millie on June 15, 1949, at St. John Bosco Rectory, the ceremony attended by family and a few friends. Jim Brophy was his best man. Although Hef had been reared as a Protestant, Millie came from a strict Catholic family. That was not a problem for him. He had long ago quit attending church, and to the shock of his mother, he referred to himself as an agnostic, perhaps an atheist. The wedding ceremony was officiated by a Catholic priest, but in the rectory, not inside the main church.

After the wedding, a reception was held in the neighboring American Legion Hall. Since money was scarce, it was not a catered affair. Family members and their friends brought along a main dish or desserts for the buffet. Hef remembered a lot of potato salad and plenty of baked goods.

In a car borrowed from his father, Glenn, Hef and his new bride drove to the Birchwood Lodge at Hazelhurst, Wisconsin, where they spent a week.

As he later confided to Brophy, "The honeymoon was not satisfactory, and I received the most devastating news of my life. Millie confessed she was not a virgin, that I was not the first. That dubious honor belonged to her athletic coach, a real jerk. Since I'd been saving myself for her, I viewed her betrayal as playing me for a chump. Her confessing to me would have far-reaching consequences. Just you wait and see."

After the honeymoon, and because of the postwar housing shortage, the couple returned to Austin, Illinois, and moved in with Hef's parents. In their two-story, red-brick home, they occupied what had been the room of Glenn and Grace when he and Keith were growing up.

On their first night back, Millie promised that she would never sleep with another man for the rest of her life. Manifesting some kind of sexual life in the same house with Hef's parents proved to be a problem. Grace complained that she could hear their bed springs squeaking, which she could not tolerate.

"I wasn't the only G.I. who returned home to find that their wives or girlfriends had not been faithful," he said. "Many guys came back to find the girls they'd left behind had been turned into 'Victory Girl' tramps and trollops in their absence, breaking their promises to be faithful."

On reflection, it seemed amazing that one of the most sexually liberated of all American men would be so shocked by Millie's confession. But he was. In the months ahead, he used her indiscretion as his excuse "to go wild sexually" (his words).

When he wasn't hunting for a job, he created the cartoons for two separate comic strips, each of them inspired by such successes as *Dick Tracy*, *Little Orphan Annie*, and girl reporter *Brenda Starr*.

The first one, *Freddy Frat*, was based on his college adventures, and the other, *Gene Fantas, Psycho-Investigator*, depicted a detective in pursuit of a homicidal, Jack-the-Ripper-style maniac who darts out from alleys at night and stabs women to death with a butcher knife. Hef had not lost his appreciation for horror. He sent the prototypes for these comic strips to various syndicates, and each rejected him, as did such magazines as *Esquire, the Saturday Evening Post, Judge,* and *Gags*.

Faced with such failure on the job market, he looked elsewhere and enrolled at Northwestern in January of 1950. He decided to major in sociology, hoping to become a college professor somewhere in Illinois. "I didn't want to leave the state."

Postwar fantasies and the baby boom: The upper photo shows the ideal and the dream of a soldier's return to home and hearth in the years after World War II.

The lower photo demonstrates the demographical crush of babies born in the aftermath of the postwar courtship and mating games.

Hef's preoccupation with intimacy, sex, and its social and moral fallout was perfectly timed.

He drove to Northwestern's campus at Evanston in his newly acquired 1941 Ford coupe with a rusty fender.

During his first year, he was assigned to write a term paper on the subject of his choice. In the thesis he researched and compiled ("Sex Behavior and U.S. Law"), and to some degree inspired by his exposure to *The Kinsey Report*, he chose to attack the repressive sexual stigmas and laws of the United States.

"Why should men and women having some fun be subject to arrest? They are just heeding the call of nature in their loins."

Depending on the state, there were laws even outlawing "premarital sex" and "lewd co-habitation," whatever that was. Fellatio, even between a man and a woman, was illegal in some states, as was (believe it or not) masturbation.

He suggested that most of these laws be eliminated in the cases of two consenting adults. He also advocated the dismissal from the books of any law regulating homosexuality between two adult men or women.

His professor defined the conclusion of his thesis as "an abomination," giving him a B-minus for his advocacy, but an A for his extensive research.

*[A few years later, in the 1950s, the American Law Institute would publish* The Model Penal Code. *Its recommendations would virtually agree with those of Hef's document.]*

After only a semester at Northwestern, he dropped out. "I didn't want to be a teacher after all. I wanted to be a creator. But of what?"

He found work as a copywriter at the Carson Pirie Scott Department Store. Every morning he headed for his $40-a-week job on the Chicago Loop. "It was the most satisfactory job I'd ever had to date, as I was allowed to do illustrations and layouts. I even considered a career in advertising."

At long last, what he thought would be the dream job of his life opened up. He was hired by *Esquire,* a magazine whose Vargas Girls and Petty Girls had intrigued him since he was a teenager, at $60 a week, with the understanding that he'd be assigned to its art or editorial departments. He was bitterly disappointed when his duties evolved into producing copy for the subscription department and assigned the task of attracting new readers.

*Esquire* seemed less and less exciting to him in its depiction of pinup women. However, he did admire it as a pioneer in articles of interest to the urban male, devoted to men's fashion and style. He also credited *Esquire* for buying essays from such noted authors as André Gide, Alberto Moravia, and Julian Huxley. He told Brophy, "If I were the publisher of *Esquire,* I'd run lifestyle essays for the guys, and articles from famous writers. I'd also feature pictures of beautiful nude women."

It soon became obvious that he'd been hired by *Esquire* at the wrong time, as it was rapidly moving its offices out of Chicago, heading for Manhattan. He was invited to go along with the move. Knowing that his expenses would increase dramatically in a far more expensive location, he asked for a five-dollar weekly raise, a proposal that was rejected by his boss.

*Esquire* would live to regret that decision, as in the 1950s and beyond, *Playboy* would become its major competition.

Preferring to stay in Chicago, he found another job with Publisher's Development Corporation for a salary of $80 a week. Every month, it released issues of *Modern Man*, *Modern Sunbathing*, and *Art Photography*. Because each of them featured nudes, they were not allowed to be shipped to subscribers through the U.S. Postal Service, and therefore depended entirely on newsstand sales for their survival.

He was assigned to *Modern Man*, established as recently as 1951. Again, he would have preferred the editorial department, especially the position of the male editor who rounded up nude models and had them pose for the magazine. Instead, he was assigned a job in the circulation and sales department.

Perhaps in the back of his brain during his gig at *Modern Man* Hef may have conceived *Playboy*. *Modern Man* featured soft-core pornography, articles on sex, humor, the latest in automobile design, and essays on popular culture. In addition to nude models, it also ran sexy pictures of the emerging "Popcorn

Hef's magazine-publishing Alma Mater was *Modern Man*, a publication whose ideas inspired his later creative statement (and erotic style) at *Playboy*.

The upper photo, published in 1954, shows a buxom and very blonde strumpet in the style of what was later emulated by celebrity celluloid queen Jayne Mansfield.

The lower photo, published in 1957, showcases the charms of Sophia Loren with the banner headline, "HOW ITALIAN MOVIES BEGAN THE BIG BOSUM BOOM."

Hef and thousands of pre-feminist American men were enthralled.

Blondes" of the 1950s, notably Marilyn Monroe, Jayne ("letting it all hang out") Mansfield, and Mamie Van Doren, plus an array of their other big-busted imitators.

The publisher of *Modern Man* was George von Rosen, whom critics labeled as "a smut peddler," long before the term was applied to Hef himself. Von Rosen was a controversial figure, writing and publishing articles about "The Bazoom Girl" or "The Red-Headed Panther." He even published an interview with a stripper-prostitute, who earned her living disrobing for conventioneers in Chicago. Another featured story in his magazine was about "How Stag Films Are Made."

Von Rosen later became America's chief advocate of the 2nd Amendment, publishing a magazine called *Guns*. It later morphed into *American Handgunner,* which ran an article entitles "How to Shoot a Man."

Later in life, although it was clearly an inspiration, Hef would not admit that he was inspired to launch *Playboy* by *Modern Man,* or that he owed a debt to Von Rosen, whom he loathed. Hef dismissed the magazine as "a titty rag for horndogs, something for Neanderthals to jerk off to."

Finally, he could no longer tolerate the ferocious Von Rosen and his arrogant harangues. He resigned and stormed out of the office. Early in 1953, he found another job, one hardly suited to his aspirations. No more nude models. For $120 a week, he joined the staff of a magazine called *Children's Activities.* It reached a readership of 250,000. His highest salary to date enabled him to buy a new TV set for Millie and himself.

"The theme of the magazine bored me, and I soon began writing movie reviews for *Dale Harrison's Chicago.* "I was a film addict, and now I was getting paid to write critiques. Hollywood was releasing some of the finest films in its history."

Hef gave rave reviews to Bette Davis for *All About Eve,* to Gloria Swanson for *Sunset Blvd.,* to Judy Holliday for *Born Yesterday,* to Olivia de Havilland for *The Heiress,* to Loretta Young for *Come to the Stable,* and to Susan Hayward for *My Foolish Heart.*

As much as he loved his new job, he was still far from his goal of becoming a cartoonist. He continued submitting applications to newspapers and magazines but received only rejection slips. Ultimately, he decided to go into self-publishing with monies he'd saved.

In the spring of 1951, he published *Hef's Toddlin' Town: A Rowdy Burlesque of Chicago Manners and Morals.* For its cover, he selected a cartoon he'd drawn of a big-breasted stripper being ogled by three horny men.

The book became his biggest success to date, generating sales of $2,031.35. It was reviewed in the Chicago press, and he appeared for interviews on radio shows.

The *Chicago Herald-Tribune* raved, "It will make you laugh if you know Chicago After Dark. I hope it makes a pot of money."

The *Chicago Daily Tribune* gave it a glowing review "for its depiction of cartoons satirizing Chicago nightlife and mores."

He was invited to appear on radio in a show hosted by Hugh Downs on the NBC radio network at WMAQ. He was quite respectful of Hef's book. After leaving Chicago in 1954, Downs would go on to become a household name in America. *[Downs was the co-host of the NBC News Program from 1962 to 1971.]*

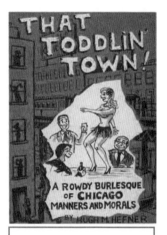

Authored by Hef, this *risqué* but well-reviewed travel guide to the raunch centers of Chicago, published at the dawn of the sexual revolution, was one more experimental step on Hef's road to Bunny-hopping glory.

Hef appeared on another radio show, this one for CBS. Called the "Mike and Buff" interview show, its hosts were Buff Cobb and her husband, Mike Wallace. Wallace would go on to greater glory, reigning for nearly forty years as the host of *60 Minutes*. In the future, Wallace interviewed Hef as the publisher of what Wallace called "that dirty magazine."

He was also invited to appear on *Ernie Simon's Man on the Street* interview show. In *Toddlin' Town*, Hef had drawn a picture of a mammoth ape carting off a scantily clad woman. To gain publicity both for his book and for his appearance on the show, he hired an actor to put on a gorilla outfit and to appear on the sidewalk beside a stripper screaming for help.

In the autumn of 1951, pleased with the success of *Toddlin' Town*, he drew up the prospectus for a new magazine called *Pulse*. He began shopping it around, hoping to find financial backers. His magazine would be about high-profile figures in Chicago, featuring nudes and articles aimed at the urban male.

He found no one interested, and the magazine died, but many of his ideas for *Pulse* about urban sophistication and lifestyle ultimately found their way into *Playboy*.

As a young man still trying to find his footing in the world, he had developed cultural icons, reading the works of Charles Darwin and Sigmund Freud. For a while, his favorite reading was D.H. Lawrence's *Lady Chatterley's Lover*. Since it was banned in the United States. It had to be published abroad and slipped through customs.

With money coming in, he rented a small apartment for Minnie and himself. "It was just large enough to hold my 78-rpm collection," he said.

Its address, located in what later became a high-crime district, was 6052 South Harper Street on the South Side of Chicago. He wanted it decorated in the style of what he imagined a hip Greenwich Villager would create for himself. For their first-born, he adapted a small room, hardly bigger than a spacious closet, and decorated it as a nursery, adorning the walls with blown-up cartoons of the character known as Pogo.

He also began to keep up with the political news of the day, deploring the communist "witch hunt" launched by Senator Joseph McCarthy of Wisconsin and his "henchman," a vicious attorney named Roy Cohn, who led a secret homosexual life. Hef predicted that if America continued to threaten free speech, its political landscape would evolve into what had been depicted in George Orwell's novel, *1984*.

For a while, he came under the influence of Ayn Rand after reading her monumental *The Fountainhead*, a romantic and philosophical novel she wrote over a period of seven years. Her book centered on a young architect, Howard Roark, and his struggles and idealistic clashes with the compromises of society. Hef identified with its main character, and saw the 1949 movie version, starring Gary Cooper, three times. He would later interview Rand for *Playboy*. He interpreted her novel as inspiration for his oncoming role as an individualist not afraid to attack middle-class conformity during the early years of the Eisenhower administration.

Hefner, and many other Postwar devotees of "the good life," were fascinated by the erotic adventures of the British aristocrat, Lady Chatterley, in the arms of her studly gamekeeper, as penned by D.H.Lawrence.

During the book's obscenity trial in the U.K. in 1960, one of the most respected bookstores in London (Foyle's) consistently ran out of inventory.

In talks with his best friend, Jim Brophy, Hef told him, "I feel I'm on the dawn of doing something big, but I don't know what it is yet. A lot of ideas are buzzing through my head. I also have a sexual restlessness, a man not satisfied with his marriage, finding it dull. I crave excitement, and, by God, I'm gonna find it!"

Millie was already pregnant when she and Hef moved into their small apartment at 6052 South Harper, which in only a year would become the birthplace of *Playboy*. She had not planned on starting a family until her husband had became more established in his career, but her Catholic doctor had refused to give her birth control information and also rejected her request for a diaphragm.

Weighing six pounds, 12 ounces, Christie Ann Hefner, the future CEO of Playboy Enterprises, was born on November 8, 1952. Although Hef loved his daughter, he would become an absentee father as the girl grew up.

Right before Christmas of 1952, Hef teamed up with Jim Brophy to present a charity review for the alumni of Steinmetz High. Once again, Brophy agreed to dress in drag, as Hef sang a rousing rendition of "Walking My Baby Back Home" to him. Their comedic skits and songs received loud applause.

"It brought back good memories of our school days when we were happy, even though the world was at war," Hef said.

As 1953 roared in, Hef became obsessed with the creation of his own men's magazine.

Brophy and his wife, Muriel, were frequent visitors to Hef and Millie's "bohemian" apartment. As Brophy recalled, "They reminded me of a brother and sister, not a newly married couple setting out in life. In all the time I knew them, I never saw him hug or kiss her."

Once, when Hef was alone with Brophy, he confessed to him, "Millie has absolutely no interest in sex. It's like fucking a dead log with a hole in it. I've tried several tricks to heat her up, to no avail. She just lies there and endures it, much as I imagine my mother doing with Glenn. I hope Muriel is not like that. The idea of being a family man does not appeal to me."

"Millie and Hef must have had sex some time," Brophy said. "After all, they became the parents of a son, David Hefner, in August of 1955."

For diversion, Hef began to host parties at his apartment, inviting couples over. Ignoring Millie's objections, he screened stag movies which he'd rented from a dealer on the black market. It appeared that on one occasion, he'd rented two "blue movies" that Joan Crawford had made in the 1920s before becoming a Hollywood star. One of them depicted her engaged in lesbian sex.

To enliven many an evening, he asked his guests to join him in strip poker, each of them peeling down to their underwear. On another night, he invited his new close friend, Eldon Sellers, and his wife, Janie, to join them in a game of switching partners. Millie objected and retreated to their bedroom. Apparently, the projected foursome became a *ménage à trois* instead.

Younger brother Keith once revealed that Hef wanted to switch wives for the night. Millie objected and retreated. "It didn't happen that night, but I suspected he had sex with my wife, Rae, although I was not sure. At any rate, that caused a temporary rift between us. Talk about sibling rivalry!"

In the same apartment building that Hef occupied with his wife and daughter, he met a couple downstairs, Terry and Betsy Bloom, who had moved to Chicago from Macon, Georgia, In the Windy City, he had found a better job working in a factory.

Hef invited the Blooms to join other couples for screenings of his latest stag films.

One night, he visited them in their apartment as a prelude to a three-way. He liked it so much that he suggested he return the following evening with a male friend he knew at work, who had a movie camera. Hef wanted the Blooms and two other couples to appear in a stag movie, *After the Masquerade*. Each of the performers would wear a mask to conceal his or her identity.

The home movie was filmed the following night with six couples in all sorts of positions. This would mark the beginning of Hef's hobby of making porn films for his private collection. In time, in Hollywood, his stag movies would include some celebrated couples. It is believed that before his death, he ordered his private collection destroyed, lest a film leaked out, causing major embarrassment after the fact.

On another night, he had a three-way with his friend Sellers and "a hot, shapely brunette," Hef had picked up. "Without our wives, of course," he said.

One night, he confessed to Jim Brophy that he had engaged in homosexual sex. "I had started to advocate that homosexuality should not be outlawed by the government. I was curious about that form of sex, which had never appealed to me. Setting out one night, I visited a gay bar in Chicago, where I allowed

Hollywood Blue: A film fan and porn connoisseur, Hef spent serious "quality time" screening, among others, some of the "blue movies" starring Hollywood celebrities during their early, lean years before they were famous, when they sometimes desperately needed the money.

Pictured above is Joan Crawford, strutting her stuff for a porn movie captured during her early years on the fringes of show-biz.

61

myself to be picked up by this young musician from New Orleans."

"He was a good-looking guy, no more than twenty-two, and was very blonde and rather thin, a bit on the fem side. He seemed girlish enough for my experiment. If he had been a super macho football type, I would never have gone through with it."

"I went back to his apartment and stripped down for him. Never once did I touch his cock. But he swallowed mine right to the base, an experienced sword swallower. The guy was terrific. I mean, I blasted off twice before leaving that night. He performed acts on me I'd never experienced before, like licking balls and tonguing my rosebud. Thrilling. To my knowledge, most women back then didn't do that other than, perhaps, a prostitute. In time, other women would perform the same sexual acts on me, but that musician kid was the first to turn me on to that kind of fun."

Once, after working late and having no dinner, he stopped off at this all-night diner, ordering a coke and a juicy cheeseburger. His waitress, whose name he vaguely remembered was Miriam, flirted with him and later agreed to meet him outside when she got off from work in an hour. After his little supper, he listened to music on the jukebox until it was near closing time.

He waited outside for her to emerge from the diner without her uniform, and then drove with her to a secluded spot a few blocks away. "We did it right in the car," he confessed to Brophy. "She knew her business and showed me a good time. It ended too quickly. I hadn't given her the customary 25¢ tip at the diner, so I presented her with a ten-dollar bill, for which she was grateful."

His life was about to change the day he visited his doctor for a checkup. In the examination room, he met an attractive nurse, Phyllis Milton. "She was brash, brassy, and brittle, and very, very sexy, with dyed blonde hair, big boobs, and a free-wheeling, 'anything goes' outlook on life."

"We had sex two nights later and continued to do so for almost a year. At no time did I ask her if she had a husband. I figured that was her business."

"I like any form of sex that's illegal," she said to him one night. "I also like girls."

"As I remembered her, she may have been the first lesbian I ever had sex with. Perhaps I should call her bisexual. As far as I was concerned, she did it like any young woman, perhaps with more oral skills than most. I also recalled she never wore panties, because she'd read that Marilyn Monroe didn't bother with underwear. The word 'love' never entered our relationship. It was just a sexual affair, no more, no less."

As Hef told Brophy, "As I was to become the chief advocate for the sexual liberation of the American male, I first had to liberate myself."

***

*Playboy,* the most widely read men's magazine in the world, had humble origins. Its first words were typed on a secondhand Royal typewriter acquired for twelve dollars. That machine was placed on a ten-dollar card table in a modest kitchen in what later became a high-crime district on the South Side of Chicago. Its unprepossessing address became the birthplace of *Playboy* magazine.

It was here that Hef wrote a promotional letter to news dealers and potential subscribers, announcing the first edition of *Playboy's* original title, *Stag Party* magazine. He claimed that it was being put together "by a bunch of men from *Esquire* who stayed in Chicago and didn't move to that magazine's new offices in Manhattan." It became the most successful promotional letter in the history of publishing, generating 70,000 responses.

But he had a problem: There was no magazine.

The idea of publishing his own men's magazine had been a fussy idea in Hef's head for many years. The concept for his magazine had not existed in mainstream America before, but in 1953, it began to take shape. Most popular magazines at the time were aimed at families, or else were summaries of the week's news, as exemplified by *Time* magazine.

Hef knew that his magazine's main competitor would be *Esquire,* which had run into trouble with the U.S. Post Office. It had been charged with distributing obscene materials through the mails. Based to some degree on those troubles, the magazine had become more staid than before, eliminating its famous "Vargas Girl" cartoons.

"I found *Esquire* duller, more sterile, less provocative, and afraid of depicting nude breasts," Hef claimed. "In their cartoons, they were putting clothing on their depictions of women, right down to dressing female slaves in the Sultan's harem."

To reinforce its revised, more "wholesome" editorial policies, *Esquire's* publisher told the press, "Our magazine is ridding itself of the last vestigial traces of the girly flavor that characterized our publication during the war years. Readers of the 1950s will find a cleaner, newer, and better *Esquire.*"

Two other men's magazines on the market were *True* and *Argosy,* which mostly appealed to the sportsman, seeking outdoor adventures including camping, fishing, and hunting. "Its articles were not literary, more about how Hitler had fled to Brazil in 1945 or what the space aliens who landed in the desert of New Mexico looked like," Hef said.

"Both *True* and *Argosy* perpetuated the myth that a woman's place was

63

in the kitchen," Hef said. "A man belonged in a smoke-filled room playing poker, or else in a barroom having a few beers with his buddies. If not that, then going camping with the guys. At home, he belonged in the living room after dinner, sitting and watching a football or basketball game."

"In contrast, I was not an outdoor man, but a man of the boudoir. I was also an incurable romantic, devoted to wine, women, and song, not necessarily in that order. *Esquire* was

Hef did not launch his sexually provocative experimental magazines into a cultural void. America in the 50s was a roiling, percolating stewpot with thousands of avid readers and a long list of pulpy competitors, at least some of which influenced his editorial and business choices during the early years of *Playboy*.

Two of the most popular of these sexual and shocking weeklies included the consistently macho and swashbuckling *Argosy*.

Another was *True* magazine, a publication that was loosely associated with, and—insofar as its focus of steamy heterosexuality, at least—*True Adventures, True Crime, True Romance, True Detective,* and *True Confessions.*

losing readers, and my aim was to pick up those guys who didn't renew their subscriptions."

"After the war, a new American male had emerged," Hef said, "and I wanted to appeal to this guy who dominated the blooming, blossoming consumer economy. His dad lived through the depression, but this new man was no longer the blue-collar laborer, returning to his home to support his wife and kids in the suburbs. His evening of fun? Watching sports on his TV set."

"Other, younger and more sophisticated men had returned from the battlefield and had settled in such cities as San Francisco, Los Angeles, New York, or Chicago. After they'd seen Paree, they didn't want to return to that Puritan home in Indiana. A different lifestyle was emerging for this urban male."

"I wanted a publication that was breezy and sophisticated, freely depicting nudity without the pussy shot. My mag would be a quality publication with lifestyle articles, even by famous writers. It would have class to attract upmarket advertisers, including cigarette manufacturers and liquor distributors. We were going to give *Esquire* a run for its money, attracting males more interested in fashion, modern furnishings, fine wines, and women, lots and lots of women, the less clothes the better."

He stated his intent at the very beginning: "We need more love on this planet. We should make love, not war. And then in the process, maybe, you could also do it with a little style. That's where I come in."

By the spring of 1953, he mostly ignored his family, as he was deep at work on his concept for a magazine. Often, he worked until three or four o'clock in the morning, getting little sleep. He seemed to thrive on sheer determination, as he plotted nude centerfolds, provocative but humorous cartoons, even rough layouts and features.

He talked about his idea to all of his friends and acquaintances. "Most of them thought I was a nutbag, and many told me it would take at least three or four years, maybe more, for a magazine to become successful, and that I needed at least a million dollars in the bank, even more, to finance it during the long and lean years."

He named his magazine *Stag Party*, its symbol an elk's head transplanted over a male body. Dressed in a smoking jacket, it would be depicted smoking a cigarette (not a pipe) in a long-filtered holder, with a highball in his other hand. The setting would be ultra-modern, perhaps with a Picasso print on the wall and a statue of a bare-breasted Venus. On his nightstand would be a novel by the Russian writer, Vladimir Nabokov, and on his hi-fi would be a recording of the songs of Ella Fitzgerald.

He had purloined the title *Stag Party* from a 1931 book of cartoons, *The Stag at Eve,* which had depicted a red-colored elk on its cover. "The animal looked horny, with a gleam in his eye," Hef said.

His father, Glenn, rejected his son's request, but his mother, Grace, had saved a thousand dollars. At first, she agreed to give him $500 to purchase his centerfold art, but eventually upped it to one thousand, which was all she had in her savings account. "She didn't believe in the concept of my magazine, but she had faith in her son," Hef said.

His close friend, Eldon Sellers, had come aboard at the magazine's inception, and he man-

Hef decided to call his new magazine *Stag Party*. He took the name from *The Stag at Eve*, a cartoon book first published in 1931. Hef felt that a "horny" stag would capture the kind of sexually active male to whom his magazine might appeal.

For the symbol of his magazine, he chose to depict a stag surrounded with cocktails in his bachelor pad.

aged to raise $8,000 from 45 investors. That sum included $2,000 from a well-heeled girlfriend.

Knowing that he needed help with his layout, Hef turned to cartoonist Arv Miller for help. Although Miller had been clever with his cartoons, Hef wan't pleased with the layout of the prototype he turned in to him.

He'd heard that Art Paul was a talented illustrator and artist, a graduate of the Institute of Design, known as the "Chicago Bauhaus." Hef decided to ask him for his help with the layout. Without an appointment, Hef went to see him in his studio walk-up on Van Buren Street in the Loop.

Paul would always remember his first meeting with Hef. "He looked like a hobo wandering in from panhandling off the street. His coat was frayed, and he had a three-day growth of beard. His stiff neck evoked Igor, Frankenstein's helper."

Hef had brought along a copy of Miller's initial layout for *Stag Party*. After looking over the pages, Paul told Hef that the layout resembled screen magazines of the era and was too much of a rip-off of *Esquire*. "What you need is more of a linear and uncluttered look, perhaps almost Oriental in simplicity, even futuristic."

Paul agreed with Hef's concept for his magazine. "I want a publication that will thumb its nose at all the Puritan values, reflecting the world in which my parents were born into. I want to be a warrior against the so-called family values of the 1950s."

Paul was talked into creating a different, more innovative and sophisticated look but he warned Hef that *Stag Party* faced a rough road ahead and that the chances of its failure were awesome. Nevertheless, he signed on but only on a freelance basis. Hef didn't have the money to pay him, so he offered him stock in his venture.

He told Paul, "I had to beg and borrow every penny I could raise to pump into my magazine. If it fails, my family will be out on the streets. But a man like me who is a dreamer must reach for the stars."

Both men agreed that *Stag Party* should offer three-year subscriptions for only thirteen dollars.

That night over drinks in a local bar, Hef expounded on his dream for the magazine.

"I want to strike a blow for

Art Paul, the commercial artist whose genius steered the *Playboy* vision, firmly and early, onto a successful look, feel, and aesthetic.

cultural freedom to help young men escape from the rigid morality of the Eisenhower years," Hef told Paul. "It seems that the men who won World War II are back home but retreating to the suburbs where every one of them is expected to settle down in a modern house, get married, have some kids, buy a family car, and conform to the existing morality of the day. I want to tout the simple pleasures of leisure, where our Playboys can have fun and seek entertainment in night clubs, all the while enjoying a healthy sex life."

As each day progressed, Hef seemed more and more pleased to have Paul aboard. Writer Stephen Heller claimed, "*Playboy* would have languished in netherland between pulp and porn had it not been for Art Paul. He rode in to rescue the day."

Hef worked side by side with Paul as his new art director. He didn't object when Paul rejected all of his cartoons as "too amateurish, too high schoolish."

"For a while, I was performing too many duties, from editor to publisher, from proofreader to promotions manager," Hef said.

Just weeks before the first copy of *Stag Party* reached the streets, a letter arrived from *Stag* magazine threatening to sue Hef for copyright infringement. He had to come up with a new name...and be quick about it.

He met with Sellers and others to try to find a suitable name, and they suggested *Sir, Bachelor, Gentleman, Pan, Satyr,* even *Top Hat,* the name of a 1935 movie starring Fred Astaire and Ginger Rogers.

Sellers, who would become the co-founder and executive vice president of the new venture, remembered that his mother had once worked for the Playboy Automobile Company, which had a short life as a car manufacturer. No sooner was the new name out of his mouth than Hef beamed, "That's great! *Playboy* it will be!"

Millie didn't like the new title, telling Hef, "It sounds like some relic of the 1920s Jazz Age when college men wore raccoon coats."

Before Hef came along, the term "Playboy" usually

"*The Nation's New Car Sensation*"
THE **PLAYBOY**

PLAYBOY MOTOR CAR CORPORATION
BUFFALO, NEW YORK                    JUNE 13, 1949

DID YOU KNOW that for a brief period after World War II, THE PLAYBOY referred to a car as well as to a hedonistic womanizer?

Founded by a Packard dealer, the Playboy Motor Car Corporation was established in 1947 with the dream of providing small, cheap ($900 each) cars for postwar consumers. Plagued with distribution problems, they produced only 97 cars—each a prized collector's item today—before declaring bankruptcy in 1951.

had negative connotations, evoking a rich ne'er-do-well, chasing after women. In society in Paris, such a man might be called a *bon-vivant*. It was never applied to a womanizing poor boy, but to a man of means in pursuit of the good life of luxury cars, lavish "digs," world travel, horse racing, gambling, and lots of women.

In time, Hef became known as "The Playboy of the Western World," a term that was first used by John Millington Synge in 1907 as the title of his classic Irish drama.

The cartoon mascot designed by Miller was quickly changed to a rabbit, although the stag's hoofs remained visible in the altered drawings. The stag got beheaded, a little animal known for its sexual appetite taking its place. "Bullwinkle became Peter the Rabbit," Hef said.

In time, of course, Hef would become known as "The Czar of a Bunny Empire."

The magazine's rabbit head logo with the cocked ear and tuxedo bow tie would be developed by Paul and would appear in the January 1954 issue. Initially intended as an endpoint for the articles, Paul sketched the logo in an hour. Hef liked it so much he decided to use the logo as a symbol of *Playboy's* corporate identity.

*[After the magazine got launched and grew steadily, Paul abandoned his other freelance work and signed on as the new magazine's art director, a position he held for the next thirty years. During his tenure,* Playboy *received hundreds of awards for excellence in graphic design and illustration.]*

\*\*\*

Before the launch of *Playboy*, Hef came up with a novel idea. To his knowledge, it had never been attempted before. The 3-D craze was sweeping across American movie houses, with members of the audience being handed cardboard-frame eyeglasses through which they'd view the action and special effects onscreen. In one film, a knife was thrown right at the camera, seemingly zooming into the audience. Many viewers screamed and in some movie houses, women fainted.

"Imagine," Hef told his partner, Eldon Sellers. "A woman's big boobs in 3-D. It'll be spectacular."

Later, when Sellers figured out how expensive that would be, the plan was abandoned. The 3-D craze itself turned out to be just a passing fad for the movies.

He began his search for "the perfect female specimen" to become his centerfold. In some quarters, readers assumed that he was the first publisher to run nudes. Actually, he was not, since sleazy magazines featuring nudes had been around for decades. Most of them were underground and often mailed out, against Post Office regulations, in brown paper wrappers.

Film historian Willian Osgerby wrote that these "skin rags presented a world of swaggering machismo, prurient voyeurism, and sexual violence."

Hef's desire was to publish a magazine appealing to the middle-class male. The ideal consumer would not have to hide it in his underwear drawer but could place it on the coffee table in his living room. "I want to take *Playboy* out of the gutter and make a nude magazine respectable with noteworthy features on the *Playboy* lifestyle. Most legit men's magazines put their focus on the outdoors. I wanted *Playboy* to be devoted to indoor pleasures, including those enjoyed in the boudoir."

Hef faced the awesome task of finding the first nude, and Sellers presented him with some two hundred pictures of naked women who had posed for calendars exhibited mostly in men's toilets at gasoline stations, in locker rooms, in gyms, and on the bedroom walls of teenage boys—at least until their mothers ripped them down.

He tested Sellers' patience by rejecting dozens upon dozens of nudes, even though admitting that all of them had a certain sex appeal and that the women were "well stacked." In his words, "No Audrey Hepburn breasts among the lot."

In 1950, he had been impressed with a blonde starlet, Marilyn Monroe, whom he'd seen in *The Asphalt Jungle,* a *film noir* where she had curled up suggestively on a sofa as the mistress of the much older Louis Calhern (born in 1895).

Although Monroe faced strong competition in *All About Eve* (1950) from Bette Davis and Anne Baxter, Monroe had stood out in his mind as

the beautiful but relentlessly stupid *protégée* of George Sanders. Playing Addison DeWitt, a theater critic, Sanders sends her over to disarm a wealthy producer, presumably for some financial gain of his own. In her scene, just before sauntering off to do his bidding, she laments, "Why do they always look like scared rabbits?" as a cynical older observer defines her character as "a graduate of the Copacabana School of Acting."

In reference to Marilyn, as Hef recalled years later, "I was turned on by

Blonde Ambition: Marilyn plays a thespian adventuress in *All About Eve*, appearing with George Sanders above in 1950.

this hottie."

He'd heard that in the spring of 1949, Monroe had posed nude for a minor photographer, Tom Kelley, who paid her fifty dollars for the entire season. Her car had recently been repossessed, and she had not eaten a full meal in two days. Based on her zeal to become a movie star, she feared that the nude photos would one day be exposed.

That indeed, happened after her breakthrough appearance in films— each released in 1953—that included *Niagara, Gentlemen Prefer Blondes*, and *How to Marry a Millionaire*.

Hef learned that John Baumgarth had purchased the rights to the nudes from Kelley, and that his office was on the west side of Chicago. "How convenient for me," Hef said.

Operating on a skimpy budget, he went by to negotiate with him, fearing that he'd demand $5,000 for the rights, since Monroe had, since the photos were snapped, become a hot property.

To his surprise, the hustler of calendar nudes wanted only $600. Concealing his delight, Hef appeared like that was far too steep for him. "Make if $500," he said, "and we've got a deal."

Baumgarth agreed to that ridiculously low price, mainly because his first calendar depicting Monroe had not sold well in 1950. Sales had picked up after the release of *All About Eve* (1950) and as her fame with movie audiences grew.

"The $500 I borrowed from my mother I used to buy the Monroe nudes," Hef said. "But I never told her that."

Hef wrote, "Marilyn and I were born the same year, and we both spent a lot of time in movie houses, dreaming the impossible dream. She wanted to be the next Jean Harlow, and I wanted to be as dashing as Errol Flynn, as sophisticated as Fred Astaire, and as tough as Humphrey Bogart."

When Sellers was shown the nude, he said, "Marilyn is lightning in a bottle—perfect for us."

"She's really dreamy, drop-dead gorgeous," Hef said. "She's not a mere mortal, but a goddess. We'll show those perfect breasts of hers, not her pussy. Every male reader will want to nibble those tits."

Mark Edison in his book, *Dirty! Dirty! Dirty!* captured the essence of the Monroe allure best:

Tom Kelley posing with one of his famous Marilyn pix. "I hired her to pose for $50. It was the best investment I ever made."

> *"From the tips of her curled toes to her painted mouth, her sleepy eyes, her tangle of curly, red-blonde hair, the submissive, come-to-me curve*

70

*of her arched back, the way her hand turned out against the soft and red-velvet set, and everything in between, especially everything in between, she was the one-in-a-million* über-*doll, the Platonic, neo-Platonic, classical, Romantic, and post-Impressionistic ideal of a* dream fuck."

Before publication, Hef put through a call to Tom Kelley in Los Angeles. "Hell, I didn't know Marilyn would become so famous. I would have held onto the rights. It would be my retirement fund."

He told Hef that, "Marilyn was at first reluctant to pose, but was desperate for a few dollars. After the shoot, I asked her to go down on me and then let me fuck her. She was most compliant."

*[In time, Hef would acquire all the Monroe photographs from the Kelley estate and the copyrights held by John Baumgarth, too.]*

Monroe became *Playboy's* first "Sweetheart of the Month." Hef wrote the introduction to her nude: "*She's as famous as Dwight Eisenhower and Dick Tracy, and she and Dr. Kinsey have monopolized sex this year. She is natural sex personified. It is there in every look and movement. That's what makes her the most natural choice in the world for our first* Playboy *Sweetheart.*"

*[In the years to come, Hef would purchase the burial vault adjacent to Monroe's remains in the Westwood Memorial Park Cemetery. "I want to spend eternity beside my beloved first cover girl and nude centerfold," he claimed.]*

\*\*\*

By the time *Playboy's* January issue hit the stands, it sold even more copies than the Monroe edition, and the February issue also saw a sweep in sales.

"We were just rolling in dough," Hef said, which, of course, was a gross exaggeration.

The January issue was the first *Playboy* to refer to the woman on the centerfold as the "Playmate of the Month," that name having been suggested by Millie.

In his search for investors in his venture, Hef had solicited a Chicago businessman, the owner of a prominent local department store who hesitated, fearing that the magazine's policy of featuring nudes would doom it.

In April of 1953, Hef wrote him: "There's nothing illegal about printing and distributing nudes. Calendar, magazine, and book publishers all do a big business in the undressed female form."

Based on its increased profitability, Hef decided to move the magazine into larger quarters. A vacancy became available at 11 East Superior on the

Near North Side of Chicago, across from the landmark Catholic church, Holy Name Cathedral. *[Hef's new premises had previously housed a manufacturer of "kneeling pads" widely used during religious ceremonies.]*

Hefner gradually commandeered the building's two uppermost floors, reserving a corner room on the top floor for his office. It adjoined a small kitchenette and a "bedroom closet" with enough room for a dresser and a cot. A small shower room with a toilet opened off his tiny bedroom.

Here he lived day and night for five days a week, promising Millie that he'd come home on weekends. But by April of 1954, he rarely honored that commitment. He'd go for weeks at a time without seeing either his wife or his infant daughter.

One day he received three short stories by an unknown writer, Ray Russell, who enclosed a note: "Why not run some stories later than those published in the 19th Century?"

"After a few conversations on the phone, we agreed to meet in a bar," Russell said. "Based on his voice on the phone, I expected he would be in his sixties and look like a combined Dwight Eisenhower and John Foster Dulles. Was I ever surprised. This scrawny-looking kid shows up with a crew cut and a pink turtleneck, wearing penny loafers and Bix Beiderbeckean white socks."

Hef also appraised Russell's appearance, later comparing him to a "miniature Orson Welles."

"When Hef opened his mouth, I was won over as he talked persuasively about his hopes, dreams, and concept for *Playboy*. The next day I quit my job and signed on."

On his first day of work, Russell showed up in Hef's office with a sign pinned on his fly that declared "I TRY HARDER."

Hef was amused. Within the week was amazed at Russell's talent and suggestions. He started out as editor and was later promoted to executive editor.

Hef's longtime supporter, Eldon Sellers, was in charge of circulation and promotion. Joe Paczek was brought in to assist Paul in the art department, and Marge Pitner was secretary and bookkeeper. Hef's father, Glenn, was always available to help with the bookkeeping, too.

In the first issue, Hefner wrote about the reader he wished to attract: "*Playboy* is meant for you if you're between the ages of 18 and 80. If you like your entertainment served up with humor, sophistication, and spice, *Playboy* will become a very special favorite."

"Mothers-in-law, especially mothers-in-law, sisters, and wives are advised to stick to reading *Woman's Home Companion.*"

At the printers, Hef chose not to date the first edition, because he didn't know if there would be a second one. In November of 1963, *Playboy* hit the newsstands of Chicago. Every day, Hef walked the streets visiting various vendors to see if male readers were buying his magazine. "Seeing it on sale was one of the great moments of my life," he recalled.

His fear of failure turned out to be unfounded. *Playboy* sold nearly eighty percent of its print run, 54,000 copies

Paul was not pleased with the first issue, and set out to make it better. He cited the Marilyn Monroe edition as a "mere sketchbook for what *Playboy* is really going to be."

Because he had no money to purchase articles, Hef used stories on which the copyrights had long expired, including ones by Arthur Conan Doyle of Sherlock Holmes fame. He also ran a lusty novella about adultery by Giovanni Boccaccio (1313-1375) as it appeared in the *Decameron Tales*. Also featured was a "strip quiz," as well as The Men's Shop (a display of the latest fashions); a rave about Cuban food and *Cuba libres,* and even a recipe for "Sob-Sob chicken." *[One disgruntled reader claimed, "I tried your Sob-Sob chicken. The dish left me in tears."]*

The recycled articles also came under fire. "Can't you run anything in *Playboy* that was written after 1889?" wrote the manager of a boxing studio. Another attacked the Decameron Tale. "The 14th Century has ended," a sports equipment salesman wrote in. "As for the music, it is now 1953. Tommy Dorsey and his band are *passé."*

Sales were picking up, as news vendors across the country inquired about this revolutionary new magazine with the Marilyn Monroe nude, in glorious color, no less.

Jerry Rosenfield, head of Empire News, hailed it as "the hottest magazine we've ever distributed, even though it sells for fifty cents instead of the usual quarter."

Almost overnight, some of the leading periodicals in the nation hailed the debut of *Playboy, Time* magazine calling it "slick and sassy, the latest phenomenon in American publishing." The prestigious *Saturday Review* even wrote about it: "Hugh Hefner's *Playboy* makes the back issues of *Esquire* look like trade bulletins from the W.C.T.U."

Time was running out, and Hef had to make a decision about a second edition of *Playboy*, whose release would be scheduled for January of 1954. He knew how many copies of the December edition had been distributed, but the returns had not come in yet when he decided to forge ahead. He threw himself feverishly into turning out another issue, improving on the first one.

"We couldn't come up with another Marilyn Monroe, but for our centerfold, I found the ideal Miss January. A shapely brunette, her breasts were pneumatic." Once again, he'd found her in the studio of John Baumgarth, from whom he'd purchased the Monroe shot.

He was so devoted to his magazine that his marriage was almost on life support. He was working twelve to sixteen hours a day in his kitchen. Although he lived in the same apartment with Millie, he paid her little attention.

"I wasn't anything like a playboy, with no time for women, not even my wife," he said.

For the first three editions of *Playboy*, he still worked out of the cramped kitchen with its smell of lima bean soup. He wasn't living the life of the *Playboy* image he projected. As if to symbolize his existence, his vintage Chevy broke down and had to be towed to the junkyard. With money he'd earned from the first edition, he put a down payment on a 1954 fire engine-red Studebaker convertible with a white top.

*Playboy* had been an instant success on the newsstands, and it also had launched Hef into the role of guru for a new generation of young men. This crop of emerging readers had more money than their depression-era fathers and more amusements to pursue—not just uninhibited sex.

In February of 1955, he wrote: "What does a man say when his dream comes true? What words to use? Elation? Joy? How can a guy possibly express his overwhelming feeling?"

He knew there were pitfalls ahead, and he'd have to confront them. But he was determined to meet the challenges. "Watch me go!" he said.

One afternoon, he shared a sexual fantasy with Paul. "I saw this cartoon of a sultan in a harem surrounded by naked women. That night, I had a dream that I was that sultan. I wanted to become rich myself and able to have my own harem, at least eight naked women whose sole aim at night was to satisfy my sexual appetite. Each of these cuties would have only one purpose in life and that was to surrender to my every command and to fulfill my every desire, if it were only to peel me a grape."

"Only eight beautiful women?" Paul asked. "Why aim so low?"

That summer, he came across a quotation that he adopted for life, printing it in his own handwriting, framing it, and hanging it on the wall. It read: "Imagination is intelligence with an erection."

"I didn't know who said it, but I'm sure it wasn't Hitler."

# Chapter Three

# Hefner Meets Victor Lownes
# "THE PLAYBOY OF CHICAGO,"
### Ultimately, the Most Influential Member of His Administration

### Inspired by Postwar Europe and its Permissive Censorship Codes, Hef and His Team Define the Playboy Aesthetic.

## Building a Brand
### Hef Adds Cartoons, Editorials, Artwork, Lifestyle Tips, and Merchandising.

### Janet Pilgrim! Bettie Page! Gina Lollobrigida! Sophia Loren!

## Dating, Orgies, and Sex Before AIDS
# PLAYMATES OF THE MONTH
### Censorship & Suppression from the U.S. Mails

The hottest women of the mid-20th Century all made their way into the pages of *Playboy*.

Hef did not confine his taste in women just to blondes. He shared the charms of Bettie Page (left), Gina Lollobrigida (center) and Sophia Loren (right) with his readers.

Although he would have liked to seduce all three of them, he managed to score only with Miss Page.

With the first money he earned from *Playboy,* Hef upgraded his image. He sold his Studebaker convertible and paraded into the Chicago showroom of Cadillac. After a negotiation with a young salesman and a commitment from him to subscribe to *Playboy,* he ordered an Eldorado for $6,500. He wanted it in a shade of bronze and delivered in three days.

The salesman could deliver car and the color, but it would take three weeks. Hef agreed to that.

He also decided he needed new housing for his family and relocated them to a more luxurious apartment at 5801 North Sheridan Road, overlooking Lake Michigan.

Millie had wanted another baby, and on the rare occasion he had sex with her, she asked him to "not use a rubber."

That had resulted in the birth of his second child, a son, David, born in 1955. Hef hadn't really wanted the child, but he had fathered it. "With the growing demands on me, I knew I could not be a proper dad, either to Christie or to my infant son. But if it made Millie happy, I guess it was okay. At least I could offer my growing family a better life even if I weren't there at night to share it with them."

Millie later complained, "I had a hard time trying to convince both of our kids growing up that their father loved them. Perhaps to compensate, I gave and gave of myself. I didn't want them to feel like orphans. The painful truth was, Hugh didn't want children. It was also hard for me to explain later when they learned their father had a girlfriend, maybe more than one, a whole squadron of bushy-tailed girls."

She remained unaware of what Hef's new womanizing buddy, Victor Lownes, had said of her husband: "Hef was not just fucking the girl next door he'd invited her to the football game. He was also taking on the whole squad of cheerleaders."

"I was spending more time with my art director, Art Paul, than I was with Millie," Hef said. "I think *Playboy* would never have become the classy magazine it was without his taste, talent, and imag-

Hef was a preening proud father that day in 1995 when he gave Christie Hefner away to her new husband, William A. Marovitz. He offered the groom some good advice: "Be good to my little girl...or else!"

The absentee father of her youth, later in life, formed a close bond with his only daughter. He even made her the CEO of the Playboy Empire.

ination. Art did for publishing what Andy Warhol did for fine art, blurring the line between what hangs in galleries and what appears in magazines."

"Art's wife, Bea, was also talented, and she designed some of our covers. We always had the *Playboy* rabbit either prominently featured or else tucked away somewhere—but always there. Art even managed to get Andy Warhol to draw his conception of our rabbit in silhouette, a vision in pink and purple."

As the magazine rapidly increased its sales, it soon became obvious that *Playboy* could no longer remain a two-man operation. Editors, artists, photographers, and both promotion and circulation managers were needed, along with secretaries to handle letters and an enormous volume of mail.

"By the summer of 1954, we had become a buzzing beehive, making honey for our newly acquired male readership," Hef said.

He designated Ray Russell as his associate editor; Pat Pappangelis as his personal secretary; and John Mastro as his production manager. Hef's father, Glenn, was called in to set up a bookkeeping system which was then taken over by Marge Pitner. Hef's close friend, Eldon Sellers, who had previously worked for Dun & Bradstreet, launched the magazine's advertising department.

"It was a real team effort," Pitner said. "All of us on the small staff felt we were creating something of cultural importance, far beyond nude centerfolds."

One of the key players Hef hired was a Japanese American from Southern California, Vince Tajiri. During World War II, he had served with the U.S. 442nd Infantry. This regiment of 4,000 men became the most decorated in the history of American warfare. It was composed almost entirely of second-generation American soldiers of Japanese ancestry.

Tajiri played a key role in graphically establishing *Playboy's* identity as a lifestyle guide. He did this through the magazine's spin on fashion, cuisine, and wine. Playmates often had to pose for as many as 125 photographs before Tajiri distilled from the raw shots a carefully selected handful to show to Hef.

\*\*\*

Hef was the final arbiter in the selection of every issue's Playmate of the Month. He often rejected dozens of nudes until he found the most enticing model. "I want a girl who stirs up fantasy in my reader, a sex object to inspire masturbation until a guy can get to a real honeypot."

His first two-page centerfold featured Margaret Scott, a beautiful model with blondish hair who was Miss February 1954. Wearing strings of pearls, she was photographed within a pink-toned boudoir, her coiffure tossed to the left side of her face. It was said that she inspired the lyrics for the song, "My Angel Is a Centerfold."

At least throughout the 1950s and into the 60s, Hef ordered that no pubic hair or hint of genitalia be visible in any of the magazine's photo layouts.

"I ran into occasional trouble with my centerfolds," Hef said. "Let's face it: The 1950s were one uptight era. Back then, if you ran a cartoon of a bare-breasted mermaid, you had to snip off her nipples. The depiction of a nipple on a cover was not acceptable on newsstands."

When Hef himself came to direct nude centerfold shots, he paid special attention to a model's nipples. If they were "too brown," he made them look rosy by daubing them with rouge. He also liked them to stand up.

Hef often rubbed ice cubes across a model's nipples to "make them look like they do when a man sucks on them." *[He credited this "discovery" to Jean Harlow. It was said that before filming her scenes in the 1930s, with the intention of making her nipples more prominent, she had famously massaged them with ice cubes before donning garments crafted from form-fitting satin.]*

He always ordered that his nude centerfolds be shot in rooms chilled with roaring air conditioning, so their nipples would be prominent—"no sweaty boobs in *Playboy*."

Sexy, saucy Margaret Scott became the first two-page centerfold for *Playboy*, a format which made its first-time appearance on newsstands in February of 1954. That was the month *Playboy* featured a cover with a beauty (PLAYBOY TOURS THE HOTTEST SPOTS IN PARIS) whose charms were artfully concealed behind feathers.

In 1993, *Playboy* began manufacturing a series of trading cards as a means of "archiving" photo-spreads from as early as 1954.

For decades, his centerfolds would remain the big attraction of *Playboy* despite the laughable but widely circulated *cliché*: "I buy *Playboy* just for the articles."

Playmates, of course, reflected Hef's own personal taste in women. He wanted that All-American look, as opposed to the sleekly glamourous creatures who emerged from the makeup and wardrobe departments of Hollywood studios.

For his early centerfolds in 1954, he once again approached John Baumgarth, who had sold him the Marilyn Monroe calendar nudes that had graced the magazine's inaugural issue.

"*Playboy* legitimized nudity by embodying it in arguably the most famous woman in America," wrote film critic Roger Ebert. "The results are all around us, even to this day."

Hef also approached the photographer who had actually snapped those pictures of Marilyn, Tom Kelley, appreciating his taste and searching for more.

He learned that Kelley photographed more than nudes, having shot dozens of celebrities with their clothes on, too. He photographed such movie stars as Clark Gable, Greta Garbo, Gary Cooper, and Marlene Dietrich; and world leaders who included Franklin D. Roosevelt, Sir Winston Churchill, Dwight D. Eisenhower, and, in time, John F. Kennedy.

For a while, Kelley and Hef collaborated, as Hef liked the relaxed look of his selections.

Neva Gilbert, Miss July of 1954, recalled, "Tom even brought his wife to the studio, so I knew there would be no monkey business. He had me lie on a tiger rug with red-painted nails for $20 an hour. I didn't think my pictures were dirty, but in good taste. He made me look quite lovely."

Tiring of nudes snapped by outsiders, Hef eventually decided to use his own in-house photographers to shoot the centerfolds. He paid them $1,500 for a layout, plus another $1,000 when the magazine hit the stands.

He had no trouble finding models. Almost daily, young women across America sent him nude photographs of themselves as a way of auditioning for a layout. If Hef were turned on by one of these models, he paid her way to Chicago to pose naked.

He conveyed his personal expectations to any photographer he hired for a shoot: "I want young, fresh-faced talent, mostly in the 18- to 20-year old age range. I'm seeking that 'Baby Doll' look, a young girl ready, able, and willing to be deflowered by a dangling dick on one of our *Playboy* readers."

His new friend, comedian Lenny Bruce, applauded his choices, calling them "winning, real kissy-kissy looking chicks. Hef, keep it up (I mean that two ways). Give us more of your sweet, pink-nippled, blue-eyed spring chickens."

Hef conceived of something special for the first anniversary edition of *Playboy*, published in December of 1954. He hired a model from Milwaukee, Terry Ryan. Photographer Norwin Bigelow applied her body makeup himself, snapping some 150 pictures of her for a six-page pictorial called "Photographing the Playmate."

His photos depicted her arriving at the studio, fully clothed, and evolving through various stages of undress. After the magazine appeared on newsstands and was shipped to subscribers, mailbags of letters arrived from young men requesting her phone number.

By 1954, after the publication of his sixth edition, Hef had become increasingly aware of the cultural impact of his carefully selected nudes. Images of his Playmates were fast replacing wallpaper in college fraternity

A year had passed since Hef's debut edition with Marilyn--enough time to showcase the burgeoning talents of both Hef's art team and the concretization of the *Playboy* lifestyle.

On this, the first anniversary edition, the hip, liberal, high-class gloss of *Playboy's* image of the urban male emerged in the form of the rabbit (a mature, well-dressed man with a taste for beautiful women in luxuriantly macho settings).

houses. Businessmen hid copies of *Playboy* in their desks, servicemen in their footlockers. "My Playmates reigned as the new American Love Goddesses, replacing those celebrated pin-up girls of World War II, especially Rita Hayworth and Betty Grable," Hef said.

Writing in the *National Review,* M.J. Sobran said, "Many of Hugh Hefner's Playmates have a rather self-conscious fallen woman look about them. Breasts thrust forth, tummy tucked in, legs coyly crossed come hither, reader—chin up, mouth open, tongue between bared teeth, even half-open but gazing right at you. Off camera, this 'goddess' perhaps chews gum and says 'yeah' to any question."

Veteran editor Nat Lehrman said, "The *Playboy* of 1953 is not all that different from the *Playboy* of today: Indeed, many of the Playmates of the 1960s and early 70s evoked those of the late 1950s. Of course, in time the choice of models showed the diversification of race, as much of America is no longer lilywhite."

Hef soon became aware that some members of the public vehemently objected to depictions not just of a woman's breasts, but of her navel, too. Through the run (1965-1970) of the hit TV sitcom, *I Dream of Jeannie,* pretty, perky Barbara Eden—despite her skimpy costume—was not allowed to show her navel.

The revolutionary comedian/performance artist, Lenny Bruce, rose up to defend his friend. "If you uptight fuckers out there are offended by the human body, don't blame Hugh Hefner. Put the blame squarely on the maker himself. Tell God he's offensive."

***

Beginning in 1953, and continuing until his death, Hef had to cope with a barrage of criticism, some of it valid, but in some instances, irresponsible and reckless. One that he remembered as particularly stupid came from San Francisco, arguably the most liberal city in America. In an interview, the chief of police there made an outlandish claim: "Hugh Hefner is peddling smut to lure our youth into juvenile delinquency and ultimately into communism. Where is Senator Joseph McCarthy now that we need him?"

During his magazine's first year of publication, Hef developed a powerful enemy in Washington. In January of 1953, Dwight Eisenhower—as a reward for helping get him elected when he was delegate chairman from Michigan—had designated Arthur Summerfield as the 54th Postmaster General of the United States. Summerfield was a great admirer of the Production Code of America that since the 1930s had yielded great power over what movie directors were allowed to put on the screen. He wished to impose those same censorship standards on books and magazines, selecting Hef as a major target to destroy.

Scary Moralists from the Age of Sputnik:

This press photo from 1961 shows one of Hefner's fiercest enemies, U.S. Postmaster General Arthur Summerfield, with his formidable wife, in 1961.

In October of 1954, Hef applied for second class mailing privileges with the U.S. Post Office, knowing that it would save him thousands of dollars. He'd become aware, during his tenure with *Modern Sunbathing,* that that magazine published nudes much more provocative than those within *Playboy,* including vagina shots.

Six months went by, and no word came in from Washington, a departure from applications which were usually processed within a month, so he knew something was wrong.

Subscriptions were arriving in mailbags, and his staff was not large enough to handle all the demands. The editorial staff also couldn't keep up, which led to Hef having to skip an issue in March of 1955. In his April edition, he apologized for the delay and promised his reader an extra magazine to make up for it.

Even when he was paying for first class delivery, local redneck postmasters in such states as Georgia and Mississippi often delayed delivery of *Playboy* through their facilities for weeks at a time. In some cases, they trashed or even vandalized the magazine, or else stole it, sometimes taking it home with them for their perusal in private.

Hef worked for *Modern Sunbathing,* which published provocative nudes, including shots of female genitalia. The November 1961 issue (see above) was typical.

The magazine avoided conflicts with the post office by being available for sale only on newsstands.

Not only that, but in Chicago, the local Post Office held up the processing of the organization's mail for weeks at a time, disrupting production.

Angered, Hef declared war on the post office and fought them all the way to the Supreme Court. In November of 1955, the High Court ruled in his favor, even ordering that the organization's mail should be delivered without delay. To help defray Hef's legal expenses, the court ordered him to be refunded $100,000 "henceforth."

Victorious, Hef announced to the press, "*Playboy* will be edited in Chicago—not Washington. Furthermore, we think Summerfield should stick to what he was hired for: To deliver the mail."

\*\*\*

Hef was among the first American publishers to feature semi-nude pictures of the Italian bombshell, Gina Lollobrigida. Her voluptuous body rivaled the shapely charm of her rival, Sophia Loren. "It was the Battle of the Bosom," Hef said. "Gina was almost as well stacked as Sophia but lacking her talent."

As a tribute to her "assets," the French coined the term *lollobrigidienne*, meaning "curvaceous and with breasts in the style of Gina Lollobrigida."

Her sultry looks thrilled Hef, as they did her lovers. They were rumored to include the Cuban dictator Fidel Castro and Dr. Christiaan Barnard, the South African surgeon who pioneered heart transplants.

Hef obtained copies of some of her early movies in which she appeared semi-nude. His favorite was of Gina in a revealing harem costume in a nude bathing scene from *Beauties of the Night* (1952). "You could just see the crack of her delectable *derrière*," he said.

Although he couldn't engage either Lollobrigida or Loren as centerfolds, he became aware of the value of French and Italian (i.e., uncensored) films as a source for erotic publicity stills.

Hef had first seen Gina on the screen when she had co-starred for John Huston in *Beat the Devil* (1953), opposite Humphrey Bogart and Jennifer Jones.

"She's like a modern apartment building with outside balconies," Huston told the press. In the heated Italian-language sniping that followed, Gina's rival, Sophia, also spoke to the press. "Gina's personality is limited. She is good at playing a peasant, but she's incapable of playing a lady."

Hef also sent for stills from one of her recent films, *Altri Tiempi* (1952, *aka, In Times Gone By.*) In it, "Gina played a sexy country girl who just can't say no," he said. "My kind of woman. I wanted my readers to be

At the time Hef met her, the curvaceous Gina Lollobrigida was deeply immersed in the girlie scene of pulp magazines and movies, and so constantly in the eyes of European filmgoers that in French, a new adjective ("*lollobrigidienne*") was coined to describe a voluptuous, desirable, and undulating woman.

In Europe at the time, films were showing women displaying nudity far more than the censors of America would allow. Here, "Lollo," as the Sultan's favorite, appears in a tantalizing shot (pundits described it as "Gina Hits the Harem") from the widely publicized Franco-Italian movie, *Les Belles de la Nuit* (*Beauties of the Night*).

tantalized by glimpses of Gina's breasts, belly, and buttocks."

Loren was the other Italian goddess of Hef's dreams, and he wanted to feature her in the magazine. When he first gazed upon her exposed bosom, Hef agreed with the latter-day assessment of Alan Ladd, her bisexual co-star in *Boy on a Dolphin* (1957; aka *Ombres sous la mer; aka Il ragazzo sul delphino*). "It was like being bombed by watermelons."

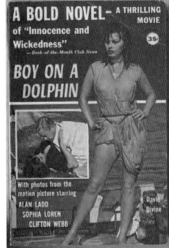

In researching Loren's early film roles, Hef discovered that at the age of seventeen, she had appeared in the 1951 Italian film, *Era lui…si! si!*, (aka *It's Him…Yes! Yes!*) and been billed as Sofia Lazzaro. In the French-language release of that film her amble but teenaged bosom was topless.

He read her amusing quote in the press: "I am not just another cheesecake pot. Everything you see, I owe to spaghetti."

After reviewing her photos, Hef recalled that he said, "Sophia should be sculpted in chocolate truffles so that the world can devour her." [*Actually, he stole that line from Noël Coward.*]

\*\*\*

In preparation for the release of *Playboy's* December 1954 "First Anniversary" issue, Hef wanted "something special." He conceived the idea of a six-page feature he entitled "Photographing a Playmate." He hired photographer Norwin Bigelow to depict Terry Ryan, a model from Milwaukee,

Hef could not get Gina Lollobrigida to pose for a centerfold. Neither could he get Sophia Loren, who was emerging fast as the greatest export from Italy since pizza.

He found her a sexy turn-on when she appeared scantily clad in *Boy on a Dolphin* (1957) with Alan Ladd. But he got to see a lot more of her in the movie *Era lui…si! si!*. In English, that translates as *It's Him! Yes! Yes!*.

for a behind-the-scenes look at what went into the creation of a *Playboy* centerfold.

Ryan is seen fully dressed, arriving for her photo shoot. She is then photographed stark naked, wearing only what was known as "Joan Crawford fuck-me high heels." The feature included views of Bigelow applying body makeup to her nude, voluptuous, and shapely figure.

Two shots have her topless, wearing an open *negligée* and later, a robe. In each shot, her legs are discreetly crossed to cover her crotch. The final picture is of Hef and Bigelow making their final selections from dozens of photos.

By the end of 1954, *Playboy's* circulation had soared to 175,000 readers and figures were climbing daily. The magazine was becoming a household word to millions of Americans who had never seen a copy of it.

Critics had already begun to evaluate it as a cultural phenomenon of the 1950s. All across the country, a windstorm of cultural and social change was blowing in. *Playboy* had clearly "struck a nerve" (Hef's words) in the American male. He wanted to wage war against the archetypal concept of the male of that era as "a mechanized, robotized caricature of humanity, a slave in mind and body."

Writer Barbara Ehrenreich had already claimed that magazines such as *Reader's Digest, Look,* and *Life* had already asserted that "Gary Gray (the conformist in the gray flannel suit) was robbing men of their masculinity, freedom, and sense of individualism." *[Gregory Peck, in* The Man in the Gray Flannel Suit *(1956), had famously depicted a struggling Madison Avenue wannabe searching for meaning in life.]*

*Playboy* continued its role as a gadfly that criticized the numbing effects of postwar American repression. Within a decade, *Playboy* even suggested that "the American man is being worked so hard by his wife that day after day, week after week, he was being invited to attend his own funeral."

\*\*\*

When Hef worked for *Esquire,* he had shared an office with copywriter Burt Zollo (nicknamed "Zoot") whom he described as "a real promoter." Although Hef finally convinced his friend to work for *Playboy,* he was reluctant to make the switch during the magazine's planning stages.

Later, Zollo said, "Hef oozes creativity. He's gangbusters in ambition, and I predict he'll make it to the top, with a lot of road blocks thrown in his path."

One of Zollo's articles ("Miss Gold Digger of 1953") appeared in the very first issue of *Playboy.* In it, he attacked the institution of alimony. "It's a weapon that women use to strip men of their livelihood and to prevent them from establishing a happier home with another spouse."

By the spring of 1955, Zoot had written another article, "Open Season on Bachelors" in which he stated: "The modern American woman is perfectly willing to crush man's adventurous, freedom-loving spirit to obtain economic and social security above all else." He suggested that readers take a good look "at the sorry state of regimented husbands trudging down every woman-dominated street in this woman-dominated land." He warned men to beware of the marriage month of June when women "become more heated, more desperate, and more dangerous."

He called himself "a true Playboy, a well-dressed, sophisticated guy who enjoys the pleasures of the female without becoming emotionally involved."

He sent out a call for the playboys of America to become free-wheeling spenders and upmarket consumers, seeking the good life in fashionable clothes and enjoying the fine wines and beautiful women. He promoted the mantra "*Love 'em and leave 'em.*" [*Hef would hear that call to arms and follow its dictates for the rest of his life.*]

Almost from the beginning, women voiced strong objections to those views as stated in *Playboy*, attacking them as "anti-women." *Playboy* was sometimes condemned for its depiction of the American woman "as a creature known for her greed, her power over men, whom she manipulated and controlled by overly domesticating them, leading to their emasculation."

Privately, Hef told his male staff members, "I want to appeal to male readers devoted to pussy and Picassos. On a typical night, I picture him in his chic apartment with a beautiful doll. While hearing mood music in the background, they drink champagne while consuming Iranian caviar. The talk is of jazz, sex, and Nietzsche in that order."

His story editor, Ray Russell, weighted in with a controversial but perhaps realistic, opinion: "Hef and I could have all the Nabokovs in the world and the best articles on the proper attire without attracting hordes of men. Let's face it: They buy *Playboy* for its tits and ass. If we remove the sex, the magazine will die like an old dog of twenty years."

***

The nude centerfolds not only launched *Playboy* but sustained it through the remainder of the 20<sup>th</sup> Century," Hef admitted. "Of secondary, yet vital, importance were our cartoons, often satirical, drawn by some of the best cartoonists or artists in America. Sometimes I wrote their gag lines.

I don't like to confess this, but many readers bought our magazine just to gaze upon our centerfolds and enjoy our cartoons. Those guys didn't bother to read our classy articles written by some of the biggest names in American literature."

"I called our cartoonists 'my cultural warriors,' satirizing and poking fun at the sexual hypocrisy of the 1950s."

"As the decade moved on, some of the biggest cartoonists in America wanted their work to appear in *Playboy*," Hef said. "They supplied the spark to ignite the oncoming sexual revolution."

"We also paid special attention to the findings of *The Kinsey Report*, which suggested that women were as sexually voracious as men. Over the decades, I published the best cartoonists in America. Nothing like our output has ever been equaled."

Cartoonist Jack Cole became known for some of the cartoons he crafted for *Playboy*—some of which depicted beautiful but dim girls with rich but equally dim old men—and also for his creation of the satirical superhero "Plastic Man."

"His line drawings of sexual stereotypes such as the Spinster became classics," Hef said. "His full-page color renderings of women were luscious."

Cole's biographer, Art Spiegelman, wrote, "Cole's goddesses were estrogen *soufflés* who mesmerized the ineffectual saps who lusted after them." *[One of the alltime best sellers within Playboy's inventory of novelty items was were cocktail napkins emblazoned with "Females by Cole."]*

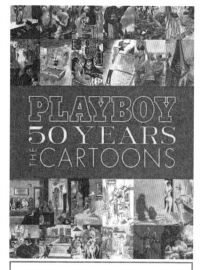

When Hef had worked for *Esquire*, he'd met and befriended Richard Loehle, admiring his talent. Later, after evolving into the publisher of *Playboy*, Hef asked him to submit cartoons. "Dick's talent never failed him," Hef said, "and his career with *Playboy* would span the latter half of the 20th Century. In World War II in China, as a member of the U.S. Army Air Corps, he was a cartographer. His cartoons appeared in

With the possible exception of those that appeared within *The New Yorker*, no other publication became as well-known for its cartoons than *Playboy*. Satirical, bawdy, amusing, eccentric, quirky, and very very funny, they're collectively interpreted as one of the magazine's most important contributions to the self-assessment of the 20th century.

Individual artists who entrenched their names within the American psyche, based on their illustrations, included Jack Cole, Shel Silverstein, Richard Loehle, and John Dempsey.

the first edition of *Playboy* and met with wide approval."

Other collaborators on the emerging magazine's staff included Al Stine. "A multi-talented artist, he could work from many easels," Hef said. "In addition to his brilliant cartoons, he became America's foremost water colorist and oil painter." For *Playboy*, he illustrated the hugely popular "Babs & Shirley" cartoons. "They were inspired by a pair of showgirls my promotion director, Victor Lownes, and I were dating at the time. Well, more than dating...."

For more than a half-century, the cartoons of John Dempsey lampooned America's sexual foibles. He submitted a batch of cartoons to Hef, and as an inaugural example, one of them appeared in *Playboy's* First Anniversary edition (December 1954). "After that, I was in the groove with *Playboy*," Dempsey said. "Hef really dug my work."

In reference to Dempsey, *Playboy's* cartoon editor, Michelle Urry, said, "Jack was the most California of our artists, drawing would-be starlets, out-of-work actors, and raunchy Bible thumpers. He did some incredibly hip cartoons...He was basically the Gary Cooper of cartoonists—a slow-talking, long drink of water. He lived on the beach and loved beach life. He was never politically correct and didn't have to be with us. Sex for him managed to be so nuanced, so full of life, that he really got Everyman, but it was a California version of Everyman."

Larry Klein was another of Hef's favorite cartoonists. His work appeared in several issues. One of Hef's faves depicted a pajama-clad male in bed with a luscious blonde. He asks, "Am I supposed to be the bird and you the bee, or is it the other way around?"

A mainstay in *Playboy* for decades, Phil Interlandi sold his first cartoon to Hef in 1955. Chicago-born of Sicilian immigrants, he served as one of the cartoonists for *Yank* magazine during World War II. He later became known for "Queenie," a syndicated cartoon strip about a voluptuous blonde secretary. "This guy had an acerbic wit," Hef said. "He rode roughshod over all those sacred cows. He told me, 'I don't give a fuck about taboos.' He could draw gorgeous gals yet make them cartoon funny."

A native of Chicago like Hef himself, bearded Shel Silverstein "was a bald-headed man who looked like the kind of guy you didn't want to meet up with in a dark alley," Hef said. "He always came into my office wearing blue jeans and a big cowboy hat."

In 1957, he became one of Hef's leading cartoonists, producing some two dozen installments of a feature, "Shel Silverstein Visits." It documented his experiences at such locations as a nudist camp in New Jersey. These essays were later published in a book, *Playboy's Silverstein Around the World*," with a forward by Hef.

Silverstein's cartoons remained a feature in *Playboy* from 1957 to the mid-'70s. "The guy was a true Renaissance man," Hef said. "You name it— country music hits, children's books, plays, even black comedies."

Bronx-born Jules Feiffer became the most famous cartoonist Hef ever published. He was also an author, playwright, and screenwriter, and by 1986, he had won the Pulitzer Prize as America's leading editorial cartoonist. "I was damn lucky to get him," Hef said.

Beginning in 1956, Feiffer was the staff cartoonist for *The Village Voice,* and during his time there, he produced a weekly comic strip titled *Feiffer* until 1997. His cartoons became nationally syndicated. After he left the *Voice,* he created the first op-ed comic strip for *The New York Times.* Among his films he critiqued was *Carnal Knowledge* (1971), directed by Mike Nichols.

Feiffer once submitted a nine-page cartoon story to Hef entitled *The Lonely Machine.* Hef accepted it, but wrote back a nine-page, single-spaced typewritten memo to the artist with suggestions about how it could be improved. Feiffer later claimed, "Hef is the best cartoon editor in America."

Ben Denison, a graduate of the Chicago Art Institute, was asked to illustrate an installment of Ray Bradbury's classic science fiction classic, *Fahrenheit 451.* "Ben came aboard *Playboy* at its inception," Hef said. "In the 1950s, he launched himself as one of the best illustrators, and I liked his cartoons. One of my favorites depicted a semi-nude girl asking another, 'What's the past tense of virgin?'"

Jules Feiffer, seen at work in 1958, became one of the leading cartoonists of America. "He was without mercy in depicting human hypocrisies and foibles," Hef said.

As a showcase for his work, *Hef* introduced what became a hit feature within *Playboy*, "The Sick Little World of Jules Feiffer."

E. Simms Campbell of St. Louis was the first African American cartoonist whose work was printed in nationally distributed magazines such as *Playboy.* He was the creator of Ésky," the familiar pop-eyed mascot of *Esquire.* His cartoons were featured in *Playboy* and in *Ebony,* and his gag panel, "Cuties," was syndicated by King Features to some 150 newspapers.

As a boy in California, Eldon Dedini first subscribed to *Esquire* when he was only thirteen. Five years later, he sold his first cartoon to that magazine. In time, his work appeared in such magazines as *Playboy* and *The New Yorker.* He became well-known for illustrating editions of Max Schulman books, including *Rally Round the Flag, Boys!* (1958).

Julius Dedman, a Yale man, class of 1948, was hired by Hef "to bring some Ivy League sophistication to our magazines. And he did just that," Hef said.

Illinois born and bred, Gahan Wilson became known for his cartoons depicting horror-fantasy situations. His grotesque style and dark humor invited comparisons to Charles Addams and his Addams family, but there was a big difference. Wilson specialized in atomic mutants, subway monsters, and serial killers, and both his cartoons and prose fiction became regular features in *Playboy* for half a century.

While reading *Esquire* as a boy, Hef had fallen in love with "The Vargas Girl," the creation of the Peruvian artist, Alberto Vargas. When he became "too hot to handle" at *Esquire*, Hef picked him up. Beginning in 1959, Vargas would produce 152 paintings of sensual women for Hef. Later, his paintings acquired quite a market value, his 1967 work "Trick or Treat" selling for $71,600 at Christies' in Manhattan.

***

*Playboy* turned the corner financially during its first year of publication and showed a profit before the end of 1954. By the time the New Year arrived, circulation had jumped to 185,000 readers, which by March would soar to 350,000.

"What better way to bring in the New Year?" Hef said, "than to publish a centerfold of Bettie Page?" In the 1950s, Page had been frequently described as the "Queen of Pinups."

Descended from white trash in Tennessee, "she became a trademark during the rockabilly subculture of the Eisenhower years," he said. "Sadly, she was an example of one who climbs the rickety ladder to fame only to fall off into a cesspool of horror."

On a visit to Miami, Bettie has worked with the cult photographer Bunny Yeager, who had hired her, for twenty dollars, as a model for semi-nude pictures. One showed her lounging on a leopard-skin rug, another frolicking in the ocean. Yeager also asked Bettie to pose for a possible centerfold for Hef's *Playboy*. Bare-breasted, Bettie posed putting bulbs on a silver Christmas tree. Wearing a Santa hat, she winks at the reader with a come-hither look. Her naked breasts were most enticing.

"A true Vargas girl comes to life," Hef said.

"It should have run in our Christmas issue, but it arrived too late," Hef said. "So I made her the centerfold in our January issue, a bit off, but what the hell? She proved to be the most popular centerfold since I'd gone nude with Marilyn Monroe."

"I think Bettie was one of the most remarkable ladies of the '50s," he said. "She was an iconic figure in pulp cultures, influencing sexuality and defying restrictions which got her into a lot of trouble with anti-porn politicians."

After publication, Hef received a call from Bettie at his *Playboy* offices. In his private apartment, a secret hideaway unknown to his family, she presented him with a series of bondage pictures called "Battling Babes," in which she posed with another nude female model.

During their meeting, she told him that men were turned on by women spanking each other, or, in some cases, using whips. "It sets their fantasies spinning, and they'd attract a lot of attention in *Playboy*," she said. "Sometimes, I was shown as the beater with a whip: at other times, I was on the receiving end."

He had to reject them, telling her they were too *risqué* for *Playboy* but he remained sure that there was a market for this type of erotic "bondage" photos.

His prediction came true, and the candid shots were sold underground. Somehow, the series was delivered to Senator Estes Kefauver, who was leading an anti-porn crackdown at the time.

[*A Democrat from Tennessee, Kefauver served in the U.S. House of Representatives from 1939 to 1949 and in the Senate from 1949 until his death in 1963.*] On the Senate floor, he denounced Bettie, calling her "a pervert and a lesbian. Only a lesbian would pose for pictures like that."

"Before she left Chicago, Bettie spent the weekend in my bed," Hef claimed. "She might have been a lesbian by day, but at night, she gave a man, namely me, the fuck of my life, at least up to that point in said life."

Frank Sinatra had picked up a copy of *Playboy's* January issue, and he phoned Hef, asking for a phone contact for Bettie. That led to plane tickets to Las Vegas, where she was installed in a suite at The Sands. On the first two nights of her stay there, she was visited by Sinatra, but on subsequent

In 2012, documentary filmmaker Mark Mori produced an iconic tribute to the iconic power of S&M stripper and model, Bettie Page.

Both Hef (an early connoisseur of her erotic charms) and Page herself contributed to its dialogue and narration.

91

evenings, Sammy Davis, Jr., arrived, followed by Dean Martin and Peter Lawford, the latter preferring only oral sex.

"Before I flew East, Frankie gave me $2,000," Bettie later reported to Hef.

Sinatra stayed in touch and a few months later, he flew Bettie to Palm Springs, where he promised to introduce her to the next President of the United States.

As she revealed to Hef on a subsequent visit to Chicago, she was introduced to John F. Kennedy swimming nude in Sinatra's pool. "I had never heard of him," she confessed. "But before too much time had passed, the whole world knew who he was."

*[Regrettably, by 1959, Bettie had became a Born Again Christian and went to work for the evangelist, Billy Graham, an anti-Semite and homophobe. She studied at Bible colleges with the hope of becoming a missionary.*

*That plan did not work out, and she became subject to violent mood swings which caused her to end up in a psychiatric ward, like Frances Farmer, the former movie star. She suffered from paranoid schizophrenia, according to the psychiatrists who examined her.]*

*\*\*\**

"Spring came early to Chicago in 1955," Hef said. "Believe it or not, I was offered a million dollars to sell *Playboy.*"

Over lunch, he met with three businessmen, all of them representatives of a financial syndicate in Chicago. In return for that bundle of cash, they wanted 100 percent control of the magazine's stock. If he agreed to that, Hef was informed that he'd be awarded a lucrative annual salary and complete editorial control.

"We'll also let you continue to select the Playmate of the Month, and privately audition her if that is your desire," one of the potential investors said.

That night, without consulting anyone, neither his wife or his *Playboy* associates, he decided to turn down the offer, even though it was tempting. He was hoping to make millions off *Playboy* in the future. "Why settle for just one mil?" he asked.

Hef's optimism was well-founded. By December, monthly sales of *Playboy* had risen to 1.1 million copies, and within a few months, it would surpass the circulation of *Esquire,* its chief rival.

*\*\*\**

During the first months of *Playboy's* publication, Hefner had turned down a major source of revenue: Many pages of advertising. Companies had approached him, but he'd rejected their products.

"In the beginning, they were hawking sleaze, nothing appropriate for the *Playboy* image. I would tell them, 'No way!' We wouldn't accept an ad whose primary appeal was for sex. We wanted Commander Whitehead of Schweppes, or else the Man in the Hathaway Shirt with the eye patch, perhaps a Playboy behind the wheel of a shiny new Jaguar with the Playmate of the Month in the front seat with him, both of them heading for an off-the-record weekend in some secluded, luxurious retreat."

"If Jesus Christ came to Chicago to ask for pages in *Playboy* to advertise his message, I would reject him," Hef vowed.

"I drew up a list of ads I'd reject. Anything promoting guns, correspondence courses, hair restoration products, trusses, and a cream that 'guaranteed an erection lasting for one hour.' I turned down three-fourths of the businesses approaching me."

He had a distinct preference for ads that promoted dinner jackets, liquor such as Bacardi Rum, auto ads for BMW, hi-fi speakers, Max Factor crewcut hair dressing, Coty perfume, English Leather aftershave, and a new credit card then sweeping across the nation, Diners Club."

His advertising department crafted slogans and scripts touting "What Sort of Man Reads *Playboy?*"

"It's a young man going places," the copy proclaimed. "A man who likes the challenges and excitement of new things, new places, and new ideas." This promotion revealed that seventy percent of *Playboy* readers were in the 18- to 34-year-old age group, a demographic with a preference for luxury goods and high disposable income.

In the beginning, some big-name advertisers were reluctant to advertise in *Playboy*, viewing it as a porn magazine. But as 1955 came to an

As the fame of *Playboy* grew, and as the value of commercial associations with its elegantly macho image strengthened, Hef was frequently confronted with decisions about what products to endorse, and what to turn down.

Replicated above is an ad for men's clothing from the early 1960s. The spiffy, well-dressed male model in the "corporate uniform of his day" who's depicted in the ad has no troubles or inhibitions about seductively interacting with the Playboy bunny in the background.

end, advertisers had lost their fear and began clamoring to buy full-page ads.

By the end of the 1960s, *Playboy* had become one of the darlings of Madison Avenue, prompting the publication of articles in ad-industry magazines entitled, "*Playboy* Puts a Glint in the Admen's Eyes." An executive at J. Walter Thompson, the nation's largest advertising agency, said, "Today, running an ad in *Playboy* is routine."

However, on some occasions, Hef faced stormy tensions with advertisers who sometimes felt that he'd "gone too far" in both his depictions of semi-nude women and in the themes and wordings of some of his articles. One in particular in the July 1962 issue stirred up a lot of controversy, and some newsstands in conservative areas of the country refused to stock it.

Calder Willingham was a popular novelist of his day, writing fiction filled with steamy sex scenes. His short story, *Bus Stop*, featured a seventeen-year-old girl getting raped by a brute of a man, who ordered her, under threat of violence, to "open your legs."

Ford Motor was one of the many companies which protested. Faced with advertisers threatening to cancel contracts, Hef wrote a letter of apology to leaders of major corporations, agreeing to meet with them. "I had a dilemma. I had to face the ire of advertisers who tried to censor me, but at the same time, I didn't want to lose readers who turned to *Playboy* for stories of sexual titillation."

In his letter to advertisers, Hef described the *Playboy* reader: "He can be a sharp-minded young businessman, a worker in the arts, a university professor, an architect or engineer. He can be many things, providing he possesses a certain point of view. That is, he sees life not as a vale of tears, but as a happy time. He must take joy in his work and be alert and aware, a man of taste, sensitivity, and pleasure, a man who is not a dilettante, but one who lives life to the hilt."

In a 1955 interview with a Chicago newspaperman, Hef admitted that *Playboy* was "a magazine for the escapist, one that projects the kind of life a potential reader would like to lead. The *Playboy* reader escapes into a world of wine, women, and song," a recurring theme for him in many an interview.

When it was revealed that thousands of high school boys were avid readers of *Playboy*, many critics attacked Hef, charging him with "corrupting America's youth."

He denied these accusations, although admitting he could not control who actually acquired copies of his magazines. "Of course, my intention is not to appeal to the level of a thirteen-year-old boy experiencing puberty."

In 1955, he launched "Playboy After Hours," reviewing restaurants in both Chicago and Manhattan. "We also review records of Frank Sinatra, as well as those of my favorite singers, Mabel Mercer and Billie Holiday, both African Americans. We recommend the sexy novels of Harold Robbins and some of my favorite movies of the year, including *Mister Roberts* (1955) starring Henry Fonda and James Cagney."

***

Back when he was working for the Carson Pirie Scott Department Store in Chicago, Hef met LeRoy Neiman at an office party. He was an illustrator who had attended the Art Institute of Chicago on the G.I. Bill.

"All I remember was seeing this guy who looked like Ernest Hemingway," Hef said. "He wore a black turtleneck sweater and had a cigar dangling from the corner of his mouth. He had an 'Ernesto mustache,' a shock of jet-black hair, and bushy eyebrows."

"It wasn't one of those evenings like the popular song of the day went. I didn't see a stranger across a crowded room, and our eyes met—and it was love at first sight. Actually, I thought no more about him until months later when I ran into him on the street and invited him for a chat in a local tavern. It stretched out for four hours. At the end, he agreed to become an illustrator for *Playboy*. LeRoy was more than that. He became one of my best buddies and confidantes, our friendship surviving over the decades and into the next century. He saw me go through a lot of women."

Specifically crafting it for the *Playboy's* Party Jokes page, Neiman created the Femlin character—an elegant beauty with midnight black long gloves and black stockings. And over a period of fifteen years, he also created illustrations for *Playboy's* "Man at His Leisure" section, crafting scenes of the Playboy at the most glittering places and events in the world, including the *belle époque* splendor of Maxim's in Paris, the Cannes Film Festival, the Grand Prix de Monaco, the bullfights in Madrid, and such major sports events as Wimbledon or the National Steeplechase in England.

During one of his safaris in Africa, Neiman wrote and illustrated articles whose names included *Portrait of a Black Panther, Portrait of an Elephant, Resting Lion,* and *Resting Tiger.*

Neiman described his years at *Playboy* and other adventures in an autobiography, *All Told: My Art and Life Among Athletes, Playboys, Bunnies, and Provocateurs.* He died on June 20, 2012, about two weeks after its publication on June 5 of that same year.

***

LeRoy Neiman was in Hef's office in early May of 1955 when a special delivery package arrived for him from Los Angeles. It was from a soon-to-be famous film producer and director, Russ Meyer. Inside were candid photographs he'd taken of his girlfriend (later his wife). She was Evelyn Turner (a.k.a. Eve Meyer).

"She's a blonde modern-day Scarlett O'Hara from Atlanta, Georgia with a 39" bust," Hef said to Neiman. "I've got to have her. She'll be our June 1955 centerfold."

In that centerfold, she was depicted in an open-to-the-navel *négligée* in front of a roaring fireplace, lying on a carpet with two glasses of wine in front of her. It is implicit that one of those glasses belongs to a Playboy, who will no doubt seduce her.

"Hef was so hot to trot with this beauty that he flew her to Chicago," Neiman said. "Russ was obviously plugging her, but Hef figured that if he were willing to show off her nude charms to readers of *Playboy* that he wouldn't mind letting him crawl be-

With his handlebar mustache, LeRoy Neiman, one of *Playboy's* leading illustrators, was hip, irreverent, and influential. Through his art work, he rendered the *Playboy* brand into something elegant, desirable, classy, amusing, and chic.

The middle photo replicates a large painting he crafted of a Bunny playing pool.

The lower photo depicts an espresso cup from one of the Playboy Clubs. The user gets a mouth-level overview of one of Nieman's "Fremlins," a saucy, voluptuous, adventurous, and amusing young woman who seems absolutely delighted with her role as a Playmate.

tween the sheets with her. By the way, his laundry loved our Playboy. He must have sent them for laundering at least two sets of sheets a day."

"As it turned out," Neiman said, "this Eve was no dumb blonde. She was becoming a motion picture actress herself and later a film producer."

Hef became so enchanted with her that he later hired her for another layout in *Playboy*. Included in the March 1956 issue, it was titled "An Evening with Eve: A Modern Bedtime Story." In it, Russ depicted what a girl could do in bed: read a book, play solitaire, eat a grapefruit or crackers, write a letter, smoke a cigarette, paint her nails...even go to sleep.

Hef began a long friendship with Eve and Russ and watched as their film careers progressed. In 1959, *The Immoral Mr. Teas*, directed by Russ, became one of Hef's favorite movies, depicting a clumsy, shy man who has X-Ray vision, enabling him to see what women look like nude beneath their clothing.

Although *Variety* called the film "as funny as a burning or-

---

It was rare that a *Playboy* centerfold (in this case Eve Meyer) graduated into a more influential role as an assistant producer. In association with her husband, Russ Meyer— a producer of "sexploitation" films—she emerged as a player in her own right.

Upper Photo: Poster for *The Immortal Mr. Teas,* a film that was top-heavy with gratuitous nudity, bad acting, and broad innuendo. Russ Meyer produced and directed it, and Eve starred.

Likewise, *Eve &The Handyman* was a comedy of errors whose vulgarity and All-Amerian sleaze directly contrasted with the poised classiness of what Hefner was doing at *Playboy*.

*Faster, Pussycat! Kill! Kill!* Although Eve didn't appear in it, she co-produced it alongside her husband, emerging with a campy sexploitation classic about what happens when bad girls REALLY set loose on a rampage in the desert.

phanage and a treat for the emotionally retarded," Hef loved it.

Russ and Eve worked together on their most famous film, *Beyond the Valley of the Dolls* (1970) which became a cult classic. Written by film critic Roger Ebert, it was a satirical take on the bestseller by Jacqueline Susann, *Valley of the Dolls. [In this instance, the word "Dolls" being a slang term for barbiturates (downers).]*

Over the years, Hef and Russ maintained a long-term friendship which intensified after Hef's move to Los Angeles. "His favorite topic of conversation was breasts, in which I also have an acute interest," Hef said.

"Most of my fans feel I'd go ape shit over Jane Russell or Sophia Loren," Russ told Hef. "But their perfectly balanced bodies don't mesh with my precise aesthetic preference. Instead, I prefer Gina Lollobrigida. My alltime fantasy would be to photograph Dolly Parton in the nude. I got Anita Ekberg to pose nude for me. She has 39DD breasts, the biggest I ever photographed. She let me suck on them for an hour before I went below her navel for dinner.":

Russ told Hef amusing stories from his past. After the liberation of Paris in 1944, he met Ernest Hemingway in a French brothel. "After Papa Hemingway found out I was a virgin, he offered to buy me any whore in the house, and I chose the one with the biggest breasts."

In time, Russ divorced Eve. On June 27, 1970, he invited Hef to attend his wedding to Edy Williams. "The bride wore history's shortest wedding

During *Playboy's* early battles with censorship and in its frenzied campaign to project an image of classy good taste, huge attention was paid to what are viewed today as "vintage" magazine covers. Displayed above are two of them, June, 1955 (left) and March 1956 (right).

Eve Meyer (center photo), a Georgia-born southern magnolia with a head for business, appeared as a model in each of them, working in collaboration with her filmmaker husband, Russ Meyer, during their lengthy marriage before her tragic early death in an airplane crash in the Canary Islands in 1977.

dress, coming to an end in 'cooze country,'" Hef said. "On her left leg, she wore a garter. I thought she was hot. For our March 1973 issue, I made her Playmate of the Month."

"As for poor Eve, her life came to a tragic ending."

He was referring to the March 27, 1977 plane crash at the Tenerife Airport in the Canary Islands. The disaster became the worst accident in aviation history.

***

During his lifetime, Hef personally selected many a centerfold, but none seemed to generate the acclaim of his first choice, the Marilyn Monroe "Red Velvet Nude" that ran in his first issue.

His chief rival, *Esquire*, also published a sexy picture of Monroe, but although she was skimpily dressed, she was not nude. That caused *Time* to quip, "*Esquire* can't keep 'abreast' of *Playboy*."

Many a picture of a delectable beauty passed across his desk for review, but he kept searching for something "new and different." He finally decided, "All I had to do was turn over in my bed and absorb the loveliness of the most beautiful blonde, the most enchanting, charming, and sexy Charlaine Karalus, with measurements of 36-24-36."

When not pleasing Hef, her official job was as "subscription fulfillment manager" for *Playboy*.

When he first proposed that she pose nude for a centerfold, she'd objected. For weeks, she'd been asking him to invest in a new Addressograph machine for her, claiming that her department was desperately in need of such a machine because of the increasing volume of their subscriptions.

He promised he'd get her one if she'd pose nude for that centerfold. "I wanted my readers to take delight in what I was seeing every night stripping down in my bedroom."

Finally, she agreed.

For her feature, Hef decided to assign a pseudonym, "Janet Pilgrim," to the woman he described as "My Betty Grable Blonde." Staffers thought he was making a pun on the Pilgrims and their moralistic roots. "Actually," he said, "I took the name from one of my favorite Grable movies, *The Shocking Miss Pilgrim* (1947)."

His art director, Art Paul, disagreed with his choice. "She's a doll, but not right for our centerfold. Our choice of a Playmate should have an air of mystery about her, not some girl who works in the office handling the mail."

Hef strongly disagreed, feeling that Charlaine's "girl-next-door allure

99

would generate sexual fantasies."

He was right.

"I saw her as creamy and delectable, a sex doll who'd bring satisfaction to any red-blooded male. A woman who looked vulnerable to male advances...Definitely hard-on material. Yet still respectable and ladylike, a full-figured blonde who could satisfy almost any man's sexual desires."

Hef personally supervised the shoot, dressing in tie and tails to appear as a blurred figure in the background of one of her best and most provocative shots. She was seated at her vanity table in lingerie, holding a powder puff, with most of her ample breasts exposed.

"Janet Pilgrim" went over so big with readers that Hef asked her to pose for two more centerfolds, designating her for the second and third times as Playmate of the Month in December 1955 and again in October 1956.

The December 1955 issue revealed her in her modern apartment on the North Side of Chicago. Exposing her breasts, she was depicted wearing the tops of a man's set of pajamas—"no need for the bottoms,"

Her celebrity was such that he sent her on promotional tours. Sometimes, she'd appear at business conventions in Chicago, at other times on college campuses with late

Happy Holidays, December, 1955: Charlaine Karalus (aka, Janet Pilgrim), appears on the cover (depicted above) as *Playboy's* semi-nude "Office Playmate."

It was true: Designated as the person in charge of renewing magazine subscriptions, she sustained an affair with Hef while working innocuously, cheek-by-jowl with him in *Playboy's* Chicago offices until she was plucked from obscurity and thrown into the limelight.

It became one of the most widely publicized "office affairs" in the history of publishing.

Charlaine died in 2017 in Norwalk, Connecticut, at the age of 82.

teenaged boys who were often devoted readers of *Playboy*. The male students at Dartmouth crowned her Queen at its annual Winter Carnival.

When she wasn't posing, Charlaine was frequently seen driving around in the front passenger-side seat of Hef's bronze Cadillac. "She represented the kind of gal I wanted in *Playboy*. The models in magazines vying with me for readers looked like broken-down whores who might ask a man, 'Are you in yet?'"

Often dressed in a form-fitting black sweater (with a Bunny logo on it) that showed off her breasts, Charlaine also made appearances wearing a cheerleader's short and perky white skirt.

"She was my personal cosmopolitan cupcake," Hef said, "as well as *Playboy's*. Whether it was flirting with the comic pianist, Victor Borge, or with the mayor of Atlanta, she was at ease with all sorts of men who adored her."

As time marched on, and as Hef turned to other Playmates, Charlaine did too. In 1958, while appearing at a business convention representing *Playboy*, she met and fell in love with an airline executive from Houston. She married him and settled down to become a wife and mother.

***

Throughout 1955, Hef paid increasing attention to his concept of a Playmate as "the girl next door."

Many of his readers wrote in asking: "What neighborhood do you live in? The girl next door to me is fat, pimply faced, wears thick glasses, and farts in class."

Hef told his editors and photographers that he was no longer interested in the mainstream-style nudes posed by professional models. "No typical pin-up or cheesecake shots that hang in barbershops. We want our models more sophisticated, semi-nude, no pubic hair showing. We want them to be sexy but with class."

He had each of his models sign an agreement that they would not appear in any other magazines, at least until two years after their appearance in any issue of his magazine.

Anne Fleming posed as Playmate of the Month in the September 1955 issue. She represented the kind of woman Hef was seeking for his centerfolds. Topless, but attired in black lace leggings, she was photographed climbing a staircase, obviously to bring sexual fulfillment to the nude Playboy waiting in bed at the top of the stairs. "Her breasts were barely exposed. It's not sex but titillation, suggesting she can bring sexual fulfillment to any male," Hef said.

His judgment was confirmed when the *Playboy* office was flooded with several hundred letters, some describing what they would do to Fleming if the sender of the letter got her in bed. "She became one of my most popular models by suggesting sexual pleasure without getting down and dirty before a photographer," Hef said. "Keep our models alluring without looking whorish," he ordered.

Photographer Dwight Hooker claimed, "So many young women between Alabama and the Pacific coastline of Washington State were sending nude photographs to us. We had to fight them off with a baseball bat."

Many urban legends about Hef and his Playmate of the Month were

101

started because of the markings (between 1955 and 1975) that appeared on the front covers of *Playboy*. The "P" in *Playboy* had stars printed in or around it.

According to legend, that indicated the rating Hef gave to his model based on how attractive she was, or else on the number of times he had slept with her—or else how good she was in bed. *[Actually, the stars, from zero to twelve, indicated the domestic or international advertising region to which that particular print run had been assigned.]*

\*\*\*

A casual invitation to a party in the spring of 1954 changed Hef's life forever. "I walked into the world of Victor Lownes III, which plunged me into a whirlwind that became bad, beautiful, glorious, and, at the end, tragic," Hef said.

Lownes was born on April 17, 1928 in Buffalo, New York, which made him two years younger than Hef. His rich family soon moved to a mansion near Palm Beach, which had a full-time chef and three servants, plus a nursemaid, seventeen-year-old Essie Klopfer, assigned to look after him and his younger brother, Tom. "Essie taught me that there was a lot a gal could do to pleasure a ten-year-old dick. As my nursemaid I did a lot of nursing on those breasts of hers."

Tragedy occurred when he was twelve and was getting ready to go with his father on a hunting expedition into the Florida Everglades. He was outside, playing with a .22 rifle that he had been given and was told that it was unloaded. He was with his best friend who was riding on his bicycle. Pointing the gun at him, with a mock threat that he was going to shoot him, he fired the rifle. It was loaded, and he shot his friend in the heart, the boy dying instantly.

After the shooting, Lownes' father, Winifred, shipped him off to the New Mexico Military Institute. Located in Roswell, New Mexico (famous for its much-disputed sightings of UFOs in the late 1940s), it boasts other alumni who include actor Owen Wilson, hotelier Conrad Hilton, and news reporter Sam Donaldson.

Lownes' roommate turned out to be Nicky Hilton, the son of Conrad Hilton. Within a few

Victor Lownes was savvy, classy, and cosmopolitan, an *éminence grise* whose influence on Hef and his emerging magazine was incalculable

years, Nicky would marry the violet-eyed young vamp and movie star, Elizabeth Taylor. The two young men bonded immediately, and often talked about futures that would include seducing the most beautiful women in the world.

After only two weeks, Lownes learned one night that Nicky was bisexual. "I took advantage of that, since I was always horny. He serviced me, but I didn't return the favor. He had to settle for masturbation. My God, he had a dick on him that was the size of two Budweiser cans stuck on top of each other."

Their weekends were spent at his suite at El Paso Hilton, where they often crossed the border to this "red hot Mexican whorehouse." At the hotel, Nicky ordered various maids, often Mexican, to come to their rooms to service them.

In 1944, after telling Nicky goodbye, Lownes enrolled at the University of Chicago. At a local jazz club, he met Judith Downs, the campus beauty queen, who was two years older than him. They began to date, and at the age of eighteen, he married her. Her father, a rich cattle rancher from Arkansas, gave them a De Soto from Detroit and a stylish, recently constructed home in the suburb of Evanston, near Chicago. One year, they gave birth to a son, the following year, a daughter.

He was given a high-paying executive position at his grandfather's firm, the Silent Watchman Corporation, which manufactured industrial time locks.

By the early 1950s, he had become tired and bored with family life in suburbia. "I decided I was not the home-and-hearth type," he confessed. "I wanted to be a free man enjoying the decadent pleasures of Chicago. I soon deserted my family to pursue extramarital affairs and, ultimately, a divorce."

Having left his wife and children, Victor rented a bachelor pad

***OOOH-LA-LA!***
SCANDALS FROM THE VERY RICH AND VERY GLAM, PLAYBOY-SOAKED "AGE OF SPUTNIK"

The forever enticing Zsa Zsa Gabor was married to hotel heir Conrad Hilton.

Unknown to dear ol' dad, his son, Nicky, regularly *schtupped* his father's movie star wife. "Do you call it incest when it's your stepmother—not your real mother?" Nick wanted to know.

During her brief marriage to Nicky, Elizabeth Taylor learned of the affair and confronted Zsa Zsa at a party. "How could you?" Elizabeth demanded. "Have you no shame?"

"Shame is for the little people," Zsa Zsa responded.

on North Wells Street in Chicago. An old coach house had been converted into a luxury apartment with one extremely large all-purpose room, ideal for parties, plus a curtained-off bedroom in an alcove, where he slept with his favorite combo, usually two or three young women, a configuration which Hef himself would prefer later in his life, too.

Having escaped from the "bondage" of marriage, he became known as "the swinging bachelor of Chicago," hosting at least three parties a week at his bachelor pad. When word got out about his parties, which often became orgies, a diverse group of young men and women, without any specific gender preference, turned up as guests.

"When I turned off the lights, except for a candle or two in the corner," Lownes said, "I never knew who I was penetrating or who was sucking me off. It really didn't matter. I was mainly concerned with my big blast-off before retiring to sleep with a redhead, blonde, and brunette (my preferred combo). I could never make up my mind about women. Even as a boy, I had trouble deciding which flavor of ice cream, and often asked for three scoops of different flavors—yes, even chocolate. I soon learned that beautiful women come in all colors."

"I became the chief porker of Chicago, not wanting to leave any vagina unattended," he bragged. "That often meant three at a time. I give these wild parties, often playing strip poker. One night I was with about fifteen guys, and we attended this drag show on the south side of Chicago. We invited all the queenies back to my flat to give us blow jobs. Holy shit! If there's one thing a drag queen can do, it's give a man a great blow job."

Sometimes, he had a steady date, but always had "plenty on the side." For a while, he dated Mary Ann La Joie, a showgirl at the Empire Room of the Palmer House Hotel in Chicago. She was appearing in a review with a newly emerging comedian, Jonathan Winters. Lownes became friends with that comedian and decided to throw a party for him after the show. He asked Mary Ann to invite the entire cast, and all of them showed up. About two dozen unrelated strangers dropped in, too.

One of those strangers was Hugh Hefner, who was still in the early stages of publishing *Playboy*. Lownes had become an avid reader of the magazine, having purchased a newsstand copy of its first edition.

Although Hef showed up with a date, he spent the early part of the evening talking to an attractive woman named Shirley, who was the roommate of Mary Ann, Lownes' girlfriend.

He also chatted with Winters, finding him "zany, even crazy, but damn amusing." After only fifteen minutes, Hef became a lifelong devotee of the comedian and, beginning in 1960, began to purchase his comedy albums which he made for the Verve Records label.

At last the busy host of the party came over to chat with Hef. Lownes would later recall, "He looked like a senior from a college campus, and was dressed like one, too, white socks and all. In appearance, he certainly wasn't the hip publisher of an avant-garde men's magazine. But right from the start, we bonded at the hip, drawn to each other by our love of music and beautiful women (not necessarily in that order). I soon learned that, like me, Hef had deserted wife and family to become a playboy, but it would take some work on my part to turn him into the actual *Playboy* he hyped in his magazine."

In contrast, Lownes was the ideal image of the swinging playboy roving about Chicago after dark—suave, handsome, sophisticated, rich, debonair—a sybarite and connoisseur of the finer things of life, including beautiful women, wines, and men's fashion.

His own role models were the two most famous playboys in the world, Prince Aly Khan, who had married love goddess Rita Hayworth; and "The Stud of the Dominican Republic," the heavy-hung Porfirio Rubirosa, who had married the two richest women on the planet, tobacco heiress Doris Duke and Woolworth heiress Barbara Hutton.

"It was Victor himself who soon became my own role model," Hef confessed. "Almost from the beginning, we saw each other every day, but mostly at night. We even slept in the same bed together, but always with a woman—maybe more than one between us. From watching Victor in action, I learned some of the finer techniques of intercourse."

"Even though he was publisher of *Playboy*, Hef in the summer of 1954 was raw and unpolished," Lownes recalled.

He set out to transform Hef's image, taking him shopping at three of the most fashionable men's stores in Chicago, one tailor of whom fitted suits and tuxedos for Frank Sinatra. First, he had to rid Hef of those 1950s zoot suits with their wide lapels, and then discard those penny loafers with those "god damn Bix Beiderbeckean white socks," Lownes said.

Early in their friendship, Hef decided that Lownes was the perfect image of the *Playboy* fantasy he promoted in his magazine. A notorious seducer and philanderer, he was tall and handsome with a debonair aura of sophistication. He was also rich enough to enjoy what he called "the good things of life—beautiful women, vintage wines, luxurious 'digs,' and a sleek sports car."

Right from the beginning, Hef began to double date with him. He dated Shirley, the young woman he'd met at Lownes party. Soon, Mary Ann was out of the picture, and Barbara Cameron was in as Lownes' date. Both men saw other women on the side.

Barbara and Shirley ended up on the cover of the October 1956 edition of *Playboy,* and both of them became the inspiration for the popular cartoon series, "Babs & Shirley," that ran in the magazine.

After the first month of hanging out with Lownes, Hef knew him very well, because his newly minted swinging bachelor friend filled him in on his past. "He was very candid about his life and pursuits, even admitting to stuff most men wouldn't confess," Hef said. "I admired him for that."

Often, Lownes waited for Hef around his office, sometimes until 3AM for him to take off from work. "I always had a surprise for him when he got to my apartment. I was the one man who really taught Hef the glories of group sex."

Perhaps out of jealousy, many staffers at *Playboy* resented Hef's new friend, even labeling him "Machiavellian." He was rumored to have introduced Hef not only to group sex, but to drugs and bisexuality.

Lownes urged Hef to hire only bachelors or divorced men on his staff—"no happily married men unless they have some special editorial talent or photographic talent."

"Hef and I fucked any Playmate willing to disappear into the night with the both of us. We wouldn't let her get out of bed until she had satisfied both of us."

"We also had some Satanic orgies, which we later learned how to stage with our new friend, Sammy Davis, Jr., who became a frequent visitor to Chicago. That little bastard was ugly as shit, but he claimed he'd fucked everybody from Ava Gardner to Marilyn Monroe—and I believed him. So did Hef."

"Sometimes late at night, Hef entertained our guests with a bongo drum concert to wake up our sleeping neighbors. Sammy joined in."

"Our lifestyle was lavish and lecherous," Lownes said. "Hef and

**HIGH ART AND SUBTLE EROTICA FROM THE ALL-AMERICAN GIRLS NEXT DOOR.**

Barbara and Shirley. They weren't technically twins, but clever hair and makeup managed to address any fetish issues the male readership might have harbored for biological lookalikes.

Catering to the postwar allure of the All American and wholesomely sexual, Hef's marketing department defined it as "The Collegiate Edition" in October of 1956.

I were two of a kind."

"I started out posing as a model for *Playboy* ads, and he called me the perfect model to hawk certain products. One thing led to another, and within a few months, I became the production manager for the upcoming *Playboy* enterprises. I was soon second in command, the job of a lifetime. The world was ours, or so we thought at the time. But sometimes reality fucks up the best-laid plans of man, including those of playboys like us."

**VICTOR LOWNES' ROLE MODEL #1**
*aka*
**Stylish EuroCelebs in the Age of Sputnik**

# PRINCE ALY KHAN

shown here with Hollywood's "sex and love goddess" Rita Hayworth (his unhappy wife from 1949-53) in a publicity photo for *Champagne Safari (1954).*

*Hailed as the world's greatest lover, "Aly just loved women too much," said actress Kim Novak. His conquests ranged from Zsa Zsa Gabor to Joan Fontaine. Juliette Greco said, "I didn't know any women who did not have an affair with Aly."*

*Lownes met him one night in London, and they talked about women. "He told me his success was because of his staying power—he could go for hours of constant intercourse."*

*According to the Prince, "I was trained in sexual stamina, an ancient Persian and Arabic technique called Imsák, something that later spread to Moghul India, when I was a teenager in Cairo,"*

*His greatest conquest involved marrying the love goddess of the world, Rita Hayworth, beautifully vivacious, sexy, and desirable. She once visited the Playboy Mansion in Los Angeles. "She gave me that 'come hither' glint in her eye," Hef said. "I told her she'd once starred in a wet dream I had."*

**VICTOR LOWNES' ROLE MODEL #2**
*aka*
**Studmuffins Every Playboy Tried
—for a while at least—
to Emulate**

# PORFIRIO RUBIROSA

Before feminism had a chance to critique him as male chauvinist, his social and sexual adventures were widely admired by playboy wannabes starved for glamour in the gray landscapes following World War II.

Admired by both Hef and Victor Lownes, Porfirio Rubirosa was known as "The Playboy of the Western World." The size of his penis, as discussed by many socially connected women, became legendary. Waiters used his name as a moniker for the oversized pepper mills then in vogue in restaurants at the time. Lownes once stood next to him at a urinal at "21" in New York, and later evaluated his genitalia as "It looked like Yul Brynner in a black turtleneck."

He was married to the two richest women in the world—tobacco heiress Doris Duke and Woolworth heiress Barbara Hutton. (He's seen kissing her hand in the photo above. She later claimed, "It cost me $65,000 a day for every day I was married to him.)

His social and sexual adventures were also widely admired by Hef. The *Playboy* publisher told him, "We both, so I hear, have something in common. We like to take two or three women to bed at the same time."

Unattractively associated with selling exit visas to wealthy Jews desperate to escape from Europe during the peak of the Nazi regime, he was infamously associated with the repressive Dominican dictator, Rafael Trujillo.

"I'll tell you the secret of my success as a lover," Rubi told Hef. "To maintain my virility, I drink Japanese tea."

# Chapter Four

# HEF & THE AMERICAN LITERATI
### AFTER HE INCLUDES THE WORKS OF CRITICALLY ACCLAIMED WRITERS , *PLAYBOY* RIDES THE WAVES OF
# LITERARY CHIC
### YET DESPITE ITS LITERARY AMBITIONS,
# PLAYBOY'S SOARING SUCCESS
### SPAWNS A HOST OF "SMIRKING, LEERING, STAG-MINDED" COMPETITORS "TRADING ON THE FEMALE TORSO"

# HEF DIRECTS A PORNO FLICK
### CO-STARRING THE BLONDE BOMBSHELL
### JAYNE MANSFIELD
### & HER FUTURE HUSBAND, MR. UNIVERSE,
### MICKEY HARGITAY

Mickey Hargitay & Jayne Mansfield, justifiably configuring themselves as a sexually hip and very liberated couple in these publicity pix from the glory years of early Hugh Hefner. Center photo: Doing the Twist at the Candy Stik Lounge in 1962

**A towering figure** in the literary and editorial world, Auguste Comte Spectorsky (*aka* "Spec") entered Hugh Hefner's world in the spring of 1956, when he became the editorial director of *Playboy*. He was hired for $35,000 a year, plus benefits that included stock in the company. His salary continued to rise during his tenure at *Playboy*. There, for years to come, he'd make the magazine more highbrow. "With your instinct and my literary taste," he told Hef, "there's no way we can't succeed."

At first, the idea of deserting Manhattan for the "wilds" of Chicago was difficult for Spec. He viewed anything in the Midwest as prairie country. He asked Hef, "Do buffalo still roam the streets of Chicago?"

Spec knew virtually every major writer in America. After joining the staff of *Playboy*, he began hosting—in league with his wife, Theo (a book editor)—literary *soirées* in Manhattan during which he'd introduce Hef to A-list writers, the cream of the literati in 1950s America.

Spec was an imposing figure, standing six feet two inches, with eyes large enough to challenge those of Joan Crawford. He ordered his barber to give him a close crop—"but not a crewcut"—as he detested men with shaggy hair, claiming "They all look like violinists." An aura of urbanity encased him. He was the most well-read editor Hef would ever know. "If I haven't read

Spectorsky (left) with Hefner in 1956. As described by Jay Livingston, a professor of sociology at Montclair State University in New Jersey, the man who "mounted" this otherwise rare photo: "One tiny fun fact that you probably won't find in the Hugh Hefner obituaries this week: The brains behind *Playboy* was a sociologist, A.C. Spectorsky.

Spectorsky did not have a sociology degree. He had a BS in physics from NYU, and he worked in media. But his writing had a sociological bent. His 1955 book *The Exurbanites* (he coined the term exurbs) was reviewed by C. Wright Mills.

In 1956, he became associate publisher of *Playboy*, and I suspect that it was Spectorsky's ideas that transformed *Playboy*, surrounding the photos of bare-breasted women with pages that proclaimed the cultural sophistication of the magazine and its readers. With Hef, he moved *Playboy* from the nudie-mag periphery to a more central place in the culture, with circulation numbers to match.

His byline was A.C., and most people called him Spec. But the initials stood for Auguste Comte.He was named after the man often credited with coining the term sociology."

an author, he (or she) isn't worth reading. That leaves out Harold Robbins, Ian Fleming, Gore Vidal, and that little faggoty bitch Truman Capote. The plays of Tennessee Williams are vile, an insult to the fine traditions of Broadway. Arthur Miller is a playwright after my heart and soul."

Born in Paris of American parents in 1910, Spec spoke only French until he was four years old. In time, he became not only a writer, but an editor, anthologist, and publisher. Involved in mass communications since 1929, he referred to himself as a "communicator," writing book reviews for *The New York Times* and becoming the editor of such periodicals as *Living for Young Homemakers, Park East, Charm,* and others.

At the time, Spec was best known for his acerbically witty book, *The Exurbanites.* Published in 1955, it examined the "horrors" of life in the post-war American suburbs.

Critic Charles Poore hailed it as a "probe into the dwellers of suburbia who come back to live in New York, leaving 'Exurbia' to the tattersall weskit tycoons, the real estate developers, the experts on the pecking order of country club dances and on station platforms, the recurring flood disasters and other awesome aspects of gracious country living."

Spec once suggested to Hef that he change the name of his magazine to *Smart Set.* Hef refused. "We've got a good thing going. I don't want to tamper with success."

The oldest member of Hef's staff, Spec stirred up resentment from some of the other editors, especially Ray Russell, who—before Spec's arrival—had been buying and editing articles from writers.

Throughout his term at *Playboy,* Spec often clashed with Victor Lownes, who once admitted to him, "I doubt if Hef reads more than ten books a year, if that. Your buying fiction from the big boys will introduce him to writers he's never read before. I don't mean to put Hef down. He has a native intelligence and is very smart, as you'll soon find out."

Hef showed a slight jealousy toward his new editorial director and didn't want to give him too much credit for bringing "class" to *Playboy.* "I admit he has brought a greater editorial excellence to us, but if it weren't him, it would surely be somebody else of equal merit. In the end, it is my own insights that have upgraded *Playboy.*"

Although to his face, Spec was always respectful of Hef, behind his back, he sometimes unleashed a more negative view. "Our Boy Wonder is forever the Frat Boy, gawking over nudes." And occasionally, Spec made disparaging remarks about Hef to other staff members. "He has so little talent as a publisher that no other magazine would hire him, so he had to start his own. He's a man of extremes, very selfish and self-centered, egocentric, anally retentive, and suspicious of others and their motives to the point of paranoia. He often suffers fools but castigates those whose opinions actually matter."

When reporters contacted Spec to set up an interview with Hef, Spec sometimes trivialized and dismissed them. "In an interview, Mr. Hefner clams up. He doesn't know what makes good copy. I suggest you abandon your hope of getting a good interview from him."

Around the office, Spec became known as Hef's "egghead editor."

Unlike Victor and Hef, Spec was a faithful and loving husband to his wife. Theo, the hostess of many a literary tea, was just as urbane and sophisticated as her husband. She once remarked, "The last thing one of these writers drinks at one of my *soirées* is tea. Most of them go for hard liquor and lots of it."

Knowing how devoted Spec was to his talented wife, Hef told Spec, "I finally realize why you and Theo make such a great couple. You two practice fidelity for kicks."

Taking time off from his administrative duties, Hef sometimes flew from Chicago to New York to attend their literary soirées. They introduced Hef into literary circles as "the new Harold Ross," a very flattering (and somewhat exaggerated) reference to the distinguished founder of the deeply respected *The New Yorker*.

Hef quickly formed sketchy opinions of the many writers he met, sometimes fearing that they regarded *Playboy* with a certain concealed contempt. "Although they'd rather be published in *The New Yorker* or in *Esquire*, they were (nonetheless) willing to cash my checks."

Quite possibly, it was money instead of prestige that attracted writers to *Playboy*. *Esquire* and other magazines often paid no more than $400 for an article, but Spec, with Hef's permission, sent them at least $2,000 per article.

***

Privately, Spec was skeptical of the young women who came and went so quickly through the lives and beds of Hef and Victor, whom he referred to as "budding Don Juans." Then, after a few months in his orbit, Spec grew increasingly alarmed by Hef's addiction to amphetamines. "Sometimes, he goes for two days and nights without sleep. He suffers from a kind of megalomania, excessively and compulsively editing and re-editing, a nightmare for some of our writers. He goes crazy debating where a comma should go."

Spec said, "I enjoy my work at *Playboy*, but at times, I feel that my role here is beneath me. My dream was to become the editor of *The New Yorker*.

At least Hef is more editorially oriented than many publishers, whose main goal is profit. At times, I hate him so much it might mean that I really love him. You know that thin line between love and hate?"

Ultimately, Spec became unpopular with the other editors at *Playboy*, especially when he mocked their literary style, or lack thereof. He came down hard on Thomas Mario, the food and drink editor. At times, in the office, he read aloud his references to food. Mario referred to clams as "mischievous mollusks with piquant personalities" and wrote a "Paean of praise to the luscious lily"—in other words, an onion.

As the 1950s moved on, three men were running *Playboy*, each with a nickname: "Hef," "Vic," and "Spec."

\*\*\*

Early in his broadcasting career, back when both men were just getting started in their respective fields, Mike Wallace interviewed Hef on his radio show. Since then, Wallace had risen to national fame with his hugely popular TV show, *The Mike Wallace Show*.

Although Hef had long interpreted Wallace as a hostile interviewer, he agreed to appear on his show during one of his visits to Manhattan.

He was waiting, ready to go on, when he heard Wallace introduce him. "Tonight, our guest is the thirty-year-old brain behind the hottest property in the publishing world. We'll try hard to find out why Hugh Hefner really did start *Playboy* and whether or not it's just a smutty magazine."

Once he was seated, Hef had to respond to Wallace's volley of hostile and off-putting questions. "Since you present women undraped, do you enjoy the profits from this oversexed endeavor?"

Hef admitted that sex was obviously an allure of *Playboy*, but claimed that his magazine was more than that, presenting articles on food and drink, men's fashion, the latest in auto design, apartment furnishings, and features on music, plus articles by some of the finest and best-known writers in America.

"Aren't you, in fact, just selling a high-class dirty book?" Wallace asked, not disguising the edge of hostility in his voice.

On TV's hugely popular *The Mike Wallace Show*, Hef had to defend himself against charges that *Playboy* was a smutty magazine. The photo displays Wallace in 1957.

"There's nothing dirty about sex unless you make it dirty," Hef responded. "A picture of a half-clothed beautiful woman is something that a fellow of any age ought to be able to enjoy. It's the sick mind that finds something loathsome and obscene in sex."

As the interview progressed, ("detoured," in Hef's words), Wallace continued to push his smut agenda through his questioning.

"I estimate that only five percent of the contents of *Playboy* is devoted to sex," Hef protested. "Yet we seem to be devoting an entire half hour of this program to it tonight."

Anxious to leave the show, Hef rose quickly at the end of the broadcast, heading for the exit.

Backstage, he spoke to a reporter from the *Daily News*. "Many young women are beginning to accept the sexual attitude of a bachelor who seeks physical pleasure without having to sign up for a lifetime," an obvious reference to sex without benefit of marriage.

Other forms of media were responding to Hef's *Playboy* with more sophistication than Wallace. At the time, the broadcaster was an admitted homophobe, and would soon air a program on "the evils of homosexuality creeping across the American landscape."

An article in the *Nation* noted the success of *Playboy*. "Starting bawdily and naïvely, it has grown progressively subtler with its photographs of fresh, attractive young women from ordinary avenues of American life. We must applaud a brand-new invention in eroticism which grew out of the free-wheeling, ebullient attitude of *Playboy* editors, notably one Hugh Hefner."

By the late 1950s, many observers claimed that the rumblings of the ongoing sexual revolution could be heard, although it would not reach its full impact until the mid-1960s.

"I was sending out a call for Americans to re-examine old morality standards," Hef said. "I wanted to publish a magazine that suggested that sex was not a work of Satan. I wanted to encourage young men to have sex free of guilt. In effect, I was attacking stiff-necked, repressive Victorians originating in England more than America's puritan roots."

"America was changing before my eyes," he claimed. "Elvis Presley with his gyrating hips has arrived on the scene, shaking his clothed but undulating hillbilly pecker before audiences of screaming teenage girls who looked like they were in the throes of orgasm. Any man who believes that sex should only be an instrument of procreation is an idiot."

He wrote articles such as "The Gentle Art of Laying Hands on Lasses All About You." Once, he suggested, "Many young men may not know this, but there are hordes of virgins out there who want to be relieved of that condition. Tomorrow, all of us may be destroyed by Soviet atomic bombs, so why not have fun tonight, instead of never?"

He accused homosexual fashion designers of de-sexing women, "creating *Vogue* mannequins with no breasts, the Audrey Hepburn look."

"*Playboy* promotes straight sex," he claimed. "We are against androgyny or the transgender status. We stand against suppression of sexual desires that can lead to child molestation among so-called celibate priests. We prefer a healthy heterosexual sexual appetite."

\*\*\*

"If Marilyn Monroe was the blonde sex goddess of the 1950s, Jayne Mansfield was at least her lady-in-waiting," Hef claimed.

Although he had never heard of her, in February of 1955, he selected her as his magazine's Playmate of the Month,. At the time, he had no way of knowing, of course, what a big role she would play in his future.

Her posing nude for Hef helped launch her movie career, which would be short-lived. Like the Monroe calendar shot, Mansfield as the nude centerfold increased circulation of *Playboy.*

One of the most enduring of the Playmates, Mansfield evoked the sexuality of the 50s when big breasts were in. As a movie star, her career was short, peaking in 1956 and 1957, during which time she posed for 2,500 photographs which appeared in newspapers and magazines.

As a star, not known for her acting but for her body, she was one of the screen's "bad girls" along with Monroe and Jane Russell. *[The "good girls" of filmdom were Doris Day, Natalie Wood, and Debbie Reynolds.]*

Dennis Russel in the *St. James Encyclopedia of Popular Culture* wrote, "Most people had not seen her movies, yet Mansfield, long after her death, remains one of the most vivid and best known icons of 1950s celebrity culture." Bill Osgerby claimed, "Marilyn Monroe, Jayne Mansfield, and Brigitte Bardot popularized the skimpy bikini from the French Riviera."

**THERE IS NOTHING LIKE A DAME**

Jayne Mansfield described her brief fling with Elvis Presley to Hef:

"I felt something wiggling around down there, teasing me, but to achieve orgasm, I require a deep, thick penetration from a man like Mickey Hargitay."

Comedian Lenny Bruce appraised her breasts: "Her cleavage matched the Grand Canyon and should have been landmarked by the National Park Service." When she appeared on Jack Paar's *Tonight* Show, he introduced her by saying, "Here *they* are!"

Mansfield held various titles: Miss Nylon Sweater, Miss Electric Switch, Miss Geiger Counter, and Miss Négligée.

Evangelist Billy Graham lamented, "Americans know more about Miss Mansfield's measurements of 40-21-36 than they do the Second Commandment."

Mansfield only pretended to be dumb, as she had an IQ of 163. She later claimed, "JFK screwed me when I was pregnant."

According to Hef, "Only the 1950s could have produced a blonde bombshell like Jayne. Like Marilyn, she wanted to be taken seriously as an actress, but then she came out on stage on Broadway wearing cellophane. To my readers, she was a living, breathing sexual fantasy, the star of many a nighttime wet dream."

"Every red-blooded male wanted to get to know Suzi," he said. "That was her nickname for her much overworked pussy."

David Niven referred to Mansfield as "Miss United Dairies."

Reporters could always rely on her for a quotable quote. "I'm a big girl, and I have to have a big guy to satisfy me…one who's big all over. Men—I just love 'em! They are wonderful creatures with one penis, two legs, and eight hands. Men want women pink, helpless, and capable of deep breathing, They love it when you scream out, 'Stop it! You're hurting me! Take it out! No, no, keep going, buster.'"

When *Playboy's* edition with her nude centerfold was published, Hef received bags of mail praising her attributes. There was the occasional dissenter. Director Pal Wendkos wrote Hef: "Shame on you! Mansfield is just for truck drivers. Your centerfold of her should be placed over the urinals in some smelly toilet along the turnpike. She's cheap looking. You let us down. You could have done better."

In *Popcorn Venus*, her book on Hollywood stars, Marjorie Rosen wrote: "Jayne Mansfield launched an all-out campaign to steal Monroe's crown. She jumped at every chance to display her vast proportions and embraced a lifestyle rivaling that of Mae West. Publicists delighted in her Pink Palace, her pink heart-shaped pool, her pink poodle, and the Hungarian muscleman she married," a reference to "Mr. Universe," Mickey Hargitay."

The centerfold was such a big hit with *Playboy* readers that he did additional layouts of her in February of 1958 and again in December of that same year as a "Christmas gift" to his readers. And then in 1960, he published additional provocative pictures of her with the headline THE BEST

OF JAYNE MANSFIELD.

But the best and worst was yet to come.

\*\*\*

Throughout 1956, Hef continued his relentless search for the ideal Playmate, finding her more often than not. Many centerfold candidates, numbering in the hundreds, were presented to him by eager photographers, only to have him reject them.

As was typical of many encounters, photographers Carlyle Blackwell, Jr. came to him with provocative photographs. After studying them, Hef pronounced them as "too nude. Her face looks like she's been around the block too many times. In fact, she looks like a hardened stripper. I want young women whose reputation is as unblemished as her body."

For the July issue, he found what he was looking for in a bright lovely girl, Alice Denham, who had emerged from a conservative Southern family without adopting their values. She told him that as a girl, she had fantasized about being a boy.

"That is one ambition you'll never achieve," Hef said, as he studied her enticing bosom.

She had graduated from the University of Rochester as a Phi Beta Kappa and had come to New York seeking literary fame and romance. "Manhattan in the 1950s was like Paris in the '20s," she said. Soon, she was making her way through the literary salons of the city, with plans to bed any famous author who came into her focus. "Manhattan was a river of men flowing past my door, and when I was thirsty, I drank."

She pitched a short story to *Playboy* entitled "The Deal" about a young woman, an aspiring artist in Las Vegas, who agrees to sleep with an aged gambler for $1,000. Meeting with Hef, she assured him that the story was not autobiographical, but based purely on her imagination.

She also told him she was writing a novel

*sleeping with* **BAD BOYS**

A JUICY
TELL-ALL OF
LITERARY
NEW YORK
IN THE 1950s
AND 1960s

*alice denham*

Alice Denham, America's ultimate literary groupie. When it came to American writers, she appealed to their minds, their sense of literary worth, their brains, and their dicks.

117

portraying the passionate conflict between a young (female) painter and her macho husband—a composer. It focuses, she said, on her rage, his brutality, and her struggle for self-realization as an artist. Hef, however, seemed more interested in getting her to agree to pose for a centerfold than he was in her literary achievements.

At first, although Denham refused to pose for him, criticizing him for "building an empire based on a woman's nude body," he finally won her over. She eventually became one of the most popular of his many centerfolds of the 1950s.

By the 1960s, Denham had evolved as an early feminist, a strong supporter of women's rights, including a woman's right to an abortion, in the 1960s. "*Playboy* advanced the sexual revolution, but it was a double-edged sword: Sexism vs. freedom," she wrote. "I have no regrets in exposing my body—in fact, it advanced my career. I got calls from publishers who wanted to print my novel."

In 2006, she published her lusty memoir, *Sleeping with Bad Boys: A Juicy Tell-All of Literary New York in the 1950s and 1960s,* in which she admitted that Hef had seduced her. "As a proper Southern girl, I was bred to be good to men—and I was," she wrote.

"Hef reached for my hand and embraced his organ with it. I was curious and disliked him enough to start playing with it. After a while, he rolled over and began kissing my breasts. Hef had a spare muscular frame, a good body. He was quite substantial and provided a hard, undeviating plunge, rhythm as unvaried as a metronome. He had staying power. A good ride, a steady canter. But I was left with no particular feeling, no personal feeling of connection, of uniting."

She also wrote of other affairs with other men, none of them more famous than her dalliance with the doomed young actor James Dean.

"Before we tumbled into each other's arms easily, without haste, tasting and feeling, Jimmy had smoother, baby-smelling, rosy white skin with very little hair except for the blondish-brown pad around his privates. He was lightly muscled, his high school sports muscles turning into longer, slimmer dance muscles because he studied ballet. Jimmy smelled like vanilla. We were lusty, we fit. His dimensions were neither disappointing nor thrilling. They were average, perhaps the only thing about him that was."

"Philip Roth," she continued in another passage of her book, "was a sex fiend. He moved from tits to—*aaaah!*—so fast I was breathless. Speeded up like his talk and his head. But once he got there, he hung in long and steamy. Tepid men move me. Philip was on fire."

Denham wrote of the time she went to bed with James Jones, author of *From Here to Eternity*. [*A stark overview of the men and machinery of World War II, it was published in 1951. Later, it was designated by the Modern Library Board as one of the 100 best novels of the 20th century.*]

Denham recalled looking down at Jones' crotch and asking him if he wanted her to try to make his penis hard, only to be informed that this was what it was like fully erect. "Never have I seen a penis so small. But I showed no shock. It was the size of a man's thumb, no longer and no thicker. When he entered me, I couldn't even feel it."

Norman Mailer invited her to his parties in Greenwich Village, although she considered him, the author of *The Naked and the Dead*, "a freak."

It was at one of Mailer's parties that Denham met the man of her dreams, the literary critic, Anatole Broyard, who enjoyed a reputation as "The Great Lover of the Village." She called him, "the very image of the Bohemian dandy, as handsome as a shirt ad." She wrote of his "mad, passionate endless tongue-lashing. We kissed torridly, he clasped my breasts and licked them remorselessly, we dallied and twisted like eels into a nice-fitting *ying-yang*. I was so moist. Nothing happened. He had a soft-on."

Denham admitted to arriving at literary *soirées* with one purpose in mind: "to snare the most famous writer in the room into getting him to fuck me." *The New York Times* called her pursuit "phallictropic."

Denham's ultimate conclusion? "What horsey male writers know about love is *nada*."

***

In some instances, beginning in the mid-1950s, famous or well-connected men would meet and marry the magazine's Playmate of the Month. Such was the case with the former Miss Denmark, Elsa Sørensen, September 1955's Playmate of the Month.

She married the pop crooner and movie star, Guy Mitchell. He had become a household word in 1957 when he stared on TV in ABC's *The Guy Mitchell Show*. He went on to sell 44 million records with such big hits as *"My Heart Cries for You (1950)"* and *"Singing the Blues (1956)."* Born in the U.S. to Croatian immigrants, Mitchell appraised Sørensen's charms as "my own Danish pastry."

For Miss November of that year, photographer Hal Adams submitted an alluring Arkansas-born model "Betty Blue." Hef liked the photographs, but said that with a name like that, "She's got to be a stripper." After an investigation, it was revealed that she was a sweet and innocent girl, and that the only time she'd ever pulled off her clothes for a photographer was for the above-mentioned centerfold.

Lisa Winters was the Playmate for the issue of December of 1950. In reference to it, Hef said, "I was Santa Claus to the readers of *Playboy* in bringing to our centerfold this pert and perky All-American girl, the type who lives up the street from where you live. She is the kind of fresh young beauty that photographers from across the country are forever in search of."

"Winters is also smart, reading Ernest Hemingway, Edgar Allan Poe, and Rudyard Kipling—and quoting the poetry of Elizabeth Barrett Browning. She is our Sunshine Girl."

He posed her in what he referred to as his "Knoll Womb Chair." His favorite picture of her was emerging from a swimming pool. Many readers thought that it was an image of Marilyn Monroe. Bunny Yeager, the photographer who had discovered Bettie Page, had also gotten Winters to pose in the nude.

Hef commented on his *Playmate* centerfolds: "I tapped into the male *Zeitgeist*. Post-war males were free agents, restless, not willing to be tied down to the model of family togetherness espoused by magazines like *McCall's*. Men carried that energy into the urban night, listening to jazz in smoky clubs, enjoying the revolutionary humor of a new kind of comedian like Mort Sahl or Lenny Bruce. *Playboy* created that heady mix for the newsstand and coffee table."

In 1955, Hef reached out to Jack Kessie, naming him associate editor. A former trumpeter, he had been advertising manager of Coronet Instructional Films. He came to Hef's attention when he submitted an article, "The Well-Dressed Playboy—Playboy's Position on Proper Attire."

Going to work for *Playboy* that June, he was still the arbiter of taste in men's fashion for the magazine, continuing to write about men's attire under the pseudonym of "Blake Rutherford." His work met with Hef's praise, and by 1960, he had named him managing editor of *Playboy*.

When Hef saw *Playboy's* sales figures for 1956, he was elated to learn that earnings had gone beyond $3 million. In magazine circulation, it had risen from 80th to 49th in the nation.

Hef answered his growing legions of critics, mostly women. "The protesting feminists don't get it. Attitudes are changing about nudity, and more and more young women are willing to appear *déshabillée*. More than any woman's magazine, *Playboy* has removed the girdle and allowed women to appear in the bikini and the miniskirt, even nude if that is their desire."

"There's something wrong either psychologically or glandularly with some guy who isn't interested in nude pictures of pretty girls. If the pictures replace the girls themselves, the guy has problems."

"I don't believe the world should be divided into virgins and non-virgins. Of course, there remain a lot of butch women who like to castrate men. They seem unhappy with the male-female relationship that exists in society. They want to expose men as impotent in bed and in the workplace, plus in a thousand and one other ways. Instead of a love relationship, it's degenerated into a battle of the sexes."

*** 

In the world of magazine publishing, the success of *Playboy* attracted—in Hef's view—a "greedy wolf pack of wannabe imitators." He was delivered each new copy of any competing magazine as soon as it reached the newsstands of Chicago. "Most of them looked like we did in our first edition, only worse," he said. "Amateur night! Models looking like yesterday's tired burlesque queens."

*Playboy* continued to attract nationwide media attention, including an article that appeared in the November 1955 edition of *Newsweek:* "For 20 years, the late David A. Smart's *Esquire* has dominated the men's indoor field. Last week, Smartmen were appearing uneasily over their shoulders. A rival, younger by a generation, was appearing uneasily over their shoulders. Bolder by several shocking inches of neckline, it is attempting to get its way into the old gentleman's hunting grounds. *Playboy,* the new magazine, is a hefty circulation success."

The April 1957 issue of *Time* defined *Playboy* as "the biggest, bawdiest, and bestselling collection of men's magazines in publishing history."

The May issue of Henry Luce's other magazine, *Fortune,* proclaimed, "Hugh Hefner has toned down the smoking room jokes and upgraded the art. In brief, *Playboy* has begun to grow up."

*** 

*Fortune* also took note of the other "roguish bachelor magazines appealing to adolescent males of all ages."

Some of those magazines competing for a share of *Playboy's* circulation included the following:

The first issue of *Tiger* hit the newsstands in 1956. Its publisher, G. George Fox, trumpeted, "Every man is a tiger," and defined his centerfold model as "Miss Tiger of the Month." It was also the first of the men's magazines to highlight "that country boy singer," Elvis Presley.

Fox didn't like his magazine being compared to *Playboy.* "Tiger is like no other magazine in America," he said. "It is a new concept, not a nudist

magazine, but a periodical for the man of destiny. In other words, TIGERS!"

He cited as his typical readers heroic men who evoked such legendary figures as General George S. Patton, George Armstrong Custer, and Napoléon.

"The comparisons of his readers to those legends is laughable," Hef said. "Who is he kidding? Himself, no doubt."

*Rogue* also rolled off the presses in 1956 as a distinct challenger to *Playboy*. It, too, offered nude pictures and sex advice to men. Like Hef, the editors turned to articles by distinguished writers such as Hunter S. Thompson, Graham Greene, and Philip Wylie.

Its publisher, William Hamling, remembered meeting Hef during his pre-*Playboy* days. "He came into my office a poor and struggling cartoonist with a passion for fantasy. I felt sorry for him and bought some of his cartoons, although they were too amateurish to publish. Later, when he had such a big success with *Playboy*, I threatened to publish those cartoons to embarrass him."

"You can't sell sex to the American public," Hamling warned Hef. "My immortal words should be engraved on my tombstone. He wanted me to back *Playboy* financially, and, like a fool, I turned him down, the biggest mistake in publishing history."

"When I launched *Rogue,* I, too, ran a picture of Marilyn Monroe, but she was hiding her goodies behind a towel," he said. "I admit I was an imitator of *Playboy*, as were 90 percent of all the other girlie magazines. Hef used the horny rabbit as his logo, so I adopted a libidinous wolf as my mascot."

*Satan* magazine originated in 1957 and was immediately labeled as a "*Playboy* clone but with a devilish beat, with a drawing of Satan on its cover with a semi-nude model. It featured pin-ups and articles for the urban male bachelor lifestyle devotee. It also specialized in occult-themed erotica, with such titles as 'Black Magic.'"

The public wasn't buying it, and it folded after only six issues. Before its demise, one of its highlights involved running pictures of Bettie Page, the Queen of Pin-Ups. As Hef said, "Been there, done that."

*Swan* was a pornographic magazine that had been around since 1941, featuring scantily clad beauties on its cover and touting articles such as "Tight Young Pussy." Inspired by Hef, it rebooted itself in the 1950s, featuring upscale writers like Norman Mailer and Ian Fleming.

*[Magna Publishing acquired the magazine in 1993 and turned it into a periodical of hardcore sex, featuring lesbian love, sex toys, and depictions of men and*

## Amid All This Competition (Tigers & Rogues & Satans & True Detectives), Where's the Bunny?

In the face of rising competition from less erudite and less discreet skin-flick mags, Hef and his team worked hard to stay on the right side of both aesthetics and political factionalism. Note the model on the cover of *Satan* magazine, one of the five below, is the pre-eminent S & M diva of her age, Bettie Page.

*women*

*engaged in sexual intercourse.]*

    *Escapade* didn't pretend to be anything but an imitation of *Playboy*—in fact, its December 1956 issue featured one of the nude calendar shots of Marilyn Monroe (not the one run by Hef). It also published a profile of the white jazz *swooshmeister*, Stan Kenton.

    The gay beat poet, Allen Ginsburg, was an early feature in *Swank*, as was William Saroyan, whose writing had previously been published by Hef. In contrast to *Playboy*, it also ran raunchy articles such as "The Life and Loves of a Girl Hound."

*Relax* magazine billed itself as a "Prescription for Pleasure" for men, and *Jackspot* hailed itself as "The Cad's Home Companion."

Oddly enough, when *Playgirl* first appeared on the market, it featured female nudes. But within months, it began to appeal to an audience of straight women and gay men by running centerfolds of male nudes.

Jean-Paul Sartre wrote an article for *Gent* magazine, causing one critic to ask, "What in the fuck is he doing in such a magazine? It's not every man who wants a dose of existentialism with his D-cups."

"Tits and ass" were a feature in such magazines as *Life Study*, and *Camera*. Those words were later used in the lyrics to a key song in *A Chorus Line*, that long-running Broadway musical.

Another magazine hitting newsstands at the time was *Dude*. Aimed at the African American male, it featured nude pictures of beautiful black women. In time Hef, too, would publish nude black models in *Playboy*.

George von Rosen had once employed Hef to work on his magazine, *Modern Sunbathing*. He came out with a new magazine called *Men's World*. Unlike the stylish urban male featured in *Playboy*, he aimed at "the beer-swilling, blue collar male. Forget the high-class fiction and those articles on men's fashion," he said. "I wanted to appeal to men who like to see a big pair of jugs. You know the type, a hairy-chested Tarzan running through the jungle to pork Jane."

*Jem* was a magazine for "The Masterful Man," and *Hi-Life* was the "Live It Up Magazine for Gentlemen."

*Cavalier* was yet another *Playboy* wannabe, running such articles as "The Guilt Free Art of Maori Love Making," a reference to the Polynesian people of New Zealand. *Adam* came onto the scene featuring "The Strip Tease Queens," and *Mister* appeared with a story about the current fad of "wife swapping."

These were only some of the magazines being hawked on newsstands. After surveying the lot of them, Hef said, "I will survive all of them, including competitors to appear in *Playboy's* future."

\*\*\*

"In 1957, on June 22, I knew I had arrived when *The New Yorker* printed a full-page cartoon showing a sultan in his harem, ignoring all the luscious damsels around him to read the latest copy of *Playboy*," Hef said.

"That bit of joy was followed by an invitation from my centerfold,

Jayne Mansfield, and her new boyfriend, Mickey Hargitay, the former Mr. Universe, to visit Los Angeles. I eagerly accepted, not knowing that Los Angeles would become my future home."

"Once there, I met Jayne's muscle-bound bodybuilder, Mickey, and found him a delight, very personable. She would marry her 'hunk of man' (her words) in 1958," Hef said. He had already seen their movie, *Will Success Spoil Rock Hunter?*

"Jayne had called to tell me that Mickey had agreed to pose for a centerfold of the two of them in the next issue of *Playboy*," Hef said. "I thought it over and—as tempting as it was—I rejected the idea but very politely. In the future, many of our competitors would pose men and women to-

Filmed in Italy in 1960, and released on television in the U.S. in 1966 as a Movie of the Week *The Loves of Hercules* (aka, *Hercules vs. the Hydra*) bombed at the box office, even though Jayne Mansfield and Mickey Hargitay heated up the screen.

Hef saw it twice, but wasn't really satisfied. "I want to do a stag film showing Jayne and Mickey making love, just for my private viewing pleasure."

On the lower left, Hargitay, a former Mr. Universe, proudly displays his muscled physique on the cover of *Iron Man*.

On the lower right, in 1959, "America's hottest couple" arrive in Paris to woo the French.

gether in sexual situations, but I felt that was against the image I was promoting for *Playboy*."

Mansfield, as Hef later learned, had spotted Hargitay when he was performing in *The Mae West Show* at the Latin Quarter, a nightclub in New York City. From her table, Mansfield had instructed her waiter, "Bring me a steak. And the handsome, tall devil on the left," a reference to Hargitay. At the time, he was West's "property," performing not only in her show, but in her boudoir, too.

"I immediately fell for Jayne," Hargitay told Hef. "She relieved me of my stud duties. After all, Miss West was born in 1893, not a big turn-on for me."

"In Hollywood, Jayne and Mickey were wonderful hosts to me. The next night, they paraded me into Romanoff's, former haunt of Humphrey Bogart. They created a sensation. I don't think anybody knew who I was."

The following night, the well-stacked couple threw a party for Hef at the famous Garden of Allah Hotel, the former abode of James Dean, F. Scott Fitzgerald, Nazimova, and Errol Flynn.

"I met Edd ("Kookie") Burns," Hef said. "He was soon to become famous in the 1958 hit TV series, *77 Sunset Strip*. Dean Martin showed up and was a real gas, jokingly agreeing to pose for a centerfold, providing I dug Italian salami."

It soon became clear to Hef that Hargitay and Mansfield were exhibitionists. They entertained him around their swimming pool, both of them completely nude. Hef pulled off all his clothes and frolicked with them in the water. "It was an obvious invitation for a three-way, and I choose not to tell what happened later that night. I left two days later."

Liz Renay, the ultimate Hollywood "star fucker" and Marilyn Monroe lookalike, claimed that Hargitay and Mansfield like to "ball in the middle of the floor, often entertaining as many as thirty to forty *voyeurs*. Jayne told me she likes to have people see her get fucked by a big stud like Mickey."

Victor Lownes flew into Los Angeles to join Hef and was entertained by Mansfield and Hargitay in more ways than one. During his visit, he got them to agree to have sexual intercourse on camera for a 20-minute clip.

According to Lownes, "After both Mickey and Jayne feasted on each other below the belt, they reverted to the missionary position for their climaxes, and I mean climax in two ways. I gave them a thousand dollars for their performances. "These two movie stars had their best alltime director, Hef himself, directing all their moves."

Regarding their physical attributes, Mansfield told Hef, "I can't help if I attract undue attention. It is just what God gave me, and I wouldn't want to interfere in the handiwork of the Lord."

While in Hollywood, Hef received an invitation to a wild party in the Hollywood Hills hosted by photographer Earl Leaf. Leaf photographed him cavorting with two beauties, Jean Bradshaw and Suzanne Sidney. In his biography scrapbook, Hef noted, "The party ended in an orgy—my first."

*[Hef's statement about how the party ended was true, but it wasn't his first orgy.]*

Later, back in Chicago, Hef called the popular columnist, Earl Wilson, and asked him to write an article, "Will Success Spoil Jayne Mansfield?"

Wilson referred to himself as "The Boswell of Bosoms," and in his article, he claimed "Jayne is the girl to make men forget Marilyn Monroe."

Hef was well aware that Mansfield was becoming one of the most talked-about stars in America. In his February 1958 issue, he ran a spread called "The Nude Jayne Mansfield" in which she is naked with her large breasts exposed. She also poses on her belly so Playboys could preview her succulent *derrière*.

In the past, except for the nude calendar shot Marilyn Monroe had posed for, such exposure would have destroyed a movie star's career

But times were changing, and Mansfield's studio, 20th Century Fox, released these photographs taken by William Read Woodfield. At Fox, it was determined that such exposure would boost Mansfield's box office allure.

"Not only that, but these hot, hot photographs caused our circulation to soar," Hef said.

\*\*\*

Any survey of the history of censorship in America would at least have to include a chapter, maybe more, on Hugh Hefner and *Playboy* magazine. He was one of the major cultural warriors of the 20th Century, battling the government and other forces for freedom of the press.

To fortify himself for his oncoming battles, he reviewed the history of censorship in the United States.

He found the chief villain was Anthony Comstock, a U.S. Postal inspector and moral crusader whose punitive effects on sexual expression in America were virtually incalculable.

Born in Connecticut in 1844, and dedicated to upholding the tenets of Victorian morality, he campaigned to censor periodicals he viewed as indecent and obscene. He developed a particular hostility toward any publication dispensing information about birth control. For his efforts, the terms "Comstockery" and "Comstockism" were applied to all future attempts at suppression.

By 1873, he'd become head of the New York Society for the Suppression of Vice, and, as such, he succeeded in getting the U.S. Congress to pass the Comstock Law, making it illegal to deliver through the U.S. Mail any material judged "obscene, lewd, or lascivious." He even opposed material about how to prevent venereal disease and tried to block the mailing of books on anatomy to medical students. He labeled George Bernard Show a "smut puddler" and tried to prevent his works from being staged.

He called himself "the weeder in God's garden." When D.M. Bennett published "An Open Letter to Jesus Christ," Comstock had the editor arrested for mailing "a free love pamphlet." Bennett was tried and sentenced to prison in Albany, New York.

Margaret Sanger denounced Comstock as "a moral eunuch," but a young J. Edgar Hoover was captivated by his message.

In all, Comstock was credited with destroying 15 tons of books and nearly four million photographs, plus building cases against writers and publishers, leading to 4,000 arrests. Had he lived in the 1950s, and been in a position of power, he would have buried Hef in his deepest dungeon.

In vivid contrast to Comstock, the "Sage of Baltimore," H.L. Mencken, was a journalist, satirist, and cultural critic. Because of his fights against the "blue-nosed Puritans of the 1920s," he became a hero to a latter-day Hef, who viewed himself as a warrior taking up the banner of Mencken in the 1950s. [Hef was willing to overlook the fact that Mencken was a racist and an anti-Semite.]

Hoover, as head of the F.B.I., was a passionate advocate of censorship, having kept Hef and *Playboy* under investigation since the release of the magazine's first issue. "The old toad seemed more interested in any reference to himself or the F.B.I. than he was in our centerfolds," Hef said. "Actually, as it was revealed, he was a major consumer of pornography, preferring nude males with erections."

It was only through the Freedom of Information Act that Hef learned that Hoover for years had kept an intensive file on him. Once, F.B.I. agents arrived unannounced at Hef's *Playboy* offices in Chicago, searching through files to find if he were involved in any "subversive" activities.

"They found nothing to indicate that," Hef said. "I was not a part of the so-called communist conspiracy that was destroying careers back in the 1950s."

Hef angered Hoover when he published an article attacking him "Hoover's campaign against pornography is only a ruse to distract the public from his inability to rub out organized crime."

Milton Jones, head of the F.B.I.'s crime division, ordered one of his G-men to read every page of *Playboy*. That order came down from Hoover himself.

Dubious arbiters of sexual morality, Clyde Tolson (left) and J. Edgar Hoover were closeted homosexuals, running the F.B.I. and persecuting homosexuals in a cynical tsunami of hypocrisy.

Jones finally wrote a memo to his boss: "I have determined we are wasting the time of our G-men by having at least one of them read *Playboy* every month. Often, the men pass it around the office. Hugh Hefner is nothing but a garbage collector of filth. I think the best way for the F.B.I. to move is to ignore his slime. Any attempt to suppress the magazine will only generate publicity for him and increase his sales."

***

Hef usually worked until midnight and then during the pre-dawn hours became a "bachelor-at-large." At this point in his marriage, he rarely visited Millie and his children.

After work, he and Victor Lownes patronized the hottest clubs on the North Side of Chicago, gathering material for their column, "Playboy on the Town."

"The horny duo," as they were called, were familiar faces at such clubs as The Black Orchid, Chez Paree, The Cloisters, Mr. Kelly's, and the Gaslight, the latter becoming the role model for the first Playboy Club Hef opened in Chicago.

Almost nightly, Lownes and Hef picked up at least two companions, always the most beautiful young women at whatever venue they visited, and invited them back to their hideaway apartment, which Lownes called "the love nest." Sometimes, they invited five or six girls there after work, and when two or three of their male buddies came along, the venue devolved into an orgy. "The name of the game is girls, girls, and more girls," Lownes said. "Bring 'em on. The orgy wouldn't end until dawn's early light."

Hef patronized the clubs not just for the pickups, but to hear some of the best jazz in America and to listen to the raunchy humor of some of the country's best comics, many just coming into prominence. Appearing to entertain the clientele in these various clubs were not only Sammy Davis, Jr., but also Mel Tormé, Buddy Rich, Don Adams, and Hef's alltime favorite singer, Tony Bennett.

With the owners of The Cloisters, Hef flew to San Francisco, which he visited as often as he could, since that city, along with Chicago, was featured in the "After Dark" columns of *Playboy*.

On his first night there, he was taken to Ann's 440 Club where he first met Lenny Bruce.

As Hef recalled, "On stage, Lenny was fearless. No words were *verboten* in his vocabulary."

Bruce appeared on stage spitting out a litany of the most forbidden words: "*Ass, balls, cocksucker, fuck motherfucker, piss, shit,* and *tits.*" Then he asked, "Are there any niggers in the audience? I think I saw one nigger couple in the back. Seated with those niggers are three kikes, two spics, one mick, two dykes, one spunky funky honky, plus six guineas and seven WOPS."

"*Playboy's* Hugh Hefner is in the audience tonight," Bruce said. "Welcome to San Francisco, home of pirates and pansies. If you didn't bring your favorite Bunny to fuck, I can line you up with some hot stuff: Three drag queens, the best cocksucker in San Francisco, and one big-busted har-lot who has a pussy the size of the Grand Canyon. Everything is legal in our fairy city."

After that, he went into the throes of faking an orgasm shouting, "I'm coming! I'm coming! I'M COMING!!"

Bruce related why he'd been discharged from the Navy in May of 1945: "To celebrate the Allied victory in Europe, I dressed in drag and put on a riotous show for my fellow sailors. The next day my commander called me in and informed me that the show revealed I had homosexual tendencies. I got the boot."

"I never got to suck one sailor dick, but I got kicked out anyway. On the subject of cocksucking, I always thank God that its practice is not confined just to homosexuals."

After that hilarious show, Bruce joined Hef at table. It was the beginning of a beautiful, yet turbulent, friendship that traveled down many a rocky road.

Lenny Bruce, onstage and under arrest.

"I ran a story on Lenny, the most outrageous comic in America, and it was his first national exposure," Hef said.

"The question I had to face was this: Is America ready for this true provocateur? Lenny pushed the envelope as far as it could be pushed."

***

Hef's alltime favorite comic was the Canadian-born Mort Sahl, with Lenny Bruce running a close second. "He was the best satirist in America," Hef said. "The first modern stand-up comic since Will Rogers. But he was Rogers with fangs."

Hef first exposure to Sahl's comedic style was at The Compass Players, a group whose name later changed to the Second City, when it featured performances by Mike Nichols and Elaine May. These young men and women satirized the stodgy reincarnated Victorians and tossed grenades at the hypocrisy of mainstream America.

Calling himself "America's only living philosopher," Sahl came on stage dressed simply in a V-neck sweater and slacks, holding a rolled-up newspaper.

Hef first saw his act at Chicago's Black Orchid. "Right from the beginning, I knew Sahl was going places. He broke new ground in satirizing politics and politicians. He also inspired a new generation of comics, even Phyllis Diller. One night Woody Allen told me that Sahl's revolutionary style of humor opened doors for people like him."

The British film critic, Penelope Gilliatt, aptly compared his routine to a circus act.

Mort Sahl. Almost as provocative as Lenny Bruce, but less prone to censorship and arrest.

He even made the cover of *Time* magazine, a rare honor for a comedian.

"He freewheelers a bike on a high-wire tightrope with his brain racing and his hands off the handlebars."

Hef soon learned that in spite of his "revolutionary mouth," Sahl was a clean-living comic. Unlike Bruce, he didn't smoke, consume liquor, or experiment with drugs.

Soon after meeting Hef, Sahl became an avid reader of *Playboy*. He quipped, "My entire generation grew up thinking that women fold in three places and have a staple in their navels." [*He was referring, of course, to the page layout of Hef's innovative three-page centerfolds.*]

Hef became so addicted to Sahl and Bruce that he featured them heavily in the pages of *Playboy*. "Sahl's fame was growing, and I'd like to give myself some credit for that," Hef said.

"In 1960, Sahl met one of his greatest fans, John F. Kennedy. JFK would have a great but destructive impact on Sahl's life."

***

As Hef faced the new year (1957), he was eager to meet the challenges—and he knew there would be many—but he was also thrilled at all the pleasures he thought he'd have.

He was gratified by his sales figures, hovering at around 690,000 per issue, but not quite the equal of *Esquire's* at 780,000. For the moment, at least, *Playboy's* chief rival was ahead of it in circulation, but Hef was determined to change that.

PLAYBOY. No other magazine, anywhere, managed to combine high class literature with high class consumer goods and high class conceptualizations of sex.

This edition from March 1962 includes articles by screenwriter Ben Hecht and futurist Arthur Clark; Playmate Pamela Anne Gordon; and a photo spread about Bunnies on display at the Playboy Club in New Orleans.

In synch with its literary focus, the lower half of the cover is a wry tribute to the reality of many writers' lives: discarded beer and whiskey bottles. Hovering above them is an erotic fantasy, a cooperative goddess draped in *haute, deep-décolletage* evening couture.

# THE PUBLISHING INDUSTRY'S LITERARY ELITE

AN OFT-REPEATED, SELF-JUSTIFYING REFRAIN FROM WANNABE PLAYBOYS:
"SURE, I LIKE THE CENTERFOLDS. BUT MOSTLY, I BUY *PLAYBOY* FOR ITS ARTICLES!"

## CELEBRITIES OF THE WRITTEN WORD

HERE ARE THUMBNAILS OF THE LITERARY SUPERSTARS
WHO HELPED PLAYBOY "RAISE THE BAR" IN ITS WAR AGAINST
COMPETING SKIN-FLICK MAGAZINES OF ITS ERA

**VLADIMIR NABOKOV** Nabokov was trilingual (English, French, and Russian) and scion of an aristocratic White Russian family in exile, He is considered one of the most cosmopolitan writers in literary history, as well as a renowned expert on butterflies.

Although many of his other novels were lauded as elegaic masterpieces, his most famous and profitable work was *Lolita* (1955), an aesthetically subtle overview of an adult man's sexual and emotional passion for a twelve-year-old girl.

Nabokov had captured Hef's fertile imagination with *Lolita*. According to Nabokov "My novel was turned down by about six major publishers, most of whom agreed they would publish it if I made my hero lusting for a young boy like Thomas Mann's *Death in Venice,* but I refused."

According to Hef, "Lolita was evidence of the new liberalism that swept America in the 1960s."

Thoughout much of his life, he was virtually inseparable from his ferociously protective Russian-Jewish wife, Vera, who acted as his agent, editor, business manager, love object, and bodyguard. Both were widely publicized residents of Switzerland's French-speaking Vaud region, near Montreux, One influential critic praised Nabokov for his "playfulness and the ravishing beauty of his prose." *Playboy* and its editors appreciated him for the undeniable literary cachet associated with his high-profile name.

***

**RAY BRADBURY**  Before he met Spec, Hef had discovered a few writers on his own. One of them was Ray Bradbury, an author and screenwriter turning out fantasy, science fiction, horror, and mysteries. Like Hef, he was a native of Illinois.

For "very little money," Hef published, as a three-part series, Bradbury's dystopian novel, *Fahrenheit 451*. In it, he depicted a society where books are outlawed and frequently burnt. *[According to Bradbury, "I really became concerned about book-burning during the McCarthy era."]* Published in 1953, it contained replicas of illustrations by Picasso, from whom Hef had not acquired permission.

On his death in 2012, *The New York Times* called Bradbury "the writer most responsible for bringing modern science fiction into the literary mainstream"

In a 1982 essay, he wrote, "People ask me to predict the Future, when all I want to do is prevent it"

***

**IAN FLEMING**  Fleming was an English naval intelligence office whose father was a member of Parliament from 1910 until his death in the trenches of World War I in 1917. Educated at Eton and Sandhurst, he made "spymastering" both glamourous and commercially successful, bashing out many of his works from his house, Firefly, in Jamaica. A heavy smoker and drinker for most of his life, he died of heart disease in 1964 at the age of 56.

Fleming's creation of James Bond 007 has been interpreted by seven different actors and appeared as film adapations twenty-six times.

Hef was an early admirer of Fleming. His creation of the debonair James Bond, the master spy, "was the *Playboy* ideal" (Hef's words). He serialized several of Fleming's novels, notably *On Her Majesty's Secret Service* (April, May, and June 1964), *The Man With the Golden Gun* (1965); and *Octopussy* (1966).

Hef would once again communicate with Fleming during his search for a location for a Playboy Club in Jamaica, where the novelist had a home.

***

**KENNETH TYNAN** Spectacularly bitchy and flamboyantly acerbic, the theater and literary critic Tynan was denounced by his daughter, Tracy, in her 2017 memoir as "violent, drunk, and sex-crazed." He was, according to his daughter, "obsessed with being famous by association with the stylish and avant-garde of the 1950s and 60s.

In 1967, Tynan's insightful interview of Orson Welles, "grown fat from spreading himself thin," appeared in *Playboy*, and is still remembered as a good example of the lucid, free-thinking style that Hefner was promoting in what became a regular feature, "The Playboy Interview."

"Tynan was my kind of guy," Hef claimed. "He was the first to utter the word 'fuck' on British television, and he once sucked off Marlon Brando. I definitely wanted him to write for *Playboy*. He drifted between men and women, showing no real sexual preference."

As a young man in school, Tynan entered into debates, advocating the repeal of British laws about abortion and homosexuality. He frequently spoke to his classmates about the pleasures of masturbation." Later, he shared such pleasures with Laurence Olivier when he wasn't seducing his wife at the time, Vivien Leigh.

The writer, Paul Johnson, recorded his early impression of Tynan: "He was tall, beautiful, and epicene, with pale yellow locks, Beardsley cheekbones, a fashionable stammer, plum-colored suits, lavender ties, and a ruby-red signet ring."

When Hef met him, Tynan told him: "My motto is, 'write heresy, pure heresy.' I'm a devotee of extramarital affairs and sado-masochism. I can get off by caning a woman's nude buttocks. My favorite sex is with two men in bed with one woman, or two women in bed with one man."

"When you come to London, sport," he said to Hef, "we'll cross dress and head for this bar on the East End that attracts lorry drivers. We'll pick up three or four blokes and get them to fuck us until dawn breaks over the skyline above Big Ben."

***

**BUDD SCHULBERG** The very essence of Hollywood Hip, and closely linked to movers and shakers of he entertainment industry since childhood, Schulberg was an screenwriter, sports writer, television producer, and novelist. Schulberg's articulated cynicism and ferocious independence dovetailed neatly with Hefner's assessment of what would appeal, in terms of provocative reading material, to the American men on the move.

"Budd was a guy I understood to my toenails," Hef said. "I read only one of his books, *What Makes Sammy Run?* (1941). He revealed the hard-core reality of Hollywood, and his Sammy Glick Cinderella story didn't have a happy ending."

*[Many critics found the novel anti-Semitic.]*

"He told fascinating stories of World War II," Hef said. He was one of the first Americans to liberate a Nazi concentration camp, and also gathered evidence on war criminals. He arrested the legendary Nazi, Leni Riefenstahl, famous for her propaganda films, at her chalet in Kitzbühel, Austria.

In 1954, Schulberg won an Oscar for his screenplay, *On the Waterfront,* which also brought an Academy Award to its star, Marlon Brando.

He also wrote the screenplay for the 1957 film, *A Face in the Crowd,* starring Andy Griffith as an obscure country singer who rises to fame and fortune. Schulberg told Hef he based it on Arthur Godfrey.

According to Hef, "Budd knew where all the bodies were buried in Hollywood, and he told me incredible behind-the-scenes crap: Who fucked who, who murdered who…Who was queer? He was the son of B.P. Schulberg, head of Paramount Studio. Budd claimed that he once fucked Mae West and denied rumors that she was a biological male, a drag queen impersonating a woman."

"Mae has a pussy just like Betty Grable and Marlene Dietrich," Schulberg said. "I should know. I had them all."

***

**WILLIAM SAROYAN** Winner of the Pulitzer Prize for Drama in 1940, and of an Academy Award for the film adaptation of his novel *The Human Comedy*, Saroyan was born in Fresno, California, to Armenian immigrants from Bitlis, Ottoman Empire. Many of his literary themes deal with the rootlessness of the immigrant, often based on observations he made as an optimistic stranger in the strange new world of Depression-ravaged America.

Raucous, irrepressible, Rabelaisian, and nonconformist, Saroyan's advice to a young writer seemed to correspond to Hugh Hefner's definition of his emerging readership: "Try to learn to breathe deeply; really to taste food when you eat, and when you sleep really to sleep. Try as much as possible to be wholly alive with all your might, and when you laugh, laugh like hell."

"I was a bit intimidated to meet Saroyan," Hef said. "Spec told me he was one of the most prominent literary figures in America but might be interested in writing an article or two for *Playboy*. Actually, I found him anchored to this earth, a sort of figure in the Hemingway, Steinbeck, and Faulkner tradition."

"I'd never read anything by him, but had seen his film adaptation of his novel, *The Human Comedy* (1943) with Mickey Rooney. Spec told me he'd earned pretty good money but went through most of it gambling and boozing. He said that his advice to all young men was to do everything with great intensity, intense when you taste watermelon, intense when you laugh, and intense when you fuck. Lose your zest for life and you're a dead man," he claimed.

"At the time I met him in the 1950s, his popularity had fallen off," Hef said. "He was attacked by guys like Hemingway for being too sentimental."

"My idealism is considered out of step with the times we're now living in," he said to Hef. "Perhaps I'll write about unrequited love affairs—that's something I know a lot about. The theme is eternal in any era."

***

**JAMES BALDWIN** The works of Baldwin, a self-described homosexual son of a poor black family in

Harlem, explore racial, sexual, and class distinctions in mid-20th-century America. Firmly associated with the Harlem Renaissance, the protest movements of the 1960s, and the nation and culture of France, where he lived in semi-exile from the U.S. for long periods of his life. In addition to works published in *Playboy*, he was widely featured in *Mademoiselle, Harper's, The New York Times Magazine,* and *The New Yorker*, too.

Baldwin's second novel, *Giovanni's Room*, written in 1956, was widely influential and avant-garde years before the gay lib movement otherwise became widespread.

The first black writer of note whose work Hef published in *Playboy* was Baldwin. "He was gay as a goose and had come out with a book in 1955 called *Notes of a Native Son*. I was interested in his stuff on racism, but also in his advocacy of gay and bisexual men. I particularly liked his gay *Giovanni's Room* which came way before the Stonewall Riots of 1969."

"Baldwin wed Henry James to the Bible and to Harlem," Spec told Hef.

***

**SAUL BELLOW** Winner of a Pulitzer Prize, the Nobel Prize for Literature, the National Medal of Arts, and the National Book Award (three times), Bellow wrote about (as described by the judges at the Nobel Committee) "the outer and inner complications that drive us to act, or prevent us from acting, and (in the words of one of his own characters), "the big-scale insanities of the 20th century."

Accurately assessing his literary voice as a perfect fit for the contained neuroses of hip urban men during of the nuclear age, the editors at *Playboy* loved him.

Spec was a great friend of Bellow. In Chicago, he introduced him to Hef. "He was major league," Hef said, "and spoke in lofty concepts, a bit over my head. I finally broke through to him, learning that he had arrived in our 'Windy City' as an illegal immigrant from Québec."

Hef read only one novel by him, the abstract and cerebral *Herzog*, published in 1964.

"In our first talk together, Bellow told me that Chicago was vulgar but vital, more representative of America than New York," Hef said. "I knew Philip Roth, Bellow's *protégé*," Hef said. "He told me that Bellow and William Faulkner were the backbone of 20th Century literature, high praise indeed."

"Not everyone liked Bellow," Hef said. "Spec once made a bad choice on his guest list, bringing Nabokov together with Bellow. The Russian publicly defined Bellow as "miserable mediocrity." In response, Bellow, who had obviously read *Lolita,* called Nabokov 'a pedophile.'"

***

**ERSKINE CALDWELL**   Caldwell's overviews of poverty, social stagnation, and race bias in the Deep South were artfully, sometimes brutally, expressed. They also won him critical acclaim, and a place in Hollywood historty, thanks to their adaptation into films. Hefner and his literary editors appreciated his unvarnished grit a very American voice writing about very American subjects.

"No one ever accused me of reading too many books, especially Spec," Hef said. "But I could not resist picking up copies of Erskine Caldwell's *Tobacco Road* (1932) and *God's Little Acre* (1933). That horndog from Georgia was once arrested at a book signing on charges of obscenity. His first book, *The Bastard* (1929), was banned. I admired Erskine very much and was honored to have him write for *Playboy.* He was the voice of the downtrodden, and what a compelling voice it was."

***

**JOHN STEINBECK**   The controversial and much-contested winner of the 1962 Nobel Prize for Literature, Steinbeck set many of his novels near his birthplace in Salinas, central California, configuring them as explorations of social injustice, especially as applied to the poor, the dispossessed, and the desperate. In 1943, he served as a war correspondent for the *New York Herald Tribune* and worked with the Office of Strategic Services (predecessor of the CIA).

In June 1957, Steinbeck took a personal and professional risk by supporting playwright Arthur Miller during his refusal to "name names" during the House Un-American Activities Committee trials. His stance against government censorship and repression endeared him to Hefner, who published some of his work, as well as excerpts from his novels, in *Playboy*.

"Steinbeck could be a prick sometimes, but he was a literary giant in American letters," Hef claimed. "And he wasn't shy about letting you know that."

Hef's favorite work by Steinbeck was *East of Eden* (1952). It was later adapted into a movie starring James Dean in his feature film debut.

"I never read his multi-million bestseller, *Grapes of Wrath* (1939), but I went to the movie which starred Henry Fonda," Hef said.

"A lot of people thought Steinbeck was a commie, since he didn't seem to care for capitalism all that much," Hef said. "His politics didn't matter to me. I was a bit of a revolutionary myself."

"I once asked Steinbeck what writer or writers he admired," Hef said. "He startled me by claiming that he considered the cartoonist, Al Capp, the creator of *Li'l Abner*, the best writer in the world. He showed me this book of cartoons he had that was filled with porn depictions of Li'l Abner. It showed Abner with the biggest dick in the world, fucking his way through all the hillbilly chicks in Dogpatch."

"Steinbeck confided in me his favorite form of sex," Hef said. "He liked to seduce the mistresses—not the wives—of his best friends."

Hef read *The New York Times'* reference to Steinbeck's death on December 20, 1968. Charles Poore wrote, "Steinbeck's literary inheritance came from the best of Mark Twain and the worst of Cotton Mather. He didn't need the Nobel Prize, the Nobel judges needed him."

\*\*\*

**PHILIP WYLIE** A New Englander, Philip Wylie, in Hef's words, "was a strange bird," but he liked his science fiction, mysteries, and diatribes about the threat of nuclear annihilation.

Hef was especially intrigued by two of Wylie's works, including *Generation of Vipers* (1942), a bestseller denouncing many American mothers as devouring vipers.

Hef was more intrigued by Wylie's later novel, *The Disappearance* (1951).

A saga exploring women's rights and homosexuality, it describes a (fictional) morning when men around the world awaken to discover that all women have disappeared. "Men would have to get along without females. No pretty boy would be safe on the streets," Hef said.

***

**LAWRENCE DURRELL** Hefner deplored the conventional, emotionally hidebound bourgeoisie, and in the rebelious author Durrell, he found an iconoclastic voice that embodied some aspects of what he envisioned as that of his magazine.

A poet, journalist, and the most famous travel writer of his day, Durrell fled from the "spiritual sterility" of his native U.K. for prolonged residency in exotic climes that included Greece, India, and Egypt.

His early work was condemned for "four-letter words... grotesques," a disturbing sense of the pornographic and the apocalyptic. Thanks to his collaboration with Arthur Miller and his mistress, the narcissistic feminist, Anaïs Nin, Durrell earned an avant-garde reputation that made him lots of money and a radical-chic niche in publications that included, among others, *Playboy.*

In 1957, he published the first novel (*Justine*) of what was to become his most famous *oeuvre, The Alexandria Quartet,* a "metafictional" work that was ultimately rejected by the Nobel Committee in favor of a work by Steinbeck.

Years later, when the reviews from members of that committee were made public, it was revealed that one member of the committee had rejected it, probably based on the same bourgeois censorship that Hefner was fighting as publisher of *Playboy:* "[Durrell] gives a dubious aftertaste ... because of [his] monomaniacal preoccupation with erotic complications."

"Perhaps I shouldn't admit this, but I had never heard of Lawrence Durrell when Spec introduced him to me in Manhattan," Hef said. "Later, I came to know a hell of a lot about him and found him fascinating. After all, how many men did I know born of British colonial parents in Punjab, India?"

Durrell's obituary in *The New York Times* defined him as "the British novelist and poet whose sensuous and exotic fiction, especially in the 'Alexandria Quartet' novels, made him a sort of prophet of the sexual revolution of the 1960's." He was greatly influenced by Henry Miller's 1934 novel, *Tropic of Cancer*, which he had discovered left in a toilet stall of a men's room. Labeled at the time as pornographic, the novel was banned in both Britain and the United States.

As Durrell told Hef, "My first novel, *The Black Book: An Agon* (1938), was heavily influenced by Miller and it, too, was banned. Both Henry and I weren't afraid to use words like 'fuck' and 'cunt.'"

According to Hef, "Durrell didn't seem in the best of health and smoked one cigarette after another and kept lighting up. He suffered from emphysema for many years. A decade or so after I met him in 1957, he became one of the most celebrated of English novelists in the latter part of our century, although he wrote in a voice that never connected to me or my desires."

***

**STUDS TERKEL**   Hefner became familiar with Terkel through his long-running status as a talk-show host, beginning in 1952, on a Chicago radio station, and for his poignant   oral histories of workaday Americans. Years later, Terkel credited his exposure to the rooming house which his Russian-Jewish parents ran, from 1926 to 1936, for  his understanding of humanity, its hopes, and its frailties.

One of many memorable volumes on the American experience was *Hard Times: An Oral History of the Great Depression*, for which he compiled recollections of the Great Depression by representatives of every social class, from the bottom to the top.

Terkel's deep-rooted origins in Chicago, his taste in music (Bob Dylan, Louis Armstrong, and Woody Guthrie), and his yen for liberal politics (he sued the U.S. government in 2006 in a bid for privacy rights), jibed neatly with the core values of Hefner, who replicated excerpts of his work in *Playboy*.

"Perhaps it was his first name that drew me to 'Studs' Terkel, who spent most of his life in Chicago as an author and broadcaster," Hef said. Hef used to listen to his radio show (an ongoing staple from 1952 to 1997) where he interviewed every celebrity from Martin Luther King, Jr. to Tennessee Williams.

After Terkel published his first book, *Giants of Jazz* in 1956, Hef wanted him to write about all the great jazz artists descending at that time on Chicago, although Terkel was too busy to contribute a lot.

***

**JAMES JONES**  Jones has been defined as one of the most articulate writers to emerge from the horrors of World War II and the havoc it wreaked on the servicement who returned home. His first published novel, *From Here to Eternity,* made cinematic history and was revered my many survivors of World War II in the Pacific. Hefner published some of his stories, accurately appraising their soulful and macho content about men under pressure as deeply interesting to the archetypical *Playboy* reader.

Spec introduced Hef to the macho writer. One of Hef's favorite novels was *From Here to Eternity* (1952), which was adapted in 1953 into a movie starring Frank Sinatra and Burt Lancaster. "When Jones met me, he asked if I could hook him up with some Playmate pussy," Hef said. "He was a real man's man except for some nights when he wasn't." Hef never explained what that enigmatic statement meant.

***

**ROBERT RUARK**    Macho, mysterious, and very much a child of the Depression, Ruark was described by *The New York Times* as "sometimes glad, sometimes sad, and often mad—but almost always provocative."

He's best remembered for his description of his months in Africa on safari, where he emulated the blood-soaked hunting exploits of his hero, Ernest Hemingway. From that emerged his best-known novel, *Something of Value*, a description of the Mau

Mau uprising against British rule in Kenya, later adapted into a movie in 1957 starring Rock Hudson and Sidney Poitier.

Shortly before his death, he wrote a final article ("Nothing Works and Nobody Cares") which later appeared in *Playboy.*

"That Tarheel from North Carolina, Robert Ruark, was both an author and a big game hunter," Hef said. "Perhaps he was too much under the influence of Hemingway. I wanted to publish something by him, and he'd already been discovered by *Esquire* and *The Saturday Evening Post.* Although Ruark was not one of the greats, he was a highly competent writer."

"In 1965, Robert died young in London, age 49, of cirrhosis of the liver." Hef said. "Because of my reckless lifestyle, I feared that would become my fate, too."

***

**MAX LERNER**  A Russia-born syndicated columnist whose work was widely distributed through the *New York Post*, Lerner was a strong advocate of the New Deal during the 1930s, a prominent name of the master list of Richard Nixon's enemies, and later a staunch supporter of Ronald Reagan.

He taught at Sarah Lawrence College, Harvard University, and Williams College.

He was also known for such poignant quotes as "The turning point in the process of growing up is when you discover the core of strength within you that survives all hurt."

Hef found him a provocative columnist who could always be counted on for hot copy. "He was an ugly toad, and I hardly thought of him as a lady killer, but he was rumored to have had an affair with Elizabeth Taylor during her marriage to Eddie Fisher."

***

**W. SOMERSET MAUGHAM**  Trenchant, acerbic, and sometimes savage in his critiques and in the characters he crafted, Maugham was, according to some sources, the most highly paid writer in the U.K. throughout the 1930s, and later, "the Grand Old Man of English letters."

His first novel, *Liza of Lambeth* (1897), a gritty story about the working-class consequences of adultery and unwanted pregnancy, was inspired by his medical internship in a London slum. It was so successful that Maugham abandoned his medical studies and became a writer, fitting into it "as a duck to water."  In 1926, Maugham bought the Villa La Mauresque at Saint-Jean de Cap Ferrat, where he presided over one of the great literary and social salons of the 1920s and 30s. Modest in regard to his own literary merits, he described himself as "in the very first row of the second-raters." Most critics agree that his masterpiece is *Of Human Bondage*. Initially greeted with bad reviews (the *New York World* described the romantic obsession of its lovesick hero as "the sentimental servitude of a poor fool"), it was later rescued and adapted into one of Bette Davis' most famous films.

"In Manhattan, Spec and Theo introduced me to an aging Maugham, England's stateliest homo," Hef said. "We got a piece he'd written for a reasonable price."

He said that one day, Maugham was considering writing an article, perhaps for *Playboy*. He found it a daring magazine, "except I wish the centerfolds were of nude men, not women. Both Noël Coward and I find all that open plumbing objectionable for our tastes. As a nonbeliever, I consider the idea of future punishment after death, or else rewards, an outrageous conceit. All of us will end up rotting in the ground, never to be heard from again."

Maugham also confessed to Hef, "As a young man, I tried to persuade myself that I was three-quarters normal and only one-quarter queer—whereas really it was the other way around."

***

**IRWIN SHAW** Born in the South Bronx, forever associated with Brooklyn, and remembered as one of the most financially successful writers in publishing history, Shaw produced novels, short stories, plays, and filmscripts which have sold an estimated 14 million copies worldwide.

Early in his career, after a wartime stint loosely associated with a filmmaking unit in the army, he scripted radio programs that included the long-running *Dick Tracy, The Gumps and Studio One*. He described his early years as that of a quasi-hack, grinding out scripts and wondering if the number of words he'd crafted would equal the amount he owed in rent. It was an effort he later cited as useful for his later success in Hollywood, and appropriate to Hef's vision of him as an appealing voice for American men during **Playboy's** peak.

Although contributions to later TV series added to his fame and fortune, an early break derived from screenplays for *The Young Lions* (1948), a story about a trio of soldiers during World War II. In 1958, Marlon Brando, Montgomery Clift, and Dean Martin brought it to the screen.

Shaw was a bit lowbrow and too much of a bestseller for Spec's literary tastes, but Hef liked his work. "I was among the many who praised Shaw's talent as a short-story writer, as did the editors of *Esquire* and *The New Yorker*," Hef said. "One of my favorites was 'The Man Who Married a French Wife.' I told Irwin that if I married a French wife, it would be Brigitte Bardot."

***

**JOHN UPDIKE** Updike specialized in clear, sometimes devastating dissections of the American small town and the Protestant middle class. Winner of two separate Pulitzer Prizes, Updike was acknowledged as a major-league literary critic who could significantly increase the sales of a book he favorably reviewed.

One of his most memorable characters was Harry "Rabbit" Angstrom, a bulwark of middle-class respectability and a former high school basketball star who appeared in four of Updike's novels. One of them, *Rabbit, Run* is sometimes cited as one of the 100 Greatest Novels of all time. The rabbit, of course, caught the fancy and imagination of Hefner, whose *Playboy* included Updike's short stories whenever it could.

Hef billed Updike as one of the most promising upcoming "rabbits" in America. He'd worked for *The New Yorker* since 1954 and was now available to write an article or two for *Playboy.* In the years to come, Hef only read one of his Rabbit novels, *Rabbit, Run.* During his first chat with Updike, he told Hef, "I try to give the mundane its beautiful due. It seems that you're as much addicted to bunnies as I am."

***

**BEN HECHT** One of the most successful screen writers in the history of Hollywood, Hecht ran away at the age of 16 to Chicago, where, in his own words, he "haunted streets, whorehouses, police stations, courtrooms, theater stages, jails, saloons, slums, madhouses, fires, murders, riots, banquet halls, and bookshops." Macho, realistic, and gritty, his work was appreciated by the editors at *Playboy* as embodying the tough but sensitive labyrinths of the American male.

Hef had long been impressed with his reputation as a literary giant of sorts, who was accomplished in fields that included playwriting, journalism, and screenwriting.

His 1920s play, *The Front Page,* had been a big hit both on stage and screen. Later, he won an Oscar for his original 1927 screenplay, *Underworld.*

"I told Spec I would buy anything by Hecht," Hef said.

\*\*\*

**CHARLES BEAUMONT** In 1954, *Playboy* selected Beaumont's story "Black Country" as the first work of short fiction it ever published. A specialist in science fiction and horror, he developed some of the early themes for the TV series, *The Twilight Zone,*

His avant-garde short story "The Crooked Man" (also published by *Playboy* in 1955) depicted a future society in which heterosexuality is penalized in the same way that homosexuality then was.

As its plot unfolds, a heterosexual man meets his female lover (she had disguised herself in male clothing) in a gay orgy bar. They break away to have sex in a curtained booth. When they're caught, they are punished.

A Chicago writer, Beaumont submitted his short story to *Playboy*, *The Crooked Man,* for publication. "He had offered it first to *Esquire,* but they rejected it," Hef said. "I got it next, and I bought it, and it became the most controversial short story we ever published." Some readers denounced it, one referring to it as "an absurd hypothetical topsy-turvydom, a paper tiger enemy."

Hef responded, "I saw it as a plea for tolerance, a shoe-on-the-other-foot piece, a reverse on the fact that homosexuals at the time were being persecuted, even jailed, by a straight society which did not tolerate their love."

Beaumont became one of his era's seminal influences on writers of the fantastic and macabre. He also penned some classic *Twilight Zone* episodes for TV, including *The Howling Man* in 1954.

\*\*\*

**P.G.WODEHOUSE**, born in 1881, impressed Hef with his humor. "He made Edwardian slang fashionable again," Hef said. "I really dug many of the characters he created, especially that jolly gentleman of leisure, Bertie Wooster, and his sagacious valet, Jeeves. A lot of snobs, even Spec, considered him flippant but I took delight in his bibulous bishops and megalomaniac movie moguls (read that Darryl F. Zanuck)."

***

**NELSEN ALGREN** "Detroit turned out more than automobiles when it produced Algren," Hef said. "He was a sort of Bard for the down and outer: Drunks, pimps, prostitutes, freaks, drug addicts, prize fighters, corrupt politicians, and hoodlums."

Today, Algren is best known for his 1949 novel, *The Man With the Golden Arm.* The protagonist of that book, Frankie Machine, is an aspiring drummer who is trapped in *demimonde* Chicago, having acquired a morphine habit during his service in the Army during World War II. Frank Sinatra brought it to the screen in 1955 in a brilliant performance as the addict.

Algren became the love of the French writer, Simone de Beauvoir, when she was not engaged with her other lover, French author Jean-Paul Sartre. She featured her affair with him in her novel, *The Mandarins* (1954).

In time, Algren became disenchanted with De Beauvoir after a trip he took with her and Sartre to Algeria and Morocco. In an article for *Playboy,* he wrote that De Beauvoir and Sartre "were bigger users of others than a prostitute and her pimp in their way."

***

**ARTHUR C. CLARKE** A British science fiction writer, Clarke, also entered Hef's world. "He was a real futurist talking about space travel and all that shit," Hef said. "Critics put a moniker on his The Prophet of the Space Age." Hef published his article, "The Hazards of Prophecy."

Today, most of Clark's fame rests largely on his status as co-writer of the screenplay for the 1968 film, *2001: A Space Odyssey,* hailed as one of the most influential movies in the history of cinema.

***

**VANCE PACKARD** "Packard was more than a jour-
nalist and author," Hef said. "He was a social critic
attacking consumerism. "In the late 1950s, he
warned Americans about the excesses of advertising, social climbing, and planned obsolescence."

"Many of us are being influenced and manipulated
far more than we realize," Packard said, drawing references "to the chilling world of George Orwell and
His Big Brother in his novel, *1984.*" In 1957,
Packard's own novel, *Hidden Persuaders,* "became
all the rage," Hef said. "I wanted him to write articles for *Playboy,* and Spec
got him for me."

# POP CULTURE, *PLAYBOY*, & THE *AVANT-GARDE*

As *Playboy* matured, its cover art and photo layouts became bellweathers for the staggering changes sweeping with every new edition through America.

As the magazine's aesthetics changed, so did the literary focus of the articles it included for the alert, open-minded, intelligent, and sexually experimental hipsters at whom they were aimed.

| "The Holiday Issue" (January 1954) | "The Hippie Issue" (September 1970) |

# Chapter Five

# IT'S A PLAYBOY WORLD

## Everyone Wants to Be One! Disneyland for Adults!

### *Playboy* Gets Televised! Ella Fitzgerald! Brigitte Bardot! Anita Ekberg! Frank Sinatra! Lenny Bruce! Playboy's Mansion in Chicago!

## Free at Last from the "Shackles of Marriage," Hef Launches One Affair After Another with the Playmate of His Choice.

## As a Promotion for His Magazine and Its Lifestyle Image, Hef Stages the Greatest Three Days of Jazz in the History of Chicago

## The Playboy Bunny Becomes an International Icon of Sexual Liberation

### She Has a Fluffy Cottontail and Bunny Ears…and a Satin Costume Cut High Up the Crotch and Low in the Bazooms.

Brigitte Bardot: In the late 1950s, her name became synonymous with the sexually uninhibited freedom of French cinema in such films as *And God Created Woman* (1957).

Anita Ekberg: This tall, icy Swedish bombshell burst onto the screens of the 1950s as a hot-blooded goddess of European sexuality, most notably in *La Dolce Vita* (1961).

"**I hit the jackpot** with *Playboy,* and foolish virgin that I was, I decided to launch a glossy magazine of satire and humor in January of 1957." Hef said "For our mascot, I chose a trumpeter herald in the style of John Tenniel's *Alice in Wonderland* illustrations."

"At first, I called the magazine "X" but soon switched to *Trump,* little knowing that the man I'd meet in the 1970s would, by 2016, become the most famous person on earth."

Hef was clearly inspired by the success of *Mad* magazine, which came on the market in 1952, featuring as its cover boy "Alfred E. Neuman."

He learned that Harvey Kurtzman was the inspiration for *Mad.* Kurtzman had personally crafted almost all the illustrations for the magazine's first 28 issues. When he learned that Kurtzman was breaking with *Mad,* Hef hired him as the editor of *Trump.*

In reference to its almost surreal penchant for satirizing every aspect of American life, rock singer Patti Smith said, "After *Mad,* drugs were nothing." Hef wanted to have an equivalent impact with *Trump.* One critic linked Hef and Kurtzman "as the two men corrupting the minds of America's youth."

"I got off to a bad start with *Trump* magazine," Hef said. "It originated in New York, and I could not oversee it since my work on *Playboy* consumed all my time."

He also had another stroke of bad luck, this time in association with his new magazine's distribution, arranged through the American News Company.

*[Founded in 1864 and based in New Jersey, it dominated the market for distribution of newspapers and magazines beginning around 1875. In 1957, its sudden bankruptcy forced many magazine and pa-*

### NOT EVERYTHING HEF TOUCHED TURNED TO GOLD

"In 1957, my ill-fated launch of *Trump* magazine (no relation to The Donald) was ahead of its time," Hef said. "It became too expensive to produce, and it was plagued with distribution problems from the start. I pulled the plug after only two issues."

Some of the editors and the creative team Hef hired for its launch had begun their careers as "Madmen" at *Mad* magazine, a cover of which appears below.

From a cover of *Mad* magazine, founded in 1952, the iconic cartoon character of Alfred E. Neuman ("What, me worry?") flashes his goodies on a nude beach.

perback publishers out of business. Trump magazine was one of the publications mortally wounded by the distribution network's demise.]

Hef managed, with Kurtzman, to release a second edition of *Trump* in March, but when its deficit exceeded $100,000, he shut down the magazine.

At the time, even *Playboy* was experiencing financial difficulties. Hef had invested heavily in editorial offices on Ohio Street, and in the middle of his oncoming financial setback, his bank yanked his line of credit.

Finding himself with no working capital, Hef asked his executives to accept major pay cuts, and fired a lot of his staff. Although he was finally able to secure another $250,000 from a bank for the continuation of *Playboy*, the arrangement did not include the survival of *Trump*.

By the end of 1957, Hef had righted his financial house, and money was coming in on a regular basis.

After the collapse of *Trump*, Kurtzman remained with Hef working for *Playboy* for the next three decades. Eventually, he created what became an ongoing feature there, "Little Annie Fanny." [*Loaded with sexual innuendo, it had nothing to do with the more "innocent," cartoon strip, "Little Orphan Annie."*]

PLAYBOY'S
*Little Annie Fanny*
$2.50

BY HARVEY KURTZMAN
AND WILL ELDER
THE SATIRICAL MISADVENTURES OF
PLAYBOY'S SEXY, COMIC HEROINE

Luminously rendered in a then-innovative combination of oils, watercolors, and tempura, and developed by corporate refugees from *Mad* magazine, *Little Annie Fanny* became a regular comix-style feature in *Playboy* for more than 2½ decades beginning in 1962.

Annie Fanny, its wide-eyed and spectacularly buxom protagonist, innocently finds herself nude at the end of every episode.

Annie's picaresque, politically incorrect *faux pas* enraged militant feminists, but somehow managed to raucously amuse thousands of *Playboy* subscribers.

***

Bob Preuss had been Hef's roommate at the University of Illinois. He remembered Hef describing the impact he'd have one day on American culture: "If my dream comes true, fine, but, if not, I'll be a miserable failure. I know that for me, there will be no in-between. I'll be either on the top of the world, or in the pit of hell."

After college, Preuss became a certified public accountant, got married, became a family man, and settled in suburbia, the very image of the kind of man Hef was aggressively rebelling against.

They had stayed in touch, but only infrequently, until one day Hef phoned his former roommate, asking him to drop by his offices at *Playboy*.

Preuss showed up the next day and was startled when Hef offered him the position of business manager of *Playboy Enterprises*. *[Originally established just to publish its namesake magazine, it eventually branched out to encompass many other ventures, including clubs, casinos, and Playboy TV.]*

Preuss accepted and went to work immediately, finding *Playboy* in a state of financial chaos. It was bedlam, and there was not enough capital to keep up with operations. "I had to decide which bills to pay and which to hold off on."

"If you could imagine Bob as James Cagney, then you've nailed him," Hef said.

According to Preuss, "Every day, new offers

Bob Preuss was Hef's roommate when both of them were students. Hef later hired him to manage *Playboy*'s business affairs.

"Hef changed since our school days. He would talk about the feeling a man has when he comes, or else the pleasure of anal penetration over vaginal intercourse."

arrived at our office, and I had to evaluate them, finding most of them worthless, many of them just trying to hook in with the *Playboy* Logo for financial gain."

From one day to the next, Preuss never knew what his exact duties would be. Once, a few hours before a crucial deadline, a vital layout was missing and as it turned out, both it and Hef were locked away, *incommunicado*, in his apartment.

"We couldn't get him to answer the phone," Preuss said. "He'd probably passed out. Using a passkey, I sneaked into his apartment and picked up the layout on his living room floor. I aroused him, and he stormed in, kicking me out. I made off with the missing layout, and the magazine went to press."

Preuss remembered how, as Hef's fame grew, many reporters wanted to interview him. "He walked around barefoot in the office, wearing soiled pajamas and always swilling a bottle of Pepsi. His hair was tousled, and he looked like he'd spent most of the night screwing. But before a reporter arrived with a camera, Victor Lownes was on call to rush in and get Hef camera ready."

A stylish Playboy himself, Lownes knew what to do. Sometimes, he summoned a barber to touch up Hef's crewcut. "Vic would attire him in Ivy League clothes, making him trim and smart-looking, perhaps with a luscious blonde out of focus in the background," Preuss said.

"For some reason, Vic liked to pose Hef with a hand in the pocket of his trousers," Preuss said. "What was that for? Fingering an erection?"

The office had a back stairwell, and it was used by Lownes to ship Playmates or other models up to Hef's bedroom. "Sometimes, these were girls that Vic and Hef had picked up at the Black Orchid or at other clubs they patronized. Many club dancers frequented Hef's bedroom, because he claimed they had better body movements. Those from the Black Orchid seemed to be the most desirable."

Lownes often used girls introduced to him by photographers who hoped to have their models cast as Playmates. "Hef liked 'em young as I did, but of legal age, of course," Lownes said. "No underaged Lolitas for us, which meant no lawsuits. It's called 'the age of consent.'"

Many members of the staff were aware of the ledger that Hef kept of his conquests. "Most of the girls were just one-night stands, but if he had a particular favorite, he'd have me invite her back," Lownes said. "He rated girls in several categories, such as 'B.J.' for blowjob, and his rating of them ranged from one to ten. Girls with an eight or more might get invited back. Under that, never!"

Occasionally, he was asked if he were still married. He usually answered that he and his wife had unofficially separated during the summer of 1957, although their actual divorce wouldn't get finalized until 1959.

"All in all, I was on my way to becoming F. Scott Fitzgerald's Jay Gatsby...without the tragedy," Hef claimed.

***

Hef continued to dwell excessively on his selection of *Playmate of the Month*. For the "Ringing in the New Year" centerfold of January, 1957, he ordered his staff to find a young woman who was very special.

June Blair, a model and minor actress from San Francisco, was his final selection, having turned down more than a hundred other submissions. A redhead with a Cupid mouth, she had first appeared on TV in 1954. For her centerfold, she was posed seductively on a sofa, with a red blanket demurely draped across her vital parts. Her left arm concealed a direct view of her luscious breasts.

Her exposure in *Playboy* didn't lead to an illustrious career, but she did win the attention of some high-profile men.

At the time she posed for *Playboy*, Blair was engaged to the singer, Nino Tempo. Later, she broke off that engagement to hook up with Lindsay Crosby, in whose orbit she attracted the attention of his celebrated father, Bing. The senior Crosby, on several occasions, was known to have seduced the girlfriends of his abused sons.

The Adventures of *Ozzie* and *Harriet* ABC-TV

Later, after teen idol David Nelson entered Blair's life, she deserted her previous suitors and on May 21, 1961, she married him, with his brother, Ricky Nelson, serving as best man.

After that, Blair joined the cast of the long-running (1952-1966) TV family sitcom, *The Adventures of Ozzie & Harriet*, appearing in 28 episodes as David's wife, June Nelson. *[A representative episode? "June Is Always Late (1963)," in which she's late for a dinner date with an important client with a passion for punctuality.]*

In time, Ricky's wife, the former Kris Harmon, would also become a TV wife on the series.

June Blair with her TV boyfriend and later, real-life husband, David Nelson are shown in the lower photo, a publicity pic.

What was one of the titillations associated with June's appearance as a centerfold?

"PSSSST!! David Nelson's wife gets naked!! How will we break the news to Ozzie? And what will Harriet do to her?"

\*\*\*

For the magazine's Playmate of May 1957, Hef came upon another winner, Dawn Richard. Her centerfold exposure would also lead to her marrying a famous man, David L. Wolper, the TV and film producer of such epics as *Roots* and *The Thorn Birds*. After salivating over Richard's centerfold in *Playboy*, Wolper met and married her in 1958, their union lasting for a decade and producing three children.

As his own marriage was all but over except for finalizing the divorce, Hef continued to engage in sexual dalliances with at least a dozen women a week, sometimes as many as fifteen. Most of them were gone and forgotten soon after he'd experienced orgasm.

But in the late 1950s, although he continued to pursue (and consummate) other amorous adventures at his leisure, three women in particular played especially important roles.

Betty Zuziak was a cute, perky brunette an eighteen-year-old coed at Northwestern University. She wanted a job at *Playboy* and was interviewed by Charlaine Karahus, who was working at the time in the magazine's subscription department. Karahus had once been both a centerfold and Hef's number one girlfriend.

Zuziak got the job and later met Hef at the office Christmas party, where he was immediately attracted to her charm and beauty. After the Yuletide season, she confessed, "I lost my virginity to Hef. I also fell madly in love with him, my first serious romance."

His affair with her endured for four years. "Betty was a warm and comfortable companion, and I visited her at her apartment three or four times a week. There was no place to park outside her building, so I parked illegally. During my affair with her, I accumulated more parking tickets than any driver in the history of Chicago."

Their evenings together were spent quietly, often listening to the recordings of Duke Ellington or Ella Fitzgerald. They watched TV, focusing on the popular sitcoms of that era, including Lucille Ball and Desi Arnaz in *I Love Lucy*.

"I cared for Hef very much," Zuziak said, "even though I knew he was seeing other women. He liked my home-cooked meals—in fact, I gave him at least a preview of what a happily married man might experience with a loving wife, who was there for him to satisfy his needs. But those needs were greater than those of most men, except for his friend, Victor Lownes."

According to Hef, "With Betty, I escaped from the problems in the office and used her as a shelter from the

**Dawn Richard:** Before her affair with Hugh Hefner, before her designation as Playmate of the Month (May 1957), and before she married (and divorced) mega-producer David Wolper, SHE HAD A LIFE!

Here are two views of Miss Richard as a teen vixen in the 1957 cult classic, *I Was a Teenage Werewolf*, one of the most financially successful "teen movies" ever made.

storm," Hef said. "She brought me great joy in simple pleasures, and I was attracted to her both emotionally and physically."

According to Zuziak, "At times, Hef had this charming 'little boy' quality to him—not the women-crazed publisher of *Playboy*. He was a very romantic guy, always sending me boxes of candy, flowers, and gifts, even jewelry on occasion."

"*Playboy* promoted the image of a man on the town, a connoisseur of women and wines, the best cars, the best clothing, the finest cuisine. But Hef in his heart was really a simple man with ordinary tastes like fried chicken consumed with one endless bottle of Pepsi after another."

In 1958, he flew to Miami where Lownes had arranged for him to live in the elegant home of Harold Chaskin, a real estate developer. Lownes had told him that *Playboy* wanted to use his home as the setting for a layout called "Playboy's House Party." Chaskin readily agreed, thinking it would increase the value of his "lavish pad" if and when he ever put it on the market. Chaskin's home—it included a sunken bathtub big enough for five Playmates at a time and a master bedroom that opened directly onto an indoor pool—was perfect for both romance and Hef's upcoming photo shoot. Hef would find inspiration in it during the design of his upcoming Playboy Mansion in Chicago.

Bunny Yeager, the photographer who had helped Bettie Page morph herself into "The Queen of the Pinups," was living in Miami at the time. It was Yeager, in her search for models who might be of interest to the editors at *Playboy*, introduced Hefner, at a house party he was hosting, to seventeen-year-old Joyce Nizzari, a beauty contest winner and aspiring model.

He was immediately taken with her youth, charm, and beauty, and began a sexual relationship with her that lasted until 1961.

Deeply involved in the photo-career of Bettie Page was Bunny Yeager, a "hot pin-up and a hot pin-up photographer."

***

She has emerged, since her heyday in the 1950s, as a genius at capturing both the physicality and psychology of her (sometimes undressed) subjects.

Hef had read in *The Miami Herald* that Frank Sinatra was also in Miami at the time. A long-time performer on Miami Beach, Sinatra at the time was

Depicted above is Yeager's self-portrait, conceived "in the style of Jean Harlow."

filming *A Hole in the Head* (1959), co-starring Edward G. Robinson and Eleanor Parker. [*The film was Sinatra's first and only collaboration with the noted director, Frank Capra. Lackluster and uncelebrated, it featured Sinatra singing his Oscar-winning hit song,"High Hopes."*]

Hef had attended several of Sinatra's club dates in Chicago, and he had grown up listening to Sinatra records. "I succumbed to the power of 'Swoonatra' like all those bobbysoxers of the early 1940s. By that, I don't mean I was queer for him, but I dug him and his music. His songs supplied the words and music to our dreams and yearnings. Ol' Blue Eyes was the voice of our time." Through a mutual contact, Hef asked if he could visit Sinatra on the set of his film, and when he agreed, Hef invited his newly acquired teenaged beauty, Joyce Nizzari, to accompany him. She was thrilled.

Sinatra was most gracious to Hef and the teenager, welcoming them to Miami. He had long been a performer on Miami Beach.

Nizzari later told him that after Hef was called away for a while, Sinatra had tried to pick her up, inviting her to come to his hotel suite when she "could escape the clutches of Hef." She turned him down.

Frank Sinatra in a publicity photo for the unsuccessful feel-good romantic comedy, *A Hole in the Head*, released to mediocre reviews in 1959.

It was shot within a frenzied 40 days on Miami Beach during one of the lowest points of Sinatra's troubled relations with the press.

Sinatra, laden with baggage from the recent breakup of his marriage to Ava Gardner, ferociously attacked some of the journalists for seizing on every scandalous rumor they could find.

Some of them involved his interactions with women associated with Hugh Hefner and *Playboy*.

This would not be the only time Sinatra tried to move in on one of Hef's girlfriends. "There was a competition between them," Lownes said. "Frank could arrive in Miami and get almost any girl he wanted. But that time in Miami, he seemed to go for Hef's jailbait, who wasn't of age yet."

When he learned about it, Hef had no ill feelings toward Sinatra. "I admire the music of the man, not his character," Hef told Nizzari.

Over the years, Hef tried to be philosophical about Sinatra's attempts to poach his girl *du jour*. "If someone is going to try to hustle one of my ladies, it might as well be Ol' Blue Eyes, the Chairman of the Board—and not the bartender."

When Nizzari turned eighteen, Hef arranged for her to pose partially dressed as a centerfold. Before that, when she was still too young to appear in a state of undress, she posed as a model for the July 1958 front cover.

"Hef and I spent many an evening together, imagining we were falling in love," Nizzari said.

According to Hefner, "I often went for blondes, but I didn't rule out brunettes. Blondes are dangerous and forbidden, even when they come out of a bottle. Redheads are a variation of blondes and also dangerous. With brunettes, there is almost a wife-and-mistress look. Those dark-haired beauties seem more respectable than blondes or redheads. Not only do they evoke home and hearth, they often arouse deeper feelings in a man, more romantic. Dare I call it love?"

Artfully undraped images of the beautiful and cheerful Joyce Nizzari, whose charms were shared by both Hefner and Sinatra, would grace several editions of *Playboy*.

"Discovered" as a model by the legendary Bunny Yeager, she's depicted here on a field of rabbit ears on the cover of the "Picnic Capers" edition of July, 1958.

"I was not a born exhibitionist," Nizzari said. "My father was a stern Italian, and I feared he would be horrified at my posing for *Playboy*. But I did it for Hef because he wanted me to pose."

Even after her affair with Hef ended, Nizzari and Hef remained friends, and she became a longtime employee of *Playboy*, working in the mansion in Los Angeles. "When I got married and had a son, he called Hef 'Uncle' because *Playboy* was such an important part of our lives."

In time, Nizzari would become his companion, accompanying him to Cannes on the French Riviera and to John F. Kennedy's Inaugural Ball.

The third important element in Hef's love quadrangle arrived on the scene in 1959 in the form of Joni Mattis, a would-be model wandering around Chicago looking for work. Since posing gigs were few, she took a job at a local movie house where, as a novelty, the female ushers dressed in the uniform of a French maid. When she met Hef, Joni jokingly said, "You can call me Fifi."

"What struck me first about Joni was her white skin, almost porcelain, like the fabled Mexican movie star, Dolores Del Rio."

"Of all the women I seduced, she came from the most tortured background," he said. "She had endured a horrific life and had grown up in a Baptist orphanage after her mother died and her father was away fighting during World War II. When he returned to civilian life, he noted that his daughter had grown up. He repeatedly raped her and invited his poker-playing buddies over to enjoy his daughter's charms, too."

When Joni became pregnant, her father kicked her out of his house. After giving birth, she put her infant son up for adoption.

To survive, she became the young mistress of a "religious nut" who preached against sin in public and involved himself in it at night. "He forced me into unspeakable things," she confessed to Hef.

When he asked her to pose as Playmate of November 1960, she willingly agreed.

Joni once asked Hef why he didn't seduce more movie stars, since several luscious beauties from Hollywood had signaled they might be available. "I turned them down because in a relationship, they take charge. I want to be in control of who I fuck, not surrendering my power to a woman. I keep on my *Playboy* armor because I don't want to be betrayed emotionally, as I was with my wife, who cheated on me with another man. For that, I'll never forgive her."

"Hef had this double standard," Joni said. "He wanted his woman to belong to him exclusively, while he dated any girl he chose to."

"At first, it was heartbreaking," she said, "but I sorta got used to it. Sometimes, he'd parade his girlfriends in front of me like he was taunting me. At other times, he could be so sweet, but that didn't last long. I'd say he was very insensitive to a woman and her hopes and dreams for a real relationship."

"I finally decided to get even with Hef one night," she said. "He threw this big party in Chicago for his new friend, Frank Sinatra. I wanted to make Hef jealous, and I flirted shamelessly with

The undeniable beauty and allure of Hef's Playmate, Joni Mattis, appeared in undraped splendor within *Playboy*'s November 1960 edition. Its artfully whimsical cover is depicted above.

Adding to its commercial appeal were new analyses of the gothic horror of Edgar Allan Poe; a feature about Playboys on the town in Acapulco; and insights into Hollywood nostalgia by scriptwriter Ben Hecht.

Ol' Blue Eyes. I only did that when I noticed Hef coming on strong with Ann Richards, a singer in Stan Kenton's band."

"Toward the end of the party, Frankie invited me to come back to his suite with him, and I agreed. He let me stay there for three nights and banged me a lot except when I was going down on him. He really had something dangling to make a gal gag. His endowment could put a lot of other Playboys to shame."

Even after the breakup of their romance, Hef and Joni Mattis remained friends. She became an employee of *Playboy*, a job she held until her death in 1999.

***

There arose in the mid-1950s a revolt from the "Beat Generation," a bohemian counterculture attacking middle-class conformity, something Hef had already been doing throughout most of the decade. But, as it turned out, there would be a big difference between Hef's own rebellion against conformity and that of the Beatniks.

Like all national magazines, including *Time, Playboy* had to comment on this generation as a means of staying competitive. Its cool, hipster alienation had become almost a national obsession.

Novelist Jack Kerouac, along with two gay writers, William S. Burroughs and poet Allen Ginsberg, became the literary spearheads and spokespersons of the Beatniks. Eventually, Kerouac evolved into one of the most visible and influential progenitors of the hippie movement, too.

Kerouac's "Bible of the Beats," *On the Road*, was published in 1956. *[Kerouac had begun working on it in the late 1940s during what he called "a three-week amphetamine jag."]* Many critics denounced it as a "rambling, prose-jazz jumble," but the Beat Generation devoured its testimonials to a nomadic life on the road.

The word "Beat" originated as a kind of underground slang, evoking a world peopled by drug addicts, thieves, and hustlers. It was a reference to the beaten-down or downtrodden in society, many of them rejects from the mainstream.

Kerouac's vision for the Beat Generation was more optimistic and sanitized. He interpreted it as something more akin to "crazy, illuminated hipsters roaming America, serious, bumming, hitchhiking everywhere, ragged, beautiful, and beatific, a graceful new wave of young people."

In the June 1959 issue of *Playboy*, Hef ran an article called "The Origins of the Beat Generation," in which he wrote about Kerouac.

"We made Hefner and his *Playboy* cronies pay some attention to our hepcat culture," Kerouac said.

He later articulated a sense of betrayal when the movement seemed to have been taken over by what came to be called "jazzniks, bobniks, or bugniks." Hef wrote of beatnik parties on Saturday night in suburbia, "which were held mainly as an excuse for drunken men to feel up the wives of their neighbors."

The stereotype of a female beatnik was a woman with long, straight hair wearing a black leotard. As the Beat Generation devolved, young men often emulated the bebop look of trumpeter Dizzy Gillespie by wearing horn-rimmed glasses, goatees, and berets, visibly rolling their own Mary Jane cigarettes.

"A new vocabulary came in, using such words as "cats," "cool," "dig," and "square."

In an article entitled "The Beat Mystique," *Playboy* defined the movement as "a new nihilism of cultural warriors battling the conformity, passivity, and boredom of middle-class America."

*Playboy* also ran a feature article, "The Best Poems of the Beatniks," including works by Kerouac, Ginsberg, and Gregory Corso. Photographers snapped photos depicting beats as "hep kittens and jive cats from the New York Islands to the Pacific Coast."

For that particular issue (July 1959), Hef personally selected what he

Tragic, lamentable, and surreal, the death and metamorphosis of Yvette Vickers corpse reflects the most gruesome aspects of the movies in which she starred.

On the left, she's depicted as a rampaging, oversized Amazon, appealing both to the fetish instincts and the sense of camp of many of her fans.

The publicity headshot on the right shows the kind of vulnerabilities which might have contributed to her death.

defined as the magazine's "Beat Playmate," Yvette Vickers. The magazine asserted that she had been "discovered" at a hippie coffee house in Los Angeles.

"She has an interest in serious acting, ballet, and the poetry of Dylan Thomas," her brief bio asserted. "Another of her interests is classical music. ('Prokofiev drives me out of my skull.') A bit more than a rebel, she frowns prettily at conformity."

A movie hopeful, Vickers had first appeared on screen in an uncredited part in that classic, *Sunset Blvd.* (1950). Her first major role was in a film released the same year as her centerfold. In *The Attack of the 50-Foot Woman*, she plays Honey Parker, who has an affair with a married man.

For her centerfold, photographer Russ Meyer shot her lying face-down on a sofa, her breasts concealed by a man's blue shirt. Her naked bum rears up for all the male Playboys to enjoy, along with her shapely legs. On the floor beside her is an open bottle of wine and an ashtray filled with crushed cigarette butts. A record player and an LP album are positioned nearby.

*[Vickers was last seen alive in 2010. Years before that, she had dated Jim Hutton, a minor movie star. During the last years of her life, she had withdrawn from family and friends.*

*On April 27, 2011, a neighbor and fellow actress grew suspicious and visited her front door, finding it covered with undisturbed spider webs. Months of decaying and mildewed letters and newspapers lay undisturbed on her stoop.*

*The neighbor phoned the police, who broke in and found Vickers mummified remains. Apparently, she had died a year before of heart failure, and no one had disturbed them since her demise.*

*"Poor, poor gal," Hef said after hearing the news. "Her life just didn't work out. She was our first Playmate who became a mummy."]*

After only a few months, Hef became disenchanted by the Beat Generation, finding its devotees incompatible with the lifestyle he was promoting in his magazine. "Their beards, their sandals, their dirty feet, their dingleberry-coated assholes...It was all too much. These unwashed freaks don't want to pursue the American dream. They were all going up in smoke, living life in a daze, wallowing in despair."

He went on to define the demographic he wanted to cater to. *[He called it "The Upbeat Generation."]* "We don't want to drop out of society, but to embrace its pleasures and sample the best aspects of life, not the downbeat in some crashpad. Like the Beats, *Playboy* readers reject conformity but want the life well-lived, where men work hard, then play hard, enjoying their rewards, which must, of course, include a beautiful woman. Jack Kerouac has got a few Beat guys piled up all drugged out in a corner. *Playboy* has nabbed the rest."

Although still a married man, at least technically, Hef continued to promote the free-wheeling bachelor lifestyle in his magazine.

One night, a reporter from a Chicago newspaper confronted him with a question when he was nightclubbing at Chez Paree at a table where three beautiful women were seated: "Would you like your sister to marry a member of the *Playboy* staff?"

"Frankly, I'd like it if one of my men didn't put a wedding ring on any girl's finger. They might get their noodle filled with a lot a crap, you know, a happy life of togetherness with a lot of kids and a devoted wife cooking supper every night before the family gathers around the TV set. And all that jazz."

"As for me, I married far too early when I was still green behind the ears, with a lot of living to do before settling down—that is, if I ever settle down with just one woman. It's not my style. I need many women in my life."

In 1959, after many delays, Millie filed for divorce. It was uncontested. The court awarded her $1,417 a month, which included both alimony and child support.

"The reason the marriage dive-bombed was my failure," Hef said. "I was married to the magazine for the past few years. When I had any free time, I didn't go home to her, to David, or to Christie. Victor Lownes told me that Millie had not grown as I had."

"I loved my children in spite of my long absences from them. Also, I never want the friendship I had with Millie to disappear completely. She is a good mother to our kids, and I'm grateful for that. She and I will go on to other loves, maybe even other marriages, but I trust that our kind feelings for each other will not turn hostile."

After the divorce, Hef beamed with happiness at his sudden freedom. "Tonight, I'm free to do what I want to do without checking in with anyone. Free to be able to go where I want and, once there, to do what I please. It's nobody's god damn business but Hugh Hefner's."

*[Millie later met, dated, and married an attorney, Edwin Gunn, settling down in Wilmette, Illinois. "I watched in astonishment as my first husband created a global empire, neck deep in glamour, women, and worldwide publicity. As for me, I prefer the quiet life with Edwin, a man I truly love, who comes home to me at night for dinner."*

*Millie's new husband adopted both Christie and David, and changed their last names to Gunn, but reports surfaced that the children did not like their new step-*

*father.*

*Eventually, Millie divorced Gunn, and David and Christie petitioned the court to have their last names changed back to Hefner.]*

\*\*\*

In 1956, the African American singer, Mabel Mercer, recorded an album, *Midnight at Mable Mercer's*, and Victor Lownes, one of her fans, presented a copy of it to Hef, who played it frequently.

In 1959, Lownes decided to produce a concert for the cabaret singer in Chicago at the Blue Angel. He invited Hef, assigning him the best table in the house.

Born in England in 1900, Mercer, a most ladylike woman, had a white mother who performed in English music halls, and an African American father, a musician, who died before Mercer was born.

In the 1930s, Mercer was the toast of Paris, performing at the chic Bricktop's, the gathering place at the time for the elite. She made friends with F. Scott Fitzgerald and his wife, Zelda, along with Cole Porter, Ernest Hemingway, and Gertrude Stein and her lover, Alice B. Toklas.

When Mercer began performing in America, Sinatra had become one of her most devoted fans. She had a throaty, story-telling style with a strong emphasis on the poetic nuances of the lyrics. *[Latter-day critics credit her precise vocal styling to the diction she learned as a student at a convent in Manchester.]* Sinatra later credited her for the deep influence she exerted on his own phrasings and story-telling techniques.

Mercer even became a favorite of Ronald Reagan, who defined her as "a singer's singer."

After the concert at the Blue Angel, Hef came backstage to meet Mercer, embracing her. "You were fantastic." Their paths would cross many times in the future, and she credited Hef with getting her better known in America.

*[That night, he ordered Lownes to write an article about Mercer for publication in Playboy, but after reading the piece, the staff mutually agreed that Lownes should do no more writing for the magazine, but stick to his original duties of handling production of the magazine.]*

"Mabel Mercer sings from the heart," said Ernest Hemingway in Paris.

"Even a cocksucker like Cole Porter appreciates her music, as does Princess Tiny Meat" (F. Scott Fitzgerald).

166

By 1959, *Playboy* had at long last overtaken *Esquire* in sales, which Hef viewed as a great victory. "I bet those bastards are still wishing they'd given me that five dollar raise I asked for."

*Playboy's* circulation had rapidly climbed past the one-million dollar mark in monthly sales, and its net revenue for the year came in at $5.5 million. He had big plans for the magazine, and in December of 1960, he had increased the page count of each monthly edition from eighty to 150, usually with twenty-eight ongoing features.

With this growth, many members of his staff urged him to move to Manhattan to be at the epicenter of the publishing industry. He consistently refused, claiming, "In New York, we'd be just another magazine."

His editorial director, Spec, agreed. "We'd become jaded very quickly by the nihilism of the Manhattan publishing scene."

With this new success and with money flowing into *Playboy's* coffers, Hef devised new schemes, and he needed Lownes to bring each of them to fruition.

One night at a club, he rejected three women attempting to interrupt and/or meet him and focused his attention on Lownes instead. "Let's talk business. How about staging the world's greatest jazz festival? Also, how about we purchase a fabulous old mansion in Chicago and convert it into a pleasure palace?"

"I'm your man!" Lownes answered.

For the August 1956 issue of *Playboy*, Lownes brought Hef a fully nude photograph of the "Swedish bombshell," Anita Ekberg. Years before, she'd been on the dawn of international fame. The Miami-based sculptor and *bon vivant*, Sepy Dobronyi, had snapped a candid photo of her, nude, when she was modeling for him as the subject of a bronze sculpture.

The photograph revealed her extremely large bosom and the triangular patch of her vagina. Hef wanted to buy the rights to the photo, with the understanding that he'd have to crop out its depiction of her pubic hair. *[At the time, he was years away from publishing pubic hair in* Playboy.*]*

With the exception of Marilyn Monroe and Jayne Mansfield, Hef was not accustomed to running nude centerfolds of movie stars, not that he could get that many name actresses to pose for him. Nearly all of his 1950s-era centerfolds depicted young women one writer referred to as "anonymous toys," mere playthings that Hef often seduced in his private quarters. On many an occasion, he attended the shoot of a model, and nearly always applied rouge to a woman's nipples, as he preferred them "rosy pink," both for his centerfolds and for rounds within his boudoir.

When Hef was presented with the nude photo of Ekberg, he was not familiar with any of her minor appearances in film. He ordered the screening of two of her movies, *The Golden Blade* (a swashbuckler from 1953 with Rock Hudson in which she played a handmaiden); and *Abbott & Costello Go to Mars,* also released in 1953. In it, she played a shapely intergalactic alien.

In time, she would star in other movies and be seduced by a series of leading men: Hudson, Bob Hope, John Wayne, Dean Martin, and Jerry Lewis.

"All of those guys had me," she later confessed to Hef in Los Angeles, where he had a one-night stand with her. "I didn't invent the casting couch, but I was one of its inhabitants." She also confided to Hef, "In spite of his public *persona,* Hope is a dirty old man."

Over the years, Hef kept abreast of Ekberg's other affairs, mainly through attentively reading about them in the scandal magazines. The A-list males who became involved with her included Frank Sinatra, Tyrone Power, Yul Brynner, Rod Taylor, Sterling Hayden, and Errol Flynn. "Frank was the only straight male on that list," Hef said. "All the others were bisexuals without a rigidly defined gender preference. I might have included Hayden among the 'exclusively straight' guys, but I was told that during his youthful career struggles, he hustled homosexuals in Hollywood, including movie stars like Cary Grant and Clifton Webb. So I guess that makes Sterling bisexual, too."

The Italian director, Frederico Fellini, was a faithful reader of *Playboy.* He had never seen one of Ekberg's minor appearances. But he became so intrigued with her nude body that he cast her in his classic, *La Dolce Vita* (1960), a worldwide hit.

When she waded into the waters of the Trevi Fountain in Rome, it became one of the most iconic scenes in the history of film. Ekberg, who was always outspoken in interviews, said, "Lex Barker *[former screen Tarzan, and the former husband of Lana Turner]* played my husband in the film. During the filming, I demanded that he perform his duties as my spouse."

After the release of *La Dolce Vita,* Ekberg told Hef, "Fellini owes his success to me, not vice versa. He tells everyone he discovered me, but I was the one who made him famous."

***

Ever since he'd watched Roger Vadim's movie, *Et Dieu...créa la femme (And God Created Woman; 1957),* Hef had been fascinated by the alluring French sex kitten, Brigitte Bardot. He had run a sexy picture of her as she appeared in the film, and quickly realized she had no problem stripping down for the camera. He figured she might be an ideal candidate for a centerfold, and he made several attempts to reach her by transatlantic phone but failed to do so.

He had heard that she'd be at the 1959 Film Festival in Cannes, on the French Riviera, so he decided to meet her there to make his proposal in person, thinking he might win her over with his charm.

He invited his current girlfriend, Joyce Nizzari (who had by now reached the age of legal consent), to fly to France with him. First, they stopped over in Paris for two nights before heading south to the Côte d'Azur.

On their second night in the French capital, he invited Nizzari to Au Mouton de Panurge, *[17 rue de Choiseul, Paris 2e. Demolished in 1977, it had, for decades, been a fashionably permissive restaurant frequented by wealthy members of the avant-garde. Covered with Rabelaisian frescoes, it was known for waiters who would request permission to politely fasten a garter onto the shapely thigh of an occasional female customer—if she were young and beautiful and if her com-*

Three views of Anita Ekberg: Left, on the cover of *Life* in January of 1956 for her role in *War and Peace.*

Middle, in a still from a spaghetti western released by Cinecittà Studios, *Deadly Trackers* (1972, aka *La lunga cavalcata della vendetta*) and...

Right: a poster with her image as the iconic symbol of Federico Fellini's most famous film, *La Dolce Vita* (1960), a movie that immortalized the Trevi Fountain internationally.

*panions were amused.]*

In Cannes, after establishing the very chic Hotel Carlton as his base, Hefner may have had second thoughts about having brought a companion with him. As he moved through the festival and along the beach, he found many a budding Bardot eager to meet, bed, and pose for the publisher of *Playboy*.

To his regret, he learned that "the real thing" *[Bardot]*, had—after years of association with Cannes and its film festival—rather quixotically announced that she would not be present that year.

Despite his disappointment, he mingled through the crowds and the galas, meeting a number of American and foreign movie stars. A major encounter was with Gene Kelly, one of his screen favorites. After an hour on the beach with him and his companion—an attractive male who looked like Alain Delon and who was attired in a semi-transparent *"cache-sexe,"* Hef learned that Kelly was bisexual.

He also met Cary Grant, who may or may not have been having an affair at the time with Kim Novak. On one other occasion, Grant, too, retreated to his suite with a beach boy hustler.

On his second night on the Riviera, Hef hosted a party at the Carlton for Novak, Grant, and Kelly. That night, he convinced Novak to pose for a future issue of his magazine, a layout that was eventually

### BRIGITTE BARDOT
THE CAT'S MEOW, POSTWAR FRANCE'S REIGNING "SEX KITTEN"

BARDOT: She was voluptuous, juvenile, and psychologically uncomplicated, an apparition who seemed to blossom under the blue skies of either Normandy or Provence, the subject of detailed examination from some of the greatest intellects of postwar France. They invented a word to describe the religion in whose name she was worshipped: *La Bardolâtrie.*

In part because of her roles as a woman who refuses to fit into conventional niches, Bardot remains, in the words of a French critic, "a symbol of cinematic fascination as viewers get first an appreciation, or lust, for her body, then for the nuances of her face, and then for her soul."

published in December 1963.

*[When the photo shoot for that layout unfolded for Novak in Hollywood, she arranged herself on a red sofa wearing a sheer white négligée, her large bosom revealed through the fabric. Her picture was so seductive that Hef featured her again for a final time in 1965.]*

He had long been a fan of "the ice blonde," having seen her in some of his favorite movies: *Picnic* (1955) with William Holden; *The Man with the Golden Arm* (also 1955) with Frank Sinatra; *Pal Joey* (1957), also with Sinatra and Rita Hayworth too; and *Vertigo* (1959) with James Stewart, who always brought a certain class to other pictures he made with her, too.

Hef had heard that she was involved in a romantic and sexual affair with his friend, Sammy Davis, Jr. In circumstances which appear non-newsworthy today, it profoundly shocked and enraged many white people in the 1950s.

In Chicago one night, Davis revealed to Hef the finale of his sexual liaison with Novak: Perhaps with the endorsement of Harry Cohn, head of Columbia, some members of the mob kidnapped Davis one night in Las Vegas and drove him deep into the desert. He was told to drop Novak…or else. One of the mobsters said, "You've got only one eye. Wanna try for none? Drop Novak!" Davis was then thrown out of the car about a mile outside of town.

Hef also heard a rumor that Novak had posed for nude pictures when she was an unknown late teenager. In 1954, during the peak of her film career, Cohn was said to have purchased (and suppressed) them for $15,000 with the understanding that their publication would damage his star's appeal. "Monroe got away with it," Cohn told her,

## KIM NOVAK
### HOLLYWOOD'S
### "LAVENDER BLONDE"

(Middle photo) Publicity for her role in *The Man with the Golden Arm*. Set in a seedy neighborhood of Hef's home town of Chicago, she plays the traumatized love interest of a morphine addict.

(Bottom photo) The cover of the February 1965 edition in which she was tastefully centerfolded.

"but I doubt that you'll be so lucky."

Hef never got a crack at the nudes of Novak, but in America, in the November 1959 edition of *Playboy,* he featured semi-nude photos from *And God Created Woman* as illustrations for an article entitled "Bardot Peeka-boo."

With tongue in cheek, Hef claimed that he was running the semi-nudes of Bardot "as a public service" for those not fortunate enough to have seen one of her sexy movies in France. In one picture, she shows cleavage, but it's of her *derriere.* Another still photo from the film exposed her right breast, except for the nipple. Yet another depicted her in an erotic dance.

Hef noted that in her film, Bardot "never got completely jaybirdsville, but in it, *'The Compleat Brigitte'* is depicted semi-nude top-to-toe, fore-and-aft, clockwise-and-counterclockwise."

Hef published more photos of Bardot in his July 1964 issue. Then, in April 1969 and again in a layout in the 1970s, he ran updated layouts of the by then somewhat faded but still alluring French star.

***

Ominously, during the normal course of his business affairs, Hef learned that the U.S. Post Office was about to refuse to distribute *Playboy* through the mails. He rushed lawyers to Washington and was successful in getting the impending ban lifted.

The Post Office then petitioned the U.S. Court of Appeals to re-establish the ban, but their complaint was rejected by judges. In part because of the controversy associated with its release, the November 1958 issue became one of his alltime bestsellers of the 1950s,

In San Francisco, the chief of police, Malcolm McDonnell, also tried to get *Playboy* banned from the city's newsstands, but for reasons associated with the configuration of beds in a movie scene. The ruckus derived from Hef's publication of still photos from *Cry Tough* (1959), a crime film starring the handsome Italian American, John Saxon, and Linda Cristal.

It was the story of a Puerto Rican gang in Spanish Harlem. As critics noted, Saxon, "did an obvious imitation of Marlon Brando." He was depicted in bed having sex with Cristal, a beautiful long-haired Argentinian actress, cast as a Cuban dance hall girl.

In films released before *Cry Tough,* a man and woman were required, during their bedroom scenes, to be filmed separately and apart, modestly attired in nightgowns or pajamas, and in separate (usually twin) beds. Even married couples like Lucille Ball and Desi Arnaz had to be filmed in twin beds throughout the course of their long-running TV sitcom, *I Love Lucy.*

*The San Francisco Chronicle* ran a story about the police chief's attempt to suppress *Playboy* because of its coverage of the sex scene in *Cry Tough,* referring to McDonnell as a "smut vigilante." *The Chronicle's* focus ignited a riot of protests in support of Hef. McDonnell had stupidly claimed that young men looking at *Playboy* may be tempted to "become immoral."

Hef shot back, "I can't think of anyone less qualified to judge what people can read than the police chief...He should not make the mistake of confusing ninety percent of his prejudices with the laws of the community."

Before Hef's lawyers shot it down, the ban had spread to neighboring communities that included Menlo Park, Mountain View, Palo Alto, and San Mateo.

\*\*\*

Violence, forbidden sex, and cross-racial conflict were depicted in the controversial film, *Cry Tough* (1959), which was featured and favorably reviewed in *Playboy*.

John Saxon and Linda Cristal played steamy scenes that caused the San Francisco police chief to remove *Playboy* from that city's newsstands.

Although he'd succeeded at handling threats from San Francisco's police chief, Hef faced a roster of much more formidable foes. Among the most dangerous was Kathryn O'Hay Granahan.

*[A high-profile, long-term Democratic Congresswoman from Philadelphia, she served, beginning in the early 1960s, under JFK, as Director of the U.S. Treasury. In 1960, to huge acclaim, she received an Award of Merit from the Philadelphia County Chapter of the Catholic War Veterans for her campaign against the sale and distribution of pornography.]*

"There are many things we don't allow our juveniles to do," she told an interviewer. "We don't allow them to drink, carry guns or drive vehicles. So why allow these filth merchants *[according to insiders, that was aimed directly at Hugh Hefner]* to sell youngsters material which is a contributing cause of juvenile delinquency?"

During elections in her home state of Pennsylvania, Granahan had insisted that all juvenile mental patients "without exception" lost their minds because of lewd literature. "American democracy and its institutions are under threat by the smut racketeers bagging millions of dollars, all part of a communist conspiracy. I have not the slightest doubt that the Soviet Union is behind this mass assault, which is turning young American males into communists."

Granahan and her anti-smut vigilantes began to zero in on magazines, books, and movies. *[The very conservative Motion Picture Production Code was still in force but weakening.]*

Glenn Ford's gritty *Blackboard Jungle* (1955) came under direct fire. Ford played a soft-spoken ex-serviceman who becomes a teacher in a widely diverse and unruly classroom in New York City, where he has to remind his students not to call each other "spic, mick, or nigger."

Ford's struggle as a teacher in a rough urban school is set against a musical score that featured Bill Haley & the Comets singing "Rock Around the Clock."

*Blackboard Jungle* attracted hordes of U.S. teenagers. Screenings often ended in violence and vandalism.

*[The U.S. was not alone in this. The same rowdy vandalism occurred in England. At its premiere in London, members of the rowdy audience, some of whom self-identified as members of the very radical "Teddyboys," cut up the seats with switchblades and danced in the aisles. The same violence occurred during screenings in other parts of the U.K., too.]*

American conservatives and "smut vigilantes" cited this film, with its many disruptions, as a strong selling point for their anti-smut campaign. Their petitions to have it banned even cited "the heaving breasts of the juvenile girls in the movie."

Foremost among its censors was Granahan: *"Blackboard Jungle* promotes juvenile riots," she asserted.

One of her opponents was a popular columnist, Herb Caen, who wrote: "The do-goodniks who have tried to keep *Playboy* off the stands are now known as the Anti-Smut Society. Their initials (A.S.S.) tell the tale."

By the end of the 1960s, A.S.S. was losing ground in the courts. Judges were upholding the First Amendment. Although they fomented outrage, even the works of the Marquis de Sade *[the 18th- century libertine whose*

Congresswoman from Pennsylvania (and later, Secretary of the U.S. Treasury) Kathryn O'Hay Granahan was a stern and judgmental American puritan who organized a national campaign against pornography, singling out *Playboy* as the worst of the offenders.

She publicly attacked Hef as "a smut racketeer, part of a communist conspiracy to corrupt American youth." Later, she was instrumental in passing the Granahan bill "to seize and detain the mail of anyone suspected of trafficking in obscenity.

Hef called her "an uptight bitch, a psycho from the extreme right who had probably never had a good fuck in her whole miserable life."

*name inspired the term "sadism,"]* were being discussed and becoming available, although some bookstores sold his works under the counter.

In the book world, a historically ferocious battle had already been waged against James Joyce's *Ulysses*. First published in 1918, it's hailed today as one of the pivotal works of modernist literature. It chronicles the peripatetic appointment and encounters of Leopold Bloom in Dublin throughout the course of an ordinary day.

Its first obscenity trial opened in America in 1921 and came to be known as "The Joyce Wars." When Americans who had been traveling abroad tried to bring the book into the United States, copies were seized by customs and burned, but by 1934, courts ruled that Joyce's masterpiece was not obscene.

"I managed to get through seventy-five pages of it," Hef said, "and that was that. Too damn dense for me. I defy any *Playboy* to get a hard-on reading this murky tale."

As the 1950s ended and a more freedom-loving America moved into the riotous 1960s, even Henry Miller's long-banned *Tropic of Cancer* became available in certain bookstores, although many outlets still refused to distribute it. First published in 1934, it detailed Miller's sexual odyssey through Paris of the 1930s, When it was released in America, it, too, had to face charges of obscenity, which went all the

The anti-smut vigilantes not only attacked *Playboy*, but turned on Glenn Ford's 1955 film, *Blackboard Jungle* about a teacher's harrowing experience in the New York public school system.

Hef was one of the chief defenders of this movie. "It is not pornography. It is a serious movie about a growing problem in the United States, juvenile delinquency."

way to the Supreme Court before the book could be made available without restriction. Hef viewed that as a victory and read the book, calling Miller "the original Playboy, but in a down-trodden way."

Hef also read the long-banned *Lady Chatterley's Lover* by D.H. Lawrence, first published privately in 1928 in Italy. Banned in Britain and the United States, the story was of a workingclass male and his affair with an upperclass woman with explicit descriptions of sex and the use of then "unprintable" words." The book also had to face and ultimately triumph over obscenity charges in court. Senator Reed Smoot [*Republican Senator from Utah, 1902-33*] defined *Tropic of Cancer* as "the most damnable, written by a man with a diseased mind and a soul so black that it would even obscure the darkness of Hell!"

In a comment he made reflecting his role as a cultural warrior, Hef said, "There was a fight for freedom of what we could read and watch raging, and I felt I was one of the leading warriors battling for a much-needed change in our culture. From the Salem Witch Trials to the Comstock suppressions to the Monkey Trial in Tennessee, to the ridiculous Motion Picture Code, I, along with others, had the damn puritans and their 19th Century mindsets on the run. With the oncoming 1960s, with its sexual liberation, men and women more and more were coming to realize you could even have sex for real pleasure and without a marriage certificate."

***

Hef had been to many of the jazz clubs of Chicago and had come to know a number of the artists who played there. *Playboy's* jazz critic, Leonard Feather, ran an article about jazz in almost every issue of *Playboy*.

[*In vivid contrast, Hef was NOT any particular fan of rock 'n roll, as exemplified by Elvis Presley. He agreed with Feather who wrote: "Rock 'n roll shares a common beginning with jazz, but it has evolved no further than the primitive, gibbering ape."*]

"There is not a night in my adult life that I pass without listening to jazz," Hef claimed. "So why not have *Playboy* sponsor the greatest jazz festival ever held in the city of Chicago?"

That is just what he did, defining its dates as August 7, 8, and 9 of 1959. To pull it off, he turned, as always, to Victor Lownes.

There would be a number of hurdles to cross. Lownes came to Hef and told him he'd booked Soldier Field for the event. They moved rapidly forward, immediately signing $100,000 worth of contracts, with more to come.

Yet suddenly, and without notice, city officials pulled the plug on their lease of Soldier Field, citing falsely that use of the stadium would damage the cinder tracks needed for the upcoming Pan America Games.

When Hef heard the news, he shouted, "That's bullshit! Some bluenose fart is behind this outrage," placing the blame on the Rev. Msgr. John M. Kelly, editor of the Catholic Church's *New World* magazine.

Hef protested to the Pan American Games Commission, whose upcoming games had been scheduled in Chicago, and to the city's mayor,

Richard Daley, finding both of them unsympathetic to his protests. "*Playboy* is not a fit sponsor for such a major event," Daly announced. "The quality of the magazine would dishonor the festival and its many great artists."

Befuddled at first, Hef and Lownes turned to the owners of the Chicago Stadium, which opened that venue to them. To garner favorable publicity, Hef announced he would donate $100,000, the estimated gross of opening night, to the Chicago Urban League. At the end of the festival, Hef would proclaim, "I went about $50,000 in the hole for our sponsorship, but it garnered a million dollars of publicity."

Announcements went out across the country that "The Giants of Jazz Blowing" would all be starring at the Chicago Stadium in early August as a celebration of the fifth anniversary of the birth of *Playboy*. Comedian Mort Sahl was selected as the event's emcee.

"I used to hang out with Vic and Hef every night after my last show," Sahl claimed. "We hit the hot spots of Chicago, most often until five in the morning. Girls and more girls. It was a case of 'one for all and all for one' like the Three Musketeers. To show how long ago that was, Hef was still wearing three-piece suits before he switched to pajamas."

Although commitments were wangled from many of America's greatest jazz artists, some high-profile stars weren't available. They included Charlie Parker, who had died in 1955. Billie Holiday, another of Hef's favorites, died weeks before the Festival began. Nat King Cole had prior commitments to a tour of South America, and a dialogue with Frank Sina-

tra revealed that he'd be in Hollywood filming *Can-Can*, set for a release in 1960.

Sinatra's most successful impersonator, Duke Hazlett, was hired instead. During his performance at the festival, Hazlett would make his entrance onto the stage dressed like Sinatra right down to the trenchcoat casually slung over his shoulder. He opened his gig by singing "Come Fly With Me" to loud applause. At the end, the crowd cheered wildly, most of them thinking it was the real Sinatra.

But when Sahl came onstage and announced that the singer had been Duke Hazlett, he was loudly booed.

Louis (Satchmo) Armstrong performed brilliantly at Hef's event and to wild applause, but he had been in poor health since he'd suffered a stroke onstage in Spoleto, Italy. "I was afraid he couldn't blow that horn, but he did so superbly," Hef said, "right down to when the saints came marching in. He also performed a show-stopping number with Ella Fitzgerald. Too bad Vic didn't record that."

"The festival was a great breakthrough for civil rights," Lownes said. "Black and white performers were on the stage and in the audience. It was totally inter-racial."

As one critic noted about Ella Fitzgerald, she "is acclaimed for the purity of her tone, her impeccable diction, phrasing, and intonation, and her horn-like improvisational ability, best reflected in her scat singing."

According to Hef, "Lady Ella was not only the Queen of Jazz but the Queen of our Festival, too. Her performance was greeted with a roar louder than that of any championship boxing match." Most of the time, she appeared on stage as a solo artist, but on occasion, she teamed with Armstrong, Duke Ellington, or the Ink Spots.

Dizzy Gillespie, a native of South Carolina, a very segregated state at the time, was one of the world's greatest jazz trumpeters, He was also a composer, bandleader, and singer. According to Hef, "Gillespie's appearance was a bit bizarre. His cheeks were so puffed out it looked like he had tiny balloons in his mouth. He wore a beret and horn-rimmed specs. He did a lot to popularize behop, and he became known for his scat singing like Lady Ella...His unique sound came from a deliberately bent horn."

Gillespie introduced Lownes and Hef to Coleman ("Hawk") Hawkins, who made the first behop recording back in 1944. "He was a jazz tenor saxophonist," Hef said, "one of the first artists to use a sax, which was more in the Glenn Miller style."

"Miles Davis was a legend," Hef said. "He was talented as a jazz trumpeter, composer, and a bandleader too. Over the decades, he rose to become one of the major figures in the history of jazz. We were lucky to get him for the festival. His career might have gone even better were it not for his dependence on heroin. He became such a druggie he was nicknamed 'Prince of Darkness.' He wasn't the most sociable musician in town."

Dave Brubeck, a pianist, composer, and the foremost exponent of "cool jazz," became Hef's first celebrity journalist. In an article he wrote for *Playboy* ("New Jazz Audience") he defined American jazz as the equivalent of European classical music.

A critic claimed, "Brubeck's music is best known for employing unusual 'time signatures,' with contrasting rhythms, meters, and tonalities." If all that sounds confusing, it's best to understand the technique by listening to his recording of "Pick Up Sticks," or "Unsquare Dance."

What would a major jazz festival from that era have been without the music of Count Basie? A regular in the clubs of Chicago, he had launched his 50-year career as a teenager, playing the piano at movie houses showing silent films. A native of Red Bank, New Jersey, he was famous, in the words of a critic, "for the use of two 'split' tenor saxophones, emphasizing the rhythm section."

In another career that eventually spanned half a century, the composer and bandleader Duke Ellington was already a legend for his performances in Harlem at the Cotton Club. A prominent feature during Hef's event in Chicago, "He had elegance and charisma. In fact, he elevated jazz to an art form," Hef said. "He even won a Pulitzer Prize for his music." Regrettably, he was dead when the prize was announced." [*Although Ellington died in 1974, he won the Pulitzer, posthumously, in 1999.*]

Also appearing at *Playboy's* Jazz Festival was Canadian-born Oscar Peterson, who had long been a favorite entertainer in the smoky jazz joints of Chicago. Hef, perhaps inaccurately, always took credit for naming him "The Maharaja of the Keyboard." Peterson's career would span six decades, incorporating successes in jazz, bebop, hard bop, "third stream," and, of course, the blues. He was especially attracted to boogie-woogie and played several ragtime pieces, where he earned the reputation of the "Brown Bomber of Boogie-Woogie."

Also present was Stan Kenton, "the pride of Wichita," leader of an innovative and influential jazz orchestra. Beginning in the early 1940s, this jazz artist, pianist, composer, arranger, and band leader had been credited with several pop hits, later establishing his reputation for progressive jazz. Hef referred to his sound as "testosterone-driven."

Barry Ulanov, writing in *Metronome*, claimed, "Kids are going haywire over the sheer noise of Kenton's band. A generation is growing up with the idea that jazz and the atomic bomb are essentially the same natural phenomenon."

In 1955, Kenton had married the young and very beautiful Ann Richards, a singer from San Diego. Hef flirted with her, and Kenton finally relented, granting his consent for his wife to pose nude as a centerfold for the June 1961 issue of *Playboy*.

In an interview in *Billboard*, Lownes later recalled, "Our main object in staging the festival was to improve the image of *Playboy* in the eyes of advertisers, who hadn't yet read our magazine, considering it a dirty publication. I wanted to show we were more than just our centerfolds, since we covered a range of interests appealing to the smart young American male on the rise."

Hef said, "I didn't want to festival to end. I had the time of my life." He paused a moment. "Perhaps that was an exaggeration. There was at least one orgy staged by Vic that topped it."

***

Hef received some of his greatest public recognition not as publisher of *Playboy*, but as the host of a variety talk-and-music show, *Playboy's Penthouse*, first broadcast on October 24, 1959.

In *The New York Times*, Vincent Copgrove recorded his impressions: "Cigarette smoke drifts above elegantly clad cocktail-shaken guests. Cy Coleman sits at a piano and sings his hit, 'Witchcraft,' although Sinatra does it better. [*The reference to Sinatra was removed from the final copy.*]

"Not far away, Lenny Bruce chats up two Playmates of the Month. *Playboy* magazine's publisher, Hugh Hefner, nervously patrols the party, making sure the jazz, liquor, and conversation flow. It's 1959 and the syndicated TV series, *Playboy's Penthouse*, is in full scotch-and-soda groove."

When he was on camera, Bruce was the life of the party, attacking such subjects as TV censorship and segregation. For the broadcast, he had to clean up his act, eliminating his penchant for four-letter words.

From its inception, it was clearly understood that *Playboy's Penthouse* would not be broadcast in America's Deep South, partly because black performers, after the conclusion of their acts, remained as part of the party, chatting with other (white) guests. Viewers saw Nat King Cole sitting on a sofa, chatting with a white woman, a context viewed in some quarters at the time as "unacceptable for television."

"There will always be stupid people," Hef said.

Although *Playboy's Penthouse* parties appeared to be unfolding within Hef's private bachelor quarters, they were actually being recorded on a stage at ABC's Chicago affiliate, WBKB, with plenty of "Bunnies" on site to mingle with the guests.

"My aim in the show was to promote the lifestyle of a typical Playboy, projecting a fantasy existence of how a roving bachelor-at-large might live," Hef said. "I was hoping to become the very symbol of Mr. Playboy."

With his familiar pipe and outfitted in a tuxedo, Hef welcomed distinguished guests to "his pad." Gin martinis flowed freely, and cigarettes dangled from the mouths of stars who included Tallulah Bankhead, who had usually started drinking long before the filming actually began.

Lownes claimed, "The show helped us to improve *Playboy's* image, showing we were not just a magazine of filth and obscenity, but a periodical of an elegant life."

"Hef was not a very good host. He was no Noël Coward," wrote one reporter. "More like Gary Cooper."

To those remarks, Hef responded, "I knew I wasn't the best host and was so dull I made that stoic Ed Sullivan look like Liberace. I was never good at party chatter and small talk. But since I was surrounded by beautiful women and celebrities, I figured they would keep the show going."

Guests included his friend, comic Don Adams, along with another comedian Bob Newhart. Sarah Vaughan appeared to sing, as did Tony Bennett, Hef's favorite male entertainer. Ella Fitzgerald sang, but seemed uncomfortable being interviewed. Count Basie and Stan Kenton were most entertaining as music men, and sometimes Hef brought on a famous author like Carl Sandburg.

Real liquor was served to guests, and as one viewer noted, "Many of them were ready to be hauled off to Zonksville by the end of every broadcast."

At the time, neither Bobby Short nor Mabel Mercer was familiar to TV audiences, but Hef invited them on. Short performed the Bessie Smith blues song, "Gimme a Bigfoot," while Mercer, with her elegant style, sang the Cole Porter number, "Looking at You."

Cool, classy, only slightly stilted, and very good at building his brand: Two views of Hefner on the set of *Playboy's Penthouse*

Dizzy Gillespie had been such a hit at the Jazz Festival that Hef invited him to perform his bebop love song, "Oo-Shoo-Be-Do-Be."

"I refused to do a segregated show, which definitely limited our appeal," Hef said. "Our sponsors want us to bring on Judy Garland, Doris Day, Pat Boone, Tab Hunter or Rock Hudson. In many ways, we were like the first reality show. Our first season ran slightly more than a year, with a second season launched on September 9, 1961, with such guests as Anita O'Day, Buddy Greco, and Jack E. Leonard. Sammy Davis Jr. always went over big, although controversial as hell."

\*\*\*

One of the first "big-name entertainers" that Hef befriended in Chicago was pint-sized Sammy Davis, Jr. Born in New York and a former child star, Davis in time became one of the most dynamic performers in show business, overcoming physical and racial barriers. He'd lost an eye in an automobile accident. But that didn't stop him, and he forged ahead, becoming one of the charter members of Frank Sinatra's "Rat Pack."

Hef came to know Davis intimately through his performances at Chez Paree, across the alley from *Playboy's* editorial offices. *[Years later, Hef housed the star in his penthouse suite above the Playboy Club when Davis took his stage play,* Golden Boy, *to Chicago before moving it on to London.]*

Once, Hef attended a scandalous party Davis was hosting. *[It later degenerated into an orgy.]* Davis stood near the entrance greeting his guests, clad in white boots, black silk panties, and a black bra, each borrowed from one of his many girlfriends.

During his sojourns in Chicago, Davis, along with such singers as Mel Tormé or Johnny Mathis, would suddenly appear at *Playboy's* offices to take Hef to lunch.

Hef sometimes arranged for Davis to hook up with certain Playmates, noting his preference for blondes. As one of them told Hef, "He has the stamina of a bull. I was in his suite for only five seconds before he whipped it out, demanding a blow-job. He could go all night."

Davis once told Hef, "If God ever took away my talent, I'd be just a nigger again."

He also claimed, "Complete ugliness, utter ugliness, like mine, is most attractive to some women."

Whenever he flew in from Hollywood, Davis brought the latest stash of porn films to share with Hef.

Hef so admired Davis' talents that he asked him to lead off the second season of *Playboy's Penthouse*, the TV series. "He was the most explosive entertainer we ever had on our show," Hef said.

Before *Playboy Penthouse* was launched, Hef had watched and been inspired by a roughly equivalent show called *The Big Party*, hosted by a drunken Tallulah Bankhead and a wooden Rock Hudson, who were having a brief fling at the time. *[The tall, handsome actor was known at the time for throwing "mercy fucks" to a lot of older Hollywood divas.]* "Sammy saved the TV show for those two," Hef said.

Hefner had become one of the staunchest defenders of Davis' marriage (1960-1968) to the blonde Swedish movie star, May Britt. When Davis met her, she'd just starred in *The Blue Angel*, the original version of which had made Marlene Dietrich a star in the 1930s.

"May was viciously attacked in the press for her role in that film," Hef said. "Perhaps the remake should never have been made. How in the world could any actress top the legendary Dietrich?"

Davis was a strong vocal supporter of the presidential run of Senator John F. Kennedy and had appeared on stage at the Democratic National Convention of 1960. It was rumored that Robert Kennedy himself had asked Davis to postpone—as a personal favor to the Kennedy family—his marriage to Britt until after the election. Davis acquiesced to that, marrying her only a few days after JFK won.

Britt's contract with 20th Century Fox was immediately canceled. Davis was worried that he, too, would be blackballed, but his career flourished despite his position at the center of a controversy that one reporter claimed "was so explosive it made the atomic bomb look like a firecracker."

Traveling together, Britt and Davis often could not book themselves into the same hotel. In 1960, interracial marriages were banned in thirty-one states. According to Davis, "In stores, May drank at the white fountain, and I slurped water from the one marked 'colored.'"

When Davis starred at the Lotus Club in Washington, D.C., neo-Nazis picketed it with signs: "YOU

Sammy Davis, Jr. on-stage in 1966.

"I popped out of the womb in Harlem, a born mugger," Davis said. "My Pop told me so."

May Britt in a still from the Italian romance, *L'ultimo amante.*

After her marriage to Sammy Davis, Jr., her studio told her, "We have no more films suitable for you."

KOSHER COON GO BACK TO THE CONGO." *[Davis had converted to Judaism.]*

Hef told him, "Live your life on your own terms, as I do, and marry the woman you love. The bigots be damned!"

\*\*\*

The Playboy Mansion, at 13040 North Side Parkway in Chicago's Gold District, was a vast brick-and-limestone monument to "conspicuous consumption" and "the good life." Built with seventy rooms, a mansard roof, and *beaux-arts* details during the closing months of the 19th Century, it had been the lavish home of a socially connected surgeon, Dr. George Swift. Inside, he had entertained the "Rough Rider," Theodore Roosevelt, and Admiral Richard E. Byrd, the explorer of the North Pole.

Hef bought the house in 1959 for $400,000, a much more vast sum back then than today, and began renovations immediately. There would be no other interior like it in all of Chicago. "I want to make it the center of the *Playboy* world," he claimed.

He ordered a bronze plaque displaying a phrase in Latin for installation near the entrance: *"Si Non Oscillas, Noli Tintinnare* ("If you don't swing, don't ring")

Guests would always remember their arrival at the mansion: After ringing, a mammoth door would swing open, and a liveried butler attired in black and white would greet prospective guests and—if they were on the list—let them into the "sanctum sanctorum." Others were turned away, including on one occasion, thirty horny male college students from the University of Illinois. As they stood in the reception hall, within sightlines of a seven-foot abstract bronze, *Modern Woman*, by Abbott Pattison, male guests often wondered, "Where's the orgy?"

An open staircase covered in thick opera-red carpeting led up to an ivory-colored door opening onto a long hall lined with modern paintings by, among others, Jackson Pollock, Willem de Kooning, and Franz Kline.

Two medieval suits of armor guarded the entrance to the mansion's ballroom. Playmates had long suspected that Hef positioned male members of his security staff to conceal themselves inside the armor. Once, it was said, a Bunny wearing sunglasses and a leopard-skin bikini—thinking there were men inside—seductively danced the Watusi in front of one of the suits of armor.

No guest was ever immediately greeted by Hef, as he tended to remain out of sight until long after everyone else's arrival. In some cases, he wouldn't come out of his bedroom at all, unless it was to welcome a VIP.

A contemporary journalist, Jonathan Perdue, described Chicago's Playboy Mansion like this:

*"At last, a guest enters the cavernous ballroom, the center of gravity, measuring sixty feet long and thirty feet wide. At the far end, flames rise in this vast seigneurial arena from a Roman marble fireplace. Over it hangs a 'Reclining Nude' by Pablo Picasso.*

*"The ceiling is beamed and inlaid with flowery frescoes. In contrast to the antique décor, the furnishings are in extreme modern, as if ripped from the pages of* Playboy *for the bachelor-at-large. Overstuffed armchairs are large enough to accommodate a playboy and at least two playmates on either side of him.*

*"At the center is a huge stereo console where music is played 24 hours a day. There is a vast number of electronic gadgets,* and at least 3,000 records from Hef's vast collection.*

**"Playboy could not have happened anywhere else but Chicago."**

— Hugh Hefner in the *Chicago Tribune*
April 21, 2012

Positioned at 1340 North State Street Parkway, Chicago's Playboy Mansion hosted visiting celebrities who included Bill Cosby, Warren Beatty, Frank Sinatra, and the Rolling Stones.

Inside, its most famous component was Hef's circular bed. It was described as "having more controls and gadgets than a Boeing 747."

After his move to Los Angeles, Hef's visits to Chicago became infrequent. In August 1984, Playboy Enterprises leased the monument to the school associated with The Art Institute of Chicago for five years at $10 annually. Renamed Hefner Hall, it operated as a student dormitory until 1990.

In 1993, what had become famous as "the most decadent mansion in Chicago" was converted into condos.

*"Guests soon learn his taste in music, such as 'As Time Goes By,' from his favorite movie,* Casablanca *(1942).*

*"On and off throughout the night, Hef's other favorites are played. From Peggy Lee, he prefers 'Is That All There Is?' and his preferred Frank Sinatra records are 'One for My Baby' and 'In the Wee Small Hours of the Morning.'*

*"The voice of Billie Holiday forever enchanted him, especially 'If You Were*

*Mine,' and 'It's Like Reaching for the Moon.'*

*"He also had some hip-hop records, which, in Hef's peculiar words, were 'Head down, ass up, if that's the way you like to fuck.' Late at night, he ordered the staff to play Vera Lynn's 'We'll Meet Again.'"*

Columnist Art Buchwald was an early visitor to Chicago's Playboy Mansion. Buchwald had asserted that Hef had made Chicago the sex capital of the world, "the home of the most enviable bachelor on the planet. Getting an invitation from Hef was more coveted than one to Buckingham Palace."

The sometimes belligerent author, Norman Mailer arrived and announced, "I'm here on a bunny hunt. Show me the way to those hot and horny dames."

Novelist Nelson Algren wrote: "I haven't seen anything like it since Joan Crawford threw that lingerie party in *Dance, Fools, Dance"* (1931).

The most luxurious bedrooms for special guests were on the main floor, and doors were always locked. The Red Room and the Blue Room were the best furnished and equipped.

On the top floor, Hef installed private offices for his magazine and bedrooms for his staff, which numbered about fifty men and women. Dormitory rooms with bunk beds housed about two dozen Bunnies, and every four occupants shared a bathroom. Many of them slept bare-assed on their beds. In the on-site cafeteria, all plates cost $1.50, be it a big steak dinner or a hamburger.

Sometimes late at night, a young man was slipped into the "harem," as one Bunny recalled, "By the time we finished with some poor guy, he wouldn't want sex for a month…at least."

Hef wanted to create a South Seas atmosphere, evoking one of those "Dorothy Lamour in a sarong" movies he'd seen as a child. He even installed a bowling alley and an Olympic-sized swimming pool, where it was recommended that men and women swim together in the nude. Otherwise, bikinis were available. Some men didn't want to wear swimwear that was too revealing and put on a pair of swimming trunks.

Such was the case when singer Ricky Nelson came to visit. One playmate recalled, "At least five of us were after him, trying to get him out of those damn trunks. I finally succeeded when I sneaked away with him. He was very shy about stripping down. It was the cutest little thing you ever saw—not too big."

In contrast, Anthony Quinn showed up and stripped naked in front of the Bunnies. His former lover, actress Evelyn Keyes, said, "There was just too much of Tony—yes, down there, too."

Behind a cascading waterfall, and reached by swimming under it, was the Grotto, with waterproof cushions for heavy petting or sexual encounters. "If there were an orgy going on, it was likely to be here," Victor Lownes said. "Soft lighting, romantic music. When you got off three times and needed a rest, you could retreat to a pool table or stash yourself at one of the pinball machines. Or, to recover with your Bunny of choice, there was always the steam room."

"Under the pool was an underwater bar where you could look up and take in the swimmers over your head. It was like a large aquarium. All that was missing was Esther Williams. You might even see Hef with his eight-inch hard-on having sex with a Playmate."

"A lot of screwing went on in those underground chambers," said *Playboy* writer Reg Potterton. "There really wasn't much else to do in the mansion except have sex. I got laid plenty of times in the underwater bar, but only once in the Grotto."

The actor, Lee Marvin, came and stayed for three nights," Lownes said. "You could see him on occasion in the steam room with that uncut dick of his dangling. God certainly wasn't fair when he assigned dick sizes."

Before she entered Hef's bedroom, a Bunny had to leave her shoes at the door. "You could always tell the number of girls Hef was seducing that night by the number of shoes left outside the entrance," Lownes said. "Guest had to walk barefooted on the snow-white carpeting where they could feast their eyes on a Brobdingnagian circular bed rotating at 360-degree angles."

Hef's famous round bed was the most written-about piece of furniture at the mansion. It was described in the April 1965 issue of *Playboy* as a "contemporary Morpheus-in-the-round, a wonderfully electronic, indolently sybaritic, ingeniously equipped sleep center."

Writing in the now-defunct *New York Herald Tribune*, author Tom Wolfe—notable for his association with the literary style known as "The New Journalism" described the marvel:

> It was a bed and a half, the biggest, roundest bed in the history of the world. It's eight and a half feet in diameter, and it fits into a bank of curved cabinets that are equipped with a refrigerator, bar, Dictaphone, and remote control switching for radio, stereo, and television. A Rapidial phone, programmed with 200 telephone numbers, that can be dialed by pressing a single button, is also built into the cabinet. Hefner can sit in bed and set the bed vibrating or rotate it to change, in effect, his immediate environment."

*"He can be the undisputed hero himself," Wolfe wrote. "The contemporary recluse, the Consumer King, at the center of the world, amid the dials. The great bed starts turning into an orbit of its own. It is the perfect moment, renewed with every revolution of the bed, every revolution of a controlled universe, with one's own self dropped not out but in to the perfect rotation, around and around, in ever-decreasing concentric circles, toward nirvana, ambrosia, while following one's own perfect orbit, out there, for all to see, the Playboy Beacon, sweeping the heavens of America with its two-billion candlepower beam of Hefnerism—and the perfect bliss rrr rrr rrr."*

Hef also confided to Wolfe that "in case something very beautiful happens in bed," he was able to film it with his $50,000 Ampex videotaping console.

Lownes claimed that Hef liked to watch himself having sex, recording it for posterity so he can view the act again or else watch the action in all the mirrors around the bed. "It's fun watching myself and a *Playboy* bedmate making mad, passionate love on closed circuit TV," Hef said.

Near the bed in a cabinet were found what Hef called instruments "vital for the ultimate sexual experience." These included chains, vibrators, studded leather harnesses, and dildoes ranging in size from five and a half inches to fifteen. Overhead, psychedelic lighting drenched his Playmates in an ever-changing pattern of swirling colors like a disco in the psychedelic 1960s.

When he wasn't having sex, the bed was covered with photo layouts and page proofs of the next issue of *Playboy.*

Once, Hefner ordered his cleaning staff to remove most of the room's sexually explicit materials and invited his son, David, to try out the bed during one of his early visits to the mansion. On another occasion, he invited his stern parents to lie on the bed with him, watching television.

Above the bed was his favorite poster. Formatted with large letters, it said, "HEF IS A VIRGIN."

Equaled only by the porn collection of King Farouk, the exiled and very decadent King of Egypt from 1936-1952, Hef owned at least 1,000 stag films, including a particularly infamous lesbian "blue movie." It had starred Joan Crawford during her struggles to stay alive in 1920s Hollywood.

Adjacent to Hef's bedroom was a marble-sheathed Roman bath big enough to accommodate Hef and up to a dozen companions in total comfort.

*[In time, Hef's round bed was spoofed on television. On* The Tonight Show

*in 1968, Johnny Carson appeared on a round bed as "Hef Handsome," alongside Angela Dorian, the Playmate of the Year.*

*In a segment on* **Laugh-In,** *Hef himself was a guest, appearing alongside comedian Ruth Buzzi, who impersonated a Playmate wannabe with a bushy tail.*

*In the 1966 film,* The Silencers, *Dean Martin starred as secret agent Matt Helm. In one of his scenes, he was hauled away from a round bed and dumped into a swimming pool full of comely "Slaymates."]*

\*\*\*

"Food and drink at the Playboy Mansion was available twenty hours a day," Frank Sinatra remembered. "If you wanted Polish vodka with fresh pomegranate juice, it was yours—that is, if you downed such crap."

"For Americans, there was *chili con carne,* Texas style," said designer Oleg Cassini. "But if you were a Frenchman and preferred duck breast stuffed with *foie gras,* that, too, could be ordered, but you had to allow more time, of course."

"If you wanted ice cream made with South Carolina yams, you could order it," said frequent visitor Tony Curtis. "That might take three hours to create. While we were waiting, Hef and I, both horndogs, retired to his round bed with two hot pieces of ass, but never more than four Playmates at a time."

According to Lownes, "Even though Hef had a *Cordon Bleu* chef, our publisher was a man of simple tastes. He ordered fried chicken with gravy almost every night, and the gravy had to be exactly like his mother made it. If a chef got creative and added a special touch to improve the flavor, that was grounds for firing him on the spot. Hef also liked pot roast like mama made. As for sandwiches, he ate only two types—one with peanut butter, the other with ham. His two favorite vegs were creamy mashed potatoes and corn on the cob. He washed everything down not with wine but with Pepsi. I'm not exaggerating. He drank thirty bottles of Pepsi a day. I'm sure if some waiter gave him a Coca-Cola, he'd toss it back into his face. I think Hef created the 'Pepsi Generation.'"

"He also had this special tobacco he kept in a cabinet," Lownes said. "I was told it came from the Bright Leaf tobacco country of North Carolina. *Bright Leaf,* that 1950 movie starring Gary Cooper and Bogie's baby, Lauren Bacall, about the tobacco industry, was one of his favorite films."

"Forgive the vulgarity," Lownes said, "but Hef's semen must have been the tastiest in Chicago. Throughout the day, he ate Butterfingers, Clark Bars, chocolate chip cookies, Twinkies, and taffy apples—and only those sweets—none other. It's a wonder he didn't die a sugar addict or weigh 400 pounds."

***

"Since Hef was a boy, he'd been in love with the movies, and he remained star struck all his life," claimed Keith, his younger brother. "Once he became a celebrity himself, he attracted a wide array of other celebrities to the mansion. As you know, celebrities flock together. More than movie stars showed up. If you were a celebrity in any field, you got an invite. You might even be a civil rights leader like Martin Luther King, Jr., or Jesse Jackson. Perhaps a mayor like John V. Lindsay of New York."

"Boxers, singers, athletes, producers, people from all fields were invited, including the literati: William Saroyan, Saul Bellow, Kenneth Tynan, Jules Feiffer, James Baldwin ("he preferred Bunny Boys"), and Ray Bradbury. He also entertained dancers, notably Rudolph Nureyev. "Rudi liked to exhibit his wares around the pool," Lownes claimed.

"Johnny Carson dropped in on occasion, a real pussy hog," Lownes said. "He never left without seducing three Bunnies."

Actor David Janssen was a particular favorite of Hef, who admired his brooding presence on the screen. Hef confessed to him one night, "Of all the actors in Hollywood, I most wanted to look like you."

Even Tiny Tim, that ridiculously campy entertainer with the ukelele, visited Chicago's Playboy mansion, confessing to Hef, "I'm tiny all over."

Jane Fonda, whom Hef referred to as "Hank's daughter," showed up. She told him, "When I learned that men found me attractive, I went wild, but not wild enough to pose for your Playmate of the Month." She also told fascinating stories of her experiences working in the movies. "Being a star in Hollywood gives you a certain expertise in the field of prostitution."

He wanted to ask her if the rumors circulating about her and the Black Panthers were true but didn't dare.

"When Bob Hope was in Chicago, he visited the mansion," said Hef. "Before he left, I think he 'Bunny-hopped' at least three times. Bing Crosby had warned me that Hope 'was a fast man with a squaw, but a slow man with a buck,' so I told the girls not to expect a tip."

Hope confessed to Hef, "I've bedded a lot of Las Vegas showgirls, but, on occasion, I sleep from the A-list. Betty Hutton and Paulette Goddard come to mind. All of them and countless others have raided my 'Hope Chest.'"

Danny Kaye had always amused Hef on the screen. "He could mug and cavort hilariously," Hef said, "but in person, he was filled with doubt and was forced to live in the closet, venturing out on occasion to seduce

190

his longtime lover, Laurence Olivier, and Louis Jourdan—a man once voted the handsomest man on earth."

"Kaye worried a lot about his sex appeal, telling me that his producer, Samuel Goldwyn, once told him he had none. His exact words to me were, 'No one in the audience would want to fuck you.'"

"Kaye was also worried about his physicality," Hef said. "When he made *The Court Jester* (1955), the director said that his legs were too skinny and bony."

"I had to wear leg falsies, to fill out those green tights—yes, there, too," Kaye claimed.

"Groucho Marx showed up one night, hoping to get laid," Lownes said. "But I couldn't find any Bunnies who wanted to lie down under him. I had to call this madam I knew to send over two hookers. One of the whores told me, 'The tiniest meat, but the fastest action.'"

"In contrast, Hugh O'Brian, TV's Wyatt Earp himself, visited us," Lownes said. "For him, the lines formed on the left and right."

Sidney Poitier was also a guest at the Playboy Mansion. "I'm not sure if he made it with any of my Bunnies," Hef said. "But I knew many of my girls found him appealing. He was from The Bahamas and in time, made the movie-going public realize that a man of color could be good-looking, talented, smart, and complex."

Dean Martin, without Jerry Lewis, visited the Mansion every time he flew to Chicago. His seductions took place in the Blue Room behind locked doors. "Hef and I envied him a lot," Lownes said. "After all, he'd seduced two of the screen's alltime luscious blondes: Lana Turner and Marilyn Monroe."

"Martin was known to be very romantic at night," Lownes said. "But the next morning, he gave his Bunny a pat on the ass and hurried off. If any girl wanted to talk, he told them, 'Call a priest.'"

One night, Jerry Lewis showed up. He told Lownes, "In truth, I fuck more gals than Dean, but all they want to do is burp me."

\*\*\*

Installed in his Chicago mansion, Hef earned a reputation for Friday night *soirées* which became the most coveted invitations in Chicago. These "Rabelaisian orgies" began at midnight and lasted until the noon lunch hour, when guests lined up to restore their energies at a lavish buffet. After that, they staggered out into the daylight.

These "get togethers" were followed by tamer fare every Sunday, usually defined as movie night at the mansion. "As a kid," Hef recalled, "mother would not let Keith and me go to the movies on a Sunday. So guess what? I made 'Sunday at the Mansion' movie night."

Seated with his *Bunny du Jour*, cuddling in an overstuffed armchair, Hef saw the best of films, all of them flown in from Hollywood.

"My alltime favorite movie was *Casablanca*" (1942), Hef said. "It has everything: Love, redemption, friendship, patriotism, humor, adventure, and a great musical score, including 'As Time Goes By.'"

"Bogie was always my favorite actor," Hef said. "I saw *Casablanca* many times, but also loved *The Maltese Falcon* (1941) with Mary Astor and *To Have and Have Not* (1944), where Bogie met his Baby," (Lauren Bacall).

His favorite musical was *Singin' in the Rain* (1952), with Gene Kelly and Debbie Reynolds. Charlie Chaplin's *City Lights* (1931) was his first choice of all the Chaplin films.

"Elizabeth Taylor was never more beautiful than she was in *A Place in the Sun* (1951)," he said. "Rita Hayworth was never sexier than in the classic *Gilda* (1946). Marilyn Monroe gave her best performance in *Some Like It Hot* (1959). For haunting romantic dramas, I preferred Gene Tierney's *Laura* (1944). That beauty got plowed by John F. Kennedy."

"Of the Bond films, *Dr. No* (1963) can't be beat," Hef said. "Ursula Andress is the ultimate Bond Girl."

His favorite western was *Shane* (1953), starring Alan Ladd and Jean Arthur.

"I always got an erection watching *King Kong* (1933) when that beastly gorilla kidnaps Fay Wray," Hef said. "I worried that their sexual equipment wouldn't match up, though."

\*\*\*

Hef and Lownes were each lying nude on his satin-covered round bed, discussing their dream of opening a Playboy Club in Chicago. Both men had just finished taking turns seducing a Playmate of the Month.

Eventually, the subject arose of a costume design for the waitresses who'd be serving food and drink.

Hef came up with the idea of some "boudoir attire," perhaps a form of lin-

Hef was not particularly well-versed in literature, but he had read F. Scott Fitzgerald's *The Great Gatsby* when fans started comparing him to the mysterious hero of that jazz-age novel. Soonafter, he ordered that Alan Ladd's 1949 film adaptation be screened at the Chicago Mansion.

Later, he asked for an in-house screening of the 1926 silent screen version, too, but was told that it had been lost to history.

gerie. Lownes did not consider that as a practical costume for a server. At the time, Hef was dating Ilsa Taurins, whom he'd met when she appeared on *Playboy Penthouse*. The following night on a date with her, he asked her suggestion for a costume, something to complement the *Playboy* Logo of a horny rabbit.

Although Hef would be condemned by feminists for forcing women into bunny costumes, it was actually a woman who originated the idea. Taurins claimed that the rabbit concept could be extended to include costumes for waitresses. Hef reminded her that the *Playboy* rabbit was "the copulatory, not the copulate."

Nonetheless, in the morning, she visited her mother, a seamstress, and worked with her on the creation of a bunny costume with rabbit ears and a bushy tail.

When it was ready, Lownes approached Cynthia Maddox and asked if she'd model the costume for Hef. Maddox agreed and that night, Lownes stripped down and joined a nude Hef in bed, promising that a surprise was on the way, and that they should be "dressed" for action—meaning without clothes.

A discreet knock on their door led to Maddox's entrance, modeling the scarlet-colored bunny costume, complete with ears and a bushy tail and towering high heels.

"Cynthia looked gorgeous, and in time would appear on five *Playboy* covers," Lownes said. "But Hef didn't immediately go nuts like I thought he would."

"It looks too much like a swimsuit, something you could see on any beach," Hef said, "except for the ears and tail."

He gestured for Maddox to approach and began to tuck at the material around her thighs until he had completely ex-

*Casablanca*, the 1942 wartime movie about an ill-fated romance, starred Humphrey Bogart and Ingrid Bergman.

"It is my candidate for the best movie ever made," Hef said, "beating out that longtime favorite, Orson Welles' *Citizen Kane*. I saw it time and time again with different Playmates cuddled up beside me. It won three Oscars: Best Picture, Best Director, and Best Screenplay. It deserved more."

Ingrid denied it at the time, but later, she revealed that she, indeed, had a real-life affair with Bogie."

posed them, leaving just enough fabric to cover her crotch.

Lownes looked skeptical. "Some Bunnies will have to borrow my razor unless you want vagina hair peeking out."

Hef made another suggestion or two before Maddox faded for the night.

"I don't think I'm gonna get hot when Cynthia comes in tomorrow night modeling those alterations," Hef said. "That was some surprise."

"I've got another one," Lownes said. "Tonight, to put some variety into your diet, I've invited two *café au lait* beauties from Paris. They're in Chicago appearing at Mr. Kelly's. Let's call it two guys putting their cream into some black coffee."

And thus, on that rainy night in Chicago, the *Playboy* Bunny was born. In time, it would become an international icon, the very symbol of sexy, liberated women of affairs.

Lots and lots of affairs.

# Chapter Six

# "MY KIND OF TOWN, CHICAGO IS!"

## MARKETING TO A NEW BREED OF CONSUMER, HEF LAUNCHES THE FIRST PLAYBOY CLUB. IT BECOMES THE BUSIEST NIGHT SPOT IN THE WORLD

## *PROMISES! PROMISES! & POLITICS! POLITICS!*

### AFTER *PLAYBOY* RUNS NUDE PICTURES OF JAYNE MANSFIELD, POLICE INVADE HEF'S BEDROOM & HAUL HIM OFF TO JAIL

## CENSORSHIP MANIA

### BOURGEOIS OUTRAGE, WIDESPREAD CONDEMNATION

## NOBODY EVER SAID THEY WEREN'T CHAUVINISTS

### FRANK SINATRA & HUGH HEFNER—EACH A SWINGER, COMPETE FOR THE AFFECTIONS OF THE SAME WOMEN

*COSMO'S HELEN GURLEY BROWN LAUNCHES SEX & THE SINGLE GIRL*

Carroll Baker

Ursula Andress

Arlene Dahl

Susan Strasberg

Susannah York

Elsa Martinelli

"A beautiful woman—often an actress—could pose for the pages of *Playboy* without showing all her goods," Hef said. Stellar examples of what he meant are reflected in the fabled faces of the stars above.

**As Hef moved deeper into the tumultuous 1960s**, he became the chief honcho of one of the most successful publishing empires in the United States. The circulation figures of *Playboy* would soar to four million readers, with annual advertising revenues topping $2.3 million.

Yet even with all this newfound success, Hef wanted to establish some newer ventures, too. Beginning with Chicago, he envisioned a string of Playboy Clubs throughout America. On a map, he plotted cities that might sustain one, eventually selecting New York, Atlanta, Los Angeles, Miami, and New Orleans. *[Later, he included Lake Geneva, Wisconsin, and the Caribbean nation of Jamaica, too.]*

Throughout the 1960s, Hef carefully fine-tuned his *Playboy* myth through the sale of sexual fantasy. Never again would he devise a nude centerfold that equaled the allure and star power of Marilyn Monroe, but he found other movie stars willing to pose seductively for him, but never in poses too flagrant or completely nude. They included Carroll ("Baby Doll") Baker, Ursula Andress, Arlene Dahl, Susan Strasberg, Else Martinelli, and Susannah York.

"Every issue of *Playboy* must be laced with sympathy," Hef enigmatically said.

A writer for *Time* turned out to be even more enigmatic, but with a colorful choice of words: "While there may be a *scherzo* of cartoons, a *largo* of literature, a *rondo* of reportage, the *allegro* in each edition is still the girls… and *molto con brio*."

***

"The first idea of a Playboy Club might have lodged in the back of my brain when I was watching Bogie in *Casablanca,*" Hef said. "In the movie, he was the owner of Rick's Place. Why not me having my own club, Hef's Place? Of course, the world didn't know who in hell Hef was, but I could call it the Playboy Club. I would fill it with beautiful girls, the best since Flo Ziegfeld's beauties entered the old age home. He was surrounded by the most gorgeous girls of his day. The same thing could happen to me."

Hef was also inspired by one of his favorite clubs in Chicago, the Gaslight, a members-only enclave where each guest was given a key. The staff was dressed in costumes inspired by the Gay Nineties. In some ways, Hef was also inspired by the legend of the Speakeasies of the Chicago in the 1920s.

"I wanted the atmosphere of my club sexually charged, tapping into the male *Zeitgeist*. Of course, I could expect the usual attacks, perhaps charges that the Playboy Club was, in essence, a secret bordello. But I'd have it patrolled carefully—no prostitution or else I'd lose my liquor license."

"I wanted a club which had great entertainment, good yet inexpensively priced food and drink, and lots of scantily clad hot tamales in Bunny tails—in fact, the best night club that Chicago has ever seen," Hef said.

While he labored over the layouts for the latest edition of *Playboy*, Victor Lownes scouted the town for a suitable location. Among those he consulted was Arthur Wirtz, the real estate developer who had rented the Chicago Stadium to Hef and himself for their jazz festival.

Lownes was escorted to an impressive five-story building at 116 East Walton Street. It had been the venue for four earlier nightclubs, each of which had failed. He inspected all five of its floors, finding each of them ideal for a different type of club or bar. The asking price for the entire building was only $100,000, but Hef didn't want to invest that much. Consequently, a lease was signed for its rental, guaranteeing Wirtz a percentage of the profits. As it turned out, it would have been far cheaper to have purchased the building outright. "Arthur made a god damn fortune off of us," Lownes said, years later.

With the lease signed, Hef drew up a plan for the renovations of the building, with a night club venue designated for all five floors. Each would evoke an elegant bachelor pad, with different areas designated as the Playroom, the Library, the Living Room, and—on the fifth floor and most "exclusive" of all—the Penthouse for late-night dancing. In the Playmate Bar, downstairs from the lobby, the décor would derive from back-lit photos of his favorite Playmates of the Month.

The building's exterior was renovated, too, configured into a series of rectangular spaces inspired by Mondrian, the focal point for which was a Rabbit Head

Behind its Mondrian inspired façade lurked a palace of "forbidden pleasures" (well, not really).

On opening night, the owner of a nearby shoe store expressed his delight: "I'm gonna come here every night to gawk at the half-dressed broads."

That same night, Victor Lownes faced a near mutiny. Many of his Bunnies were "earless," having removed their rabbit ears, complaining, "They're killing me."

He handled such mutiny by issuing an order. "If I see a bunny without ears, *out she goes!*"

logo—no actual sign.

Guests would migrate from room to room, from floor to floor, experiencing excitement on every level as Bunnies darted about, serving food and drink. A party atmosphere with a theme based on wine, women, and song would—at least in theory—be prevalent throughout the building, and some areas would be venues for musical performances or comedy routines.

Every food item, from a steak to a chef's salad, was priced at $1.50. So were drinks, and so was a package of cigarettes. These low prices prevailed throughout the 1960s.

"Décor be damned," might have been its dominant decorating concept at the time. The understated furnishings tended towards autumnal colors, solidly crafted teakwood, and macho-looking leather. Visual interest derived almost entirely from beautiful girls and/or their photos, the originals of which had run in previous editions of *Playboy.*

Hef even published a magazine for members, *VIP: The Playboy Club Magazine.* It included previews of coming attractions, which often featured big-name entertainers. His goal was to attract the urban elite among males, who paid either a one-time fee of $50 for a lifetime membership, or else an ongoing annual membership fee of $25.

Before the club opened, Hef put his kid brother, Keith, a failed actor, in charge of Bunny training. Rising to the challenge, Keith wrote a manual that laid out management's official guidelines. According to Keith, "My job was to take a beautiful waitress and turn her into a Bunny with a bushy tail and make her the sex symbol of the 1960s." He solicited models, out-of-work actresses, and dancers, offering salaries of between $200 and $300 a week. With tips, that enabled some Bunnies to pull in a thousand dollars a week.

He wrote, "Men are very excited about being in the company of Elizabeth Taylor, but they know they can't paw her or proposition her."

Included as an unassailable warning among his advice tips for Bunnies: "You must be sure your Bunny Tail is white and fluffy at all times."

Hef cited a motto ("Gape, Don't Touch") and maintained a strict rule: Bunnies could not give out their phone numbers or arrange dates on the premises. Of course, he had no control over what they did during their private, off-duty hours.

According to one Bunny who might have exaggerated a bit, "The most difficult part of being a Bunny was to keep smiling while an infuriated and jealous wife stubbed out a cigarette on your thigh."

A sometimes contributor to *Playboy,* author Norman Mailer, writing in *The Presidential Papers,* described the scene at the Playboy Club in Chicago:

*"The Bunnies went by in their costumes, electric blue silk, Kelly green, flame pink, pin-ups from a magazine, faces painted into sweetmeats, flower tops, tame lynx, piggie, poodle, a queen or two from a beauty contest. They wore Gay Nineties rig that exaggerated their hips, bound their waists in a ceinture, and lifted them into a phallic brassiere—each breast looked like a big bullet on the front bumper of a Cadillac. Long black stockings—up almost to the waist on each side—and to the back, on the curve of the can, as if ejected tenderly from the body, was the puff of chastity, a little white ball of a Bunny's tail that bobbled as they walked. The Playboy Club was the place of magic."*

Before she became one of the nation's top models, Lauren Hutton worked as a Bunny in the Chicago Club.

In the 1974 photograph above, her closed lips conceal the gap in her front teeth.

The strapless satin-and-rayon one-piece garment was mounted on a "Merry Widow" corset.

John Dante, a bartender at the club, said, "The sheer black panty hose added to the overall clean sexuality. Completing the costume was the bushy Bunny Tail, a puff of combed fluffy white cotton that was snapped to the *derrière*, and the Bunny Ears, which were attached to a satin headband, the same color as the costume."

Some Bunnies went on to fame elsewhere, notably Lauren Hutton, a Southern belle from Charleston, who signed a modeling contract with Revlon in 1973. At the time, it was the biggest such contract in the history of the modeling industry—and she did that in spite of the signature gap between her front teeth.

Miami-born Debbie Harry, the American singer, became famous as the lead singer of the New Wave band, "Blondie." With her distinctive photogenic features

"The Blonde Bombshell of Florida," Debbie Harry also began her career as a Bunny in Chicago.

She went on to greater glory as the lead singer in the New Wave band "Blondie," as reflected in the album cover above.

and bleached, two-tone hair, she soon became a punk icon.

One of the first *Playboy* Bunnies was Carol Ann Bongiovi ("Sharkey"), who went on to enlist in the U.S. Marines. There, she met her future husband, and in 1962, they gave birth to the singer Jon Bon Jovi. His mother became president of his fan club.

Chicago's Playboy Club was an immediate hit, with prospective patrons lined up around the block, trying to get admitted. "You had to join and be given a key if you wanted to get a whiff of what the fantasy world of *Playboy* was all about," Keith claimed.

During the last three months of 1961, some 135,000 guests visited the club, making it the busiest nightclub in the world.

As the 1960s moved on, every celebrity who visited Chicago came through its portals. They included singers such as Bob Dylan and John Lennon. In the 1971 thriller, *Diamonds Are Forever* (1971), master spy and ladykiller James Bond appeared there to check out the Bunnies.

***

In the beginning, Victor Lownes booked most of the talent—mostly singers and comics— at Chicago's Playboy Club. Many of the acts he hired were on the verge of great success, and many managed to leverage their association with the Playboy Club into other gigs.

To lead off the first performance in the Library, Lownes hired one of his favorite singers, the lyrical Mabel Mercer, who had also become one of Hef's favorite entertainers.

She always attracted relatively sophisticated Playboy Club members, the ones who appreciated cabaret acts almost as much as the Bunnies themselves.

Lownes also booked another African American singer, Aretha Franklin, who was relatively unknown at the time. And whereas Keith appreciated Mercer as a performer, he did not like Franklin at all. In fairness to that artist, she was a long way from being the performer that she morphed into. Fusing jazz with gospel, she became the "Queen of Soul."

In time, Bobby Short, a master of the piano and one of the most polished of all

Victor Lownes was one of the first to see the talent in a young Aretha Franklin, the future "Queen of Soul." He told Keith Hefner, "This gal is going places."

"Yeah," Keith said cattily. "Out of town on the road to nowhere."

How wrong he was

200

performers, performed here, too. He'd go on to attract a cult following in Manhattan, drawing, among others, heiress Gloria Vanderbilt.

The first comic Lownes booked into the club was Professor Irwin Corey. Billed as "The World's Foremost Authority," he's viewed today as a pioneer in the unscripted, improvisational art of hilarious absurdity.

Lenny Bruce told Hef, "Irwin is one of the most brilliant of the stand-up comedians, but I must warn you that politically, he's far beyond left field."

"If I had a problem with Corey," Keith said, "It was that he was constantly chasing after our Bunnies, trying to grab their bushy tails and other attractions."

Writing in *The New Yorker*, theater critic Kenneth Tynan said: "Corey is a cultural clown, a parody of literacy, a travesty of all that our civilizations hold dear, and one of the funniest grotesques in America. He is Chaplin's Little Tramp with a college education."

During the 1960 presidential election, Corey was a third-party candidate, running against Senator John Kennedy and Vice President Richard Nixon.

Also on location as a performer, George Carlin was a brilliant, witty entertainer, a specialist in black comedy, who performed a "seven dirty words" skit. In time, he became known as "The Dean of Counterculture Comedians."

The younger brother of Dick Van Dyke, Jerry Van Dyke appealed more to mainstream audiences than many of the acts booked into the Chicago Club. As more and more Playboy clubs opened around the country, he became a regular performer, moving from one venue to another. "If you like your comedy not too political, not too controversial, then Jerry was your guy," Hef said.

"I began to think for a while that all Jewish comedians were named 'Jackie,'" Hef said. "The run of Jackies began with the very controversial Jackie Mason. You could always count on him to be politically incorrect. *Time* magazine claimed he spoke to an audience "with the Yiddish locutions of an immigrant who had just completed a course in English...by mail."

At many of the Playboy clubs,

PROFESSOR IRWIN COREY

The World's Foremost Authority

"Hef and Victor Lownes were among the first to appreciate my outrageous humor," Irwin Corey said. "I became the first star comedian associated with *Playboy*."

"Hef even backed my mock run for President of the United States."

Jackie Gayle was the opening act for either Frank Sinatra or Tony Bennett. "He was from Flatbush and his humor reflected his origins," Lownes said.

Jackie Vernon was hailed as "The King of Deadpan," distinctive for his gentle, low-key delivery and his self-deprecating humor.

A native son of Chicago, Ramsey Lewis became one of the best jazz composers and pianists in America, a winner of seven gold records and three Grammy Awards. In 1965, Lewis landed on the pop singles chart with "The In Crowd," a funky groove-driven number well-suited for either dancing or listening.

Flip Wilson was one of the most celebrated entertainers Lownes ever booked, and Hef made it a point to see his show every night he was at the Playboy Club in Chicago. In time, he became a household name when he starred on TV in *The Flip Wilson Show,* the second-highest rated show on network TV. In 1972, *Time* magazine named him TVs first black superstar. Wilson's most popular character was Geraldine, a role he played in drag. *[Geraldine often referred to her boyfriend as "Killer" as part of a schtick—"The Devil made me do it!"— that evoked raucous laughter from the audience.]*

GERALDINE
*don't fight the feeling*

Of all the African American comics Hef hired, none appealed to him more than the outrageous Flip Wilson.

"He was never better than when he dressed in drag and came out as Geraldine," Hef said. "I asked him if he had a gay streak. He told me, 'I've streaked in every direction.'"

Lou Alexander, another comedian, had a hard time getting his first booking at Chicago's Playboy Club, but in time, he became a regular, appearing at associated clubs across the country. "It was my bread and butter for quite a while," he said.

"Hef's original club in Chicago was the hippest damn place in the country," Alexander said. "But Hef diluted its value by opening too many other clubs. In time, almost any bozo comic could be hired for a gig at one of his clubs. They sprouted up even in jerkwater towns. Bunnies were multiplying like a population bomb."

Lownes met the controversial African American comic, Dick Gregory, at a car wash in Chicago and auditioned him. Finding him unique and brilliantly funny, he hired him.

That same day, he also hired a Jewish singer from Brooklyn, Barbra Streisand, but by the time of her much-anticipated club date, she'd become too famous to accept the engagement. *["Before she became a star on Broadway, you could get Barbra for $1,500 a week," Lownes said. "Same price for Woody Allen and the Smothers Brothers. Hard to imagine, right?]*

Unlike Streisand, Gregory, however, did appear and was an immediate success. "When Vic (Lownes) approached me, I didn't know he was going to book me for a white audience. I thought he was coming up to me to say, 'Come and pick my cotton, boy.' He hired me for fifty bucks a night, and I'd never seen that much dough in my life. There had always been black comics, but white folks weren't exposed to them until Hef came along and put them on stage. He waged a lifelong battle for racial equality, and I give him a lot of credit for that."

"Hugh Hefner didn't care if I were scarlet, magenta, Kelly green, a sickening purple, or rosy red," said comedian Dick Gregory.

"Because of him and exposure on the Jack Paar show, my salary went from $1,800 a year to $3.5 million."

Gregory became the first black comic to work in a mostly white night club before a mostly white audience. Although membership was open to everyone, during the early stages of its existence, very few African Americans joined.

Born in St. Louis, Missouri, Gregory became a civil rights activist, social writer (he entitled his autobiography *nigger*), and a conspiracy theorist. For his outrageous performance, he was arrested several times, but Hef always stood by him. Near the end of his career, he pronounced Hef "one of the finest human beings on the planet."

\*\*\*

*[The Chicago Playboy Club moved over the years, ending up on the second floor of a high-rise apartment building. The final incarnation of the club was called "Rabbits," the male version of the former Bunny reference. This was an attempt to attract women and gays, perhaps couples.*

*The club in Chicago closed for good in 1986.*

\*\*\*

Frank Sinatra had long been a frequent visitor to Chicago and it had seemed inevitable that over the years, he and Hef would gradually get to know each other. Comedian Mort Sahl had been the first to introduce them by taking him to the Playboy Mansion. Since that time, Hef had showed up at Sinatra's various club dates and had visited him on a movie set in Miami.

"Hef and 'Ol Blue Eyes were sorta friends," said Lownes. "But they kept each other at arm's distance and were never close. There was some obvious jealousy there, as one womanizer faced off against another womanizer."

Bill Zehme wrote, "Frank Sinatra would never quite fathom what Hefner had created for himself. Sinatra wooed like few others in human life, and rarely failed to get that which he wanted, female-wise, and all else wise. But now, there was this Hefner cat, with the big house in Chicago, which was Frank's kind of town, and in this big house were all these chickies he saw before him and those spread on Hefner's magazine pages, too. The two preeminent swingers of the 20th Century engaged, as such, in tender combat over female flesh."

In 1960, Sinatra flew into Chicago to perform at a benefit concert for the Urban League. Hef invited him to the Playboy Mansion, and Sinatra arrived late with a retinue of men, many of whom looked like hoodlums from New Jersey. Hef extended a warm welcome, nonetheless.

Lownes sat in on the long talk Sinatra had with

Snapped in front of the Cal-Neva Lodge one bright desert morning when it's presumed that all the subjects were hung over, this photo, especially the billboard in its background, demonstrate the enormous allure and fame the "bromance" of the Rat Packers generated.

Hef. The singer complained of the treatment he'd received in such show biz newspapers as *Variety*, which had run many negative stories about him. At some point in the evening, there arose the possibility that these two supercharged egos might start their own show biz weekly.

"With their quick tempers, I strongly suspected that they would not survive the first issue without knocking each other off," Lownes said. "After all, Sinatra was known for throwing plates of spaghetti into a waiter's face if he didn't like the way it was cooked."

In contrast with other publications, Sinatra always appreciated the worshipful tones used to describe him in previous issues of *Playboy*. In a profile in 1958, Hef had called him "the most potent figure in show business today, the most spectacular singer of popular songs, the most sought-after movie star, the most successful wooer of women."

During his first interview with *Playboy*, Sinatra had said, "An entertainer can be the most artistically perfect performer in the world, but an audience is like a broad—if you're indifferent, it's Endsville."

The idea of their West Coast newspaper never survived that drunken night.

On his next visit to Chicago, Hef invited Sinatra to a lavish party in his honor at the Mansion. Sinatra accepted, but only with the provision that the guest list be limited to fifty—"I don't like being gawked at—and the guest list must consist of only those I invited."

Hef set about providing a lavish bar and buffet, a setup capable of mixing every drink Sinatra was rumored to have ever ordered, and his favorite foods, accompanied by his most beloved melodies. Twenty Bunnies were hired, as were an equivalent number of extra bartenders and waiters.

Hef watched in agonized anticipation, but by midnight the Sinatra party had still not arrived. Time seemed to slow down—1AM, 2AM, 3AM—Hef was bitterly disappointed. Sinatra did not appear...nor did he call.

Finally, at around 4AM, the doorbell rang and the comedian Phyllis Diller was ushered in to meet Hef. "Frank threw this bash at the Ambassador, and everybody's

The cackle of Phyllis Diller became her trademark. "She knew how to make fun of herself and her beau, 'Fang,'" Hef said.

"I loved her act. Off stage, she was always asking some guy to fuck her. She asked not only me, but all the members of the Rat Pack except Joey Bishop. No one took her up on the offer. Poor, neglected Phyllis."

drunk," she said. "Dean Martin is crawling on the floor."

At dawn, Hef dismissed the staff, thanking them for showing up for work at "the most high-class party that never was."

Despite the snub, Hef continued to invite Sinatra to the Playboy Mansion or Club. Sometimes, he would show up with members of the Rat Pack, notably singer/actor/comedian Dean Martin, comedian Joey Bishop, actor Peter Lawford, and Sammy Davis, Jr., who was already a friend of Hef's.

Author Gore Vidal claimed that the Rat Pack had come into existence after "that long nap of the 1950s when America went to bed with Ike and Mamie at 10PM. It was also an excuse for men to act like adolescents."

Sinatra told Hef his own reason for the Rat Pack. "I formed my gang because it was my desperate attempt to avoid loneliness."

Humphrey Bogart was the original leader of the gang, and his wife Lauren Bacall was rumored to have first labeled them. Sometimes, they were known as "The Summit" or "The Clan."

When females hung out with the gang, they were called Rat Pack Mascots. Judy Garland was designated as vice president. Other stars included Marilyn Monroe, Angie Dickinson, Juliet Prowse, and Shirley MacLaine. Occasionally, associates included Ava Gardner, Nat King Cole, Robert Mitchum, Elizabeth Taylor, Janet Leigh, Tony Curtis, Mickey Rooney, and Lena Horne. David Niven claimed that he and Errol Flynn were among the original members.

On January 20, 1961, Sinatra invited Hef to attend John F. Kennedy's Inaugural Ball in Washington, D.C. He arrived with his girlfriend and *Playboy* Playmate on his arm, Joyce Nizzari.

Lownes also attended with a "hot date." For the occasion, Hef rented a Georgetown home, in which he staged a late-night party. He later flew to New York with Nizzari to attend a tribute to Martin Luther King, Jr., at which Sinatra and his Rat Pack cohorts, including Sammy Davis, Jr., entertained.

***

Hef had met actor Tony Curtis when he was asked to make a guest TV appearance on *Playboy's Penthouse*. After the show, Hef invited him to the Playboy Mansion, and the two of them bonded almost immediately. Or, in Hef's words, "It was the case of one horndog meeting another Bunny-sniffing bloodhound." Rumors of Curtis' bisexuality didn't bother Hef a bit.

Curtis had completed Hef's favorite movie comedy, *Some Like It Hot*, in which he'd appeared in drag during most of the scenes. He told Hef amusing stories about working with his co-star, Marilyn Monroe. "It was like kissing Hitler."

Over the first of many weekends that Curtis would spend with Hef, they'd discussed working together to create a feature film based on Hef's remarkable life. "I was flattered by Tony's idea and promised my complete cooperation."

After that weekend, Curtis came to stay at the Mansion every time he flew east. Sometimes, he mingled with other celebrities, including Barbra Streisand, "Slugger Joe" DiMaggio (divorced from Monroe), Tony Bennett, and author James Baldwin. He wanted Curtis to make a movie based on his gay-themed novel, *Giovanni's Room*.

Curtis was in the audience to watch the cabaret performances of such artists as Paul Anka and Rich Little. One night, he was seen with Eddie Fisher and Elizabeth Taylor during happier days of their marriage.

"After you dumped Debbie Reynolds, I fucked her when we made two movies together," Curtis confessed to Fisher.

Playmate Linda Gamble remembered meeting Curtis one night at the Playboy Mansion. "I always had a crush on Tony in the movies. One night, he picked me up

Tony Curtis, along with Rock Hudson and Robert Wagner, was one of the chief "pretty boys" of 1950s cinema.

From their first meeting, he and Hef bonded. Curtis admitted later in life, "The two of us explored our hidden bisexuality."

In the lower photo, Curtis is seen in drag with Jack Lemmon, appearing in Hollywood's alltime best comedy, *Some Like It Hot* with the formidable Marilyn Monroe.

and threw me over his shoulder and carried me into the Blue Room. We ate breakfast with a bunch of people the next morning."

Once, Curtis—emerging from the shower and wearing a ten-gallon hat—posed for *Playboy's* camera wearing only a towel, showing off his perfect chest with leg akimbo and one hand reaching toward the ceiling.

In the meantime, plans to shoot a movie based on Hef's life moved ahead when Columbia agreed to finance it, with Stanley Margulies set to produce it. Tentatively, it was to have its premiere late in 1961.

Bernard Wolf was assigned the job of scriptwriting. He'd had a colorful background, serving for two years as the secretary and bodyguard to the exiled Leon Trotsky in Mexico. Later, he wrote eleven pornographic novels in eleven months, working with Henry Miller and his mistress, Anaïs Nin.

Later, Wolf would attempt to bring Miller's long-banned *Tropic of Cancer* to the screen.

During the early stages of pre-production on the movie about Hef's life he began to disagree with Curtis and the producers about the storyline. Curtis wanted a light comedy about his trying to balance three girlfriends at the same time and all the complications that entailed.

Hef had a very different idea for the movie, as outlined in the detailed memo below:

*"It is the middle 1950s in Chicago, and a young man in his mid-twenties, a rather down-at-the-heels Brooks Brothers type, with button-down shirt frayed at the edges and buttons coming loose on his overcoat, is working for $60 a week for a big, plush men's magazine. The young man is unhappy—but he has wild dreams for the creation of a magazine for the urban man....[He successfully launches the publication and a national do-good group says the magazine is obscene; the Playmate of the Month is little better than a streetwalker. The group sues and there is a dramatic trial.] We get a chance for a wonderful court scene that has many of the emotional values of the beautiful court ending in* Mr. Deeds Goes to Town, *and a similar judicial-type climax set in the Washington Senate in* Mr. Smith Goes to Washington. *This climax offers all the opportunities for the evils and hypocrisy of censorship, prudery, and the bluenose view of life pitted against freedom, youth, a notion that sex is beautiful rather than dirty...Through the stress and strain of it all, our hero has come to his senses and realized that it is truly the little secretary that he loves, and they wander out of that courtroom to live happily ever after."*

"Hot damn!" Curtis said. "My good buddy wanted the entire 'Playboy Philosophy' to be depicted in a script that would run at least six hours or more. It would be longer than *Gone With the Wind*. There was no way that Columbia would go for this. He sent in one single-spaced memo after another. I didn't bother to read them. I found it easier to weigh them."

To pacify Hef, Columbia brought in two new writers, Norman Lear and Bud Yorkin. But Hef rejected their script, too. Finally, late in 1963, with no agreement forthcoming, the project faded into oblivion like so many other movies never made.

*[In 1984, Curtis checked into the Betty Ford Clinic, battling his drug addiction. After his release, Hef invited him to come and live with him at the Playboy Mansion in Los Angeles. According to Curtis' memoirs "I had a back room which was very quiet during my final recovery. Sometimes, I played pool with Hef, a game requiring great concentration, which was good for me. There were days when I couldn't get out of bed. I was so inundated with substance abuse, my body just*

*screamed. 'Give me a hit!' At times, I'd stay in bed day and night. On the weekend, I'd get up enough energy to clean up a bit, socialize a little, and then head back to my room again."]*

***

A big disappointment and a major failure in Hef's ever-expanding Playboy Enterprises was his attempt to launch a new magazine, *Show Business Illustrated* (*SBI*). Before publication of the first issue in September 1961, he announced, "I want to print a magazine that will do for show business what *Sports Illustrated* does for sports, what *Time* does for news. We will avoid the cotton candy, press agent pap of the fan magazines or the sanctimonious peeping tomfoolery of the exposé magazines such as *Confidential*."

Its retail price would be fifty cents a copy, which made it the most expensive bi-weekly magazine on newsstands at the time. Hef promised advertisers a circulation of 350,000.

Frank Gibney, formerly of *Life* and later, *Newsday*, was brought in as its editorial director. He hired Leonard Jossel, who had held a similar position for *Time, Inc.,* books.

Almost from the beginning, Gibney and his staff failed to get Hef's vision. Gibney wanted to create *"The New Yorker of Show Business."*

Hef wrote a memo about what he saw as the editorial direction of the publication. "I want it to catch the thrills, excitement, humor, pathos, color, and glamour of show business itself. We need to feature a beauty in every issue—no nudes but wearing very few clothes. Show business is a wonderful fairyland, and I'm not referring to any of the sexual leaning of its inhabitants. It's a world of make-believe, colored lights, tinsel, and sequins. That glamour has to be reflected on every page."

Throughout the course of its brief life, Hef continued to bombard the staff of *Show Business Illustrated* with written instructions. "He sent out more damn

Dated September 5, 1961, this is the cover of the first issue of Hefner's ill-fated magazine, *Show Business Illustrated.*

"I just had to put Frank Sinatra on the cover of the first edition," he said. "After all, he was Mr. Show Business."

memos than David O. Selznick in Hollywood, the alltime memo guy," said Lownes. "Regrettably, most of them were ignored."

"I wanted a magazine with a lofty goal," Gibney said. "Time and again, Hughie and I butted heads over butts." *["Hughie" was Gibney's contemptuous nickname for Hef.]*

A special issue of *Show Business Illustrated* would eventually feature four color pages of scantily clad Las Vegas showgirls, along with profiles of Frank Sinatra or Marlon Brando. As he did in *Playboy*, Hef insisted on running stills from European movies so explicit that as films, they'd been either banned from the U.S. market or heavily censored before their U.S. release.

Around the same time, another playboy, Huntington Hartford, the A&P heir, decided to offer a slicker and better-illustrated rival showbiz magazine, *Show*. With access to virtually unlimited funds from the sale of all those groceries, it sounded a virtual deathknell for SBI.

After a meeting in New York, Hef sold his fledgling magazine to Hartford for only $250,000, a fee representing a loss of $1.5 million.

Right before its transfer, Hef gave a very misleading interview to *The Wall Street Journal*. "After only eight issues of wandering and wobbling, *SBI* is beginning to show life. Our editorial approach is going in the right direction. With any meaningful upturn in circulation, *SBI* could go into the black this fall."

*[Actually, Hef was delivering the magazine's epitaph.]*

With the competition eliminated, Hartford continued to pour millions into *Show* until it became known as the 'most fabled moneypit in the history of magazines."

Hef reflected on his own failure. "I hired a lot of squares to run a hip magazine."

\*\*\*

The mailroom at *Playboy* was more and more inundated with letters from readers with burning questions on their mind. Having no one to turn to, many men brought their problems to *Playboy*. Reacting to their sense of urgency, Hef ordered the creation of a *Playboy Advisory* column.

"It was a sounding board where our readers could deal with their sexual insecurities, anxieties, and neuroses as they moved into the turbulent 1960s."

The questions were not just confined to sex but embraced a number of other topics too: Fashion, food, drink, hi-fi, sports cars, and dating dilemmas.

# LETTERS TO 🐰

Every week, Hef was presented with intriguing questions. He became personally involved with choosing the ones he felt would interest the most readers. Not surprisingly, he found most questions centered on the size of a man's penis.

A reader from Toledo, Ohio, wrote in with: "My cock measures twelve inches, but my girlfriend consistently complains that it is too small. What does she compare me to? A horse?"

Another expressed an opposite concern: "My penis is abnormally small, measuring only three and a half inches when fully erect. I'm a virgin afraid to have sex. Do you think I can satisfy a woman?"

ANSWER: "You can try but avoid anything that resembles the Grand Canyon."

The staff wrote back that any penis from five and a half to six inches was quite average and was capable of satisfying a woman. A prostitute of twenty years' experience with soldiers and Marines, truck drivers, and construction workers claimed, "Size has no bearing whatsoever in giving a woman pleasure."

*[Of course, some women didn't agree with her.]*

The most frequently asked question also concerned the penis: "I have a curved penis. Will that greatly affect my sexual performance?"

*Playboy* advised, "There is nothing to fret about if you have a curved penis, as that is as normal as possessing a straight one. Men all over the world with a curved penis number in the millions. There are many claims that a curved penis has advantage over straight ones. Some women are of the opinion that a bent penis has the ability to reach the coveted G-spot. What's more, a curved penis covers a larger space compared to a straight one, and the person of the opposite sex feels that one entering her is actually double its actual size."

One woman concerned with her weight wrote in that she liked to per-

211

form fellatio on many men in the toilet of a truck stop along a California turnpike. "I don't want to put on pounds. What is the caloric intake of the average explosion of sperm?"

One letter with photographs was brought in to Hef for his own enlightenment. It was an illustrated article praising the joys of fist-fucking, which he did not think was physically possible until he saw the graphic evidence.

Some letters might have been sent in as a joke yet got a truthful answer anyway.

"Which animal has the largest penis in relation to his body size?"
ANSWER: The flea.

By 1963, Hef launched another popular feature, the *Playboy Forum*, which became an exchange of ideas among readers. The forum dealt with a large number of issues that included lesbianism, masturbation, abortion, impotence, penis envy, lack of sexual drive, breast feeding, even civil rights. One question that appeared with some frequency was, "Will I be able to obtain an erection when I'm sixty-five?"

\*\*\*

The strikingly beautiful Cynthia Maddox was only eighteen and a dropout from a junior college when she came to work as a receptionist and secretary for *Playboy*.

She first attracted the roving eye of Lownes. Seated beside him at a luncheon table, he kept trying to feel up her dress under the table. She continued to slap his hand down and resist further sexual overtures from him. He finally gave up in disgust. "Cynthia is the company virgin, the only such living thing in the entire building."

Maddox soon attracted Hef himself. He, too, had a roving eye for every young woman who came to work for *Playboy*, providing, of course, that she was gorgeous. "I was never into the Marjorie Main Ma Kettle type," He said.

He described Maddox as "a beautiful blue-eyed blonde, with pink satin skin and a knockout body that you mooned over at your

The charm and curves of Cynthia Maddox adorned what became one of *Playboy's* most iconic covers, the issue of July 1964.

"She was my girlfriend #1 during the turbulent years from 1961 to 1963, more or less marking the presidency of John F. Kennedy," Hef said.

desk in high school"

"Hef could have any girl in the world he wanted, but he went for the one I had picked out," Lownes lamented.

Hef began dating her in 1961, their romance lasting for two and a half years. "She made it very clear to me at the beginning," Hef said. "She planned to remain a virgin until she got married, and I made it clear from the beginning that I never planned to marry again."

"I turned on the old Hef charm and finally got her hot enough to surrender the pink," he said. "For this major event, I flew her to Los Angeles, where I had booked a cottage in the gardens of the Beverly Hills Hotel, the same cottage where aviator Howard Hughes took his boy or girl of the moment to seduce them."

During that sojourn in Hollywood, Hef also took her to the set of the latest Frank Sinatra picture, *Come Blow Your Horn* (1963). In it, Ol' Blue Eyes played a free-swinging bachelor with wall-to-wall girls. "Is this the story of your life?" Hef asked him.

Hef and Maddox had posed together for an ad for the Hat Institute of America. "Yes, Hef wore a stylish hat, something you would never see him in," Maddox said. "But Sinatra always seemed to have a hat on. The Institute should have used him instead of Hef to hawk their *chapeaux.*"

On the West Coast, they entertained many celebrities, including Mel Brooks and Anne Bancroft, a couple Hef labeled as "The Beauty & the Beast."

"We hung out with Lenny Bruce, who was a riot, along with such diverse people as Danny Kaye and Rod Serling," Maddox said. "Never a dull evening."

In Chicago, Hef and Maddox held their own premiere of Paul Newman's latest film, *The Hustler* (1961). It had been adapted from a story by Walter S. Tevis that had first appeared in *Playboy.*

"I never told Hef this," Maddox said, "but if that handsome hunk Newman had just flickered an eye, I would have dumped Hef at once."

"I was crazy about Cynthia," Hef said, "but I wasn't the marrying kind. I had been burned once—that's enough. We were both interested in modern art and movie classics. Both of us got off on those Jeanette Mac-Donald/Nelson Eddy musicals of the 1930s. We loved cartoons."

She said she often reviewed as many as 200 to 250 cartoons submitted to *Playboy* every day. "I would discard most of them and select no more than twelve, which I would take to Hef's round bed for him to review in his pajamas after dark."

Throughout the course of their stormy relationship, Hef and Maddox had many a blow-up over his double standard. "He could screw around with other women, but if I so much as kissed a boy, he went ballistic."

\*\*\*

When the Playboy Club opened in Manhattan, Hef and Maddox were photographed there with Franchot Tone (the former Mr. Joan Crawford) and the German-American actress, writer, and Baroness, Betsy von Furstenberg. Maddox chatted with the very dull Ed Sullivan before meeting those singers, Steve Lawrence and Eydie Gorme. Lawrence whispered in Maddox's ear, "If I didn't have Eydie, I would surely lure you away from Hef."

On another occasion, Maddox and Hef were snapped by photographers in Manhattan at the 1962 Playboy Jazz All-Stars Ceremony, where Benny Goodman and Duke Ellington were designated as the winners. Later, they attended a party hosted by Ella Fitzgerald for the winners at Basin Street East, a then-famous jazz club on Lexington Avenue at 49th Street.

Hef was so entranced by Maddox's beauty that he featured her on the covers (but never as the centerfolds) of five different issues of *Playboy*: February 1962; March 1963; February 1964; July 1964; and April 1966.

By the time the photo for the final cover was shot, Maddox had ended the sexual aspect of her relationship with Hef. "Our friendship remained, but I had to move on. Yes, I found a man who wanted to marry me."

\*\*\*

In the early 1960s, Hef began committing to paper what he called his Playboy Philosophy. Collectively, it reflected his point of view about the oncoming sexual revolution. An informal manifesto on politics and government, with insights into his vision of the modern age, its first installment appeared in the December 1962 edition of *Playboy*.

Hef claimed that a healthy heterosexual life would restore the American vitality that had long been suppressed by religious bigots, who

Hef spent weeks and weeks formulating his Playboy Philosophy.

He was often mocked for it, but his art director, Art Paul, said, "If anybody actually read it, he'd find that it was an intriguing manifesto about sexual expression and censorship."

seemed to think that sex was too closely allied to procreation—and not to enjoyment.

He surveyed the prevailing women's magazines of the day, including *Cosmopolitan* and the *Ladies' Home Journal,* and found them lacking, labeling their staff and editors "The Pious Pornographers." He deplored many of their articles, including "Virginal Wives" and "Jealousy-Crazed Mates," feeling that many of them dwelled on "the sadistic aspects of a man's sex life."

Late one night, he issued a statement about the sexual culture of America in the 1960s:

> *"There is a transition taking place in society today. This is very evident in movies and in books and magazines, too. The nation is becoming more mature and able to view openly what was taboo years ago. Playboy isn't interested in being sensational—it never was. If we took the sex out of* Playboy, *we would be a fraud. We are concerned with staying well within the bounds of good taste."*

At the beginning of his manifesto about the sexual culture of America in the 60s, he stated one of his goals: "I'd rather be damned for what I believe than have people damn me for what they *think* I believe."

Hef's ultimate aim was to provide a kind of Baedeker *[a popular travel guide at the time]* of *savoir faire,* a great organ of communication to campaign for social justice and against deplorable prison conditions, outmoded divorce laws, and more human tolerance for abortion (which should be legal). Homosexuality (which should not be against the law), and greater tolerance for drugs, especially marijuana.

In all, his sententious opus consisted of a quarter of a million words, appearing in twenty-five issues of *Playboy.*

Eventually, his philosophy swelled to more than a thousand pages, taking three years for all of it to be published in sequential editions of *Playboy.* Although his point of view about sex and sexuality was certainly a part of it, it eventually branched out to encompass legal issues and cultural and political concerns, too.

Hot topic issues dealt with the controversial abortion issue as well as birth control and divorce. His ideas were debated on university campuses and at religious forums, too.

He attacked marriage as an institution, especially early marriages, which he claimed often ended in disaster and divorce. He blamed Puritan antagonism against sex outside wedlock for these ill-fated unions.

His guiding principles and editorial credos also became a hot topic of talk around office water coolers, in campus dorms (both male and female), at cocktail parties, and in fraternity house bull sessions.

Defending freedom of expression, he attacked "prudes and the prigs, the censors, and the bluenoses," accusing them of trying to suppress great literature and suggestive art.

"There are those who would destroy not simply the body, but the very mind of all humankind. If a person can look at the picture of a beautiful woman and find ugliness there, even obscenity, then it can only be that he carries that ugliness and obscenity within himself."

Feminists bitterly attacked his assertion that "girls are the grandest of all consumer goods. A girl is something, like a sports car, a bottle of wine, or an Ivy League suit, that is meant to be used and enjoyed by men. Girls are playthings, and, once enjoyed, can be set aside and replaced with others newer and fresher."

*Playboy's* continued support of abortion drew the harshest critics. An (unnamed) woman wrote to *The Washington Post* that she later regretted having had an abortion. This letter drew a response from James Nichols of Cincinnati, who wrote to Hef: "May you live to regret your words advocating abortion as much as that woman who killed her baby."

Richard Green of Los Angeles wrote: "There is evil in killing a human fetus. Once a nation becomes callous and indifferent to human life, there may be no hope for humanity."

Hef was far more dedicated to his *Playboy Philosophy* than most of his key editors or many members of the literati who bothered to read it. He told his staff, "I intend for it to be a living statement of my beliefs, insights, and yes, I admit it, my prejudices."

For a while, Nat Lehrman, one of his most influential editors, tried to help him sharpen both the prose and the insights. "Many of the pages he handed me were muddled and repetitive. The ideas emerged from his head in some haphazard arrangement, a sort of organic approach. If an idea popped into his head, however disjointed, he typed it. He resisted my editorial changes, viewing every comma, every word he typed as sacred as the Sermon on the Mount."

During the compilation of his Philosophy, Hef sometimes never left his bedchamber. *[In one instance, he didn't emerge for a period of three uninterrupted weeks.]*

Hef sometimes took time out from his hysterically busy work cycles for Sharon Rogers, the Playmate of the Month for January 1964. She worked in the room with him, compiling his papers and photographs until he needed her to take care of other needs.

According to Rogers, "I was introduced to Hef when I was eighteen, and I fell in love with him. Most of our love affair took place in his bedroom, but once or twice he took me out. The most memorable occasion was a nightclub near the O'Hare Airport in Chicago. We were entertained by Rat Packers Frank Sinatra, Sammy Davis, Jr., and Dean Martin. My oh my, what a lusty trio of horndogs. No woman was safe in their company."

He did take other sex breaks, too, as noted by his girlfriend, Joni Mattis. At the Playmate House Party right before Christmas of 1961, he seduced eleven of the twelve Playmates of the month. The party lasted for four nights.

Working around the clock, sometimes for three days at a time, and "fueled by Dexies," Hef was compared to Jack Kerouac, author of the bible of the Beatniks. *[Kerouac was said to have written that novel, fueled by Bennies, in three grueling weeks. Hef preferred Dexies to Bennies. The drug references, of course, were to Dexedrine and Benzedrine.]*

His increasing dependency on Dexies took a physical toll. Richard Rosenweig came to work for Hef in 1963 as an editorial assistant. "I was shocked by his appearance. He looked like one of those Jewish refugees discovered by Allied armies in 1945 at the Dachau death camp." He seemed to exist on a diet of Pepsi and Dexies."

"His memos to the staff grew longer and longer each passing month," said editorial director Auguste Spectorsky. "I think some of them were the equal of Tolstoy's novel, *War and Peace*. The staff often called him 'Hitler in his bunker.' He would work to the end of human endurance and then savagely crash and sleep for twenty-four hours straight. He'd get up, swallow some more pills, down bottle after bottle of Pepsi, and start writing that god damn manifesto again, which I had to read. He wrote on every subject from Renaissance sex to nocturnal emissions."

Although he had attracted millions of supporters, his critics were also numerous. *Life* denounced his philosophy as "a pretentious marathon outpouring."

Journalist Helen Turner attacked his royal use of the word 'we,' a usage which had been made famous by Queen Victoria: "The *Playboy Philosophy* reeks of defensive pomposity, in a numbingly and breathtaking naïveté. Many readers find it boring and turn to the centerfold."

Author Tom Wolfe labeled Hef as "King of the Status Drop-Outs," after he visited his bedroom at the Playboy Mansion. "He was surrounded by research material, everything labeled according to subject matter, which ranged from 'Heterosexual Sodomy' to 'Homosexuality,' from 'Adultery' to 'Premarital Sex.'"

Wolfe claimed, "A mantle of sepulchral reverence descends on his bedchamber when he is writing. Even the Playmate of the Month can't distract him."

In one of Wolfe's more awkward assessments, he criticized the Philosophy, which to him "seemed like a naïve and tedious set-to with a colossus somebody or other must have killed off forty years before."

Editors at *Time* magazine weighed in with their view, defining his manifesto as "often pretentious and relatively conventional. Hefner is a kind of oversimplified Enlightenment thinker with what comes out as an almost touching faith in the individual's capacity for goodness. Release a man from repression, thinks Hefner, and he will instinctively pursue a 'healthy' life in business and sex alike. He also exhibits a tendency to 'situation ethics,' which calls for judging acts within their special context rather than by a more fixed morality. Some use this formula to justify homosexuality, but Hefner firmly draws a heterosexual line. He does not endorse extramarital sex, though he approves of the premarital variety."

Author Mike Edison claimed, "The *Playboy Philosophy* was a sprawling mess of proclamations and pseudo-egghead broadsides lobbed against the usual suspects: Organized religion, and the Puritanical, hysterical, hypocritical, societal mores that strive to keep America's pants on."

***

Ever since he'd been a young man, Hef had protested against the restraints that organized religion placed on men's sexuality. In doing such, he met strong counterattacks from priests and pastors used to rousing a crowd. It seemed inevitable that religious leaders from both the left and the right would blast Hef from their Sunday morning pulpits.

Hef wrote that over the centuries, "Religious conflicts have led to bloody wars at the cost of the lives of millions. Religion has promoted the tyranny of man over his fellow man."

Roy Larson, who cited "the world as my pulpit," attacked Hef in *motive* magazine, charging him with "leading young men down the wrong path."

*[Founded in 1941, and officially spelled with a lowercase "m," motive was the official magazine of the Methodist Church's Liberal Student Movement and, later, for the University Christian Movement (UCM) too. It was noted for its avant garde social and artistic vision, and for its then-radical opinions about gender issues and Vietnam. In 1966, Time magazine wrote that it stood out among church publications "like a miniskirt at a church social."*

*Although motive's life as a magazine ended in 1972, it's believed in some quarters that an entire generation of religious activists were shaped by its editorial opinions.]*

Professor Benjamin De Mott, who taught English at Amherst, was no admirer of Hef or of *Playboy* either. In 1962, in an issue of *Commentary,* he wrote, "The Playboy world is first and last an achievement in abstraction: History, politics, art, ordinary social relations, religion, family, nature, vanity, love, whatever the subject, Hefner offers a vision of the whole map reduced to its private parts."

*[Founded by the American Jewish Committee in 1945, and edited by Norman Podhoretz from 1960 to 1995,* Commentary *focused, and focuses, on religion, Judaism, politics, and cultural and social issues.]*

A noted theologian, Harvey Cox, professor at the Harvard Divinity School, started out by attacking Hef, but later bonded with him, even though their respective views of religion were markedly different. He began by denouncing *Playboy's* advocacy of "recreational sex" in the then-influential periodical, *Christianity and Crisis.*

Eventually, their barking at each other grew less shrill. They even appeared as Op-Ed spokespersons at forums on religion together, most visible at the 1967 Conciliatory Playboy Panel, where they referred to each other as "sparring partners in the ring."

Cox even became a contributor of articles for *Playboy,* beginning with "Revolt in the Church," in which he maintained that many theological doctrines had outlived their usefulness. In another article, "For Christ's Sake," he urged his followers to "embrace the revolutionary spirit of Jesus."

Cox told *Time* that *Playboy* is basically antisexual. Like the sports car, liquor, and hi-fi, girls are just another *Playboy* accessory. Hefner works to spread the gospel of pleasure with a dogged devotion that would do credit to any God-given missionary."

The *National Review* interpreted Cox's unexpected role as a contributor to *Playboy* as "the most remarkable since Saul set out for Damascus."

Hef admitted to Cox that he didn't believe in "a biblical God, although I do accept the existence of a possible Creator. In fact, I'm so religious that I am giving a heavy discount to all religious leaders like priests and ministers who subscribe to *Playboy.* The mailroom has been inundated."

"I'm a spiritual person, although not a believer in the supernatural. An afterlife would be a great deal if it exists. In the meantime, a man should not live his life anticipating a reward when Gabriel blows his horn. It would be more rewarding if a man left this world a better place than he found it in."

A copy of *Catholic World* was mailed to Hef by the chaplain of the Southern Methodist University. In it, he compared the Playboy Philosophy to the First Epistle of John. "It may surprise the reader to know that John was wrestling with many of the same problems which *Playboy* confronts in the contemporary World."

Like his counterparts at *Catholic World*, Allen Moore, of the Claremont School of Theology, also contributed to Playboy's documentation of religious thought in America: "Because of Mr. Hefner and his *Playboy* magazine, theologians are traveling to the last frontier and facing up to the challenges of talking about sex and the Christian man. Because of his influence, discussions are becoming frank about a once *verboten* subject."

In addition to the dilemmas being raised by theologians, dissent even began emerging from the rank-and-file of Playboy readers. A young man of twenty-three, who worked as a carpenter in Boulder, Colorado, wrote to Hef with a question: "Gee whiz! Do we *have* to have a Philosophy?"

Yet despite the moral pressure aimed on him and his publication for the remainder of his life, Hef maintained that "true religious freedom means freedom *from* as well as freedom *of* religion."

***

Early in 1963, Hef hired Nat Lehrman as associate editor of *Playboy*. He became a key player, specializing in articles about human sexuality and social activism—or, as he described it, "I was *Playboy's* sex editor."

He put an enlightened progressive stamp on the content of the magazine. "He was one of our earliest and best editors," Hef said, "and he had a lot to do with the heart and soul of the magazine. He was also a wordsmith, and he added a great deal to *Playboy* in terms of its editorial sophistication."

Lehrman had many duties, including editing the *Playboy Forum* and interviewing key figures in the sexual revolution, including William Masters and Virginia Johnson. He even answered questions sent in to *Playboy Advisor*.

Hef jokingly referred to him as a "real life Hawkeye Pierce character" as portrayed in the hit TV series, *M\*A\*S\*H.* (1972-1983).

"He had a rapier wit," Hef said, "but watch out that he doesn't turn it on you. He could make fun of almost anything. He was a left-wing radical and wasn't obsessed with naked girls and all that, like most of my male staff members."

Lehrman admired Norman Mailer's writing and continued to publish him, although Hef brought in other, newer voices too. He agreed with Mailer in that conservatives such as William F. Buckley were a "contradictory stew of reactionaries, fascists, and libertarians."

One of the writers whose work was selected by Lehrman and which later appeared in *Playboy* was the London-born Sir Julian Huxley, who had long been defined as an "evolutionary biologist, eugenicist, and internationalist." Much of his work towered over the heads of the average *Playboy* reader, but Hef liked his article "The Age of Overbreed." In it, he predicted the oncoming disaster of overpopulation that would drain the overtaxed resources of a much-abused planet, causing social upheavals and revolutions.

\*\*\*

Another writer whose then very *avant-garde* work appeared in *Playboy* was Paul Goodman. With the sometimes radical ethos of Greenwich Village permeating his philosophies and figuratively "stamped" on his forehead, Goodman was a novelist, playwright, and psychotherapist. Hef termed him "an anarchist philosopher." Credited as one of the founders and original practitioners of Gestalt therapy in the 40s and 50s, *Playboy* ran an article by him which in vehement terms denounced America's school system.

[*Goodman was mostly known for his 1960 book* Growing Up Absurd, *a tract widely read by student protesters during the mid-to-late 1960s. He had once been on the faculty of the University of Chicago but was fired because of his affairs with both male and female students. A recent documentary on his life defined him as "the most important influence on modern sociology you might never have heard of." He told Hef, "To get fucked makes you a well-rounded man."*]

\*\*\*

Likewise for the writings of Terry Southern. Hailing from Texas, and known for the role he played in changing the style and substance of American films in the 1970s he was much admired by Hef for his friendships with counterculture figures in Paris, "Swinging London" of the 1960s, and New York. A player in the postwar literary movement of Paris and Greenwich Village in the 1950s, he'd befriended such writers as Jack Kerouac of the Beat Generation.

Southern excelled as a screenwriter, and his novel *Candy* was adapted into a movie starring Marlon Brando and Richard Burton in 1968. Southern worked on many famous movies, sharpening the dialogue, as he did for other films that included *Dr. Strangelove, The Loved One,* and *The Cincinnati Kid.* His work on *Easy Rider* helped define the independent film movement of the 1970s. In an article for *Playboy,* he claimed that films had supplanted the niche previously occupied by "The Novel" because of the sensory capabilities and potentialities of filmmaking.

***

On June 4, 1963, two armed Chicago policemen invaded the Playboy Mansion to arrest Hugh Hefner. Told that he was in his bedroom, the officers barged in, one with a pair of handcuffs, to inform him that he was under arrest. They did not specify the charge.

The found him wearing a pair of red silk pajamas smoking his pipe in bed with a nude Playmate who appeared to be in a post-coital glow.

Hef was allowed to change into street clothes before being hauled away, passing by his gawking staff on his way out. A top editor got on the phone immediately, soliciting help from Hef's lawyers, presumably with the intention of learning what charges had been filed, and to post bail. Circumstances eventually led them to Chicago's municipal court, as presided over by Judge Norman N. Eiger.

Inside the courtroom, Hef learned that he'd been busted "for publishing and distributing an obscene magazine." The charges derived from *Playboy's* focus on nude or nearly-nude stills of Jayne Mansfield from her latest sex comedy, *Promises! Promises!* The charges had been filed by a Catholic group, the Chicago Citizens for Decent Literature.

The judge had been presented with a copy of *Playboy*—apparently, he was not a subscriber—and he told Hef and his attorneys that he was satisfied that there was, indeed, probable cause for the issuance of the warrant. He made it plain that that was the only issue he

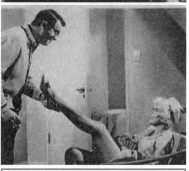

Sure, Hefner was being provocative by running the nude pictures of Mansfield from her film in *Playboy*, but as he argued, he was merely reflecting a general trend in moviemaking.

The middle and lower photos depict stills from the film. Though relatively tame by today's standards, "All Hell broke out" when they were released in 1963.

would rule on. "The matter of whether Miss Mansfield's pictures are art or obscenity must await judicial determination at the trial scheduled for November."

Back at the Playboy Mansion, Hef said, "At first, I thought the arrest was a bad dream, the result of my drinking too many Pepsis and eating too many hot dogs the night before."

*Promises! Promises!* had not yet opened in movie houses, but already, posters had been printed advertising it. Bold letters proclaimed: "YOU READ ABOUT IT IN *PLAYBOY*. NOW SEE ALL OF JAYNE MANSFIELD UNCUT! UNCENSORED!

The unrated film was shot during the final months of the rapidly expiring Hays Code that had once held enormous power over what could or could not be shown on America's movie screens. *Promises! Promises!* was the first motion picture to feature a mainstream star—in this case, Mansfield—in the nude. However, had Marilyn Monroe lived, and had she finished her last film, *Something's Got to Give,* she would have been entitled to that dubious nude photo distinction too.

What seemed to spark rage was the juxtaposition of a naked Mansfield with her fully dressed (male) co-star. Whereas Mansfield was shown with her breasts exposed in some shots and with a tantalizing view of most of her *derrière* in another, Tommy Noonan, spiffily wearing a suit and tie, looked down at her through horn-rimmed glasses.

Before he had to face a jury, Hef received a lot of irate mail, as certain members of the public denounced him as a "moral leper" and a "rotten moron." An investigation by *Playboy's* staff discovered that many of these outraged protesters had

*3 Nuts in Search of a Bolt*, released in 1964 and starring Mamie Van Doren, was directly inspired by the success of *Promises! Promises*. It played on the fascination of that era for sex and psychiatry.

PLAYBOY reviewed it widely as "A zany comedy of Freudian tomfoolery."

never read a copy of *Playboy*. Their judgments were based on what they had read in the newspapers. In one letter, a woman lectured, "At last this law is catching up with you."

Hef shot back, attacking his accusers (and the Chicago Citizens for Decent Literature) noting that at one time, such authors as Ernest Hemingway and William Faulkner had also, in some quarters, been judged as obscene.

A copy of *Promises! Promises!* was personally delivered to the Playboy Mansion for a screening by Mickey Hargitay, who had been cast in the film as the husband of Marie ("The Body") McDonald.

*[The Plot? Affected by the stress of his job as a television scriptwriter, Jeff (played by Tommy Noonan), is unable to make love to his wife, Sandy, who wants to get pregnant. Assuming that a departure from their daily routines will change the dynamic of their marriage, they go on an extended cruise. On board, they meet another couple, portrayed by Mickey Hargitay and Marie McDonald, and indulge as a foursome in an uninhibited, alcohol-soaked wife swap. When both women determine that they're pregnant, it seems to become crucially important that they determine who the respective fathers are.]*

Hargitay told Hef, "There was no danger that Tommy *[i.e., Tommy Noonan, the film's producer and Jayne's co-star]* would make a play for her. As it turned out, I had to worry more about my own chastity than hers. He followed me around like a panting dog. He wanted my Hungarian salami, and he got plenty of it. He even trailed me into the urinal. I gave in to him, since he was the producer." *[Today, Noonan is best known for his role as the rich fiancé of Lorelei Lee (Marilyn Monroe) in* Gentlemen Prefer Blondes *(1953).]*

Also in the film was T.C. Jones, playing Babbette, the hair stylist to the character played by Mansfield. At the time, he was the most famous female impersonator in America.

Up until the moment Mansfield got Hefner involved in a jury trial, he had done very well revealing pictures of her. He'd first exposed her in *Playboy* in February of 1955, which he followed with a shot of her partially covering her bosom with her hands.

Based on Mansfield's status as a hot seller, *Playboy* featured her every February from 1955 to 1958, and once again in 1960. Rather chauvinistically, and much to the rage of feminists, Hef asserted, "She has developed more of an acting talent than might be expected from her proportions of 40-21-32."

*[In February of 1958, Playboy had run the nude Jayne Mansfield as "our vivacious Valentine in her first full-figure study. For the first time in print she poses au naturel, showing everything but pubic hair."]*

When she learned of the *agita* Hef was enduring because of her photos, she wrote him a letter: "I've just finished reading the October installment of *Playboy Philosophy.* I am in complete accord that Jayne Mansfield *per se* is not the issue. This is a matter of censorship, in that a few are trying to govern the tastes of the many. I strongly support you in your efforts to keep the press free, and in your championing each individual's right to make up his own mind."

Before the trial, Hef's lawyers battled with the prosecution in the selection of a jury.

The prosecutor tried to stack the jury with members of Charles Keating's Citizens for Decent Literature, but Hef's attorney lodged strong objections.

At the trial, Hef testified that the pictures he ran of Mansfield, for which she was not paid, were actually candid publicity shots for a movie in the making.

To beef up his case, Hef cited two towering figures in American history. He quoted Mark Twain: "Man is merely and exclusively the Immodest Animal

At least some of the fury of moral arbiters of that era was based on their perception of Mansfield as an irredeemable slut.

That opinion was reinforced by her appearance on the covers, around the same time, of a wide assortment of porn rags less classy than *Playboy.*

The top and middle photos show Mansfield in all her suggestive glory, with headlines even suggesting that "she'll swallow."

In contrast, the cover of *Playboy* from June of 1963, in which Mansfield's face plays "peek-a-boo" from the lower right corner, looks positively demure.

for he is the only one with a soiled mind, the only one under the dominion of a false shame!"

He also quoted from a letter written by Benjamin Franklin in 1745, "Advice to a Friend on Choosing a Mistress." In it, one of America's founding fathers counsels a young man about channeling his sexual urges. He suggested that an older mistress is preferable to a younger one, citing better conversations, and the corporal enjoyment that an older, more experienced woman might be better able to provide than a younger counterpart. "All cats are grey, and there is less risk of pregnancy. The face first grows lank and wrinkled; then the neck, then the breasts and the arms; the lower parts continue to last as plump as ever."

Dr. Ner Littner, a member of the Chicago Police Censor Board Appeals Committee, defended Hef's decision to run the photographs. "I do not believe the June issue [of Playboy] was obscene, and in my opinion, it does not appeal to the prurient interests of the average person."

In the end, the jury deadlocked in a decision of seven members who found Hef guilty, and five who did not. Consequently, Judge Nicholas J. Matkovic declared the case a mistrial.

Copies of the June issue of Playboy featuring Mansfield were grabbed up by avid consumers and collectors for as much as ten dollars each. In all, Hef sold two million copies of the Mansfield edition.

In reaction to the Mansfield nudes, three mailbags of letters arrived, voicing two radically different opinions. Most men found Mansfield "the most perfect specimen of womanhood since God created Eve."

A Baptist minister interpreted things differently, and denounced Mansfield as a "gourd-breasted, slack-jawed, slack-hipped broad with grotesquely protruding, gnarled and becorned feet."

One irate woman from Indiana called her "a shameless hussy, worse than a harlot like Elizabeth Taylor." And in yet another "sent-through-the-mail" comment, a male reader from Baltimore wanted to know, "When can we see the triangle of this busty yeh-yeh-rah sexpot?"

When the Beatles arrived in the U.S. as part of their first visit to Hollywood, John Lennon told the

**SOLID AS A $100 BILL.**
**BEN FRANKLIN**

What did Ben Franklin and Hugh Hefner have in common? Both dispensed liberal advice about sex, morality, and manhood.

press, "Jayne Mansfield is the one movie star we want to meet." Her press agent quickly arranged a rendezvous with Mansfield and the Beatles at Whiskey à Go Go, a then-famous nightclub on Sunset Boulevard. After their inaugural meeting there, she disappeared for the night, returning to Lennon's suite. He later called her "the undisputed champion of the in-the-altogether brinksmanship."

Paul McCartney had a dissenting opinion. He told *Playboy*, "Mansfield is a clot! Really an old hag!"

Critic Roger Ebert reviewed the film, claiming, "Finally, in *Promises! Promises!* Jayne Mansfield does what no Hollywood star ever does except in desperation. She does a nudie. In 1963, that kind of box office appeal was all she has left."

In spite of Ebert's snarky attack, within seven years of Mansfield's ground-breaking movie, major female Hollywood stars were also doing nude scenes in A-list features.

For its American release in 1963, *Promises! Promises!* was edited and heavily cut, although its original (uncut) version was widely distributed throughout Europe. A photograph of a completely nude Mansfield, with her pubic hair visible, appeared in Kenneth Anger's book, *Hollywood Babylon*. It was not until 1984 that the full uncut version of the film appeared on television. *[Naturally, it was broadcast on the Playboy Channel.]*

Mansfield, down on her luck, died tragically in a car accident in Louisiana in 1967. The following year, a documentary was released, *The Wild, Wild World of Jayne Mansfield*. It included both the nude scenes from *Promises! Promises!* and pages from *Playboy's* pictorial.

***

A new day was dawning when *Promises! Promises!* opened in Chicago. Theaters booked it as part of a double billing, an accompaniment to a Canadian documentary entitled *The Most*. Crafted in Chicago in 1961, it focused on the life of Hefner himself.

With a hint of satire and in black-and-white, it depicted Hefner as preening, proud, self-satisfied, and just a bit smug. As he told the camera, "I have come to be seen as emblematic of the 1960s."

The film opens as Hef is driving his white Mercedes convertible through the rainy streets of Chicago *en route* to the Playboy Mansion. He identifies himself as a thirty-five-year-old publisher of *Playboy*, the focal point of his $20 million empire. "You get only one time around in this old world, and if you don't make the most of it, you have no one to blame but yourself."

The camera then invades the Mansion itself, where a party is going on, with a mixed, multi-racial bag of guests, some fully dressed, others less so. Most of the women are in bikinis, twisting and shaking their way across the floors. Guests are also seen cavorting in the underground swimming pool. Later, the camera reveals a view of two men asleep in armchairs, ignoring the seductive frenzy swirling around them

Although Hef was known for relatively simple tastes in food, the camera reveals a lavish buffet laid out for his guests. The camera then zooms in once again on Hef, who admits to leading the good life. "I consider myself to be, quite possibly, the luckiest human being in the world."

If *The Most* has a leading lady, it's Cynthia Maddox, Hef's cover girl. *[He had launched an affair with her the year the documentary was made.]* In the film, she confesses that she prefers to keep Hef for herself, but that she's aware that he gets involved with other partners as part of other seductions. She doesn't come off as too bright, stumbling over the word "intelligent."

Although the film shows frequent views of the *Playboy* offices, the aura is that of a party. The music of Duke Ellington plays in the background.

Although it won some awards, the film was widely denounced in the media. *Newsweek* wrote: "Hugh Hefner is strutting, preening, posing, and spouting nonsense in this new kind of animated cartoon, a sort of mental Magoo."

\*\*\*

From 1966 to 1976, Robie Macauley, a novelist and critic from Grand Rapids, Michigan, served as the fiction editor of *Playboy*. During his tenure in that job, he raised the literary profile of *Playboy* to the point where it was hailed as second only to *The New Yorker* as a prestigious showcase for serious writers. They included works by Saul Bellow, a prevailing member of the *literati* of that era, and author of such works as *Herzog* and *The Adventures of Augie March*.

*[Bellow would go on to win the Nobel Prize for Literature in 1976 "for the human understanding and subtle analysis of contemporary culture that are combined in his work." Self-described as "an insolent slum kid and thick-necked rowdy," he appealed to Hef's sense of counter-cultural chic.]*

Macauley was not an untested, unseasoned innocent. During his stint during World War II with the U.S. Counterintelligence Corps (CIC), he had experienced horror, including the liberation of the Flossenburg concentration camp. He became friends with Captain Kermit Beahan, bombardier of the Boeing B-29 Superfortress *Bockscar* which had released the atomic bomb over Nagasaki on August 9, 1945, an attack that ended America's war with Japan.

Other writers whose work appeared in *Playboy* included Chicago-born Michael Crichton, the astonishingly successful science fiction guru who became known for selling more than 200 million books worldwide. *[One of his most famous works, published in 1990, was* Jurassic Park.*]*

*Playboy* also published the fiction of John Cheever, the New England-born specialist in  short fiction of his era, who'd been hailed as "The Chekhov of the Suburbs." His *The Swimmer*, a surrealistic exploration of the association of wealth with happiness in suburban America, was originally published in *The New Yorker* in 1964 and later adapted into a movie (1968) starring Burt Lancaster.

Also included in *Playboy* were the works of Roald Dahl, a Welshman who'd been a fighter pilot during World War II. He had once been famously married to movie actress Patricia Neal. In the postwar era, he sold more that 250 million books, some of them darkly comic books for children, making him one of the leading authors of the world.

A Georgia boy from Atlanta, James Dickey, poet and novelist, became the 18th poet laureate of the United States in 1966. A novelist, he wrote *Deliverance.* Published in 1970, it was adapted two years later into a controversial film starring Burt Reynolds and Jon Voight.

Brooklyn-born J.P. Donleavy, novelist and playwright, is best known today for his novel, *The Ginger Man.* Shortly after its publication in 1953, it was banned on charges of obscenity. Today, Modern Library ranks it as one of the one hundred best American novels.

Macauley also reached out to women writers, introducing many of them, through *Playboy,* to American audiences. Among them was a South African writer, humanitarian, and political activist, Nadine Gordimer. Her body of work focused on apartheid in her native South Africa. According to the Nobel Committee, which awarded her their prize for Literature in 1991, "Her epic writing is a very great benefit to humanity."

Another talent favored by Macauley was John Irving, a New England-born novelist and screenwriter who, in 1978, won international acclaim for his *The World According to Garp.* Eventually, he won an Oscar *[Best Adapted Screenplay]* for his authorship of the screenplay for the 1999 film, *Cider House Rules,* based on the novel he'd released in 1985.

Other elite members of the literati whose works appeared in *Playboy?*

Emerging from Budapest, Arthur Koestler joined the Communist Party in 1931, but later became disillusioned and dropped out. His 1940 novel, *Darkness of Noon,* an anti-totalitarian work, brought him international acclaim. Diagnosed with Parkinson's disease, and later with terminal leukemia, he and his wife committed suicide together at their home in London in 1983.

John le Carré, a British author of espionage novels, published his best-known work, *The Spy Who Came in from the Cold* in 1963, and it became an international bestseller. Richard Burton starred in the 1965 film with the same name, playing the embittered Cold War spy.

Ursula K. Le Guin of Berkeley was a novelist known for writing in the genres of science fiction and fantasy. *The New York Times* called her "America's greatest living science fiction writer." She died in 2018.

Born to British parents in Iran, Doris Lessing was a novelist, playwright, and biographer. She was awarded the 2007 Nobel Prize for Literature, mainly for her sequence of five novels collectively known as *Children of Violence* (1952-69) and another five novels collectively known as *Canopus in Argos* (1979-1983).

*Playboy* backed a winner when it published Bernard Malamud who, along with Saul Bellow and Philip Roth, are three of the best-known Jewish writers of the 20th Century. One of Malamud's best-remembered and most symbolic works was *The Natural* (1952). In 1984, it was adapted into a film starring Robert Redford.

Author of some forty novels, Joyce Carol Oates, from New York State, also writes short stories, poetry, and nonfiction, and has won many honors, including the National Book Award. There are so many of her books out there that an article in 2003 was called "Joyce Carol Oates for Dummies." If a reader has time for only one book from her daunting *oeuvre*, the author herself has suggested *Blonde* (2000).

Anne Sexton, known as a "confessional poet," was a daughter of Massachusetts. She won the Pulitzer Prize for poetry in 1967 and for her book *Live or Die*. Her poetry reflects her troubled bipolar life as she battled depression and suicidal yearnings. Critic Maxine Kumin said, "Sexton wrote openly about menstruation, abortion, masturbation, incest, adultery, and drug addiction when none of these subjects were viewed as proper topics for poetry.

Isaac Bashevis Singer, a Polish-born Jew, was awarded the Nobel Prize for Literature in 1978. He wrote and published only in Yiddish. Fleeing from Hitler's Germany, Singer came to the United States in 1935.

He was bold in his subject matter, surprising many readers when he wrote about female homosexuality, transvestism, and rabbis "corrupted by demons." Some of his stories depict the yearnings and hopes of immigrants pursuing the American dream. Singer's story, *Yentl, the Yeshiva Boy,* was adapted into a film in 1983 starring Barbra Streisand.

\*\*\*

In the mid-1960s, Hef was confronted with the formidable press and PR machine of a self-described "Little Girl from Little Rock," Helen Gurley Brown. With single-minded precision, she embarked on a mission to transform *Cosmopolitan* into a magazine "that does for the single girl what Hefner does for playboys-at-large."

She had already won acclaim for her authorship of *Sex and the Single Girl* (1962), a manifesto that encouraged women to become financially independent and to enjoy sexual relationships before or even without "the benefit of marriage." A runaway two-million-copy bestseller, it was published in 28 countries and stayed on *The New York Times* bestseller list for more than a year. In 1964, Natalie Wood and Tony Curtis adapted it into a film with the same title.

In 1965, Brown was designated as editor of *Cosmopolitan* (a.k.a. "Cosmo.") Originally launched in 1886 as a family magazine, it later evolved into something more fashion-oriented and more literary. Brown set about revamping it as a "must-read" for hipster urban women ("Cosmo Girls"), focusing its image on advice that included frank discussions of sex.

Once at a party, Brown ran into Hef, telling him, "Women have sexual desires, too."

"My dear woman, don't you think I discovered that years ago?"

*The New York Times* described "The Cosmo Girl" as "self-made, sexual, and supremely ambitious. She looks great, wears fabulous clothes, and has an unabashedly good time when those clothes come off."

In her magazine, Brown even pitched

First the book, then the movie starring Tony Curtis and Natalie Wood.

Both attested to the changes in morality sweeping across America of the 60s.

the advantages of sleeping with married men. No major publication had ever dared do that before.

She became critical of the Don Juan image promoted by *Playboy*: "His sole aim is to prove his masculinity, about which there may be a great deal of doubt in his mind. Most literature indicates he doesn't love women at all. He really loves only himself. Far from really loving, the modern Don Juan exploits. He's a sick character." *[Brown denied that she had Hef specifically in mind when she wrote that.]*

Whereas Hef had created a sensation in 1953 with the first issue of his famous magazine when he'd run that nude of Marilyn Monroe, Brown made headlines after persuading a rising young actor, Burt Reynolds, to pose nude for a centerfold in *Cosmo*. His left hand covered his genitals, but that's all that was covered. The headline read: AT LAST A MALE NUDE CENTERFOLD—THE NAKED TRUTH ABOUT GUESS WHO!

Cosmo's centerfold turned Reynolds into a sex icon of the 1970s. Brown later revealed that she'd tried to get Paul Newman to pose nude, but that he had rejected her offer.

According to Brown, Hefner showed the world that men liked to look at pictures of nude women. Well, I showed them that women like to look at naked men."

Although *The New York Times* hailed her for "playing a key role in helping young women redefine their roles in society," Brown attracted many critics. One of them called her "a bad girl, a pioneer in Prada, a revolutionary in stilettos."

Another of her critics was Betty Friedan, author of *The Feminine Mystique,* who famously accused Cosmo of promoting "an immature teenaged-level sexual fantasy."

According to Hef, "I didn't feel jealous of Helen because we weren't competitors since we appealed to different readers. There is no doubt she was inspired to transform *Cosmo* by my creation of *Playboy*. In a way, we were comrades-in-arms, as both of us were accused of being anti-feminist. As for Betty Friedan, she can go fuck herself. Let's face it: No one

Burt Reynolds, one of the top box office draws of the 70s, is shown here in his most successful film, *Smokey & the Bandit* (1977). Five years before that he had posed nude for *Cosmopolitan*. Later, he confessed that it had probably damaged his image as a serious actor.

else will."

***

By the end of the 1960s Hugh Hefner—the only publisher in America with massive name recognition—had become one of the most talked-about, praised, and/or attacked men in America.

He was profiled in all the national magazines and even in such publications as *L'Espresso* in Italy or *Queen* in London. *The New Yorker* hailed him as the "Playboy wonder of the publishing world."

The *Saturday Evening Post* called him "The Czar of a Bunny Empire. Hugh Hefner is a fraud, dealing in sleazy nudes while professing high-minded ideals."

*Time* called him a "living promotional stunt."

*Saturday Review* condemned Hef's "Bunny-tailed Utopia," attacking his readers for "their arrested adolescence, a perpetuation of teenaged fantasies they never outgrew."

By the mid-1960s, his fortune had spiraled up to $100 million, with the magazine grossing about $30 million of that. Writing in *Life* magazine, Diane Lurie said "In Hefnerland, a woman is simply another aspect of the stats symbol mania stamped all over *Playboy*. She is no more or less important than the sleekest sports car or the most expensive bottle of Scotch. A woman becomes depersonalized, an object of man's pleasure, someone to pour his drinks, inflate his ego, and look gorgeous on his arm as he parades her in front of his pals."

"*Playboy*, with me as its publisher, has certainly made its mark on the world," he said. "But we are more than sex and parties. *Playboy* has always been a wish book, a dream book, a book of aspirations and fantasies."

But as Hef's fame increased, so did his notoriety: Almost everyone had an opinion about his magazine, even people who had never seen a copy: "I don't need to look through its filthy pages to know that it's a publication written and photographed in Hell itself," wrote Betty Anderson of Macon, Georgia.

Hef admitted, "Like a woman, I, too, wanted to be a sex object. Why do I smoke a pipe? Why do I wear a smoking jacket? Why do I wear cologne? Why did I purchase that rotating round bed? It was because of my wanting to be a sex object."

In an assessment of his future at the time, Hef said, "As *Playboy* moves into the second half of the 1960s, the world is rapidly changing around us, almost daily," Hef said. "The sexual revolution that I launched is galloping ahead beyond my wildest dreams. The goal for me now is to come up with

233

new and innovative challenges for *Playboy*. Where do I go from here? That is the question."

In the fall of 2011, NBC tried to recapture the early 1960s in an ill-fated series, *The Playboy Club*. Hef, as a narrator who's seen in the series only in silhouette, describes his club as a respite from the corruption of Chicago in the 1960s. Eddie Cibrian starred as the male lead.

Critics reviewed the plot as a rip-off of *Mad Men*, with Cibrian interpreting his role as "a shameless Don Draper." *[Mad Men, from AMC, which focused on a Madison Avenue ad agency, was also set in the 1960s.]*

A murder, a cover-up, and a love triangle kept the series bustling along, but not fast enough. It attracted very few viewers, faced angry critics, and disappeared after only three episodes.

It did, however, budget many thousands of dollars for replication of the clothes, auras, and accessories of the Playboy Clubs during their creative early heydays, as shown in the larger of the two images above, a publicity photo from NBC.

# Chapter Seven

# GROWTH & DIVERSIFICATION
## PROMOTING THE PLAYBOY PHILOSOPHY
# HEFNER BECOMES A LIFESTYLE GURU

### IN A MAJOR INTERNATIONAL EXPANSION
HEF OPENS MORE NIGHTCLUBS AND A CHAIN OF THE "SWINGINGEST RING-A-DING DINGIEST" RESORTS IN THE WORLD

### MORALISTS DEFINE HEF AS DESTRUCTIVE TO AMERICAN VALUES

## FEMINISTS PROTEST, & A DETRACTOR DEFINES HIM AS "THE GODZILLA OF SLEEPY HOLLOW"
STRESSED OUT FROM BUSINESS & LEGAL CONFLICTS, HIS MANSION'S REPUTATION AS A "MECCA OF HIP," AND ALL THOSE FREELOADING CELEBRITIES, HEF SURVIVES ON A DIET OF PEPSI AND DEXEDRINE.

Ironically, *Playboy's* greatest expansion happened during an era when it was under attack from feminists, who scapegoated it alongside publications far more lurid, more explicit, and far less classy.

Some of the critiques were from unheralded women across America, as, for example, the photo on the left held by a protester holding a sign declaiming "Porn Makes All Women Whores."

Others derived from the cream of the American intelligentsia, including Gloria Steinem, the respected feminist who went undercover as a Bunny in one of Hef's Playboy clubs as part of what became a widely influential assignment and exposé.

Steinem went on to become one of the founders of MS magazine. The cover of its first edition, in 1970, is replicated on the right, advocating Wonder Woman, or any contender with a platform for women's rights, as the next U.S. president.

**Whether it was true or not,** Hugh Hefner liked to fancy himself "The Father of the Sexual Revolution" that swept across America in the 1960s, particularly in the latter years of that tumultuous decade.

Its roots were planted during the nation's the first sexual revolution, in the 1920s, when the silent screen created the two most famous stars of the era, Clara Bow, the "It" girl, and Rudolph Valentino, the great lover in the seminal silent film, *The Sheik* (1921).

Flappers emerged with their short dresses and bobbed hair, dancing the Charleston, none of them doing it better than Joan Crawford in such then-scandalous films as *Our Dancing Daughters* (1928). Of course, the grim Great Depression that began in 1929 put an end to that frivolity, and by the end of the 30s, another World War threw more cold water on the wannabe party-goers.

The 1960s saw not only changing morals, but the Vietnam War, social unrest, the rise of civil rights protest, plus three major assassinations: John F. Kennedy, Robert Kennedy, and Martin Luther King, Jr.

Sexual behavior was greatly affected, including that of young men and women taking on larger numbers of sexual partners than ever before in American history. Couples were also engaging in premarital sex with greater frequency. On the rise were births out of wedlock, births to teenaged girls (often very young ones), and an increase in such afflictions as gonorrhea.

Facilitators of change in the 1960s included feminists (most of them anti-*Playboy*), long-haired hippies, gay rights advocates, and political upheavals, including anti-Vietnam War protests.

"The Pill" came into vogue and was wisely used by women wanting to have sex for fun without the burden of an unwanted pregnancy. By 1962, an estimated

Sex, subliminal or explicit, had been a part of the American landscape since the days of vaudeville. The loud recriminations that Hefner faced in the 60s had already been expressed by the repressive censors of the 1930s.

One venue that particularly enraged the censors of an earlier day had been the 1928 film, *Our Dancing Daughters*, wherein Joan Crawford, depicted above, played a flapper whose dancing was particularly explicit.

1,200,000 women were taking the pill, which was heralded as one of the society's most influential triumphs over nature.

As amazing as it seems, birth control was illegal in some states, including New York and Connecticut, generally the two most advanced states in the nation for individual rights.

Hef called the pill a major advance toward sexual equality. "It frees women to use their bodies for pleasure, not procreation."

By the 1970s, an aftermath of the sexual revolution of the 60s had become painfully apparent: The number of marriages in America had declined by a third; the divorce rate had doubled; and the number of children living in single-parent homes had tripled.

\*\*\*

On Hef's business front, marketing for his brainchild was booming by the end of 1964. *Playboy* was selling 2.4 million magazines every month, with the expectation that circulation would increase to three million copies a month before spring. Advertising sales were on the rise, and more and more mainstream businesses, which had once dismissed *Playboy* as a "nudie mag," began showcasing their products within its pages, companies such as Goodyear and Fabergé.

Hef also authorized the *Playboy* logo to appear on all sorts of merchandise: Clothing, jewelry, key chains, golf clubs, and bar accessories, including instructions on how to make the perfect martini. For prospective Playboys on the make, vacation package tours were hawked. Calendars showcasing various Playmates of the Month became hot items on the market, too.

\*\*\*

As the 1960s moved on and as Hef faced the prospect of becoming forty, he did not stop dating Bunnies and bedding Playmates.

**MERCHANDISING THE BUNNY**

Around this time, both as an income-producing device and as a (sometimes dubious) means of increasing *Playboy's* visibility, Hef's administration began hawking the rabbit head and *Playboy's* association with the good life to manufacturers.

Vendors hyped air fresheners (see above), jewelry, shot glasses, wine glasses, pillows, shower curtains, pillows, cigarette lighters, and bed linens.

If anything, he increased his "immersion" in the *Playboy* lifestyle. Throughout the 1960s and into the 80s, he continued to take on steady girlfriends and eventually two more wives.

He had one inviolable rule: He could cheat on them, but they had to remain faithful to him for as long as he wanted them to stick around. "Sometimes it would be just the two of us in my round bed, but on many occasions, I'd have to have a number of girls. For example, what would Christmas be without at least three Bunnies in my bed? My steady girl had to understand and accept that about me—or else no dice."

In 1960, Hef was still conducting his affair with Joni Mattis, although that was winding down.

The coming year of 1961, found him balancing a number of relationships at the same time, although some of the young women engaged in jealous disputes over him. "I'm the kind of guy women fight over," he boasted to Victor Lownes, who concealed his jealousy. He continued his affair with the previously previewed Cynthia Maddox, managing to work her into his busy schedule. Maddox was the first woman to model, and show off, a Bunny costume.

A German import, Christa Speck, entered Hef's orbit after one of his cohorts "discovered" her working for Bank of America as a secretary.

[Hef and Lownes personally supervised a photo shoot of Speck in the nude, delaying running it for months before eventually designating her as Playmate of the Month in September 1961, and as Playmate of the Year in 1962. *[She was the first foreign-born model awarded with that title.]* Christa worked as a Bunny in Chicago's Playboy Club and was eventually featured in many of the magazine's 60s pictorials about life at the Chicago Mansion. Later, in a retrospective, she was designated by *Playboy* readers and editors as one of their "ten favorite Playmates from the magazine's first decade."

Whereas Hef mostly conducted his affairs with women without ever leaving

Charming and beautiful, Christa Speck was artfully depicted on the cover of the April 1962 issue of *Playboy*, and even more artfully depicted in the semi-nude layouts inside.

Born an ethnic German in Gdańsk, Poland during the darkest days of World War II, she died, fully Americanized, the first foreign-born Playmate of the Year, in Los Angeles in 2013.

his bedroom and its rotating round bed, with Speck, it was different. With her as his companion, they went on occasional night club binges in Chicago, driven to and from the venues in a chauffeur-driven limousine.

One memorable night, they attended the performance of an emerging African-American entertainer, comedian Bill Cosby. From the stage, Cosby introduced them as "Hugh Hefner and the Playmate of the Year, Christa Speck." She was thrilled.

After a year of living in the Playboy Mansion at Hef's beck and call, Christa opted for a break in California for rest, relaxation, and sightseeing. Hef did not accompany her.

During her vacation, she attended a performance of *Les Poupées de Paris (The Dolls of Paris)* a musical puppet show that toured the United States throughout the 1960s, associating some of its marionettes to stars who included Greta Garbo, Joan Crawford, Dean Martin, and Mae West. Created, produced and directed by a brother-sister team from Canada, Marty and Sid Krofft, and

## GIRLS, GIRLS, GIRLS: IT WAS, INDEED, A SEXUAL REVOLUTION

In synch with the generalized permissiveness in which *Playboy* thrived was a risqué, adults-only puppet show, *Les Poupées de Paris (The Dolls of Paris)* whose sometimes topless marionettes were modeled after their human likenesses at the Lido and Folies Bergère in Paris.

Conceived and produced by members of the Krofft family, and eventually headquartered within a dinner theater in Los Angeles, it featured artfully risqué likenesses of, among others, Judy Garland, Sammy Davis, Jr., and Mae West, who is depicted in this publicity photo.

The show was a success, and became a key attraction at the Seattle World's Fair in 1962, the New York World's Fair in 1964-1965, and San Antonio's Hemis-Fair '68. Lavish and amusing, the show cost an estimated $200,000 to produce; and included a revolving stage, an ice-skating rink, a waterfall, elevators, and a review of girls, girls, girls, each campy and/or beautiful, and each a novelty for its era.

The Rev. Billy Graham attended one of the shows and immediately denounced it, complaining that the "women don't wear bras," failing to mention that the "women" in the show were puppets. This negative endorsement, which appeared at around the same time as a review in *Time* magazine, resulted in record-breaking attendance.

As explained during an interview by Marty Krofft, who married Christa Speck, Playboy's Playmate of the Year for 1962. "Be sure to mention it's dirty—that will give them the picture."

aiming its *risqué* references as "for adults only," it survived attacks from, among others, the Rev. Billy Graham. As *avant-garde* performance art with lots of humor and sexual innuendo, it eventually attracted an estimated 9.5 million visitors.

Christa—Playboy Bunny and Hef's sometimes girlfriend—and Marty Krofft met, fell in love, and got married, their union producing three daughters and lasting until her death.

Although Christa disappeared from Hef's life, he retained some aspects of the German-speaking flavor she left by taking up with Austria-born Heidi Becker, designating her as Playmate of the Month in June 1961. Their affair lasted as long as a plucked wildflower before it wilts.

He also had a brief and torrid affair with Donna Michelle, whom he called "My Prima Donna." When he first met her, she told him she was eighteen—actually, she was only seventeen. Although it was illegal because of her then-status as a minor, she posed for pictures in her capacity as Playmate of the Month for the December 1963 issue of *Playboy*.

Michelle boasted measurements of 38-22-36 and weighed 118 pounds. Her age wasn't all that was unknown to Hef when he chose her as a mistress. She had married David M. Ronne, but he was nowhere to be seen.

"She was very unpredictable and most ambitious," Hef said, "dreaming of a big Hollywood career. This azure-eyed beauty could light the night. She was like a triple flowering, blossoming as a grade school piano prodigy, a bantam ballerina, and adept on stage as an actress"

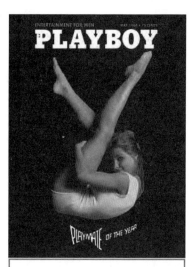

"She demonstrated her flawless form as a *premiere danseuse*," Hef continued, "looking gorgeous in ballet tights or a leotard. Her arabesques could bring a standing ovation and talk about those leaps through the air…she was a female Nureyev. Yes, I was smitten."

When she moved into the Playboy Mansion, she was an immediate hit, spending a lot of her time playing recordings from Hef's vast collection—"anything but Montovani and his musical molasses," she said. He purchased a new Triumph for her to drive, and she said she'd like to go on a record-setting race

Donna Michelle with (Hef's words) "nipples that could topple empires," appears here on the cover of *Playboy*'s May 1964 edition, contorting herself, perhaps uncomfortably, into a human replica of the magazine's "rabbit ears" logo.

with Stirling Moss "both on or off the track."

*[Not just Donna Michelle, but a bevy of international beauties were attracted to Stirling Moss, a British inductee into the International Motorsports Hall of Fame and one of the most recognized celebrities in the U.K.. He won 212 of the 529 races he entered across several categories of competition. He preferred to race only British cars.]*

"When it comes to a *beaux*," Michelle told a reporter, "I like a guy who's been around the block and looks it. Hef is a perfect specimen of that kind of guy. I like a man who is worldly wise but not world weary. You can, after all, be too sophisticated. I was drawn to Hef because he is skeptical of sacred cows. He demands the right to be himself, no Mr. Milquetoast for me, following some outdated moral code best buried with Queen Victoria."

Michelle accompanied Hef to court when he was brought up on obscenity charges for having run those nude shots of Jayne Mansfield from *Promises! Promises!*

He also flew her to the north coast of Jamaica when he was scouting for a suitable property for transformation into the latest Playboy Club, the only one projected for the Caribbean. She was even his escort when he taped *The Steve Allen Show* on television.

She was also in his bedroom when news came over the TV that President John F. Kennedy had been assassinated in Dallas in November of 1963. He remembered her constant complaining that her favorite shows had been preempted because all the channels had been taken over by news being broadcast about the assassination and later, the funeral.

She didn't remain for long at the Playboy Mansion, eventually bolting for Hollywood in hopes of a movie career.

During her brush with media fame in La-La Land, she managed to nab some very minor roles and didn't mind lying on the casting couch. She was alleged to have had a lesbian affair with Barbara Stanwyck during Michelle's brief stint on *The Big Valley* (1965-69).

On one of Tony Curtis's visits to the Playboy Mansion in Chicago, he informed Hef that he'd seduced Michelle on the set of *Goodbye Charlie* (1964), a movie he'd made with Debbie Reynolds. "That Donna is one hot piece," Curtis said.

"Been there, done that," Hef responded.

"Donna had a lot of animal magnetism, and I never understood why she didn't go over in Hollywood," Hef said. "She was willing to lie on any casting couch for an agent, producer, director, male or female—it didn't matter to her. I predicted she would become the Marilyn Monroe of the 1960s. That goes to show you: Even Hugh Hefner can be wrong."

By late November of 1963, JFK wasn't the only thing dead. So was Hef's affair with Donna Michelle.

A new Bunny had entered his life, Mary Warren. Hef first spotted her when she was working as a "Door Bunny" at Chicago's Playboy Club, welcoming visitors.

At the time of their first meeting in August of 1963, she had just turned twenty, and he was mesmerized by her sparkling green eyes and sexy figure. "Are you still a virgin?" he asked, in lieu of a formal introduction.

"I still am, Mr. Hefner," she said in her rather shy, demure way.

"I can certainly remedy that," he said, "and I'm the man to do it."

"So I hear," she said.

The first night he met her, he told Victor Lownes, "I vowed never to marry again, but after meeting Mary, I might change my mind, although I can be very stubborn."

Lownes recalled, "When I met her, I found she was unlike other Playmates I had known and usually fucked. Most of these hotties want to use Hef and *Playboy* as a stepping stone to a movie career or else as an introduction to some future husband, but only if he were a millionaire. Mary was very sweet, genuine, fresh, and unspoiled, just waiting to be deflowered. It was inevitable that Hef would have the honor of popping her cherry. The next thing I heard, she was known as the Grace Kelly of *Playboy* because of her regal blonde looks."

In an article in *Life* magazine, she was pictured waiting patiently in his bedroom until he got off from work, which most often was during the wee hours of the morning. She told a reporter, "I never dare to interrupt his work—nothing is more important to him than that. I never have anything vital enough to say that couldn't wait. She avoided answering the question of whether or not the relationship was fulfilling. "To be his companion is a great honor for me. More than that, it's a great experience."

Like all the other young women who had gone before her, she could not convince Hef to "remain true blue" in her words. "On many a night, I spotted some woman slipping out of his bedroom. I

Emulating "The Girls of Texas," and looking better than most of the gunslingers who helped make the state famous, Mary Warren, photographed by Barry O'Rourke, appears on the cover of *Playboy's* June 1966 edition.

called them 'rotten god damn bitches' for going after my man with his cheating heart."

There was one regularly scheduled event where she could always count on Hef belonging exclusively to her, and that was on Sunday movie night at the Mansion. In its profile on Hef, *Time* described the details of one of those screenings:

"In walks a man and a woman—he, casual in slacks and a cardigan sweater; she, blonde and wearing a black dress. Simultaneously, a full-size movie screen begins a silent descent down a side wall. Hefner, 40, swings down into a love seat saved for him beside his 15-foot-long stereo console. His girlfriend, *Playboy* Cover Mary Warren, 23, slips in alongside him, putting her head on his shoulder. A butler brings popcorn and bottles of Pepsi, The light dims and the movie begins."

The featured movie that night was Michelangelo Antonioni's *Blowup* (1966). Starring Vanessa Redgrave and David Hemmings, it was Antonioni's hypnotic pop culture parable of a photographer caught up in the freewheeling and very permissive lifestyle of Swinging London in the 1960s.

Bobbie Arnstein, Hef's assistant, said, "Mary was different from the other girls. She really seemed devoted to Hef and attended to his every wish. She even went into the kitchen to make sure the chef fried his nightly chicken and made the gravy just like he demanded it. She went shopping and bought silk pajamas for him, selecting color schemes such as scarlet pajamas with a Halloween orange robe. She was the most devoted girlfriend he ever had."

"On occasion, he took her out to a Chicago night club, nearly always the Playboy Club. One winter, he invited her to go skiing on the slopes of Aspen and once to New York to see the latest shows on Broadway."

During her relationship with Hef, Mary changed her hair color twice, getting rid of the blonde in favor of chestnut and later, brunette.

In 1965, Hef told *Look* magazine, "Mary Warren is my special girl in spite of other young women who come and go through my life. She knows I cheat on her, and that is difficult for her to accept, but she seems to understand my needs. I have this motto I live by—'So many girls, so little time,' but none of the women who pass in and out of my bed challenges my thing with Mary."

The most frequent witness to their affair was a big, lumbering St. Bernard named Humphrey after Hef's favorite movie star, Bogart.

By 1967, Warren seemed resigned to the fact that Hef would never settle down with her and make her his wife. She left *Playboy* and became a secretary for a medical research firm. Her last note to him read, "Love, forever, Mary."

Weeks after Warren "escaped" from the Playboy Mansion, she made a call to her friend, Milda Bridgewater, a secretary at the Mansion and the keeper of Hef's scrapbook of key events in his life. An arrangement was made to slip her back into the building when Hef was out of town.

On the appointed day, Warren appeared and was allowed into Hef's bedroom, where, with Milda, she searched for a sex film he'd made of them making love. It was found near a blue-covered logbook that detailed his sexual relationships. There were almost 1,000 names in that book, many of them Playmates or Bunnies from the Playboy Club, others those of random females who had attended parties at the Mansion.

Bridgewater told her of a surprise discovery: Although Hef had seen little of his son and daughter since divorcing his first wife, Millie, he hosted a "Sweet Sixteen" party for his daughter, Christie, allowing her to invite her young friends, both male and female. He arranged for a lavish buffet and hired a band so that they could dance.

Apparently, a young friend of his daughter, who had just turned sweet sixteen herself, was attracted to Hef for whatever reason. Before leaving the mansion that night, she had left an envelope filled with 8" x 10" photos of herself in various nude poses.

When Bobbie Arnstein, Hef's assistant, showed the pictures to him the next day, Hef admitted that he was turned on, but wondered if it would be the right thing to take advantage of a girl who was (presumably) a virgin and underaged and a friend of his daughter.

Arnstein advised against it, but Hef responded that the temptation was just too great. "Send for her, advising her to be very discreet," he said. "How often does a man of my age get to break in a virginal young teenager to the glories of getting plugged by a man? If not me, her deflowerer might be some inexperienced football jock who will knock her up."

Bobbie Arnstein, Hef's confidential secretary *(depicted above)*, kept the Playmates coming and going from his bedroom. He also directed her to provide girls for his VIP visitors, including the British movie star, Anthony Newley, once married (1963-1970) to Joan Collins.

One typical memo from Hef to Arnstein read as follows:

*"Please get word to all the girls in the House, plus all the Bunnies in the Chicago Club, that Anthony Newley will be my house guest Wednesday and Thursday."*

*"We would enjoy having as many of the girls hanging out in the evening, and after work, as possible."*

*"Hef."*

***

The Playboy Club in Chicago became the most written about, debated, vilified, and/or lauded in America. In the wake of its success, Hef plotted opening new clubs in many of the key cities of America, especially those with a wide coterie of free-spending and adventurous bachelors-at-large.

In the press, it had generated such new expressions as "ring-a-ding-belles," or "feminine fauna." Bunnies were glorified, spoofed, rhapsodized, revered, and reviled in various media that included comic strips, records, books, movies, and television commentaries.

A Playboy Keyholder once compared his visit to the Chicago club "to a kid given *carte blanche* in a candy store."

*Paris Match,* the French-language weekly news magazine, wrote: "The Playboy Bunny is the best known animal in American mythology." *The New York Herald Tribune* stated, "Bunnies are *Playboy's* Americanized version of the Japanese Geisha Girl."

The Playboy Bunny was viewed as a "contemporary cross between an airline stewardess and a Ziegfeld Girl." Reporter Mike McGrady referred to the Chicago club as "Disneyland with broads." The magazine itself, in the words of one critic, was "a nationally circulated publication aimed at young homewreckers."

Early in the life of the club, Hef shared with a reporter his vision for future clubs, which he saw extending across North America from New York to the Pacific Coast. He even envisioned the creation of a "Caribbean Playboy Paradise" on the north coast of Jamaica.

"I want to open a club in Honolulu, one in Toronto, perhaps Montréal. In Europe, we're considering such capitals as London, Paris, Rome, Copenhagen, and Berlin. We're even thinking Tokyo, Manila, Hong Kong, San Juan, Mexico City, and such South American capitals as Buenos

Hef's best friend, John Dante, was sent out on a "Bunny Hunt" across the American landscape.

"I was the chief recruiter for the Bunny Clubs," he said. "Before I hit town, I'd take out an ad in the local newspaper, touting the glamourous life and the high pay that a Bunny could make. Everywhere I went, at least two hundred girls would show up wanting to become Bunnies."

Replicated above is the cover of *Barmate,* a mixologist's guide from Southern Comfort that was distributed with the December 1964 issue of *Playboy.*

245

Aires and Rio de Janeiro.

***

His first launchpad was Miami, where he opened a club in May of 1961. That would be his beach resort for Playboys who wanted to escape the harsh winters of the north, like those he'd experienced in Chicago.

Although the Mondrian-inspired exterior of the Playboy Club was similar to the one in Chicago, its interior was more glittery. Its address was at 7701 Biscayne Boulevard, part of a waterfront estate with its own dock. Parts of the inside were equivalent to the one in Chicago—its Penthouse, its Cartoon Club, its Playmate Bar, its Piano Bar, its Living Room, and a lavish buffet in another room that featured Florida lobster and stone crab.

Throughout the club darted bushy-tailed Bunnies in their skimpy costumes and rabbit ears. At least two of them, Joni Mattis and Joyce Nizzari, were former girlfriends of Hef.

On its opening night, he was photographed with a luscious blonde Playmate, Lisa Winters.

For entertainment, Martha Raye, who had made a fortune using her big mouth, had been hired. She spent the night bellowing, cackling, and mugging. She sang all her hits, which included "Mr. Paganini," and performed her strip-spoof "It's On, It's Off." Many of the ex-servicemen whom she'd entertained during the war showed up to cheer her on.

*The Miami Herald* reviewed the club, calling it "The swingingest ring-a-ding-dingingest hot spot in Miami."

As part of their frequent visits to Miami, a familiar roster of celebs showed up to be entertained, none of them more notable than John Wayne, Frank Sinatra, Sonny Liston, Shelley Berman, Steve Allen, Peter Lawford (who waited around for one of the bartenders to get off from work), Harry Belafonte, Tony Curtis, Danny Kaye, and Johnny Carson.

"We've conquered Chicago and Miami," Hef said. "Now it's on to New Or-

Born into a vaudeville family, big-mouthed Martha Raye, one of Hef's favorite entertainers, was always a hit at Playboy Clubs.

Sometimes compared to Joe E. Brown, she was one of the first female clowns in the movies, and a widely recognized comedian during the early days of television.

leans."

*[The Miami Club eventually moved to 150 NW LeJeune Road and closed in 1984.]*

***

In 1970, Hef established yet another club, this one on Collins Avenue in Miami Beach. For $13 million, he bought the Hilton Plaza Hotel from Conrad Hilton, renaming it the Playboy Plaza. According to Stephen Byer, "Hef's ego forced him to buy a hotel from Hilton because this was an affirmation that *Playboy* had hit the big time."

What set the Miami Beach club apart from other *Playboy* venues at the time was the caliber of its entertainment. Regrettably for Hef, his resort opened during the dying gasps of the Golden Age of entertainment on Miami Beach, when it was known as "Las Vegas of the East."

Stan Musick, a talented musician, was designated as the club's musical director. *[Musick had played in the orchestra associated with the 1960 television event,* Welcome Home, Elvis, *during its taping at the Fontainebleau Hotel. It had marked Presley's return from his military tour of duty in Germany. Musick, who was keenly aware of America's rigorously segregated nightlife during the 1950s, applauded Hef's policy of racial tolerance, telling him that he had once been arrested at a little jazz joint when he'd showed up with a black girlfriend.]*

Musick booked some of the biggest names of his day, including an opening night that featured Frank Sinatra and members of his Rat Pack. Other performers during the life of its venue included Steve Lawrence and his wife, Edyie Gorme, Liza Minnelli, Diahann Carroll, Sonny & Cher, and "Mr. Television" himself, Milton Berle.

*[One night backstage, when Uncle Miltie had had too much to drink, he bet the stagehands a thousand dollars if they felt they had a bigger dick than he had. He told them he'd unzip and take it out and let Musick be the judge. There were no*

According to Hef, "Christmas came early to Miami Beach when the great Marlene Dietrich, the *femme fatale* of the 20th Century, appeared on stage at the Playboy Club."

"She said '*Helloooo*' to the audience in the longest two-syllable drawl in nightclub history. The audience rose to its feet and applauded hysterically. Even though it concealed her world-famous gams, her Jean-Louis designed dress created a sensation."

247

*takers, since Berle's endowment was legendary within show biz circles.]*

The most memorable artist Musick ever booked into Hef's Miami Beach Playboy Club was Marlene Dietrich, the German *femme fatale,* in her seventies at the time. Hef flew in for her opening night and found—despite the reputation that had preceded her—that she was not an "imperial diva." Instead, she was "a very down-to-earth human being. Back in her suite, she even prepared me her famous omelet."

On stage, wearing a gown by Jean Louis, Dietrich was accompanied on the piano by Burt Bacharach, her much younger lover. There were tears in the eyes of many members of the audience when she sang "Lili Marlene," the favorite song of both the Allied and Nazi armies during the war.

Another memorable gig at the club on Miami Beach was Mitzi Gaynor, the singing and dancing star of all those sentimental musicals of the 1950s. *South Pacific* in 1958. For the *Playboy* audience, she sang her hits from that show, "Some Enchanted Evening," and "I'm Gonna Wash That Man Right Out of My Hair." The *Playboy* audience loved her.

"Mitzi had that rare quality," Musick said. "Wholesome yet seductive. She barged on through with a brassy, hard-sell show biz pizzazz as long as there was one table full in the audience. Those legs of hers will live forever."

Ironically, long before Hef had "muscled in" on Miami Beach, Conrad Hilton had recognized that the neighborhood was downsizing. Despite Hef's armada of big-deal nightclub acts, they wouldn't be enough to sustain his Miami Beach property for long. It lost $2.2 million in the ten-month period between August of 1970 and June of 1971. Its occupancy level never went above 55 percent.

*[Even before he sold it to Hefner, Conrad Hilton had decided that it was time to dump the property one evening when he entered the 350-seat dining room and found only four tables occupied during what should have been the dinner rush hour.*

*The Playboy Plaza continued to be a finanial drain, having lost millions of dollars during its operation. In 1974, Hef sold it for book value, $13.5 million.]*

\*\*\*

"There is a house in New Orleans," so the song went. As it applied to the business ambitions of Hugh Hefner, it was a 19th-Century carriage house complete with its former slave quarters. Hef inspected the property at 727 Rue Iberville, off Bourbon Street, in the city's historic French Quarter, eventually deciding that it would be ideal for the third Playboy Club. It was with the understanding that it would be operated as a franchise. Elaborate restorations continued up until a few days before the club's widely publicized opening on October 13, 1961.

Its location as an emporium of food and drink faced stiff competition from its immediate neighbors. Across the street was the Acme Bar, said to serve the freshest and most succulent oysters in the city. Also very close nearby was the Creole restaurant, Moran's, one of the best in New Orleans.

The décor of the New Orleans Playboy Club was different from the other members of its chain. There were crystal chandeliers, shuttered windows, slate floors, and bubbling fountains. A Bunny logo embedded in the stained glass doors led into the standard Playboy Club subdivisions, which were spread across five floors. They included a Playmate Bar, and a "Living Room," site of some of the best live jazz in the South.

Hef could not come to terms with the franchise owners, so he bought them out so he could run the club as he pleased. "Their price was highway robbery," he said, "but I paid it."

From the beginning, the club ran into problems with the segregation issue. As was his custom, the racially tolerant Hef wanted to book black artists, and have a membership roster open to all colors, despite the fact that that racial mixture was against the Louisiana laws that prevailed at the time.

Racial issues derived from more than just prevailing legalities. "There was always some redneck yelling the 'N' word," he said. Whenever that happened, "I had my boys throw him out of the club."

The Bunnies who worked there reported the worst conditions, and some of the worst harassment, of any club within the franchise. One Bunny claimed, "Some of the drunks liked to pour their liquor down our tops, and others pulled at our Bunny Tails."

"New Orleans was the best and the worst Playboy Club," claimed Howard Beder, singer and comedy writer. "There was a big outcry—protests from local members that it wasn't right—when Hef opened it to blacks."

"Hef just said, 'Then leave. Just go. Forget it. Don't even come back here.' He was quite a man in that regard.'"

One of America's most talented saxophonists, Al Belletto, was brought in to manage the club and book the talent. Still a young man, he had recorded for Capital Records in the 1950s. As manager, he hired some of the best jazz artists in New Orleans, and brought in top artists from New York and Chicago, too. Ella Fitzgerald, after delivering a concert at the New Orleans Playboy Club one evening, introduced what she called a rising young star: Stevie Wonder. Other artists such as Gerry Mulligan, Kenny Rogers, and Dave Brubeck appeared to entertain too.

Belletto also hired the politically controversial black comic, Dick Gregory, who managed to stir up even more controversy at the club. Ellis Marsalis, the son of one of Louisiana's finest jazz families, became a regular. "The law didn't allow us to play with white performers," he said. "We played downstairs, and then we backed up black performers that came in. By the time of my second gig at the club, the law, happily, had changed."

Years later, a former Bunnie, Laura Misch, remembered her days at the club: "I married a cop of easy virtue, posed nude for Hef's *Playboy*, drank all night after work at Lucky Pierre's, a former whorehouse, and appeared in the worst movie ever made, where I played a prostitute."

*[She was referring to the controversial* Mandingo *(1973), starring James Mason and Perry King, a trashy potboiler based on Kyle Onstott's bestseller.]*

***

Hef returned in 1999 for a gala at the Chaos on Miami Beach. He paid $100,000 to rent the club for four hours. According to a reporter for the *Sun Sentinel,* he was mobbed by a bevy of blonde women.

He'd ordered the doorman to allow only women into the event. By midnight, more that 400 women were inside, many of them vying for Hef's attention. Never in his entire life had he ever been the focus of so many females. Inside, to handle the women he couldn't manage, Hef had invited fifty of his male friends and business associates.

***

Victor Lownes was initially in charge of booking talent into the Playboy Clubs, and he was credited with having a sixth sense about hiring up-and-coming singers and comics on the dawn of fame. Since the clubs paid relatively low salaries to its performers, he had to hire these artists while they were still affordable.

Whereas he couldn't afford big names such as Frank Sinatra or Barbra Streisand, he did book Bette Midler during the early days of her career, as well as Billy Cristal, Steve Martin, and Peter Allen, who made a pass at Lownes. Phyllis Diller said, "The Playboy Clubs were a good launching pad for a lot of entertainers, who were getting started in the business. Lownes had a nose for sniffing out major talent on the rise."

*Playboy* employee Noel Stein claimed, "Victor didn't always have to see the act, especially if it were out of town. He was an avid reader of *Variety*, and he scanned the reviews. If a critic called a performer 'a socko,' he would hire him for $300 a week. But if a review of his act asserted that he was 'wowsy,' Victor gave him $500 a week. The same deal worked for women entertainers too, though there were far fewer of those back then."

For weeks, Hef and Lownes talked over making Manhattan the setting for their next Playboy Club. Lownes finally flew into New York to scout for locations, completely unaware of all the illegal troubles they would face. "Hef and I had screwed dozens of women, but we were virgins about how to operate a club in New York City. It was a question of who to bribe. I nicknamed Manhattan 'Sodom.' Everything and everybody were up for sale."

"We were told we'd have to bribe certain *politicos* in Albany to get a liquor license. I met with Martin Epstein, the Commissioner of the New York State Liquor Authority, and he came right to the point. He wanted $50,000 in cash for his help in getting me a license. He warned me that key clubs *[i.e., clubs, often segregated, which demanded that members pay dues and/or an inaugural membership fee]* were illegal in the state, and clubs had to grant membership to all."

"Hef and I hated paying bribes," Lownes said. "In his own way, he was still a Puritan with roots in Nebraska. He was not a sleazeball, even though he had many critics because of his adoration of the undraped female form."

Backroom negotiations for the acquisition of the club's liquor license floundered for several months. In the meantime, Lownes found a six-story building whose location and layout were suitable. With offices on the top floor, and an art gallery at street level, it was near the exclusive Sherry Netherland Hotel on 59th Street, east of Fifth Avenue. Even though he had not yet acquired that liquor license, Hef ordered that renovations should begin, allocating an initial $2.15 million for their costs. *[Before the club opened, he would have to shell out something approaching $7 million for hidden "extra costs."]*

In January of 1961, Hef flew to New York to meet with Lownes and to attend a secret meeting with Epstein. His demand of $50,000 in cash had not changed, and he still warned that "clubs cannot grant keys to its members."

The meeting between Epstein and the Playboys didn't go well. *[Later, after ratcheting up the corruption quotient even higher, Epstein dismissed Hefner and Lownes as "boy scouts."]*

Epstein's (also corrupt) boss was an attorney, I. Judson Morhouse, then-chairman of New York State's Republican Party. Morhouse's influence had significantly contributed to the election of NY State Governor Nelson A. Rockefeller.

Morhouse would eventually demand $100,000 in cash for his legal help in obtaining a liquor license for the NYC Playboy Club. Morhouse also raised another condition: He demanded to be allowed to purchase $100,000 of *Playboy* stock and to have exclusive rights to operate the gift concessions within the club. Hef agreed to pay the money but couldn't grant the stock request because that would be subject to public disclosure.

After leaving Morhouse's office, Hef told Lownes, "The creep is a blackmailer." At this point, Hef had already collected a $25 annual membership fee from 60,000 future key holders.

Unknown to Hef, the New York County District Attorney's Office was conducting a secret investigation into corruption within the NY State Liquor Authority. In December of 1961, subpoenaes went out for information about *Playboy's* efforts to acquire a liquor license in New York. Hef's lawyer worked out a deal with the Attorney General for immunity by revealing everything they knew about the Liquor Authority's previous attempts at extortion.

In time, Epstein avoided prison because he was ill. Morhouse, however, was indicted and found guilty. Because he, too, was ailing, Governor Rockefeller commuted the sentence of his long-time friend and ally.

As if all this weren't enough, Hef faced more trouble, this time from Bernard J. O'Connel, the head of the New York License Commission, who refused to grant him a cabaret license. A staunch Catholic, he claimed that the appeal of the club was not to hear singers or comics, but for its members to gape at scantily clad waitresses with bunny tails. Hef appealed the decision to the New York Supreme Court and won.

A judge ruled, "It is not necessary for a club owner to dress his female employees in middy blouses, gymnasium bloomers, turtleneck sweaters, fishermen's hip boots, and ankle-length overcoats to satisfy the commissioner's personal moral code."

Making Hef's life at the time even more complicated, Lownes was engaged in personality conflicts with both Keith Hefner and Bob Preuss, who called him "a son of a bitch." Keith referred to Lownes as "a pain in the ass."

"Lownes' management style was that of a madman out of control, yelling and screaming at employees," Preuss said. "On a personal level, he often made sexual advances to the Bunnies and harassed them if they turned him down."

Both men urged Hef to fire Lownes, but he was reluctant to do so, owing to their long-time friendship that dated from 1955.

Keith and Lownes also battled over the talent he booked, as both men had widely different taste in music. According to Lownes, "Keith thought he knew more than I did, because originally, he wanted to be an actor himself. He got a role on a kiddie program and played Johnny Jellybean. Need I say more?"

*[Finally, Hef decided to let Lownes go, but made a sweetheart, "golden parachute" deal with him, paying him a retainer of $75,000 a year and naming him manager of the New York Playboy Club. He would, however, no longer make decisions that affected the magazine.*

*Hef wanted to buy back Lownes' stock, which was worth a million dollars, and he agreed to give Lownes $300,000 a year until he was paid for all of it.]*

\*\*\*

Lownes had staged the opening night ceremonies at the New York Playboy Club with klieg lights and celebrities, the event evoking a Hollywood premiere. Its stars arrived in limousines and Rolls Royces. Rock Hudson was the hit of the evening. All the Bunnies wanted his autograph.

Kia Winding, a talented trombonist and arranger, was specifically designated to book acts for the club. Among the artists he hired were Jamaica-born Monte Alexander, later a leading figure in the bebob revival; singer Jack Jones; and comedian Lily Tomlin who sometimes sang about "muff diving" and "beating your meat."

Woody Allen proved himself a first-rate talent, as did Nipsey Russell and Dionne Warwick.

Patrons at the NYC Club eventually included Eddie Fisher and Elizabeth Taylor (not at the same time). Tony Bennett was a frequent visitor, arriving with such guests as Ella Fitzgerald, Dean Martin, and Tony Curtis. "Don Rickles insulted everyone from the stage," Lownes said. "Paul Anka and Rich Little went over big, too."

Food was a big attraction at the New York City club, with a filet mignon priced at $2, a large lobster going for $6.

One night, a drunken Frank Sinatra arrived with his party just before the 3AM closing. "Since it was Sinatra, I kept a skeleton staff to attend to them," Lownes said. "About six Bunnies were resting at a nearby table when Sinatra began to taunt them. Finally, he came over and tossed a lit cherry bomb under their table. Three of the girls screamed as their legs were burnt. I had to threaten to sue Sinatra, but he coughed up $10,000 the next day to pay off the girls until the sores on their legs healed and they could return to work. That Frankie! What a guy!"

Lownes had rented the penthouse at the St. Moritz Hotel on Central Park West. According to legend, the greatest orgies in Manhattan took place there at the rate of three or four a week. "Bunnies showed up after work along with an assortment of international playboys," Lownes said. "Sometimes I staged exhibitions, starring this Brazilian stud Ramon with his 15-inch penis. He put John C. Holmes to shame."

"Word reached Hollywood, and many visiting stars wanted to come to my orgies, knowing it would be very discreet. I got to see a lot of my favorite stars in action, things they couldn't show even on the liberated screen. They brought out the *voyeur* in me. Sammy Davis Jr. took the prize for the fastest action."

***

One day, a job candidate who identified herself as Marie Catharine Ochs showed up for an audition at the Playboy Club in Manhattan and was hired. "Marie Catharine Ochs" was her cover: Her actual name was Gloria Steinem, a Phi Beta Kappa graduate of Smith College. She had gone underground to write a two-part exposé on the Life of a Bunny for *Show* magazine. Entitled "A Bunny's Tale," it became widely read and caused Hef great *angst*. Two decades later, it was made into a television movie.

Steinem virtually destroyed the glamorous image of a Playboy Bunny. She exposed the low pay, the harsh working conditions, and an unending struggle with indecent proposals from boorish customers. She claimed eight hours in high heels led to long soaks of aching feet at night. The tight costumes caused red welts. As if to destroy the glamour quotient completely, she claimed the Bunnies padded their bras with 'Bunny Bosom Stuffers"—Kleenex, plastic dry cleaners' bags, absorbent cotton, cut-up bunny tails; foam rubber, lamb's wool, Kotex halves, silk scarves, and gym socks.

Before Steinem was hired, she was forced to submit to a gynecological exam and test for venereal diseases. She was presented with a brochure that read, "When you become a Playboy Bunny, your world will be fun-filled, pleasant, and always exciting. You might even get to meet Tony Curtis."

"Bunnies are overworked, exploited, and exhausted," she charged. "You get pinched as you serve." She also revealed that management took half of what the Bunnies made in tips, and despite promises of $200 to $300 a week, during her first week, she earned only $35.90."

When Hef read her article, he exploded in anger. "Would you believe that some jerk I know once tried to set me up on a blind date with this Gloria Steinem?"

Steinem's article caused many Bunnies to try to form a labor union. They were tired of the "Saturday Night Massacre" when many of them could be routinely fired for the slightest infraction. Often the women weren't even told what they were doing wrong but got their Bunny tail ripped off on their way out the door.

Unlike the relatively docile women working in other Playboy clubs, Bunnies in Manhattan picketed Hef's club, protesting their working conditions. Their struggle, never very successful, continued into the 1970s.

In one picket, a sign read—HUGH HEFNER IS A MALE CHAUVINIST RABBIT.

Hef's response? "Really, Bunnies. I'm not a male chauvinist rabbit, and I love and respect all of you. Maybe I've just been a wee bit overprotective."

\*\*\*

"The Playboy Interview" became one of the best-known and most widely read features in the magazine. It was launched in the September 1962 issue when author Alex Haley, fresh out of the U.S. Coast Guard, interviewed the acclaimed jazz trumpeter, bandleader, and composer, Miles Davis.

Haley was relatively unknown in 1962, but by 1976, he would write *Roots: The Saga of an American Family*, which ABC adapted into a TV minis-

In 1969, *Time* magazine described Gloria Steinem as "one of the best dates to take to a New York party these days — or, failing such luck, one of the most arresting names to drop...She has legs worthy of her miniskirts, and a brain that keeps conversation lively without getting tricky."

According to Steinem, "To this day when people don't like me, they introduce me as a former Bunny as a put-down. On the other hand, I did improve the working conditions for those women."

"I don't know how she does it," said Susan Brownmiller, an ardent feminist who opposed Steinem at multiple levels, at multiple times, in public, for almost forty years. "She's still so totally beautiful. When women went to see her, they were just relieved, because she was so calm, and she could be funny. She made a lot of women feel, 'Oh, that's what the women's movement looks like. I can be part of that.'"

Depicted above is Steinem from around the era she was emulating a Bunny.

eries. It reached a record-breaking audience of 130 million viewers.

Davis was dubbed "the Prince of Darkness" in the jazz world. Haley found out why when he pursued Davis for an interview. The prickly musician was the most recalcitrant and off-putting in the music industry. Fortunately, Haley was African-American, as Davis held white journalists in contempt. Complicating matters, Davis viewed *Playboy* magazine as "disgusting—their naked women are all blondes with big tits and flat asses—or no asses. Hefner never runs a black woman as a Playmate. For that matter, he also boycotts brown women, even China dolls."

Time and time again, Davis rebuffed Haley's attempts to interview him. Haley approached Davis' press agent for access, as well as Davis' wife, but without luck. Night after night, Haley showed up for Davis' performance at the Village Vanguard in New York City's Greenwich Village, but he was consistently rejected.

Finally, Haley learned that Davis went several afternoons a week to a black gym on 135th Street in Harlem, where he boxed in a ring mainly for exercise. Haley was no athlete, and he was short and wore glasses. Spotting him, Davis decided to teach "that pestering nerd a lesson" and invited him into the ring for a bout.

Willing to make any sacrifice for an interview, Haley took off his glasses and stepped into the ring. It was a fast, one-sided match, as Haley could hardly see the blows coming his way, but he certainly felt them.

Davis admired his guts and even invited him to join him in the communal showers, where they soaped up and

The *Playboy* interview became a milestone in American journalism.

Alex Haley, the future author of the international bestseller, *Roots*, helped launch the feature by gaining access to some of the most controversial people in America.

Alex Haley's interview with the spectacularly temperamental trumpeter Miles Davis, known in music circles at the time as "The Prince of Darkness," was a landmark insight into race relations in America at the time.

During the interview, which entrenched *Playboy's* controversial reputation as a liberal voice for social change two years before the passage of the Civil Rights Act, Davis talked bitterly and at length about Jim Crow and "the agony of being black in America."

bonded as brothers. That was followed by an invitation to Davis' house on West 77th Street, where Haley finally got his interview.

As it turned out, the topics they discussed were mostly about race relations, not music. Race-related turmoil was on everyone's mind at the time. In the South, African American churches were being bombed, and KKK crosses were burning on the lawns of black families in Georgia, Alabama, and Mississippi.

Davis spoke with bitter passion, telling Haley that when he was a senior in high school, he played the best music in his class. "But the prizes went to the boys with blonde hair and blue eyes. I decided right there and then that I would outdo any white boy on the horn. Jim Crow is not dead. It lives in the heart and soul of the white man."

After committing the interview to paper, Haley showed up at the office of *Show Business Illustrated*, the original commissioner of the interview, only to be told that the magazine was folding.

Shortly after its demise, and as part of its bankruptcy proceedings, Murray Fisher, an associate editor at *Playboy*, was told to scan the files of the defunct magazine to see if there was anything worthy of publication from among the unpublished manuscripts left behind. Because race relations was the hot topic of the day, he schlepped the texts of Haley's interview with Davis over to Hef, who approved it for publication in *Playboy*.

Hef was so pleased with Fisher that he put him in charge of a new feature, *The Playboy Interview*. Thus began a monthly series of insights into some of the most famous and/or controversial figures of the era. They included Bertrand Russell, Jean Genet, Jean-Paul Sartre, Ayn Rand, Cassius Clay, Jimmy Hoffa, Albert Schweitzer, Ingmar Bergman, Dolly Parton, Timothy Leary, George Wallace, Princess Grace, Henry Miller, Ralph Nader, Arthur Schlesinger, Jr., Fidel Castro, and inevitably, Frank Sinatra, "the Chairman of the Board."

Ironically, before the end of the decade, Haley's three most widely read interviews (each of them published in *Playboy*) would be with a trio of controversial personalities, each of whom would be assassinated: Malcolm X; George Lincoln Rockwell, head of the American Nazi Party; and the also-doomed Martin Luther King, Jr.

***

As his *Playboy* empire expanded, Hef had to hire new executives. Whereas some did not fit in, others stayed on for years. Such was the case of Stephen Byer, who in the 1960s was named vice president and marketing director. Before that, he had worked for Cowles Communications, publisher of *Look* magazine.

He was lured away from *Look* when Hef offered him a salary of $100,000 a year. Within a few months, his compensation had increased to $200,000 a year, making him the highest-salaried employee at *Playboy*, second only to Hef himself.

But by the time Byer turned 28, he was out the door. In 1972, he described his experiences at *Playboy* in an autobiography provocatively entitled, *Hefner's Gonna Kill Me When He Reads This...*

His tell-all exposé marked the first time a former executive had shared, in print, his opinion of Hef and his enterprise. Byer labeled Hef a "loner," claiming that he had no close friends or family ties. He painted him as a recluse, living in a bedroom that was like a "sealed capsule," except when Playmates visited, which they did frequently. "Daylight is banished from his impenetrable fortress." Byer defined Hef as "a male chauvinist who feels women are merely objects and of lesser intelligence than men."

"I had a long-standing and deepseated bias against *Playboy*," he claimed. "I viewed Hef's empire as one of the most negative and immoral in the country. My meetings with Hef and the rest of the *Playboy* brass somewhat softened my prejudice but failed to dispel it."

Byer revealed that on his first day on the job, he learned not to open a door before knocking and receiving permission to enter. Having violated that rule, he encountered a scene "straight out of a Henry Miller novel," as an executive was getting a blow-job from his secretary. Reacting to the sound of the opening door, the executive whirled around during his ejaculation, spraying Byer's navy blue suit with semen. Embarrassed, the executive offered to pay for its cleaning before Byer hastily retreated from the room.

In his exposé, Byer also revealed

Stephen Byer was a highly paid *Playboy* executive until Hef fired him.

To get even, Byer became a *provocateur extraordinaire*, writing a tell-all exposé of what really went on at the Playboy Mansion in Chicago. Its cover depicted him on a Hefner-esque "throne," holding a bunny captive on a leash.

"I seriously pissed off Hef." he said.

that 60 to 80 percent of the magazine's male staff, including Hef, had been divorced, some of them several times. In his words, "The swinging atmosphere at *Playboy* was somewhat on the high side of whoopee," a phrase that suggested that members of the staff, both male and female, were frequently engaged in sexual encounters during working hours within the building.

"Spying was also deeply entrenched," Byer charged. "Everybody was spying on everybody else, with word getting back to the boss. Hef soon learned who was loyal—and who was not."

Byer made it a point to explode a number of what he called "myths" about *Playboy* and its executives. "Some of them were appalled at the number of black men who frequented the *Playboy* clubs. Their patronage drove some of these guys crazy. They were public liberals but private bigots."

He attended two *Playboy* parties at the Mansion in Chicago—one for about a half hour, the second for fifteen minutes. He never went back. "To me, these parties were screamingly dull and obnoxiously loud. People of all ilk went there."

He was no doubt referring to such movie stars as Robert Mitchum, who showed up one night completely nude but with catsup slathered across his hairy chest. He announced, "I've come as a raw hamburger."

Even Senator Eugene McCarthy, an unlikely guest by anyone's estimate, showed up at the Mansion. He would run against Robert F. Kennedy for the Democratic Party's presidential nomination in 1968. The famous British model Jean Shrimpton also appeared there one day, as did most of the cast, both male and female, of the musical, *Hair*. "These actors stripped down like they did on stage and jumped into the pool."

Bill Cosby was a frequent party-goer at the Mansion, "always on a Bunny hunt."

Shortly after his arrival at one gathering within the mansion, Sammy Davis, Jr. disappeared into a bathroom with a Bunny for a quickie blow-job.

Byer also alleged that Hugh O'Brian, TV's Wyatt Earp, often went around with his trousers unzipped, inviting Bunnies to reach in for a feel.

Byer did attend a few photo shoots for nude Playmates of the Month. "Some of these sessions took on the aspects of a pornographic film being shot on 42nd Street in Manhattan."

Most of the executives at *Playboy* fell into line, agreeing with almost every proclamation that issued from Hef's typewriter, some of his memos stretching thirty single-spaced pages. "Think Tolstoy's *War and Peace*," Byer said.

Byer, however, was markedly different, often challenging Hef and coming up with a very different opinion. He even told Hef that the Bunny costume then prevalent in the Playboy Clubs was "silly," and presented him with three competing designs, two of them from well-known designers. *[The best of them, he alleged, was submitted by a 78-year-old fat lady.]*

Byer also maintained that the ads for "What Sort of Man Reads Playboy?" had been running for fourteen years without any substantial changes. He desperately wanted to update the image for the *Playboy* of the 1970s, and submitted ideas for major changes to the look of the magazine's marketing campaigns, all of which Hef rejected.

Finally, that "day of reckoning" came for Byer, when he was summoned into Hef's office. The meeting was tense and brief, as Hef puffed nervously on his pipe. Finally, he spoke: "One of us has to go," he said.

"I guess it won't be you," Byer retorted.

"You got that right, good buddy,"

A few moments later, Byer was escorted from the building, never to return, except in his memoir, published two years later.

***

Famous guests visiting Chicago still showed up at the Playboy Mansion for the three or four parties hosted there each week. On several occasions, Hef never made an appearance, but remained locked in his bedroom, often directing his closed-off world from his round bed.

Bob Hope came to inspect the Bunnies. In spite of his public image, Hope was an almost obsessive womanizer. During his rare visits and because he was such a big name, Hef allowed him to slip away to The Blue Room with the girls of his choice.

Larry Gilbert, a screen and TV writer, had

HUGH O'BRIAN as the famous marshal

# Wyatt Earp

It took brains and a Buntline... to tame the "TERROR TOWN"!

GUYS YOU WERE LIKELY TO MEET AT THE PLAYBOY MANSION

## WYATT EARP
(AKA, HUGH O'BRIAN)

"I think I was the most sought-after stud visitor to the Mansion. The Playmates went apeshit over me, and so did the waiters, half of whom were gay."

260

warned Hef: "Bob beds a lot of Las Vegas showgirls. He fools around with anyone who is young and mobile and guest stars on his show."

Hope told Hef, "I'm lucky, I guess. The money is good, and I bed all the girls I want." After his first visit, he told a reporter in Chicago, "It's Hugh Hefner's world. He merely lets the rest of us guys inhabit it."

Norman Mailer remained a sometimes visitor, comparing the Mansion to "a timeless, spaceless sensation like an ocean liner traveling to the bottom of the sea."

On more than one occasion, Hef decided that as a means of improving his image, he should invite "celebrity ministers," beginning with Dr. Martin Luther King, Jr., who accepted the invitation. On site at the Mansion, he and Hef "rapped" until four in the morning, talking through a number of issues, mostly civil rights.

The Rev. Malcolm Boyd, author of *Are You Running With Me Jesus?*, showed up too. Shortly after he got there, a scantily clad Playmate of the Month asked him, "Do you like sex?"

The Mansion's party atmosphere and frivolity masked a rather dark secret: Hef had become dependent on drugs, and from time to time, they had clouded his judgment. It was Victor Lownes who first recommended Dexedrine when he noticed Hef falling asleep at his desk, unable to concentrate on massive piles of editorial work which he refused to delegate to other editors. He often worked until dawn.

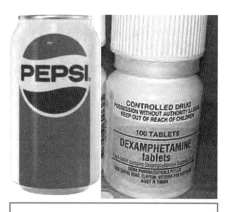

"Before I knew what was happening," Lownes said, "Hef was gobbling Dexies. My God, he went one time for four days in a row without sleeping."

Hefner himself confessed, "By the early 1960s, Dexies were supplying the fuel to keep the *Playboy* image powered."

Spectorsky (Spec), behind Hef's back, also began to question his editorial judgment. "Fortunately, he didn't interfere in the selection of fiction, but he wanted to run everything else. Although we were acquiring articles by some of the top writers in America, he

### NEUROSES, A BAD DIET, AND THE IRONIES OF CELEBRITY

As his troubles mounted, Hef began—much to the alarm of his staff, lovers, and friends—to subsist on a diet of Pepsi, dexamphetamines, and candy.

His health suffered, but according to some of his Playmates, his appetite for sex continued, undiminished.

didn't bother to read the fiction he published. He was more obsessed with the Playmate choice, the Party Jokes, and the cartoons."

Staffer Ray Russell resigned in 1963. "Those damn pills were fucking up Hef's mind. Was I working for him or under the control of Dexies?"

Richard Rosenzweig joined the staff in 1963 as an editorial assistant. "I noticed that Hef was reluctant, almost afraid, to leave the Mansion, as if the outside world was fraught with untold dangers."

"Hef hated to delegate authority, and his empire was growing daily," Lownes said. "He could no longer handle it by himself, yet he insisted on making nearly all major decisions. That meant his chief editors had to consult with him. But he was never available. Sometimes we had to make a decision. If he didn't like what we decided in his absence, he threw tantrums."

As the 1960s moved on, Hef began to look gaunt, his weight dropping to 135 pounds. One staffer said, "He evoked an inmate released from Dachau in 1945."

"He thrived on candy bars and on 35 Pepsis a day. That soft drink was rotting his teeth," Lownes said.

Once, Hef's mother visited the Mansion and was shocked at his appearance, comparing her son to a skeleton. She brought along the family doctor who examined Hef. He told him, "At the rate you're going, you will not live to be fifty."

LeRoy Neiman, Hef's illustrator, said, "In spite of his weakened condition, his interest in sex continued. He had a steady girlfriend or two, but still insisted on variety. He confessed to me that his one-night stands bored him. Once he had his orgasm, he wanted them to get the hell out of his room."

"I almost never call for repeats," Hef confessed. "Nothing these dumb Bunnies has to say interests me. If they do say something, it's a remark I've heard countless times. Momentary relief, that's all I get."

Relentlessly, *Playboy* continued to promote Hef's glamourous image. One cartoon depicted a world-weary traveler climbing a mountain peak. There, he meets a bearded guru who tells him, "In a place called Chicago, there is a man who lives in a Mansion filled with beautiful women. He wears pajamas all the time. Sit at his feet and learn from him, for he has found the secret of true happiness."

Actually, he wasn't feeling happy at all, telling his aides, "I feel I created this monster called *Playboy*. I am no longer running it. It is running me, at times devouring me."

Spec ended up referring to him as "The Godzilla of Sleepy Hollow."

***

At Hef's request, the controversial comedian, Lenny Bruce, compiled his autobiography, *How to Talk Dirty and Influence People* — a title that deliberately mocked and satirized Dale Carnegie's bestseller, *How to Win Friends and Influence People*. It was published in book form after it was serialized in *Playboy* in 1964 and 1965.

The book begins with a description of Bruce's rocky career, launched in the late 1940s, and morphs into an attack on the social, sexual, and racial hypocrisies of the era. Along with Hef, Bruce, throughout the 60s, was one of the most outspoken advocates for free speech.

The police continued to harass Bruce for the obscenities that peppered his performances in Chicago, San Francisco, and New York.

Only months after the publication of his book, Hef received a call from Hollywood informing him that Bruce, only forty years old at the time, had died of a drug overdose. His last trial on charges of obscenity had been in Manhattan in November of 1964, in which he was found guilty. Coming to his defense was an array of famous Americans. In addition to Hef, they included Woody Allen, Bob Dylan, Jules Feiffer, Allen Ginsberg, Norman Mailer, William Styron, James Baldwin, and columnist Dorothy Kilgallen.

Bruce had been sentenced to four months in a workhouse but was set free on bail during the appeals process. He died before a ruling came down on his appeal. Eventually, based on political pressure and the uproar from his fans and from liberals across the nation, he received, posthumously, a full gubernatorial pardon.

*[It was revealed later that Bruce's autobiography had actually been ghostwritten by Paul Krassner, a key player in the counterculture movement of the 1960s as an associate of Ken Kesey's "Merry Pranksters," a group notorious for its prankster activism. Krassner was also a founding member of another social activist group, the Youth International Party (a.k.a., "the*

LENNY BRUCE

Preface by
LEWIS BLACK

Foreword by
HOWARD REICH

HOW TO
TALK DIRTY
&
INFLUENCE
PEOPLE

An Autobiography

Hef's alltime favorite comedian was the controversial Lenny Bruce, who published an outrageous memoir, *How to Talk Dirty and Influence People.*

"Poor Lenny became the first major casualty in the war against censorship in this country," Hef said.

"When he died, it was up to me to pick up the banner and carry on the fight."

*Yippies.")*

*In 1958, Krassner became the editor and publisher of* The Realist, *a pioneering magazine of social-political-religious criticism intended as a grown-up version of* Mad *magazine and Lyle Stuart's anti-censorship monthly,* The Independent.

*Krassner's most notorious article, "The Parts That Were Left Out of the Kennedy Book," was a grotesque and fake exposé that came out in the wake of the (heavily censored) William Manchester overview of John Kennedy and his assassination.*

Paul Krassner was the author of a piece in a publication, *The Realist*, that was viewed as among the most controversial ever printed during the 1960s.

It was intended as an obvious satire, but "thousands upon thousands of sane people actually believed it."

*In his article, Krassner made the flagrantly fake claim that Lyndon B. Johnson, flying back to Washington from Dallas aboard the same plane that carried the corpse of the slain president, went to the rear of Air Force One. There, behind locked doors, amid the chaos and uncertainty associated with the horror of JFK's assassination earlier that morning, Krassner alleged that Johnson sexually penetrated the bullet hole in JFK's neck as a means of showing his contempt for the assassinated president, whom he hated.*

*Although such a disgusting claim—even if interpreted as a grotesque attempt at satire—seems inconceivable, writer Elliott Feldman asserted afterward that "Some members of the mainstream press and other Washington political wonks, including Daniel Ellsberg of* Pentagon Papers *fame, actually believed that the incident was true."*

*Thirty-two years later, in an interview that appeared in* Adbusters *magazine in 1995, Krassner stated, "People across the country believed, if only for a moment, that an act of presidential necrophilia had taken place. It worked, because Jackie Kennedy had created so much curiosity by censoring Manchester's* The Death of a President. *There was another reason: What I wrote was a metaphorical truth about LBJ presented in a literary context. The imagery was so shocking, it broke through the notion that the war in Vietnam was being conducted by sane men."]*

\*\*\*

In February of 1994, Hef granted an interview to the *Chicago Tribune.* Within its context, he said: "One of my most important and symbolic connections with Chicago was the beacon on top of the building at 919 North Michigan Avenue. My kid brother and I, at night, could see that beacon sweeping across the skyline of the city. For me, it was like the wail of a railroad train passing by, part of that mystical yearning of youth and adolescence. I think that's the reason the Palmolive Building, in time became the Playboy Building."

*[Completed in 1929, the skyscraper was topped by the beacon, which was named the Lindbergh Beacon to honor the historic 1927 flight of aviator Charles Lindbergh from New York to Paris. From the beginning, the two-billion candlelight revolving searchlight needed two full-time electricians to maintain it. Pilots flying into the Chicago area could see it for 250 miles away, motorists headed toward Chicago could spot it 80 miles away.]*

In 1965, Hef signed a 63-year lease on the 37-story structure for $2.7 million, a decision that put him in control of the 37-story building. The location was prime, only three blocks from Lake Michigan at the corner of the exclusive North Michigan Avenue and near the high-rent district known as "The Gold Coast."

After Hef's takeover, the Chicago Press dubbed the searchlight "The Bunny Beacon." Under the beacon, Hef ordered nine-foot tall neon letters to flash PLAYBOY along the top of his new headquarters.

*Playboy's* offices would be located on floors four through twelve, each with an elegant modernist lobby and a receptionist who might have easily qualified as a "Playmate of the Month" centerfold. Renovated and beautifully furnished, the offices were ready for occupancy by the *Playboy* staff in 1967.

As amazing as it seemed, Hef had never emerged from his cocoon in the Playboy Mansion to inspect his new location, although he'd issued detailed single-spaced memos about its décor, the location of its various departments, and the artwork, much of which focused on illustrations or photographs from previous editions of *Playboy*.

Unexpectedly and without warning, one rainy morning at 2AM when Hef couldn't sleep, he finally left his bedroom. He was unshaven, his hair tousled, as—still clad in

The famous "Bunny Beacon" atop 919 North Michigan Avenue in Chicago was photographed sending light out and into the Middle West in 1969.

Everyone in Chicago, including airplane passengers flying in and out of town after dark, soon realized that Hef was King of the Bunnies and that this building was now the headquarters of his empire.

his silk pajamas and bathroom—he donned a Humphrey Bogart trenchcoat and headed out into the rainy Chicago night. During his walk to the new headquarters of his now very famous magazine, he got soaked, because he had not taken an umbrella.

At his building's front entrance, he confronted a security guard, who thought he was a homeless bum wanting a handout or shelter.

After being refused entrance to his building, Hef protested, "But I'm Hugh Hefner. I own the fucking building. If you don't let me in, I'll have you fired tomorrow, you bastard."

"If you're Hugh Hefner, I'm Nelson Rockefeller," the guard answered. It is not known what transpired after that, but somehow "drowned rat" Hef convinced the guard that he had better let him inside the building.

Still not trusting him, the guard unlocked the door to the building's main entrance and followed Hef from room to room during his inspection tour. Hef carefully surveyed the newly installed teak-and-marble furniture, the Art Deco bas-reliefs on the elevator doors, the framed illustrations, even the wastepaper baskets emblazoned with the Bunny logo. In all, he'd spent $2 million on renovations and furnishings.

After two hours, Hef left the building. The rain had stopped, and he headed back to the safety of his cocoon, having confronted what he called "life in the real world."

When the morning guard appeared for his day shift a few hours later, the night guard headed immediately to the office of the building's manager, where he described the strange events (and the strange visitor) of the night before: "I still can't believe that was Hugh Hefner, the stylish Playboy and Man about Town. But just in case it was, I let him in but was always two feet behind him in case he tried to steal something."

"Don't be an idiot," the manager told him. "I've been alerted. That was THE Hugh Hefner. If you'd refused him, he not only would have fired you, but he'd have kicked me out on my ass for being stupid enough to hire you."

***

In 1964, Hef acquired the Playboy Theater at 1204 Dearborn Street in Chicago. It had begun showing silent pictures during the dawn of the movie industry in 1913.

During Hef's ownership, it featured a mixture of offbeat films personally selected by him. At the same time, he continued his weekly screening of movies every Sunday night at the Playboy Mansion. In reference to the movies he selected for showcasing, both at home and in his theater, he said, "If I like it, Joe Six Pack will dig it, too."

Often, he was wrong, as his tastes were sometimes markedly different from those of the general public. In reference to Hef's taste in movies, film critic Gene Siskel once noted, "Management was a haphazard affair over the years, in spite of the fact that Hef was a movie buff and should have known better."

After Chicago's Playboy Theater was sold in 1976, its former manager, Ron Lichterman, was outspoken and critical of Hef's selection of films. "We could have run *American Graffiti* (1963), a monster hit, for three years, but Hef demanded that we shut it down and feature his own movie, *The Naked Ape*, instead. That turkey was both an artistic and financial failure."

*[In 1973, Playboy Enterprises crafted and produced a film adaptation of Desmond Morris' book* The Naked Ape, *which had first been published in 1967. Morris, a zoologist and former caretaker for mammals at the London Zoo, wrote it as a means of "popularizing and demystifying science." Serialized in one of the U.K.'s largest newspapers (the* Daily Mirror*), it became a worldwide bestseller, translated into 23 languages.*

*The widely publicized star of the book's money-losing film adaptation was Johnny Crawford, an ex-Mousketeer who went on to play the son of the rancher played by Chuck Connors on the hit TV series,* The Rifleman *(1958-1963). In Hef's film, Crawford stars as a modern man, who—despite centuries of evolution—is still a "naked ape."*

*Victoria Principal, early in her career before her involvement in* Dallas, *was the co-star, playing a mini-skirted, go-go booted cutie. Naturally, Crawford goes "ape" over her.*

*The director, Donald Driver, who also wrote the screenplay, tried to compare human mating rituals with those of the animal kingdom. There is even talk of monkey orgasms. The viewer will get to see horny cave people lust after each other as they hunt for big game.*

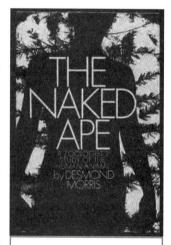

*The film critic for the* Chicago Tribune *found it "convoluted, heavy-handed, and, worst of all, a tame (PG!) story, a train wreck on every level. It combines varied lead characters, stale insights, sappy Jimmy Webb tunes, and is of a painfully ponderous self-importance."]*

Most critics agreed that although Hugh Hefner was a major league magazine publisher, "he was a lousy film producer."

After he financed a movie adaptation of *The Naked Ape*, the public stayed away in droves.

\*\*\*

In 1965, a letter came in to the Playboy Forum from a Donn Caldwell, who was serving a one- to ten-year term in the West Virginia State Penitentiary for being the recipient of fellatio during a heterosexual encounter. Bobbie Arnstein, Hef's assistant, passed the letter to Hef since she considered the sentence outrageous, and she knew that he would, too.

"What fat-assed judge passed down such a sentence?" Hef asked, telling Arnstein, "I'm god damned outraged and want to do something about it. The poor guy has already wasted two years of his young life serving an unjust sentence imposed by an idiot old judge who had probably never been laid." Through Hef's efforts, attorneys obtained Caldwell's release in 1967.

*[As it was later quipped by insiders, "Thus was established the Playboy Foundation, an organization that came into being because of a quickie blow-job."]*

The Playboy Foundation, under Hef's guidance, set out to award grants to nonprofit groups which were either fighting censorship, protecting the freedoms of the First Amendment, or researching human sexuality. One of those was the research team of William Masters and Virginia Johnson, who were pursuing the theories originally launched by Kinsey.

His foundation also sponsored groups seeking "rational" sex and drug laws—"not the draconian and antiquated laws on the books. In all, the foundation is an extension of the articles of the Playboy Philosophy advocated in my magazine."

Hef also awarded grants to filmmakers who produced documentaries advocating points of view dear to his heart. These included *The Times of Harvey Milk* (1984), the San

*Time* magazine defined the work of sex researchers William Masters and Virginia Johnson as "Sex Education for Adults."

Hefner supported, emotionally and financially, the enlighted good sense of this extraordinary research team.

The draconian Production Code of Hollywood made it illegal to even refer to homosexuality on the screen.

But in 1981, Vito Russo revealed in his book, *The Celluloid Closet*, that it had been there all along, hidden except to the most hip.

Francisco city official slain because of his homosexuality.

Hef also helped finance *The Celluloid Closet* (1995), narrated by Lily Tomlin, who lined up on-camera interviews with Tony Curtis, Shirley MacLaine, Tom Hanks, Susan Sarandon, and others. Movie clips were sandwiched between interviews showing how Hollywood had to mask homosexuality because of the draconian Production Code in effect since the 1930s.

Later, in the mid-1990s, Hef also backed *Heart of the Matter*, a documentary that followed an African woman's struggle with AIDS.

Hef was such a believer in freedom of expression that he even provided legal fees to defend protesters against *Playboy's* policy of exploitation of women through its publication of nude centerfolds. At Grinnell College in Iowa, students, male and female, had stripped nude to protest *Playboy's* alleged exploitation of women, leading to their arrests on charges of indecent exposure. Hef's attorneys successfully defended their right of protest. In fact, one of the shapely female protesters later agreed to pose for a nude centerfold herself, forgetting her former objections against *Playboy's* policy.

Grants from the Playboy Foundation also went to groups campaigning for a woman's right to an abortion. Hef was horrified to learn of the case of Shirley Wheeler in Florida, who was convicted on a manslaughter charge for aborting her child. Hiring lawyers, he battled her sentencing, which he called "a sadistic act of vindictive moralism."

He also provided seed money to help launch NORML, a group dedicated to those "unjustly" sentenced for smoking marijuana. He was told that half a million Americans, mostly young men, had been arrested and sometimes sent to prison for possession of weed. "These guys are rotting in jail, often just for smoking a joint," he said. Starting with a modest grant of only $5,000, Hef increased his underwriting of that group in 1971 to $100,000 annually.

*[Although in the beginning, Hef had banned the use of marijuana at his parties in the Playboy Mansion, but over the years, he modified that stance, claiming, "Marijuana increases sexual pleasure, I have discovered. A reefer spotlights the difference between just fucking or making love."]*

In an interview, Hef was asked to summarize exactly the stated goal of the Playboy Foundation: "It is to foster open communications about human sexuality, reproductive healthy and rights, protecting and fostering civil rights and civil liberties for all people, and protecting freedom of expression. In essence, the Foundation's aim is to pursue,

perpetuate, and promote the principals of freedom and democracy."

\*\*\*

When he wasn't watching movies, Hef was addicted to television, and he became a fan of the hit TV series, *I Spy*. Running from 1965 to 1968, it starred Robert Culp and Bill Cosby, who played U.S. intelligence agents. Assigned the task of chasing villains, spies, and beautiful women, they traveled undercover as globe-trotting "tennis bums."

What had initially impressed Hef about *I Spy* was that it was the first major TV drama to star a black actor (Cosby) in a leading role.

The series was also a trailblazer in its use of locations, as the cast and crew flew to such film sites as Venice, Morocco, and Hong Kong. Obviously, the writers were inspired by the James Bond espionage movies.

Hef arranged for his assistant, Bobbie Arnstein, to invite Culp and Cosby to a lavish party at the Playboy Mansion. For Culp and Hef, it became a "bromance," long before that word came into general usage. Cosby, too, became a regular visitor after that initial invitation, though he never developed the close bond shared between Culp and Hef.

Playing detectives disguised as tennis players, Bill Cosby (left) and Robert Culp were the stars of one of Hef's favorite TV series, *I Spy.*

Cosby began a somewhat formal acquaintance with Hef that would stretch over decades and involve several return visits to the Playboy Mansion and ultimately, dozens of allegations of rape.

Culp, on the other hand, became a more intimate friend of Hef's, getting involved in escapades in his sex life.

During the course of his life, Culp would marry five times. When Hef met him, he was the father of three sons and one daughter, all born in the early 1960s. But he was hardly a faithful husband. On his first chat alone with Hef, it was arranged that there would be future invitations for the sharing of Bunnies on Hef's round bed. Culp seemed to have no objection to seducing women in front of Hef, and actually seemed to look forward to it.

Throughout the years to come, Hef, with Culp, indulged in a number of self-styled "fuck-a-thons," with two or three Bunnies at a time.

One of the most notable of these seductions was a *ménage à trois* among Hef, Culp, and the African American singer, Eartha Kitt. She was cast as a drug-addicted singer in one of the episodes for *I Spy*. Entitled "The Loser," its script was written by Culp himself, and it won an Emmy for Kitt that year as the most outstanding single performance by an actress in a leading role in a drama.

A CIA dossier, later made public, characterized Kitt as a "sadistic sex nymphomaniac, rude, crude, shrewd, difficult." She was known for involvement in affairs with partners who included film producer/director Orson Welles and Porfirio Rubirosa, the Dominican playboy known for his huge endowment and marriages to two of the world's richest women, Barbara Hutton and Doris Duke.

"Rubi introduced this cotton-pickin' 'yallah gal from South Carolina' to the High Life," Kitt said. "Champagne, caviar, stylish parties, *haute couture,* and diamonds."

Two of Kitt's most significant lovers included James Dean and Arthur Loew, Jr., an heir to the cinema chain. Sometimes, however, those two young "objects of her affection" were in bed with one another.

In 1977, Kitt was in Key West, shooting *The Last Resort,* a film based on Darwin Porter's bestselling novel, *Butterflies in Heat.* At a party hosted by a wealthy Key West businessman Bill Johnson, she discussed her visit to the Playboy Mansion in Chicago: "Bob *[Culp]* and I had been having a little fling, and I was eager to meet Hefner. Actually, my aim was to be booked for singing engagements in some of the Playboy Clubs. I knew that Hefner was a key player in promoting black entertainers, and, frankly, I wanted to get in on the action."

"By midnight, things were getting out of hand, and I sensed all three of us were heading for his notorious round bed for a sleepover. Well, it wasn't exactly a snooze. We didn't get much sleep that night."

"Hefner never lured me into doing a nude centerfold," Kitt said. "However, I agreed to put on a bikini for the editors of *Jet* magazine. The staff there posed me with two other beauties, Freda Paine and Jayne Kennedy. We were chosen as the three most beautiful black women in the world."

Kitt summed up her own life in six words: "Rejected, Ejected. Dejected. Used. Accused. Abused."

\*\*\*

Both Robert Culp and Bill Cosby, especially Culp, popped up, on and off, in Hef's life during the decades to come.

After *I Spy,* Culp went on to appear in both feature films and TV, giving hundreds of performances as part of a career that spanned fifty years.

Of all of Culp's movies, Hef preferred *Bob & Carol & Ted & Alice* (1969), a glossy look at sexual choices and lifestyles of that era. Rightly or wrongly, Hef felt that the inspiration for the movie's "sexually liberated" plot [*it revolved around two married couples swinging in the same bed together*] was a direct offshoot of the experiences Culp had shared with him at the Playboy Mansion.

From *I Spy,* Cosby went on to star in his own TV sitcom, *The Bill Cosby Show,* from 1969 to 1971. But it was in the 1980s that he achieved his greatest fame, producing and starring in the TV sitcom *The Cosby Show.* Airing from 1984 to 1992, it was eventually rated the Number One TV show in the U.S. for five years.

Hef selected Cosby in 1970 to join a panel of judges in the selection of the "Bunny of the Year," Gina Byrmas, an African-American beauty from Baltimore, who was voted the winner. In the aftermath of her designation, she was frequently photographed with Cosby.

On some occasions, Cosby turned up at unexpected times, as he did in December of 1968 in an episode on TV's *Playboy After Dark.* Hef spotted him as the cigar-smoking tambourine player in Sammy Davis, Jr.'s backup band. Later that same evening, Davis' lovely rendition of "The More I See You" was interrupted when "two cut-ups," Peter Lawford and Jerry Lewis, came out to ruin the singer's act.

In April of 1977, both Culp and Cosby starred in ABC's televised *Playboy's Playmate Party.* "Cosby always dug our Bunnies," Hef quipped, "and not just their bushy tails, although he appreciated those, too."

Beginning in 1982, Cosby was designated as host of the Playboy Jazz Festival, a gig he would retain for thirty-one years.

"So far as it is known, Cosby never had to drug a Bunny to go to bed with him," Victor Lownes said. "Most of them went willingly. Of course, he was a hell of a lot better looking then. He aged badly. I mean REAL badly."

Cosby and Culp were also near the top of the guest list when Hef threw a lavish reception at the Playboy Mansion in Los Angeles to celebrate Hefner's marriage (his second) to Kimberley Conrad in July of 1989.

*[Bill Cosby, a once-beloved actor, sullied his reputation when some sixty women lodged numerous complaints against him, accusing him of giving them drugs before sexually assaulting them. These charges, which covered decades, erupted into the public eye in 2014, but the statute of limitations prevented nearly all of them from going to court. However, there was one that fell within the chronological limits of the law. On April 26, 2018, Cosby was found guilty on three counts of aggravated indecent assault.]*

\*\*\*

Although Hef had already fired Victor Lownes, the two men remained friends, and he was still remotely involved in the operation of the New York Playboy Club. They spoke frequently on the phone, as Hef remained in Chicago, appearing only rarely in New York.

Lownes never admitted he'd been fired, claiming, "I took a sabbatical from *Playboy,* and especially from Keith Hefner. We weren't brothers, but you might say that I shared a sibling rivalry with Hef's kid brother."

Late in 1963, Hef decided the time had come to open a Playboy Club in London. Of all the available candidates, Lownes seemed the idea choice to scout for a location, as he had done in Manhattan.

As the epicenter of the "Swinging Sixties," London was a hot destination, attracting high rollers, from the Middle East. At the time, oil-rich Arab sheiks were flooding in, many of them in search of business deals, upscale consumer goods, *laissez-faire* morality, and blondes.

Lownes flew into London just as the city was celebrating its Christmas season. He read in *The Times* of London that at least 1,500 casinos, most of them quite small, were open. Hef was not a gambler himself, calling it "a sucker's game, attracting rich men with more money than sense."

"I phoned Hef and told him that hawking Bunny Tail was one thing, but the big pounds were to be made in gambling. It took about an hour, but I talked him into it. He greenlighted my ambitious plan, dreaming of heaps of pounds being shipped from England."

Lownes' search for a suitable building took six months. In the meantime, he enjoyed the London scene, and he rented a fashionable residence on Montpelier Square, where he began to host "the hottest parties in town."

He invited local celebrities and those visiting from America to his lavish gatherings. Slim models and actors who included Peter O'Toole and Peter Sellers dominated the scene, and the Beatles showed up on several occasions. Lownes could be seen chatting with John Lennon and Ringo Starr.

"I went after the Birds (young women) by the flock," Lownes said. "To my parties I invited the world's most adventurous ladykillers—where is Errol Flynn now that I need him?—and matinee idols such as Louis Jourdan visiting from Paris, where he had been voted 'the world's handsomest man.'"

Guests at his residence agreed on one thing: Lownes added a high-octane swing to Swinging London. That sentiment was echoed by Roman Polanski and his wife, Sharon Tate (whom Lownes secretly bedded), along with a slightly drunk Judy Garland, who was also lured into his bedroom. "Two fellow horndogs, Warren Beatty and Michael Caine, loved my parties," Lownes claimed.

He agreed with *Time* magazine's assessment of the city: "London has burst into bloom. It swings. It is the scene. The city has switched on ancient elegance with a new opulence, all tangled up in a dazzling blur of op and pop. London is alive with Birds and the Beatles, battling with minicars, miniskirts, and telly stars."

In a manner entirely befitting a *Playboy* emissary, Lownes had a different woman every night. One weekend it was a pair of beautiful twins, which one London tabloid defined as a "three-in-a-bed sex romp."

After rejecting many lesser contenders, he finally acquired a suitable building at 45 Park Lane) as the site of London's Playboy Club & Casino. Designed by Walter Gropius, an internationally renowned master of modernist architecture, it rose seven floors overlooking Hyde Park between The Dorchester and the London Hilton on Park Lane. Hef agreed that it was the right choice and signed a 63-year-lease at £80,000 annually.

*[He later regretted the decision to lease when he could have purchased the entire building for a million pounds. By the 1980s, London realtors told him it was worth at least forty million pounds, perhaps a lot more.]*

To the London Club, Lownes added an innovative touch. He taught and trained Bunnies as *croupiéres,* and insisted that most of them be blonde, either bleached or natural, as a means of catering to what he perceived as a then-prevalent preference of the clientele he wanted from the floods of oil-rich third-world moguls in London at the time.

*[In time, however, British gambling authorities demanded that the Bunnies wear some sort of cover-all bib so as not to unfairly distract the gamblers who might be concentrating more on décolletage than on the money they might be losing.]*

As a nod to the rules that influenced the staff within other Playboy Clubs, Bunnies were forbidden to date the customers, but with one exception. That exception, of course, was Lownes himself. "I plan to bed each and every one of them," he asserted. "Maybe two at a time."

He planned, however, to dismiss any Bunny who gained weight or started looking "wilted." Usually, by the time a Bunny reached her 28th birthday, Lownes considered her wilted. "Men like young flesh, not mothers," he said.

At long last, opening night came, and Hef was flying to London from Chicago to attend the gala event.

\*\*\*

Disembarking from his airplane on British soil, Hef was soon to discover a city that *Time* magazine likened in many ways "to the cheerful, violent, lusty town of William Shakespeare."

He was immediately sucked up into the scene on his second trip ever to Europe. Three dozen Bunnies showed up at the airport to welcome the man who by now was hailed as "The King of the Bunnies." His detractors referred to him as being "horny as a jackrabbit."

Young girls paraded along King's Road in Mary Quant miniskirts. And there seemed to be action around every corner, with thriving sales—especially on boutique-lined Carnaby Street—of the latest hip fashions. Young men strolled along in haircuts inspired by Vidal Sassoon.

Hef wanted to be a part of the scene, although he felt a bit old for it. Aware that he needed to get into better shape, physically, he flushed his Dexies down the toilet. "I went cold turkey," he said.

His first daytime outing involved a visit Savile Row, the centerpiece of men's fashion, to order chic, custom-made Edwardian suits. "I planned to be a Casanova-style fop."

Driven by young and nubile Londoners, a Renaissance in art, music, and fashion was unfolding before Hef's eyes. Key elements of the Swinging London scene included the Beatles and the Rolling Stones.

Model Jean Shrimpton and Twiggy posed in the latest fashions, and stars like Terence Stamp appeared in a new wave of movies demonstrating freedom of expression, as did stage plays, plus films that included *Darling* (1965) and Michelangelo Antonioni's *Blowup* (1966), which played to packed movie houses.

David Bailey, to some degree, became almost the official photographer of the icons and legends of that era. His subjects included John Lennon, Mick Jagger, and Michael Caine. The Union Jack became the symbol for the new movement.

London's Playboy Club opened on June 28, 1966, as some 1,500 cele-

Motivated by the fame he generated during his widely publicized trip to Europe in 1966, *Time* magazine featured a bizarrely disjointed image of Hefner on the cover of its edition of March 3, 1967.

In it, they headlined his role in what they defined as "The Pursuit of Pleasure."

Hef was now one of the most famous celebrities and trendsetters in the world, and to many sexual conservatives, one of the most dangerous.

brated guests—the men wearing black tie, and many of the women in *haute couture*—showed up for the event. TV cameras were on hand to record the event.

Lownes said, "Hef was in his glory. He still gets excited by stars as much as the man in the street."

The "Bond Girl," Ursula Andress, turned up, as did the British ballerina, Dame Margot Fonteyn with her dancing partner, Rudolph Nureyev. London resident Lee Radziwill, Jacqueline Kennedy's sister, was among the honored guests, as were Rex Harrison, Ringo Starr, the Earl of Suffolk, Woody Allen, Julie Christie, Vanessa Redgrave, Jean-Paul Belmondo, James Garner, Lee Marvin, and the Marquis and Marchioness of Tavistock. Sidney Poitier was there, too, talking to Sean Connery, and Henry Luce III chatted with Peter Lawford. Seated at a piano, Bobby Short provided musical entertainment.

Also on hand to greet Hef were British actors Peter Sellers and Laurence Harvey, film director Roman Polanski, and Grand Prix racer Stirling Moss.

Keith Hefner said, "Our club became a mecca for the hip. Many movies were being shot in London, and the stars came to our club to unwind. It was the place to be in 1966."

Not all of the entertainers present were mop-topped pop stars. "We also had elegant ladies like Mable Mercer," Keith said.

Profits at the end of the first year exceeded more than a million U.S dollars, a good return on an initial investment of $1.5 million.

As they celebrated their success, neither Hef nor Lownes was aware of the trouble and heartbreak that lay ahead.

# Chapter Eight

# HEF'S PLAYBOY CLUBS MULTIPLY & THRIVE
## AS AMERICAN HORNDOGS CATCH
# BUNNY FEVER

## HEF AS 007: HE PERSUADES THE BOND GIRL TO POSE AS A SEMI-NAKED CENTERFOLD, LATER CITING IT AS ONE OF HIS GREATEST ACCOMPLISHMENTS

## HEF DEVELOPS THE PLAYBOY INTERVIEW CONFIGURING IT AS A STANDARD FIXTURE IN THE CULTURE WARS OF THE 1960S

# HIS BATTLES WITH "IRRATIONAL CHICKS"
# "I AM NOT A MALE CHAUVINIST PIG."

## IN A MOVE CONSIDERED DARING AT THE TIME, HEF INTEGRATES HIS PLAYMATES OF THE MONTH
## "BLACK IS BEAUTIFUL. SO ARE 'CHINA DOLLS.'"

| | |
|---|---|
| Ursula Andress, the Swiss-born cover girl for November 1965. Her "faux" tattoo reads "James Bond's Girls." | In this iconic scene from the James Bond thriller, *Dr. No,* (1962), Ursula Andress—like a primeaval goddess—rose "magically" from the sea, accessorized only with a knife and a white bikini. It became one of the most famous garments in the history of fashion. |

**In the 1960s, as head of Playboy Enterprises**, Hef set out to create a cross-country network of Playboy Clubs, offering scantily clad Bunnies serving good food and drink in elegant, sophisticated settings. Hef told the press, "We're not a strip club, but a deluxe night club with excellent entertainment, often from major stars, all featured in a soothing atmosphere for the devotee of the *Playboy* lifestyle."

"Most of our customers treated our Bunnies with respect," said Victor Lownes, "Unless, of course, they had too much booze. If a man must drool over our Bunnies, let him mop it up with a silk handkerchief."

In his rush to establish other clubs, it was inevitable that Hef would turn his gaze toward the West. There, in the clichés of previous generations and old movies, ranch hands and old coots like "Gabby" Hayes or Hopalong Cassidy would drink too much at a street-level saloon, then head for the ladies on the second floor for "saddle relief."

That kind of raunchy rusticity was not visible in Hef's clubs. He went to great lengths to "outlaw" prostitution, demanding "a safe, clean fantasyland for keyholders." This concept for his clubs lasted throughout the 1960s and into the early 1970s. At their peak, Playboy keyholders numbered more than a million.

The Playboy Clubs of the 1960s still remain the most successful night clubs in history, before jazz clubs gave way to the rock 'n roll era.

Titty bars, burlesque houses, and joints showing "blue movies" in the backrooms, even scantily clad waitresses, had existed before the advent of the Playboy Clubs.

As one reporter claimed, "Along comes Hugh Hefner, who took the sex club out of the gutter and made it respectable. It became okay for the guy next door to have the hots for the girl next door. Since he couldn't ask her out, he could always go to the local drugstore and gaze upon a nude centerfold in *Playboy*."

Or he could go to a Playboy Club and check out the *décolletage*. Many men diverted their eyes to that small skimpy little bit of satin covering the crotch of a Bunny. The most frequently asked question from keyholders was, "Do they shave? How else do they hide the hair down there?"

After opening clubs in Chicago, Miami, New Orleans, and New York, Hef granted franchises for clubs in St. Louis (a city that had always promoted itself as the "crossroads of America) and Phoenix in 1962.

Robert Goddard, columnist for the *St. Louis Globe Democrat*, reviewed the opening of the club in his city at 3914 Lindell Boulevard: "Hugh Hefner's multi-level Playboy Club is 'Early Fabulous,'" he wrote, "with its

Japanese garden and bubbling fountain. I don't like to use the word classy, any more than I can help, but let's face it. The club in St. Louis is class with a Capital C. Its unusual feature is a suspended balcony seating a dozen customers hanging out over the bar."

In St. Louis, the club had the usual *Playboy* features, including a Playmate Bar with pictures of centerfolds on the walls and a Cartoon Corner.

Many of the Bunnies here actually had husbands who were babysitting for otherwise unsupervised children at home. Bunny Sheilah Foster said, "I brought home the bacon."

Another Bunny, Gwenn Markham, said, "We got used to entertaining horny conventioneers and out-of-town salesmen. Mostly, we got middle-aged men bored with their wives. I met the famous Victor Lownes one night when he popped up in St. Louis. He invited me to his hotel suite when I got off from work, an invitation I declined."

The club in Phoenix became a mecca for the Playboys of Arizona. Located in the Mayer Central Building, the club became a chic rendezvous, especially its Penthouse and Library, each of them an entertainment venue. Some of the best food and drink were served here by "succulent Southwest Bunnies," in the words of one reporter.

Dick Lord, a former drummer who became a stand-up comic, said, "Many an up-and-coming entertainer got their start in these early Playboy

High-cut in the legs, and low-cut in the bazooms, with a fluffy cottontail that moved alluringly across whatever Playboy Club they graced, "The Bunny Costume" became an iconic symbol forever associated with standards of female beauty and bounty in the latter half of "The American Century."

Clubs. Lonnie Short, Jerry Van Dyke, and I called it 'working the trenches,' hoping to go on for appearances in New York and Chicago. It was like paying your dues as you hoped to rise through the ranks until you hit the big time. Often, we had to do two, three, or four shows a night, depending on the house count."

\*\*\*

The state of Michigan is still filled with relics of mostly forgotten *Playboy* Enterprises. In 1963, on East Jefferson Street in Detroit, a Playboy Club opened, replacing the once popular Stockholm Restaurant.

It stood directly across the street from Christ Church. On Sunday morning, as parishioners began to arrive, the club was still partying. It drew some of the best jazz musicians in the country, and such celebrity singers as Tony Bennett.

Even though the Detroit Club failed and had to shut down in 1974, a second Playboy Club opened in 1974 along the Lodge Freeway, an eight-mile drive north of Detroit's center. It had been owned by Ivan Boesky, who made national headlines when he went to prison for insider trading in the 1980s. That club lasted until 1978.

Hef, it seemed, couldn't give up on Michigan, and in 1982, yet another club opened in Lansing in the Hilton Hotel. When it eventually closed in 1988, it was the last remaining Playboy Club in America.

\*\*\*

In the era when Playboy Clubs were flourishing (1964), Hef approved a massive expansion, both domestic and foreign. A club was launched in the Philippines, another in Los Angeles, a premises that would include a penthouse apartment for his own private use.

The Baltimore Playboy Club flourished from 1964 until it drew its last breath in 1977. Star performers included such African American entertainers as Flip Wilson and Richard Pryor. Bunny

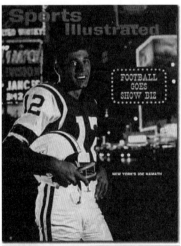

One of the most famous athletes in football history, "Broadway Joe Namath" appeared on the July 19, 1965 cover of *Sports Illustrated* with the banner headline "Football Goes Show Biz."

Namath was a regular and very popular client at the hippest and most sought-after chain of nightspots in the world, the Playboy Clubs.

Frieda Merkel remembered Wilson begging the manager to give him a cash advance because he couldn't pay his hotel bill. "I saw Pryor in the kitchen crying because his act didn't go over."

Jets quarterback Joe Namath, then at the height of his fame, arrived wearing a white mink coat featured in magazine ads. A drunken Robert Mitchum showed up, too, bumping into an older woman on the staircase. She apologized, "for shaking you up."

"Madame," he told her, grabbing his crotch. "You can shake anything of mine you want."

Sharon Bernstein Peyton was a Bunny cocktail waitress during the "Mad Men" era of the three-martini lunch. She remembered serving leading sports figures, an occasional movie star, and the local politicos.

"One time, Hefner showed up in Baltimore, flying in on his Bunny plane," she said. "I tried to talk to him, but he was very shy. Engaging him in conversation was like pulling teeth."

During his visit, about 150 women showed up to picket the club, conveying the familiar slogan about exploitation of women.

That protest surprised Hef, since his club was only blocks away from a notorious night spot, "The Block," where strippers like Blaze Starr showed everything. "The Block" also contained darkened booths where the waitresses fellated men who shelled out fifty bucks.

The *Baltimore Sun* covered the protests in front of that city's Playboy Club. "How could a city like ours be corrupted by about fifteen young ladies encased in their tight satin corsets? In contrast to some other clubs in Baltimore, the Bunnies aren't even allowed to sit down with the paying customers."

\*\*\*

Initially, the Kansas City Playboy Club was packed every night, mostly with local politicos and businessmen, and prosperous farmers in town to make deals for their summer crops.

Bunny Eileen Benton said, "We had other items on the menu, but nearly all of my customers ordered steaks: The pay was good, enough to support me and my two kids. Hubby had bolted. Mother warned me not to tell any of her friends where I worked."

"Hefner showed up one night to inspect the club and surveyed the Bunnies," she said. "He looked me over but passed me by. I guess he didn't consider me Playmate material."

\*\*\*

As a relatively prosperous state, Ohio was filled with businessmen, and after some research, Hef decided that Cincinnati was a potentially profitable location for one of his clubs.

Betty Greene worked there as a Bunny, and she recalled that the club attracted would-be playboys from all over the state, including Toledo, Akron, and Cleveland. "My fellow Bunnies came from all walks of life. One beautiful blonde girl—bleached, that is—turned out to be a prostitute but was eventually found out and fired."

"The pay was good, and I needed it since I was paying my husband's way through dental school. Alas, when he became a dentist, he dumped me for another woman."

"Not only that, but at the age of 29, I was fired," she said. "Too old, they told me. I got a job working as a waitress at a roadside diner. What a comedown. I got more passes from the truck drivers who patronized the diner than I did from the keyholders at the Playboy Club. At least the truckers didn't consider a 30-year-old woman too old."

\*\*\*

In a surprise move, Playboy Enterprises went international, invading the Philippines by granting a Playboy Club franchise to the owner of an existing club in Manila. Hef referred to it as "our first international Bunny hop."

Positioned in the penthouse of the E.I. Katigbak Building, the club offered a panoramic view of Manila Bay. Small private rooms were rented for parties or business meetings. But months later, Hef learned that these rooms were often venues for prostitution. Although that had been expressly forbidden in the club's franchise agreement, Hef was too far away to control what was going on.

The club became known for its beautiful "Asian Dolls," many of them imported from Japan and China.

Unique in the history of Playboy Clubs, the Manila branch also made beautiful young boys available to men who wanted more variety in their lives. Some of these young men performed in drag before disappearing later into the night, most often with customers.

\*\*\*

For New Year's Eve, 1964, the Los Angeles Playboy Club opened to spectacular newspaper and television coverage. It was a celebrity-studded night, evocative of a movie premiere. Fans waited outside to see who would emerge from limousines.

Stars that evening included Milton Berle, a long-standing devotee of Playboy Enterprises. Hef's longtime friend and Bunny lover, Hugh O'Brian, attended, as did Julie Newmar, famous, among other roles, for her role as Catwoman in two seasons (1966-67) of the TV series Batman.

Stars included Don Murray [known for his starring role alongside Marilyn Monroe in Bus Stop (1956)]. Shirley Jones, [noted for her starring roles in Oklahoma (1955) and Carousel (1956), the last of Hollywood's "musical sweethearts"] also made an appearance.

Once they were inside the club, many customers gravitated to the Penthouse. A cabaret-style venue with a panoramic view of Los Angeles by night, it soon became a desirable venue for top-rate performers.

In addition to the West Coast offices of Playboy, the ten-story building also housed a 200-room hotel, with private quarters where Hef "auditioned" Bunnies and other hopefuls, many from western states such as Colorado and Montana, a swimming pool, and a shopping arcade.

Such big names as Bob Hope and Johnny Carson were seen dining here during the weeks to come. Always prospecting for Bunnies, they were frequent patrons of other Playboy Clubs, too, especially those in Chicago, New York, and Miami.

Bunny Gloria Harris said, "On rare occasions, Hefner dropped in to check on the business. He didn't show up unless it was a press conference or some big event. Our food was very good, but when he stayed for dinner, he always brought his own chef to prepare his meal."

Actor Bob Forrest reported what he saw on his one visit to the club: "It was late at night and a drunken Shelley Winters had come into the club with two young men. As the night wore on, both of these guys crawled under the table and presumably performed cunnilingus on her. That Shelley!"

A reporter from the New York Daily News, on a trip to Los Angeles at the time, visited to see how the club stacked up against the one in Manhattan. "A lot of middle-aged men were there, each trying to prove he was as hip as Hugh Hefner."

By 1972, the club had relocated to the ABC Entertainment Center in Century City, under the Shubert Theater. In reviewing the new location, a reporter for Variety didn't give the entertainment even one star. "The shows I saw evoked that 'Springtime for Hitler' look."

He was referencing the legendary production number of Mel Brooks' film, The Producers (1968).

Faced with stiff competition in the entertainment center of the world, the club eventually went belly-up. "There was no one around to record its passing," said a nearby restaurant owner. "No one cared at this point. *Playboy* Bunnies were a tired joke by the 1980s. I visited the club on its final week. Only four tables were occupied in the VIP Room."

In an ironic touch, in the 1990s, the site once occupied by the Playboy Club became a lesbian bar named "She," a symbol of changing times.

\*\*\*

Right after the launch of the Los Angeles Playboy Club, Hef flew to the north coast of Jamaica for the opening of the first Playboy Resort hotel, a new type of venture (and adventure) for him.

Originally, he had been "turned on" to the site by his friend, an occasional contributor to *Playboy*, Ian Fleming, the creator of the James Bond character. Fleming maintained a vacation home in Jamaica, and told Hef that the north

News of Hefner's expansion into Jamaica caused news flashes and ripples throughout the tourism industry, and—as was their wont—the Jamaica Tourist Board snapped immediately to attention.

Taken at Dunn's River Falls, a popular day trip organized from Ocho Rios' "Bunny Bay," as the locale was named during Playboy's heyday in the region, the photos above are elements from the ad campaigns which Playboy commissioned to publicize Jamaica and its romantic potential to jackrabbits and their mates. .

coast of that island nation would be ideal for a resort.

Fleming died in August of 1964 and never got to attend the opening of the resort he had envisioned for Hef.

Built for a cost of $7 million, the Jamaica Ocho Rios Playboy Hotel had 204 guest rooms with sunken Grecian baths. It was set on ten lush acres fronting a white, sandy beach. Bunny lifeguards watched over the guests at the Olympic-sized swimming pool, the largest in the Caribbean at the time. Other resort features included an 18-hole golf course, limbo dancing on the poolside patio, champagne brunches, and Jamaican calypso bands performing at night in a showroom that seated 400 guests.

The multi-racial roster of on-site Bunnies was an added attraction. Since the climate was too hot for the typical satin "Bunny uniform," the women at the Jamaican resort wore specially designed bikinis.

For those who wanted to explore the countryside, there were excursions to Dunn's River Falls and cruises in glass-bottomed boats. The adventure lover could be escorted on a crocodile hunt in waters near the mouth of the island's Black River.

\*\*\*

After Jamaica, Hef continued to open clubs, riding high on the popularity of his concept of a night club, even though times were beginning to change. Of all the city options, he selected locations in Boston, Atlanta, and San Francisco. "I'm sure those cities are filled with hare devotees,"

Although construction of the Playboy Club in Boston was delayed because of local opposition, the venues in Atlanta and San Francisco opened on schedule.

Drenched in suave 1960s chic, and located within the Dinkler Hotel on Luckie Street, the Atlanta Playboy Club premiered in March of 1965 as the 15th member of the international chain.

A winding staircase led from the hotel's elegant lobby to the club's main floor. Consistent with a theme that permeated the other Playboy Clubs, framed photos of former Playmates adorned the walls of the bar. Adjoining it was a bumper pool table where men could challenge a Bunny to a game. The customer often lost, since these Bunnies were skilled pool players, having played the game night after night.

A flight of stairs led to the Penthouse Show Room, which became known for its first-rate entertainers, including some of the best jazz artists in the South. Star acts included Dean Martin, George Catlin, Steve Allen, Sid Caesar, and Steve Martin. Mel Tormé and Tony Bennett entertained with their comedy and their music.

Once, an aging George Burns moved through the motions of his one-man act, but because he was losing his eyesight, he had to be escorted onto the stage by a Bunny.

The Atlanta Playboy Club was a big success throughout the 1960s, but as the 1970s swept in, customers migrated to other spots. After a fire swept through the building in 1975, it never reopened.

***

By the time the San Francisco club opened in 1965, Bunnies were no longer considered as *risquée* as they'd been. Only three blocks from the club was Big Al's, run by a man who resembled the gangster, Al Capone. For his customers, he featured a studly young man having sexual intercourse on stage with a beautiful blonde who tried to make herself look as much as possible like Marilyn Monroe.

When Hef heard this, he told his aides, "We'd better start looking for other towns less sophisticated than San Francisco—perhaps Buffalo, New York; Omaha, Nebraska; or Columbus, Ohio."

Because of the huge gay population in San Francisco, one of the franchise holders suggested that instead of female Bunnies, the club should hire male Bunnies wearing jockstraps with the Bunny logo on their pouch. Hef rejected such a suggestion. "It's against our image."

He visited the San Francisco club on several occasions. "The highlight for me was hearing my good friend, Tony Bennett, sing, 'I Left My Heart in San Francisco.'"

During his visits, he often seduced some of the Bunnies, showing a special interest in the women who'd come south from Canada. "The hottest little number, I recall, came from the cold dark winters of Alaska."

***

At long last, the Boston Playboy Club opened in 1966 on Park Square, having been delayed for three years because local authorities would not grant Hef a liquor license. One of the city fathers told the press, "The Playboy Bunny costume is a bit too *risqué* for Boston."

As in all the clubs, live entertainment was a permanent feature of the Penthouse, and as such, drew a chic clientele that included lots of visiting celebrities. They included Gloria Swanson when she was in Boston performing in a play.

A former Bunny, Shirley Howe, remembered the night Joe DiMaggio came in alone. "He caused quite a stir," said bartender Terry Bradley. "It

286

was strictly against the rules, but several Bunnies slipped the slugger their phone numbers. I guess they wanted to find out what had turned on Marilyn Monroe."

Occasionally, protesters—most of them women—picketed the club. However, a group of fraternity men arrived to protest the MIT inter-fraternity conference meeting at the Playboy Club, considering it "not an appropriate venue."

On several occasions, women's liberation groups arrived to protest, the president of one of the clubs claiming, "Hugh Hefner is turning young women into whores."

In 1969, the club in Boston made national headlines when both of the co-managers were fatally shot during a robbery attempt. Hef offered $10,000 to the person who fingered the killer. Finally, a 25-year-old man from Georgia was arrested. After a trial, he was sentenced to life in prison.

Boston Bunny Jean Hill said, "Many Bunnies in Boston considered ourselves feminists in spite of the liberation protests. Feminists were fighting for equal pay and equal opportunity. As a Bunny, I was making more money than my husband, my brother, and my father. Many Bunnies used their gig at the club as a stepping stone to another career, especially those women who wanted to break into show business."

Although the club was packed throughout the 1960s, during the 70s, patronage diminished year by year until, in 1977, the club shut its doors forever.

***

The only club to open in Canada was the Montréal Playboy Club, throwing open its doors in July of 1967. Since the location was within French-speaking Québec, Bunnies were required to speak both French and English. When Hef landed, he was treated like a superstar, facing the paparazzi from the moment he arrived at the airport.

*[A few months later, when Donald Trump flew in from New York, he didn't generate much publicity, as he was virtually unknown in Montréal at the time. One Bunny, Lauren Peterson, said, "Trump came into the club. It turned out he was chasing this model named Ivana, although she already had a boyfriend. But money talks. He got his woman."]*

"Our entertainment budget sucked because we were such a small, intimate club," Peterson said. "Our manager hired Bunnies who could also sing and dance, and often, they provided the entertainment unless we booked an occasional singer."

***

Since Playboy's resort in Jamaica had already opened and seemed to be running successfully, Hef conceived another resort closer to home. Instead of beach-goers in winter, this one on Lake Geneva in Wisconsin would attract skiers. He ordered the installation there of a chairlift, one of the first resorts in America to do so, and authorized construction of a landing strip for private airplanes, many of which would eventually fly in from Chicago.

Set on a 1,350-acre site, the resort lay only a 30-minute drive from the Playboy Club in Chicago. Built at a cost of $18 million, and opened in May of 1968, it featured two golf courses, a wildlife refuge, horseback

It was a more innocent age:

Though racy and much gossiped about at the time, many aspects of Playboy's Lake Geneva Resort seem vintage-tame by today's standards—especially the note (*Come and get it all!*) that a complete dinner and show (*Live music! Girls! Steak!*) cost only $11.95.

During the frantic years of Hefner's accelerated expansion of *Playboy* into the tourism business, an armada of writers, graphic artists, and advertising executives labored day and night to promote its enterprises. The illustration on the right, conceived in 1968 by Larry Frederic, showed an idealized vision of Hef's year-round resort in Lake Geneva, Wisconsin.

On the left is a view of the *Playboy*-sponsored hot air balloon high above two of that destination's golf courses, THE BRUTE and THE BRIAR PATCH, whose inauguration featured an impressive array of golf pros, including Jack Nicklaus.

riding, both indoor and outdoor pools, and a 15-acre lake for fishermen.

Tony Randall flew in to host its opening night, and the resort booked entertainers who included Buddy Greco and Lorna Luft, the daughter of Judy Garland.

The Playmate Bar featured the Russ Long Trio, and the Showroom employed a 32-piece orchestra that provided dance music every night. Sam Distefano was the resident pianist.

The club was never picketed like its counterpart in Boston, but many right-wing local residents resented what some of them called "bringing decadence to our peaceful community."

\*\*\*

In 1971, Hef embarked on the greatest resort challenge of his life, with no idea that it would ultimately emerge as his biggest dud. On a scenic, wooded site near MacAfee, New

## Leave the canyons.

## Come to the Gorge.

Leave Manhattan's cold skyscrapers and sunless canyons behind. And escape to the Playboy Club-Hotel at Great Gorge.

You'll find yourself in a valley so unspoiled, even Mother Nature would be pleased. With trees and horseback trails, 27 holes of championship golf and tennis courts that blend right into the green landscape.

When the snows fall on our valley, we've got some of the best skiing in the East right outside our door. Plus great ice skating. And when

night comes, the whole valley comes alive. With famous entertainers on our Penthouse stage. Dancing. And the best food and drink from our smorgasbord of bars and restaurants.

The Playboy Club-Hotel at Great Gorge. Less than 60 miles from the canyons of Manhattan. But a world apart. For more information and reservations, see your travel agent or call, toll-free, 800-621-1116. In New York call (212) 565-3435. In New Jersey call (201) 827-6000.

**playboy club-hotel at GREAT GORGE - McAFEE, N.J.**

Long before gambling was legalized in Atlantic City, and perhaps because of Hef's belief that it might one day be legal throughout New Jersey, his massive investment in the Playboy Resort at Great Gorge, 75 miles northwest of New York City, was one of the most expensive flops in the history of tourism. It was a regrettable tale of mismanagement, misperception, and corruption.

Manhattanites, for whom the resort was intended, greeted its opening with a big collective yawn.

Depicted above are (top) a postcard displaying some of the staff members a playboy might meet, and an ad defining its allure to the traveling public.

Local legends cite the embarassment the resort faced when a nudist group, assuming that nudity would be acceptable at any resort associated with *Playboy*, wanted to stage its annual convention on the grounds here. Management, defining the place as a "family friendly" resort, had to turn them down.

Jersey, a 2 ½-hour drive northwest of Manhattan, he opened the Great Gorge Playboy Resort for a cost of $30 million. Staffed with, among others, 90 Bunnies culled mainly from New York and New Jersey, it boasted a whopping 600 rooms. Ann-Margret flew in as a featured entertainer for opening week.

Hef envisioned his resort as a lure in both summer and winter. It would require a sixty percent occupancy rate to break even, but it never met that quota. On many nights, the house count didn't exceed thirty percent.

There were many attractions, including lavish banquets in the Duke of York ballroom, catered gourmet picnics, and horseback rides. But the hordes of New Yorkers Hef had hoped for never showed up.

He later blamed the location and poor management. "In the end, we went bust. I decided no more money should be pumped into it. I called Great Gorge "the Money Trap.""

*\*\**

Even though Playboy Clubs were failing across the country, Hef responded to a group of Japanese entrepreneurs who flew to Chicago from Tokyo. After some intense negotiations, he agreed to grant them franchises to open a quartet of Playboy Clubs in Japan: Tokyo in 1976; Osaka in 1978; Nagoya in 1979; and Sapporo in 1980.

As a novelty for the black-haired men of Japan, club owners imported a bevy of blondes, mostly from Britain and America. Wearing regulation Bunny uniforms, they were trained in the conventional waitressing services provided in other clubs worldwide.

On the side, private rooms were staffed by geisha girls. Although Hef continued to outlaw prostitution, these geishas were discreetly made available by club managers "to cuddle" male clients in need of such attentions.

*\*\**

Beginning around 1980, most of the Playboy Clubs had closed across America. Nonetheless, from his headquarters, Hef entertained groups of government officials from The Bahamas. They proposed the construction and franchise of a Playboy Club in Nassau. Hef would put up no money, as they would build it, with the understanding that Hef would be granted a management contract.

He agreed to their terms.

When the Bahamian resort was finished, he appointed Val Lownes, Victor Lownes' son, to run it.

On opening night, Dionne Warwick was the featured entertainer. After that the government insisted that only Bahamian musicians be hired. Likewise, they demanded that the Bahamian resort's "Bunny Corps" be recruited from the ranks of local women.

Business flourished for a while, mainly from cruise ship passengers and from gambling junkies visiting from Florida.

Before the Playboy Clubs went out of business, Hef also managed to open a series of rather lackluster clubs in Des Moines, Denver, Buffalo, St. Petersburg, Columbus (Ohio), and Omaha.

As surprising as it sounds, Playboy Clubs would be reconfigured (some said "rebooted") in the 21st Century.

***

Stephen Byer, Hef's marketing director, claimed that he and the *Playboy* publisher often studied fifty transparencies, maybe a lot more, to determine which picture would become that month's centerfold. "In his search for perfection, Hef could detect the slightest flaw—horror of horrors, it should be a pimple."

Hef always cited Katharine Hepburn's policy when it came to blemishes: "When she ordered call girls to come to her home, she would send them back if she discovered the slightest blemish or discoloration on their flesh."

"Far more than a blemish, the one thing Hef never wanted was one of the Playmates to look like a slut," Byer said. "From my experience of knowing many Playmates, I concluded that they might appear like the innocent girl-next-door in the centerfold. In reality, they often drank, took dope, and fucked like rabbits."

One of the Playmates told him that she had aborted her baby. The child's father, she claimed, was a movie star and frequent visitor to the Playboy Mansion in Chicago.

Hef's standing direction to his editors and photographers was, "All Playboys deserved to have the perfect Playmate."

"Becoming a Playmate of the Month is a very natural thing for a pretty girl to do," said Lisa Baker, voted Playmate of the Year in 1967.

Feminists did not agree. Beginning in the 1960s and continuing into the 1970s, Hef and *Playboy* endured an endless array of denunciations in articles, on television, and often in anti-*Playboy* demonstrations.

Hef was accused of "objectifying women," and Playmates were seen as "dehumanized products of patriarchy."

Maria Elena Ruszek wrote that "The Playmate is nothing more than a pliable toy meant for straight male consumption and gratification."

At the 1968 Miss America pageant, a group of angry feminists tossed copies of *Playboy* into "a freedom trashcan."

The following year, Hef held a casting call for would-be Bunnies hoping for a job at the Chicago Playboy Club. Feminists infiltrated the Playboy Mansion and handed out leaflets to wannabe Bunnies: "Sister, know your enemy. Hefner has made us into lapdog female playthings to be sold on the open market like shaving lotion."

Hef denied that his magazine "put down" women, as so many had suggested. He asked, "Did Goya's nude portrait of the Duchess of Alba dehumanize her—or glorify her?"

Meeting with his art director, Art Paul, Hef conceived the idea of having eleven major artists transform the Playmate into fine art. For centuries in art, beginning in ancient times, the undraped female form had been the subject of painting and sculpture, an inspiration for Velázquez, Raphael, Vermeer, and Goya, among many others.

Several artists were eager to respond to Hef's request, notably Salvador Dalí, the *enfant terrible* of Surrealism. He depicted a languorous Playmate in a 20" by 30" watercolor.

Bronx-born Larry Rivers, a leading artist of American abstract expression, created a five-foot Plexiglass and metal Playmate.

Andy Warhol, the country's crown prince of Pop Art, came up with a three-foot silk screen, revealing a double Playmate torso. But her nudity, "to keep the police at bay," was only visible when the artwork was illuminated with ultra-violet light.

Hef did not read all the articles published every month in his magazine, but he always had time to obtain what he conceived as "the perfect centerfold."

He viewed as one of his greatest achievements getting "The Bond Girl," Ursula Andress, to pose for a centerfold that appeared in his magazine in June of 1963. He called her "a

Whereas the rare Italian-language poster displayed above is an ad for the 007 Ian Fleming derived film *License to Kill (1989)*, and despite that fact that other actors eventually starred in it, it borrowed the image that Sean Connery and Ursula Andress had immortalized together many years before in their iconic pairing in *Dr. No* (1962).

Such was the power of her white bikini.

creature of classic grace and sensual allure, the quintessence of all that is female, a true sex goddess."

After Andress's appearance with Sean Connery in *Dr. No* (1963), a critic claimed, "She is the most awesome piece of natural Swiss architecture since the Alps." Hef devoted twelve pages to her nude layout, the most extensive he'd ever devoted to a single model.

She was photographed exclusively for *Playboy* by John Derek, her husband, and the screen's former "pretty boy."

Andress told *Playboy* readers, "I am not opposed to nudity in films when it is used for a purpose and is done with a maximum of taste, style, and class."

When she starred in *What's New, Pussycat?* in 1965, Hef had a copy rushed to him in Chicago.

He always preferred Playmates with large busts like Andress. However, to his surprise, his own taste in women did not always parallel that of some of his readers, who found his selection of women "too busty."

A Philadelphia mechanic wrote in, "You can go too far with a good thing. You don't want a Playmate looking like a cow. Don't feature so many women with big jugs, not breasts." Another reader, a garage station owner from Hartford, had found Miss March of 1962 with her 39" bust "vulgar and disgusting." Another man, a deli owner in Brooklyn, called that same model an "udder disaster."

Max Eastman, a writer, sent a personal letter directly to Hef. "You're running nudes that are too full bosomed. Some of your recent Playmates give me the feeling I must cultivate my mother complex rather than my sense of beauty and adventure."

However, the majority of male readers were bust aficionados. A motel

Whereas the cover shots and photo layouts of Ursula Andress were relatively demure within *Playboy's* American edition, as dictated by company policy, their equivalents within *Playboy's* Italian edition were less restrained.

Above are replicas of the cover shots of Ursula Andress in *Playboy's* Italian Editions of (top) November 1975 and September 1981, released in Europe to *Ooooh-la-la* public acclaim.

293

owner in San Diego wanted to know which movie star had the largest bust, Jayne Mansfield, Jane Russell, or the late Marilyn Monroe.

Hef's answer was, "Neither. The honor goes to that former MGM songbird, Kathryn Grayson."

He had his own special point of view about breasts. "An infant baby boy begins his sex life by sucking his mother's breasts, a passion that most of us continue until the day we croak."

***

As *Playboy* left the 1960s and headed into the dawn of a new decade, anti-*Playboy* feminists were growing increasingly militant, and Hef had begun to feel their sting. Women seeking "liberation" were reading Betty Friedan's seminal book *The Feminine Mystique,* and some were even burning their bras. As Hef quipped, "Personally, I have always preferred women without bras."

He visited Grinnell College a private, co-educational, nonsectarian, liberal arts school in Iowa. A dozen or so students, both male and female, removed their clothes during the protests they staged at the event, greeting Hef completely nude. He was urged to join them in the removal of his own clothing, but he politely rejected their offer.

During his speech in one of the college's auditoriums he was frequently booed. "*Playboy* has come to the aid of women by decontaminating sex," he told the unruly students. "We are responsible for the non-girdle look, the miniskirt, and the bikini. My magazine is a celebration of sexuality, not an exploitation of women. Feminists should be grateful to us."

Later in the decade, Shelly Schlicker, a secretary working out of the *Playboy* offices in Chicago, intercepted and copied a memo that Hef had composed and sent to Spectorsky, one of his chief editors. She leaked copies of it to women's liberation groups, and it was widely reprinted in various publications.

"I want you to commission an article that will take female militants apart. I'm interested in the highly irrational, emotional, kookie trend feminism has taken. These chicks are our natural enemy. It is time to do battle with them, and I think we can do it in a devastating way. If you analyze it, you'll find that feminists are unalterably opposed to the romantic boy-girl society that *Playboy* promotes. It is up to us to do a really expert, personal demolition job on these bitches."

The free-lance article was eventually written by Morton Hunt and published under the headline, "Up Against the Wall, Male Chauvinist Pig!"

The memo inflamed and infuriated feminists. In response to their growing outcry, he agreed to appear on Dick Cavett's TV talk show. He later claimed, "The fucker set me up by having these Amazon warriors on to oppose me."

Among the women confronting him was the feminist activist, Brooklyn-born Susan Brownmiller, later known for her authorship, in 1975, of *Against Our Will: Men, Women, and Rape.* According to Brownmiller, "When Hugh Hefner comes out here with a cottontail attached to his rear, then we'll have equality."

After his lackluster defense of *Playboy* on *The Dick Cavett Show, Glamour* magazine published an attack on him entitled, "The Article I Wrote on Women that Playboy Would Not Publish," by Susan Braudy.

"Why can't a magazine written to titillate men present a full picture of real women to these big, brave men. Why must she be a fantasy figure so dehumanized as to be really desexed—hairs plucked, smells replaced, pores filled with makeup, smoothed to unthreatening blandness? Is the *Playboy* male so weak, so ultimately unable to cope with reality that the fantasy creature of his glossy *Playboy*-inspired reveries must be mechanized, passive, manipulable, and controllable."

Other magazines joined in the attack on *Playboy.* In *Life,* editors published a critique: "In Hefnerland, a woman is simply another aspect of the status-symbol mania that is stamped all over *Playboy.* She is no more or less important than the sleek sports car or the most expensive bottle of Scotch." *Cosmopolitan* also ganged up on Hef, falsely claiming that he viewed a young woman as "no more than an accessory for the well-heeled and well-dressed bachelor-at-large. She is discarded when she reaches twenty-five or before that, if she shows the slightest bit of intelligence."

"Even though Hef boasted how he liberated women, he never viewed them as having an intellect the equal of a man, much less (as) a person of superior intelligence," said Victor Lownes.

"I never met a woman who was my intellectual superior," Hef boasted to a reporter. The most stimulating people are men, not women. Women are stimulating in other ways,"

Gloria Steinem continued her assault on *Playboy,* at one point claiming, "A woman reading *Playboy* must feel a little bit like a Jew studying a Nazi manual."

Hef once admitted to a reporter that he liked young girls (but only those at least eighteen years old). "I prefer virgins who have not yet been broken in by a man. I picked good-looking girls because I get something very good out of their innocence and sweetness that exists at a tender age. Most of the girls I have gone out with have benefitted from me because I give them an identity. Often, they don't even know who they are. They are better off having enjoyed the pleasures of my round bed. Many go on to settle down with a fine young man and raise a family."

"I am very much the alpha male," he said, "the dominant partner in a relationship. I prefer very feminine women who are submissive, giving in to the desires of a man. An intelligent woman who tries to be superior to a man leaves me cold. No erection for her. I don't like female castrators."

Hef had his defenders among women, notably the prolific novelist, Joyce Carol Oates, who had published articles in *Playboy*. She once wrote, "My personal belief is that worship of youth, flesh, and beauty of a limited nature is typically American and is fairly innocuous. The anger by ardent feminists over *Playboy* and its hedonistic philosophy is possibly misdirected."

As regards the evaluation of his magazine by militant feminists, Hef announced, "If girls were the only motivation for purchasing a copy of *Playboy*, it wouldn't sell. People would buy sheer smut on the newsstand. We, on the other hand, are Taste City."

\*\*\*

The aesthetics associated with the beauties selected by Hef to reign as

Ironically, the first photos of an artfully undraped black woman appeared in the edition of March, 1965, behind a cover (by Vargas) that displayed the ultimate blonde, blue-eyed goddess.

The blonde was a replica of the Hollywood *ingénue*, Carol Lynley, that edition's centerfold, who showed off her *Baby Doll* good looks in an issue that also featured literature by Vladimir Nabokov and Calder Willingham.

The African-American model was Jennifer Jackson, whose alluring, doe-eyed likenesses were replicated on the left and right half *(center and right-hand photos above)* of a widely distributed *Playboy Playing Card*.

Playmates of the Month underwent significant changes in the late 1960s and 70s. For the first time, an African American woman became a Playmate, as did the first of what Hef called "A China Doll."

Hef broke through the color barrier in the March 1965 issue of *Playboy* based on his centerfold of a black beauty, Jennifer Jackson, who was said to like progressive jazz and "the joys of trying something new."

According to author Thomas Weyr, "Hefner was always blind to color bars, but he agonized over black sex. He understood the ambivalence in black communities about depicting their women for white delectation."

Hef said, "Black women were always viewed as sex objects and made welcome in a white man's bedroom—and not much good would be done for civil rights with that."

Jackson later stated her opinion of Hef: "Clearly, he was a glorified pimp, although I liked him personally, but he's still a pimp."

The most famous African American woman to appear as a Playmate (October 1968) was Barbara McNair, a singer and TV, film and theater actress. She became well known during her world tours with Nat King Cole. Shortly after posing for *Playboy,* she would make a series of films, none more notable than *They Call Me Mr. Tibbs* (1970) with Sidney Poitier.

*[In October of 1972, McNair was arrested on a charge of possession of heroin at the Playboy Club in New Jersey. Her husband, the Chicago businessman Rich Manzie, was later charged with the crime, and charges against her were dropped. On December 15, 1976, Manzie was murdered at their mansion in Las Vegas.*

*As time moved on for McNair, her life, to Hef's regret, took a downward turn. She filed for bankruptcy in 1987, declaring nearly half a million dollars worth of debt.]*

In October of 1969, Jean Bell became yet another African American Playmate of the Month. Hef claimed that "the eyes of Texas" were upon this popular model, a native of the Lone Star State. She told readers that she was a

Two views of music-theater star, Barbara McNair, the top photo dating from 1964.

Also a regular feature in JET magazine, McNair's appearance in *Playboy* helped solidify it as a venue for beautiful celebrities appearing in widely distributed and artfully undraped venues.

And it helped pay the bills, too.

"fanatic" about bowling, and that she'd actually considered becoming a professional bowler.

Hef broke down another racial barrier when he selected China Lee, a "China Doll," (his words) as Playmate of the Month for August 1964.

In his review of Hef's choice, critic Sheridan Prasso referred to the "Asian Mystique," and suggested that Hef had successfully tapped into a fantasy associated with "the exotic, indulging, decadent, sexual Orient." He went on to suggest that the tens of thousands of war brides brought home by returning Allied soldiers reinforced the allure of Asian women. In the magazine's description of the Playmate that month, it informed readers that China Lee always wore basic black and had a "wicked" softball pitch on the field.

CHINA LEE #32
Miss August 1964

CHINA DOLL

A street view of *Playboy's* first Asian-American playmate, designated as such in August 1964, Miss China Lee, as depicted on Playboy Trading Card #32.

Eventually, Ms. Lee developed such a fan base that Hef hired her to appear at the opening of more than a dozen Playboy Clubs. In 1967, she married Hef's favorite stand-up comic, Mort Sahl.

Another "China Doll," Gwen Wong, became Miss April of 1967. She was described as a "startling blend of six nationalities: Scottish, Spanish, Australian, Chinese, Filipino, and Irish. In *Playboy,* she was billed as "Spice from the Orient."

For the most part, the designation of African American and Chinese women as Playmates met with approval from *Playboy* readers, although in the beginning, Hef received letters of protest from very conservative readers, some of them from the South, for his inclusion of black women in the nude.

\*\*\*

In London in the early 1960s, Hef met with J. Paul Getty at an exclusive restaurant. The British-American industrialist, founder of the Getty Oil Company, had been named by *Fortune* as "the richest living American," and by the *Guinness Book of Records* as "the world's richest private citizen."

Whereas Hef showed up in a brown sports coat and a white turtleneck, the billionaire wore his usual conservative business attire: a black suit, white shirt, and black necktie. In spite of their differences, the two men bonded and almost unbelievably, Hef got Getty to agree to write a series of articles for *Playboy* about finance. One was entitled "The Vanishing American."

In 1965, Spectorsky gathered these articles and published them in book form, *How to Be Rich,* issued by the Playboy Press.

As surprising as it might seem, this oil-rich industrialist was impressed with Hef's business sense—especially in his launching of his string of Playboy Clubs. He called Hef in 1964 to discuss the possibility of a management contract and the re-designation of his Pierre Marques in Acapulco as a Playboy Resort.

The richest man in the world, oil tycoon J. Paul Getty, once considered a business venture with Hef.

It involved the transformation of a resort he owned in Acapulco into a venue managed by *Playboy*.

The deal fell through, but not before Getty told an aide, "Mr. Hefner and I have a great appreciation for the undraped female form, although personally, I find money more alluring."

Hef responded awkwardly, but with interest, in correspondence which read, "You may be assured that any of a great number of directions that might be mutually advantageous in a business alliance of the sort that has been suggested will be viewed with the greatest possible initial interest from this side."

However, shortly after Getty received this letter, the value of the oil tycoon's stock took a plunge, and he dropped the idea.

\*\*\*

The February 1965 issue of *Playboy* ran a candid interview with the Beatles, labeling them "England's mop-topped millionaire minstrels." Each of them admitted to being avid readers of *Playboy*.

John Lennon was asked if he thought the Playboy Club in London would go over, and he claimed he thought it would. "London is full of dirty old men," he said, "Enough to make the club a success. We Beatles are dirty young men."

George Harrison told interviewer Jean Sheppard, "Ringo and I are getting married to each other. But that's a thing you'd better keep a secret. Otherwise, people will think we're queers."

Lennon said, "If you say you're non-religious, people will assume you're against religion. We're not sure what we are, but we're more agnostic than atheist."

Ringo Starr claimed, "We used to get in the car, and I'd look at John and say, 'You're a bloody phenomenon,' and then laugh, 'cause it was only him.'"

Paul McCartney weighed in: "We'd be idiots to say it isn't a constant inspiration to be making a lot of money. It is to anyone. Why do business tycoons stay tycoons?"

A far more provocative interview was given by Lennon in 1980 at his exclusive Manhattan apartment in the Dakota complex, where he was living with his wife, Yoko Ono, and his young son, Sean. The reporter was ushered into the kitchen and told to wait for Lennon to appear.

When Lennon finally arrived, he was *au naturel*, "stark jaybird naked," as he called it. He sat down and placed his feet on a butcher block table, telling the interviewer that he was baking bread—hence the choice of the kitchen as the venue for their meeting.

The interview was long and wide-ranging. Ironically, it covered assassinations. Lennon asserted that all celebrities lived in fear of that. "I receive death threats from psychopaths."

He spoke about the assassinations of both Robert F. Kennedy and Martin Luther King, Jr., in 1968. "Who in hell cares who murdered a nigger?" Lennon asked. "In my opinion, I think James Earl Ray was framed."

He seemed deliberately trying to be as provocative as he could, knowing that *Playboy* would not print some of his more dangerous comments. At one point, he called Mick Jagger "a son of a bitch."

He revealed that Yoko Ono giving birth to their son, Sean, nearly cost her her life. "She was going through convulsions, almost death spasms. A doctor had given her the wrong blood transfusion. I called for the doctor, and he got there immediately. He told me he had always wanted to meet me and tried to shake my hand. 'I always enjoy your music,' he said."

"I started screaming, 'My wife's dying and you wanna talk about music?'"

With tongue-in-cheek, he sati-

Leading the British invasion, "The Fab Four," as the Beatles were called, admitted that they were horndogs when they arrived in America to wow their fans.

"No good-looking girl will be safe from us," John Lennon warned.

rized his image, depicting himself as a "housemother' while Ono was away tending to business. "I'm home baking bread and changing Sean's diapers."

He was spinning that yarn when Ono came into the apartment and picked up on their conversation. "Many men with good reason have penis envy. But men also have womb envy, regretting that they cannot give birth to a child. I feel that it is good for John to indulge in this yearning to be a woman."

He was asked why he had bolted from the Beatles: "When Rodgers worked with Hart and then worked with Hammerstein, do you think he should have stayed with one instead of working with the other? Should Dean Martin and Jerry Lewis have stayed together because I used to like them together?"

Ironically, that installment of the "Playboy Interview" would not hit the newsstands until the night of Lennon's assassination in 1981. He was shot by Mark David Chapman, a fat, bespectacled, baby-faced security guard, who worked at a condo beside Waikiki Beach in Hawaii.

It was later discovered that Lennon was at the top of this list of a number of celebrities that Chapman planned to assassinate. Hef was horrified when the list was published: Ronald Reagan, Jacqueline Onassis, Elizabeth Taylor, Hugh Hefner, Johnny Carson, David Bowie, and George C. Scott.

Shortly after that, the officers of Playboy Enterprises met with Hef and suggested he buy a $300,000 armor-plated limousine. Even with Chapman imprisoned, it was obvious that there were a lot of other psychopaths out there who might want to replicate the publicity that surrounded Chapman after he murdered Lennon.

Victor Lownes had flown in for that meeting. Of the several officers present, he was the only one who objected to spending money on the type of limousine used by presidents of the United States. "Hef doesn't need such a limo," he said. "Why does he need such protection? He never leaves his bedroom!"

*** 

Hef may be the only man in history who hired scantily clad "Bunnies" as flight attendants to serve food and drink aboard his custom-designed "Big Bunny," the Douglas DC-9 plane he purchased in 1967 for $4.5 million.

Of course, the jet had to be redesigned according to his desires, one of which was that the aircraft be painted midnight black with the Bunny Logo on its tail.

He hired two designers, both from Chicago, Gus W. Kostopulos and

Dan Czubak, to outfit the aircraft's interior. They relied heavily on deep orange carpets and sofas. "I want everything push-buttoned," Hef instructed them. Most of the attention focused on an intricately designed bedroom outfitted with all sorts of gadgets.

As he told Czubak, "I'll need everything for seduction. The only thing you don't need is the tool. I'll supply that." His bed was like no other, upholstered as it was in Himalayan goat leather and covered with a spread of Tasmanian opossum pelts.

Deep into the retooling of its interior, Hef came aboard to inspect, but didn't like how a section of the plane's interior was progressing. He called it "garish, stupid, and cheap," and ordered that it be ripped out and reconfigured for a cost of $500,000.

During the staffing of his new plane, he recruited technicians and pilots from Purdue Airlines in Lafayette, Indiana, and he personally selected its flight attendants from various Playboy Clubs. For the design of their Bunny costumes, he specified the use of black nylon with a "wet look" (his words).

When the components of his new aircraft had been installed and completed, Hef took an inaugural flight. A "Jet Bunny" greeted him at the entrance with a Jack Daniels and a Pepsi.

On this flight, guests were treated to oysters Rockefeller and lobster or a thick, juicy steak. A reporter from *Newsweek* called it, "The most mind-boggling display of sensual opulence ever assembled on a flying machine."

Hef, however, rejected all the fancy food and ordered his personal chef to make him fried chicken with gravy.

"I think the Big Bunny was the second best-equipped plane in America," Hef said. "Its only equal was Air Force One. I even had a disco for dancing, plus an Ampex 600 color video machine. We could see movies, even porno."

"I wanted a private plane since I hated to fly on commercial jets with strangers and all those crying babies. My plane could seat 39 passengers and sleep 15 (not counting the Bunnies in my bedroom. I quickly became the unofficial president of the Mile High Club." [*His reference, of course, was to those men and women who had experienced sexual intercourse aboard an aircraft in flight.*]

When word of this decadence reached the press, his enemies dubbed the Big Bunny "Satan's Chariot."

In July of 1971, Hef set out with girlfriend Barbi Benton on a world tour, stopping first in London. At Heathrow Airport, some 300 reporters, photographers, and the idle curious turned out to greet him, along with dozens of "Cottontails" from the London Playboy Club.

As part of his tour, he landed in Nairobi for a photographic safari, witnessing migrations of wild animals across the Serengeti Plain. He also journeyed to Tasmania, the birthplace of Errol Flynn.

Then it was on to Rabat, the capital of Morocco, where General Moahmed Oufkir, that country's interior minister, entertained him in his private palace, featuring a bevy of belly dancers from Egypt.

For the final leg of the tour, he visited some of Europe's most historic cities, including Rome, Venice, Málaga, and Munich.

In Paris, paparazzi recorded his entrance into the historic and exclusive symbol of France's *belle époque*, Maxim's. Earlier that day, he'd sent his valet, Jodie MacRae, to instruct the head chef at this deluxe restaurant to prepare his fried chicken. Hef's excuse was, "I was pretty horny for some home-cooked chicken."

*[The owners of Maxim's weren't insulted by this outrage. In fact, they tried to sell the landmark restaurant to him before the night ended.]*

Eight years would pass before he took another trip abroad. He told a reporter, "Places in themselves hold little interest for me. I could visit the most historic city like Rome or experience the glamour of Paris, but they would have no meaning for me unless I was with the woman I loved, however temporary that union might last."

\*\*\*

In 1963, Alex Haley had conducted an indepth interview with the controversial Malcolm X. In time, that extended interview emerged as a prelude to Haley's ghostwriting of *The Autobiography of Malcolm X. [The African American men had met before, in 1960, when Haley had written an article about the Nation of Islam for* Reader's Digest.]

At Malcolm's insistence, Haley met him in Harlem at a restaurant run by Black Muslims, who Malcolm predicted would one day seize control of the American government. His reason for not getting personal, he said, was his belief that a "white devil" like Hugh Hefner would never publish his heretical views in his magazine.

According to Malcolm X, "The all-white boys who read *Playboy* can't face the fact that

Malcolm X was the most controversial and revolutionary African American in the United States.

Despite resistance from his literary editors, who considered his work too inflammable for insertion in *Playboy*, Hefner accepted it and promoted it within his magazine.

we'll be wearing their wardrobes, living in their fancy apartments, and driving their sports cars. The only thing we won't take is their women, who are the color of paste. We have thousands upon thousands of our own black beauties. Black women are far more beautiful than any white bitch who ever walked the planet."

Haley submitted his uncensored version of the interview to Auguste Spectorsky, who rejected it. Haley then went directly to Hef, who accepted it, although warning that several of Malcolm's more "heinous" points of view would have to be edited out. "We'll leave in enough to enrage at least half of our fans. But I think *Playboy* readers should be aware of this growing threat. As you know, I want an integrated, interracial society. I don't want to see whites and blacks go into battle against each other."

Spec heavily edited the article and inserted a warning, defining the interview as a "damning self-indictment of one of the noxious facets of rampant racism."

Before his rise to power, Malcolm as a young man had been a dining car steward. He later claimed, "I would spit into the plates of food before serving the white devils. There was one fat capitalist pig who treated me like a slave when I served him. I jerked off in the toilet and inserted my semen into his mushroom soup."

Malcolm was fired from that position and became a bootlegger, pimp, and dope pusher before landing in prison in 1946 at the age of twenty. There, through contact with certain militant prisoners, he converted and became a member of the Nation of Islam, which advocated separation of black and white Americans. However, by 1964, he disavowed the Nation and embraced Sunni Muslims, a fatal decision on his part that would in time lead to his assassination.

In *Playboy's* interview, he charged that the white devil wanted to keep the black man always dependent on him for jobs, food, clothing, shelter, and education. He accused the Christian church for giving the world two heresies: fascism and communism.

He denounced Hef, claiming he had wanted the interview "just to exploit my views and sell more magazines. No white man, regardless of what they say, wants to see a black man advance. The white devil wants to keep us in bondage. Thoughtful white people fear us because they know they are inferior to black people. They realize in their hearts that we will rise up and rule the world one day. We will overthrow them and subject them to white slavery to pay for the sins of their fathers."

"The world of tomorrow will be black," Malcom claimed. "Black and righteous. In the white world, there has been nothing but slavery, suffering, lynching, colonialism, and the rape of our women with their tiny dicks. In the black world of tomorrow, there will be true freedom, justice, and equality for the black race. That day is coming sooner than the white devil thinks."

Malcolm X never lived to see the Armageddon he had forecast, or the extinction of "the white devils." In 1965, at a rally in the Audubon Ballroom in Washington Heights (Manhattan), he was gunned down by three members of the Nation of Islam.

*[Published in 1965, the year of his death,* The Autobiography of Malcolm X *has been a consistent bestseller. By 1977, it had sold six million copies. In 1998,* Time *ranked it as one of the ten most influential books of the 20th Century. More than a decade later, Haley would produce his own bestseller,* Roots: The Saga of an American Family.*]*

***

For his next major interview, Haley selected a radically different subject, one at the opposite political spectrum from Malcolm X. He somehow arranged an interview with George Lincoln Rockwell, the commander of the American Nazi party.

When Hef phoned Rockwell to ask if he'd sit for a Playboy Interview, the Nazi asked, "Is your reporter a Jew?"

Hef assured him that he was not, leaving out the fact that Haley was an African American. His editor (Spec) speculated that Hef's sending a black man to the Nazi headquarters "was a deliberate act of provocation on Hef's part. I suspected that Rockwell might chase him out of the Nazi headquarters with a gun."

As agreed, Haley drove to the American Nazi Party's headquarters in Arlington, Virginia. Across one of the upper stories of the building

George Lincoln Rockwell (center) the commander of the American Nazi Party, is flanked by two of his henchmen. Hef himself was considered radical at the time for covering the evils and dangers of Rockwell's propaganda in *Playboy*, an act that in some cases cost him some readership at the time.

Rockwell had called African Americans "the lowest scum of humanity," but was intrigued with the idea of a coalition.

"Nazis and Black Muslims can be allies, since both of us seek the same goal—separation of the races."

was a large sign: WHITE MAN FIGHT THE BLACK REVOLUTION.

A pair of armed security guards were posted beneath a portico to which were affixed a half-dozen Swastika flags. One of the guards seemed concerned with Haley's color, and phoned Rockwell with the information that his interviewer was black. Rockwell, nonetheless, agreed to follow through with the pre-arranged plan.

Haley was ushered into the building's large foyer, which was illuminated with flickering red candles. On the walls hung portraits of George Washington, Adolf Hitler, and Rockwell himself. On one of the walls hung an eighteen-foot flag emblazoned with a huge Swastika.

Finally, two stormtroopers arrived and directed Haley into the back of a black Cadillac. "We'll take you to the home of our Supreme Commander," one of them said.

The winding road led to a large remote farmhouse in the countryside. It, too, had Swastikas flying above its entrance, and more security guards, plus two enormous, flesh-devouring Dobermans. "I felt like I might be dog food." Haley said.

He was ushered into Rockwell's office, where he stood beneath an enormous portrait of Hitler. Rockwell removed a pearl-handled revolver from his holster and placed it on the table beside him. "I see that Mr. Hefner, perhaps as a practical joke, has sent a nigger to interview me. You know, of course, you are from an inferior race."

"I didn't know that, but I've been called a nigger many times. This time, I'm getting paid for it."

"Actually, I favor shipping all you American niggers back to Africa. I plan to become president in 1972, and I will do just that. It'll take a lot of ships because you black bastards multiply like rabbits. Rabbits—what an appropriate image for *Playboy*."

"What do you plan to do with Jews?" Haley asked.

"Extermination, that is the only solution for them," Rockwell said. "Hitler was said to have killed six million of them. What ridiculous libel! There was no such thing as the Holocaust. Jews are trying to take over the world. But I will stop them. I'll finish the job that Hitler was only rumored to have done."

"What about homosexuals?" Haley asked.

"I will have my stormtroopers round them up in every state of America. Then I will have them shipped to some remote island. There they will be tortured for their crimes against humanity. I will subject them to every form of degradation known since the dawn of time. Perhaps use them for medical experiments. Of course, after their arrival on the island, castration will be mandatory."

During the interview, Rockwell revealed some details about his background. His parents were liberal, both having careers as performers in vaudeville. They separated when Rockwell was six years old. Through his father, and as a boy, Rockwell met such big names as Walter Winchell, Benny Goodman, Jack Benny, Fred Allen, and Groucho Marx. "Groucho was repulsive," he said. "I think he set me off on my lifelong hatred of Jews."

Rockwell later joined the U.S. Navy and was greatly impressed with its sense of order and discipline. "I'll impose that on my stormtroopers."

While serving at a naval base in San Diego in the early 1950s, he became inspired by Senator Joseph McCarthy and his stance against American communists. When General Douglas MacArthur ran for U.S. President, Rockwell supported him and even adopted his familiar corncob pipe.

"All you niggers, including that swine, Martin Luther King, are protesting for civil rights," Rockwell said. "Race mixing, that's what all that rioting is about. You black bastards want to integrate into society so you can fuck white women. All niggers want to put their slimy dicks into a white pussy. You guys really know how to piss off white people."

"Actually, I plan to form a temporary alliance with the blacks," Rockwell said. "The black nationalists like Malcolm X and Elijah Muhammed have taught me how important it is to mobilize people."

"That Muhammed son of a bitch has gathered millions of dirty, immoral, drunken, doped-up, filthy-mouthed, lazy, and repulsive niggers and inspired them to be clean, sober, honest, hardworking, dignified, and dedicated. He's turned them into admirable human beings in spite of their color and ignorance."

"Once they have served my purpose, and I no longer need them, they'll still end somewhere in the Sahara Desert, where I will strip them of their clothes and abandon them to their fate."

"Racial separation will bring peace, prosperity, and harmony to America. Our chief opponents are not niggers, but the communist Jew agitators. They are the enemy. To help the black cause, I am personally donating twenty dollars to the Nation of Islam today."

"In politics, one must sleep with some strange bedfellows, at least temporarily. Like the black nationalists, I, too, believe in racial separation."

"In 1972, I will run for President of the United States and will be swept into office by the rising anger of all the white people who are pissed off. So niggers will have been of some use to me after all."

In 1996, Rockwell heard Black Panther Stokeley Carmichael utter the words "Black Power." He found inspiration in that, naming his movement "White Power," which also became an ongoing theme and battle cry within one of his party's newsletters, *Stormtrooper Magazine*.

The BBC labeled Rockwell "The American Hitler." But his grandiose plans came to an end on August 25, 1967 when he was gunned down by an expelled member of his Nazi Party.

When David Duke, white supremacist and grand wizard of the Ku Klux Klan, learned of Rockwell's assassination, he said, "The greatest American who ever lived has been shot down and killed. I, too, will run for president, and I will succeed where he failed. Our cause will never die."

Haley's interview with Rockwell was recreated in the film adaptation of *Roots* with James Earl Jones cast as Haley and Marlon Brando as the Nazi leader.

After the fallout from his incendiary interview with Rockwell, Haley would go on to interview Muhammed Ali, who spoke about changing his name from Cassius Clay. Others of his interviews were devoted to Sammy Davis, Jr., forever outspoken, along with football great Jim Brown; TV host Johnny Carson; and music producer Quincy Jones who loomed so large in the career of Michael Jackson. An odd subject was Melvin Belli, the defense attorney for Jack Ruby, who assassinated Lee Harvey Oswald as he was being transferred from one place of detention to another in Dallas following his assassination of President John F. Kennedy in November of 1963.

***

The biggest scoop of Alex Haley's career as a journalist came when Martin Luther King, Jr. granted him the longest interview of his life, with the understanding that it would appear in *Playboy*. MLK had already delivered his most famous speech ("I Have a Dream") before 200,000 civil rights campaigners at the Lincoln Memorial in Washington.

The King interview appeared in the January 1965 issue of *Playboy*. By that time, the "Playboy Interview" had become a regular and popular feature of the magazine. Readers never knew what diverse celebrity would be featured. Perhaps Dolly Parton or Fidel Castro. If not those personalities, then Timothy Leary, Albert Schweitzer, Truman Capote, Princess Grace, Bill Cosby, Orson Welles, or Woody Allen.

In the beginning, King had been unsure about the desirability of a spotlight in *Playboy*. "I don't think it's the proper forum to talk about civil right," he said. Haley pointed out that *Playboy* reached a wide audience of some three million readers, many of them well-read and well-informed. He also pointed out Hef's long promotion of civil rights and his backing of such African American writers as James Baldwin. Haley also noted the enormous promotion Hef had given to black entertainers in his magazine, on his television show, and in the *Playboy* night clubs.

Finally, King was persuaded, and Haley flew to Atlanta, where he met with King late at night after he'd returned from a Sunday barbecue and rally that had ended at midnight.

King met Haley in his office at the rear of the Ebenezer Baptist Church and talked with him until 4AM, when he began to nod off.

The publication of Haley's interview with MLK in *Playboy* was timely, as it came out only weeks before he won the Nobel Peace Prize.

In October of 1967, King visited Hef at the Playboy Mansion in Chicago, and they had another long talk about civil rights and social issues. During that meeting, Hef asked him to write an article for *Playboy*, which he agreed to do, and which he submitted for publication.

King was shot on April 4, 1968 on a motel balcony in Memphis. His assassination sparked riots throughout the landscapes of America.

The January 1969 issue of *Playboy* was specifically configured as a 202-page testimonial to the magazine's 15th anniversary. One of its articles, written by MLK himself, was entitled "Testament of Hope." It glorified both Robert Kennedy and MLK's fights for justice and social change, painting them as martyrs to the cause of civil rights.

It would be the last piece the civil rights leader ever wrote. In it, MLK claimed that "America has waited until the black man was explosive with fury before stirring itself. Black men have slammed the door shut on a past of deadening passivity. I am denied equality solely because I am black, yet I am not a chattel slave. Millions of people have fought thousands of battles to enlarge my freedom, restricted as it still is, but progress has been made. That is why I remain optimistic, though I am also a realist about the barriers before us. Why is the issue of equality still so far from solution?"

Hef's championing of liberal causes did not go unnoticed by the media. In 1972, the *Los Angeles Times* claimed, "*Playboy* is a major instrument of social and moral change in the mid-20th Century."

\*\*\*

After MLK's death, Hef shifted more of his attention to Jesse Jackson, the emerging new civil rights leader. From the beginning, he was the heaviest contributor to Jackson's PUSH (People United to Save Humanity, its name later changed to the Rainbow PUSH Coalition.)

"Long before it became fashionable for white liberals to get involved, Hefner opened the pages of his magazine to black writers and his checkbook to the civil rights movement. "His commitment to racial justice is a story that should be better known," wrote the *Los Angeles Times*.

Jackson's first interview in *Playboy* appeared in 1969, about 19 months after MLK's assassination. "It was a raw and painful time," he said. "Dr. King was dead. Bobby Kennedy was dead, and youths in Vietnam were being slaughtered. I initially thought after the murder in Memphis, that Dr. King's death ended America's last chance to be redeemed."

Hef told Jackson, "We at *Playboy* are outspoken foes of segregation. We are actively involved in the fight to see the end of all racial inequalities in our time."

According to Jackson, "In 1961, Hef catapulted Dick Gregory to success by giving him a platform to perform at his Chicago club. Three years later, he gave Gregory $25,000 to use as reward money in the search for the killers of the slain civil rights workers, Chaney, Goodman, and Schwerner, buried in the soil and misery of Mississippi."

"For Jessie," Hef said, "the Playboy Mansion became a sanctuary. He spent a great deal of time there and actually referred to it as his second home."

\*\*\*

Motivated by the national exposure of his TV show, *Playboy Penthouse,* Hef opted to emerge from seclusion for the launch of yet another TV variety show *Playboy After Dark.* It would be shot in color at the CBS-TV studio in Hollywood, where a special set had been built for its filming. During its taping, he commuted between Chicago and Los Angeles.

To prepare for the series, he spent $15,000 on tailor-made Edwardian suits, although he should have been warned by his handlers that such Mod-inspired garb was fading from the wardrobes of style-conscious men.

"I think Hef harbored a secret desire to be a film star," said Victor Lownes. "He knew that by appearing as the host of *Playboy After Dark*

Into the social ferment of 1968, Hef launched a second TV series, *Playboy After Dark*. He took a bold stance by mixing black and white guests and performers into what was conceived as a convivial and permissive late-night venue among peers.

"That meant that stations south of the Mason-Dixon line refused to air it, which severely hastened our demise. We were far hipper than anything put on by Ed Sullivan."

his image would become far better known. He envied the adulation heaped on stars. As he walked down the street, he wanted passers-by to stop and stare, saying, 'Look, there goes Hugh Hefner.'"

Once again, he recreated an apartment-style setting where singers, comics, and other entertainers, could casually drop in for a chat, followed by one of their routines.

"The camera was the third person at our party," Hef said. "In keeping with the Playboy Philosophy, we wanted to advocate more permissive behavior but still keep it within the bounds of good taste. For many, it was still too provocative, and many TV stations—in fact most stations—turned it down when I tried to launch it into syndication."

Vincent Cosgrove, writing for *The New York Times,* described the debut of the show like this: "The miniskirt had replaced the evening gown. Some men sport Chia Pet-like sideburns, others garishly colored evening jackets. Dancing couples boogaloo to rock music like refugees from 'Shindig!' Mr. Hefner, who seemed so at home with the Great American Songbook in the *Penthouse* Series, looks as if he'd rather be back at the Mansion digging the latest Dave Brubeck L.P."

Reviews were anything but raves, and some were acerbic. A critic wrote, "What was elegant and slightly cool about the earlier series now seems forced. Joe Cocker and Canned Heat share the bill weirdly with Billy Eckstine and Vic Damone. Rex Reed discusses Gore Vidal's *Myra Breckinridge,* the legendarily awful film he made with Mae West. Under his dinner jacket, Mr. Hefner wears a shirt so puffy it could have inspired a famous episode of *Seinfeld.* And the image of blacks and whites socializing on television no longer breaks ground."

Other critics were harsh, *Time* writing, "As an actor, Hefner makes a pretty good magazine publisher." Most reviewers attacked his "wooden hosting."

Hef defended himself, claiming, "I am better than *The Johnny Carson Show* and *The Joey Bishop Show,* and do a better job of hosting than Ed Sullivan."

In the style he'd previously defined during his involvement with Playboy's Penthouse, Sammy Davis, Jr. dominated virtually any episode of *Playboy After Dark* in which he appeared. "Except now," a critic wrote, "as befits the hippie era, he glimmers with enough gold chains to qualify as the Godfather of Bling. Tina Turner sings 'Proud Mary' as Ike sulks in the background. Sonny Bono beats a cowbell with the ferocity of Gene Krupa, as Cher warbles 'Take Me for a Little While.'"

During the TV series' short run, its roster of entertainers was an amazing assemblage: Johnny Mathis, Otto Preminger, Roman Polanski, Sharon

Tate, the Smothers Brothers, Buddy Rich, Mabel Mercer, the Grateful Dead, and Jack Leonard.

As before, Hef loaded each show with a lot of African Americans such as Nat King Cole, Ella Fitzgerald, Ray Charles, Sarah Vaughan, Della Reese, Dizzy Gillespie, Bobby Short, Nina Simone, Barbara McNair, and the dancer, Geoffrey Holder.

"As always, my favorite singer was Tony Bennett," Hef said. "I loved it when he came onto the show. He leaves his heart in every song he sings, including 'Blue Velvet.'"

"Basically, I tried to blend Las Vegas with Haight Ashbury, [representatives of] the latter group showing up with love beads, long hair, and bell bottoms."

As producer of a TV series, Hef's second time around wasn't as successful as his first. When he tried to syndicate *Playboy After Dark*, there were few buyers. Most stations, especially in the Midwest and the South, feared that it would be too controversial. *Playboy After Dark* went off the air in 1971.

It accounted for a big hunk of the money Hef lost in 1970 as part of what defined as "other *Playboy* ventures outside the magazine."

\*\*\*

In August of 1968, the soon-to-be notorious Democratic National Convention came to Chicago. It was during a tumultuous era when America was divided into two warring camps, battling over the war in Vietnam, and over issues related to race. There had already been rioting in more than 100 cities. Alternative lifestyles were increasingly vocal and getting more articulate and stronger. Hef liked to fancy himself as one of the leaders of this counterculture revolution.

In direct opposition to Vice President Hubert Humphrey, who had served under Lyndon B. Johnson, Hef strenuously supported "The Peace Candidate," Senator Eugene McCarthy of Minnesota, who had competed with the slain Robert Kennedy for the Democratic Party's nomination as their candidate for the U.S. Presidency. In Chicago, Hef hosted a $100-a-plate fundraiser in McCarthy's honor.

After that event, as reported in *The New York Times*, he also hosted a week-long party at Chicago's Playboy Mansion for the beautiful people of the Democratic Party. Warren Beatty and Jesse Jackson were among the celebrities who attended, and during its course. Hef chatted with the mayor of Cleveland, Carl Stokes, and the mayor of Boston, Kevin White, along with other visiting dignitaries.

During the course of his week-long party, when Hef saw rioting on television near the Playboy Mansion, he went out into the streets with friends to observe some of the violent confrontations between the Chicago police and the demonstrators. Hef was accompanied by Jules Feiffer, columnist Max Lerner, his secretary, Bobbie Arnstein, and another *Playboy* employee, John Dante.

They didn't get very far before a policeman in a squad car screeched on his brakes and jumped out onto the pavement. With billy club raised, he confronted Hef. "Get the fuck out of here! Go home or I'll arrest you. Move on!"

When Hef protested, the police officer whacked his ass with his night stick. The next day, Hef called a press conference to denounce police brutality. "Such violence doesn't separate us from countries ruled by dictators," he claimed.

Most of the press agreed with him. "America is going through an era of change. It's the decade of sex, drugs, and rock 'n roll."

During the turbulent course of the Democratic Convention, many visiting celebrities, including Warren Beatty, used the Playboy Mansion as their headquarters. Katharine Graham, publisher of the *Washington Post*, was its most distinguished visitor. Other notables who showed up included Jack Valenti, who was about to assume the presidency of the Motion Picture Association of America. State Treasurer Adlai Stevenson III was another visitor, as was Perle Mesta, "the Washington hostess with the mostest."

Outside the Convention Hall, Chicago cops battled demonstrators in full view of TV cameras. The nation watched in horror. Many reporters were caught up in the violence, including Mike Wallace and Dan Rather. Chicago Mayer Richard J. Daley was blamed for much of the violence of his

Scenes of American rage from the Democratic National Convention of 1968.

The street fighting was bloodier and more intense, and the politics more vindictive than anything the participants predicted.

Hefner, then headquartered in Chicago, very close to the fighting, opened the doors of his Playboy Mansion as a refuge for liberal movers and shakers from across the American landscape.

313

police force. Some left-wingers denounced the cops as "Nazi stormtroopers."

The worst violence occurred on August 28 at Grant Park as police battled Yippies who were chanting, "Pigs are whores."

Demonstrators converged on the Hilton Hotel where Humphrey was staying in a suite. As he was taking a shower, he was overcome by tear gas seeping through his windows from the street below.

On the floor of the National Convention, Connecticut Senator Abraham Ribicoff delivered his nominating speech for McCarthy, denouncing the "Gestapo tactics in the streets of Chicago."

Daley rose from his seat, exploding in anger and shouting at Ribicoff, "Fuck you! You Jew son of a bitch!"

After the devastating TV coverage, many talking heads publicly speculated that by the end of the convention that had fitfully nominated Humphrey as the Democratic candidate, Americans would elect the Republicans' "law and order" candidate, Richard M. Nixon.

*[In the aftermath of the convention and the eventual election of Nixon as President of the United States, Hef continued to publish articles by left wingers who shared his political agenda. Notables included Jesse Jackson, Allen Ginsberg, Eldridge Cleaver, and William Sloan Coffin. Spectorsky opposed this policy, but Hef prevailed.*

*Spec warned that publishing left-wing articles would lead to a massive decrease in the sales of* Playboy, *"Nixon fans will not buy us. Descending to being politically partisan, no matter how slightly we stoop, is like pregnancy—there's no such thing as a little bit. You are or you aren't."]*

***

As the highly contested 60s came to an end in 1969, Hef was presented with a financial overview of Playboy Enterprises. The December issue that year sold 3.7 million copies at $1.50 each, and advertising revenue for that year topped $4 million. Some twenty Playboy Clubs were in operation. Playboy Enterprises, totaling every venture they were involved with, grossed more than $100 million.

With courage, Hef faced the 1970s eager to see what the future held— perhaps additional financial successes.

Dare he wish for love to enter his life?

# Chapter Nine

# HEF'S SHANGRI-LA

SET IN LOS ANGLES IN A GARDEN OF EDEN,
IT BECOMES A BRANDING TOOL AND AN ORGY SITE
FOR FILM STARS.

PLAYBOY GOES PUBLIC IN A NATIONWIDE STOCK OFFERING

LOVE HURTS WHEN BUNNIES BITE:  NAVIGATING HIS WAY BETWEEN THE BEDS
OF SEPARATE PLAYMATES—ONE IN CHICAGO, THE OTHER IN L.A.—
HEF VOWS ETERNAL LOVE TO EACH

HOW HEF AND VICTOR LOWNES PLAYED CHESS
FOR THE FUTURE OF PLAYBOY'S CASINO TRADE
STAFF MEMBERS NICKNAME HIM "JAWS" AFTER FEELING THE BITE OF HIS TEETH

SHOW-BIZ MANEUVERS FROM BARBI BENTON,  ROMAN POLANSKI,
& THE ROLLING STONES. THE RISE AND FALL OF *OUI* MAGAZINE.
FUN AND GAMES IN THE GROTTO
& THE LAST HURRAH OF PLAYBOY'S LITERARY EDITOR, COMTE SPECTORSKY

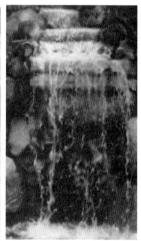

Left:     Hef with Barbi Benton on the cover of *People* magazine, Dec 2, 1974.
Center:  An aerial view of the Playboy Mansion in L.A.
Right:    Entrance to The Grotto, where a LOT of good-looking (or not) people got laid.

**The final months of the 1960s** were coming to an end. "And what a decade it was," Hef said. "So much happening, my head was spinning. I was both thrilled and awed to be facing a new decade. Will it bring as many surprises as the '60s had?"

He would eventually interpret the early 1970s as "the time I climbed Mount Everest. After that, it was all down the slopes for me on just one ski...From 1970 to 1972 was *The Best Years of Our Lives*," a reference to the William Wyler movie.

By 1972, *Playboy's* circulation peaked at 7.2 million copies a month. By 1973, pretax profits amounted to $20 million; the company's advertising revenue reached its zenith; and with only a few exceptions, *Playboy's* hotels, resorts, and casinos were profitable. In synch with the ebullient profitability of the times, a Braille version of *Playboy*—without the nudes, of course— was launched.

Hef later recalled, "It was the most difficult decision of my life when I began to debate with my executives if we should go public and place 30 percent of my shares of *Playboy* stock on the market."

Half of his executives favored going public. The others opposed it, mainly because they viewed Hef's management style and his idiosyncrasies as unsuited to a publicly traded company.

"I view opening myself up to public scrutiny as an anathema," he said.

But despite his reservations, he urgently needed to raise some cash, based on the terrible losses of his Great Gorge Resort in New Jersey.

Victor Lownes estimated that most of the money derived from the sale of *Playboy* shares would be used to pay off existing debts. "We at *Playboy* were competing with Disney, but our Bunny was no match for Mickey Mouse."

After rejection from several Wall Street Firms, Loeb, Rhoades & Company, a New York investment firm, agreed to underwrite Playboy's initial stock offer.

As one Wall Street reporter noted, "Before that, *Playboy's* finances were like a rabbit warren known only to a few Bunnies."

Loeb, Rhodes objected to the illustration that Hef wanted replicated on *Playboy's* stock certificate. *[Sprawled*

According to Hef, "As an entrepreneur, I was often compared to Walt Disney. But my bunny had to compete not only with a duck, but with a mouse, too."

across it was an image of the nude, reclining body of Willy Rey, Playmate of the Month for February 1971. Loeb, Rhodes eventually persuaded Hef to agree to let her coiffure cover her otherwise naked breasts. When he acquiesced to their "suggestion," Hef said, "I don't want to assault the financial world's sensibilities."]

Finally, on November 3, 1971, *Playboy* went public, offering 1,586,812 shares of common stock to outside investors. By doing that, Hef's ownership of the company was reduced from 80 percent to 71 percent.

He had predicted that a *Playboy* share would trade at $40, but the initial offer priced each share at $23.50. Within a few months, the per-share price had fallen to $14. Later, it rebounded to $19.

Going public added $7 million to Hef's bank account, a supplement to holdings which netted him $800,000 annually, plus an annual salary of $303,874. According to *Forbes,* Hef had become one of the richest men in America, with an estimated worth of $157 million.

"It was my world back then," Hef said. "But by the mid-1970s, that world would undergo some radical changes, all for the worse. Those shareholders, hoping to get rich quick, were deeply disappointed, as they were forced to endure a history of poor management and missed opportunities."

Early in the 70s, Hef had dreamed of an expanding empire. He'd purchased 500 acres on Spain's Costa del Sol for the construction of a sprawling beach and golf resort. He had also been negotiating a resort on the outskirts of Tangiers, Morocco.

Playboy Casinos were envisioned at locations that included both Las Vegas and in Provence, France. He was also huddling with "the fourth richest man in Japan," about franchising hotels and clubs across that island nation, too. "We'll blitz Japan with *Playboy,*" Hef predicted. "We'll make the biggest blast since we dropped those atomic bombs in 1945." *[Then he turned to an attentive reporter saying, "Don't print that!"]*

In collaboration with representatives from the Levitt Empire, builders of, among others, Levittown, Playboy Enterprises also planned the construction of apartment colonies for single people in locations ranging from Santa Monica to Miami.

None of these grandiose plans ever came to be, as *Playboy* and its fortunes, year after year, continued to nosedive.

Throughout the 1970s, Hef endured many attacks on his managerial style, either secretly from current executives or publicly from executives who had either quit or been fired. Stephen Byer, a former vice president, claimed, "The organization is full of incompetents promoted to jobs far over their heads. The few able executives of Hef's are reduced to subservient 'yes men'"

Byer was replaced as Playboy's marketing Veep by Robert Guttwillig, a refugee from New York's literary world. He became known around the office as "The Man in the Gray Flannel Suit."

He immediately began extinguishing "brush fires" in New York, Washington, and Europe. He launched new foreign-language editions of *Playboy*, organized the Playboy Book Club, and developed new kinds of merchandise that included greeting cards, puzzles, and bartop accessories.

"Playboy's biggest asset is that it feeds off itself, building one project on top of another, meshing them together so that they reinforce each other," Guttwillig said. "Hef can do that better than Disney. Why limit ourselves to just one market? We've got to be always on the lookout to exploit new markets."

In the 1970s, *Playboy* had to face severe competition from other men's magazines, especially *Penthouse*. Profits for Playboy Enterprises dropped. Offsetting the losses, casino profits from London kept rising, covering many of the deficits generated by *Playboy's* other venues.

Some of the most glaring of those deficits derived from, among others, Hef's filmmaking endeavors (especially Roman Polanski's *Macbeth*) and properties that included the Miami Plaza Hotel & Casino, and Playboy Towers in Chicago, both of which continued to lose money.

Making matters worse, and refusing to heed warnings, Hef forged ahead with the expansion of *Playboy's* book publishing as well as venues associated with music and the recording industry.

In London, Lownes was deeply alarmed, since in his view, "Hef was moving ahead with the confidence of a foolish jerk who thought he could do no wrong. He did not have the Midas Touch."

\*\*\*

As the 1970s lumbered on, Hef noted to his surprise that the Sexual Revolution he took credit for launching had moved far beyond his wildest dreams.

"The Playboy Bunny, with her perfumed cottontail, was no longer racy stuff," he said. "She looked tame, indeed, especially when compared to the raunchy entertainment that sex clubs were featuring, even fucking right on stage."

"Often—just a few doors down from a Playboy Club—would be a rival nitery boasting tits, ass, and strippers who showed everything. Some of them even showed off their butts, opening their cheeks to display their rosebud for men who liked to enter through the back door."

"Even small towns had seen the rise of the singles bar," Hef said. "'Singles bar' was just a polite name for a pickup joint. If a visiting businessman from, say, St. Louis or Cleveland, had the dough, he could get laid for the night—that was almost guaranteed. As for me, I was still touting my untouchable Bunnies."

He complained, "Whereas city authorities were always gunning for me over the most minor violation, some other club owners were getting away with not exactly murder, but with gross indecency, everything except perhaps a woman-and-dog show."

"For my Bunnies, I stuck to my 'look, don't touch' policy. I wanted to hire unspoiled girls from the boondocks, not hardened strippers who'd had a hundred men before they turned sixteen. As time rolled on, customers in our clubs became far more aggressive. Many Bunnies referred to them as the gropers. In some clubs, against my wishes, I heard that Bunnies were allowing horndogs to slip a twenty-dollar bill into their satin-covered crotches."

Not only were the hotels losing money, but so were the Playboy Clubs.

## GUIDEBOOKS to THE GOOD LIFE
### RETRO, VINTAGE, & RECYCLED

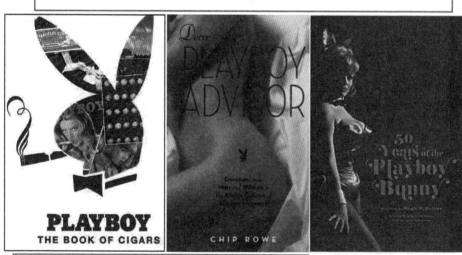

**PLAYBOY'S PUBLISHING AMBITIONS
FROM THE GOLDEN AGE OF BOOK-BUILDING.**

In their relentless search for new profit centers, the fertile imaginations of Hef's editorial team worked hard to re-package their images and ideas into books directly aimed at the sexual and lifestyle-related yearnings of their readers.

Here are only a few of the many titles churned out by Hefner's occasionally dysfunctional but very productive team.

In 1975, word reached Victor Lownes that in the second quarter of that year, *Playboy* suffered a loss of $2.7 million. It was time for belt tightening—no more lavish lunches with lobster, a delicacy replaced by turkey sandwiches.

By 1975, *Playboy's* troubles—Lownes, from his base in London, referred to them as an "economic blizzard"—had become glaringly obvious. He was ordered to attend an emergency meeting of Playboy's Board of Directors in Chicago, knowing that most of them were vocally opposed to his flashy style of administering.

In Chicago, Hef shocked Lownes by offering him full control of the *Playboy* empire in both the United States and in England. "I'll give you a free hand," Hef assured him. "You'll have to fly from Miami to Los Angeles, from New Orleans to Chicago, and San Francisco to London. Just remember to bring a sharp axe with you. You'll need to put the heads of worthless employees on the chopping block."

"I had been given a license to kill," Lownes later quipped.

After the steering of Lownes into his new, much-expanded role, Hef flew back to the comforts and security of his newly acquired Los Angeles Mansion.

During his time in Chicago, Lownes noticed that the Chicago Mansion was operating at full staff, even though Hef, now ensconced in new digs in Los Angeles, was there only three or four times a year. As his first order of business, he took steps to reduce some of its scope and scale.

"Not only that," Lownes said, "but he was aboard the 'Big Bunny' for only about three or four flights a year, yet it cost $1.5 million in upkeep. To park the Bunny at a major airport, we were hit with a $350,000 annual fee. Hef put up a struggle but I finally convinced him to sell the 'Big Bunny' for $4 million. Of course, the sexy Bunny flight attendants weren't part of the deal."

"I soon discovered," Lownes continued, "that most of the managers of the Playboy Clubs in America would be better off operating a hamburger joint, and the hotels were being run by men who'd be challenged in operating a roadside motel for truckers where beds rented by the hour. In desperation, I turned some of the hotels into time-share units."

"I was firing and devouring employees at such a rate I earned the nickname 'Jaws.' Every time I turned a corner in the *Playboy* operation, I discovered massive waste. Some idiot at the New York Club had shelled out $4 million to redecorate it, a worthless investment since the club was deeply in the red. Many keyholders were running up massive bills, then never showing up again."

Lownes instructed *Playboy's* entertainment director, Sam Di Stefano, to book entertainers who were cheaper and less famous than the acts from days of yore. "No more Ella Fitzgerald or Duke Ellington. Bring in a cheap Doo Wop act, some black jazz group, or some country western singer, even an Elvis impersonator."

"I meant business, even if it meant firing my own son, Val," Lownes said. "He had been managing our club in The Bahamas. The final straw, the event that led to my firing him, was his arrest by U.S. Customs agents, who caught him with a bag of pot during a flight from Nassau into Miami."

Lownes shut the doors of one *Playboy* Club after another—first, San Francisco, then Kansas City, then Atlanta. Likewise for the clubs in Montréal and St. Louis, both of which were suffering losses because the neighborhoods in which they were located had become dangerous at night.

American tourists had stopped going to Jamaica after the socialist Manley government took over, and because of riots, crime, and political unrest, Lownes closed the resort in Ocho Rios, too.

"Many neighborhoods across America had undergone big changes, mostly for the worse, since we had first opened clubs there," Lownes said. "Population shifts had led to some clubs standing in a depressed area of the city, which had devolved into high crime areas with a lot of drugs. Our upmarket Playboys didn't want to wander into these districts at night. They could pick up girls at safer clubs than ours."

"If a club had the potential of drawing good business, I moved it to a better area. In Los Angeles, I reopened a Playboy Club in Century City. I shut down our club in Phoenix and shifted it to a better location in Scottsdale. Other clubs I shut down for eternity."

The Playboy Club in the Philippines, which secretly promoted prostitution, lasted only a few months in 1964, establishing itself as the franchise with the shortest lifespan.

On many occasions, Hef wasn't even consulted about the closings, having told Lownes, "You are the captain of the ship, but I'm the admiral of the fleet, to be called in for only the really atomic decisions."

The cutbacks affected *Playboy* merchandising, too, dampening some of Hef's initial enthusiasm for an expansion into new types of branding.

URBAN BLIGHT. In the 1960s and 70s, it galvanized partisan politics, shifted demographics, and prompted major shifts in the way Americans opted to entertain themselves and where.

It also contributed to the decay and decline of many of the Playboy Clubs. Originally centered, by company policy, in core urban neighborhoods, they were either moved or closed as the decades, and the blight, advanced.

"I don't plan to put a *Playboy* Logo on a man's shirt. Nor on his shorts. Certainly not on his dog. We don't want our readers to live in some *Playboy* bubble. We already have our ideal Playboy carrying around our logo on his key chain: He fastens his tie with our *Playboy* clip, and he lights his cigarette with one of our lighters."

"He pays his bill by reaching in for his *Playboy* wallet, and he plays golf with one of our balls (no, not that kind). He sleeps between our *Playboy* sheets with a wannabe Bunny. For winter chills, he dons our *Playboy* parka. But merchandising can be carried too far. We don't want our logo on the toilet paper a playboy uses to wipe his ass."

In print, Hef was often compared to Walt Disney. "Both men are playing out their boyhood fantasies," wrote Peter Shrag in *The Decline of the WASP*. "Hef and Walt are two great Puritan entrepreneurs of culture in the 20th Century. Those boys are extreme expressions of white, Anglo-Saxon, Protestant cultural values."

It was noted that whereas Disney at times displayed a certain anti-Semitism, that was absent in Hef's character. He employed dozens of Jews in top management posts throughout the *Playboy* hierarchy. Even so, Shrag and others claimed that "the tone and feel of Hefner's world was intensely WASP."

According to *The New York Times*, "Walt Disney sanitizes his rodents, and Hefner sanitizes his Playmates—no warts, no wrinkles, no other blemishes, just ivory skin perfection."

Scholars and academics sometimes tried to analyze *Playboy's* initial success. Rollo May, a psychotherapist, writing in *Love and Will,* said, "*Playboy* got its dynamic from a repressed anxiety in American men that underlies their fear of involvement. This is an anxiety about possible impotence. Everything in the magazine is beautifully concocted to bolster the illusion of potency without ever putting it to the test or challenge."

In the beginning, Hef approved of all of Lownes' cutbacks, although reporting, "Every closing of a Playboy Club was a stab in my gut."

*[Later, in 1977, after many months of the aggressive cutbacks for which he'd become respected, reviled, and feared, Lownes received a package from the Playboy Mansion in Los Angeles. When he opened it, he discovered a mounted set of shark's teeth on a trophy board with a plaque that stated: "TO JAWS WITH LOVE FROM HEF AND BARBI," a reference to Hef's then-girlfriend, Barbi Benton.*

*Soon after that, however, the affection was abruptly withdrawn.*

*"Hef betrayed me," Lownes said. "The axe, in time, came down on my neck in one swift, clean cut."]*

\*\*\*

At long last, in 1969, love found Hugh Hefner.

Born in New York in 1950, Barbara Klein "was a nice Jewish girl and a virgin" when she met Hef. Green-eyed, she stood 5' 3" and was a former beauty queen who grew up in Sacramento. When she came into Hef's orbit, she was eighteen years old and a co-ed at UCLA.

Hef had been captivated by her ever since she'd been cast as an extra on his TV series, *Playboy After Dark*. After only about two episodes, he elevated her to the position of co-host because he had learned that she wanted to be a singer and actress. "I thought that would win her heart," he told LeRoy Neiman. "She was still wearing a chastity belt, although we'd gone out on a few dates. At least I got a kiss or two for my efforts, but I wanted more. The chase was on."

When Hef had first asked her out, she said, "I don't know. I've never dated anyone over 24."

"I haven't either," he shot back. At the time, he was 42.

He convinced her that if she wanted to make it in show business, she'd have to change her name. Henceforth, she'd be known as Barbi Benton, the "Barbi" having been inspired by the Barbie Doll.

One night at the Chicago Mansion, the reluctant Barbi "surrendered the pink" to this middle-aged man. The next morning, while she was still asleep in his round bed, he put on his pajamas and a robe and hurried to the office of his secretary, Bobbie Arnstein. "We did it," he exclaimed. "We did the dirty deed!"

"What do you want me to do?" Arnstein asked. "Announce it on the Goodyear Blimp?"

Dick Rosenzweitz, Hef's executive assistant, heard the news, too. "You could always tell when Hef had fallen in love, because he was bright and bubbly. Very up. That was unusual for him. He seemed to feel that all was right with the world, or at least with his part of the universe."

In almost every case, Hef didn't mind displaying the body of his current love interest within the pages of *Playboy*. He told his aides that "Barbi has a spectacular body." It had taken some convincing to get her to surrender her virginity. It took even more to get her to disrobe in front of a photographer, but she did several times, showing off her wares and her "Ultra-Brite smile."

She made appearances on the covers of *Playboy* in four different issues: July 1969; March 1970; May 1972; and as late as December 1985. And although he never designated her as *Playmate of the Month*, she was also featured in two nude layouts in the December 1979 issue.

Hef was often challenged for dating a girl so young. "It's not that more mature women frighten me. It's just that I find young women sexier, just as everything has begun to blossom and nothing has sagged. If you get them young, you can break them in to what you prefer."

That was a sentiment he'd often expressed. "Having an affair with a young girl helps me recapture my lost youth, or at least remember it."

"I don't need women for intellectual stimulation," he said. "I'm surrounded by some of the brightest bulbs, all men, in the publishing business. They give me all the intellectual stimulation I can handle."

One day, he invited Gloria Steinem by to meet Barbi. He had apparently forgiven her for that devastating piece she'd written after her gig as a Playboy Bunny.

Barbi Benton, Hef's beautiful and very charming girlfriend from 1969 to 1976, appears both on the cover and provocatively inside *Playboy's* edition of March 1970.

Cynics and her competitors gossiped bjtchily about how sexual intimacy can help a Playmate get ahead.

When Barbi left the room, Hef asked Gloria, "What do you think?"

"She's awfully young," the feminist responded.

"A girl needs a man with my vast experience to break her in," he answered.

Steinem was horrified by that remark, later describing it to her editor as, "The utterance of a male chauvinist pig if I ever heard one."

Since Benton liked to travel, she was occasionally able to lure Hef from his den. In fact, he'd chosen her to accompany him on the world tour that included the safari in Africa. She often succeeded in getting him to fly her to vacation retreats in Hawaii, Las Vegas, Aspen, and Acapulco. He even went parasailing with her, warning her in advance, "I can't swim."

To the surprise of his friends and the *Playboy* staffers, his relationship with Benton would be long enduring, at least for him, which meant five years. However, on occasion, he slipped around and hopped a Bunny whenever he wanted variety from his heavy diet of sex with just one woman.

In the spring of 1974 when Benton appeared on *The Tonight Show,* she told Johnny Carson, "I think Hefner will be ready for marriage in about four years. When I'm ready, he'll be ready."

When he realized she was serious about a recording career, Hef had her cut both singles and albums for Playboy Records.

\*\*\*

Celebrity psychic to the stars, the deeply respected John Cohan came into Hef's life during his involvement with Barbi Benton. [*Hollywood stars turned to Cohan both for his spiritual advice and for his insights into their futures. Many A-list personalities have been clients of Cohan: Elizabeth Taylor, Elvis Presley, Julia Roberts, Burt Lancaster, Merv Griffin, and Lana Turner. Sandra Dee also came into his world and became "the love of my life." For decades, Cohan's yearly forecasts have appeared in Cindy Adams' widely read column in the* New York Post.

*Many vignettes from Cohan's fascinating star-studded life are found in his memoir,* Catch a Falling Star. *Among his many revelations, he names who really killed Nicole Brown Simpson, the murdered former wife of O.J. Simpson. He also writes about the final moments in the life of Natalie Wood. Married at the time to Robert Wagner, she drowned off the coast of Catalina Island in 1981.*

*Even Debbie Reynolds shared her troubled life with Cohan, interpreting him as "a gentle soul and an insightful visionary.]*

When Hefner moved into his Playboy Mansion in Los Angeles, he, too, became a client of Cohan. After his first (disastrous) marriage, Hef had vowed that he'd never marry again. But the entrance of Barbi into his life made him seriously consider abandoning that vow. He turned to Cohan for some guidance.

The psychic found him "more and

"Barbi and Hef" seemed to have a lot of fun together. Inspired by her ambitions as a Country-Western star, she posed here, with Hef, as country bumpkins on an episode of the TV series, *Hee-Haw.*

Despite their costumes, these hip and sophisticated media players were anything but country-rustic.

Celebrity psychic and advisor to the stars John Cohan.

He told Hef, "True love is the one infallible shield against all the ugly and harsh things in the world. Once you find it, hold onto it and cherish it carefully, forever."

Of course, he knew in his heart that Hef would not do that, perhaps could not do that.

more smitten" (Hef's words) with this beauty and her voluptuous body. His relationship with Barbi had begun in 1969, and it would last until 1976, even though he cheated on her throughout the course of their affair.

He may not have told Hef at the time, but Cohan sensed that a possible marriage to Barbi would be a disaster. More likely, it would never take place.

It was more than the wide difference in their age. A young woman with a middle-aged, rather jaded playboy, Barbi was very career oriented, and her goal extended far beyond being Hef's Playmate. She'd already received a lot of attention when she'd co-hosted the TV series, *Playboy After Dark*. She'd gained additional exposure through her appearances on four *Playboy* covers.

Pursuing her ambitions as an actress and country singer, she began to get minor roles, including spots on such TV series as *The Love Boat* and *Fantasy Island*.

Her first three albums hit the Country Music charts: *Barbi Doll* (1975), *Barbi Benton* (1975), and *Something New* (1976). That made her the second biggest country star at Playboy Records, right after Mickey Gilley.

Her biggest single was "Brass

Barbi Benton's career was not limited to gigs associated with *Playboy*, even though few, if any, of them would bring her the exposure provided through Hefner.

In the upper photo, Barbi is seen in a 1978 skit with entertainer Minnie Pearl on CBS's hit, corn-porn variety show *Hee Haw*.

The lower photo is an ad from 1977 touting the premiere of a TV sitcom, *Sugar Time*, promoting Benton as one of a trio of adorably engaging girl band singers during their rocky debut in show-biz.

Despite its good intentions, its endorsement by Hef, and moments of genuine post-adolescent charm, it ran for only 13 episodes.

Reviews described it as "the heyday of jiggle television," and " a cross between *The Monkees* and *Three's Company*."

Buckles," about an innocent country girl corrupted by fame and money. Autobiographical? One lyric in the song had her posing as a centerfold for *Playboy*.

Benton also appeared in a movie produced in West Germany and released in 1970, *How Did a Nice Girl Like You Get Into This Business?* Hef himself appeared in a cameo.

As Cohan predicted, her marriage to Hef never materialized, and although they remained friends, the affair between Barbi and Hef drifted. By 1979, she'd married George Gradow, a real estate developer. They settled into married life, rearing two children and dividing their time between houses in Los Angeles and Aspen.

***

On some nights, Cohan recalled that Hef spoke with nostalgia about Marilyn Monroe. On occasion, he teared up when revisiting her sudden death, which deeply troubled him. He rejected the theory that she had committed suicide and firmly believed that she'd been murdered because she'd become too explosive, having threatened John F. Kennedy, his brother Robert, and mob boss Sam Giancana.

To some degree, Hef credited Marilyn for his successful launch of *Playboy* in 1953. *[On its cover, he'd run a sexy picture of her, and in the centerfold, he ran her nude calendar shot with her sensual body posed against a lush background of red velvet. With her on its cover, the newsstand inventories of the first edition of* Playboy *almost sold out.]*

Hef revealed to Cohan that during the years since the launch of *Playboy,* he'd made several attempts to get in touch with her, but she never acknowledged his invitations to visit him in Chicago. He'd heard that she had resented his exploitation of her, since she had been paid only $50 to pose for that nude calendar by its photographer, Tom Kelley.

"At first, I felt that Hefner had destroyed my career, just as I was getting a good start with *All About Eve* (1950) and *The Asphalt Jungle* (also 1950)," she told her friend, Jeanne Carmen.

She revealed to another close friend, the columnist Sidney Skolsky, that she'd gone to a lawyer and asked him to contact Hef, seeking a "retroactive" fee of $25,000, even though he was under no obligation to pay it.

"I heard from him all right," Marilyn said. "No check, just another invitation to visit Chicago. He wanted to fuck me more than he wanted to pay me. Had he mailed a check, I'd have gone to Chicago, providing he sent the ticket. As far as he was concerned, I would keep on my chastity belt. I don't go for men who are cheap."

The exposure of her nude photo in *Playbay* did not destroy Marilyn's career, as so many Hollywood insiders had predicted. For the most part, the response, especially from men, was favorable. Marilyn's salary as an actress skyrocketed, and from then on, she played lead roles. "So I guess in some roundabout way, I got even with Hefner. I had the last laugh all the way to the bank."

Despite Marilyn's rejection of Hef's romantic overtures, he continued his life-long fascination with the blonde star. "Like Romeo and Juliet," he told Cohan, "We will be reunited in death. I bought the gravesite next to her tomb."

In a 1987 retrospective on Marilyn, Hef defined her as "a celestial enigma with which every incandescent blonde has been (usually unfavorably) compared. Her style was both timeless and matchless, her elegance ineffable."

Neither Cohan nor Hef was thrilled when it was announced that Connie Stevens, the former wife of Eddie Fisher, had been cast as a Marilyn clone in *Sex Symbol*, released as a TV movie in September of 1974 as part of ABC's Anthology Series.

Its plot focused on the erratic behavior that was contributing to the erosion of Marilyn's career. Hef complained to Cohan, "Connie doesn't have that much in the bust, and her bottom is too big. What was the director thinking?"

The critics agreed with Cohan and Hef. One of them wrote, "Connie Stevens cries, coos, snots, and coddles her way through this one, trying to elicit sympathy but only succeeding in being disagreeable. Her decision to go nude (though with crossed legs) cements this one that will be remembered in the darkest cobwebs of the Internet."

Boobs, lesbianism, frigidity, and rape were among the topics previewed in the film.

Connie Stevens is
**The Sex Symbol**

ABC TUESDAY MOVIE OF THE WEEK
8:30 PM

**CAT FIGHT**

Aside from highlighting the highs and lows of the life of Marilyn Monroe, the focus of *Sex Symbol* is a grudge match between "The Symbol" (as played by Connie Stevens) and gossip maven, Agatha Murphy (as played by Shelley Winters).

Aggie is a "mashup" of Hedda Hopper and Louella Parsons.

***

Hef had formed a close bond with Roman Polanski, the avant-garde film director who had been born to Polish-Jewish parents in Paris. Their friendship had begun after Hef saw his first feature-length film, *Knife in the Water,* in 1962. Hef invited him to stay at the Playboy Mansion on his next visit to Chicago, and Polanski accepted the invitation. As could have been predicted, both men discovered that they shared an interest in beautiful young women, although the director, as subsequent events revealed, liked them perhaps a bit younger than Hef.

Hef didn't think Polanski would settle down and was taken by surprise when he married the budding actress, Sharon Tate in 1968. That was the same year he'd shot his best-known film, *Rosemary's Baby*. He had wanted Tate to play the lead, but the producers had gone for Mia Farrow instead.

Here is the doomed Sharon Tate in a pill-swallowing publicity still from *Valley of the Dolls* (1967).

Most critics attacked it as being terribly written and acted, and filled with scattered unintentional laughs. It was a tawdry adaptation of Jacqueline Susann's tawdry bestseller.

The opening night party for the movie was held at the New York Playboy Club. Among the many celebrities attending was the veteran English actress Hermione Gingold. After a quick glance at the club's showroom, she turned to Andy Warhol saying, "Tacky, tacky, tacky."

When she met Hef, she told him, "Dearie, I can't pose for any centerfold for you, because I live in London, but my tits are in Canterbury."

It wasn't Gingold but Tate that Hef wanted to pose for a centerfold, but she consistently refused. He was taken by her natural beauty and charm.

He had long been alert to her regular appearance in fashion magazines. Later, he'd been captivated by her performance as Jennifer North in the 1967 cult classic, *Valley of the Dolls,* based on Jacqueline Susann's bestseller. She was seventeen years younger than Hef.

Unknown to Polanski, but according to Bobbie Arnstein, Hef had had sex with Tate on three separate occasions. He even brought up the subject of marriage, telling Victor Lownes, "I shocked myself when I spoke of wedded bliss, but the words just spewed out of my mouth. That was how taken I was with this beauty, the hottest number who ever came out of Dallas."

Whereas Tate did not love Hef, she fell in love with Polanski. Hef was invited to their widely publicized wedding in the Chelsea district of London on January 20, 1968. At the ceremony, Polanski appeared in "Edwardian finery," with Tate attired in a white minidress.

Earlier, Polanski had allegedly told Hef that it would not be a traditional marriage, and that he'd continue to seduce other women. He referred to Tate's desire for fidelity as "her hang-up."

Victor Lownes, who hosted their wedding reception at the London Playboy Club, was also a friend of Polanski. To thank him, he presented Lownes with a gold phallus.

Although Hef was jealous of Polanski for snaring a beauty like Tate, his friendship with the director continued, and they often talked about Playboy Enterprises backing films.

In a strange coincidence, on August 9, 1969, Polanski was in London with Hef and Barbi Ben-

Decades after the personal, professional, and legal horrors that had traumatized him in the U.S., Roman Polanski continued his work as a film director and documentarian from a base in Europe.

ton at Revolution, a discothèque, when he learned that Tate had been murdered along with three of her friends, including Jay Sebring. Eight and a half months pregnant at the time of her death, she'd been stabbed in the belly sixteen times.

The killers had scrawled the word PIG in Tate's blood on the front door of the murder house. In time, it was learned that the killers, each of them arrested and imprisoned, were part of the crazed Charles Manson cult.

Devastated and in a state of shock, Polanski flew from London back to Los Angeles. Hef told Benton, "This horrible death could destroy Roman. He adored Sharon. My God, if we'd been in Los Angeles, we might have been invited to that party at their home."

In the aftermath of the hideous murders, Hef said that "to restore Roman's sanity, I thought he should direct a film for Playboy Enterprises."

During their meetings, he learned that the director had long wanted to make his own film version of Shakespeare's *Macbeth,* which he claimed would be far superior to Orson Welles' rendition of 1948.

Hef was intrigued by the idea, informing Polanski that any film associated with *Playboy* would be immediately interpreted as erotic or semi-pornographic. "If we take on the Bard, it will show the world that *Playboy* is serious about making movies."

Kenneth Tynan, author of the notorious *Oh! Calcutta*, a stage play featuring nudity, had agreed to adapt Shakespeare's stage play for the screen.

Hef authorized a budget of $1 million. He told Polanski, "I want you to show them that *Playboy* can do more than a tits-and-ass movie."

When word spread through the *Playboy* staff about *Macbeth,* Hef's top executives were strongly against it, predicting a financial disaster, based on its cost and its "inevitable" failure at the box office.

Spectorsky correctly assumed that the movie would go way over budget. Before it was completed, a year behind schedule, *Macbeth* cost Hef $2.5 million.

"Roman will lead us down the garden path and leave us there," Spec predicted. Bob Preuss, who had always given Hef good business advice, also predicted a financial disaster. Ignoring them, Hef pressed ahead. Polanski began shooting the film in London.

On Hef's 45th birthday, April 9, 1971, his friends tossed a small party for him at his Chicago Mansion. Polanski sent rushes of the famous opening scene on the heath, in which witches gather around a bubbling cauldron, chanting "Bubble, bubble, toil and trouble."

Polanski had cast "the ugliest old hags in Britain," and filmed each of them topless, with sagging breasts. At the end of the scene, and as a joke, his filmed preview showed them standing

Top photo. Jon Finch, a relatively unknown actor selected by Polanski for the role of Macbeth, is shown between scenes on location in Scotland prominently displaying *Playboy's* logo. At the time, tensions were high between the Playboy organization and the hard-to-control, high-spending Polanski, even before the release of what emerged as a spectacular, much-ridiculed flop.

In the lower photo, Jon Finch and Francesca Annis, in the words of one critic, "brought a fierce hunger and loyalty to their roles. These two were like proto-Thatcherites—ruthless, cunning, and determined to carry out their most basic desires with a disregard for the folly of their actions."

up and singing, "Happy Birthday, Hugh Hefner."

The staff remembered Hef breaking into hysterical laughter.

When Polanski's *Macbeth* was released, most critics panned it. Some reviewers even suggested that the director's emphasis on blood and gore was his way of exorcising the horrible death of his murdered wife. Nonetheless, the National Board of Review of Motion Pictures voted it the best movie of the year.

When asked what he thought of the film's failure at the box office, Hef said, "Let's face it: Making any film is a crap shoot. Only a fraction of the movies made show a profit after all the expenses are deducted."

In a statement later interpreted by *Playboy* executives as a major act of betrayal, in the VIP Room at London's Playboy Club, Polanski was interviewed by Stanley Edwards of the *Evening Standard.* "I really don't like it here," Polanski said. "I feel the money that Hefner used to finance *Macbeth* was tainted."

"When I heard what he'd said, I hit the roof," Lownes claimed. "To say that was lousy business for both my club and Hef's movie. We deserved better, and Roman's reference to our dough being smelly was undeserved."

Lownes was so angered when he read about it in the *Evening Standard* that he fired off a note the next day to Polanski. "I no longer care for your full-length, life-sized portrait in my house. I am sure you will find no difficulty getting some friend you can shove it up."

\*\*\*

*[In 1977, Polanski was arrested and charged with drugging and raping a 13-year-old girl. He pleaded guilty to the charge of unlawful sex with a minor and spent 42 days undergoing psychiatric evaluations in prison in preparation for sentencing. He had expected to be put on probation.*

*But when he learned that the judge was going to order him jailed, Polanski immediately fled to Paris to begin many long years in exile from the U.S.]*

\*\*\*

It was Hef's #1 girlfriend at the time, Barbi Benton, who discovered the sprawling property that would become Hef's final home. A 30-room Gothic Tudor mansion on six acres of landscaped gardens, it stood in the exclusive Holmby Hills district of Los Angeles, only a block from "The Boulevard of Broken Dreams," Sunset Boulevard.

Hef claimed that the residential neighborhood was still haunted by the ghost of Humphrey Bogart, who had lived nearby until his death in 1957.

Close to the northwestern corner of the Los Angeles Country Club, near the University of California and the Bel-Air Country Club, it had been built in 1927 by Arthur Letts, Jr., the son of the founder of the Broadway Department Store. Letts had ordered his architects "to spare no expense." That meant the inclusion of such features as Botticini marble floors, a ton or so of carved oak paneling, and a Prohibition-era wine cellar with a hidden entrance.

Benton arranged for Hef to escort her on a tour of the property. At the time, it had been configured by the City of Los Angeles into a hospitality center for visiting dignitaries. In that capacity, it had housed ambassadors, prime ministers, and the Kings of both Thailand and Sweden.

Hef spent an entire day inspecting the property, asserting, "At last I've found my Shangri-La." By nightfall on February 3, 1971, he had agreed to pay $1,050,000 for the property, which was the most expensive price ever shelled out in the history of Los Angeles for a private home. *[The price he paid seems paltry in terms of today's skyrocketing real estate values.]*

Hef would spend more than $13 million in renovations of the interior and landscaping, adding both a swimming pool with a Grotto and tennis and basketball courts.

After its purchase, Hef brought in landscape architects to redesign the grounds and gardens, creating what he called "a veritable Garden of Eden with waterfalls, carp-filled ponds, and a variety of birds and animals flying or running free—in other words, "a Disneyland for Adults."

To inform the elite that there was a new man in town, Hef threw a party on November 20, 1971. It evoked those fabulous days of the Roaring Twenties when film stars staged lavish galas. A fleet of Rolls-Royce, Bentleys, Jaguars, and Mercedes-Benzes rolled along the winding ivy-banked drives that accessed the entrance.

"Film stars and models, along with members of the Hollywood gentry, including producers and directors, arrived. A pipe-smoking Hefner in pajamas and a silk robe greeted them in the marble-clad hallway, holding an open bottle of Pepsi. By his side was a high-collared princess in a low-cut blouse and tailored, spangled "blue denims." Or so wrote Gay Talese in his book, *Thy Neighbor's Wife*. He was referring to Barbi Benton.

The guest list included Burt Lancaster, Anthony Quinn, Ryan O'Neal, opera diva Beverly Sills, Richard Widmark, Yul Brynner, Russ Meyer, Shel Silverstein, Angie Dickinson, Walter Matthau, Senator George McGovern, Jerry Brown, Milton Berle, and Arthur Schlesinger, Jr.

No one captured the scene better than Anthony Haden-Guest, writing in *Rolling Stone:* "Hugh Hefner's Playboy Mansion West is a mullioned slab of Old Englishry, a gray gleam of ersatz granite in the Southern California sunlight. To the back, the image dissolves, re-forms. Sexy vicarage meta-morphoses to miniature Versailles. Gibbons swing and chatter in the trees, while a couple of house guests foozle with croquet hoops; a quintet of East African cranes lope up a handmade hill, and an associate movie producer hopefully pursues a trio of cuties. Mottled Japanese carp float on one side of a bridge, and on the other, in the bathing pool, another cutie, with the left cheek of her bikini bottom cut into a heart shape, floats on an air mattress."

There are few houses on the globe as famous as their occupants, but examples include Buckingham Palace, Neverland Ranch, and the Playboy Mansion in Los Angeles. Many visitors compared Hef's lifestyle at the mansion to that of Jay Gatsby, the fictional hero of F. Scott Fitzgerald's classic, *The Great Gatsby.* Like Gatsby, Hef, too, was a romantic figure, enigmatic, and mysterious.

"I always wanted my own parties, like Gatsby's, to evoke the Roaring Twenties. One of the most famous lines from the author was that 'There are no second acts in American lives.' How wrong he was on that. Ronald Reagan had a second act when his Hollywood career faded. And I turned my turbulent life into a veritable mini-series."

Guests were dazzled the moment they entered the Great Hall. Dominated by a mammoth chandelier, it boasted a double staircase layered with oaken garlands of vines and grapes. Near the Great Hall was the Mediterranean Room, floored in green marble with a lavishly sculpted fountain. Paintings by Salvador Dalí, Jackson Pollock, and de Kooning lined the walls.

The dark-paneled living room featured an Aeolian organ installed deep into a wall (it played 'Moonlight and Roses"); a 20-foot film screen, and state-of-the-art projectors. *[Movie nights were Friday through Monday.]* On site was a reproduction of a topless woman by Picasso and a collection of antique Bunny figurines.

In advance of some of his interviews, Hef would often meet reporters here. Wearing black silk pajamas and a red silk bathrobe, he'd make a dramatic entrance through black velvet draperies.

The Game Room was Hef's favorite. With a pool table in the center, it contained both vintage and modern games that included pinball machines, a player piano, jukebox, TV, and stereo. He became obsessed with backgammon. Billy Eisenberg, a champ of the game, remembered that once Hef played for three days and nights, surviving on "Dexies" and Pepsi. When not playing that game, he preferred Monopoly, using custom-made pieces to move across the game's real estate "landscape."

When he wasn't playing board games, he devoted most of his time to sexual pursuits. As girlfriend Benton said, "When I was on tour pursuing a career, Hef just could not keep his pants zipped."

His "pit of seduction" was, of course, his bedroom, which contained "every gadget invented by mankind," (his words) along with vibrators, dildoes, chains, studded leather harnesses, and large bottles of Johnson's Baby Oil. Most of his sexual conquests ended up with an oily massage.

There were six screens for watching TV, as well as video cameras if he wanted to film the action on his bed. Like a 1970s disco, psychedelic lighting provided an ever-changing rainbow array of colors.

Next to the bedroom was a library containing 350 volumes of the never-ending serial of his life. It included virtually everything ever written about him, both positive and negative. The room even contained the cartoon that Larry Flynt had run in *Hustler* magazine when he named Hef as "Asshole of the Month," and depicted him emerging from an anus.

An animal lover since he was a boy, Hef was finally able to fulfill a long-held dream of having a menagerie on the grounds of his Mansion. In essence, he set about to create an animal park with so many animals he had to register it as a zoo with the City of Los Angeles.

Flamingos and peacocks strutted across the grounds. A topless Playmate could be seen hugging Lambert the Llama as a Wooley Monkey showed off for visitors. They might also be introduced to Lucy Goosey, or else see Peter Sellers feeding the koi in the Japanese pond.

At almost every turn, one could encounter African cranes, macaws, rabbits, or dogs running wild. The gardens also encompassed a citrus grove, mostly orange trees, and the largest stand of redwoods in Southern California The landscape contained a bathhouse where nudity prevailed, plus a guest cottage, a large jacuzzi, and a game room which once a week was converted into an orgy den.

The most dramatic feature was the man-made Grotto, entered by swimming through a waterfall. Inside, a visitor saw a series of Jacuzzi baths or else secluded "islands" for making love. This was the site of Roman-style orgies where as many as one hundred naked bodies could

One of the most appealing of the thousands of exquisite objects in the gardens of L.A.'s Playboy Mansion is this replica of an ancient Roman monument—the Wishing Well.

It's been said that more futile wishes and unanswered prayers have been uttered into the recesses of this receptacle than anywhere else in Los Angeles—a city overflowing with broken promises and unfulfilled dreams.

satisfy their lusts.

The décor of the Grotto was modeled on the prehistoric caves of southwestern France. Embedded in the glass ceiling were decorative panels with tableaux of, among others, giant insects trapped in amber.

A *Playboy* editor, Larry Dietz, said, "An invitation from a beautiful woman to visit the Grotto was a euphemism for saying, 'Let's fuck!'"

Leon Isaac Kennedy recalled his first visit when he swam into the Grotto and found a bevy of beautiful women. Resting on an "island" overlooking the scene below, he spotted three men, each of whom he recognized: Peter Lawford, Warren Beatty, and Jim Brown, each "jaybird naked. Lawford shouted down 'C'mon up and join us!'"

Animals weren't the only creatures roaming the property. On a typical Friday night, a celebrity spotter might encounter George Raft, Groucho Marx, Jack Nicholson, Clint Eastwood, John Derek, Don Adams, Don Rickles, Tony Curtis, Bob Culp, Bill Cosby, James Caan, Harry Nilsson, Dean Martin, Sally Kellerman, Ursula Andress, Dean Martin, and Sammy Davis, Jr.

After Tommy Smothers surveyed the scene, he quipped, "If somebody set off a bomb, Hollywood would have to relaunch itself all over again."

On any given night, Peter Lawford might show up, perhaps with Yul Brynner and/or Glenn Ford. Eva Gabor, with whom Ford was having an affair at the time, might also visit.

One afternoon, Hef showed the property to Peter O'Toole, Paul Newman, and Joanne Woodward. At the end of the tour, the star of *Lawrence of Arabia* said, "This is what God would have done if only he had the money."

When his zoo was fully stocked, Hef invited a fellow animal lover, Doris Day. Before accepting his invitation, she asked, "Will I have to disrobe?" During her tour of the grounds, she spotted Sonny and Cher entranced by a gold and blue macaw.

Hef also staged "Fight Nights," inviting macho boxing fans such as Robert Mitchum, Mick Jagger, Jim Brown, Clint Eastwood, and James Caan. The bout was televised to the watching guests.

Hef seemed fascinated by boxing, despite his claim that "I abhor violence."

The most memorable boxing match broadcast to Playboys at the Mansion was between Mohammed Ali and George Foreman in 1974. Hef was amazed when Ali, at the beginning of the fight, said hello to him on camera and in front of the world.

No host in Hollywood, before or since, fed his guests as well as Hef. His lavish buffets featured everything from bowls of caviar to homemade mango ice cream. The kitchen operated 24 hours a day, and both Bunnies and movie stars could order as much as they wanted. Naturally, most guests went for the expensive items. One particularly larcenous glutton entered the kitchen and ordered fifty lobster sandwiches, telling the staff, "Don't be stingy with that lobster!" He then packed them up and took them to his own home in Brentwood to feed a party he was hosting later that night, his blue-collar guests from the B-list.

In January of 1975, Hef was ready to show off his Mansion and its grounds to the readers of his magazine. He authorized a 14-page pictorial of his abode, saying, "I'm preening proud of it."

In his new abode, Hef spent little time editing his magazine, relegating the tasks to others. He paid close attention every month, however, to the selection of the Playmate. One editor remembers him going over 500 nude photographs of young women before making his choice.

He was coddled and pampered by his staff of 90 servants. They included a butler in tails who stood ready to serve his breakfast when he arose every day at around four in the afternoon.

The "Prince of Pleasure," as the media dubbed him, rarely left his lavish estate, thereby inviting comparisons to Samuel T. Coleridge's Xanadu, as expressed in that poet's early 19th Century reverie, *Kubla Khan; or, A Vision in a Dream: A Fragment.*"

He had created a citadel of sensualism, where his every request was met. One that his staff soon became familiar with was for a cold bottle of Pepsi and a package of M&Ms. Often, however, his demands were more daunting, perhaps the procurement of a young woman who was ready, willing, and able for some mock bondage and the use of a 14-inch dildo.

\*\*\*

By 1975, the financial anguish of Playboy Enterprises became acute when it suffered a downturn in sales. Executives were told to take a 25 percent cut in salaries, and there were numerous other cutbacks.

Throughout all this financial turmoil, the London casino operation remained the brightest bulb in Playboy's financial chandelier. Lownes was still in charge at the London Club, and also directing additional Playboy casinos in Portsmouth and Manchester, too. In all, he was running the most successful club in *Playboy's* empire.

From January 1975 to June of 1981, some £600 million were exchanged for chips at England's Playboy Casinos. Many stories about losses by Arab sheiks became legendary, including that of a Riyadh prince losing £2 million in just three nights playing roulette in London.

A setback had come in 1968 after the passage of the British Gaming Act that mandated that all casinos in the UK had to be owned by local citizens. Foreign ownership was prohibited, and that directly applied to *Playboy*. Lownes met the challenge presented by the new law by establishing Playboy Club of London, Ltd, whose bylaws demanded that 75 percent of its stock be transferred to permanent residents of Britain.

\*\*\*

Lownes became the sybaritic frontman for the British casinos, and his lifestyle reflected his elevated position. His financial success led to his move to a more upscale address: 1 Connaught Square, a house which had previously been the home of Mary Augusta Ward, a 19th Century novelist who used to sell millions of copies of her books. Lownes came into possession of a mammoth painting by Francis Bacon. It was considered so "hideous" that he moved it into the hallway of his new home, where it was displayed near a surreal depiction of a grandfather clock painted by Timothy Leary, the LSD guru.

In 1972, Lownes acquired the most prized possession of his life, the country estate of Stocks, in Hertfordshire, near the hamlet of Aldsbury in the Chilterns. Mentioned in the Domesday Book, the present estate dated from 1773. The 42-room Georgian mansion had been owned by Earl Grey, Britain's 19th-Century prime minister. It had also been owned by Mary Augusta Ward, who, coincidentally, had also owned Lownes' house in London.

The property once had been a school for proper young ladies, and Lownes had been warned that the interior smelled of "cabbage and pencil boxes." He set about to change that and pumped a million dollars into renovations, having acquired the estate for £115,000.

A former private chapel was converted into a training school for Bunny *croupières*, for which he charged Playboy $250,000 a year. He also installed a disco, unique among elegant country estates.

He spent most of his weekends at the country estate, arriving there from London in a

Stocks, the historic manor house at Aldsbury, near London, where Victor Lownes threw some of the hottest, sexiest, and most sought-after country house parties since the English Restoration.

The neighbors ran the gamut between amusement and horror.

chauffeur-driven Rolls Royce. In the rear of the car, he often nestled with one, two, or three Bunnies chosen from the staff at the club.

On weekends, and dressed in raffish tweeds and Wellington boots, he paraded around the grounds. Because of his elevated position in London, he also mingled with the aristocracy, attending parties with Princess Anne or fox-hunting with her brother, Prince Charles.

***

With his newly acquired fortune (thanks to Hef), Lownes became an avid collector of modern art, acquiring some lesser-known paintings by, among others, Picasso. He also developed a passion for pornography and, other than King Farouk of Egypt, was said to have acquired the world's largest collection of porn movies.

Once his country estate was restored and "ready for prime time," he hosted a series of parties that became notorious throughout England. They attracted press attention as "the most decadent in Britain."

Neighbors still remembered his first New Year's Eve Party, where naked women were running across the grounds in spite of the cold weather. "They weren't singing 'Auld Lang Syne,'" claimed one of the local landlords.

A lot of movie stars, including some from America visiting London, came to his country weekend parties, which most often morphed into orgies. His guest list included four Peters: Lawford, Sellers, O'Toole, and Cook. Warren Beatty and Woody Allen came to see the action, as did Jack Nicholson, Gene Hackman, George Segal, and Lee Marvin.

"One thing one could count on at one of Victor's parties," Sellers said, "was that by midnight, panties would be hanging from the chandeliers."

Using Hef as a role model, Lownes had dreams of becoming a producer of both films and stage plays in the West End of London.

"I backed some losers from time to time, but I had my successes, too."

He decided to invest in the Monty Python film series, despite his fears about whether British humor would go over in America. For £200,000 he invested in the first Monty Python movie, a 1971 release called *And Now for Something Completely Different,* based on their hit TV comedy series. The situations referred to in the title included being roasted on a spit or lying on top of a desk clad in a small pink bikini.

Lownes named himself executive producer, and he conflicted with the performers. The director, Ian MacNaughton, found that Lownes was trying to insert himself into every facet of production.

The movie made money for me," Lownes said, "and I could almost

339

live on what was coming in for years to come. In the States, Monty Python became a cult favorite."

He sent frequent invitations to Hef, praising the sex appeal of his international array of beauties, whose countries of origin ranged from Finland to Italy. He informed Hef that some of his Bunnies performed specialty acts which he might want to interact with personally.

"I am not a screaming sex maniac," he told a reporter. "Neither is Hugh Hefner."

When asked if he were promiscuous, he said, "A promiscuous person is some other bloke getting more sex than you are."

Privately, he told his friends, "I have Bunnies for breakfast, Bunnies for lunch, Bunnies for dinner, and Bunnies for a midnight snack. I had no idea that with all these Bunnies hopping about, Hef and I would get into a jealous feud over the same Bunny."

***

From the historic city of Portsmouth (England), a 21-year-old beauty quit her £12-per-week job as a supermarket clerk, packed her sole suitcase, and rode the train to London. Her mother had fried a chicken for her and given her a loaf of home-baked bread to eat along the way.

The goal of Marilyn Cole was to become a Playboy Bunny. She'd already submitted a cheesecake picture of herself and had been accepted for an interview at the Playboy Club in London.

She checked into a "bedsit" in Muswell Hill, and nervously waited for the days to pass before she was allowed to enter the offices of the Playboy Club. Once there, she was interviewed and hired as a trainee for a Bunny job. She didn't know where such a position would lead her, no doubt she'd have to fight off a lot of creeps, but she was willing to do just that. At the time, it was beyond her wildest dreams that she would come between two of the world's most notorious playboys, Victor Lownes and Hugh Hefner.

Born in 1949, she just knew she'd look great wearing that satin costume with a Bunny tail. She already had long legs and hair like silk. By the time she was fourteen, she was said to have the biggest and most beautiful breasts in Portsmouth. All the boys in school, and a lot of grown men, were after her.

"Being a Bunny, I found out, was hard work," she said. "You had to do more than look beautiful. You had to carry a damn tray serving food and drink and learning the 'Bunny Dip' in ways that wouldn't make your breasts fall out. It required you to be an exhibitionist. But for the most part, it was bloody good fun. It sure as hell beat working in that dull supermarket where I was employed."

Within a week, her beauty and charm had been noted by the staff, and the following Monday morning she was asked to ride in a chauffeured limousine to the home of the club's manager, Victor Lownes. The "Bunny Mother" who supervised the girls warned her, "You may be asked to pose with your clothes off."

"No problem," Cole answered. "I'm not the shy type."

Within an hour, she was ushered in to be greeted by the lascivious eyes of Lownes himself. Instead of using his own photographer, he wanted to photograph her himself in total privacy.

"Within fifteen minutes, I had heeded his request to strip bare-assed naked," she said. "How could I have known I'd spend decades getting naked in front of him since this was my future husband?"

In the studio were very sexy erotic paintings by Egon Schiele and Balthus. "Victor did not seduce me right away. That would come later."

"He later showed me a set of my nude photos, and, if I say so myself, I looked both sexy and gorgeous. He told me he was air-freighting my nudes to Hefner at his Chicago Mansion."

"As it turned out, Hef learned that I, too, was dating Marilyn. More than dating, you might say. She was not a virgin when she met both of us. In those days, no one belonged to anyone else. We traded freely on the flesh market. I never thought I owned a woman, and I thought Hef and I were on the same page about that."

As Cole herself admitted, "We were all promiscuous back in those days."

She had been impressed with Lownes the day she met him, and she had also found Hef attractive. "Vic was a swashbuckler who had discovered Brooks Brothers suits when he was in diapers. He was a 'man about London,' indulging in libertine pastimes unknown since

As the centerpiece (and centerfold) of *Play-boy's* edition of June 1973, British-born Marilyn Cole is depicted within what looks like an homage to a Pre-Raphaelite English Garden.

Known as "the gilrl who married the Boss," she made a spectacular marriage, and remained happily married for many years, until his death, to Victor Lownes.

341

the Restoration."

A charismatic philanderer with three goals—sex, beautiful women, and parties—Lownes told her, "I am the true avatar of the *Playboy* image."

He once confessed that he let gay men enjoy him below the belt provided he had a beautiful young woman feeding him her breasts. His tongue was rumored to be "devouring."

When he first met Cole, he had no intention of marrying her. "I never want to tell a girl I love her and get her hopes up."

She later revealed to Lownes that on her first night at the Chicago Mansion, Hef had invited her for dinner. "Later that night, I became his dinner when he lured me into the round bed."

His affair with her continued on and off, as did her more torrid affair with Lownes. Hef did not

Less restrained than the Americans, the French editors of *Cinerevue* magazine positioned Marilyn Cole, bare-breasted and newly "discovered," on the cover of its September 26, 1975 edition.

It helped her ride the craze of fascination with the Brits *(la folie anglaise)* then in vogue in Paris.

want his friend to go with Cole to any party he attended. "I'll be so jealous I'll be burning up," he warned Lownes.

On his next trip to London, Hef was the escort of Barbi Benton, but he nonetheless managed to seduce Cole in Lownes' bedroom when Benton was out shopping along Bond Street.

Cole became Playmate of the Month in January 1972, and the following year, she was designated as Playmate of the Year, the only Briton to hold that title. She worked as a Playboy Bunny from 1971 to 1974.

As the first model whose full frontal, jaybird-naked nude was published in *Playboy*, Cole caused outrage in some quarters of America. Take, for example, Macon, Georgia. There, Mayor Ronnie Thompson ordered three of his cops to go to the drugstore to arrest the hapless pharmacist who sold copies of *Playboy*.

[In time, Hef's interest in Cole waned, but Lownes still found her captivating. "I even did the unthinkable. I asked her to marry me."

His male friends asked if he wanted to have them throw a stag party. He turned

342

*them down. "My whole life has been a stag party."*

*At the time of Lownes' death at the age of 88 in 2017, he was still married to Cole. He had, for a while, been a multi-millionaire, but his estate had dwindled to about $600,000, which he left to her.]*

\*\*\*

In 1972, Swinging London of the 1960s had ended, and Lownes was in the mood for expansion. He was told that historic Clermont House on Berkeley Square was up for sale. With a Palladian interior, marble columns, a very grand staircase, a Grand Salon, and glittering crystal chandeliers, it was England's most elegant casino. In its basement was Annabel's, the most exclusive disco in London, a favorite of Princess Margaret.

John Aspinall, the building's owner, was a gambler himself and had run into financial difficulties and wanted to bail out. Lownes to the rescue! He offered to buy it for £357,000.

It took only nine months for Lownes to recoup the investment for Playboy.

Before he departed from the property, Aspinall told Lownes, "Clermont is the kind of casino where English gentlemen can ruin themselves as elegantly and as suicidally as did their ancestors 300 years ago."

Under new management by Playboy, Clermont House began welcoming an odd blend of clients, as English aristocrats mingled with oil-rich businessmen from the Mid-

**Supremely posh**: The Clermont Club, 44 Berkeley Square, Mayfair, London W1, was the most elegant casino in London.

With a Palladian interior dating from 1742, it was noted during the 1960s for visits from Princess Margaret, Giovanni Agnelli, and lots of high-profile show-biz personalities. According to one addicted gambler, "It had gaming tables squeezed into a pair of small rooms, and it resembled neither Las Vegas nor Monte Carlo. It was more like a library, really, where fortunes changed hands discreetly."

In the early 70s, it fell under the ownership of Playboy Enterprises, attracting oil-rich, well-connected Arabs, who, when they weren't throwing petro-dollars around, told each other a secret:

"Dangle a diamond bracelet or a Cartier watch at her, and the blonde Bunny is yours for the night. Of course, you can also achieve the same result with a mink coat."

dle East. On any given night, you might encounter such society figures as David Stirling, Lucian Freud, Lord Lucan, Lord Derby, Lord Boothby, the Duke of Devonshire, or even Ian Fleming, the creator of the James Bond thrillers. Within this odd mixture, the Arabs were the biggest spenders, often losing vast fortunes in just one night.

"If the Israelis wanted to get the Arabs to the peace table, all they had to do was cover it in green baize," Lownes told Hef. "The Arabs are gambling addicts. One sheik came into the casino and lost £1.2 million. He begged me to lend him another $100,000, which I foolishly did. By 3AM, he not only won back his loss but left the club with an extra £300 in his pocket. That was the poorest investment I ever made."

Another sheik lost £65 million one night. Before the evening was over, he asked a staffer to show him the checks he'd written. When they were presented to him for his inspection, he ripped them into shreds and rushed out of the club, heading immediately to the airport and boarding the next flight to the Middle East.

The Arabs also patronized the high-priced hookers who hung out at the club. According to Lownes, "Hef didn't allow prostitution, but there was no way I could really stop it," Lownes said. The girls were elegantly dressed in evening gowns, and whereas the Arabs awarded them with gold, diamonds, and mink coats, an English gentleman sent a girl flowers and candy.

In London, Hef learned that Lownes had taken up with two beautiful young twins, Mary and Madeleine Collinson. "They like to do everything together," Lownes said to Hef. "If you get my drift, and I know you do, the girls made it clear they came as a two-way package, which turned them into a three-way package. Call it 'double your pleasure.'"

Hef became so intrigued with the twins that, in a daring move, he had them pose nude together in October of 1970 for *Playboy*, the one and only time he'd ever done that. He followed that innovation in October of 1971 when he made Darine Stern the first African American cover girl.

*** 

Hef called her "My Yellow Rose of Texas." Hailing from Dallas, her name was Karen Christy, and she had large, succulent breasts, and a slim figure encased in buttermilk skin. Her head was topped with a peroxided blonde coiffure.

She'd grown up in Abilene, Kansas after the death of her parents, her mother from kidney disease and her father, shot to death in a hunting accident.

During one of his semi-annual "Rabbit Hunts" across the American landscape, Hef's aide, John Dante, picked Christy out of a line-up of 200 local beauties, each hoping to be selected as a Playboy Bunny in a club or perhaps a centerfold in the magazine.

Dante invited her to the Chicago Mansion and wanted to show her around, "perhaps make a conquest before Warren Beatty arrived to snare her away." He took her on a tour of the Mansion, including the dormitory, where she'd be lodged with a lot of other Bunnies.

At the end of their tour, she asked to see Hef's bedroom. After checking with him and finding him awake, Dante escorted her for a meeting with Hef, who was still clad in pajamas. He showed her around his bedroom, demonstrating how his round bed operated, vibrating and revolving around.

Dante knew it was time to go. "I always surrender a woman to the boss man if he desires her. That was the pecking order at the Mansion."

That night, Christy appeared in a pair of skimpy, shocking pink hot pants. After dinner with Hef, he took her to the Grotto for a nude swim before retreating, alone, to his bedroom. Although he was mildly disappointed that she was not a virgin, he later informed Dante, "The best sex I ever had. What man in America can judge good sex better than me?"

He later made her Playmate of the Month for December 1971 and moved her from the dormitory into a private apartment at the Mansion.

"Karen is the Jean Harlow of my schoolboy fantasies of the 1930s," he told Dante.

DID YOU KNOW? That among the dozens of objects "branded" with the Playboy Logo was a series of *"Playmate of the Month Centerfold Jigsaw Puzzles?"*

A wannabe Playboy could buy it, assemble it over a period of weeks, or months, in a prominent position in his living room, asking friends to insert a missing piece, should they be so inspired.

The puzzle whose image, still in its original can, is displayed above is a replica, when assembled, of Karen Christy's centerfold, as it appeared in the December, 1971, edition of the magazine.

An alluring emigrée to L.A. from Abilene, Texas, she became, for a while, one of Hefner's personal playmates, but only after some power plays and competion with another member of his staff.

Hef and Karen became lovers, and both of them admitted to falling in love with each other. Soon his gifts to her began to arrive in abundance: A five-karat diamond ring from Tiffany's, a diamond-encrusted gold wrist watch from Cartier, a full-length, ivory-colored mink coat, a white Lincoln

Continental, even a white Persian cat with green eyes that matched her own.

There was one major complication: He was already in love with Barbi Benton, who was living at the time in Los Angeles. He became the third leg of a love triangle, and he began to divide his time between Los Angeles and Chicago.

His cover was blown in a *Time* magazine article that called him "a two-of-a-kind consumer, with Barbi Benton stashed in Los Angeles and Karen Christy in Chicago.

"When I was in Los Angeles, I called Karen every day and told her how much I loved her. When I was in Chicago, I phoned Barbi every day. Same message. But my cover was blown by *Time*. I lost both women, as they moved on to other lovers, even husbands."

\*\*\*

In mid-June of 1972, in the midst of a tour of America, the Rolling Stones, including Mick Jagger and Keith Richards, were invited to the Play-boy Mansion in Chicago. The band accepted Hef's invitation, though he later regretted extending it.

As one *Playboy* staffer remembered it, "It was a four-day orgy of constant partying, Bunny hopping, nude romps, and massive consumption of drugs."

At poolside on his first night, Jagger appeared in his bathrobe. He was nude underneath. A former Playmate, a model from Georgia, came up to him and said, "I'd love to bite your ass."

Jagger flipped open his robe, exposing himself nude and fully erect. "Go to it, luv."

Milda Bridgewater was at the scene, and she remembered "the wild, rollicking stay of the stoned Stones. They were screwing everything in sight and running around naked. The air was thick with the smoke of weed. My God, they were even climbing the draperies. It was a sight I'd never seen before."

On their second night in residence, Bobbie Arnstein bowed out of the revelry and retreated to her room, ordering something from room service. She remembered finishing her dinner with a slice of Brie cheese.

Jagger opened the door and walked in. He was shirtless, wearing a pair of skin-tight white leather pants. Suddenly, he began licking and kissing her, and she worried that her breath smelled of Brie. She wished she'd rinsed her mouth before trying to satisfy his lust.

She pushed him back, and he fell into a chair on which rested a gooey chocolate cake. "Sorry, luv," he said, heading out the door with globs of chocolate icing dripping from the seat of those once white leather pants.

One nineteen-year-old from Maryland showed up in Chicago to be photographed by Alexas Urba. When she arrived at his studio at 10AM, he discovered that her breasts were black and blue from bruises inflicted the night before with the Rolling Stones. Parts of her skin were discolored, and he drove her to the hospital. It took two weeks before her skin had cleared and she could be photographed in the nude.

As Hef's guests of honor, the Stones had been given the best guest accommodations in the Chicago Mansion, including both the Red and the Blue Rooms.

Before their eventual departure, the rockers had trashed

Mick Jagger's abusive treatment of hotel suites became a legend worldwide. With members of his entourage, there was so much damage inflicted on some of the accommodations within the grand hotels of Europe that some of them refused to house him or any other members of the Stones.

It was a lesson Hef learned, to his regret, after Jagger trashed one of the accommodations at the Playboy Mansion.

Jagger is depicted above on the cover of this souvenir from his 1987 tour of Australia

their quarters, inflicting serious damage. Razor blades had been washed down the drains of some of the washbasins, and plumbers had to tear into the walls for access to clogged pipes. Bedroom fixtures, especially rugs and upholsteries, had been ripped or burned with cigarette butts.

Broken mirrors had to be reinstalled and carpets replaced. Eventually, Hef ordered that the decimated rooms be radically redecorated.

***

In an attempt to compete with the up-and-coming porn magazine, *Penthouse*, Hef decided to meet the competition with the takeover of *Oui*, a French magazine widely known for its explicit, full-frontal female nudes. The first issue had appeared on newsstands in Paris under the name of *Lui* in 1963, a decade after *Playboy* had made its debut.

"I was placed in the awkward position of copying a magazine like *Penthouse* that, in essence, had been a rip-off of *Playboy*," Hef said. "But if *Penthouse's* publisher, Bob Guccione, wanted to slug it out as to who could print the most filth, then welcome to the race, fucker."

In a memo addressed to his new staff at *Oui*, Hef wrote "I am hoping to lure a younger reader than the average reader of *Playboy*. Most of our guys are over 35. I want a more rambunctious editorial slant in both the articles and most definitely in its depictions of nudes. We'll follow *Penthouse's* example when it comes to photography."

Hef manufactured an astonishing 750,000 copies of the first American edition of *Oui*, and nearly all of them sold within two weeks. Young men

This is the cover of the first American edition of *OUI* magazine, released in 1972 as one of Hef's "experiments,"

When it didn't take off, he sold it.

literally grabbed them off newsstands, even though many in the mainstream press attacked Hef. "Hefner has gone too far with *Oui*. What country does he think he lives in? France?"

Zsa Zsa Gabor was given a copy of *Oui* to peruse. She said, "Dahlink, in its centerfold, you can see all the way to Honolulu."

The articles were also "hair-raising." Beneath a photo of a native of New Guinea was this headline: THIS IS THE MAN WHO ATE MICHAEL ROCKEFELLER.

*[The story had derived from a reporter who, as part of an anthropological expedition, had wandered into the wilds of New Guinea, buying artifacts. There, he met a native who relayed, through an interpreter, that he was the hungry man who had eaten the Rockefeller heir for dinner.]*

Another heated controversy associated with *Oui* magazine involved the then-29-year-old bodybuilder Arnold Schwarzenegger, who gave an interview about sex, drugs, and bodybuilding. When he ran for governor of California, this explicit interview was republished to embarrass him.

To his horror, Hef eventually learned that, contrary to his forecasts, *Oui* was stealing more readers from *Playboy* than from *Penthouse*. He decided that the time had come not to say "*oui*," but to say "no." He sold the magazine in 1981.

*[Reconfigured and under new ownership, Oui continued to generate news. Its editors focused on celebrity nudes: Demi Moore, Linda Blair, and Pia Zadora.*

*By the 2000s, Oui went even farther in its depiction of explicit sex, publishing pictures of couples having intercourse, depicting the actual penetration.*

*The magazine struggled along for survival until 2007 when it folded. By then porn had reached the Internet, and the market for printed nudes was in decline.]*

\*\*\*

According to *Playboy's* Literary Editor, Auguste Spectorsky, "In November of 1972, I set out to upgrade *Playboy's* image with a class act." I invited the 71 most distinguished writers, academics, journalists, scientists, politicians, and opinion makers to Chicago for a cross-pollinating conference about the state of the nation. The press dubbed them "The Chicago 71."

"I wanted to elevate the magazine and turn it into a periodical that people weren't ashamed to read," he said. "After all, *Playboy* was the kind of magazine to which a man of letters like Jean-Paul Sartre would grant interviews to. The highlight of the conference would be a sneak preview *[hopefully followed by lots of favorable reviews]* of Roman Polanski's *Macbeth*, the one that had been financed by Hef."

Writers articulated in advance why they'd agreed to attend the conference: Max Lerner arrived to "study youth" at the Playboy Mansion; Gay Talese to play tennis; Arthur Schlesinger, Jr. to see *Macbeth*; Dr. William Masters "to talk about the future of sex." Some scribes were blunt in expressing hopes of being able to fool around with some of the Bunnies.

Hef remained surprisingly uninvolved. As Spec recalled, "Most of the time, he preferred to stay in bed with a Bunny."

He was, at least, symbolically visible in the form of an inanimate stand-in. According to Art Buchwald, who attended the conference, "He sent this dummy stand-in who looked remarkably like him."

The guest list included a spectacular array of talent: John Clellon Holmes, John Kenneth Galbraith, Arthur C. Clark, V.S. Pritchett, Michael Arlen, Kenneth Tynan, Tom Wicker, Garry Wills, Larry King, Murray Kempton, Harvey Cox, James Dickey, Bruce Jay Friedman, Nat Hentoff, Calvin Trillin, John Cheever, John Skow, and Nicholas von Hoffman.

The press generated by this conference was generally unfavorable, with critics evaluating it as "boring, pretentious, sheer extravagance with little substance, and a waste of time."

Hef's strange words to his departing guests were, "You writers are *Playboy's* real sex objects."

In a depressing afterthought on his way out of the conference, Murry Kempton, later a winner of the National Book Award, told a reporter, "The grace has gone out of our lives."

***

*Playboy's* writers' conference might be defined as "Spec's Last Hurrah." He died of a heart attack on January 17, 1972 at his island home in St. Croix. During the final two years of his life, he had been quite ill and had performed many of his editorial duties from his sick bed.

His replacement at *Playboy* was Arthur Kretchmer, who was only thirty-one years old and had already worked at *Playboy* for five years. He was tall and thin, a New Yorker who had graduated from City College. Under a head of black curls and behind a beard, he viewed the world through horn-rimmed glasses.

Radical in his politics, he often showed up for work provocatively dressed in outfits that included a "Trotsky Youth" T-shirt, faded blue jeans, and black cowboy boots.

Kretchmer was strong-willed and opinionated, telling *The New York Times,* "We know we're publishing the best magazine in America. As the new editor, I have to keep the same level. We don't have to prove anything."

With bitchy intent, a rival editor said, "In spite of what Arthur told *The Times,* I'm sure he'll be innovative, perhaps publishing the genitals of America's most famous writers. For James Jones, readers will have to use a magnifying glass."

Reporter Charles Leroux described Kretchmer as "tall, soft-spoken, and erudite, looking like a professor of anthropology."

According to Kretchmer, "In my first year as editor, I endorsed a story about how lesbianism was ruining the women's movement. It caused an outrage among feminists."

He worked hard to bolster Hef's image. "He has never gotten enough credit for inventing the world," Kretchmer said. "Here is this finger-snapping hipster who spotted where society was going better than the sociologists and the politicians."

Kretchmer had read his first article in *Playboy* way back in the 50s. Entitled "Things We Can Do Without," the writer had listed "bad martinis, Boston, and virgins."

"After reading that, I thought Hef and his editors were the coolest guys on the planet. My dream was to join them one day."

Both Hef and Kretchmer came to feel that after the turbulent 1960s, the era of war, revolt, and sexual revolution had ended. "Things have cooled off so much, I fear *Playboy* may be losing some of its original bite. We've got to guard against that," Hef warned.

"We are seeking to define and embody the cutting edge of the mainstream," Kretchmer told the press.

When Hef read that, he asked his editor, "Exactly what does that mean?"

"I mean that I want to make *Playboy* more contemporary, more integral to life in the 1970s. We need to get over the malaise that set in after the '60s passed us by. The Age of Aquarius is over. We should appeal to today's urban male, at least to his psyche."

At a meeting, Hef conveyed the newest incarnation of his editorial desires to his editors: "I want a lifestyle mag devoted to how a playboy spends his leisure time—not only with women, but with foreign cars and European fashions. Let's even give our reader advice on how to survive a tax audit. Tell our boy that if the IRS agent is gay or a woman, to wear tight pants and no underwear. That's our candid advice."

Assisted by Kretchmer, Hef reached out to the now-matured Baby Boomers, consumers who had rebelled in the 1960s and who were now trying to become a part of the business world, earning enough money to buy the luxuries of life. "For these men, the day of the smelly, long-haired hippies in a crash pad was over," Hef said.

Kretchmer launched a "Lust for Life" campaign, suggesting that the new *Playboy* wore faded jeans and soft leather boots, sitting out on his "vodka martini" front porch at his summer vacation home watching the sun set in the Golden West.

Hef wanted *Playboy* to stay abreast of rapidly changing political developments. With Hef's permission, Kretchmer serialized *All the President's Men* by Carl Bernstein and Bob Woodward. The articles exposed the crimes of the Nixon administration in ways that led to the president's resignation.

Kretchmer never cultivated links to the literary world as impressive as Spec's, yet he brought in some of the brighter bulbs in the chandelier of American writers and journalists, figures who included Joan Didion, Tom Wolfe, and the spectacularly liberal (sometimes zany) Hunter S. Thompson—seemingly everyone's favorite writer—as freelancers.

After Spec's departure, Kretchmer steered the magazine down a rocky, left-handed road. He published articles written by such liberals as Senator Gaylord Nelson or writer Michael Harrington. Tom Hayden and his wife, Jane Fonda (aka "Hanoi Jane"), were given a literary platform to air their views. Simultaneously, much-beloved "people of faith," including evangelist Billy Graham, came under attack.

Hef also ordered his new editor to introduce romance into *Playboy*. "When there is romance," he said, "the sex link is difficult to assault." Romance creeped into articles about travel, fashion, and food. *Playboy Advisor* ran letters that agonized about romantic entanglements. "What can I do?" wrote a recently married man. "I had never met my wife's Maid of Honor until the day of the wedding. I fell in love with her and married the wrong woman."

One feature, "The Rousing Return of Romance," urged readers to reconsider the allure of candlelit dinners, hand-holding in the moonlight, and consumer products such as massage oil, Hef still preferring Johnson's Baby Oil for massaging his Playmates.

Other articles published by the new editorial board focused on the "Me, Decade" of the '70s. Hef claimed that *Playboy* had endorsed the tenets of that decade long before its arrival. "We're already totally in step with the 'Me Decade'—that is, in our appreciation of living one's life and getting the most out of every day…and most definitely the night when even more pleasure is possible."

The results of a 1971 survey among college students revealed that with the closing of the 60s, young people had become more involved with personal pursuits, including self-realization and the quest for one's own desires, than they were about social change, abortion, and civil rights.

Hef finally concluded in his magazine that the "Me, Decade was about doing one's own thing. We at *Playboy* have made it acceptable to care about oneself, first and foremost."

# Chapter Ten

*PENTHOUSE* (BOB GUCCIONE) VS. *PLAYBOY* (HUGH HEFNER)
VS. *HUSTLER* (LARRY FLYNT) VS. *SCREW* (AL GOLDSTEIN)
BATTLING OVER THE BOUNDARIES OF FEMALE NUDITY

# "THE PUBIC WARS"

## LINDA LOVELACE,

RIDING HIGH ON HER PORN CELEBRITY,
GETS DEEP, THROATY, & STAR STRUCK AT
THE PLAYBOY MANSION

THE ARNSTEIN AFFAIR
(HEF'S EXECUTIVE ASSISTANT COMMITS SUICIDE)

HEFNER'S DAUGHTER, CHRISTIE—"HARE APPARENT TO THE PLAYBOY
EMPIRE"—BEGINS A COST-CUTTING "REIGN OF TERROR"

PLAYBOY LOSES ITS GAMING LICENSES IN BRITAIN
HEFNER LAMENTS: "MY CASH COW NO LONGER GIVES MILK"

Looking sweet and demure, a symbol of virginal innocence, Linda Lovelace, star of the porno flick, *Deep Throat,* was hailed by Sammy Davis, Jr. as "America's best cocksucker."

In the center is a cover of *Penthouse*, the first (September 1969) of its American editions.

Bob Guccione, displayed on the right with his open shirt and gold chains, was a world class sexual predator.

**During Hefner's heyday,** "skin rags" that were more explicit and less firmly entrenched than *Playboy* appeared only rarely in "front and center" positions on newsstands. More frequently, they were stealthily sold from "under the counter," and only if they were specifically requested. Consequently, Hef didn't pay them much attention—at least not at first— since they did not seriously affect *Playboy's* circulation.

One challenger, however, became threatening, since it virtually declared open warfare on *Playboy*. A playboy himself, Bob Guccione had founded *Penthouse* magazine in Britain in 1965. At first, he had wanted to call it *Playgirl*.

His new magazine became a big success, mainly in London. Its content included material appealing to "urban lifestyles" like those within *Playboy*, but with a big difference. Guccione introduced softcore pornographic pictorials that in direct contrast to *Playboy*, showed the pubic hair of his (completely nude) models, whom he hired for £5 an hour.

In September of 1969, *Penthouse* began appearing on U.S. newsstands, its logo incorporating the symbols of both Venus and Mars. Instead of a Playmate of the Month, it featured a "Penthouse Pet," an undraped woman usually wearing a necklace with the distinctive logo of the magazine.

There was no doubt about it: *Penthouse* was clearly a rip-off of *Playboy*, hoping to capture Hef's readers with photos more explicit than what *Playboy's* in-house policies allowed.

When accused of plagiarism of *Playboy's* business model, Guccione defended himself: "We took no more from *Playboy* than Hefner stole from *Esquire*."

Brooklyn-born Guccione had become Hef's chief rival. Five years younger than Hef, he was a skilled photographer who, in the beginning, took his own pictures of the nudes he published. His magazine always contained erotic content more extreme than that within *Playboy*, as well as more in-depth reporting on one of Guccione's favorite topics, government corruption and scandal.

As ironic as it seemed, Guccione had once considered training to become a priest, but eventually rejected the idea. He did not think he could practice celibacy. Like Hef, he was also a cartoonist.

Ignoring the under-the-counter skin magazines, *Penthouse* became the first major American magazine to show pubic hair on its models. Within months, that was followed by even more intimate shots of the vulva and the anus.

*Penthouse* also featured both authorized and unauthorized photos of

Madonna and Vanessa Williams, the first black Miss America. One layout depicted porno queen Traci Lords. It was later that Guccione learned that she was only fifteen when she had posed for these candid shots.

As its circulation increased, *Penthouse* became more explicit, publishing photos of women engaged in urination, various forms of bondage, and "facial penetration."

A street fighter, Guccione had grown up as a tough kid battling his way through the alleyways of Brooklyn. He drifted around Europe for years as a painter, making a meager living as a fortune teller, later as a dry cleaner.

This tough guy was willing to take off his gloves to battle Hef in a series of anti-*Playboy* ads. One of them depicted the Playboy Bunny shedding tears over a sign that depicted *Penthouse's* circulation figures. The *Wall Street Journal* asked, "Is there room at the top of the totem pole for two smut twins?"

Robert Gutwillig joined *Playboy* as its marketing director and vice president. Before that, he had worked for the Time-Mirror Company in Manhattan, which helped launch the American version of *Penthouse*. During Gutwillig's stint with Time-Mirror, executives there designated him as "Bob's keeper," with instructions to brief them about how Guccione was handling their investment.

In his new post at *Playboy*, Gutwillig attended the monthly board meetings over which Hef presided. He was the first to sound an alarm about Guccione and the growing threat from *Penthouse*, warning, "The Redcoats are coming! The Redcoats are coming!"

"Perhaps because I was the new kid on the block, no one, especially Hef, seemed to pay me much attention," Gutwillig said. "I reported that *Penthouse* sales had shot up to 1.5 million copies monthly, all at the expense of *Playboy*."

"Hef kept calm like a steady commander during these meetings, just sitting with his Pepsi," Gutwillig said. "He let me blow off steam before heading back to his pinball machines and more Bunny business. He always had this look on his face. To me, it said, 'I've done my duty and sat through all this alarmist shit. Now I can go and I won't have to listen to more of it until another month.'"

In April of 1976, the *Wall Street Journal* ran an article entitled "Playboy's Slide." In the eyes of that paper, *Playboy* had become "a little frayed when compared to *Penthouse*." The article concluded, "For years, the transfusions—*Playboy* magazine's profits—have kept the company alive, but now are diminishing. Without radical surgery, the life of the body is in danger."

In the summer of 1969, Guccione made it obvious who he was gunning after. He ran ads across the country depicting the *Playboy* Bunny in the crosshairs of a telescopic rifle with a caption that read, "WE'RE GOING RABBIT HUNTING!"

Another ad depicted the *Playboy* Rabbit lamenting "Penthouse Envy." That ad asked, "Has the aging *Playboy* gone soft?"

As its sales rose, *Penthouse* became even more daring, depicting women fondling their private parts, engaged in lesbian scenes, enjoying three-somes and adventures associated with dildo masturbation.

"We will present our pin-ups without *Playboy's* hangups," Guccione promised his readers. "The *Playboy* reader today is hobbling around on a cane while the *Penthouse* reader is climbing an alpine peak before coming down again to bed a Penthouse Pet in a cozy Swiss chalet."

He referred to Hef in his silk pajamas and Japanese silk robe as "a closet queen." In vivid contrast to Hef's dress code, Guccione wore tight leather pants revealing his endowment ("my pride and joy") and encased his feet in cowboy boots. His shirts were open-necked and deeply unbut-toned, displaying an abundance of flashy gold chains from which dangled, among other ornaments, a depiction, in gold, of his penis—"the exact size."

Guccione and Hef came together only once, and that was at a gala sponsored by their mutual friend, Bernie Cornfield, head of the Investors Overseas Service. When Cornfield brought Guccione over to meet Hef, he was escorting his girlfriend, Barbi Benton.

As Guccione remembered it, "Hefner licked his little pink lips and gave me a limp handshake, muttering something that sounded like a hello."

"How are you?" Guccione asked of both Hef and Benton but got no response.

Two days later, Hef used Cornfield to send a message to Guccione: "Fuck you!"

In spite of the rising competition from *Penthouse, Playboy* was slow to change. Hef held to his "girl-next-door" standards of female nudity, de-picting only breasts, until he felt the time had come to become a soldier in what came to be known as "The Pubic Wars."

But he proceeded with caution, fearing new charges of obscenity that might be brought against him in court.

In August of 1969, *Playboy* offered its readers their first glimpse of pubic hair. It was seen fleetingly in a strobe lit photo of Paula Kelly, a dancer in the musical *Sweet Charity*. Several images of her graced (or dis-graced) the pictorial, and in two of them, her pubic hair was clearly visible.

That led to *Playboy* being charged with racism, since Kelly was African-American. Civil rights leaders charged that "a black woman is being ex-ploited for the white man's delectation."

"Hef proceeded with extreme caution," said his art director, Art Paul. "He wanted to test the waters and try to gauge reader reaction."

He waited a few months, later noting that "the world did not explode when pubic hair appeared in *Playboy*."

In January of 1971, *Playboy* ran pictures of model Liv Lindeland, revealing her back-lit blonde tuft in a layout. A year later, in the January 1972 issue, he published a full frontal of Marilyn Cole, the British model involved with Victor Lownes. "At last, I was reconciled to the urgent need for our readers to see the Playmate of the Month display all of her charms," Hef said.

Writing in *Rolling Stone*, Anthony Haden-Guest said, "The Marilyn Cole picture was set up in Chicago where Hefner was in a negative mood. He was very indecisive at the beginning of the shoot, ambivalent about what was about to transpire. At the last moment, he finally said, 'Let's go for it and see what happens.'"

Even though he'd authorized a display of pubic hair in his own magazine, Hef still denounced *Penthouse* as "cheap pornographic crap!"

After the Cole feature, it became *de rigueur* for Playmates to show their frontal anatomy; and on occasion, even a flaccid penis in the background, never a semi-erect or an erect one. He'd sent a memo "outlawing one organ penetrating another organ."

Even *Playboy* covers changed in June 1974 when one of the model's nipples appeared in the photo selected for the cover.

Guccione was rigorously tracing these new developments at *Playboy*. "The difference between Hefner and me is that he's still fighting the sexual revolution, whereas

Deliberately more lurid than *Playboy* in almost every instance of both its cover art and the views inside, *Penthouse* played the provocation card, as illustrated on the cover of its April 2003 edition.

Also, in a striking departure from the artfully demure presentations in *Playboy* which Hefner had choreographed and steered, *Penthouse* was always more glaringly obscene.

For example, within the pages of the edition depicted above was a bluntly phrased recommendation for a then-new brand of masturbation cream which *Penthouse* endorsed.

Rated best in the Penthouse Survey was Gun-Oil Stroke 29 Cream. According to Martin Downs, author of *Penthouse* magazine's review, "The first few strokes were unpromising, and (like the first time you got high) you wonder if it'll really work. Then suddenly you'll be like 'Damn, this shit feels awesome on my dick.'"

It was a turn of phrase that Hefner and his editors at *Playboy*, it was argued, would have avoided.

we at *Penthouse* know the war has already been won."

Guccione proclaimed himself as "The Liberator of the Loins," contrasting himself with "Granny Hefner hiding under his 19th Century sun bonnet."

Hef did admit to *Time* magazine that "*Playboy* is not nearly as *avant-garde* as it used to be. We are not in the forefront any more in the battle for sexual freedom. But as far as *Penthouse* is concerned, I see it as an old-fashioned sex machine with a bit of frosting. Guccione is no more than a Victorian Peeping Tom." Hef did, however, acknowledge the "libidinous appeal" of *Penthouse*.

Depicted above is Bob Guccione evoking a Renaissance-era Medici Prince, outdoing anything Hef might have presumed to have accomplished within his Playboy Mansion.

By 1975, Hef came to realize what Guccione had long known: That straight men get off on looking at pictures of two women engaged in lesbian love. Considered novel for *Playboy* at the time, its multigirl extravaganza issue was released as *Playboy's* October 1975 edition. Retailing at the time for $1.25, it was subtitled "Stunning Portraits of Sappho Women in Love."

In 1982, much to Hef's envy, Guccione was listed by *Forbes* as one of the 400 richest men in the United States, with a net worth of $400 million. That same year, Guccione summoned architects and artisans from Italy and France to build the largest private residence in Manhattan. With thirty rooms, it cost $7 million a year to maintain it and its staff.

Guccione's vast wealth also allowed him to assemble one of the country's largest private art collections. It contained works by El Greco, Chagall, Dalí, Picasso, Léger, de Chirico, de Kooning, Pissaro, Renoir, Rouault, Van Gogh, Botticelli, and Dürer, among many others.

According to Guccione, "I not only have more money than Hefner, but I'm a better lover. I've seduced some of the same bitches he has, and all of them tell me I'm much more skilled in the sack, the master of the multiple orgasm. Girls fight over me."

\*\*\*

In newsstand sales, *Penthouse* peaked in 1984 when it beat out *Playboy* and published the first nude photos of Vanessa Williams, who had become the first African-American Miss America. The issue in which she appeared sold 3.5 million copies, earning Guccione a profit of $1.5 million. *[On that edition's front cover, she appeared demurely, and fully clothed, with the octogenarian comedian George Burns, with a caption exclaiming "MISS AMERICA! OH, MY GOD! SHE'S NUDE!"]*

The photographer, Tom Chiapel, had first approached Hef and offered the pictorial to him, but he rejected it. He did not want to run the blatantly erotic photographs without Williams' consent, and she was avidly opposed to it. When she'd worked as a makeup artist for Chiapel, she had agreed to pose for erotic shots with a white model, but never realized that they would be seen by millions of readers. She'd foolishly signed a release.

Even though Hef wanted to run her pictures, he understood that many African Americans had been proud of her status as the first black Miss America, and he did not want to taint her reputation.

After viewing the layout, author Mike Edison wrote: "Miss America's labia were

MADONNA: Not Like a Virgin

The competing magazines sometimes shared the same vision about who should appear on their respective covers.

pretty and perfect and right for the whole world to see. Her white partner licked her from every direction. You could practically hear them purr."

Many African Americas were outraged against Guccione, and he received numerous death threats.

Williams was pressured to give up her crown, surrendering it to Suzette Charles, Miss New Jersey, the first runner-up.

Although Guccione relished his success with the dethroned Miss America, he soon wondered where to turn for his next triumph. "What frontier was left for me to cross? There remained full-fledged fucking and fisting."

As for Williams, she rebounded from the scandal and went on to have a successful career as a singer, actress, and fashion designer. In 2012, she published a memoir, *You Have No Idea*, in which she revealed that she had been sexually molested by a woman at the age of ten, and that she'd had an abortion when she was in high school.

In 1974, *Penthouse* sued *Playboy* for allegedly disseminating "false and fraudulent information about its circulation figures among advertisers and ad agencies."

*[Reacting to that, Robert Preuss, VP of Playboy, retorted with alleging basically the same charge against* Penthouse, *which had claimed that in December of 1973, it had sold 4,637,933 copies. A survey by the Audit Bureau of Circulation revealed that the figure was high by 613,416 copies. Guccione was embarrassed.]*

*Playboy* countersued, alleging that *Penthouse* had infringed on its trademark in its advertising. Eventually, both cases were thrown out on technicalities. "Too god damn bad," Guccione said. "I had Hefner by the nuts. It was an open-and-shut case of libel."

A final insight into the effect of the Pubic Wars between *Penthouse* and *Playboy* was revealed in a survey of returning U.S. prisoners in the aftermath of the Vietnam war. Many of them, including Arizona Senator John McCain, were asked "How has America changed during your absence?"

The overwhelming response was that Hugh Hefner, since the

Vanessa Williams being crowned at her coronation as the first African American woman to become Miss America.

But when nude pictures of her surfaced, the crown was taken away and awarded to the first place runner-up. Hef had been offered the very explicit photographs, but turned them down, not wanting to humiliate either Williams or the pageantry and pride associated with the Miss America contest.

Guccione had no such concern.

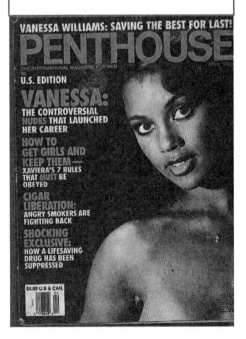

prisoners' return, was now showing pubic hair in *Playboy*.

It wasn't just the Pubic Wars that had caused conflict between Hef and Guccione. It was the battle for readers. To make that war all the harder, both publishers had to deal with the rising tide of religious fundamentalists who collaborated during the 1980s to challenge them.

At one point, these religious zealots persuaded some 18,000 stores to discontinue their sales of both magazines. In the aftermath of that resistance from fundamentalists, *Playboy* lost an estimated 700,000 readers, a loss that compelled it to lower its advertising rates by 17 percent.

*Playboy's* new art director, Tom Staebler, suggested that these outraged fundamentalists had not read the magazine recently, or had perhaps never even seen a copy of it. "We are trying to take some of the sex out of the magazine—for pragmatic reasons, not philosophical ones."

Young adult males had become a shrinking audience for both magazines, preferring to get their sexual kicks, if not from the real thing, then from watching video cassettes and adult cable TV. "They offer more explicit sex than *Penthouse* or *Playboy* ever did," said Phil Beach of San Diego. "To think that when I was in college I got off by looking at a *Playmate of the Month* exposing her tits. Now I prefer looking at either vaginal or anal penetrations."

\*\*\*

In 1974, at the Playboy Mansion in L.A., Hef had been delivered the first issue of *Playboy's* competitor, Larry Flynt's *Hustler* magazine. Hef's first reaction was, "I think this Flynt guy wants to be a gynecologist more than a magazine publisher. Frankly, I don't see much future for it."

Then, after thumbing through it, he tossed it into a corner of his office along with such sleazy, under-the-counter magazines as *Hot Hole Detective Woman, Mouth Fucking, Muff Diver, Pussy Lickers, Swallow,* and *Surrender the Beaver.*

On that hot, sunny afternoon in California, based on his first view of the first edition of *Hustler,* Hef misjudged its publisher, a controversial, outspoken, and gutsy guy who was utterly fearless about being perceived as scatological, tasteless, and crude.

Flynt seemed to take pride in the attacks that the media hurled at him. The *Chicago Sun-Times* used harsh terms to describe him: "a beer-belly macho," a "sex pervert," a "filthy degenerate," and "just plain white trash." Columnist Bob Greene nicknamed him *"El Scummo."*

The son of a sharecropper, Flynt was born in Kentucky in the poorest county in America. He grew up in abject poverty, living for most of his early life in a one-room shanty. At the age of 15, he used a fake birth certificate to join the U.S. Army. After military service, he returned to Kentucky and survived as a bootlegger until he heard that IRS agents were on his trail. He rushed to join the Navy in 1960, rising to the rank of radar operator aboard the USS *Enterprise.*

After his stint in the Navy, he returned to Dayton, Ohio, where he put his entire savings ($1,800) into buying his mother's tavern. Working twenty hours a day, and fueled by amphetamines, he prospered and used the profits to invest in more bars, becoming the first in the area to feature nude hostesses and dancers. He called his string of taverns "Hustler Clubs," with outlets in Toledo, Cincinnati, Columbus, Cleveland, and Akron. They were so hotly patronized that each grossed between $250,000 and $500,000 a year.

In January of 1972, *Hustler* magazine originated as a two-page *Hustler Newsletter* about his clubs. In time, however, revenues from his clubs declined drastically, as newer competitors challenged him.

Looking with envy at Goldstein's *Screw,* Hefner's *Playboy,* and Guccione's *Penthouse,* plus all the other "skin rags," creeping their way onto the market, Flynt decided to enter the magazine publishing field, issuing his first edition of *Hustler* in July of 1974.

Goldstein related an incident

Larry Flynt published the first edition of *Hustler* magazine in July of 1974, daring to be far more provocative than either *Playboy* or *Penthouse.*

As one critic said, "*Hustler* became the most eye-popping, vile, officious, and wonderful sex magazine of the 1970s."

Larry Flynt, publisher of *Hustler* magazine, as he appeared on CNN. He was denounced as "the personification of evil and a nightmare of a degenerate."

when Larry Flynt showed him some secret pictures snapped of Hef having oral sex in a "69" configuration with a Playmate. According to Goldstein, "Flynt urged me to publish them in *Screw*, but I turned him down. I was impressed, however, with the size of Hef's dick. It sure beats mine."

"I brought Hef and Larry together, and he agreed to turn over the purloined photos, which had been smuggled out of the Playboy Mansion," Goldstein said. "But later, Larry told me he'd had copies made and might one day publish them in *Hustler.*"

In his book, *Thy Neighbor's Wife,* Gay Talese wrote: "We need a free society, and freedom is not won by literary tea parties and well-meaning, virtuous publishers. It is won by disreputable people like Al Goldstein."

*Rolling Stone* was the unofficial magazine of the counterculture.

Its editors claimed that Hefner's world was "one of adolescent fantasy. "

Hef's chief rival, Bob Guccione, told *Rolling Stone* that "Hugh Hefner is the closest thing to a closet queen that I know of."

\*\*\*

At the time, *Playboy* and *Penthouse* were seemingly preoccupied with their respective "Pubic Wars." Unphased and uninvolved with the fine points of all that, *Hustler* "trumped" both of them by publishing the first "pink shots" of open vulvas in a nationally distributed magazine. "Right from the beginning, I wanted to make Hefner and Guccione look like Sunday school teachers."

Flynt's big break came from Jacqueline Kennedy, then married to Aristotle Onassis. As a team, they were known as "Beauty and the Beast."

In isolation on his Greek island, she sometimes sunbathed in the nude. During a sojourn there in 1971, she had been snapped, nude, by paparazzi. Four years later, during *Hustler's* second year in business, in its August 1975 issue, Flynt was granted permission, for a fee of $18,000 to include the four-year-old nude shots of the former First Lady. The magazine sold a million copies in just a week. *Hustler* was launched.

It became obvious that Flynt was imitating *Screw* more than *Playboy* or *Penthouse*. One of his columns was entitled "Asshole of the Month." A public personality was selected—once, Hef was named—and a replica of his head was shown during its release from the anus of a cartoon donkey.

To compete against Hef's "Little Annie Fanny," or Guccione's "Wicked Wanda," Flynt created a comic strip entitled "Honey Hooker." She supplied graphic details of her sexual encounters with both women and men, even invading the locker rooms at the Super Bowl for access to sex.

The most controversial feature in *Hustler* was "Chester the Molestor" cartoon strip, in which Chester, a middle-aged pedophile, gleefully raped underaged girls.

As the months went by, *Hustler* became more and more hard core, depicting sexual penetration, sex toys, and "group fucking." At its peak, it reached three million readers, nearly all of them male, although a few thousand lesbians bought the magazine, too.

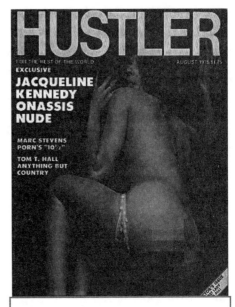

During Jacqueline Onassis' post-JFK heyday, the nude photos of her snapped on a Greek island with a telephoto lens were the most controversial images in media, provoking indignation on talk shows nationwide.

Replicated thousands of times since then, and widely visible today from a fast search on the internet, they're infinitely less incendiary than when they appeared in this edition of *Hustler* from August 1975.

As an ardent and often provocative liberal, Flynt infuriated the leading figures, both spiritual and political, of his day. A two-page illustration in his magazine depicted Nelson Rockefeller, President Gerald Ford, and Henry Kissinger collectively "gang-raping" the Statue of Liberty. Called the "Bicentennial Ball," the illustration was a satirical condemnation of the government's abuse of power.

Whereas *Playboy* had its interview column, with insights into some of the most powerful and/or creative personalities on the globe, Flynt sought out more colorful figures, many of them barely, if at all, on the fringes of mainstream life.

One controversial article was an interview with "The Biggest Black Cock Ever," with a subhead—"The Most Sought After Piece of Meat in the Western world."

Flynt's motto became, "Anyone can be a *Playboy* and have a *Penthouse*, but it takes a man to be a *Hustler.*"

It took only two years for Flynt to aim his guns at *Playboy.* He published an article that infuriated Hef. It was called "Going Down in Bunnyland: The Decline and Fall of the Playboy Empire."

In it, Flynt attacked Hef's staff as "a pack of cronies who did not know how to run a business." He cited figures, claiming that the value of *Playboy's* initial stock offering had declined from $21.1 million when it went public in 1971 to about $3.5 million in 1976. The article also made the claim that Playboy Clubs were draining Hef's bank account at the rate of $4.5 million a year in losses. "Hefner's resorts were a big mistake," *Hustler* charged, "the misconception of egomania."

In the meantime, *Hustler* was taking a "shark's bite" out of *Penthouse* and *Playboy.* "Not bad for a redneck Kentuckian hillbilly who never went beyond the ninth grade," Flynt said.

"Minority stockholders could bring a class action suit to depose Hefner for his gross mismanagement and for raiding corporate funds," *Hustler* charged. "Hefner doesn't give a damn about being an editor or publisher. Ask him to name a hero, and it will be Arthur Godfrey, not Henry Luce. He's just an upright, starstruck guy. When he got married, he was a virgin, not his wife."

In summation, Flynt concluded "*Playboy* has become a hospice for old men and tired ideas."

\*\*\*

The worst day in the life of Larry Flynt occurred on March 6, 1978 in Lawrenceville, Georgia, small backwater where he was charged with obscenity for shipping copies of *Hustler* into the county.

He showed up for battle at the local courthouse with his lawyers. At 11AM, a lunch recess was called, and Flynt and one of his attorneys, Gene Reeves, Jr., went across the street for a bite. As they were returning to the courthouse for the afternoon skirmish, an unknown assailant, hiding in the alleyway across the street, fired at them. It was obvious that he wanted to hit Flynt, but the attorney also got shot in the arm.

Flynt narrowly escaped death. As he recalled, "It was like a hot poker pushed through my abdomen."

As he gasped in pain, a second bullet tore into him, too. The sniper had fired two .44 Magnum bullets, mangling his internal organs and causing Flynt to collapse onto the sidewalk. A court reporter described the scene: "Larry Flynt looked like a pile of intestines. As I learned later, his spinal cord was nearly severed, and his stomach was ripped apart."

The shooting would leave him paralyzed for life, which he was forced to spend in a wheelchair. He experienced excruciating pain, which he described as "agonizing suffering like being suspended in a vat of bubbling water."

"I had been disemboweled and hung on a meat hook like a ham in my grandpa's smokehouse in Kentucky."

The judged declared a mistrial, allegedly saying, "Mr. Flynt has suffered enough for one day."

The local hospital didn't have the equipment needed, and Flynt was rushed to the more advanced medical facilities in Atlanta. A nicked artery near his heart would not stop bleeding. "In Atlanta, my life was saved by a miracle," Flynt said. "although I knew I would never walk again. I was a casualty in the war to preserve the First Amendment."

Even though he did not admire Flynt, Hef was devastated at the news when he heard about it in Los Angeles. He told his staff, "It could have been me."

Initially, it was reported, perhaps falsely, that Flynt thought that either Hef or Guccione had hired a hit man, a ridiculous accusation.

After he recovered, Flynt decided it was time to move away from Ohio and settle in Los Angeles. There, for $375,000, he bought a Mediterranean-style mansion once inhabited by Errol Flynn, Robert Stack, Tony Curtis, and, more recently, Sonny and Cher.

Flynt's assailant remained unknown for many years until his arrest in Missouri as a serial killer who had murdered eight victims. During his interrogation, Joseph Paul Franklin, a white supremacist, confessed to having shot Flynt because he'd run photos of an interracial coupling in *Hustler* beneath a headline "Black cock with a blonde."

Franklin was tried and convicted of murder. He was executed by lethal injection in November of 2013.

Oliver Stone, the producer of the film *The People vs. Larry Flynt* (1996), wrote: "He is the late 20th Century version of Horatio Alger pursuing the American dream, but with a perverse twist of building his empire from pornography. I find him more in the rapscallion tradition of Mark Twain's Huckleberry Finn—the country boy, misunderstood by many, trying to figure it all out, rafting down the American psyche of a country gone wacko."

\*\*\*

In the 1960s, Hef said, "Without question, love in its various permutations is what we need more of in this world." For him, a celebration of sexuality meant a celebration of all types of sexuality.

As the 20th Century neared its end, he even entered the debate over same-sex marriage. "The fight for gay marriage is, in reality, a fight for all of our rights. Without those rights, we will turn back the tide of the sexual revolution and return to an earlier, puritanical time. People practice discrimination disguised as religious freedom."

"What makes Hefner really important is the combination of his belief in the First Amendment and his Playboy Philosophy," said Charles Francis, president of the Mattachine Society of Washington, D.C. "He was an early supporter of LGBT equality. *Playboy* gave a platform where the first serious consideration about homosexuality could take place, well before the Stonewall Riots in Manhattan in 1969."

At that time, most psychologists viewed homosexuality as an "illness and perversion." Hef advocated that gay men should be treated as human beings, not as perverts or deviants.

WOODY HARRELSON COURTNEY LOVE EDWARD NORTON

THE PEOPLE vs. LARRY FLYNT

A MILOS FORMAN FILM

"THE BEST PICTURE OF THE YEAR!"

DVD

Mike Edison wrote that *The People vs. Larry Flynt* is a cartoon—as fancied up, condensed, and idealized as most Tinseltown biopics.

"If the Larry Flynt film had actually shown what was in *Hustler*—the vicious, no-holds-barred ghetto humor and colossal hyperexplicit pornography, that made *Playboy* look like propaganda for a new Disney theme park—I think most movie-goers would have been appalled."

Obviously, although Hef's primary allegiance was aimed at heterosexual masculinity, the magazine took a strong stand on gay and lesbian issues even before Stonewall. Editors reported legal and political developments relevant to the gay community in the popular *Playboy Forum*.

Finally, as a culmination of the personal evolution he'd experienced since the 1950s, Hef said, "There is room to expand the accepted definition of manhood to include gay men, too."

Mattachine founder Frank Kameny introduced his famous slogan, "Gay is Good" in the Playboy Forum, and in March 1969 issue of the magazine, he expressed his outrage at the anti-gay attitudes and policies then prevalent.

Hef paid close attention to the implications of the Stonewall Riots. Spontaneous and widely publicized demonstrations by members of the

LGBT community on June 28, 1969, they sparked an increase in public awareness of gay rights. They were followed by a revolution by gays campaigning for their rights in ways that approximated what African Americans had done in the 1960s.

***

With deep disappointment, Hef watched *Playboy's* circulation fall from its peak of seven million in 1972 to only 3.5 million in 1986. To contrast, *Penthouse* had reached its peak of 4.8 million in 1978, tumbling to 2.7 million in 1986. The other rival, *Hustler,* went from 3 million in its top year of 1976 to about 800,000 readers a decade later.

The change in readership forced *Playboy* to enter the field of video cassettes. Larry Flynt, the editor of *Hustler* magazine, predicted that the age of video would make men's magazines *passé.*

Gary Cole, *Playboy's* new photo editor, admitted, "We are getting depressed around the office with all that's happening in the magazine field. Lifestyles are changing, and there are more leisure options than ever before."

The magazine's art director, Tom Staebler, claimed that *Playboy* covers were becoming more fashion conscious than sexy, as were its contents. Articles featured men's skin care products, new styles in fashion, more coverage of sporting events such as football, and interviews with leading male movie stars. "We have long since retreated from those so-called Pubic Wars," Staebler asserted.

"Our hearts were never in those pussy wars," Hef claimed. "For a while, we at *Playboy* lost our compass, but we've found our way back."

Behind the scenes at *Playboy,* the staff gossiped among themselves, suggesting that Hef, now in his 60s, "had lost touch."

He wanted to be brought up to date with how Guccione was diversifying after the loss of readership. He was told that Guccione was now distributing dried milk to the Arabs in partnership with Muhammed Ali.

Asked about "the clean-up" at *Playboy,* Guccione said, "Hefner's girl next door moved away a long, long time ago. His trouble is, he's never faced that fact."

"Our culture today needs *Playboy* much more than it did in the 1950s— and more than it did in the 1970s," said Arthur Kretchmer, who was now the chief honcho, as Hef had more or less faded into his bedroom, arising on occasion to dictate some memos.

***

Among the "smut peddlers" in the publication field, no one—certainly not Bob Guccione of *Penthouse* or even Larry Flynt—sank lower than Al Goldstein. He was the most daring publisher in America, taking risks that no one else dared. One that caused probably the most fury, with the greatest personal risk to himself and to his magazine, was his outing of F.B.I. director J. Edgar Hoover "as a cross-dressing faggot."

Goldstein was the publisher of *Screw,* a scandalous weekly tabloid that had exploded onto the scene in November of 1968. Promoting itself as "Jack-Off Entertainment for Men," it sold 140,000 copies a week during the peak of its success.

It reached its zenith in 1973 when it published unauthorized nude photos of Jacqueline Kennedy Onassis, secretly

This interpretation of The Last Supper was obviously not the work of Leonardo da Vinci.

It was authorized by Al Goldstein, publisher of *Screw*, who was known as "the Scumbag's Scumbag."

*Screw* was a protest rag. "We burst onto the scene as a direct reaction to Hugh Hefner's false fantasies in his so-called *Playboy*," Goldstein claimed.

snapped by paparazzi on Skorpios, the Greek island owned by her husband, Aristotle Onassis.

*The New York Times* defined Goldstein as "a cartoonishly vituperative amalgam of Borscht Belt comic, a free-range social critic, and a sex-obsessed loser who seemed to embody a moment in New York cultural history—that is, the sleaze of decay of Times Square in the 1960s and 70s." Another writer called him "a hairy, sweaty, cigar-chomping, eczema-ridden fatso."

Near the end of his life, he boasted of having had 7,000 sex partners of various genders, colors, and sizes.

Although Hef never considered Goldstein a serious rival worthy of great amounts of respect, he nonetheless ordered that twenty-five "hot off the press" copies of *Screw* be delivered to him every week as a bellwether for what the competition was printing. He'd leave most of them in the foyer of his Los Angeles Mansion for visitors to read, or at least gape at.

Because Hef had himself been the victim of obscenity charges in his battle with censors, he watched the unfolding of Goldstein's raft of legal troubles with intense interest.

In 1977, Alabama governor George Wallace sued Goldstein for $5 million after the publisher's charge that he learned how to perform sexual acts by reading *Screw*. The case was eventually settled for $12,500.

"No one had a vocabulary to match Goldstein's," Hef said. "Not even my good buddy, Lenny Bruce, who went to jail for the words spewing out of his mouth. Goldstein was never afraid to speak of 'dykes, cocksuckers, niggers, WOPS, and kikes.'"

"As I was growing up on the tough streets of Brooklyn," Goldstein told Hef, "I learned my vocabulary from the local gangs, who sometimes beat the shit out of me. We often put down each other's mothers, calling dear ol' mom a dicksucking whore who even fucks dogs. It was a Brooklyn thing."

In his memoirs, Al Goldstein did what no other autobiographer had ever done: He published a photo of himself getting fellated.

Reporter Lili Anolik wrote: "Al Goldstein was straight out of Central Casting. Out of your worst nightmare. He was fat. He was hairy. He was covered in cigar ash, eczema flakes, and flop sweat. *Screw* wasn't just dirty. It was gross."

"Trying to survive over the years, I did almost anything to make a buck, even selling my blood," Goldstein said.

"For reasons known only to him, Hef seemed to like to hang out with me," Goldstein said. "Every now and then I got invited to one of his parties, even to orgies in his Garden of Eden. At the first party I attended, I got to fuck two Playmates, both of them sisters. The only reason I got laid was that I had a $200 bag of coke, which I found was the key to many a Playmate's spuzz box—certainly not my manly physique."

"At another party, I met this former girlfriend of Hef's," Goldstein said. "He'd dumped her. That time I screwed her right on one of Hef's pool tables. I'm sure he had to pay to have it recovered. I loved eating the analytical pussy of this bitch, but she dumped me when I refused to buy her a Rolex."

"One night at one of those *Playboy* parties, I met this little heifer named

Toni," Goldstein claimed. "After we left the Mansion, she and I went to this real seedy part of town, an after-hours S&M hangout for both men and women. We got to see guys torturing guys, guys torturing girls, whatever. That night I hung this gal upside down and screwed her—a lot of fun. Try it sometime if you can find a willing bitch."

"The following night, I told Hef about that place, and he slipped out of the comfort and security of his Mansion—and we were off into the night. Hef didn't participate in any of the acts of torture, but he took it all in like a wide-eyed stranger in Babylon. The one act he did join in was as a fellow pisser. He stood next to me and urinated with me and five other guys over this naked redhead in a bathtub. She was the Queen of the Golden Shower addicts. After she got up, a nude young teenaged boy got into the tub, but reinforcements had to be called in, since Hef and I and the other piss dudes, had already emptied our bladders."

"Although Hef preferred eating at his Mansion, contrary to his legend, he did go out on occasion," Goldstein said. "For a while, he spent a few nights on and off at a restaurant, Spago. He would show up with the same boyfriends—Robert Culp, Robert Blake, James Caan, and Tony Curtis. I don't mean to suggest anything by the use of the word 'boyfriend.' If anything was going on in that group, it was between Tony and Hef. They always sat together and seemed to share a lot of secrets."

According to Goldstein, "Once, after Tony returned from the men's room, he told us that a guy had followed him in, stood next to him at the urinal, and looked down at his dick as he pissed. Curtis asked him, 'Are you cruising me?' and the guy said, 'No, but I wanted to look at the piece of meat that plugged Marilyn Monroe.'"

As surprising as it sounds, Goldstein also pursued friendships with both Larry Flynt and Bob Guccione. "I used to crawl into bed with Bob and his wife at their Manhattan brownstone. I knew Flynt from way back when he used to run this seedy bar and stripper joint in Columbus, Ohio. Larry's wife and I used to wash the pussies of his strippers before they went on stage. From there, they'd invite guys from the audience to go down on them. Most of them had dirty twats and needed to be cleaned before beginning their act."

"Actually, it was Hef who made me famous on a national scale by running an interview with me in *Playboy*," Goldstein said. "Before that, I was just known to the raunch crowd in New York City. But even though he increased the circulation of *Screw*, I got pissed off at him because of the headline he wrote himself—A CANDID (UGH!) CONVERSATION WITH AL GOLDSTEIN."

"He didn't have to write that. It wasn't necessary. But you couldn't go to him and say, 'Hef, what in the fuck are you doing?' He was just so controlling, like a choreographer. Nonetheless, that damn interview put me on the radar screen. I became a national star and a hero to all smut lovers."

In his *Playboy* interview, Goldstein claimed, "I really believe I'm doing something good in demythologizing sexuality—Okay, the way I do that is raunchy (my favorite word), obnoxious, and disgusting."

In March of 1974, Goldstein launched another new magazine, appropriately called SMUT, and evaluated it as follows: "It was so filthy that you had to take a bath after reading it, using a lot of disinfect solutions. SMUT was just not dirty…more scummy."

"Let's face it. During my reign in the 1970s, I was the leading 'porner' in America, the master of the vulgar, the prince of tastelessness. I made no effort to make our filthy material look artistic, like Hef did in his nude pictorials. I liked to see a man's cum running from a *puta's* mouth, dripping down to her tits. My stock in trade was sex in the raw."

"Hef got a lot of artsy-fartsy writers to contribute to *Playboy,*" Goldstein said. "Not me, brother. I published reviews of erotic massage parlors, brothels, peep shows, and porn flicks, the dirtier the better. I also ran pictures of nude movie stars, all of them snapped when they were trying to get a break in show business. I ran nudes of Marilyn Monroe but also such stars as Burt Lancaster in all his uncut glory."

Using press and PR devices never before seen in the history of publishing, Goldstein threatened to fire members of his staff if they did not write and include within *Screw* unflattering copy about him. "I wanted to be attacked regularly in print," he said. "I told my editors to give me everything negative about me they had. They could make fun of my tiny cock or call me an overweight, penny-pinching Jew fag." Goldstein—in a way that he believed, correctly or not, contributed both to his notoriety and to the sales of *Screw*—seemed to revel in his negative publicity.

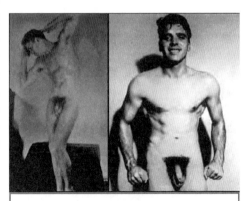

Al Goldstein in *Screw* was the first publication to run these notorious nudes of a young Burt Lancaster. "I thought our readers should get to see what Elmer Gantry's dick looked like. Burt, in case you didn't know, was bisexual."

\*\*\*

In time, Hef and Goldstein parted company over some minor dispute. "He banished one of my closest friends from attending movie night at the Mansion," Goldstein said. "I got pissed off."

In *Screw,* Goldstein fought back and for a time made *Playboy* its "whipping boy," as he called it. He launched his war of words with an article headlined, "PLAYBOY: A MAGAZINE FOR FAGS?"

He charged, "Hefner's *Playboy* is written and edited by a pack of cockhungry homos who often throw up when having to work with pictures depicting female genitalia." *[Before publishing those lines, he had a rewrite man soften them a bit.]* Nonetheless, he still asked, "Can *Playboy* or its publisher, one Hugh Hefner, actually get it up for a woman? I doubt it!"

In another article, Goldstein wrote, "The words that spill out of Hefner's glossy dream factory cushion the *Playboy* reader against the constant fear that his latent homosexuality will spring forth one day, as he seeks hungrily to gobble up every cock within swallowing distance."

"The *Playboy* world is peopled by hairless women and cockless men, a world of hypocrisy, sham, and deceit," Goldstein maintained.

"*Screw* is anti-*Playboy*," Goldstein said. "I hate Hefner's air-brushed nudes that come out of his fantasy factory, which is only a fancification of fucking, not the real thing."

"I was the one who made *Deep Throat* a success, not Hugh Hefner," Goldstein claimed. "Of all the skin publications, we are the only one not inspired by *Playboy.* Of course, *Playboy* itself is the naughty stepchild of *Esquire.* Without *Esquire,* Hefner would never have come up with the idea of *Playboy.* He lacks such imagination."

"*Playboy* just pretends to be for the urban male," Goldstein claimed. "Its true origin, its real sensibilities, have roots in the Midwest. Hefner's stern parents are American puritans who came from Nebraska where they had sex in those days with their clothes on. In contrast with *Screw,* I bring a sense of post-Kinsey sexual awareness. Hefner is just a spectator to the *Zeitgeist.* Fuck, don't I sound erudite!"

"Picture this," he wrote. "Hefner in his luxurious mansion fucking some porcelain-skinned Playmates. Me, in this seedy hotel on the Lower East Side of Manhattan, plugging some nigger whore transvestite in the ass."

"Do you get my point?" he asked. "I am god damn tired of Hefner's attempt to sanitize sex. *Screw is a direct reaction to* Playboy. Even John Lennon told me so."

"I added the names of John and Yoko to my masthead. I call them 'My Bedfellows.'"

Growing even more daring in subsequent issues of *Screw,* Goldstein wrote: "Hugh Hefner is afraid to admit that he likes cock. But I'm not afraid to admit that I do. I've experienced thrills sucking off a man or being serviced by a man for my own big blast-off. The message from *Screw* is this: If it's love between two people, who cares what gender it is?"

"I've written about my own bisexuality," Goldstein asserted. "I've even run pictures of myself with a black girlfriend. Color and gender never stood in my way when it came to having a good time. I've always marched to a different drummer. I even started a gay tabloid called *Stag*, which was written and edited by two gay activist pals of mine."

"But as the clock moved on, I grew tired of attacking Hefner," Goldstein said. "I'd made my point. I turned to Tricky Dickie instead, even exposing the fact that he has a small dick."

*[Of course, he was referring to the nickname that the enemies of President Richard Nixcon had given him.]*

"As president," Goldstein said, "Trickie Dickie spent more time getting plowed by the Cuban sausage of his longtime lover, Bebe Rebozo. He hadn't slept with Pat in years. The first time he seduced her, she asked, 'Are you in yet?' I also ran a centerfold of the two Nixon daughters licking each other's tasty bits. I depicted Nixon's attorney, John Dean, fucking the First Lady. After all, somebody had to do it. Pat wasn't getting anything from Tricky."

"In revenge, that bastard Nixon ordered the Feds to go after my ass." Goldstein said.

***

Historian Mark Stein wrote that the *Playboy Forum* created "what may have been the country's most influential forum for public discussion about homosexuality during this period."

It wasn't until 1999 that Carrie Leigh, Hef's steady girlfriend from 1983 to 1988, told a reporter for the *Washington Post* that Hef's "infamous and misogynistic sexual swinging also included men."

The reporter wrote, "Leigh and other Hefner girlfriends from the 1980s say they were also disturbed by Hefner's propensity for sexual encounters with men. Leigh claims that she interrupted Hefner's liaisons with men a couple of times. The irony of this symbol of heterosexual virility being also involved in homosexuality was not lost on her. But her real fear was that Hefner's only true interest in women was exploitative."

"His homosexuality bothered me," she said. "I tried to accept it. He thought it was all okay."

Indeed, in an interview with the *Washington Post*, Hef acknowledged having many bisexual trysts. "There was some bisexuality in the hetero-

374

sexual, swinging part of my life," He added that Leigh, "who also had lesbian dalliances, was 'obsessed' with gays and her suspicion that I preferred men was only a 'projection' on her part. At that time, I was testing boundaries, just knocking down walls. That period of sexual experimentation is long gone."

Carrie Pitzulo, writing in *Bachelors and Bunnies,* claimed, "Apparently, Hefner's early sexual experiences with men did not necessarily challenge his heterosexuality. Nor, however, did it guarantee unconditional support for gay men in the pages of *Playboy.* While he publicly expressed sympathy for the homosexual community, he likewise believed that there was the possibility that a gay male might find his way back to a predominantly heterosexual lifestyle."

*[And that just goes to show you that the "Father of the Sexual Revolution" could be naïve at times.]*

\*\*\*

Although both men remained relatively secretive about their affair, it appears that the one man Hef had an ongoing and rather long-lasting intimate relationship with was the actor, Tony Curtis. At times, he came to live with him, occupying his own quarters within the Mansion in Los Angeles.

Hef became intrigued with the New York actor during his marriage (1951-1962) to the screen star, Janet Leigh, when they were hailed as "America's

Actor Tony Curtis, one of the so-called "Pretty Boys" of the 1950s, became Hef's closest friend in the movie colony. He frequently occupied Hef's round bed, "with or without Playmates."

The lower photograph is a scene between Curtis (left) and Burt Lancaster in *Trapeze* (1956).

The role of a trapeze artist was easier for Lancaster than for Curtis, as Lancaster had once been a circus acrobat and a gymnast. Curtis told Hef that he and Lancaster had had an affair during the making of the movie.

375

Sweethearts."

Hef had long heard of his affairs—many admitted to him by Curtis himself—with a string of actors in the 1950s, especially with his sometimes co-star Rock Hudson. Curtis's most serious gay affair was with Burt Lancaster, with whom he had co-starred in the *film noir, Sweet Smell of Success* (1957), which brought him his first sensational reviews. Lancaster and Curtis re-teamed in *Trapeze* (1956), showing off their masculinity in the tight-fitting uniforms of circus acrobats.

No film of Curtis had a greater impact on Hef than his co-starring role with Marilyn Monroe in *Some Like it Hot* (1959), hailed today as the greatest Hollywood comedy ever made. In the film, Curtis and his co-star, Jack Lemmon, appear in drag. Even though *Some Like It Hot* was one of Marilyn's greatest successes, she detested the role. "How dumb did they want me to be? C'mon, don't you think I realized that Tony and Jack were men in drag?"

During the shoot, Curtis told reporters that "Kissing Marilyn was like kissing Hitler." He explained later that he was angry at her for being so temperamental and causing endless delays and disruptions during the shoot.

He told Hef, "The Marilyn I seduced in the late 1940s, when both of us were struggling to break into movies, was not the big star I co-starred with in 1959."

"In those early days, her pussy tasted like champagne," he said. "I have many beautiful memories of falling in love, and the most beautiful moment was going down on her. What's the bad thing about oral sex? I mean is, when you're down there, what can you see?"

In those long-ago days, Marilyn and I had a lot of fun," Curtis said to Hef. "A friend of mine had a little house on the beach in Malibu, and Marilyn and I would sneak off there to make love. Often, we'd screw right on the beach under the glow of the moon. She started to learn about men from me, and I about women from her. By that, I don't mean we were virgins—far from that."

"At the same time, I was getting plowed by another newcomer, Rock Hudson," Curtis continued.

Hef was very fond of the amorous and notorious scene that Curtis had played opposite Laurence Olivier in *Spartacus* (1960). "It was so hot," Curtis said, "that censors cut it out of the original release, but it was restored in later versions of the movie. I've always had a profound relationship with gay actors like Lord Olivier. In fact, I've had profound friendships with most gay men I came to know. There were so many in my life back in the 'pretty boy' heyday of the 1950s."

Curtis waited until the 21st Century, near the end of his life, before "Outing" himself in a London-based gay newspaper. He admitted that he was bisexual, and spoke of his long-ago intimacies with Hudson, Olivier, and Lancaster, among others. He claimed he'd had sex with Hef on many occasions, most often when there were two women in bed with them at the same time.

"Hef doesn't perform oral sex on a man, but he doesn't object if a good-looking guy does the favor for him. He told me his favorite form of sex, with both a woman and a man, was anal. He's good at it. He's had enough practice."

"On looking back, you might say Hef and I were asshole buddies, a term used then by straight men to describe an intense friend-ship with a man. Today, I think they call it a 'bromance,' or some shit like that."

***

Hef had long been fascinated by the ex-ploits of "The Superswinger," quarterback Joe Namath, both on and off the field. In 1969, he ordered his editors to craft a long feature article on him. It was just after the Superbowl win of Namath's New York Jets over the Bal-timore Colts, previously hailed as "the great-est football team in history."

In the *Playboy* feature, Namath was called "the most flamboyant and premier quarterback in football. "Transmogrified from grid superstar into cult hero, he now finds himself cast as a kind of Jean-Paul Bel-mondo with a jockstrap. And Namath's off-the-field activities, centering mostly on his sexual conquests, have assumed the dimen-sions of modern myths. He is already said to have bedded more women than Casanova in his prime."

Namath's reputation as a playboy began during his college years in Tuscaloosa, Ala-bama. "He could think like a fox, run like a deer, and drink like a fish," according to rep-

Though he's most widely asso-ciated with football, Joe Namath got around to film deals and product endorsements, too.

In the upper photo, a publicity photo shows him interacting with Ann-Margret in *C.C & Com-pany* (1970).

In the bottom photo, he's en-dorsing shampoo.

utation.

For his *Playboy* interview, a photographer was allowed to invade his bachelor penthouse apartment in Manhattan, where he found an oval bed, a black leather bar, and a wall-to-wall white llama rug.

A media darling, he was seen cavorting with Mamie Van Doren, a Marilyn Monroe clone, and with Raquel Welch.

Namath told *Playboy*, "I like my girls blonde, my Johnnie Walker Red."

He was asked about "the thousands of sexual conquests" attributed to him.

"It wouldn't be a number that high," he said. "Actually, I had achieved about 300 conquests before I graduated in Alabama. The older I get, the more I like sex. I really go for the broads."

"I'm more of a leg man than a chest man," he revealed. "I prefer Southern girls, as they are sweeter, gentler, not like hardened New York gals. I get tons of mail from horny females wanting me to screw them."

Provocatively, he was asked if he were as good in bed as he was on the field and couldn't really answer that.

"You're only at your best if a girl really turns you on. You certainly can't measure your performance by the number of climaxes you reach. After the first few times, you just can't expect to go on having orgasms."

He admitted that many coaches advise their athletes to refrain from sex the night before the big game. He doesn't follow that advice, finding that seducing a woman before tomorrow's game "makes me mentally and physically fit."

He didn't plan to get married, because he did not feel he could be faithful to a wife. "I like playing the field, a good expression for me in football or in the boudoir."

Namath's reputation extended far beyond being a football hero. Although no one ever accused him of being Laurence Olivier, he became an actor, starring with such sexpots as Ann-Margret in the 1970s "biker film," *C.C. and Company*. He also appeared on Broadway and was always popping up on television, including frothy, good-natured appearances on *The Love Boat*.

Mostly because of his very hip ability to self-satirize, his commercials became some of the most popular ever aired, especially in 1974 when he shaved his legs and posed seductively for a Hanes Beautymist Pantyhose commercial. His shapely gams were hailed as "the most beautiful in football history." He also posed lathered up with Noxzema shaving cream, where he was shaved by the then-unknown Farrah Fawcett.

He became somewhat notorious for wearing floor-length fur coats. In November of 1971, he showed up at Shea Stadium in a stunning white fur coat crafted from coyote and Norwegian fur. The *New York Daily News* asserted that "The Namath fur attracted more attention than the game." It also inspired a massive upturn in fur sales for men.

Others ridiculed it as "a caveman coat" and denounced him for wearing fur, citing it as "disgusting and cruel."

Nonetheless, Blackglama Mink hired Namath to pose in fur for its ad campaign, adding him to a roster of celebrities (including Judy Garland and Bette Davis) in "What Becomes a Legend Most?".

Namath ended the *Playboy* interview by stating his philosophy of life. "As long as you don't hurt anyone, and don't hurt yourself, do what you want to do. That's just what I plan to do."

When Hef read that, he said, "Joe is a man after my own heart. We live by the same self-imposed rule."

\*\*\*

Over the years, many Playboy Bunnies and/or Playmates have written about their experiences within the clubs or at either of the Playboy Mansions. Such was the case with Miss Virginia of 1971 who, when she arrived in Hollywood, billed herself as "Bunny Bee-Jay."

She'd come hoping to find work as an actress but got only a small part in the Jack Nicholson film, *The Last Detail* in 1973. She did find work, however, at the Playboy Club in Century City.

She recalled attending her first party at the Mansion, and of going home with one of Hef's best friends for a night of sex. After that, she claimed that she started sleeping around with other friends she met at Hef's parties.

She was at the Mansion one night when it was announced that Cher would be arriving. She heard Hef telling his cronies that he'd like to seduce Chastity.

"I was shocked," Bee-Jay said. "Cher's daughter was only ten years old."

On another occasion, she attended a special party at the Mansion with her roommate, Libby. Hef invited her to go with him for a nude swim in the Grotto, along with Libby, two hookers, and three of his male friends. The swim led to an invitation to an orgy in his bedroom. It began with all of them sitting around watching the porn flick, *The Devil and Miss Jones* (1973).

After that, Hef invited her onto his bed for anal sex, telling her, "That is my preference." Beside them on the bed were Libby and one of his male friends. His two other male friends were on the carpeted floor seducing the hookers.

"I learned there was a protocol," Bee-Jay said. "The other three guys could not have their orgasm until Hef shot off inside my ass. Then they, too, could blast off."

Driving home as the sun came up over Los Angeles, "I felt dirty and disgusted with myself."

With her film career going nowhere, Bunny Bee-Jay began to feel "completely expendable at the Mansion—no more than a mere plaything."

After two failed attempts at suicide, she headed back to Virginia. "*Playboy* magazine should have a warning on its cover," she said, "just like cigarette advertising. It should read: HAZARDOUS TO YOUR HEALTH."

***

The moment Hef learned that the decade's most talked-about porn film, *Deep Throat* (1972), had been released, he arranged for a dozen copies to be delivered to the Playboy Mansion in Los Angeles. One of the first porn flicks to have a plot and character development, if it could be called that, it also had relatively high production values.

Produced by Louis ("Butchie") Peraino, it had been written and directed by Gerard Damiano, and starred Linda Lovelace and her co-star, Harry Reems, playing the male who is deep-throated.

As a "doctor," actor Harry Reems explores Linda Lovelace's *Deep Throat*, finding that her clitoris is centered there.

Later, he inserts another tool.

Reems starred as Dr. Young, a psychiatrist, who discovers that Linda's clitoris is in her throat. He offers to help her develop her oral skills.

*Deep Throat* was the first porn film that ever went mainstream, launching what was known as "porno chic," and drawing into movie theaters the likes of celebrities and public figures who included Jacqueline Kennedy, Barbara Walters, Johnny Carson, and Frank Sinatra. Even Vice President Spiro Agnew went to see it, as did Martin

Scorsese, Brian De Palma, Truman Capote, and Jack Nicholson.

The film even lent its name to the informant in Washington, D.C., who transmitted to journalists the closely guarded secrets of Richard Nixon and the Watergate scandal that led to the president's resignation.

On a budget of $47,500, *Deep Throat* was eventually alleged to have taken in $600 million dollars, an unprecedented gross for a porn movie and one unlikely ever to be topped again. Mafia-connected associates of the Peraino family distributed the film.

*[In time, Linda would testify that she made only $1,250 for her performance, the fee confiscated by her abusive then-husband, Chuck Traynor. She told stories of sexual abuse, rape, and forced prostitution in the porn business, claiming that she had not consented to many of the sexual acts depicted, including forced sex with a dog. She also claimed that Traynor threatened to kill her, brandishing handguns and rifles to control her.]*

\*\*\*

In a film review published in the May, 1972 issue of *Screw* magazine, Al Goldstein had written, "The star of the film has fine legs, firm tits, a not unattractive face, and the greatest mouth action in the annals of cocksucking. The girl with the deep throat is almost a *Ripley's Believe-It-Or-Not*, as she takes the whole joint down her gullet. No, it's not a small-potato penis, but a roustabout rod of ten inches that plummets into the deepest recesses of our lady's oral cavity; down, down, and down it plunges until nothing remains. It seems a miracle."

The interview with *Screw* was conducted about a month after the film's release in a cold, seventeen-dollar-per-night hotel room. Goldstein found Linda inarticulate, so Chuck Traynor answered most of his questions.

She appeared at the interview in a transparent blouse to meet Goldstein and *Screw* magazine's editor, Jim Buckley. She found Buckley rather reserved and dignified, but Goldstein, in her words, was "a cheap guy—loud, crude, rude, infantile, obnoxious, and dirty."

"My interview was about as dirty as Goldstein looked," she said.

"When I wrote that review that put you guys on the map, I couldn't get over the cum pouring out of your mouth as you sucked off Harry Reems," Goldstein told her. "Your movie gave me eleven hard-ons. That's why on *Screw's* Peter Meter, I gave *Deep Throat* a hundred. That's our max."

GOLDSTEIN: *What is the largest cock you ever sucked?*
LINDA: *Maybe twelve to fourteen inches. Once your throat opens up, it's not the length but the width. Did you know there are a few men on the planet*

that are nine inches in circumference?

GOLDSTEIN: *Give me their phone numbers. I want them to pose for Screw. Do you cum even though your clit isn't being worked on?*

LINDA: *Yeah, I do. I have an orgasm every time I get screwed in the throat, just like the gal in the movie.*

GOLDSTEIN: *Do you like the taste of sperm?*

LINDA: *Oh, yeah, I love it. It's like caviar and champagne. It's a rich vanilla malt on a hot July day. It has the power to make babies and to make a woman's face look radiant and beautiful. It should be swallowed right from the cock itself. If no cock is available, women should be able to purchase it refrigerated at the pharmacy.*

GOLDSTEIN: *How do you think shooting off in a chick's mouth makes a man feel?*

LINDA: *Like rockets going off inside his head. His whole body tingles with excitement, right down to his toenails.*

GOLDSTEIN: *Is size important to you?*

LINDA: *I can transport a man with four inches to heaven. Three inches — hard, that is — is a bit small. But once I open my throat, I can take about anything. At least, no one has successfully challenged me yet. When I get to Hollywood, I'll give you my report on Frank Sinatra, Milton Berle, and John Ireland. Rumor has it they've got all the other male stars beat. We'll see.*

Then Chuck asked, "Listen, Al, you're so interested in cocksucking, why not try Linda out yourself?

HOW FAR DOES A GIRL HAVE TO GO TO UNTANGLE HER TINGLE?

EASTMANCOLOR Ⓧ ADULTS ONLY

Linda Lovelace gets ready for action in *Deep Throat.*

"It made me one of the most sought-after actresses in Hollywood. Some of the biggest stars in the business, including the Rat Pack led by Frank Sinatra, didn't want me to appear in movies with them, but wanted to sample my fellatio technique."

He also asked Buckley if he'd like to sample Linda's golden throat, but he declined. As Goldstein later said, "Jim likes to keep his repressed cock zipped up!"

Of her experience with Goldstein, Linda later wrote, "I numbed myself to that experience."

Goldstein, however, was more articulate in his memoirs: "Here I was with the world's greatest cocksucker, and yet it was a lonely experience. I had never fucked a woman in the mouth like that. It seemed hostile. I felt alienated. Though I've often felt I was hung like a rodent, I have a slightly above average cock, seven inches, and the fact that it disappeared down her throat interfered with my concentration. I kept thinking, 'Am I *that* small? Is she *that* good? Should I cum now?' She then sat on my face in a 69 position, as I was eating her, but not bringing her any pleasure. Her pussy was hairless, which I didn't care for."

In Los Angeles, Hef was upset that Goldstein had gotten to Linda before him, but he ordered his aides to contact Chuck Traynor and Linda, extending invitations to visit him at the Playboy Mansion.

After Goldstein's blow-job, *Screw* magazine made Linda "our Marilyn Monroe," featuring her extensively as the new voice of liberated sexuality. "Had I been a faggot, Goldstein said, "she would have become the magazine's Judy Garland."

Writing in *The New York Times*, Vincent Canby said, "The film has less to do with the manifold pleasure of sex

A sensational, widely publicized overview of the dark side of the American Dream, Blood Moon's *Inside Linda Lovelace's Deep Throat*, traces the origins, the adventures, and the evolution of one of the most unwittingly consequential figures in the history of media.

*HEEERE'S LINDA,* the ultimately tragic sex goddess of the 1970s who morphed into a (disjointed and eventually unwilling) feminist icon of the 80s, emerging as a lightning rod for America's changing attitudes about sexuality and porn.

This is the story of Linda Boreman's uncomfortable stance as the Queen of the One Night Stand; the "flash in the pan" party favor of dozens of Hollywood stars; her deep-throated encounters as a status symbol in the Entertainment Industry, and her murky origins as a fetish queen from the D-list.

WInner of several literary awards, this book is packed with information you never knew about the love goddess who transformed the term "deep throat" from a noun into a verb, and who, in ways she'd never have believed at the time, turned "fellatio" into a household word.

than with physical engineering."

Porn star and porn director Fred Lincoln mocked Linda, claiming that she sincerely believed that people were seeing *Deep Throat* because of her acting. "She's not only a masochist, but a fucking moron!"

On TV, Bob Hope said, "I went to see *Deep Throat* because I'm fond of animal pictures. I thought it was about giraffes."

When the call came in from Hef, Chuck and Linda were in Florida. They eagerly agreed to travel to his Playboy Mansion in Los Angeles as part of a photo shoot whose results would appear in Hef's magazine. "I loved Linda in *Deep Throat*, but also in *The Dog Fucker*," Hef told Chuck over the phone.

With the understanding that Hef would send his private *Playboy* jet for them, Chuck, through Hef's staff, coordinated the details of their west-bound flight. Noting that Hef seemed to like bestiality movies, Chuck opted to bring Rufus as part of their entourage.

Linda agreed to pose in the nude for *Playboy*. The photographer asked her to cut her hair again, just like it had been during her appearance in *Deep Throat*.

"I think it was the call from *Playboy* that caused Chuck to respect my earning potential for the first time," Linda said. "Instead of treating me like I was trailer park trash, he began to view me as a hot property. I never knew how much *Playboy* paid for that layout of me, because Chuck took all the money and didn't tell me."

"From the moment we arrived in Los Angeles for the *Playboy* layout, Hef had ordered a limousine and chauffeur for us," Linda said. "For the first time in my life, I felt like a bigshot."

When she encountered the setup at the Playboy Mansion West, she said, "I knew this was going to be a class act—no bullwhips or dildoes. The *Playboy* photographer treated me like a lady, so courteous and courtly. He used lace—as in Love-*lace*—as a backdrop. Antique lace, that is. He'd shopped half the antique stores in Los Angeles. He put me at ease. He even made me feel I was a vision of loveliness in the sunlight. No one had ever done that to me before."

"Not all the shots were arty," she later confessed. "I had to strike some stupid poses, like sucking my finger instead of a big dick. I had to fondle my fake breasts. In one shot, I was depicted licking my lips as if I'd just tasted a load of cum."

Linda and Chuck finally got to meet "The King of the Boudoir," Hef himself.

"I liked her immediately," Hef said. "She wore a black see-through blouse to show off her tits. She was an unassuming, uncomplicated, down-to-earth woman."

"Chuck Traynor was clearly a hustler," Hef said. "When I talked privately to Linda in my Library, she told me she was his sex slave, and that he had forced her into prostitution and porn with his death threats. But no evidence of violence was visible to me at the time."

"That Traynor guy always insisted on running the show," Hef said. "I don't think Linda could take a piss without getting permission from him. He was always hovering over her. She told me that she wanted to be a serious film actress—not a porn queen. I suggested that she and Traynor move to Hollywood and leave Florida if that was her goal. A few weeks later, they took my advice, and even came to live with me at the Mansion until they found a place of their own."

That Saturday night, Chuck and Linda were invited to attend a buffet and a movie Hef was screening for about fifty guests. "I changed my view of *Playboy* that day," Linda said. "Before I came to the Mansion, I thought *Playboy* was a dirty magazine my brother-in-law used to jerk off to in the toilet."

"But when I saw all these high-class people there, I changed my mind. I learned that Hef sometimes attracted really big names like Teddy Kennedy and definitely Jack Nicholson. One night I heard that George McGovern showed up. He was that guy who ran for President against Richard Nixon. In other words, I wasn't hanging out with white trash, baby."

For her first evening appearance at the Playboy Mansion, Chuck even shelled out a hundred dollars to buy a form-fitting, dove-gray knitted dress for Linda.

Before meeting Hef that night, Chuck came up with what he called "a fun scheme." He escorted Linda around the Mansion, inviting the butlers and other servants to see how many fingers they could put inside Linda. She was humiliated by the experience, although the male staff members seemed to regard it as excitement. She later said, "I hoped they washed their hands before serving the guests food and drink."

"On my first night there, I spotted Warren Beatty and Peter Lawford. I didn't get to speak to them but would in the future. Goldie Hawn was there and so was Connie Stevens."

Blonde-haired Hawn, then in her late 20s and married at the time to

People you were likely to meet at the Playboy Mansion: Goldie Hawn—young, unformed, unsure, and at the debut of her career.

dancer Gus Trikonis, seemed to have just discovered Eastern philosophy, claiming that she was "a Jewish Buddhist," although no one seemed interested.

Stevens, who had become famous for playing "Cricket Blake" in the popular TV detective series, *Hawaiian Eye*, had divorced Eddie Fisher in 1969. She entertained guests with her tales about dating Elvis Presley, and much less so, her devotion to the Republican Party. While she was doing that, her former husband, Eddie Fisher, who was also at the gathering, discreetly obtained Linda's phone number, which he tucked into a secret compartment of his well-stuffed wallet. At the other side of the Mansion, Stevens didn't seem to notice—or even care—that her ex-husband was at the same party on a Bunny hunt.

In a memoir, Linda claimed that within the Mansion, she encountered Elizabeth Taylor, but was too afraid to speak to her, perhaps fearing that the movie diva would interpret her as a trash act. "It was Miss Taylor who spoke to me, breaking the ice. At first, she terrified me, but she was so quick to put me at ease. She looked so down to earth, although she wore a celestial hairpiece and a shimmering gown, plus a diamond-and-ruby necklace."

"Elizabeth may have looked like a regal queen, but when she spoke, she sounded more like a drunken sailor on Saturday night," Linda claimed. "Tanked up on champagne, we got right to the point."

"Hef screened *Deep Throat* for me," Taylor said, "and was I impressed. I really was. Perhaps if I pay you well, you'll give me lessons. I'm sure Richard Burton would volunteer to be our guinea pig for instructions in how to throat a cock."

"I'd be honored, but I think there are few things I could teach the Serpent of the Nile," Linda said.

"You flatter me, darling, but, believe me, I'm always learning. I usually get rave notices from my men, but I couldn't satisfy Victor Mature. He wanted me to go all the way down. But after gulping down a foot and a half of cock, I gave up."

"I bet I could handle him," Linda said.

"You know what?" Elizabeth said. "I bet you could, too, and he would love it. Would you write down your phone number? I'll have Vic call you. He'll let me know how your session turned out."

"You're not kidding, are you?" Linda asked. "THE Victor Mature?"

"Samson himself."

Linda wrote down her phone number and handed it to Elizabeth, who made a notation on it and put it into her purse. Taylor continued, "Believe me, Victor is the best. I should have married him. Rita Hayworth, Betty Grable, and Lana Turner have told me the same thing. We shouldn't have let him escape our clutches."

At this point, one of the staff approached Elizabeth, telling her that Hef wanted to see her in the library.

Before tearing herself away from Linda, Elizabeth took her hand and caressed it. "Keep up the good work, my dear. You have many fans in Hollywood. I know for a fact

Adept at playing voluptuous vixens, Elizabeth Taylor was at the Mansion, too. Linda remembered her as accessible, kind, and non-judgmental.

Here's Dame Elizabeth as she apppeared, playing an unrestrained sybarite, in *The Sandpiper* (1965).

Clint Eastwood was a formidable talent on the screen, but at the Playboy Mansion, Linda Lovelace failed in her attempt to make a conquest.

"To me, Clint was an icon of American macho, and he had a certain coolness with a hidden ferocity that might burst forth at any moment. The real Clint would always remain a mystery to me."

that half the male stars will soon be trying to get in touch with you. Don't expect to hear from the other fifty percent. They're gay."

Although Elizabeth was gracious, her all time idol, Clint Eastwood, was not. "I'd worshipped him on the screen for years. He was my dream man. In the coincidence of coincidences, he took the empty seat next to me in the screening room where Hef showed some movie. I don't remember the name of it. All I could think about was Eastwood sitting next to me."

"To my deep heartbreak, he didn't even look at me or say hello. By the time we were thirty minutes into that stupid movie, I decided to take the bull by the horns, so to speak. Slowly, I reached over and placed my delicate little hand on his crotch. I'd seen his package in some movie in which there was a bedroom scene, and he paraded around in a pair of white jockey shorts. From what little I saw, I wasn't expecting John C. Holmes. But I planned to make do with what he had."

"He really insulted me. He very firmly took my hand off his crotch and placed it back in my own lap. That was the end of my romance with Eastwood. No more fantasies about him."

Hef always made his appearance at around ten in the evening. His drink of choice was a cold Pepsi-Cola. "Joan Crawford would have been proud of him," Linda said. "After all, she was the Pepsi queen."

Hef was most gracious in greeting both Chuck and Linda. She resented that he spent most of the time chatting with Chuck about kinky sex, and she was horrified that *The Dog Fucker,* starring herself and a German shepherd, was one of his favorite 8mm loops.

Finally, he got around to complimenting her, telling her that she was much prettier in person than on the screen. "Usually, when I meet a movie star, it's the reverse. On screen, she's a *femme fatale,* but up close and personal, I greet an old hag. Incidentally, Warren Beatty freaked out over your movie," Hef said. "He wants to meet you."

After their first night at the Playboy Mansion, Hef gave both Chuck and Linda a gold card, which allowed them to come and go from the Mansion whenever they wanted. "We joined the rest of the freeloaders to see the movies, to devour the food and drink, to attend the parties, especially those Wednesday night orgies, where *Deep Throat* was a regular feature," Chuck said, as reported later by Linda.

***

For a brief period in her life, Chuck and Linda became "members of the family," as Hef labeled it, at Playboy Mansion West.

"Just from the way he approached the various girls and Bunnies, I could tell Hef was a big boob kind of guy, but I suspected that all those mammoth tits were made of plastic," Linda said.

The longest time she spent with Hef, a total of four hours, was in his library. "There was no sex," she said. He genuinely seemed interested in me, Linda Boreman, as a real person. Where I came from, what I felt, what intrigued me. No one had ever paid attention to me before. All they wanted was Linda Lovelace—or, more to the point, her deep throat."

She had taken to speaking of herself in the third person, as if the character she played in *Deep Throat* was a fictional creation and not her.

In front of Hef, his Bunnies, a scattering of movie stars, and assorted flotsam and jetsam of the sex-crazed 1970s, Chuck demonstrated a new trick, using Linda as his victim. "It's called fist-fucking." Then, to the astonishment of the audience, he inserted his fist into Linda's anus.

After gaping at the fist-fuck demonstration, "all of Hef's guests applauded, just like they'd have done for a dance by Ginger Rogers and Fred Astaire in a 1930s movie," Linda said. "At the Mansion, it was always a bacchanal—a word I'd learned only recently—and Hef was always cast in the role of Caligula. As for Caligula, all I needed to know about him I learned from that Bob Guccione movie eight years before. The hardcore stuff in *Caligula* wasn't bad, but I could have done without all those beheadings and disemboweling. To my knowledge, Malcolm McDowell, Peter O'Toole, Helen Mirren, and John Gielgud each made their first porno in *Caligula*. I started this trend of big stars doing porn."

"Chuck and Linda may not have invented fist-fucking, but they set off a new craze," claimed Steve McQueen. "It was all the rage for many years, although it put a lot of people, both gay boys and women, into the hospital."

"A lot of voyeurs at the Mansion wanted to see me get fist-fucked," Linda recalled. "When they didn't want to watch that, they wanted me to indulge in some lesbian love with one of Hef's Bunnies. No one seemed to want sex like grandma did it."

Every week, Hef staged "orgy night" at the Mansion, the sex often taking place inside a simulated Grotto near the pool. Always attired in an elegant bathrobe and/or in silk pajamas, Hef made his appearances late, after the action was al-

Fist fucking had been around for centuries, and the notorious emperor, Caligula, was said to have summoned at least a dozen teenaged boys to his side to ram them, enjoying their screams.

In front of many in Hollywood, Chuck Traynor, Linda Lovelace's husband and pimp, used his wife as a guinea pig to demonstrate the technique.

ready under way.

"Chuck virtually pushed me at Hef, but he took his time coming on to me," Linda claimed.

Before Hef jumped into the pool, she saw him strip down and apply Johnson's Baby Oil to his chest, thighs, hands, and penis. Then he plunged into the water, laughing as he did.

"When Hef finally joined us in the pool, I wanted to fuck him and give him some head," Linda claimed. "He first invited me to make out with this beautiful gal standing next to me. We started with some lesbian love, and he joined the scene. I felt his experienced tongue on my clit."

"After he'd had enough of that, he entered me from the rear. The guy really knew what he was doing. He should, after all the experience he'd had. He turned me around and began to screw me royally, down deep and dirty. He went at it for fifteen to twenty minutes. I lost count. We both had a climax together. I'd call that perfect harmony. Some of the famous names I seduced during the height of my popularity plunged in no more than two dozen times—and that was that."

"Actually, I never experienced sex with Hef the way I really dreamed it," Linda said. "I wanted him to take me up in his private plane and screw me 30,000 feet off the ground. I wanted to join the Mile High Club."

"Sure, Hef and Linda balled, usually in public and around the pool," Chuck said. "But it wasn't a romantic thing. It was more of an ego trip for him, because Linda was the sex symbol of the moment. *Playboy's* honcho was known for separating sex from romantic feelings."

Hef was said to own the largest collection of 8mm loops in the world, including porn shot by stars before they became famous. These included everybody from Joan Crawford to Marilyn Monroe. He also collected bestiality films, including loops depicting women fornicating with donkeys and horses. One particularly bizarre loop that Chuck discovered showed a young man getting sodomized by a black stallion.

She was upset to hear that Hef had seen *The Dog Fucker* several times. She heard him tell Chuck that his staff at the Mansion had tried several times "to bring a chick and a dog together, but it had not worked out."

Chuck agreed how tricky it was, and then offered to bring their dog Rufus to the Mansion the following night. "Wait until you see how Linda and Rufus go at it," he promised.

"Hef really wanted Linda to fuck a dog," Chuck claimed.

Although she said that she intended to be ready for the dog, Linda had no intention of letting Hef witness her getting fucked by Rufus. The following evening, when the dog was brought out to join them at the pool, Hef and Chuck settled back for some excitement, which they did not get.

Using techniques which had worked before, she came on aggressively toward the dog, acts which this time seemed to frighten him. When Rufus couldn't produce an erection for Linda, Hef ordered a member of his staff to take the dog to his kennel. But after only one night there, Rufus killed one of Hef's sheep dogs and nearly chewed another dog to death. The following morning, Rufus was shipped back to a kennel in Miami.

In a *New York Times* article published on September 5, 2004, a reporter claimed, "Linda gained a reputation for her enthusiasm for seducing dogs. She reportedly put on bestiality shows for Hugh Hefner and company at his Playboy Mansion in Los Angeles." Years before, she had denied that, giving her own version of events.

Norman Mailer, the author, had heard of the various entertainments provided at the Mansion, and he showed up on a number of occasions. Years later, he admitted that he missed all the fist-fucking and bestiality, but that he had found other diversions.

"You never knew the sexual liaisons you'd have there," Mailer said. "One night, I met Linda Lovelace, who volunteered to give me a blow-job. I think Hef turned her on to me. Now I won't pretend that Linda had read *The Naked and the Dead*. But what did it matter? It was the best blow-job of my life."

"I'm just a nice Jewish boy from Brooklyn," Mailer told Linda. "But James Baldwin claimed I'm a real sweet *ofay* cat, but a little frantic. Allen Ginsberg said I was 'macho folly,' and Chandler Brossard claimed, 'I was an unemployed and unemployable Hamlet.' *The Village Voice* dismissed me as

A rebel, a performer, and a provocateur, the quixotic and easily enraged Norman Mailer always gave people something to talk about.

A frequent visitor to the Playboy Mansion, he's shown here during his unsuccessful run for Mayor of New York City in 1969.

WHO GIVES A BETTER BLOW JOB? The always provocative gay author, Truman Capote, at drunken parties, claimed he was the "master of fellatio and far better at it than Linda Lovelace."

So far as it is known, there was only one person in the world who had tried both throats. That was novelist Norman Mailer, who claimed, "Linda has him beat."

'a narcissistic pest.'"

She had never heard of any of the men Mailer had cited but found the assessments amusing. At the end of his recitation, he asked her, "And what do the pundits say about you?"

"That I'm the world's greatest deep-throater, although some stupid actor told the press I use too much teeth."

"That simply isn't true," Mailer told her. "You didn't leave one tooth mark on my honorable penis."

"Truman Capote always claimed that he gave a better blow-job than Linda," Mailer claimed. "That Capote was such a bullshitter. One night at a drunken party in Brooklyn Heights, I let Capote go down on me. The mincing little flamer gagged. By far, Linda was a better deep-throater than Capote. Trust the man who knows. Of course, I would have preferred Marilyn Monroe to both of them."

"I rarely went down on a famous author like Mailer," Linda said, "but during my days at the Playboy Mansion, I sucked off a lot of movie stars at some of Hef's orgies," Linda claimed. "It didn't always have to be at an orgy. On any night, there was sex going on somewhere, perhaps in the hidden corner of the Grotto or somewhere on the grounds. On orgy nights, most of the big movie stars disappeared, perhaps fearing they'd secretly be photographed. But many of the stars were very exhibitionistic, guys like Tony Curtis who didn't seem to mind parading around naked in front of people and getting it on. Tony went both ways, and one night I saw him going down on a young actor wannabe. Perhaps he promised the kid a part in his next movie."

"One of my greatest triumphs was the night I got to go down on Curtis," she said. "I met him in the pool, and we sneaked off under a waterfall into the Grotto. He had an uncut dick, not terribly big, but he knew how to use it. He literally fucked my mouth. As he did, visions of his former conquests, everyone from Elizabeth Taylor to Marilyn Monroe, bounced through my head."

"With Tony's creamy gift lining my stomach, we later put on our bathing suits and enjoyed a lobster-and-wine buffet, courtesy of Hef," Linda said. "Some of the females didn't even bother to dress for dinner. All of them flirted with Tony. I had drained that guy dry. Tony amused his admiring flock of young Bunnies by telling them that when Elvis started out, 'He copied my hairdo.'"

"I remember other movie stars there, including Raquel Welch—that stuck-up bitch, Jack Nicholson, and even Groucho Marx. I'd seen Groucho on TV and thought he was very funny. He told me his greatest wish was to be able to get it up again. 'I was born in 1890,' he said, 'but don't tell anybody.' I took his left hand and let him feel my pussy. He got quite a good feel. After he'd finished, he said, 'I can tell you've just gotten back from the barber.'"

"The orgies, of course, weren't too brightly lit, and you never knew who was piling on top of you," Linda recalled. "I was stoned a lot of the time. One night, I looked up into the face of Russ Meyer. I recognized him from the Hollywood newspapers. He'd made that campy *Beyond the Valley of the Dolls* plus a lot of other movies."

"Late in 1974, I tried to get him to cast me in his picture, *Supervixens*, but he must have forgotten about the free fuck I gave him. Of course, he was famous for casting women with mammoth boobs, so, even with the silicone, I guess I wasn't busty enough."

At this point, Linda became a bit catty. "As for Meyer the Lover, he got to the point quickly enough—a hug, a brief kiss, a touch of my breast and quick penetration, goodbye, and thanks for the memory."

"On another occasion, I ran into Angie Dickinson," Linda answered. "I came on to her, but I don't think that at that time she knew who I was. I'd heard that JFK had fucked her at one time, but my pass was subtle. She just walked away. She may not have heard me, but if she did, I think she had no interest at all in lesbian love."

"I also saw Peter O'Toole strolling the grounds with Hef, and I wanted Hef to set up something with me and O'Toole. I had fallen in love with him when I saw *Lawrence of Arabia*, but nothing came of it."

"I once saw Paul Newman wandering about, but I didn't get him that night. Blue Eyes definitely lay in my future. All Paul needs to do is ask Harry Reems if I can handle Jewish dick."

Anthony Quinn, the superstar from Mexico, had a smouldering presence both on and off the screen. Linda found him an amazing athlete..."sexually sparkling," she claimed.

"It would have been easy to fall in love with Tony, but he was gone too quickly, often to his next conquest. His stated goal was to impregnate every woman in the world."

\*\*\*

One night, she met a lusty Anthony Quinn, who came on to her rather strong. As a frequent movie goer, she had thrilled to his smoldering presence in such movies as *Zorba the Greek* (1964).

One of the first questions this Mexican-American asked her was, "Linda, now that

393

you're a movie star, who is your role model? Elizabeth Taylor, Jane Fonda, or Lucille Ball?"

"I want to be a serious actress, but the only roles offered me are in porn," she said.

"In the 1920s, I did some porn, but I think all the loops are lost today," he said. "At least nothing has resurfaced to haunt me."

"Who was your role model?" she asked.

"Believe it or not, I wanted to be Napoléon, Michelangelo, Shakespeare, Picasso, Martin Luther, and Jack Dempsey, all rolled into one," he said.

"Fortunately for those of us who go to the movies, you became none of the above...but Anthony Quinn."

"That compliment, little darling, will get you anywhere with me," he said.

"Standing before you, I'm ready, willing, and able," she said.

"Forgive me, but what I have in mind calls for you to be on your knees," he said.

"You're on!" she said. "Let's head for the game room."

After plunging down on Quinn, Linda agreed with the former assessment of his girlfriend, actress Evelyn Keyes, who had played Scarlett O'Hara's younger sister in *Gone With the Wind*. Keyes had said, "There was simply too much of Tony. Yes, down there, too."

"After giving him 'one of my best blows,' he said something strange," Linda said. "He told me that 'until tonight, I've never really felt a man's masculinity was in his penis. But it sure was tonight.'"

"I love reading about the love affairs of movie stars," she told him. "I fear unfavorable comparisons with your former lovers—Mae West, Carole Lombard, Shelley Winters, Rita Hayworth, Ingrid Bergman."

"No competition from Ingrid," Quinn said. "She doesn't go that route. You're the best, and I've been fellated ever since I was fourteen years old and passed out on L.A.'s Seal Beach. When I came to, an older woman was licking away to her heart's content."

[*At the time Linda met Quinn, he was married to Jolanda Addolori, the Italian costume designer.*]

Also at Hef's mansion in L.A., Linda had a much stranger encounter with the bald-

Great at playing exotic kings, and a regular in the gardens of the Playboy Mansion, Yul Brynner depicts a Pharaoh in *The Ten Commandments* (1956).

headed actor Yul Brynner, famous for starring in film version of *The King and I* (1956). When he heard that Linda was also at Hef's Mansion, he arranged for a male member of the *Playboy* staff to send for her. They met on the grounds, far away from the main house, in a temporary Arabian Nights tent which Hef had erected in the gardens.

She was shown inside, where Brynner was the center of attention while seated with five other men, perhaps actors, but none she recognized. He had to explain to her that they were smoking opium, and he invited her to join him, but she refused.

"Pot, or perhaps a little cocaine, are my drugs of choice," she said.

"Too bad," Brynner told her. "Opium is life's greatest pleasure."

"You didn't invite me here to smoke opium," she said in front of the other men, all of whom had remained silent and seemed to resent her presence. She suspected they were gay, since Brynner was known for his bisexual tastes.

"I've decided the two greatest pleasures in life would be to combine smoking opium with getting a blow-job," he said. "Would you oblige me in what is increasingly known in Hollywood as the Linda Lovelace specialty?"

"I'd love to," she said. She came over to him and got down in front of him. He was wearing a robe which he opened for her, displaying an uncut penis which in her mouth and throat rose to an impressive eight inches. "As he smoked, I blew," she later recalled.

"Someone had told me that that starlet in the 1940s, Nancy Davis, now married to Ronald Reagan, had been called 'The Fellatio Queen of Hollywood.' Now that she was retired from the game, I wanted to be known as the new 'Fellatio Queen of Hollywood.' During their affair, I could just imagine how many times Nancy went down on Yul, and I was determined to best her."

"Yul really blasted off to the moon, so I think I won the prize. He more or less confirmed it. I looked up into his eyes for approval. 'Better than Nancy?' I asked."

"Tallulah Bankhead was not good at it, but Nancy and Marlene Dietrich were," Brynner said. "You beat them. For your effort, I'll share a special treat with you."

A bowl of grapes rested nearby. "I'd never done this ritual before," she said. "But he put the grape in his mouth, eating half of it and inviting me to share the other half. It was all very, very sensual. I wondered if he pulled shit like that with another of his lovers, Joan Crawford."

*[At the time Linda met him, Brynner was married to the French socialite, Jacqueline Thion de la Chaume, but she was nowhere to be seen. They had adopted*

*two Vietnamese children. Linda had also read that in Switzerland in 1965, he had renounced his naturalized U.S. citizenship for tax reasons.]*

In addition to Brynner, one of the more regular visitors at the Playboy Mansion was actor James Caan. "He was a little guy, but I found him sexy," Linda said. She claimed she made it one time with Caan, "but I was with three other gals, and I don't think he even knew who I was."

Biographer Mart Martin claimed that Caan seduced "lots of *Playboy* centerfolds, including Connie Kreski, and models." Martin also quoted Caan as saying, "I balled an astounding number...*bam, bam, bam, bam*...in a row."

"Many women who like to be dominated by men fell in love with James Caan when he starred as the hot-headed Sonny Corleone in Francis Ford Coppola's *The Godfather* (1972)," said Linda Lovelace.

"But I first fell in love with him when I saw him in Billy Wilder's *Irma la Douce* (1963)."

Linda said that one night she was standing in "that row of Bunny fuckees" when one of the Playmates told her that Caan was "crazy about licking pussy. I spent hours squatting over his face."

"Caan was an amusing guy, a great friend of Hefner, and I found he had a powerful sex appeal," Linda said, "even if he didn't know, or seem to know, who I was. Once, sitting around a buffet, he amused his table by claiming that he had lost his virginity, at the age of thirteen, in a Miami whorehouse. "It was taken by a middle aged *puta*," he said. "As I fucked her, my ass was eaten alive by mosquitoes."

Sometimes, Chuck and Linda joined Hef aboard his private plane for visits to the Playboy Mansion in Chicago. "In Illinois, we didn't meet much of that movie star crowd, and the parties there were much duller," Linda said. "I couldn't believe it: Some of the jerks in Chicago didn't know who I was, and at the time, I was one of the most famous movie stars in the world. Chuck spent most of the day watching 8mm loops, and I enjoyed the world's best beef Wellington prepared by this wonderful chef.:"

"I remember meeting Shel Silverstein, the writer and cartoonist. He suggested doing an album of country and western songs with me, but greedy Chuck screwed it for me and the deal fell through."

When she first met Silverstein, Linda did not know who he was, until Hef explained that he was a singer-songwriter, musician, composer, cartoonist, and author of children's books. In books alone, he'd sold more than

20 million copies, which were translated into thirty different languages.

Years later, at his home in Key West (Florida), Silverstein told the senior co-author of this book, Darwin Porter, "I don't know what it was, but there was something that attracted me to Linda. In some ways, she reminded me of Loretta Lynn. I'd written a hit for Loretta called, 'One's on the Way.' For Linda, I somewhat envisioned her potential for a whimsical hit like 'A Boy Named Sue' that I'd written for Johnny Cash. Except in this song, as sung by Linda, she'd have a girl, whom she'd name Henry to help her fight off rapists in the Rocky Mountains."

"I tested Linda out, but she couldn't sing. But with the right—and loudest—background music, I came up with the idea of a mostly talkie song about a woman who develops a sore throat after a wild night of partying."

"Of course, there was her technique. She swallowed a guy whole and even tried to fit in his balls. As an oral artist, she was great sex. I was really turned on by her. My Jewish girl friends in high school wouldn't ever go down on me."

"Linda would have been great recording my cautionary song about venereal disease," Silverstein continued. "'Don't Give a Dose to the One You Love Most.'"

"In 1962, I wrote a song, 'Boa Constrictor,' about a hapless man getting swallowed by a snake. That folk group, *Peter, Paul, and Mary*, recorded it. I envisioned doing a sort of porno version of it—not dirty, just comedic—with Linda singing about swallowing the boa constrictor. I thought we could put together a comedy-and-song album."

"What screwed the

Linda Lovelace's face expresses her high anxiety and stress in the presence of her sadistic, domineering husband, Chuck Traynor, who pimped her for sexual trysts that would have made many sex workers cringe.

Early in her career, before she became sought after as a vogue-ish party favor suddenly infamous as a fellatio expert, he insisted she consummate a sex act with a dog for a video he later distributed.

He also rented her out, for pay (which she alleged he collected but never passed on to her) for men with genetic aberrations. One of the partners he arranged for her had two penises. Others were violently sadistic and/ or repulsive.

[Diphallia, penile duplication (PD), diphallic terata, or diphallasparatus, is a rare developmental abnormality in which a male is born with two penises.]

deal?" Silverstein asked, rhetorically. "It was that fucking Chuck Traynor. He started barging in with his demands and talks of percentages. I finally said to hell with the idea, but not until I got a final blow-job from the *artiste* herself, Linda Lovelace."

According to Linda, Chuck had more of a fantasy about Hef than she did. "He wanted to become his best pal, sharing Playmates and fluffy-tailed Bunnies," she said. "Hef, of course, was too smart to get tangled up with a sleazeball like Chuck, and he came to realize that he and Hef were not going to become fuck buddies or business partners."

Although Hef was not ready to go into business with Chuck, he did recommend a former Bunny, Delores Wells, as an ideal candidate for the management of their newly created Linda Lovelace Enterprises. Delores turned out to be a savvy choice.

When Chuck met Delores, he liked her at once, because "she fitted my chief requirement that all my female employees have big tits."

But it was to Linda that Delores was drawn, finding her unspoiled, natural, and very sweet in spite of her name and scandalous reputation. "When I introduced her to my six-year-old daughter, Linda shed a tear, confiding in me that her great dream involved having a happy marriage and children," Delores said.

When the nude *Playboy* layout of Linda was released, it did not meet with universal approval from the magazine's readers. In the opinion of

Ten years after her heyday as a Playboy Bunny, Delores Wells (lower photo) acted as a savvy business manager for Linda Lovelace, enforcing order and good business sense onto the starlet's chaotic and dysfunctional life.

Ms. Wells, (aka Miss June, 1960 and centerfold for that issue), also appeared driving a car on the cover of *Playboy* that month.

Decades later, that illustration always propels that edition onto the short list of the best covers *Playboy* ever produced.

thousands of men, Linda did not live up to the beauty, glamour, or the breasts, of previous Playmates.

A typical criticism came from Larry Wilson, who wrote: "I was always at a loss to understand the appeal of either Lovelace or *Deep Throat*. She was rather unattractive, not even the usual soft-focus airbrush photography of *Playboy* could make her appealing."

In later memoirs, Linda would present an unattractive portrait of the debauchery at the Playboy Mansion. But Hef never treated her unkindly. She concluded: "Hef was a terrific guy. A wonderful guy. He did something that Chuck could never do. He treated me like a human being."

She had a parting comment: "Hef knows how to make a girl's cunt feel real good."

Asked to recall her encounters with Hef, she said, "I think he borrowed a bit of life's philosophy from Peggy Lee and her famous song. He told me, 'If that's all there is, then let's keep dancing.'"

***

Ever since Hef had informed Linda about how engrossing Warren Beatty had found *Deep Throat*, she was anxious to meet him. When she was fifteen, Beatty, along with Clint Eastwood, had been her dream man. Her previous encounter with Eastwood had been a dud, but she was hoping for a livelier performance with Beatty, who was a frequent visitor to both the Playboy Mansion West, and to the Playboy Club that had opened on the Sunset Strip in the mid-1960s.

Beatty's reputation had preceded him. Film historian David Thomson claimed, "Warren Beatty cannot endure or dispense with the legend of Don Juan."

Linda was convinced that Beatty, according to the gossip columns, maintained the most impressive list of seductions of any male star in Hollywood, beginning with Jacqueline Kennedy and Elizabeth Taylor, with whom he'd made the 1970 *The Only Game in Town*. In 1967, Linda had seen *Bonnie and Clyde* five times and had thrilled to Beatty's good looks, calling him at one point, "The Sexiest Man Alive."

Beatty's list of conquests was legendary before and after Linda met him—

Warren Beatty, as he appeared in 1975 in *Shampoo*.

Joan Collins told Hef, "Three, four, five times a day was not unusual for Warren. And he was able to accept phone calls at the same time."

Leslie Caron, Cher, Julie Christie, Joan Collins, Jane Fonda, Angelica Huston, Bianca Jagger, Diane Keaton, Madonna, Mary Tyler Moore, Christina Onassis, Lee Radziwill, Vanessa Redgrave, Diana Ross, Jean Seberg, Carly Simon, Barbra Streisand, Goldie Hawn, H.R.H. Princess Margaret, Princess Elizabeth of Yugoslavia, Brigitte Bardot, Candice Bergen, Diane Sawyer, and maybe—just maybe—Tennessee Williams and "that other gay playwright," William Inge.

One night at the Los Angeles Playboy Club, Linda sat at Hef's table and overheard Playboy Bunny "Kevin" Lauritzen speak of her affair with Beatty. She told the table, as she'd later confide to Beatty's biographer, Ellis Amburn: "Warren is a cerebral fuck, not a great lover. He fucks your mind before he fucks anything else. He even convinced me I was a more fascinating woman—and better in bed—than Jackie Kennedy. I've had better lovers. It's not his love making, but the attention he gives a woman. More than any guy I know, he really listens to a woman, and that's a real turn-on. He's the most sought-after date in Hollywood, and the reason is not because of what's between his legs. He reaffirms your femininity, your womanhood."

Another visitor to the Playboy Mansion, Sarah Porterfield, told author Amburn: "Warren would never go to a girl's apartment, because he was so paranoid. He was terrified of hidden cameras that would show them doing it. If he wanted sex with a girl, he always went to the Beverly Wilshire Hotel. The only place he ever did sex besides the Wilshire was at Hef's Mansion. It was safe there. I remember being up at Hef's one day and Warren appeared with a Bunny on each arm. Hef said, 'Have you been robbing the Hutch again, Warren?' I think he was doing Playmates as well."

Finally, Hef introduced her to her idol, saying, "I'd like your number one fan, Warren Beatty, to meet his number one fan, Linda Lovelace."

She'd heard that Beatty had "flipped" over *Deep Throat*, "He praised my free-flowing style. Since he didn't come on to me, I believed he was sincere."

She wrote, "Just the thought of Warren touching my hand would create shivers." She also claimed that on several different evenings at Hef's Mansion, Beatty propositioned her and wanted her to go to the Beverly Wilshire with him. "If I ever faced temptation," she said, "that was the occasion."

During a "grilling" session, Linda was asked if she'd gone to bed with Ryan O'Neal, the other Hollywood Lothario of the 1970s. "She neither confirmed nor denied it, but that Mona Lisa smile on her face more or less confirmed it. Put another way, she had a look of a cat who ate the canary," Hef said._

"Everyone in Hollywood knew that Beatty and O'Neal sometimes seduced the same women—Joan Collins, Angelica Huston, Bianca Jagger, Diana Ross, and Barbra Streisand." Hef said.

Author Joy Fielding took a rather cynical view of Linda's seductions and self-promotions. "Perhaps she came to feel that ultimately, no one would believe her gruesome memoir, and that she would be dismissed as a woman only out to make a buck, out to out-confess Britt Ekland or Joan Collins, and all the others who'd slept with Warren and Ryan. Perhaps Lovelace feared she'd be laughed at as a woman clutching at the straws of fame that had long since deserted her."

\*\*\*

In the opinion of many "culture vultures in the early to mid-1970s, *Deep Throat* became the most 'in' thing since The Twist."

"Then the shit hit the fan," said its producer, Butchie Peraino. John Lindsay, the Mayor of New York *[in office from 1966 to 1973]*, turned out to have a Puritan streak in him. "I also heard from this *puta* that the mayor was a lousy lay," Butchie claimed.

Lindsay decided to wipe out pornography in New York and ordered the New York Police Department (NYPD) to confiscate a print of *Deep Throat* from the World Theater, where crowds of both men and women had been lining up around the block.

The next morning, headlines blared—MAYOR CRACKS DOWN ON DEEP THROAT. The national media picked up the story, and subsequently, *Deep Throat* made frontpages across the country.

"Al Goldstein at *Screw* was largely responsible for launching *Deep Throat* in New York," its director, Gerard Damiano, said. "But it was Mayor Lindsay who made it a nationwide success and ultimately, a worldwide hit. Demands for copies of *Deep Throat* were swamping Butchie's office in New York. Almost overnight, he had a major hit worth millions. Linda Lovelace, of all people, became a movie star."

The World Theater, where *Deep Throat* had premiered in New York, decided to fight the

Handsome, charismatic, and articulate, this photo shows New York City Mayor John Lindsay emphasizing a point at a public forum in 1965.

401

obscenity charges. "Overnight, another print of *Deep Throat* was delivered to the movie house, and showings resumed because it would take months for the battle to be resolved in the courts," Harry Reems said. Until *Deep Throat*, paying porn audiences had been mostly the raincoat-over-the-lap crowd. But here was a hard-core movie challenging the censorship laws. Plump, mink-coated matrons from Mamaroneck and Manhasset, who looked like they were heading for a matinée of *No, No, Nanette,* were lining up to plunge down their five dollars at the box office."

To strike back at Lindsay, Goldstein hired a photographer to secretly snap a picture of him in a state of undress at the New York Athletic Club. He ran the nude in *Screw,* and within hours the New York Police descended on *Screw's* headquarters and arrested Goldstein, charging him with obscenity. He was held behind bars until his attorney posted bail.

Hef avidly followed the developments associated with *Deep Throat* in New York because he believed that the same censorship forces might view a victory there as a chance to go after *Playboy.*

In 1972, a New York jury found that *Deep Throat* was not obscene. But in March of 1973, Judge Joel J. Tyler ruled that the film "is a feast of carrion and squalor, a nadir of decadence, and a Sodom and Gomorrah gone wild before the fire." He fined the World Theater $100,000 which was later reduced on appeal.

***

Of the many trials spinning around *Deep Throat,* the one that had the most far-reaching consequences took place in Memphis, Tennessee, the home town of Elvis Presley. A series of grand jury indictments began on August 15, 1974, a process that would eventually fill up 1,000 pages of court documents and testimony as various distributors involved with the filming and release of *Deep Throat* were cited. Most of the charges involved the transport of the film across state lines.

Since Linda had volunteered as a witness for the State, she was not indicted. Amazingly, in Memphis, she was not called to testify, either, because of her previous statements before juries in other states. Behind the scenes, prosecutors had privately evaluated her as "a walking time bomb liable to explode at any time." Her reputation as an opponent of censorship had also been clearly noted by all sides of the debate.

The most controversial defendant at the Memphis trial was Reems. Among other citations, he faced charges of having "committed sodomy, fellatio, and cunnilingus."

The Hollywood community in particular was outraged by the charges against him. Actor Dennis Hopper told the press, "This is the first time in U.S. history that an actor has been arrested and tried for merely playing a part."

Having earned only $250 for his participation in *Deep Throat*, Reems faced a legal bill that would grow to at least $150,000—and maybe a lot more.

Spearheaded by Hef, celebrities joined in the effort to pay Reems' legal fees. The list of supporters was impressive: Jack Nicholson, Warren Beatty and his sister, Shirley MacLaine, Richard Dreyfuss, Colleen Dewhurst, Rod McKuen, Ben Gazzara, Mike Nichols, Julie Newmar, Dick Cavett, George Plimpton, Stephen Sondheim, and Louise Fletcher.

Based on what was revealed during the trial, Reems was quoted as saying, "I started hearing about people being killed; baseball bats on projectionists' heads; money going to The Bahamas, and I soon realized that I was mixed up with the wrong crowd. Every day in court I sat on the witness bench, I'd move a little farther away from them."

At the beginning of the trial, the jury was friendly to Reems until they were collectively transported by bus to a movie house in a downtown neighborhood of Memphis for a screening of the film. When the hearings resumed, they stared at Reems with hostility, interpreting him as a sexual pervert.

Back in the courtroom, Chief Prosecutor Larry Parrish offended some members of the court by being too graphic in his questions. "Did you see Reems take his penis out and ejaculate all over Miss Lovelace? Did you see his semen run from her eyes into her mouth as she licked it with her lips?"

The Federal jury in Memphis, which Reems defined as "the buckle of the Bible Belt," convicted him of conspiracy for his role as the doctor in *Deep Throat*. He faced five years in prison and a $10,000 fine.

Harry Reems was the male star of *Deep Throat*. In the photo above, he is caught *in flagrante delicto* with the unseen Linda Lovelace.

At a court trial in Memphis, he was charged with having committed "sodomy, fellatio, and cunnilingus."

The famous attorney, Alan M. Dershowitz, a professor of criminal law at Harvard, referred to Reems' conviction as an outrage and subsequently orchestrated his successful appeal. "Here is an actor who works on a film when the type of work he was doing was constitutionally protected. One year later, the Supreme Court changes its ruling and the actor is charged with a crime."

Gerard Damiano Film Productions was also indicted, but the director, like Linda, had agreed to give state's evidence, so no charges were ever filed against him personally. Gerard Damiano Productions, however, was fined $10,000.

The defendants each appealed their case to a higher court. Their retrial was conducted in Memphis in 1978, at which time Reems was dropped as a defendant. The other defendants lost their appeal.

In the 1970s, with the lawsuits behind him, Reems was a frequent visitor to the Playboy Mansion in Los Angeles, and he and Hef bonded as friends. At times, between other porno gigs, he lived at the Mansion. He had only one complaint, which he relayed to Hef: "Every girl I meet wants my body. I can't service all of them. They don't want me to screw them, they want to give me a blow-job like Linda in *Deep Throat*."

***

For Hef's birthday in 1978, his pal, Lee Wolfberg, staged a special celebration for him, calling it *The Schlong Show*. Its theme had been inspired by the hit TV series, *The Gong Show*, hosted by Chuck Barris. For Hef's show, Wolfberg announced himself as "Chuck Bare Ass."

He booked a medley of talent, all acts in (deliberately) bad taste. Hef's mistress, Sondra Theodore, and actress Sheila Sullivan, performing as "Baby Blue and Silky Sullivan," sang a duet onstage.

The star of the show was Reems and his "Bouncing Balls." Clad in a white bikini, nothing else, he performed a juggler's act with a set of metal balls, announcing the title of his gig as "Pubic TV." Part of it was accompanied by the musical score of "You're the Cream in My Coffee."

Peter Lawford and other male guests were invited to come onstage, drop their pants, and reveal their schlongs. *[Whereas many men dropped their pants, most of them pulled down their jockey shorts to reveal their pubic hair and maybe one or two inches of their penises. Few, however, opted for "The Full Monty."]*

Hef's 52nd birthday celebration gave him the idea of hosting a very private but far more tantalizing *Schlong Show*. He turned to Reems for help in staging it in the privacy of his large bedchamber. Hef personally called six

404

# THE SCHLONG SHOW

## AKA "HIGH JINX AND EXHIBITIONISM
## AT THE PLAYBOY MANSION"

Lots of players in L.A.'s entertainment industry had gossiped about the Who's Who of big schlongs among the remaining ranks of Hollywood's Golden Age movie stars, and which of them might be exhibitionistic enough to display them at a special, adults-only event. So one otherwise uneventful night at the Mansion, some of Hefner's friends and staff members decided to make it a focal point for that night's party.

Who agreed to strut their stuff from a makeshift stage that raucous, perhaps enchanted evening?   They included, left to right in the rows below, stars who would never get away with it at family-friendly event:   John Ireland, Victor Mature, Forrest Tucker, Steve Cochran, Chuck ("The Rifleman") Connors, and Lex ("Tarzan") Barker.

of the most well-endowed actors in Hollywood and persuaded them to participate.

According to the testimonies of many females, rugged John Ireland was the best-endowed actor in Hollywood. A native of Vancouver, he was divorced from his actress wife, Joanne Dru, with whom he had made *All the King's Men*, the Oscar-winning Best Picture of 1949. Acquiescing to Hef's plan, he learned the rules of the game.

Victor Mature, who had starred alongside Hedy Lamarr in *Samson and Delilah* (1949), also agreed to "flash for Hef." When Mature had served in the Coast Guard during World War II, he had been photographed by a fellow serviceman as he lay naked on his cot. Hef had acquired a copy of that photo attesting to the star's uncut glory. Gore Vidal had told Hef, "If the Nazis had seen that picture of Victor, they would have surrendered much earlier."

One Bunny told Hef that having sex with Forrest Tucker felt like giving birth to a big baby boy. The macho star suggested that his penis, which he referred to as "The Chief," should have been immortalized in cement on the Hollywood Walk of Fame.

Steve Cochran also joined "for the hell of it." His nickname in Hollywood was "Mr. King Size," or "The Schvantz." He'd seduced everyone from Mae West to Joan Crawford. On screen or off, he was known as the Bad Boy of Hollywood, and Hef's *Schlong Show* sounded like fun.

A former star athlete, Chuck Connors also signed on. He was once a baseball player and known for "The Big Bat" he carried. When he was new to show business, he'd made a gay porn film, of which Hef had a copy. "He was definitely a contestant in any Big Schlong contest," Hef said.

Lex Barker was the last to sign on. The former Tarzan had captivated his former wives, Lana Turner and Arlene Dahl, both of whom had raved about his "Big Package." *The New York Times* said, "Lex Barker is a streamlined apeman with a personable grin and a torso to make any lion cringe."

According to Lana Turner, "Lex had to wear extra heavy jockstraps when he starred in that flimsy loincloth in all those movies where he swung from a vine. He had something else swinging, too."

Harry Reems and Hef carefully set up a room within the Mansion for the show. To enhance the ranks of its participants, he also invited 24 of the most appealing Playmates or Bunnies. Positioned vertically on a small stage were six wooden partitions designed to conceal the face and body of the actors, but each accessorized with a "glory hole" drilled through it at "scrotum height." It was understood that each of the actors, otherwise concealed from the audience, would insert his (erect or semi-erect) penis through the hole for display.

The "actresses" had to guess which penis belonged to which actor. The winner with the greatest number of correct guesses would collect $5,000.

Later, as part of their own reward, each actor would disappear into one of the nearby bedrooms with two or more of the Bunnies.

Unknown to the actors, Hef secretly arranged for sex tapes to be made of their seductions, admitting to Reems, "It takes more and more kink to really turn me on."

***

Bobbie Arnstein was only nineteen years old when she was hired to join the Chicago-based staff of *Playboy*. It was 1960, and a handsome young senator, John F. Kennedy, was running for President.

When she reported for work at 232 East Ohio Street, her former classmates at Chicago's Lake View High School were shocked that she'd taken a job at "such a dirty magazine."

Her best friend, Betty Frazer, said, "The next thing I hear is that you'll be posing for a centerfold and sleeping with Hugh Hefner."

Two months later, Arnstein met Frazer for lunch. "Only one of your predictions has come true," she confessed. "I'm not centerfold material, although several male staffers have suggested I disrobe for a photographer. However, I am sleeping with Mr. Playboy himself in his round bed. He took my virginity. A bit painful at first but now it's a smooth ride. He likes my platinum blonde hair, even though, as you know, it's bleached. However, he said I should also bleach my pubic hair. He tells me that Marilyn Monroe did that so she could be 'blonde all over.'"

Hef's affair with Arnstein lasted

## Playboy aide gets 15 years in dope case

Bobbie Arnstein, Hef's chief aide and *confidante*, was headed for tragedy.

She fell in love with the wrong man, which in time would lead to her suicide.

Hef referred to these unfolding events as "an incredible fuck-up."

only six weeks, and then he dumped her. But he liked her so much that not only did a lasting friendship develop, but he offered her the post of executive secretary. She also became his *confidante*, someone with whom he could discuss his continuing roster of affairs.

Since she couldn't have a permanent and exclusive relationship with Hef, she became in time what he called "my umbilical cord, linking me to my ever-expanding empire. While I slept for most of the day, she kept abreast of what was running smoothly and who was fucking up while I snoozed."

"In her new post, Bobbie was a real straight shooter," Hef claimed. "She was very assertive and told other executives what they sometimes didn't want to hear. She would even talk back to me when she thought I was doing something really dumb. In most cases, as it turned out, she was right."

"If I had a problem with her, it was that I had to constantly reassure her that she was a good looker and had a great body. She was always comparing herself unfavorably to all those centerfolds who paraded in and out of our lives, mostly out."

As his *confidante*, friend, and private secretary, she emulated Hef in taking amphetamines to help her cope with the many pressures of the day, fending off people who wanted to get to the boss, and protecting him from bores.

She had become so protective of him that he even had her pimp for him, procuring individual Bunnies or Playmates he fancied. She'd approach them and ask if they would have sex with Hef. "I sent her out in my place because I had come to fear rejection, especially as I aged.

After only four months on the job, Arnstein fell in love with Tom Lownes, the Harvard-educated younger brother of Victor Lownes. The summer of 1963 found him working as an associate editor at *Playboy*, since he had editing skills that his older brother did not.

For their summer vacation, he invited her to drive with him from Chicago to Florida. She did not have a driver's license, and Lownes was teaching her to drive on open country roads where there was little traffic.

On the way south, she remembered that he was optimistic about his future. Hef had told him that he was being groomed to take over the editorial duties, one day, of Auguste Spectorsky. "I'm moving up in the world, baby," he told her. "And as soon as my divorce comes through, I want you to marry me."

She promised that she would.

Behind the wheel of Tom's Volkswagen, she was still a bit nervous, especially when she encountered an oncoming car. Arnstein lost control and veered off the highway, crashing into a tree. She was thrown from the car and suffered a broken arm. Tom Lownes, however, was hurled through the windshield, which shattered, killing him and almost decapitating his corpse. Hef recalled, "It was an accident, but Bobbie never recovered from Tom's death. She blamed herself, but it could have happened to any inexperienced driver or to even an experienced driver. I tried to help her get over Tom, but it was one hard struggle. She began to drink quite a bit."

In London, Victor was horrified by the death of his younger brother and never forgave her. During the only encounter they had after his death, he accused her of murder. In tears, she ran from the building and disappeared for three days.

By September of 1971, she found love again in the arms of Ron Scharf, who was seven years younger than she was. He moved in with her at the Playboy Mansion, and she introduced him to Hef. The two men did not like each other, but Hef tolerated his presence because of his loyalty to Arnstein.

After a few weeks of living together, she discovered that he not only took drugs, but sold them, too. That horrified her, and she urged him to abandon drug dealing. He steadfastly refused, claiming that it was "easy money."

She went to great lengths to keep Hef from finding out, fearing that he would kick both of them out of the Mansion. She tried to steer him into some other line of work, telling him she could get a job for him in *Playboy's* circulation department, but he rejected the proposal as "too much labor."

At this point, she was so much in love with him that she was willing to tolerate his drug dealing, but she warned him that she didn't want to know any of the details: "Every time he left my bed and headed out into the city, I didn't know but what the next time I saw him, he'd be behind bars."

One week, he asked her if she could get Hef to give her five days off so they could fly together to Miami "for some OJ and Florida sunshine." She eagerly arranged that, hoping it would be some sort of honeymoon. Actually, she suspected that he was going to propose marriage. Maybe by becoming a married man, he would reform.

However, in Miami, she learned he'd flown there to get "some dynamite coke" from a local drug dealer, George Matthews.

"He looks like he'd sell his own mother down the river," she claimed.

After their time together in Miami, as they were packing for their return to Chicago, he put a half pound of cocaine in her purse. It is not known if she were aware of that, but she carried the stash on the plane with her back home.

At the Chicago Mansion, she met with Hef and found him very depressed. He had learned that he was on the "enemies list" of President Richard Nixon. "He'll probably order the IRS to go after me, even have Federal agents trying to get something on me. I've got to watch my step. Like I don't want to be screwing a Bunny and find out she's only fifteen and a runaway from home. You've got to look out for me."

Arnstein promised she would. It was obvious he hadn't learned about her connection with drugs.

Hef told her, "A woman of your charm, beauty, and wit could attract a better package than Ron Scharf."

Months passed, and things continued as they were. Scharf, from his base inside the Playboy Mansion, kept receiving shipments of drugs from Matthews in Florida, and Hef –despite telling Arnstein that he feared that the Feds "are after my ass"—was still unaware of the legal threat it placed him in.

On March 21, 1974, their worlds changed. As Arnstein was leaving the Playboy Mansion for lunch, three Federal agents confronted her. After establishing her identity, she was placed in handcuffs and maneuvered into the back seat of a squad car. Photographers from the Chicago newspapers had been alerted, and news of her arrest appeared the next morning on frontpages throughout the Midwest. Hef was prominently featured as part of the story, even though no charges had been made against him. "I'm guilty by association," he complained to his staff.

News of Arnstein's arrest vied for coverage with Nixon's Watergate scandal.

At the headquarters of the Drug Enforcement Administration on Dearborn Street, Arnstein faced intense questioning, mostly as the agents tried to link her drug charges to Hef. She was told that Scharf had also been arrested.

When he heard the news, Hef summoned his attorneys to rush to police headquarters, where they arranged her release on a bail of $4,500, which Hef paid.

As coverage and more investigations ensued, Hef said, "I'm the patsy. They don't give a damn about Bobbie. The fuckers want to get something on me."

Anonymous charges were received at the U.S. Attorney General's office in Chicago, perhaps from disgruntled former *Playboy* employees who had been fired. It was said that nearly all the *Playboy* executives were drug addicted. It was also alleged that "bags of cocaine" were regularly flown in on the "Big Bunny." There was even a charge that Hef himself was involved in drug trafficking.

"My troubles were mounting," Hef said. "As I predicted, the Internal Revenue Service was auditing my books. I was even being sued by a former African American employee who ridiculously was claiming that he had been fired because of my discrimination policies."

In the weeks ahead, he faced more unwelcome headlines, such as HOLLYWOOD FIGURES TIED TO PLAYBOY DRUG PROBE. Peter Lawford, the former brother-in-law of John F. Kennedy, was rumored to be one of the stars who arrived at the Playboy Mansion with stashes of cocaine.

On the frontpage of the *Chicago Tribune* was another blaring headline: FEDERAL DRUG PROBERS ZERO IN ON HEFNER. The article maintained that he had long been suspected of harboring illicit drugs at the Chicago Mansion.

In his paranoia, he ordered that the entire mansion be swept "for wiretaps, bugs, and illegal drugs."

Matthews was the first to stand trial, and he was found guilty and sentenced to fifteen years in prison. Working through an attorney, he agreed to change the testimony he'd given at first trial and be a star witness at the trials of Arnstein and Scharf. In his revised testimony, he asserted that Arnstein had been a carrier of cocaine between Miami and Chicago.

After giving state evidence, Matthews had to serve only four months of his fifteen-year sentence.

Hef had a powerful enemy in James R. Thompson, a Republican who was known as "a hard ass," fanatically devoted to cracking down on illegal drug trafficking. He had hoped to nail Hefner as a means of reinforcing his image as a champion of law and order, certain that it would enhance his chance of victory during his race for the governorship of Illinois.

It was claimed that Thompson found *Playboy* "an easy mark, much like voting against sin."

At the trial of Scharf and Arnstein, she did not take the stand in her own defense to counter Matthews' charges. Her attorney didn't want her to, fearing that she might crumble under the pressure of cross examination. An attorney informed Hef,

Peter Lawford always managed to look good in public, even while compromising Hefner with allegations of drug abuse during his visits to the Playboy Mansion.

Here, he's depicted with Ruta Lee in a scene from *Sergeants Three* (1962) in which he co-starred with other members of the Rat Pack.

411

"Bobbie is dangerously close to a nervous breakdown."

The trial lasted for three days, and on November 26, 1974, Federal Judge B.M. Decker sentenced Scharf to six years in a Federal prison. The shock in the courtroom came when he handed down a fifteen-year sentence to Arnstein. He also ordered her to undergo ninety days of psychiatric testing.

Hef was able to get her released on bail while his attorneys filed an appeal. During this time, Federal Attorney General Thompson phoned her and told her that a drug gang had put her at the top of a list of victims to be wiped out. "Your life is in danger. We can offer you protection, but you have to reveal what you know about Mr. Hefner and his drug dealing. It'll go easier for you if you do."

She rejected his offer.

Meanwhile, *Playboy* stockholders were intensely agitated about all the headlines linking Hef to a drug cartel.

Bob Gutwillig, vice president of marketing at *Playboy*, called Victor Lownes in London and asked him to fly to Chicago for a meeting of the company's top executives.

The prestigious business journal *Dun's Review* (a forerunner of *Dun & Bradstreet*) wrote: "The record of Playboy Enterprises at its 20th anniversary is one of careless squandering that promises a dismal future."

At the meeting, Gutwillig read, out and loud, a fiery memo he'd written. "Hugh Hefner is a chief executive who rules with a whim of iron, a disregard for the welfare of Playboy Enterprises, as well as a contempt for his employees. His lifestyle evokes that of Louis XIV, the Sun King of France."

Robert Preuss, Hef's longtime friend and President of Playboy Enterprises, joined Gutwillig in asking Hef to step down until the drug investigation was complete.

The next day, the First Bank of Chicago asked *Playboy* to find another lead bank.

Hef responded to all this turmoil by firing Gutwillig, which he had the power to do.

Preuss was also tossed aside during the subsequent reorganization of *Playboy* when

Long before President Donald Trump made the term "witch hunt" infamous, Hef used the same accusation against the attorney general of Illinois (later the long-term governor), James R. Thompson.

"The asshole used me as a sepping stone to advance his political goals," Hef claimed.

"The charges against me were all lies."

a seven-man "office-of-the-president" took over management of the entire operation. Angered after having served loyally for twenty years, Preuss resigned. "The place has come to disgust me," he said. "Hef brought in a bunch of phony baloneys, and the place was riddled with back-stabbers."

Hef was angered by how he'd been treated in Chicago and began to think of relocating permanently in Los Angeles. He had many supporters. Author Gay Talese claimed, "Government investigators were eager to present the Arnstein conspiracy case in an atmosphere of sex, drugs, degeneracy, and death. Unfairly, Hefner was investigated repeatedly."

While awaiting her appeal, Arnstein admitted to friends Richard and Shirley Hillman that, "I am going through the torments of the damned. I'd rather kill myself than go to jail. Also, I'm horrified that Hef's name was dragged through the courts even though he was innocent of all charges. I have not served him well. I can't even sleep, and I'm taking a lot of pills."

She dined with the Hillmans on January 11, 1975. Then, in the early hours of January 12, she checked into the Hotel Maryland on Rush Street in Chicago under the *faux* name of Roberta Hillman. On her door she posted a DO NOT DISTURB sign.

At around 3PM the next afternoon, a maid could not gain entrance and reported it to management. When the door was forced open, they discovered Arnstein's dead body. An autopsy revealed that she had committed suicide with an overdose of sleeping pills, barbiturates, and tranquilizers.

A note was found beside her body, prefaced with a headline: "Another one of those boring suicide notes."

Her message was long and rambling. "I was never part of any conspiracy to transport or distribute drugs. Hugh M. Hefner is a staunch, upright, and rigorously moral man—I know him well and he has never been involved in any criminal activity which is being attributed to him now."

Hef was in Los Angeles when he learned of the suicide. He had his aides announce that he would hold a press conference in Chicago the following afternoon. He flew there aboard the "Big Bunny."

The press conference on January 14, 1975 at 1PM drew at least a hundred reporters and photographers. Looking worn and tired, Hef appeared emotionally disturbed as he read a statement, blaming "overzealous government prosecutors for driving Miss Arnstein to kill herself." He labeled their investigation as "an anti-*Playboy* witch hunt."

He also charged investigators with giving Arnstein that harsh fifteen-year sentence "to get her to give false testimony against me."

He called her "the brightest and most worthwhile woman I've ever known." In tears, he read "Puritanism remains as formidable an opponent to a truly free and democratic society as ever. Authoritarian repression continues to threaten a free society."

Thompson dismissed Hef's accusations, calling them "...off the wall. I'm not sure that what Hefner stands for these days is all that relevant, or that any prosecution of him would mean much."

When Thompson eventually ran for governor, he resigned his position as U.S. Attorney General. He was successful in his run for the governorship, and was not only elected, but served four consecutive terms, from 1977 to 1991. "He owes it all to me," Hef said. "He rode into office attacking *Playboy* and me."

Thompson's replacement as Attorney General was Samuel K. Skinner, who ordered his agents to drop any investigations into Hef. He issued a statement to the press: "No evidence of unlawful acquisition or distribution of cocaine or other hard drugs by Mr. Hefner, the corporation, or its employees has been adduced."

Hef received the news with both relief and bitterness, calling it "a Pyrrhic victory. My name has been blackened and a young woman is dead. Thompson, however, won 65 percent of the vote in his race for the governor's seat."

\*\*\*

In 1976, Derick J. Daniels, a former top executive at Knight-Ridder newspapers, went to work for *Playboy* and ultimately became its chief executive. He was hired with the understanding that he would train Hef's daughter, Christie, and that she would eventually take over and turn the company around.

Under his direction, the company dumped unprofitable enterprises, including clubs and resorts, and cut overhead by at least 40 percent before the end of 1982. It was in that year that he ceded control to Christie.

Daniels was born in Washington, D.C., to a family with roots in North Carolina politics and newspapers. He was only 47 when he signed on with Hef. One of his private goals was "to get rid of that shithead, Victor Lownes. I hate the fucker's guts," he told other Playboy executives.

*Playboy* never had an executive as flamboyant as Daniels. Lownes, his arch enemy, thought he appeared like a foppish Beau Brummel, yet with "a Little Orphan Annie coiffure." He preferred jumpsuits, one of them crafted from gold *lamé*.

One author described him as looking like "a pinched cherub with a fluffy mop of golden curls" evoking Shirley Temple in all those lollipop movies of the 1930s. Yet another executive described him as "all Carolina charm and Manhattan flash." His thin, heavily lined face betrayed his high

414

life ways.

He shocked *Playboy* executives when he arrived at the Chicago mansion and threw a party to introduce himself. He appeared there wearing white high-heeled boots, a white *blouson* top with billowing sleeves, white skin-tight trousers, and a white scarf flung around his neck. The next day he reported to work wearing a pilot's suit with red cowboy boots.

Daniels went to work, shutting down the resort in Jamaica, the Playboy Club in Baltimore, and the financing of movies. He sold Playboy's movie theaters in Chicago and New York, and he signed a profitable record deal with Columbia Records. Then he surveyed the other Playboy Clubs in the chain, searching to see which ones were losing money. He defined his drastic cuts as "hutch cleaning."

During his first month on the job, he fired seventy employees at the Playboy Club in Chicago, defining the payroll there as "bloated."

By 1978, after cutting away all that dead weight, Playboy rebounded a bit. As *The New York Times* phrased it, "Glamour Gone, Profits Revive."

A reporter wrote, "It is not clear if the Playboy Bunny has made a comeback, but Derick Daniels has shot these frisky rabbits with oodles of cortisone."

When asked how he planned to handle the *Playboy* centerfolds, he stared back at the reporter with one blue eye, the other green. His answer was not clear. "I learned about female anatomy from reading the Sears catalogue."

That reporter wrote, "He reminds me of John Wayne trapped in Joel Grey's body."

In Miami, Daniels threw another party in Coconut Grove. A reporter from the *Miami Herald* covered it: "The male waiters were obviously selected for their buttocks, as they were attired in leather and leopard skin outfits with their ass bare. The female Bunnies attending wore black thong panties and were topless. The highlight of the evening was a stripper named Dawn Vulva, who revealed that her pubic hair had been fashioned as a Valentine heart and dyed a bright red."

*[As time went by, Daniels would be replaced by Christie Hefner far sooner than Daniels had expected. He displayed his Beau Brummel look as flamboyantly at his departure as he had when he was first hired. For his final exit, he was attired in a white leather jumpsuit, heading out the building and into a white chauffeured Mercedes limousine. In its back seat, he sipped from a bottle of champagne that had been cooling, as he headed off for a night at the opera. In his pocket was a severance check for $500,000.]*

Despite the many improvements Daniels had orchestrated, Hef continued to face a barrage of attacks from his enemies.

Mike Royko, columnist for the *Chicago Sun-Times*, asserted, "Hugh Hefner is a self-promoter whose idea of sophistication is to jiggle a case of Pepsi and play backgammon with those of his companions, often Bunnies, intelligent enough to understand the game."

In the U.K., the *Guardian* claimed that Hef "promoted consumerism run amok: expensive cars, expensive clothes, and expensive women."

Other critics suggested that Hef's outlook on sex was to "take a leering voyeur's view of what was written on the walls of men's toilets."

These were merely verbal attacks. By the 1980s, he would face far more dangerous enemies, including a newly elected president of the United States, a former actor in the movies, plus the so-called Moral Majority. "The oncoming 1980s would mark the nightmare years of my life," he said.

\*\*\*

As she was growing up, Hugh Hefner's daughter, Christie, born in 1952, saw relatively little of her famous father. It seemed beyond her wildest dreams that one day, she would be running the Playboy Empire as a sort of "Hare Apparent."

She had been reared mostly by her mother, Mildred (Minnie), Hef's first wife. By the time Christie was five, her parents had separated.

In 1974, she had graduated *summa cum laude* and a Phi Beta Kappa from Brandeis University with a bachelor's degree in English and American literature. She would not marry until 1995.

She spent her first year on the job market as a freelance journalist but joined the *Playboy* staff in 1975. Holding down various jobs within the organization, she rose to power at a swift rate. After four years, she was promoted to the rank of Vice President. By 1982, she assumed the presidency of Playboy Enterprises, shooting up to become Chairman of the Board in 1988. Hef continued as the often absentee editor-in-chief and was the majority stockholder.

As a *Playboy* executive, Christie remained aloof to Hef's libertine lifestyle as she watched his "steady" girlfriends come and go, sometimes bonding with one or two of them. She was a stylish business woman, attractive, always well groomed, showing up for work elegant and demure in Gucci business suits, usually in dark colors.

As she sat at the helm, she was the first to realize that three decades had passed since her father had launched *Playboy* with Marilyn Monroe on the cover. The Sexual Revolution had come and gone.

*Playboy* readers were more jaded and far more sexually sophisticated than they'd been during the Eisenhower era. "Naughty nudity" seemed something their fathers, or even their grandfathers, had enjoyed in a more innocent time.

Christie's task was daunting. She not only had to rescue the company's finances, she had to redefine the *Playboy* credo of "Entertainment for Men." She soon learned that it took a lot more in the 1980s to keep men entertained.

As she set about rescuing *Playboy* before it went over the cliff of financial disaster, she was soon recognized as one of America's most powerful woman executives.

It was not just the centerfolds that she focused on, but social issues. The articles she approved from leading writers were highly praised. She became known as a champion of AIDS research, gay rights, and the plight of battered women.

Her aging father told the press, "There is something fascinating and quite wonderful about the heir to *Playboy* being a woman, not a man. If it had been calculated, it could not have worked out better. If Christie had not

At the age of twenty-nine, the brightest bulb in the *Playboy* chandelier, Christie Hefner, took over the direction of her father's financially troubled empire. Depicted here in 2007, she became an instant media celebrity. The press dubbed her the "Hare in Chief."

With her business skill and intelligence, she tightened her grip, eliminating waste and reshaping the company's future.

been born to do this job, our promotions department would have to have invented her. My girl's good, really good at her job."

Although she faced the inevitable attacks, Christie was also hailed as "The Katharine Graham of the Middle West," a reference to the publisher of the *Washington Post*. Attorney Gloria Allred praised Christie as "one of the most articulate, committed, and hard-working feminists in the United States."

During the tenure of Derick Daniels, and despite his cutbacks, the empire had continued to languish. Playboy Clubs across America had gone from a high of twenty-two to only three. The loss of the gambling revenue from London was a terrible financial blow. "Our cash cow no longer gives milk," Hef lamented. Losses were in the millions.

Into this financial quagmire Christie stepped. She also had to mop up problems that emerged after audits by two government agencies.

In 1978, the Internal Revenue Service challenged the operating expenses affiliated with the tax returns of the Playboy Mansion in Chicago, and especially those associated with its counterpart in Los Angeles. After their review, the IRS, for the seven-year period from 1970 to 1976, demanded an additional $13.4 million in back taxes and penalties.

In Chicago, a *Playboy* stockholder filed a lawsuit claiming that Hef's occupancy of these lavish mansions was "a waste, a gift, and an embezzlement of the enterprise's assets."

As if that weren't trouble enough, the Securities and Exchange Commission moved in on *Playboy*, too, launching a probe of "undisclosed remuneration by officers of *Playboy* and its affiliates."

An internal audit revealed that Hef and some of his executives had received unauthorized benefits totaling $2 million over an eight-year period. *[In one item alone, Hef billed the company $75,000 for laundry and dry cleaning.]* He was asked to reimburse the company $800,000 from his personal funds for what the audit had defined as "personal expenses." He willingly paid the debt.

The most astonishing discovery was that Hef paid Playboy Enterprises a monthly rental fee of only $650 for each of his mansions. Around that time, the annual operating costs of each of the venues was made public: $9,141,000 for Chicago and $11,500,000 for Los Angeles.

Despite the closer scrutiny from Federal Agencies, in January of 1979, Hef ordered that *Playboy's* 25th anniversary be celebrated with gala events in Los Angeles, New York, and Chicago. For the magazine's 25th Anniversary Playmate, Hef found a sexy beauty, claiming that "her real name is Candy Loving."

Jerome Kern, who for a time was interim chairman of *Playboy*, summed up Christie's challenge and how she met it: "She oversaw *Playboy's* transition from a domestic magazine publisher to a global lifestyle and multimedia company, directing its entry into television and online and mobile offerings. Under her leadership, the enterprise grew from insignificance to a most profitable business, and she was only 29 when she headed the whole enterprise."

Her takeover was not universally heralded. Columnist Joan Beck wrote: "It's difficult to imagine any intelligent, well-educated woman with a smidgen of self-respect who would be willing to preside over the kind of lecherous exploitation of women that built the Playboy Empire—and now sustains what is left of it in its declining years."

As head of *Playboy*, Christie was eagerly sought out for speeches and interviews. On such occasions, she defended *Playboy*, calling it "fundamentally liberal and humanistic. I'm living in a country where the President of the United States wants to make abortion a crime, and some segments of the women's movement suggest that *Playboy* is a major enemy in society— that's crazy!"

She denied that the atmosphere at *Playboy* contributed to "a culture of harassment and toxic masculinity." She also claimed that she had never experienced any sexual harassment at *Playboy*. "Of course, once I became president and later CEO, it was most unlikely that I would be targeted."

"It was a highly sexualized environment because of the creative content of *Playboy*," she said. "But it was a culture of respect for both men and women. We didn't subject our employees to drug tests, and our models were as respected as the writers we hired."

The challenges Christie faced were daunting, since in the early 1980s, nearly every division of Playboy Enterprises was losing money, including music, film, book publishing, and a modeling agency. The magazine itself was suffering from major competition, especially from *Penthouse* and *Hustler*. She had to cut costs, lay off employees, and hold onto readership. Monthly circulation had dropped from 4.4 million to 4.1 million copies. By 1983, revenues continued to plummet.

From his Los Angeles Mansion, Hef was particularly concerned with the demise of his Playboy Clubs, but seemed only dimly aware of the decline in revenue and continued, more or less, his lavish lifestyle.

He spoke to a reporter from the *Los Angeles Times*. "I started the clubs in the 1960s, but I'll admit, they seem a bit antiquated and behind the times—you might call us camp. Our Bunny has not quite entered the realm of the Model-T, but we're getting there, having to compete with all those strip shows. I'm not planning to cut off the cottontails of our Bunnies, because they are now an international symbol. But Christie and I are looking at ways to make our remaining clubs, and even the magazine itself, more up to date in keeping with the changing times."

Christie had gone to work immediately, firing nearly a hundred executives and giving them a severance check and a farewell. In her first six months as president, she had slashed annual expenses by $8 million dollars.

*Fortune* magazine summed up her assumption of power: "In contrast to her father, she has an affinity for balance sheets, a tolerance of daylight hours, and a gregarious personality. She also shows a willingness to control people and to fire and promote without years of soul-searching."

Behind her back, some staff members, afraid for their jobs, accused Christie of "conducting a Reign of Terror not seen since the French Revolution."

"When I took over," Christie said, "the company was in a classic position of having over-diversified. So obviously, part of what we were trying to do was to figure out what was the right kind of businesses to hang onto and make a go of it, and what enterprises to drop as losers."

She flew to Los Angeles at least once a month to visit with Hef and catch up not only on their personal lives, but on the happenings within and across the Empire. She gave an interview to reporter Aurelie Corinthos in which she noted the changes that had taken place with her father over the years.

"He was not a person of regrets. He wasn't apt to have a would-have, could-have, should-have attitude about things. How he definitely changed was he found it much easier to express how important people were to him—and how much he loved them—not just with family but with other people he was close to."

"He was always a Romantic," Christie continued, "but that mostly revealed itself in his personal romantic relationships. The softer side of him didn't manifest itself as much in his professional relationships. He was always a fundamentally kind person. As he got older, he became a softer version of himself. Maybe he came to realize how fundamental and essential human relationships are at the end of the day and how they're to be treasured and honored—and part of that is expressing what they mean to you."

\*\*\*

A *Playboy* interview, harmless as it seems today, created a firestorm during the presidential race of 1976. Jimmy Carter, a former peanut farmer and later governor of Georgia, was vying for president against sitting President Gerald Ford, who had replaced Richard Nixon, midterm, after he resigned because of the Watergate scandal.

The interview that Carter gave to *Playboy* was hailed as a major journalistic *coup* of the 1970s, and it almost cost Carter the hotly contested election. After *Playboy* hit the stands and the interview was highly publicized, Carter's popularity dropped fifteen points in polling. Ford saw his election to the presidency within his grasp.

What ignited the firestorm involved Carter's telling *Playboy*, a magazine "bulging with bosoms and buttocks" about his sexual desires. "I've looked at a lot of women with lust. I've committed adultery many times in my heart."

He didn't stop there but went on to tell the interviewer that he knew that God had forgiven him. "I would not condemn a man who leaves his wife and shacks up with somebody out of wedlock. Christ says, 'don't consider yourself better than someone else because one man sleeps with a whole lot of women while another guy is loyal to his wife.'"

Carter also claimed during this soliloquy "that the Bible taught that all men are sinners, and that it was God's place—not man's—to judge."

Ferociously, the media grabbed it, *Newsweek* calling it "The Great *Playboy* Furor. Newspapers throughout the country are making whoopee with Carter's overly candid confession."

Carter was denounced for his "locker room talk," as was future president, Donald Trump. Carter was particularly criticized for using such words as "screw" and "shack-up."

Columnist Max Lerner, a frequent visitor to Playboy's Mansion in Chicago, chastised Carter for "misjudging presidential standards of decorum."

Cartoonists jumped into the campaign to ridicule Carter. One newspaper cartoon had a Playboy Bunny sitting on the lap of the leering Presidential candidate who told Miss Cottontail, "I'm Jimmy Carter, and I'm running for President."

Reporter Ted Gup wrote: "At the time of the *Playboy* interview, Carter was pressed to demonstrate that he was not so morally rigid and out of touch with the prevailing sexual and social mores, that he could not see beyond his Sunday best to the world as it was. He was baited in the interview to show that, if elected, he would not be a priggish schoolmarm wagging a moral finger in the face of the nation that had just embraced the Sexual Revolution. His challenge was to show that he was not the sanctimonious Bible-thumping Southerner many feared."

Another reporter wrote, "Before *Playboy*, Carter might have been to many people a country slicker. After *Playboy*, he comes on more as an honest Elmer Gantry, an old-time brooding Evangelist—a strange, sincere man with something of the tortured quality of the Rev. Mr. Davidson in Somerset Maugham's

The interview that the presidential candidate, Jimmy Carter, gave to Hefner nearly cost him his chance at the White House during his race against sitting president, Gerald Ford.

421

tale about the prostitute Miss Sadie Thompson," as had been depicted in several movies, one with Rita Hayworth in 1953.

In late October of 1976, with the election looming in November, Carter said, "I would not have given that interview if I had it to do over again."

Even so, the interview did not, as predicted, cost him the Presidency. He narrowly beat Ford.

\*\*\*

In an interview in 1972 with the British weekly music magazine, *Melody Makers,* David Bowie (aka Ziggy Stardust) outed himself as a bisexual. In a September 1976 issue of *Playboy,* he reconfirmed his bisexuality. That interview was billed as "An outrageous conversation with the actor, rock singer, and sexual switch-hitter," and referred to Bowie as "a bisexual balladeer."

Within the *Playboy* article, Bowie was quoted as saying, "Girls are always presuming I've kept my heterosexual virginity, so I've had all these girls try to get me to move over to the other side. 'C'mon, David, it isn't all that bad.' I always play dumb."

As if bisexuality weren't enough, Bowie also stirred up controversy with the comments he'd made about Adolf Hitler. "He was one of the first rock stars. Look at some of his newsreel films and see how he moves. I think he is quite as good as Mick Jagger. The world will never see his like. He staged a country."

Speaking as the self-styled "White Duke," Bowie claimed, "Britain is ready for a fascist leader. I think it would benefit from one. After all, fascism is really nationalism. I believe strongly in fascism."

He later retracted that interview he gave to *Playboy,* blaming it on his mental instability at time caused by his drug prob-

David Bowie's magazine coverage of 1976 included major pieces in both *Rolling Stone* and *Playboy.*

At the time Bowie gave these interviews, he suffered from an all-consuming cocaine addiction and was obsessed with the Charles Manson death squad and the Nazis.

He also believed that Satan lived in his indoor swimming pool.

lem. "I was out of my mind, totally, completely crazed."

***

From 1978 to 1979, Stefan Tetenbaum was employed as Hef's valet at the Los Angeles Mansion. He told the press, "One of my major tasks was to see that everything functioned smoothly on 'Pig Nights.' On these occasions, Hefner invited celebrities, usually movie stars, but also an occasional sports figure, to enjoy high-priced call girls. Guys like the ill-fated John Belushi showed up, but I won't name others out of fear of embarrassing them."

Some of the hookers fastened on *faux* penises and proceeded to sodomize the willing men. "This was one of Belushi's favorite sexual pleasures, or so it seemed."

"After these pig nights, I ordered the maid to round up all the sex toys and take them to the basement to sterilize them," Tetenbaum claimed. "God knows what cavities some of them had probed."

"I never saw Hefner indulge in any sexual acts on those Pig Nights," Tetenbaum said. "He was always the voyeur, overseeing a couple fornicating like the director on a movie set. While he took in all the action, he liked me to provide him with red licorice sticks to munch on—never black."

He always watched a lot of porn, and later had someone on his staff hire the most well-hung of these actors to come to the Los Angeles Mansion to fornicate before the audiences he'd invited."

His favorite star was John C. Holmes, noted for his 13½ -inch penis. This country boy from Ohio—"ugly as hell"—had moved to California in 1964, where he began making porn flicks. Partly because of his endowment, he became the hottest male porn star in Hollywood, the star of films such as *Let Me Count the Lays* and *Sex and the Single Vampire*.

John C. Holmes was the leading male porn star in America when Hef invited him to the Playboy Mansion in Los Angeles for "performances."

The picture above with all those women's hands was designed to show that it took a lot of fingers to cover up his endowment.

Some of the women who were not used to getting penetrated by such large penises complained to Tetenbaum that they were in pain. "I often had to help them stumble to bed in the dormitory. Sometimes, Hef paid them an extra bonus for enduring such brutal sex for his amusement."

Many of these encounters with porn stars were filmed by Hef's cameraman. Later, he would screen them for his male friends.

"Hefner provided plenty of cocaine at these parties, although he did not partake of the drug himself," the valet said. "He preferred to smoke weed. In fact, he liked it so much, he sometimes threw parties for the marijuana growers of California."

The valet was also in charge of Hefner's strange diet. "I had to make sure that his Pepsi drinks were chilled just right. He also preferred Campbell's chicken noodle soup and lots and lots of M&Ms."

Stefan Tetenbaum photographed in the entrance lobby of L.A.'s Playboy mansion. For about a year, he was Hef's valet at the Los Angeles Mansion.

His duties included being the producer of the orgiastic "Pig Nights," and seeing that the maids sterilized the sex toys the following day.

He was often cruel to his girlfriend of the moment," Tetenbaum claimed. "Rather brutal, as a matter of fact. If their tits weren't big enough, he'd order them to get implants on some occasions. Implants were fairly new at the time, and many of the girls who underwent the operation experienced shifting or even bursting implants. They had to be rushed to the hospital. At least Hefner paid their medical bills. But he didn't invite them back. They were disposable."

"At the end of the 1970s, when I met him, Hefner was no longer the liberation guy he'd been in his earlier days, when he advocated abortion and equal rights for gays. As he grew old in Holmby Hills, California, he had turned into a dirty old man."

\*\*\*

Outside of Nevada, gambling was illegal throughout the United States. In 1976, New Jersey voted to permit gambling within its borders, but only in Atlantic City. That did little to help Hef's failing Great Gorge (New Jersey) Resort.

424

Hef decided he wanted to open the most glamourous casino in Atlantic City, a glittering palace not only for gamblers and Playboys, but for high-end entertainment, too. "We'll be a palace, attracting high rollers to hear, say, Liza Minnelli or Barbra Streisand. I have high hopes for its success. I don't think we'll have trouble getting a gaming license."

Hef's dream of becoming "The "Golden Boy of Atlantic City" evaporated when the gaming commission refused to grant him a license, citing various past infractions by Playboy Enterprises.

A future U.S. president, Donald Trump, would later take over the premises. His management would cause yet another series of disasters for this unfortunate enterprise.

As he envisioned it, his Atlantic City casino and hotel would rise 24 glittering floors, offering 500 luxurious rooms. Since the total cost of construction and development was estimated at $135 million, he formed a partnership with the Elsinore Corporation.

Work on the glass-and-steel structure began in March of 1979. Hef was told that this new enterprise would gross at least a million dollars a day in revenue.

It was granted a temporary gaming license from the state in time for its opening on April 14, 1981, but although 10,000 pages of documents and a $100,000 application fee had already been submitted, it appeared vaguely ominous that a permanent gaming license had not yet been received.

Many of his advisors had warned Hef that as a gambling mecca, he'd face severe competition from any number of other casinos. He plunged ahead anyway.

A financier in the *Wall Street Journal* wrote, "I find it hard to believe that *Playboy* will be granted a license to operate a casino in Atlantic City." Hef should have listened.

In Hef's words, "the shit hit the fan" in November of 1981, when the Division of Gaming Enforcement denied his request for a gaming license.

Several reasons were given, including the charge that *Playboy* executives had bribed an official in Albany during his application for a liquor license for the Playboy Club in Manhattan. And once again, the drug allegations associated with Bobbie Arnstein were aired, along with unsupported data that both *Playboy* and Hefner himself were somehow involved.

Hef was stunned and ordered his attorneys to arrange for a public hearing in front of the New Jersey Casino Control Commissioners. Five officials sat on the Board. He would need four of them to vote in his favor.

Hef flew in on the morning of the hearing. Escorted by the tall and shapely Shannon Tweed, his latest sleepover girlfriend, he made a highly visible entrance. He looked in bad shape, with a day's growth of beard. He had not slept for the previous two nights, existing on a diet of "Dexies" and Pepsi.

He was ill-prepared to answer questions, later admitting "I bombed." To most questions, he replied, "I don't know," or "I don't remember."

One reporter in Atlantic City wrote, "I never have seen a prospective casino executive as ill-prepared as Hugh Hefner, the *Playboy* honcho. He couldn't even answer basic facts about his company's operation. He left the impression that he was drugged and had spent the previous night with a Bunny instead of getting ready to be questioned."

At the end of the hearing, the commissioners retired to their chambers. Their verdict came back in less than half an hour. Three of the commissioners voted in Hef's favor, but two men chose to deny him the license.

The commissioners, however, did toss an olive branch to the overall partnership, asserting that they might grant the license providing they divorced themselves completely from any association with Hef. Officers of the Playboy/Elsinore coalition were not prepared to do that and rejected the commission's offer.

Hef held 66 percent of the company's stock, and he became the first would-be casino operator forced out of Atlantic City. He met with his fellow executives and agreed to put their building up for a "fire sale." He divested his interest in the Atlantic City property to Elsinore for slightly less than $60 million. Elisinore had to post only $7.6 million in cash, the balance covered by an unsecured note.

As news became public, *Playboy* stocks virtually crashed on the stock market. Word spread around Wall Street that *Playboy* was on the verge of collapse. Playboy's cash reserves were drained, and future revenues, it turned out, suffered a severe blow. Under new management, after Playboy's rabbit logo was removed from the building, the property on Atlantic City's boardwalk at Florida Avenue became The Atlantis.

*[The property operated under the Atlantis banner until 1989, when Donald Trump bought it for $63 million, renaming it the Trump Regency. Ironically, at least temporarily, Trump enjoyed a brief reign as the Golden Boy of Atlantic City. He too, however, would face financial disaster, and his own Atlantic City fiefdom would eventually collapse.]*

\*\*\*

426

In *People* magazine, Monty Brower wrote: "Hugh Hefner has played Pygmalion to a pantheon of Playmates over the years, picking the comeliest from the pages of his magazine, then transforming them from mere pinups to living symbols of his Playboy Philosophy. Showering them with money and furs, posing before the finest photographers, offering them up for the attentive appraisal of Hollywood agents and producers, Hefner has shown his women how to turn T&A into taxable assets so that when their tenures as First Bunny ends, they do not leave empty-handed. In return, the young women have but to share his bed and hang around quietly."

When Barbi Benton lost her Bunny crown in 1976, she was immediately followed by a trio of beauties who warmed Hef's bed throughout the remainder of the 1970s and for most of the 1980s, too. In the final year of that decade, he would marry for the second time.

The Playmates who were selected during this time frame were as follows:

Sondra Theodore (1976-1981)
Shannon Tweed (1981-1983)
Carrie Leigh (1983-1988)

"All of these women were fully aware that there was little possibility that I would ever consider marrying again," Hef said.

As stated by Victor Lownes, "Hef is lousy company when he doesn't have a full-time mistress, and worse than ever when he is not in love, or at least thinks he is."

As the guest of another woman, a beautiful but rather shy Sondra Theodore showed up one evening at the Playboy Mansion in Los Angeles. The blonde beauty was twenty years old, a native of California, and a former Sunday School teacher.

"Across a crowded room" (as phrased in lyrics to the popular song), Hef spotted her and gravitated toward her. Soon they were dancing to the sounds of "Baby Blue," the Barry White song. In July of 1977, Theodore would pose as Playmate of the Month, although her mother "did not raise a daughter to show off what she's got to those *Playboy* men."

The girlfriend who accompanied her to the party at the Mansion that fateful night later claimed, "Hefner just swept Sondra off her feet. I came to the party with her, but she was not around when it was time to go, if you get my drift. I went home alone."

Hef's romance with Theodore began that night.

"As a child, I captured lizards and made them my pets," she confessed.

"Now, Hef has caged me and made me his pet. I know how those little reptiles of mine felt."

Although Hef was pledging his undying love for Theodore, he continued to seduce other Bunnies or Playmates on the side. "I was committed to non-committal," he claimed. "Sondra is a special girl, but not my only girl."

Privately, Theodore confessed to some of the women on Hef's staff, "I feel my heart is breaking when he goes off with another Bunny for the night. When I took up with him, I knew he had a reputation of having a cheating heart, but I loved him enough to tolerate it, although we did have some arguments. If he asked me to marry him, I would do so right away. Maybe, as he grows older, he'll settle down and need only a good and loving wife. I hope he chooses me."

Theodore later revealed that during the first week of their sexual relationship, Hef suffered a near-fatal mishap during sex with her. What was it all about? When he was performing cunnilingus on her, he accidentally inhaled one of her Ben Wa Balls.

*[Ben Wa Balls, also known as rin-no-tama, Venus balls, orgasm balls, or geisha balls, are hollow, marble-sized metal spheres, each containing a small weight. Their aficionados, including the (fictional) characters of Anastasia and Christian in* Fifty Shades of Grey, *maintain that when one or more are inserted into a vagina or anus they can contribute to sexual stimulation.]*

The cover of *Playboy's* July 1977 on which Sondra Theodore appeared with an inflatable toy as Playmate of the Month.

The girlfriend who "chaperoned" Sondra to the Playboy Mansion on the night she met Hefner went home alone. Later, in a testimonial to their romance, she said, "Once Hefner spotted Sondra, he was a goner—and so was she."

Sondra told the press, "His boyish charm won me over. You just want to cuddle him and love him. He's witty and a delight to be with."

Hef responded publicly that he found Sondra "fresh faced and wholesome. She makes me feel like a boy again."

Choking and gasping for air, Hef fell back on the bed, managing to dislodge the sex toy as he was on the verge of asphyxiating. After recovering he said, "If I had choked to death, just imagine the tabloid headlines."

For their first "anniversary," he presented her with a necklace that spelled out "Baby Blue" in diamonds. *[That was the name of the languorous Barry White song they'd danced to on the night they met.]*

428

As a child, Theodore, like many California beauties, had dreamed of becoming an actress. She also hoped to become a singer, imitating the songs she heard from her parents' record collection. In time, she would leave Hef's embrace to seek fame and fortune outside the Playboy Mansion.

It appeared that her big break had come when she almost nabbed the role of Pinky Tuscadero in the long-running (1974-84) hit TV series, *Happy Days*, but at the last minute, the coveted role went to another actress.

How did her career advance after that? Along with that of her fellow Playmate, Patti McGuire, Theodore's image as a Bunny was featured on the glass front of the Playboy Pinball Machine. *[Introduced in 1978 and manufactured by Bally, it eventually sold more than 18,000 units and—insofar as used pinball machines are concerned—is something of a collector's item today.]*

Even though Sondra Theodore didn't look at all like Dr. Ruth, some internet users found her soothing. Displayed above is an advertisement from the on-line magazine, *CigarAdvisor.com* for their promotion of her as the girl you want to confess to.

In one of her columns, Sondra wrote that she did not believe in cheating on one's mate. "It's one of the cruelest things you can do to someone who is supposed to love you."

Although she never became a star, Theodore made guest appearances on a number of television shows: *Barnaby Jones, Pink Lady, Fantasy Island,* and *The Bob Newhardt Show.* She also appeared on the big screen in minor roles in such films as *Skateboard* 1978) and *Stingray* (also 1978).

Near the end of her reign as Hef's Queen Bee, Theodore appeared on-stage at the Playboy Mansion in L.A. at—as described by her—"an event that will live in the anus of show business, the Fifty-Fifth Annual Calamity Awards."

Lee Wolfberg, Hef's close friend, presented her as "someone close to Hef's heart—and to his other vital organs, too. She's a lady we all loved—till Hef found out."

Theodore then delivered a humorous comment about what she defined as "the best movie ever made by a producer who does not own a magazine," a reference to *Lawrence of Arabia* (1962) with Peter O'Toole. From the stage, she said, "In the movie, Lawrence yells 'Charge!' So does Hef. The last time, he missed the bed and pole-vaulted over my oasis."

Later, also from the stage, she told the audience that Hef, just before screening a copy of *It's a Wonderful Life* (1946), told her that "the greatest experience in life is having sex with the one you love. And to prove that, he continued to play with himself as I watched the film."

By 1985, Theodore had abandoned her position as "Mistress of the Manse" and married her manager, Ray Manzella. Following their divorce, she remarried in 2000 at the age of forty-four.

As young women came and went from his bed, Hef spoke of his romantic image with the *Chicago Tribune*. "Women say they want a lover who is faithful, but do they really? Actually, in my view, they are thrilled to have a much experienced seducer bed them—take the legend of Don Juan or Casanova, for example. The more experienced a man is, the more women desire him in their boudoir. I have a lot of notches on my belt—in fact, those notches would consume several belts. Women consider me desirable. All I have to do is extend an invitation, and there's a stampede to my bedroom. It's not my nature to sound so immodest, but what I said is the truth."

*** 

"I remember it well," Victor Lownes said: "I'd wake up some fine English mornings as the Bunny King of Britain. A fleet of Rolls-Royces was waiting to take me wherever I wanted to go. I was the highest paid executive in England, with a penthouse on Park Lane in London and a half million dollars in salary coming in every year. And, lest I forget, there was a Bunny on either side of me, ready, willing, and able to satisfy my every need and desire, no matter how disgusting it may be to them. I was a man with occasional bizarre tastes. When you've seduced hundreds of girls, you keep desiring newer and kinkier diversions—that's understandable, certainly to Hef of all people. He and I were very much alike in spite of our differences."

"There was trouble on the horizon, but I didn't pay it much heed," Lownes said. "For years and years, Hef had been my trusted friend—in fact, my best friend. Women weren't the only thing we shared in common. I know he appreciated my efforts to save the Playboy Empire in America. I just didn't see the storm clouds brewing."

"But I began to take notice back in the spring of 1976 when Derick J. Daniels was recruited as second in command under Hef himself. He was taking over my former duties in the States, but I didn't seem to mind, since I liked being planted on English soil, where, so to speak, I had taken root."

On September 8 of that year, Daniels was officially named president of Playboy Enterprises. "I had once dined with Daniels at the University Club in Chicago, and I reported to Hef that I was not impressed," Lownes said. "My exact words were, 'He's not your man for the job.'"

"I had a certain security in my job, knowing that I was the hottest ticket in town," Lownes said. "In fact, I think I was supporting all their other failing enterprises. From the cold winds of January 1976 to the bright sunny June of 1981, our U.K. casinos pulled in a mammoth £661 million."

"With renewed confidence, I set out to take over the Victoria Sporting Club, which had gone on sale in 1979. The previous owners had been disastrous and had lost their gaming licenses in Britain. In fact, their offices had been raided by the London police.

"The fuckers were only too eager to accept my offer of £6 million," Lownes said.

"After making the purchase and sealing the deal, I got a whiff of news from Chicago that the other Playboy brass, perhaps even Hef himself, was not too keen on what I had pulled off."

Lownes had to face a legal challenge in London courts about the gaming license for the Victoria Sporting Club. He won the battle after a bitter fight, and the license was finally renewed. He shot off a cable to Hef: "VICTORIA VICTORIOUS. VISION VINDICATED. VALUE VERIFIED. VERILY VICTOR."

He later told Hef that in the wake of this victory, he expected that *Playboy's* British casino profits would double in the year ahead.

Much to his later regret, while serving as a member of the British Casino Association, Lownes had incurred the wrath of the gambling czar of London, Cyril Stein, the director of Ladbroke casinos. Lownes had learned of some "dangerous" corrupt methods being engaged in by some of his competitors, including Stein, and he began to air charges.

Among other accusations, Lownes claimed that Stein was bribing porters at deluxe hotels to steer gamblers to Ladbroke casinos and not to Playboy's. Lownes also charged Stein with bribery of some corrupted London police officers.

When Stein learned of Lownes' accusations, he exploded in rage. "If *Playboy* doesn't withdraw its objections, the mud's going to fly," he threatened. "I've got the goods on Victor Lownes."

Lownes belatedly learned that by bringing charges against Ladbroke, he might have inadvertently set off a probe into *Playboy's* own operation. He went to his top executives and presented them with the threat from Stein, but his officers responded that their own operation in Britain was "as clean as a hound's tooth."

Stein lost his appeal in the British courts and his Ladbroke casino gaming licenses were revoked. He set out for revenge on both Lownes and his Playboy Clubs. He began by bribing two Playboy officials, hoping to get some dirt.

He didn't discover very much, but he did learn that *Playboy* bribed hotel porters by offering them free memberships if they would steer high-rollers to their clubs instead of to Ladbroke's. But despite some challenges, Lownes—for the moment at least—emerged victorious. Playboy's U.K. gaming licenses were renewed in 1980.

But by the end of that year, and to his deep disappointment, he found out that those Arab pertrodollars were not pouring in as fast they had in the oil-rich 1970s. As he told *The New York Times*, "The bloom is off the rose."

Things didn't get better. Late in the morning of New Year's Day, 1981, Lownes was nursing a hangover from the festivities of the night before. But before the year's end, a hangover would be the least of his worries.

In February 1981, he suffered severe injuries in a riding accident on his trusty gelding. The horse had a steady record of being sure-footed on ice, but on this Saturday in midwinter, he slipped. Lownes fell from his horse and hit his head on a rock, causing severe, perhaps irreparable damage. The nerve that registered his sense of taste and smell had been severed. He'd be confined to bed for a long recovery.

The reclusive Cyril Stein was a committed Zionist , philanthropist, bookmaker, and observant Jew who never went to the race-track on the Sabbath.

He emerged as the gambling czar of London after his acquisition of Ladbroke's in the mid-1960s.

His feud with Playboy led to the loss of its gaming licenses in Britain. Later, that fight contributed to events that almost caused Stein's downfall in the late 1970s.

"When it rains, it pours," he said. "While I was bed-ridden, trying to recover from a near-death experience, I got the news that Playboy's offices in the U.K. had been raided and its records seized."

Investigators began audits of his operation and soon learned that his casinos sometimes accepted cheques from oil-rich clients drawn on banks at which they had no deposits. Two members of the Royal Family were said to have written checks with insufficient funds. Lownes refused to reveal their names to the press. "What was I to do? Go to Queen Liz and ask her to cover for her errant boys on her private bank account? Surely, no cheque from Her Majesty would bounce."

Another charge asserted that Playboy executives sometimes gambled at their own tables, which was illegal.

Lownes believed that any infractions might be minor, not enough of a violation to make Playboy lose its gaming license. He jokingly suggested, "The real purpose of the raid was for the police to get the phone numbers of our sexy Bunnies."

But in Chicago, Lownes' troubles were taken very seriously, one executive suggesting, "Playboy Bunnies are up to their ears in rabbit shit."

In a gesture of goodwill, Hef had presented Lownes with a lifetime subscription to *Playboy*. But as an ominous warning, at around this period, the magazine no longer arrived in his mailbox.

In Los Angeles, although Hef was kept abreast of this investigation, it didn't interfere with his 55th birthday festivities on April 9, 1980. He celebrated alongside his current Bunny, Sondra Theodore.

One writer covered the event, finding Hef hanging out with "fading football stars, failed film producers and directors, fawning bootlickers, Playmate clones, former Bunnies of yesterday, and bleached blondes from the beaches near San

**British Bunnies at London's Playboy Club**: They were beautiful, they served drinks like pros (and always got the garnishes right), and some of them could sing, as proven by this CD, released in 1969.

It contains a medley of then-current pop songs including "Gimme Gimme Good Lovin'" and "Build Me Up, Buttercup."

Emanating from one of the most fashionable nightspots of its era in the U.K., those days of long ago now seem retro, vintage, and quaint.

At presstime for this book, the world's busiest and most visible Playboy Club was the stylishly reconfigured branch in London. Hip, sophisticated, and aesthetically pleasing, it operates from premises at 14 Old Park Lane, London W1K 1ND (www.playboyclublondon.com).

Operated by London Clubs International in association with Caesars Entertainment, it includes a members-only casino where croupiers and dealers are outfitted as Bunnies, the "Tale" Bar (which is open to non-members), a stylish restaurant with elegant cuisine, a nightclub with live acts, and traditions directly linked to the glory days of Hugh Hefner.

Diego."

Lance Rentzel, an honored guest, said, "Hef sat on his throne, auto-graphing a number of breasts presented to him."

Despite his weakened condition, Lownes was ordered by Daniels to drive in from his estate at Stocks to the London offices of Clifford Turner Solicitors. At the meeting, he renewed his relationship with Marvin Huston, whom he had known in Chicago. He noticed that Huston seemed embarrassed to shake his hand. He would learn later that a man he thought was his friend had become the new director of Playboy Enterprises in London.

After some awkward ramblings, Daniels finally got to the point: "Victor, the feeling of this board, a move approved by Hef, is that you should step down. Your services are no longer needed. We'd like your resignation immediately. I have a paper for you to sign."

"You've got to be joking," Lownes protested. "You must have started to believe your own press notices."

"Our decision has been confirmed by Hef himself," Daniels said. "If you don't believe me, you can speak to him directly in Los Angeles."

"No need," Lownes said. "I'm sure all of you have brainwashed him against me. I will not sign any paper resigning. I'll announce to the press that I was fired!"

"Suit yourself," Daniels rose from his chair and exited the room, leaving the lingering smell of perfume in the air.

As Lownes recalled, "I knew Hef was probably still in bed in Los Angeles. I didn't expect him to come to my beheading, as he hated the sight of blood. He was Henry VIII issuing an order for the beheading of one of his wives. No doubt, he'd given the order for my execution."

Someone in the office leaked the news of Lownes' dismissal to the press, and about a dozen reporters and photographers were waiting at the entrance to his Playboy office.

Lownes decided to address them, and he chose not to conceal his anger. "Derick Daniels, the chief honcho, and his gang are really dumb, total idiots. That's not all they are: They're also dingleberry-coated ass-holes."

He then headed inside the building where he encountered a sympathetic staff, some of them in tears.

At his desk for a final moment, he placed a call to Hef in Los Angeles. His secretary answered the phone and then told him, "Mr. Hefner is not receiving calls this morning," Then she slammed down the receiver.

"On the day I was fired, I drove back to Stocks, knowing it would not be mine for much longer," Lownes said. "I took sleeping pills—no, it was not a suicide attempt—but these little 'dolls' allowed me to sleep until noon of the following day. I woke to the realization that I had joined the growing ranks of the unemployed, thanks to Daniels and my former dear friend, Hugh Hefner. He was no doubt cuddled up with some Playmate in that Los Angeles Mansion. Time was, in the good old days, when I might have been in bed with them."

Playboy needed a British citizen to replace Lownes, and Hef aimed high, selecting Admiral Sir John Devereaux Trencher, former Second Lord of the Admiralty and Commander-in-Chief of NATO's Northeast Atlantic Division. He had impressive credentials but knew nothing about the gaming laws of Britain. He told the press, "The Royal Navy isn't all just about wind and spray and *yo-heave-ho*. After all, we're taught management skills, too."

***

As charges against *Playboy* had been aired before the U.K.'s gaming commissioners, lurid tabloid headlines had appeared, including one that alleged "BUNNIES LURED INTO VICE RING."

Without any strong evidence, charges had been made that Bunnies, ages eighteen and nineteen, were hired just to service oil-rich Arabs who preferred blondes. *The News of the World*, known along Fleet Street as "The News of the Screws," published unfounded rumors about *"Playboy's* whores."

An orchestrated campaign of letters had poured into the commission, most of them repeating the now-familiar refrain that *Playboy* Bunnies were selling themselves to Arabs. Playboy Clubs were called "finishing schools in England for future prostitutes."

The end result was that the police investigation of Playboy's books revealed at least seven violations of the 1968 British Gaming Act.

Hef had lost Playboy's right to operate casinos in Britain. This was the worst financial blow of his life, because his U.K. clubs had been his "cash cow" that kept less successful *Playboy* endeavors in America operational.

On October 5, 1981, the licensing justices in London ruled that *Playboy* was "not fit and proper" to operate casinos in the U.K. All gaming licenses are hereby rescinded." News quickly hit Wall Street where Playboy shares dropped to a new low of $5.75 from a peak of $23.50.

Instead of appealing, Hef notified his executives "to cut our losses and bail out."

By November of that year, Daniels announced that Playboy had sold its gaming operation in Britain to Trident Television for $24.8 million.

Marvin Huston, who had taken over for Lownes, said, "The objections to *Playboy* were chicken shit, and everyone knew they were chicken shit."

According to Lownes, "The only good news I got at this time was that Daniels, my arch enemy, had been kicked out on his ass, just like the fate I'd suffered. It served the asshole right. At last I could dance on his grave. To my surprise, Christie Hefner, who was anything but a Bunny, was taking over the empire."

The collapse of Playboy in the U.K. led to gloomy predictions about the impending collapse of the Hefner's Empire. The *Wall Street Journal* asserted, "Earnings from the remains of the former empire would cover only a fraction of Playboy's operating costs. Domestic clubs and hotels have been unprofitable for years. The circulation and advertising pages of *Playboy* have been dropping steadily. Hugh Hefner presides over a weak and troubled company whose future in in doubt."

A November 10 meeting of Playboy's board members was addressed by Hef himself. "Rumors about our demise are gross exaggerations," he said. "We are a strong company with a very, very real and bright future."

# Chapter Eleven

# HUGH HEFNER'S HOLY WAR WITH THE U.S. PRESIDENT

How Ronald Reagan, Bolstered by the Justice Department and with Militant Feminists, Tried to Destroy *Playboy*

"Bye Bye Bunnies" Signals the End of an Era Playboy Clubs Everywhere are Shuttered and Closed

The Cottontails of Hef's Beauties Are Sent Into Mothballs

## THE MURDER OF DOROTHY STRATTEN
Why Her Lover, a Prominent Hollywood Director, Publicly Feuded with Hef in its Aftermath

Peter Bogdanovich publicly challenges: "Hugh Hefner is the Walt Disney of Porn & a Hygienic Super Pimp"

Fathering Two Sons with a Centerfold Blonde
## HEF GETS MARRIED
"His Second Time Around"

Hef claimed he'd never marry again, but along came a beautiful blonde, Kimberley Conrad.

**The 1980s brought Hef** some of the most serious challenges of his life: government investigations, feminist attacks, financial disasters, and the urgent need to update and expand his entertainment division. He also had to get used to a new cast of Playmates, both in bed and in court, since at least one of them was in a suing mood. Before the end of the decade, there would even be a new wife, his second.

In 1980, the right-wing National Heritage Foundation, with the stated intent of "cleaning up America," sponsored a series of ads attacking Hef and *Playboy.*

He was denounced as a "smut peddler," a phrase that by now was deeply familiar to him. "Those fuckers seem to blame me, or at least *Playboy,* for all the country's ills, including fatherless children, widespread teenage abortions, drug overdoses, moral decay, and sex without responsibility. My Playboy Philosophy was labeled anti-Christian. I was called the Anti-Christ and Satan."

According to one widely distributed call to arms, "Hugh Hefner and his *Playboy* magazine have encouraged self-indulgence unknown in American history. Today, we are reaping the bitter harvest of the seeds this destructive man and his periodical have sowed across the landscape."

"Perhaps most distressing of all were the reports coming in from some of the media that *Playboy* had become irrelevant in the Reagan 'Me' Decade," Hef said. "It appeared that our golden years were over, our future uncertain. Even *Rolling Stone* wrote about the 'disillusionment of Playboyism.'"

The *Conservative Digest* accused Hef of promoting homosexuality. "Will wonders never cease?" Hef asked. "Me, Hugh Hefner, the chief architect of heterosexuality. I was even accused of causing the onset of AIDS, and I had to confront all these lesbian Amazons attacking me for exploiting women. Frankly, I think they wanted to keep all the beautiful girls for themselves."

One right-wing radio announcer said, "An uncontrolled hedonism is threatening to topple our country, aided in no small part by Hugh Hefner and *Playboy* magazine. Are we, like the Roman Empire, facing our ultimate decade?"

The 1980s brought financial problems "delivered on platters straight from hell" (Hef's words).

For the rescue of Playboy Enterprises from the brink of disaster, Hef turned to his daughter, Christie, "to save us, dear one, before we fade into history."

Sadly, Hef's decade began with one of the most notorious murders of the 1980s.

***

It was not unique that a Playmate of the Month would meet an early, sometimes ghastly death. In 2009, the body of Jasmine Fiore, a former Playmate, had been discovered—strangled and stuffed into a suitcase.

In September of 1973, Adrienne Pollack, a Playboy Bunny, died of a drug overdose. Yet another Playmate, Willy Rey, Miss November of 1971, had died of a barbiturate overdose a month before Pollack's death. Her father, Johannes, said, "I wished there never had been a magazine known as *Playboy.*"

Constance Petrie had worked as a Bunny in the Chicago Playboy Club. At the age of 26, she refused to take a lie detector test when she was accused of taking drugs. That night in her apartment, she was found dead after consuming an overdose.

A beautiful blonde, Eve Stratford, who worked as a Bunny at the Playboy Club in London, and who dated high-rolling Arab gamblers, was found dead with her throat slit at her home in East London.

Hef was still haunted by the suicide of his assistant, Bobbie Arnstein, when she was facing a jail term over alleged drug smuggling.

So although other Playmates had also come to disastrous ends, none ever achieved the notoriety of Dorothy Stratten in 1980.

***

A gorgeous Canadian blonde, Stratten was born in Vancouver as "Dorothy Hoogstraten." She was employed as a counter attendant by Dairy Queen when a sleazy pimp and hustler, Paul Snider, walked in the door seeking some ice cream. What he got was the stunning late teenaged beauty whom within days he had renamed Dorothy Stratten.

It was a cold day in British Columbia, and he wore a full-length mink coat, lizard skin boots, and a jeweled Star of David on a gold chain around his neck. He was mildly attractive, with thick black hair and sideburns.

A shiny black Corvette waited outside, and within days, Dorothy was seen riding around in it with Snider at the wheel. He became her lover the day he met her and would soon become her husband and promoter.

Back in Los Angeles, Hef and his editors were searching for an Anniversary Playmate. Snider knew of the contest, and he persuaded Dorothy to pose nude in front of a local photographer who had once shot a centerfold layout.

As soon as her photos were ready, he sent prints of twelve of them to Hefner at his Playboy Mansion. Within days, Hef responded, sending Dorothy a pre-paid plane ticket to Los Angeles. Snider followed her, driving south from Vancouver in his Corvette.

At the Playboy Mansion, she posed for a nude pictorial. She did not win the Anniversary Playmate contest, the prize going to Candy Loving (her actual name). However, Hef did select her as his Playmate of the Month, and she appeared as such in the August 1979 edition. He offered her a job as a Bunny at the Playboy Club in Century City, and she moved with Snider into his apartment in West Los Angeles.

Her pictorial brought her immediate acclaim, and some of the *Playboy* editors predicted that she might become "the next Marilyn Monroe." A writer called her breasts "minor miracles, her curvature of Venus a penis-welcoming Nirvana." She was showered with gifts and invitations for sex, including a $65,000 Russian sable coat from an admirer who wished to spend a weekend with her in his bungalow at the Beverly Hills Hotel.

On August 14, 1981, the death of a blonde beauty, who at age twenty was reigning as Playmate of the Year, shocked Hollywood.

Dorothy Stratten was found nude, her body lying across the corner of a bed, her face blasted away with a shotgun blast.

She had been sodomized after her death by her estranged husband, Paul Snider, age twenty-nine.

Snider became jealous of all this attention, although realizing it was necessary for her to gain a foothold in show business. As a means of exerting more control over her career, he married her. As her husband, he determined which "casting couches" she should lie on.

His apartment was modest, but he predicted stardom for her and that both of them would soon be occupying an estate in Bel Air. Before Dorothy, Snider had survived on the sidelines of the entertainment industry, making a living with whatever scheme he concocted. He was a dubious promoter and pimp, supplying girls he picked up to wealthy men, girls who had come to Hollywood to become movie stars but who ended up on the streets, turning to prostitution.

Sometimes, he also offered his own body to rich homosexuals in the film colony. He would stage contests that catered mostly to gay men. One such contest sought to name "the Best Male Stripper in Los Angeles," another seeking "The Man with the Handsomest Face in the Movie Colony."

To stage one of his contests, he borrowed money from the Mafia, but his beauty pageant didn't make any money, and he was without funds to pay back the Mob. One night, two men burst into his hotel room and dangled him out the window, holding him by his ankles from the 30<sup>th</sup> floor. He was told to have the money in the morning—"or else."

Through various connections in the film industry, Snider managed to get Dorothy minor film roles, but despite his best efforts, her only major part was as the female lead

Stratten with then-husband Snider in happier times. She was his meal ticket, and he pimped her out.

When money was low, he sold his own body to wealthy homosexuals among the Hollywood elite.

of the low-budget 1980 movie, *Galaxina,* a science fantasy comedy shot in just twenty days. The movie had only a limited release and ended as a financial disaster. The *Washington Post* wrote: "The term 'sophomoric' seems too sophisticated to describe the level of humor in this sci-fi spoof."

Dorothy's life changed the night she met the film director Peter Bogdanovitch at the Playboy Mansion. She had seen two of his acclaimed movies, *The Last Picture Show* (1971) and *Paper Moon* (1973). He was also a writer, producer, and film historian.

Bogdanovich was enthralled by her beauty and wanted to cast her in a supporting role in his latest film, *They All Laughed* (1980), starring Audrey Hepburn and Ben Gazzara. Filmed on the streets of New York, its plot focuses on two detectives, Gazzara and John Ritter, each hired to spy on two beautiful women (Hepburn and Dorothy), both of whom were suspected of infidelity. The detectives wind up falling for the women themselves—Gazzara for Hepburn, and Ritter for Dorothy.

Offscreen passion flourished too: Hepburn fell in love with Gazzara and launched an affair. Dorothy's off-screen romance was not with Ritter, her co-star, but with her director, Bogdanovich.

He discussed his sudden love for Stratten with Hef, and said he hoped to avoid the publicity that had hounded him during his romance with Cybill Shepherd.

Snider was not allowed on the (closed) set, and he grew suspicious when rumors reached him that Dorothy was having an affair with Bogdanovich.

20th Century Fox test-marketed the film in Providence, Rhode Island and in Minneapolis. Disappointed with the results, they decided to pull the movie from release. In the aftermath of that (devastating) decision, Bogdanovich took over distribution of the film himself, spending $5 million trying to get it into theaters. That decision contributed to his eventual bankruptcy, as it resulted in only $1 million in ticket sales.

Despite the failure of the film, Dorothy came out looking good. As Teresa Carpenter wrote, "She emerges as a shimmering seraph, a vision of perfection clad perennially in white…bathed in a diaphanous light."

Other directors were hearing about how well she photographed. She was offered the role of Marilyn Monroe in a made-for-TV movie and was also considered for the role of one of *Charlie's Angels* in the hit TV series.

During filming, Dorothy had written a letter to Snider asking him to "let the bird fly." He asked her to come by his apartment in West Hollywood to discuss the terms of their divorce. What happened next became one of the most widely publicized events in the 1980s scandals of Hollywood.

\*\*\*

As it was later revealed, Snider apparently had argued bitterly with Dorothy, no doubt seeing his hoped-for meal ticket disappearing. He had then raped her and shot her in the head with a secondhand 12-gauge Mossberg pump shotgun. He'd then sodomized her, even though her face had been blown to bits. After getting off her, he shot himself with the same shotgun. Their nude bodies were found later that night by the police with black ants crawling over their corpses. The date was August 14, 1980.

News of Dorothy's brutal murder by Snider reached Hef at the Playboy Mansion in L.A. and almost sent him into a state of

# *Death of a* P*LAYMATE*

### DOROTHY STRATTEN
*was the focus of the dreams and ambitions of three men. One killed her.*

BY TERESA CARPENTER

This is a replica of the feature that the *Village Voice* published on November 11, 1980. In it, Teresa Carpenter described how *Playboy* managed the relationship between Stratten and her domineering, homicidal husband.

As headlined in the *Voice*, "In the end, Dorothy Stratten may be less memorable for herself than for the yearnings she evoked: In Snider, his lust for the score; in Hefner, his longing for the star; in Bogdanovich, his desire for the eternal *ingénue*."

shock. He ordered his staff to release a statement to the press:

*"The death of Dorothy Stratten comes as a shock to all of us at* Playboy. *As our Playmate for the Year, with a film due to be released and a promising career ahead of her as an actress, her professional future seemed bright. But equally sad to us is the fact that her loss takes from us a very special member of the* Playboy *family."*

He was told that it was too late to pull photos of Dorothy from the upcoming issue of *Playboy,* but he had time to remove her picture from the cover of the 1981 *Playmate Calendar.* He also scrapped a Christmas promotion that would have included a "Seasons Greetings" in the form of a nude Stratten with himself.

Decades later, the life and death of Playboy's most tragic Playmate remains a "True Crime" fascination.

\*\*\*

Even though he considered the charges completely unfair, Hef feared in some way that he might be blamed for Dorothy's brutal murder. Articles and films would indict him, causing him to hover on the verge of a nervous breakdown similar to what he'd suffered after the suicide of Bobbie Arnstein.

Reporter Teresa Carpenter had begun an article on Dorothy's death that would eventually be published in the *Village Voice* under the title "Death of a Playmate." Her first-rate investigative reporting would win her a Pulitzer Prize. In her article, Carpenter noted that even though Snider had pulled the trigger, Bogdanovich and Hef were also to blame.

Hef denied to her that he'd ever put Dorothy on the casting couch. "My relationship was not romantic, but more of a friendship. I was like a father figure to her. She was not a *loose* lady."

Carpenter wrote about what the police found when they discovered her body: "Dorothy's blonde hair hung naturally, oddly unaffected by the violence of her countenance. The shell had entered above her left eye, leaving the bones of her seraphic face shattered and displaced in a welter of pulp. Her body, mocking the soft languid poses of her *Playboy* pictorials, was in full rigor."

Carpenter said, "The irony that Hefner does not perceive—or at least fails to acknowledge—is that Stratten was destroyed not by random particulars, but by a germ breeding within the *Playboy* ethic. One of the tacit tenets of the *Playboy Philosophy*—that women can be possessed—had found a fervent adherent in Paul Snider. He had bought the dream without qualification, and he thought of himself as one of *Playboy's* most honest apostles. He acted out of dark fantasies never intended to be realized."

She also wrote: "Hugh Hefner has struggled to make stars of his Play-mates, and Stratten seemed destined to take him to the next level. There is something poignant about Hefner, master of an empire built on intimate nudes, but unable to coax these lustrous beauties to life in feature films. His chief preoccupation now is managing the Playmates. Yet with all these beautiful women at his disposal, he has not one Marion Davies (mistress of press baron William Randolph Hearst) to call his own."

Carpenter went on to define Hef as "the incongruous spectacle of a sybarite in mourning."

He told Carpenter, "There is still a great tendency for this thing to fall into the classic *cliché* of smalltown girl comes to *Playboy*, comes to Holly-wood, and begins a life in the fast lane—and that was somehow related to her death. And that is not what really happened. A very sick guy saw his meal ticket and his connection to power slipping away—and it was that that made him kill her."

In a 16-lage memo discovered after Stratten's death, Dorothy had writ-ten: "A lot of men were entering my life all of a sudden, and a lot of them wanted me. No one was pushy or forceful—but talk can be very powerful, especially to a mixed-up little girl like myself."

Dorothy's murder inspired two movies and a book by Bog-danovich. The first of the films was *Death of a Centerfold: The Dorothy Stratten Story*, a made-for-TV movie starring Jamie Lee Curtis as the murder victim. It aired on NBC in November of 1981. Bruce Weitz was cast as Paul Snider, with Mitchell Ryan as Hugh Hefner.

Movie critic Leonard Maltin found the film, "exploitative," but many critics praised it, espe-cially the performance of Weitz. *People* magazine said that Curtis was "just right as Stratten, and Weitz was a standout as her ex."

*Star 80* was another film ver-

*Playboy's* June 1980 Playmate of the Year. Dorothy Stratten, who was soon to be murdered by her psychotic husband.

Hef described her as "one of the few emerging film goddesses of a new decade."

sion of Dorothy's murder, with Mariel Hemingway in the leading role. Eric Roberts delivered his most brilliant performance as her psychotic husband, Paul Snider. Carroll Baker, the long-ago star of Tennessee Williams' *Baby Doll*, was cast as Dorothy's mother.

Cliff Robertson played Hefner. "I'd already been cast as John F. Kennedy, so why not Hefner, too? Both of them were Playboys!" *[Robertson was referring to his performance in the Navy drama,* PT 109, *released in 1963, playing a young JFK as a lieutenant, junior grade, in command of a PT-109 boat during World War II.]*

*Star 80* became the last film directed by Bob Fosse, and it received lackluster reviews, the *Washington Post* calling it, "Fosse's latest stylish stinker, a sad farewell to such a talented artist."

While the two movies about Dorothy were in production, Bogdanovich was at work on a book, released in 1984, *The Killing of the Unicorn: Dorothy Stratten 1960-1980.*

It dealt with Bogdanovich's love affair with the would-be star, the making of *They All Laughed,* and his version of Stratten's murder. The book was also highly critical of Hef and *Playboy's* treatment of women.

He described his first meeting with Stratten at the Playboy Mansion in 1980: "She wasn't simply beautiful, but exquisitely beautiful. Her beauty was like an extraordinary mirage, too glorious to be real." In the pages of his book, he blamed his former friend, Hef, and *Playboy's* hedonistic philosophy for her death.

Bogdanovich also charged that "Dorothy could not handle the slick professional machinery of the *Playboy* sex factory, nor the continued efforts of its founder, to bring her into his personal fold, no matter what she wanted."

Hef was especially wounded by the book's accusation that "he was a feminist if you believed that feminism is a pretty woman who will have sex with you."

An actor and film producer, Patrick Curtis, had already achieved a kind of immortality during the first year of his life. *[He had been cast in the classic film,* Gone With the Wind *(1939) as Beau Wilkes, Melanie (Olivia de Havilland) Wilkes' newborn, when he was about a year old.]*

In 1967, Curtis received added fame when he married the sex goddess, Raquel Welch, and played an instrumental role in promoting her sky-

Film director Peter Bogdanovich, depicted here on the cover of *People* magazine, had fallen desperately in love with Dorothy Stratten.

After Stratten's death, he directed his romantic intentions toward her younger sister.

rocketing career. After six years of marriage, they filed for divorce.

Curtis had been a frequent visitor to the Playboy Mansion, and Hef regarded him as a friend. But for reasons not made clear, his pass was revoked and he was banished.

Perhaps to get even, Curtis fed Bogdanovich a lot of anti-Hef and anti-*Playboy* information for his book. Much of it was later discredited, but the harm had been done. In the aftermath, Hef felt betrayed by both Curtis and Bogdanovich, each of them a former friend.

In *The Killing of the Unicorn*, Bogdanovich defined Hef as "the Walt Disney of Pornography... Doesn't *Playboy* figuratively seduce and rape young women, often teenagers? Live off them? Destroy their lives? *Playboy* and its kindred porno mills continue to grind up women and spit them out for the masturbatory pleasure of men the world over."

In his controversial exposé, *The Killing of the Unicorn: Dorothy Stratten*, Bogdanovich viciously attacked Hef.

"As I found out more and more about Hefner's role in the tragic life of Dorothy Stratten, my rage toward him grew."

The director seemed vindictive and a bit unhinged as he referred to Hef as "a hygienic super pimp." He even claimed that the Sexual Revolution had been staged as a male rule to get men laid. "The ruin of Dorothy Stratten," it was alleged, "was a direct result of *Playboy's* great con."

Bogdanovich hit the circuit on television show after television show during promotions for his book. On NBC's *Today* Show, he claimed that "Dorothy had been used by Hefner and *Playboy* who lured her into a large trap. She became disillusioned, feeling she'd been used like a game, like a pinball machine. Hefner and *Playboy* are a social poison that destroys women like Dorothy Stratten."

Hef was labeled as a "dedicated hedonist, cavorting in his Bunny-filled crash pad of vile seduction, dragging innocent teenagers into his web of deceit, only to defile them and destroy their young lives."

In its review of *The Killing of the Unicorn*, *People* magazine wrote: "Hefner is portrayed as an insensitive sexmonger and egomaniac."

In the magazine article, Bogdanovich insisted that a post-midnight interlude in a Grotto tub between Hef and a reluctant Dorothy Stratten destroyed her psyche. The author portrays himself as "Mr. Sensitive and a goody-goody."

Hef shot back, charging that Bogdanovich, "perhaps consumed by his own grief and culpability, had written this outrageous work of fiction that does a terrible injustice to me personally and to *Playboy*. The book is a total fabrication, a guilt trip on his part."

"In an attempt to portray my own dark side, he has inadvertently revealed his own dark side," Hef charged.

Hef eventually became obsessed with the charges being leveled against him. Lisa Loving, his assistant, claimed, "It consumed him day and night."

Hef's editor, Arthur Kretchmer, warned him, "Both you and Bogdanovich are going down a stairway to a dark gulf. Heed the warning: 'He who seeks revenge should dig two graves.'"

***

The daughter of a mink rancher in Newfoundland, Canada, Shannon Tweed was born in March of 1957, making her more than 30 years younger than Hef. When her father died in a car crash, she and her mother went to live in bleak Saskatoon, Saskatchewan, surviving on welfare checks.

Following breast enhancement surgery at the age of twenty, the gorgeous blonde began to enter beauty contests. In 1978, she became the third runner-up in the Miss Ottawa beauty pageant. She would go on to be named Miss Canada, having won the talent competition for her singing voice.

Her big break came when she starred on the "wish fulfillment" TV series, *The Thrill of a Lifetime*, telecast in Canada on CTV from 1981-88. Her wish was to fly to Los Angeles to pose as Playmate of the Month in a centerfold. Her wish was granted, and, as Playmate of the Month, she was the focus of the magazine's edition of November 1981.

But in August of 1981, during the buildup to her selection as Playmate of the Month, Hef invited her to Playboy's Midsummer Nights Dream Party. She'd never seen a photo of *Playboy's* publisher before, and she introduced herself to actor Hugh

When Hef had to appear before the the assembled members of the New Jersey Gaming Commission, a state agency which was balking at giving his glittering hotel a gambling license, he arrived in the company of Shannon Tweed, which caused a great distraction.

One reporter wrote, "She wore a leather suit so tight that if it had rained, she would certainly have been strangled."

O'Brian, mistakenly assuming that he was Hef. "I was disappointed," she said. "I learned later that O'Brian was a sex symbol to thousands of women, of which I was not one."

After O'Brian's identity was revealed, she was escorted to the area of the party where Hef was holding court as "King of the Bunnies." From the moment he took her hand, he seemed enchanted with her, "especially her infectious laugh and 1000-watt smile. She became a shoo-in for Playmate of the Year in 1982."

On the night she met him, he invited her to his gadget-filled "bed-chamber of love." There, she would remain from 1981 to 1983, becoming the virtual "Mistress of the Playboy Mansion." She even delivered her opinion of Hef's sexual abilities to a reporter: "He is romantic, inventive, very imaginative, open-minded, and, in spite of his years, young. He's the kind of guy who will die in bed with a smile on his face."

As their torrid affair heated up, he told his cronies, "Shannon is the love of my life," perhaps forgetting that he had uttered those same words to Barbi Benton not so long ago. "I plan to marry this gorgeous blonde goddess from the wilds of Canada."

She told another reporter that she suspected she would have a hard time getting Hef to walk down the aisle. "Marriage is not his natural state, but it is for me."

After a few months into their affair, Shannon sounded a different note when she spoke to the press: "Going with Hef and being his steady girl-friend is not my ultimate goal. I don't know if we'll marry or not. Actually, I plan to become an actress."

He decided to give her career a boost by casting her as a hostess in an TV episode ("Playboy on the Scene") which was aired on the Playboy Channel.

Film work followed, including a gig on the hit TV soap opera, *Falcon Crest*. In 1985, she landed her biggest role in yet another soap, *Days of Our Lives*. In all, she would appear in minor parts in some 60 movies.

In 1983, Shannon would begin an affair with Gene Simmons but would not actually marry him until 2011. In time, she would also star on the TV reality show, *Gene Simmons' Family Jewels*, which ran from 2006 to 2012.

During her time with Hef, Shannon was said to have urged him to run more articles that appealed to women. Perhaps taking her advice, he launched a column called "Women," billing it as a "lighthearted report from the female front in the so-called Sexual Revolution."

By 1986, he even agreed to run a male/female pictorial, something that had long been a standard feature within his rival, *Penthouse*. Hef's pictorial was called "Double Take," and it depicted Don Johnson, the star of the hit

TV series, *Miami Vice,* with his wife, Melanie Griffith, on a Mexican beach "kissing and fondling."

The relationship between Hef and Tweed drifted along, and it appeared that they had different goals. It all ended at Motown's 25th anniversary party. The tension between them was obvious to the guests at tables nearby. One guest later said, "I think he suspected she had other boyfriends and was taking coke."

"It all came to an end that night," Hef said. "It was time for me to move on to my next conquest. I wished Shannon well in her career and sent her on her way, but we've remained friends—no hard feelings."

***

Once again, *Playboy* turned to television. On November 1, 1982, Playboy Enterprises began broadcasting *The Playboy Channel,* which it franchised to MindGeek, a privately held media company headquartered in Luxembourg and operating at  the time mostly from Canada. The program's stated aim was to "reflect the wit, style, and taste" of the printed pages of the magazine. Sometimes Hef would sit for hours watching the channel, which aired from 8PM to 6AM.

At first, the offerings were rather tame, mostly R-rated films. Many early subscribers found the programming a bore and switched to more provocative channels. The producers eventually opted to dip into soft-corn porn as a lure for audiences, which at the time were mostly male.

To compound its problems, many religious fundamentalists applied pressure on local stations to cancel the channel, and many of them did.

Cable television was on the rise. At its peak, the Playboy Channel had 750,000 subscribers, but that figure had sunk to 430,000 by the end of the decade.

Christie Hefner, now in charge, replaced the channel with a pay-per-view service called *Playboy at Night.* It broadcast soft porn and Playmate videos.

It was an instant success. Before the end of the 1980s, *Playboy* would rank as the third largest nontheatrical distributor of videos, with Walt Disney firmly entrenched at the top. One of *Playboy's* best-selling videos was the massage picture, *For Couples Only.*

Originally, Hef played a hand in the channel's programming, but soon bowed out.

In 1989, the name of the channel was changed to *Playboy TV*, which saw the advent of sexier women, more graphic movies, and around-the-clock broadcasting. Featured shows included *The Truth About Sex, E-Rotic, Hot Babes Doing Stuff Naked, Naughty Amateur Home Videos, Under Hot Lights,* and *Show Us Your Wits.* Porn star Jenna Jameson hosted her *American Sex Star* episodes, which were very popular. Some films dipped into bondage and/or rape fantasies.

Other well-watched features included *Groundbreakers* hosted by the controversial filmmaker John Waters, never known for his conventional tastes. *Fantasy Flirt* suggested that beauty comes in all shades and sizes.

*Playboy* went international, broadcasting in countries that included Great Britain, Israel, and Japan.

*[In 2008, a decision was made to dip into hard-core erotica, with an appeal to both men and women. In the 21st Century, a popular feature was Mr. Skin's Year in Nudes, a look back at most of the previous year's top female nude scenes in both television and film.]*

***

The AIDS crisis of the 1980s had a profound impact on Hef's personal life and on his public stance, too. He fixated on the disease soon after it was identified and became a subject of (often terrified) public debate. He used his spotlight—that is, *Playboy* magazine—as a forum for all the latest information about the disease, and he ran the latest guidelines on how to practice safe sex. He also published an article on the origins of the disease, said to have first broken out in Africa.

He dismissed those who erroneously called it "the Gay Plague," and bitterly attacked those religious zealots who claimed that "AIDS is God's revenge on queers." He found rallies where rednecks held up signs saying "THANK GOD FOR AIDS" deeply offensive.

"God had nothing to do with it," he said.

*The Advocate,* America's leading GLBTQ newspaper, asked Hef if he were a gay rights activist. "I am a human rights activist," he answered, "and have been since the inception of *Playboy*. I campaigned against the nation's outdated sodomy laws, which criminalized certain acts. If the pursuit of happiness has any meaning at all, as it is written in the Constitution, the government's intruding into one's bedroom, into personal sexual behavior, is as unconstitutional as anything can be."

He also told *The Advocate*, "The only thing wrong with the AIDS crisis is the way our government has responded to it. Ronald Reagan, our president, won't even speak of it. The government is culpable on many, many levels. Homosexuality, and that homophobia that surrounds the AIDS crisis, are part of a much bigger picture for me. I hear a lot about that god damn 'Shining City on the Hill' that Reagan sees, but not one word about homeless veterans and AIDS."

Long before Caitlyn Jenner (once known as David Jenner) became a household name, Hef was a pioneer in transgender rights. In the 1980s, the English model and actress Caroline ("Tula") Cossey was outed as a transgendered woman by the tabloid *News of the World* after her appearance in 1981 in the James Bond thriller, *For Your Eyes Only*. Reacting to the brouhaha, Hef ordered his editors to publish a beautiful photo series of her, making her the first openly transgendered model for *Playboy*.

The magazine re-ran the spread in 2015, at which time Cossey wrote Hef, thanking him "for showing that a transgender woman can be sexy. I wanted to fight for the right of recognition. That was my goal, and *Playboy* was a great platform for me."

\*\*\*

Sondra Theodore and Shannon Tweed had left Hef's nest to pursue fame and fortune elsewhere, even though it appeared unlikely they would find either. But another Canadian woman was about to enter Hef's life in the shapely form of Carrie Lee Carmichael. *[She later re-christened herself as Carrie Leigh "because it would fit better on a marquee."]*

As Hef told a reporter from *Rolling Stone*, "I spotted Carrie one night at a party and gravitated right over to her. I decided right then and there she was the girl with whom I wanted to party. It was love at first sight. She was also the perfect age for me, only nineteen."

On her Playmate Data Sheet, she named Hef as the man she most admired. "He started *Playboy* in his kitchen with a few

Caroline "Tula" Cossey became the first transgendered *Playboy* model.

Letters from Playboys around the globe poured into the magazine, wanting her phone number.

Tula even became a Bond Girl in the thriller *For Your Eyes Only* (1981).

hundred borrowed dollars and turned it into an empire."

Carrie had first gone to the Los Angeles Playboy Mansion to pose for the April 1983 cover. "She was the perfect model," said photographer Alison Reynolds. "She was an exhibitionist—nothing shy about her. Hef was addicted to Monopoly, but if she wanted his attention, she would interrupt his game with the guys by walking in wearing only high heels and a garter belt."

*Playboy's* photo editor, Marilyn Garbowski, found Carrie "very personable but a bit crazy. Hef told me theirs was a *Romeo & Juliet* remake, but I found that it evoked Jack Nicholson's *One Flew Over the Cuckoo's Nest.*"

He referred to her as a wounded bird, but her enemies at The Mansion referred to her as "The Vulture" who was exploiting Hef. Once or twice when he tried to dump her, she threatened suicide.

Carrie Leigh was fêted and heralded at the Mansion. In *Playboy's* edition of July 1986 (see above), she was described as "The First Lady of the Playboy Mansion."

It evoked comparisons to Hefner's self-definition as "President" and to his ladyfriend of the minute as a presidential wife.

In her quest to become "camera ready," she underwent several procedures with a plastic surgeon, including breast enlargement and a facial peel. She was very temperamental, and she and Hef, right in front of others, often got into bitter arguments. They later made up through lovemaking.

Her provocative dress code was accepted (or indulged) at the Mansion, but sparked controversy during public appearances. Such was the case when Hef showed up with her at the lavish home of Barbra Streisand, who was staging a fund raiser for Democratic candidates. One reporter described Carrie's outfit as "tight as a Dodgers' hot dog."

At Hef's birthday party in 1984, Carrie decided to throw a bash for Hef that would top any of his previous parties. She rounded up 18 nubile beauties and asked them to strip naked and head for the Grotto. Then she escorted Hef down to the Grotto, requesting that he, too, strip down and join the girls in a wild romp. After a lot of group fondling and kissing, Hef selected his six favorite beauties and invited them to his bedroom. As he told Carrie, "It's always preferable to be the only cock at the party."

In 1985, for his birthday bash, he named Carrie "First Lady of the Manse." He celebrated his affair with her by featuring her on the cover of

*Playboy* with a 12-page pictorial of her inside.

Showing up for the black tie gala were his close friends, Warren Beatty and Jack Nicholson. Other guests seen chatting with Hef were Whoopi Goldberg, Vanna White, Hugh O'Brian, Lloyd Bridges, Jacqueline Bisset, and Mel Tormé.

Carrie entered Hef's life after the heady days of the Sexual Revolution of the 60s and 70s had ended. Different in tone was the Reagan era of the 1980s, permeated with strong moralistic overtones.

*Newsweek* pictured Hef with Carrie on its cover under the banner headline, "THE PARTY'S OVER."

In retaliation, Carrie made her own cover and had it enlarged. This one pictured her with Hef under a "revised" banner headline: "THE PARTY'S JUST BEGUN."

As the months dragged on, Carrie reportedly turned to others for sexual trysts, and Hef knew about those. Many an argument ensued.

"What Carrie did not comprehend," said Garbowski, "was that the party might not be over, but it was coming to an end, as was their relationship. That was obvious to many of us. What was amazing was that the affair lasted for as long as it did."

In January of 1988, when Hef was out of town, Carrie packed up her massive array of clothing and possessions, put them into storage, and flew to Manhattan. From there, she phoned Hef to tell him, "It's all over."

After their breakup, she hired a lawyer, Marvin Michelson, and held a press conference where she announced she was suing Hef for $5 million in a palimony suit. She left open the suggestion that Jessica Hahn might have been "instrumental" in her breakup.

Hahn had found a safe haven at the L.A. Mansion after fleeing from the notoriety generated by her sex scandal with the evangelist Jim Bakker.

At the age of 61, Hef defended himself, telling the press, "I'm the silliest possible target for a palimony suit. I'm the most con-

*Newsweek*, with Hef and Carrie Leigh on the cover of its edition of August 4, 1986, was among the first to herald the end of the sexual revolution.

Instructed by Hef's longtime status as a target of both anti-porn activists and the U.S. government, its headline blared: "The Party's Over."

But at the Playboy Mansion in Los Angeles, no one could convince this romantic duo that the drinking, the sex, and the partying was over. Their motto was, "Let the good times roll."

firmed bachelor of the 20th Century."

Before reporters, he detailed the once-a-month checks for $5,000 he'd given Carrie and detailed some of the deluxe gifts he'd bestowed on her, including a Mercedes limousine, diamonds, and sable coats.

Hef told his friends, "Carrie has a short attention span, so I'm surprised she stuck around for as long as she did. She has many problems, most of them emotional. During our time together, there were many sexual improprieties and an abuse of alcohol."

He admitted that because Carrie had refused to practice birth control, he had prominently posted a chart of her menstrual chart next to his bed as a means of preventing "an accident."

He dismissed the palimony suit as a publicity stunt. "It was a long and important relationship, so I feel a certain sadness at its end."

The suit never went to trial.

## JESSICA HAHN
### What Happened?

\*\*\*

Hailing from Massapequa, New York, and born in 1959, Jessica Hahn was an American model and actress. She would become notorious after working as a church secretary for the televangelist, Jim Bakker, in 1987.

She later testified that she was drugged and raped by Bakker in 1989, during her stint as a 20-year-old church secretary in 1980. She also alleged involvement by another preacher, John Wesley Fletcher.

To silence her, she was given a settlement of $279,000. [*The funds derived from the PTL Satellite Network, a global South Carolina-based evangelical Christian television network. Founded by Jim and Tammy Faye Bakker in 1974, it was at the time under Jim Bakker's direction.*]

When exposed, the sex scandal forced Bakker to resign. However, in his 1997 memoir, *I Was Wrong: The Untold Story of a Shocking Journey from PTL Power to Prison and Beyond,* he claimed, "I was set up, and the sex was consensual."

Political liberals and agnostics called it the most salacious piece of White Trash gossip in the history of televangelism.

It centered around Jessica Hahn, whose public rape allegation against televangelist Jim Bakker, and his subsequent exposure as a fraud artist, led to the ultimate downfall of the PTL (Praise the Lord) TV network

The photo is a publicity piece for a TV special which aired for the first time in October, 2017, forty years after the initial allegation that resounded like an atomic bomb through the corridors of the Born-Again Christian movement in America.

Bob Guccione of *Penthouse* was the first to contact Hahn with an offer to run her story. She visited his Manhattan brownstone with her lawyer, Dominic Barbera.

She was immediately turned off by the publisher, later telling her attorney, "Talking to him is like conversing with Satan himself. He's got these chains around his neck, and his look is one of pure evil. He wanted me to wire myself and meet privately with Bakker, recording everything he said. It was all so dirty and backhanded."

In contrast, she was invited by Hef to visit with him at his Los Angeles Mansion. "What a contrast in men," she said. "He was kind and understanding and came out casually in acqua green pajamas."

"I want your story for the November and December 1987, issues. I ask only that you tell the truth, for, as you must know, the truth will set you free."

When she confessed to him that she was receiving death threats from religious fanatics loyal to Bakker, he invited her to come and live at the Mansion, which had very good security, for a period of eight months. She accepted his generous offer.

While living there, she met and befriended Carrie Leigh. One day, Carrie told her she had the code to Hef's safe, in which he kept sex tapes of his sexual adventures from the 1970s. She claimed that she was going to open the safe and remove one of the most embarrassing tapes "to hold over his head during any future litigation."

Hahn viewed this as an act of betrayal, for she felt that Hef had been exceedingly generous and kind to both of them. She alerted Hef that Carrie had stolen the video, and he was able to retrieve it from Carrie, presumably before she'd had any copies made of it.

When last heard from, Hahn was married and living on a ranch somewhere north of Los Angeles.

Above, left: Tammy Faye and her husband, Jim Bakker, were two of the most visible televangelists in the world, operating as a proselytizing Born-Again team every day on morning television.

The scandal set off by Jessica Hahn had front-page implications. As stated in the headline on the cover of *Time*, "TV PREACHER JIMMY SWAGGART AND THE BESIEGED BAKKERS."

Three views of Jessica Hahn as a media star. Much of her celebrity derived from lingering memories of Bill Clinton and his "White Trash" affairs; the embarassment she'd inflicted on the Religious Right, and from her image as a scandal-soaked "flash-in-the-pan" denizen of the skin mags.

***

Hef continued to feel the pressure as attacks on him poured in during the aftermath of Peter Bogdanovich's charges in the media. Across the country, many former Playmates [but definitely not all of them] rallied to the side of the director, claiming that *Playboy* had "ruined their lives, their minds, their bodies, and their dreams." Although many of them had hoped for stardom, most of them entered oblivion after their centerfolds went public.

"Bogdanovich's attack hit a nerve with Hef," said Murray Fisher, a *Playboy* editor. "He just couldn't get over it and ranted about it day and night."

Hef asked, "Am I like the man he wrote about in that god damn book? I don't think so. I was Peter's friend, loyal and supportive of him. Why did he betray me like this? The publication of *Killing of the Unicorn* is like my worst nightmare come true. It haunts my days as well as my nights."

Some people watchers remember Tammy Faye Bakker as one of the most riveting and compelling crazy people in the history of talk TV.

Here she is on the cover of *People*, still making news even after her collapse as a televangelist.

Its headline blares, "While Jim Bakker serves out his 18-year prison term, Tammy Faye gets a divorce and tries out a new life, a new look, and a new man at her side."

America gobbled it up as a host of skin mags, including *Playboy*, accelerated their attempts to get Hahn under contract.

The stress began to show in Hef, as he underwent one sleepless night after another. As his health deteriorated, his editors grew concerned about his physical condition.

And then it happened at 2AM on March 7, 1985: Hef was in bed reading the *Los Angeles Times*. Suddenly, the newsprint became blurred, as he couldn't even read the headlines. He placed an emergency call to his doctor, Mark Saginor, who advised him to take some aspirin, go to sleep, and stop staying up all night agonizing about the allegations made against him.

By 7AM, his condition had worsened, as noted by his faithful assistant, Mary O'Connor, who immediately detected that something was wrong with her boss. She had praised him as the most articulate boss a girl ever had, claiming "Hef always made everything perfectly clear."

Now, he spoke in some vague terms, and she didn't know what he was trying to communicate to her on the phone. With two male staffers, she entered his bedroom. There, they saw that the right side of his face had palsied.

His doctor was summoned and a series of tests was immediately set up with a neurologist. It was decided to whisk him by helicopter to a hospital in Pasadena for more extensive testing. There, it was confirmed that he had suffered a stroke early that morning.

He confessed to his aides, "I guess I half believed what Bogdanovich was accusing me of. Perhaps it was that that brought on the stroke."

Someone at the hospital leaked word to the press that Hef was a patient there. His staff responded with a statement that he had come down with the flu. One reporter for *Variety* sardonically suggested, "Maybe he came down with a case of 'Bunny Fever.'"

Dr. Saginor later told the press what had happened: "At first, the stroke had caused an enormous impairment of Mr. Hefner's speech. This was a devastating blow to him, of course. His whole life had been devoted to speaking up…well, maybe not his whole life. I would have put any other patient of mine in the hospital, but I knew that he loathed hospitals. Therefore, I decided to move into the Mansion to be at his side day and night."

"I put him on a drug called dexamethasone. It was a bit experimental, but within days, he showed remarkable signs of recovery. The drug worked, and he quickly recovered. His life has changed. He gave up smoking that pipe of his, and he quit drinking a case of Pepsi a day. He started to exercise on a bicycle, something he had never done before. Today he is in excellent shape once again."

On March 20, Hef issued his own statement to the press, noting that one radio station had already broadcast his obituary. "I suffered a stroke two weeks ago," he said. "It was a direct result of the stress I've suffered from the release of a pathological book written by Peter Bogdanovich, in which he falsely blamed *Playboy* for the tragic death of Dorothy Stratten. My recovery has been something of a miracle. You might even call it a 'stroke of luck,' since it has forced me to change directions in my life and give up some of my bad habits like smoking."

He thanked all the thousands of people from around the world who had sent him greetings, his favorite coming from columnist Max Lerner. "Not only have you and I survived, but we have prevailed," Lerner wrote. "I think that is just god damn fucking marvelous. A few years back, I was diagnosed with terminal cancer. But the years have gone by, and here I am."

On his first day outside the main core of his Mansion, Hef was photographed in its garden wearing black silk pajamas and a cougar brown bathrobe. He was holding the hand of his current girlfriend, Carrie Leigh, who wore only the smallest white thong. *[The picture was taken just before she broke up with Hef and moved out of the Mansion.]*

When a reporter asked him how the stroke had changed him, Hef responded, "I have forgotten all the names of my former girlfriends."

He sought revenge on Bogdanovich, defining the moment as "payback time." He hired a detective agency to investigate the director's private life, since he had heard some shocking rumors. When the detective's report came in, Hef was most surprised.

Whether it was accurate or not, the report alleged that Bogdanovich was having sexual relations with Dorothy Stratten's 13-year-old sister, Louise Hoogstraten, as well as with her mother, Nelly Schaap.

After Hef recovered from his stroke, he called another press conference on April 1, 1985. About thirty reporters and photographers showed up at the L.A. Mansion. In front of the press, Hef presented the charges from the detectives about Bogdanovich's sexual relations with Dorothy's underaged sister, Louise, as well as with her mother.

To validate his claims, he introduced Burl Eldridge, the ex-husband of Nelly and the former stepfather of Louise. Eldridge asserted that the charges were true.

Louise contacted the feminist lawyer, Gloria Allred, and filed a $5 million lawsuit against Hef, alleging slander, libel, and invasion of privacy. The suit was eventually dropped.

In time, Bogdanovich issued a public apology to Hef, saying that he was sorry if he had caused his health to suffer as a result of his accusations. There was no evidence that Hef had ever forced Dorothy into having sexual relations with him.

*[Ironically, Bogdanovich married young Louise in 1989.]*

Most of Hef's friends viewed his ending of the dispute as a victory, but Hef felt that "too much damage has been done."

A reporter summed it up: "It was a sad, sad day as I watched the ultimate playboy, Hugh Hefner, maligning the reputation of a teenage girl and bickering over the bones of a Playmate five years dead."

As Hef told a reporter from *Rolling Stone*, "That whole episode in my life sickens me."

***

The time had arrived for Hef, more or less, to sing "Bye Bye Bunny." Although the cottontail had been a sex symbol in the 1960s, Playboy Clubs across the country had shut their doors. Keyholders had stopped patronizing Bunnies. As a stopgap solution, Hef had introduced a pink Playmate Keycard to attract female customers, but that innovation drew very few clients.

"We were a victim of our own success," Hef lamented. "We were so hot, so successful, that we inspired dozens of sleazy imitators who siphoned off our customers. We were a sophisticated, non-sleazy club, but so many get-rich slobs were out for quick dough in clubs that encouraged prostitution."

"Very few of our clubs were actually showing a profit, and even our flagship clubs in New York, Chicago, and Los Angeles were barely in the black. Our London enterprise was such a cash cow that it kept the other clubs afloat for a while until Britain denied us a gaming license. We were in deep shit."

He also labeled the resorts at Great Gorge and the Miami Plaza as "financial black holes. In the 60s, our clubs were riding the waves, but by the late 70s, we were hitting the bottom of the ocean."

After unrelenting attention from "Bunny Matrons" and Playboys, the cottontail was about to disappear—a playful, charming, but now vintage relic of a distant, more innocent era.

Hefner interpreted its demise with sadness.

In 1985, wearing a bunny tail that seems of riveting interest to the male customer she's serving, a young, then-shapely Kirstie Alley played a bunny on television.

It was part of a made-for-TV comedy drama loosely inspired by Gloria Steinem's infiltration of one of the Playboy Clubs more than twenty years before.

One reporter wrote, "The world had gotten used to the Bunny. Now, they were cute, not 'sin on sight.' They had become part of Americana, rather harmless, not angels fallen from heaven. More a Disneyland for adults. But that was becoming more and more a distant memory."

"The Bunny that I had loved for so long was not a sex symbol anymore," Hef said. "Her cottontail was not so white and fluffy anymore. She had faded with the music of Eddie Fisher. Even when we introduced male Bunnies in virtually see-through jockstraps into our New York Empire Club, that didn't save us from the brink."

In June of 1986, Hef had to shut down the flagship clubs in New York, Chicago, and Los Angeles. "Most of our Bunnies got married and retreated to the 'burbs with some guy to have three kids, stashing their satiny costumes and Bunny tails up in the attic."

In the decades to come, there would be some attempts to resurrect Bunny Clubs, notably with the 2006 Las Vegas "Playboy at the Palms." But for the most part, the efforts were unsuccessful. Hef lamented, "The Bunny is now a relic of America's cultural past, and especially of my own past. Oh, the happy memories. Now my bones are a bit creaky, and I don't think I'll go on any more Bunny hunts."

One reporter for the *Los Angeles Times* was unkind: "Hefner seems to float in an airbrushed dream space, a fading caricature of his former self."

\*\*\*

Defeating Jimmy Carter in the race for U.S. presidency, that "Moral Crusader," Ronald Reagan moved into the Oval Office to dominate politics for two terms in the 1980s. He was no longer the liberal Democrat of the 1940s, who had supported Franklin D. Roosevelt and Harry S Truman. Since hired as a spokesman for General Electric in the 1950s, he had swung to the far right.

For a long time, Hugh Hefner had been Reagan's target. He had the *Playboy* publisher in mind when he

In a bit—more than a bit—of hypocrisy, Nancy and Ronald Reagan, shown here in 1964, reconfigured themselves as "Moral Crusaders" after they started running the Free World.

Each of them forgot their notorious pasts in Hollywood. Among their many conquests, Nancy seduced Spencer Tracy and Clark Gable, while Ronald went for blondes like Lana Turner and Marilyn Monroe.

denounced "pornography" as a form of pollution, promising, "We will work to clean up hazardous waste sites. In the 1960s and '70s, America lost her religious and moral bearings, forgetting that faith and family values are what made us good and great."

By May 20, 1985, the president decided to go after "Hefner and hundreds of other pornographers working to destroy the moral fabric of America." He announced that Attorney General Edwin Meese would establish a special panel "to investigate the corrosive effects of pornography."

Meese said that cable TV and video recorders had made pornography available in every home, "Even children can access it by simply pressing a button."

After an investigation, the panel was to make recommendations to the U.S. Department of Justice for prosecution. Hef immediately denounced the panel for its "sexual McCarthyism."

Born in Oakland, California in 1931, Meese was the man for the job. Hef called him "so far right he's on Mars." He had joined Reagan's team during his tenure as governor of California, serving as his chief of staff. Meese became notorious when he cracked down on student protesters in Oakland in May of 1969. Hundreds of students were injured, and he asked Reagan to send in the National Guard.

Meese became Reagan's link to the evangelical community and even addressed Congress, telling the politicos that "In spite of four billion laws passed, we haven't improved one iota on the Ten Commandments." Meese survived various governmental scandals but never lost Reagan's trust.

Under Fire

*Time* magazine noted that the men on the Meese panel embarked on "a surrealist mystery tour of sexual perversity." Hauled before the panel were FBI agents, former hookers, and victims of sexual abuse. Panel members were said to have watched "tons of porn and studied hundreds of magazines, especially *Playboy.*" Members also visited sex shops to examine the latest sex toys that had come on the market, especially 14-inch dildos.

Reporter Sena Braswell wrote, "One of the primary targets of the investigation proved to be a man who more than any other had catalyzed the Sexual Revolution. That was *Playboy*

Released in April of 1984, a year that ominously evoked the title of George Orwell's dystopian novel about a heavily censored, heavily restricted nation, this edition of *Newsweek* highlighted Edwin Meese and his intentions to oppress so-called pornographers like Hugh Hefner.

Civil libertarians were outraged,

founder Hugh Hefner. The resulting political storm would lead to stranger bedfellows than even Hefner's circular bed at the Playboy Mansion had ever seen, as prominent feminists lined up alongside their frequent enemies in the Reagan administration to make the case against adult magazine publishers like Hefner."

Siding with the right wingers, feminist writer Robin Morgan claimed, "Pornography is the theory and rape is the practice." Other leading feminists such as Catharine MacKinnon and Andrea Dworkin signed on as "anti-Playboy warriors."

**Thunder on the Right**
The Growth of Fundamentalism

The Reverend
Jerry Falwell

Meese had total support from the televangelist and conservative activist, Jerry Lamon Falwell, Sr., who had founded the so-called Moral Majority in 1979. Hef called him "the most disgusting man in America today."

Hitler wanted to gas the Jews, but Jerry Falwell, the leader of the so-called Moral Majority, preferred to rid the globe from "the curse of homosexuality."

When not attacking "smut peddlers," Falwell went after gay people, calling them "brute beasts, vile agents of Satan. One day when all of them are annihilated, there will be a celebration in heaven."

Before an audience of the faithful, Falwell said, "Wouldn't it be wonderful if Hugh Hefner got saved and shut down Playboy Enterprises and became a spokesman for Jesus Christ? He could be another Saul."

Ever the provocateur, Larry Flynt—himself the product of a southern childhood—satirically attacked Falwell in an article he published in *Hustler*.

In it, he accused Falwell of losing his virginity to his mother during a moment of passion in a smelly outdoor toilet ventilated only with a half moon-shaped peephole cut through its swinging door.

In 1983, Hef watched in fascination as Falwell and his rival, Larry Flynt, battled it out in court. *Hustler* published a parody that included a mock interview with Falwell. In this satire, Falwell admitted that his "first time" was incest with his mother in an outhouse while he was drunk.

Falwell immediately filed a $45 million lawsuit, alleging invasion of privacy and libel, and intentional infliction of emotional distress. The jury rejected the claims of invasion of privacy and libel but awarded $200,000 in damages for emotional distress.

Flynt appealed to the U.S. Supreme Court, which ruled against Falwell, claiming that the First Amendment prevented public figures from recovering damages for emotional distress caused by parodies.

Hef's hatred of Falwell continued even after his death in 2007. It was reported, perhaps erroneously, that he said, "If that crackpot had been given an enema, his family could have made his coffin a matchbox. He was a fund-grubbing Bible thumper, a fat charlatan, putting Elmer Gantry to shame. He promoted hatred and intolerance."

*Playboy, Penthouse,* and *Hustler* met their most implacable critic in the shape of Dr. Judith Reisman, who had become a vicious attacker of the Kinsey Report, a survey that had partially inspired Hef to found *Playboy.*

She falsely claimed that Dr. Kinsey had relied on pedophiles in his research and that he had sexually abused children himself. Critics denounced the charges as groundless, especially her accusation that Kinsey had indulged in genital torture and had had sexual relations with some 800 children.

The Office of Juvenile Justice and Delinquency Prevention of the U.S. Department of Justice granted her $800,000 (later reduced to $734,000) to study certain men's magazines such as *Playboy* and to determine if their cartoons led to the sexual abuse of children.

Witnesses came forward to testify, including Roy Madison, who claimed that the first time he read *Playboy* had led to his raping a nine-year-old girl. Don Cohen claimed that he read a copy of *Playboy* when he was in the ninth grade and that had corrupted him so much that "I became a sex pervert and a heavy drug user."

The Reisman committee reviewed 372 issues of *Playboy,* 184 issues of *Penthouse,* and 125 issues of *Hustler.*

When Hef published nude photos of Madonna, the panel charged that the singer was an idol of youth, and that the pictorial on her would lead to an increase in child pornography. Of course, there was no evidence to connect the Madonna nudes with the child porn industry.

The baseless charges of the Reisman study were widely criticized as "a scientific disaster," "vigilantism," "paranoia," and "pseudo-scien-

Despite her attempts to look as cheery and optimistic and as emotionally generous as Dr. Ruth, Judith Reisman was condemned by liberals and civil libertarians as a dangerous, vengeful reactionary and a spokeswoman for the forces attempting to eradicate *Playboy.*

Notorious for her scary and repressive views about sex, Reisman attacked Dr. Alfred Kinsey as a "sadomasochist, pedophile, and porn addict."

Hef detested her.

tific hyperbole." Nevertheless, citing the Reisman accusations, many magazine distributors dropped *Playboy* and other skin magazines, too.

In an attempt to discredit them, sample cartoons from *Playboy* and other magazines were singled out and scrutinized—utterly without humor—for sinister intent. One cartoon was cited of a girl in pigtails, white bobby sox, and bows in her hair. It was condemned as a "call to incestuous fathers to force sex on their underaged daughters."

Another cartoon from *Playboy* called "Rubber Ducky," was said to attract pedophiles by depicting a girl tottering on oversized, red high-heeled shoes taken from her mommy's closet. It was noted that the subject had "knock-kneed, long, adolescent legs and a narrow hip line."

Hef denounced the investigation as motivated by "sexual fascists who are every bit as dangerous as Hitler."

The right-wing Moral Majority and the often left-wing female activists formed an uneasy alliance in their attempted suppression of *Playboy*. Writing for *Harper's Bazaar*, Susan Brownmiller claimed, "Pornography is propaganda against women, and propaganda is a very power spur to action—think of the anti-Semitic propaganda of Hitler's Nazi Germany."

She sent out a battle cry that attracted militant women, such groups as Women Against Pornography. This coven was the most radical of the feminist activists. Established in 1978, it drew widespread support. In Manhattan, thousands of women invaded Times Square, exposing sex shops and movie houses screening pornography. Many of their leaders testified before the Meese panel, calling for "civil rights-oriented, anti-pornography legislation."

One of Hef's chief attackers was the radical Andrea Dworkin, who argued that porn was linked to rape and other forms of violence against women. She thought of herself as a military general in the feminist sex wars of the 1980s and viewed Hef as "my natural enemy."

She wrote such books as *Pornography: Men Possessing Women* in 1981. Her book *Intercourse* (1987) was interpreted as opposing all heterosexual intercourse. She maintained that pornography violated the civil rights of all women.

Some female protesters went to extreme measures, as when Marcia Womongold, a self-described "matriarchist revolutionary," fired a bullet from a rifle into a Boston store selling copies of *Playboy* and *Penthouse*.

Author James Petersen described them as "Big Sisters straight out of George Orwell's *1984*, members of the 'Thought Police.' They seem to think sex is rape, desire, and degradation."

A former Playmate, Mika Garcia, had been Miss January of 1973. Later, from 1976 to 1982, she became director of Playmate Productions. Because of her close connection to the operation, her views were taken seriously by some. She testified that Hef furnished drugs to both his staff and to Playmates, urging them to partake of bisexual acts of depravity to satisfy his interests as a voyeur. She also charged that he operated an international call girl ring in which many Playmates were forcibly involved.

Garcia spoke of "models who were raped both physically and mentally." Her allegations spun a tale of "attempted murder, drug addiction, and prostitution leading many models to contemplate suicide."

Hef denied all her charges, claiming she was attempting to peddle an exposé book about *Playboy*. Garcia countered that she had put her life in danger by making her charges.

Brenda MacKillop had worked as a Bunny at the Playboy Club in Los Angeles from 1973 to 1976. She went on Oprah Winfrey's show to share her revelations about Hef and the activities at his Mansion, asserting that they had driven her to the brink of suicide.

After leaving Los Angeles, she became a Born Again Christian, the wife of a pastor, and an anti-porn activist, defining *Playboy* as "a filthy magazine." She also asserted that there was a great deal of homosexual activity going on at the Mansion, particularly during orgy nights.

Hef denied her charges, noting her newfound Christianity as: "The form of religion you practice is the equivalent of burning a cross on someone's front yard."

In a daring move during the spring of 1986, Meese sent letters to the corporate headquarters of 13 major drug and convenience store outlets, alleging that they had been named as major purveyors of pornography by the Rev. Donald Wildmon, chairman of the National Federation of Decency. The letter said that the government would name the retailers as pornographers unless the owners or the chains could prove otherwise. Several of the stores stopped selling

The debate continues today:

Was Andrea Dworkin's unfortunate physicality something that reinforced her ferocious condemnations of men?

She became famous for her bizarre alliances with the religious right in their stance against such "pornographers" as Hugh Hefner.

*Playboy, Penthouse,* and other magazines.

The biggest hit to *Playboy* came from 7-Eleven convenience stores, which announced that it would no longer distribute the magazine in any of its 7,500 outlets. J.C. Penney among others followed suit. Bob Guccione and Hef sued in Federal court and on July 3, a Federal District court judge ruled in their favor.

Celebrating his victory, which came after a lot of financial loss, Hef accused the Meese commission of being "a circus show of misinformation and innuendo." He called the censorship attempt "a form of terrorism," and he was highly critical of Reagan and his administration, accusing them of "porn paranoia." He was one of the backers of People for the American Way, which set out to attack and expose extreme right-wing views.

Hef drew massive support from the media, nearly all of whom opposed censorship. The *Chicago Tribune* wrote, "*Playboy* is once again thrust to the ramparts, battling the forces of ignorance and repression. Hugh Hefner is heading the charge of the anti-censorship crusaders." The *Orange County Register* defined the members of the Meese panel as "Blue-Nosed Bullies. Hugh Hefner and others are facing anti-sex feminists and fun-hating religious fundamentalists."

A Pulitzer Prize-winning columnist, Anna Quindlen, was more measured in her response. Writing in *The New York Times,* she opposed censorship and endorsed Hef's right to depict nudity in *Playboy.* However, she said, "I think the centerfolds are silly, and that all those women miming sexual ecstasy in bizarre undergarments succeed only in looking as if they had a cold."

In July of 1986, Meese called a press conference to announce the results of his report. Some reporters found it amusing that he chose to conduct the venue in the Great Hall of the Justice Department. He stood before a 12-foot "Spirit of Justice" statue. *[Crafted from cast aluminum in 1933 in the Art Deco style by C. Paul Jennewein, it depicts a defiant Lady Justice with one of her ample breasts prominently undraped.]*

The report emerged as a harsh attack on the $8 billion-a-year porn industry. It exposed a link between violent porn and acts of sexual violence, and it demanded legal restrictions on porn. Meese asserted that the panel was focused on child pornography and publications that degrade women or depict them as victims of violence.

Yet when the full degree of public opposition to his vision was made clear, he retreated from his earlier attempts to censor *Playboy,* claiming, "In my opinion, there has not been any court that has held *Playboy* or *Penthouse* to be within the Supreme Court definition of obscenity. And so I do not feel that those are the kinds of things that should be subject to prosecution under the law."

Seeming to straddle the political divisions that the Meese commission's oratory had to some degree, intensified, David J. Anderson, an attorney for the Justice Department, said, "The Meese commission never took the position that *Playboy* was obscene or pornographic. I'm not going to say that there's been a decision for all time that no issue of *Playboy* will ever be obscene. Who knows what *Playboy* will publish in its February centerfold?"

Dr. Park Elliott Dietz, a respected psychiatrist who served on the Meese panel, claimed, "*Playboy* has published the healthiest nude sexy pictures in America. It should have a larger share of the sex picture market. The commissioner's factual findings suggest that there ought to be more *Playboy*-like nudes available in our society and fewer X-rated slasher films."

Betty Friedan, author of *The Feminine Mystique,* is credited with launching the second wave of American feminism. She advocated full partnership with men, and was at first critical of Hef, feeling that he exploited women. Yet with the advent of the 1980s, she seemed to withdraw from the ranks of the more radical feminists and softened her position toward him.

A view of the late, great, Betty Friedan, author of *The Feminist Mystique.*

As a major force in the articulation of the "second wave" of American feminism, and noted for her sense of humor, she addressed issues associated with family and workplace issues, reproductive rights, domestic violence, and legally sanctioned inequalities. A book she published in 1981, *The Second Stage*, critiqued what she interpreted as extremist excesses of some feminists.

In September of 1992, Hef ordered his editors to feature Friedan in a *Playboy Interview* wherein she was cited for her more moderate brand of feminism. She still didn't like *Playboy* for turning women into sex objects, but she was not one to deny the allure of sexuality. She won Hef's heart when she said, "To suppress free speech in the name of protecting women is dangerous and wrong."

She interviewed Hef as part of the research for her book, *Fountain of Age* (1993), later reviewed as her attempt to combat the debilitating mystique of age. *["...We have denied the reality and evaded the new triumphs of growing older..."]*

In it, she wrote, "Men will live longer when women are strong enough to realize that they don't need men as scapegoats anymore. We need you, and you need us more than ever."

Hef joked, "Betty and I came to smoke the peace pipe with each other, mainly because I

According to Hef, "I was never on the same page about almost anything with Betty Friedan, but at least she and I showed that a playboy like me and an ardent feminist could agree to disagree without beating the shit out of each other."

never asked her to pose for a centerfold. Let's face it: Betty is quite brilliant but her face looks like a combination of Hermione Gingold and Bette Davis in *What Ever Happened to Baby Jane?*"

Still stung by the thousands of attacks on himself and on *Playboy*, Hef issued a statement: "I think the women's movement got sidetracked with its anti-porn, anti-sex attacks, which were very hurtful. The women's movement was supposed to be about freedom. The notion that sex itself is somehow demeaning to women is one of the saddest notions I could possibly imagine. Even radical feminists should not wind up on the same side as Christian right-wingers fighting porn. If there remains a belief that the actual sex act is degrading to women, then we are in serious trouble."

\*\*\*

Another young model from Canada, Kimberley Conrad, entered Hef's life and changed it forever. The gorgeous honey blonde made her first appearance at Hef's Shangri-La on May 22, 1987 to pose for a centerfold, which appeared in the January 1988 edition as Playmate of the Month. At the time, Hef was still living with Carrie Leigh, and Conrad did not immediately encounter him.

However, he became so intrigued with her nude images that he invited her back for another photo session on January 18, 1988. At the time she posed for one of Hollywood's most noted photographers, Helmut Newton, for a pictorial which Hef later turned into Playmate of the Year for 1989. On this occasion, Hef came out to greet her, suggesting that she "perhaps might like to spend the evening with me."

"I don't think so," she said. "I don't know you except by reputation."

"How in hell are you going to get to know me unless we spend time together?" he asked.

In the face of such logic, she said, "You've got a point there. You're on, Big Boy."

For their first dates, they spent quiet nights together weeks before the invitation came to sleep over.

He learned that she'd been born in Moulton, Alabama in 1962, but had been reared in Reno, Nevada and later grew up in Vancouver. She'd worked as a model, posing for ads for Levi Jeans and also for juicy hamburgers from McDonalds.

"Unlike Hef's behavior with other Playmates, he did not rush Kimberley to bed right away," said John Dante, one of his best friends. "He began to date her and wooed her until the day both of them fell in love. It happened so quickly, she came to me with this startling bit of news: 'Hef asked me to marry him.'"

She told Dante how the proposal had unfolded and recorded in her diary the historic date of July 22, 1988. She had just finished a winning hand at the game of "Foosball," and Hef walked out of the Game Room with her, holding her hand as they headed back to the Mansion.

"I was feeling wonderful that night," she told Dante. "We stopped by the Wishing Well, and he turned to me and asked, 'Will you marry me?'"

"I did not immediately say yes, but told him I'd have to think it over," she said. "I mulled it over for exactly three seconds before I said yes."

Later that day, Hef told Dante, "I have done the unthinkable. I asked Kim to marry me, after swearing off marriage for decades. I must have been on something. Maybe I'm just getting old, but I can actually contemplate spending the rest of my life with this gorgeous doll."

Still in residence at the Mansion, Jessica Hahn said, "They met, they developed a friendship, and both of them fell in love. I felt they were perfect for each other. He deserves to be happy. So does she. Of course, there is a difference in ages, but I'm sure they can overcome that."

During the next few days, Kimberley was going around the Mansion showing off her 3.5 karat diamond engagement ring. Hef told her that instead of Playmate of the Year, he was going to dub her in the magazine as Playmate for a Lifetime.

He even went so far as to stage a "coronation" for her, dressing her in a fur-trimmed cape and a diamond tiara. For the ceremony, he called in Prince Frederick von Anhalt of Germany, the husband of Zsa Zsa Gabor, to officiate and lend some European *gravitas* to the ceremony. Dressed in monarchical regalia, Von Anhalt took his sword and, in a mock-knighting

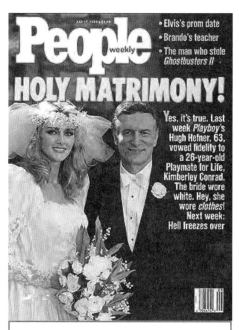

"The first time I saw Kimberley Conrad, I knew I had to have her," Hef said.

"She was blonde, which I prefer, and also strikingly beautiful, which I demand in a woman. Of course, I still had Carrie Leigh in my life when I first met Kimberley, so I had to clean out my bedroom to make way for Kim."

"Physically, we were the perfect match but we differed on our set of social values."

ceremony, dubbed her "Kimerella," a play on the name of Cinderella. In a tuxedo, Hef stood by, beaming.

On July 1, 1989, Hef relinquished the niche he'd occupied as "America's no. 1 bachelor." Kimberly Conrad became Hef's second wife in a lavish ceremony in the gardens of his L.A. Mansion. She wore a stunning white designer bridal gown by Jim Hjelm, the New York designer.

An array of Hollywood stars attended the wedding, including Bill Cosby, Angie Dickinson, Mark Hamill, James Caan, Robert Culp, and Tony Curtis.

The Rev. Charles Ara officiated. When Hef said, "I do," the pastor broke from the usual liturgy. Addressing the gathering, he said, "You heard it from his own lips. Hugh Hefner, confirmed bachelor, uttered the words, 'I do.'"

In a novel twist, Hef had invited his three most recent mistresses, who collectively posed with him for photos right after the ceremony. He found Barbi Benton "teary eyed;" Shannon Tweed in "high spirits;" and Sondra Theodore "emotionally distraught." His most recent girlfriend, Carrie

Later in his life, Hugh Hefner opted to replicate, then and now, seven of the cover photos that had, over the years, graced his magazine.

The most visible was that of Kimberley Conrad, whose original cover (left) from 1988 is positioned alongside the updated cover she shot thirty years later as well-preserved mother of his children

Hef's stated intention? "Each of them proves that beauty is timeless and women can be sexy at any age. Once a Playmate, always a Playmate".

Leigh, was not invited because at the time, she was suing him.

The lavish event was planned and orchestrated by Colin Cowie, an Englishman born in Zambia. The event was such a success that it launched him into a career as a wedding consultant, and he became known as "the Martha Stewart of wedding planners."

Hef's aging mother, Grace, showed up, taking both his hands. "Son, I'm glad you've decided to settle down."

Some 300 guests attended the lavish reception. It was staged inside a mammoth Bavarian-style tent erected in the gardens of the Mansion, its interior draped with 15,000 yards of white satin. The spaces in and around it were "accessorized" with an assortment of nude female statues.

When Kimberley was told that Hef had invited some of his former girl-friends, she claimed, "I'm not jealous. After all, I'm the young one."

The romantic highlight of the reception was when Ray Anthony & His Orchestra played "As Time Goes By." Hef and Kimberly danced to his fa-vorite song from his favorite movie, *Casablanca*, starring Humphrey Bogart and Ingrid Bergman.

The wedding received wide media coverage, Hef telling *USA Today*, "Out of nowhere, this angel from the north winged her way into my life and everything changed. She is the one woman I've searched for all my life and never found. I'm one lucky fellow."

*People* magazine ran a wedding photo of Hef and Kimberly on its cover under the headline "Holy Matrimony!" Its caption read: *"Playboy's* Hugh Hefner, 61, vowed fidelity to a 26-year-old Playmate, Kimberley Conrad. The bride wore white. Hey, she wore clothes! Next week, hell freezes over."

The "Second Coming" headline in the *New York Daily News* pro-claimed: "END OF AN ERA: PLAYMATED! NO MORE BUNNY BUSI-NESS!"

The comic strip *Doonesbury* referred to the Hefner/Conrad marriage as "the belated end of the 1970s."

***

Hef went from a bachelor seducing several different women every weekend to a husband craving commitment. "I'm at the point in my life where I've sown my wild oats, and I'm now seeking a stable relationship with the woman I love. Kim is just what I need—open, honest, straightfor-ward. It is a most serious relationship. A real marriage."

"I've spent most of my life on a romantic quest. Now I've found real happiness and fulfillment in a traditional relationship similar to that of my

471

parents. But I don't think this would have been possible if I hadn't pursued the other life first."

As the new Mistress of the Manse, Kimberley set about making some changes, and surprisingly despite her former role as a Playmate, it soon became apparent that she had rather conservative values. She wanted to rid the Mansion of many hangers-on, men who were sponging off Hef as freeloaders. "I grew impatient coming down the stairs to find 50 people there, most of whom I didn't know."

She outlawed the raucous Midsummer Night's Dream parties, with their associated nudity and orgies in the gardens, especially in the Grotto. And she made it clear that she didn't want Hef's guests walking around their home in the nude.

Hef may not have intended to start a second family, since he'd paid so little attention when his first son and daughter were growing up. But soon after they were married, Kimberley announced that she was pregnant. On Hef's 65th birthday, she presented him with a son, naming him Marston Glenn, taking his first name from Hef's middle name and his middle name from Hef's father.

A glimpse of Hef was snapped in 1978 when the pipe-smoking, tuxedo-clad Playboy of the Western World was stepping out for the night, escaping the confines of his bedroom. "I was swimming in a sea of blondes that night," he confessed.

That was the year he met another blonde, the ill-fated Dorothy Stratten, and became a fixture in her life and a key figure in the tragedy that would soon befall her.

According to Hef, "I wasn't around when Christie and David were growing up, but with the birth of my second son, I planned to become a hands-on dad."

Sex toys were replaced with kiddie toys around the Mansion. Kimberley said, "A lot of girls still come over, but I insist they wear at least a bathing suit, one suitable for a public beach."

A second son, Cooper Bradford Hefner, arrived on September 4, 1991. Kimberley wanted her boys to grow up together.

"I saw the birth of Marston and the later arrival of his little brother, Cooper, as part of my newly defined romantic dream," Hef said. "The boys are my life, that and my animals, which include ten dogs and eleven cats, most of them rescues."

Cooper was named for agent Cooper of *Twin Peaks*, a favorite TV show watched by both Hef and Kimberley.

Their early marital bliss faded as time went by and Kimberley became bored with life at the Mansion. "I didn't like living in a fish bowl. Hef followed the same old routines night after night. Movie nights. Card games that lasted until dawn. The endless buffets where tons of people showed up to gorge themselves."

"I wanted to be a wife and mother, not some hostess. I wanted to spend nights with my husband and two sons, not waste my time with all those playboys and playgirls who flocked to the Mansion."

She later recalled, "I began to feel like Lady Di must have felt when she found herself trapped in a loveless marriage to Prince Charles."

Hef found her constant complaints unreasonable. "I just didn't understand why I couldn't be a family man and still have my friends, my movies, my parties. They had sustained me for years and had continued to do so during my married life."

By the time the mid-1990s rolled around, sex between Kimberley and Hef had tapered off but not vanished completely. It was later alleged, never quite proven, that Kimberley had begun an affair with one of the handsomest of *Playboy's* security guards. Within a context of rising tension within their marriage, Hef confronted her with that. In contrast, he maintained that he had been faithful to her throughout the early years of their wedded bliss.

On December 31, 1997, guests were surprised when Kimberley did not attend Hef's annual New Year's Eve party. Publicly, Hef maintained that she had the flu. Actually, she'd flown to Hawaii with her sons.

But on January 21, 1998, when Marston was seven and Cooper six, it was announced that Hef and Kimberley would separate.

Two years earlier, Hef had purchased the spacious home next to his

L.A. Mansion and had torn down the garden walls that separated the two properties. After her return to the U.S. mainland from Hawaii, Kimberley, along with Marston and Cooper, moved into the new quarters.

Hef told the press, "With the passage of a little time, maybe Kimberley and I can recapture what we have lost."

She found some solace in her new life near to, but outside the Mansion. "I enjoyed the freedom of living next door in a house of my own, with my boys, watching them grow up. I still miss Hef on occasion, but I'm doing fine. I told him that I looked up the word 'gentleman' in the dictionary and found his picture printed along with the definition of the word."

"I think Hef came to miss the old life he once led in Chicago and in the early days at the Mansion in Los Angeles. He was very tame with me, very much so, as a father and a husband. He was good to his boys—in fact, he doted on them."

"I think he wanted to recapture his lost youth. After I moved out, I heard he was desperately trying to do that. I just hope it doesn't bite him in the butt. It would be a tragedy if something bad happened to him like AIDS. I'd miss him. So would his daughter and three sons."

Hef's second divorce did not become final until 2010. "I would have been happy to file for divorce years sooner, but she wanted to stay married, at least in name only, until our youngest son turned eighteen. She got her wish."

\*\*\*

Hef's separation from Kimberley coincided with his discovery of Viagra. In a scrapbook he wrote, "VIVA VIAGRA! Picasso had his Blue Period. I'm now in my BLONDE PERIOD with the aid of Viagra."

After his separation, he began to be spotted at certain trendy clubs in Los Angeles, most often with a different Playmate. He was known to have dated such Playmates as Jamie Farrell, Jaime Bergman, and Carrie Stevens.

He also told his friends that, "I'm a babe magnet. I can't walk into a club but what beautiful women flock to me. Is it because of my body or because I'm the multi-millionaire publisher of *Playboy?*"

Medical breakthroughs promised Hef, and millions of other men, relief from erectile dysfunction, retoring them, through association with Viagra and other substitutes, to the fountains of their youths.

474

His magazine ran a rather personal article about him in December of 1998. "After a decade of devoted family life, the legendary Playboy Mansion madness is back, replete with Playmates prowling the grounds." In a photograph, he was depicted surrounded with beautiful women, the caption reading: "Do these photos look like Hef is suffering from separation anxiety?"

The article continued, "Since his marital status has changed, he has been stepping out for retro Rat Pack nights of cocktails, swing dancing, and healthy blondes."

Once, after seducing four young women in the Grotto, Hef proclaimed, "Through Viagra, I have discovered Ponce de Leon's Fountain of Youth."

He went to a plastic surgeon, telling him to "work your magic on the sagging folds of skin around my neck"

Recuperating from surgery, he was seen dating Brande Roderick, the *Baywatch* actress who became Playmate of the Year in 2001. He was also seen with two lovely girls on each arm. They turned out to be twin sisters, Mandy and Sandy Bentley.

The former homebody who didn't want to leave his bedroom was now seen at such trendy clubs as Las Palmas, Snatch, Garden of Eden, Opium Den, Bliss, and Barfly. A buxom blonde, Tina Jordan, Playmate of the Month for 2002, often was seen with him at these joints, and he also took up with another girlfriend, the aptly named "Tiffany Holliday."

"I should write a best-selling autobio," he told John Dante. "I'll call it *The Hectic Sex Life of a Septtuagenarian.* In it, I'll raise the question: Why should a man in his 70s settle down with just one woman when he can have at least four or five a night? The girls tell me I'm a wonderful lover. Hell, I should be. I've had decades of practice."

His rejuvenation drew a mixed press, David Plotz writing in *Slate* magazine, "Hefner is the unfrozen caveman swinger, cryogenically preserved since the 1970s."

"Hef's Mansion is hopping again," proclaimed *Harper's Bazaar. Vanity Fair* published a picture of him taken by the famed photographer, Annie Liebowitz, depicting him with two beautiful women lying in bed with him as two other beauties in the background pose in a lesbian embrace. The caption read: "Hugh Hefner is presiding over the pagan splendors of his pleasure mansion."

Other critics continued to write him off as "a decaying relic of yesterday."

# NEW YORK CITY'S PLAYBOY CLUB
# IT'S BACK!

The photo above, depicting a Bunny in her youthful glory—a vision dear to the heart of an aging Hugh Hefner—is a publicity shot from the 2011 TV series, *The Bunny Club*, whose aesthetics did a brilliant job at replicating the glory days of the Playboy Empire.

At presstime for the first edition of this book, the Bunny dream and vision, presently thriving at the Playboy Club in London, is about to make another comeback—this time in Manhattan.

It's scheduled for an opening during the Autumn of 2018 at 512 West 42nd Street, in Manhattan, a brisk walk from its original (from 1962 to 1986) 59th Street address. Designed with four rooms and a scattering of ambience bars, it's adjacent to the Cachet Boutique New York Hotel.

Club membership options will "unlock" additional rooms. According to Playboy Enterprises, the space will artfully evoke the "luxurious, seductive, and playful spirit of the original Playboy Mansion." In addition to an after-work and late-night bar, the venue will also host events like "A Midsummer Night's Dream" theme party, a Playboy Haunted Mansion Halloween, a Playboy Masquerade Party, and more.

Playboy is very clear that its trademark venue in New York City will be a place where women are respected. According to a company spokesperson, "Playboy is priding itself as a brand holding women on a high pedestal, never objectifying them, and giving them a platform, a place to speak their minds. That's what the brand has always defined itself around."

Asked if they'd invite Gloria Steinem, who famously went undercover as a Playboy Bunny in 1963, and who's famously quoted as saying, "The truth will set you free, but first it will piss you off," the company said they'd be "happy to host" her.

# Chapter Twelve

# TWILIGHT
## FOR THE PLAYBOY OF THE WESTERN WORLD
### HEF TAKES HIS THIRD BRIDE
#### 60 YEARS YOUNGER AND A FORMER PLAYMATE OF THE MONTH
### PASSING THE TORCH: COOPER

Hef Launches His Portfolio of Celebrity Nudes
# FAMOUS AND NAKED!
### JOAN COLLINS ("THAT BITCH FROM *DYNASTY*") AND
### PATTI DAVIS, THE ARGUMENTATIVE, REBELLIOUS, "FREE AT LAST"
### DAUGHTER OF "JUST SAY NO" RONALD AND NANCY REAGAN

# IT'S THE DONALD!
### "PART BILL GATES, PART CASANOVA"
### TRUMP, LONG BEFORE HE'S ELECTED PRESIDENT,
### POSES FOR THE COVER OF *PLAYBOY*,
### LATER AUTOGRAPHING PHOTOCOPIES AS A CAMPAIGN TOOL

## KISS & TELLS:
### KENDRA! HOLLY! BRIDGET! ISABELLA! JILL ANN! SUZEN! STEPHANIE!

**THE CHANGING TIDES OF CONSERVATISM:** The appearance of a presidential candidate on the cover of *Playboy* alongside an undraped Playmate would have been the kiss of death in any "normal" election cycle, but for Donald Trump, it became a standard, much-bragged-about part of his campaign chest.

Even the *de facto* Emperor of the Religious Right, Jerry Falwell,Jr., shown on the upper right with his wife, managed to find it innocuous and harmless. Lower right: Moguls Hef and Trump, schmoozing and perhaps bonding.

**"We've come a long way, baby,"** Hef told his then-wife, Kimberley, as the 1990s began.

"*Playboy* readers are more diverse, more mature, and much more sophisticated. The reader of 1953, when I started the magazine, is now a grandfather or has passed on his way. Today's readers are more demanding, less uptight, more tolerant, even bisexual in many cases. Marriage is less important than ever in modern American history."

He praised the management of his daughter Christie. "She is completely in tune with the tastes and desires of a new generation."

In the 1990s, the overseas market came into sharper focus, the foreign circulation of the magazine going from half a million readers to 1.5 million. *Playboy* was now published in 14 foreign editions, including in Italian and German.

Because *Playboy TV* had gone over well in America, Christie directed that more of its programming be inaugurated in Western Europe. *Playboy TV* was also thriving in Tokyo.

"Europe was way ahead of us in the depiction of nudity," Hef said. "A boy growing up in Italy becomes accustomed to nude statues. Take Michelangelo's nude of *David*. He looks like he has a small dick, but it's fourteen inches long, flaccid."

On the homefront, *Playboy* faced more and more competition, especially from the Internet. The magazine's advertising revenue was down, but it still had a respectable 3.5 million readers.

Christie also moved ahead in the licensing department, authorizing 10 sportswear boutiques, selling tight-fitting jeans, jogging suits, dress shirts, or *attaché* cases, all with the Bunny logo.

*Playboy* even re-entered the gaming business, owning a 15 percent take in a casino operation on the Greek island of Rhodes.

Christie continued to explore new ideas for merchandising, saying, "*Playboy* still represents a high-quality lifestyle." Such items as a rabbit logo air freshener for cars and especially the porn channel provided much of the income for the parent company.

Of course, as expected, criticism of *Playboy* continued. One reporter wrote, "*Playboy* has lost its mojo. It never really survived the AIDS crisis and the backlash of the Reagan moral crusaders."

But Hef sighed with relief that most of his enemies had been silenced. "It's a new day out there. Reagan is so far gone, so 'gaga' at this point that I understand he doesn't even remember that he was President of the United States. The Bill Clinton era is upon us. He's my kind of guy to lead us into this new day."

"I refer to the 1980s as 'The Age of Repression.'"

Christie continued to expand into new markets, but also practiced cost-cutting techniques, as she had done the year she took over Playboy Enterprises. One of her major expenses was the operation of the Los Angeles Playboy Mansion, which cost $4 million annually, employing 60 servants to maintain the house and its extensive gardens.

*\*\**

To Hef, the name of *Trump* was a painful reference to his ill-fated satire magazine that had failed so terribly to attract readers late in 1953.

By 1990, Donald Trump had become such a controversial, even notorious, real estate developer in Manhattan that Hef decided he would be worth an interview. At the last minute, Hef decided to ask him to pose for the cover, wearing tuxedo pants, a cummerbund, and a bow tie. Playmate Brandi Brandt wore his jacket—and nothing else.

Hef had long been intrigued by the exploits of the real estate tycoon, both his lifestyle and his many rumored seductions. During his visits to the Playboy Club, he had always been a self-styled "babe magnet," attracting the cottontail Bunnies. "They did cluster around him and vie as to who would wait on him. I don't know if it were for his body or for his money, but I had a pretty good idea it was the latter."

"Trump was an arrogant prick but newsworthy, so I decided to feature him in the March 1990 edition of *Playboy*. I didn't plan to make him a centerfold, but I did have him photographed for the cover. We shared at least something in common: We both had a reputation of being part Bill Gates, part Casanova."

Hef sent reporter Glenn Plaskin to interview Trump, but he didn't unearth any of the tantalizing revelations Hef really wanted.

Plaskin asked him, "Are you monogamous?"

"I don't have to answer that," Trump said, meaning, of course, that he was not. "I never speak of my wife, which is one of the advantages of not being a politician. My marriage is and should be a personal thing."

At the time, he was married to Ivana Trump, but, according to the gossip of the day, he was hardly faithful to her.

The reporter pressed for more details. "Are you flirtatious?"

"I think any man enjoys flirting, and if he says he doesn't he's

Bunny with an unidentified friend

479

a liar. Or else he's a politician trying to get those four extra votes."

"How is your marriage?" Plaskin asked.

"Ivana is a very kind and good woman, and she has the instincts and drive of a good manager. She's focused and she's a perfectionist."

"And as a wife, not a manager?" the reporter asked.

"I never comment on romance," Trump said. "She's a great mother, a good woman who does a good job."

It was later learned that at the time Trump made these comments, he was involved in a torrid romance with Marla Maples, whom he would marry after he divorced Ivana.

Trump denied he was going into politics one day. "I don't want to be President. I'm 100 percent sure. I'd change my mind only if I saw the country continue to go down the tubes."

For years, Trump kept a framed copy of this racy *Playboy* cover of himself with a partially undressed Bunny hanging in his office. He viewed it as a feather in his cap, something that positioned him with the other entertainment luminaries *Playboy* had previously highlighted.

Later, he boasted to a *Washington Post* reporter, "I was one of the few men in the history of *Playboy* to be on its cover." [*During his run for the presidency in 2016, he made autographed replicas of that issue's cover available as publicity handouts.*]

Not only was Trump on the cover of *Playboy*, but he appeared, fully dressed, in an explicit *Playboy* video which featured nude women in various sexual poses. He once told a reporter, "Personally, I admire Hugh Hefner, a self-made man who took a few bucks and turned it into an empire. I heard his mother gave him $500 to start his magazine. My dad was more generous. He dumped a million dollars on me."

When Trump did run for President, Hef did not support him, sending campaign money to Hillary Clinton's campaign instead. "We don't respect the guy," Cooper Hefner said. "Hef was embarrassed that he once featured him on the cover. The *Playboy Philosophy* is about freedom. If the *Playboy* team had only known what Trump would come to embody, he would never have found his way onto our cover. We encourage all individuals to choose the life they want to live."

*Newsweek* pointed out that Trump, during his heyday as a private citizen, had been a regular at the Playboy Mansion in both Chicago and Los Angeles. "But as a presidential candidate, the magazine noted, "Trump pitched himself as a defender of the values of Christian conservatives—the very same people Hefner regarded as his chief enemies."

Hef was also horrified when Trump designated the homophobic Mike Pence his running mate, and equally horrified when both of them resolved that transgendered people should not be allowed to serve in the military.

"If I were President, I would believe very strongly in extreme military strength," Trump said. "I wouldn't trust anyone. I wouldn't trust the Russians, I wouldn't trust our Allies. I would trust a huge U.S. military arsenal. I would perfect it, understand it."

In an analysis of Trump's foreign policy, the *Atlantic* noted that many foreign leaders had read the *Playboy* interview before actually meeting the newly elected president. Trump had laid out the framework of his political philosophy, while simultaneously presenting a scathing appraisal of America. He saw the country as "weak and pushed around by the rest of the world." In the interview, he unfurled a blueprint for his hypothetical presidency.

As president, Trump was linked once again with *Playboy* in a most unflattering way.

Ex-Playmate of the Year (1998), Karen McDougal, kept a journal of her affair with Trump and sold it to the *National Enquirer* for $150,000. She said, "He introduced me to his family and showed me his wife's bedroom in the Trump Tower. Later, in Los Angeles, we had an affair that lasted on and off for nine months at the Beverly Hills Hotel."

If you want to become a household word, become *Playboy's* Playmate of the Year (1998) and the mistress of President Donald Trump.

Karen McDougal sued the parent company of *The National Enquirer*, hoping to get out of a nondisclosure pact she'd signed.

She has been threatened with financial ruin if she talks about her close encounters with the presidential penis.

"Trump would fly me across the country to have an affair while he attended various events such as the Lake Tahoe Golf Tournament," McDougal claimed.

It was at this same tournament that Trump began his far more notorious affair with the porn star who goes under the name of "Stormy Daniels."

"I was introduced to Trump's sons, but ended the affair, thinking what my mother might think of me," said McDougal, who told reporters, "I recently found God."

The exposé she had authorized about her affair, based on her having accepted payment for it and her signing of a confidentiality agreement, had been bought and paid for by Trump's pal and supporter, David Pecker. But instead of publishing her scandalous confession, he suppressed it.

*[If you're a politician, especially President of the United States, it's good insurance to have Pecker as a friend. Among other titles, he is the chairman and CEO of American Media, Inc., which publishes the* National Enquirer *and the* Star.

The New York Times, *in April of 2018, ran a story that Pecker and his media company were being probed to see if "catch-and-kill" payments had been made to McDougal. That's a reference to acquiring the rights to someone's tawdry tale, but, instead of publishing it, it's "buried," and never printed or distributed.*

*Certainly, news of Trump's affair, coming in the wake of the notorious Hollywood tapes in which he bragged about groping women, might have seriously threatened his chances of winning the election.* The New York Times *maintained that such a transaction between Pecker and McDougal might represent an undeclared and therefore illegal "in-kind" campaign donation in violation of Federal Election Commission dictates.*

*A month before that article appeared in* The New York Times, *McDougal had filed a lawsuit against American Media in the Los Angeles Superior Court. She was seeking to invalidate her non-disclosure agreement, which blocked her from talking about her alleged affair with the future President.*

*FBI agents searched the office and residences of Trump attorney Michael Cohen, seeking evidence of Trump's alleged involvement in the payment to McDougal, plus other illegal activities.*

*Another publication, the* New Yorker, *also ran a story that a doorman at Trump Tower had alleged that Trump had an affair in the 1980s that led to the birth of a child. The mother was not named. The magazine could not confirm the affair, although it alleged that American Media had all the details, including the name of the woman and the circumstances associated with the conception and birth of her child.*

*In July of 2018, Hef was dead, but his Playmate, Karen McDougal, was lead-*

*ing off the news on all channels. It was revealed that Michael Cohen had secretly recorded a conversation he had had with Trump about the McDougal affair, and prosecutors wanted to know whether that violated Federal campaign finance laws.*

*The recording's existence appears to undercut the Trump campaign's denial of any knowledge about secret money slipped to the model, the purpose of which, in essence, was to hush her up.*

*McDougal alleges that Cohen played a major role in cutting a backroom deal to silence her.]*

\*\*\*

After his many expensive and exhausting confrontations with the "porn-hating dragons of the Reagan era," Hef interpreted the arrival of Bill Clinton in Washington as "a breath of fresh air." He also believed there would be no more government repression of him and *Playboy,* suspecting that the former governor of Arkansas also "had a taste for Bunny tail."

When *Playboy* first appeared on the newsstands in 1953, Clinton was just seven years old. By the time he was thirteen, he was eagerly reading every issue. At the same time, he was knocking on the door of every whorehouse in Arkansas and getting told "to come back in a few years."

It came as no surprise that his two rivals, Bob Guccione of *Penthouse* and Larry Flynt of *Hustler,* were also backing the Democratic candidate against George H.W. Bush, who was defeated in his bid for a second term. Hef ran a picture of Clinton and himself, posing with the newly elected President's arm around his shoulder.

David Schlesinger, a distributor of video porn, said, "Bill *[Clinton]* is a supporter of the porn industry. I just know it. He's batting for our team. He's not going to go after us like the sleazy Reagan Republicans did in the '80s."

That prediction was accurate. Fed-

"Reagan wanted to return America to its Puritan roots," said Hef, "but I thought a horndog like Bill Clinton—I don't know about Al Gore—would never turn the heat on *Playboy* the way the Republican moralists tried to do to me.

"If either Bill or Al wanted me to deliver Playmates to them at the White House, all they had to do was call."

eral obscenity prosecutions during the eight Clinton years plummeted by 86 percent.

There were some conservative kickbacks to the less repressive political environment: A gala Democratic fund-raising event was announced at the Los Angeles Playboy Mansion, which provoked "moral outrage" in some quarters. Some Democratic strategists feared that staging the event at *Playboy* headquarters would give the "family values GOP" a weapon to use against them.

The event was canceled, but both Clinton and Vice President Al Gore accepted generous campaign contributions both from Hef and his daughter Christie.

Richard Rosenzweig, the executive vice president of *Playboy*, seemed surprised and a bit dismayed at the outrage. "We at *Playboy* have supported Mr. Clinton and Mr. Gore, as we have any number of other Democratic candidates over the years."

Having been severely battered, both financially and morally, throughout the '80s, Hef and his staffers greeted the 1990s with a renewed zeal. In hindsight, Hef defined the Reagan era as "a time of conservative corruption and greed."

He ran an article in *Playboy* entitled "Wake Up and Smell the Nineties." In it, he humorously listed items to be junked during the new decade: Fur coats, junk bonds, Donald Trump's *The Art of the Deal*, T. Boone Pickens, Barbara Mandrell "comebacks," and the Fox Network.

But despite his optimism, Hef did not approve of all the new concepts of the 1990s, especially the emphasis on political correctness, which he thought could be carried too far. He called it "the new form of Prohibition."

When scandals broke accusing Bill Clinton of sexual misconduct both in his past as Governor of Arkansas as well as during his tenure in the Oval Office, Hef helped morph it into a *cause célèbre*, defending the President for the most part.

He sent a letter to Clinton in Washington, giving him some advice, which, incidentally, was not heeded.

"Remind the country that many other Presidents have been accused of misconduct, including Franklin D. Roosevelt and John F. Kennedy. Yes, FDR still functioned below the belt even though confined to a wheelchair. Perhaps you should make the following statement:

*'I've lived a full-blooded life. So far as I know, no one got hurt, and I always used a condom, so there are not a lot of little Billy Clintons running around Arkansas. I urge other men, if the need calls, to do the same.'*

"Of all the Presidents," Hef told his readers, "Bill Clinton is the most like you and me."

All sorts of charges against the Clinton White House were made, many of them venomous, misleading, and false. They included so-called scandals about Hillary, the tabloids accusing her of being a lesbian. One accusation was made by investigative reporter Paul Sperry. In an article, he claimed that "a massive Internet pornography ring had been discovered within the White House." The accusations were featured and amplified on some TV news programs, especially Fox.

Hef slightly scolded Clinton for the "Monica Lewinsky scandal and the stains on the navy blue GAP dress," but he directed most of his fury at the "blue-nosed Puritans who wanted to destroy Clinton's presidency. We do not expect, nor should we, for our leaders to be the stuff of *McGuffey's Readers*. We are human beings, and, as such, are sexual. Now, let's put all these attacks on Clinton behind us, and let's get on with our own lives."

"Okay," Hef said privately. "So our esteemed President could not keep his whacker in his pants and needed Monica to lick it. That's understandable. Only in America could a blow-job from a nice Jewish girl almost topple the most powerful government on earth."

"That Monica, with her gossipy tongue, could have left out a few details," Hef lamented. "Like Bill putting his cigar in her vagina, then licking it, telling her it tasted good."

"Let's face it, a lot of those Republicans who wanted to remove Clinton from office weren't angels themselves. Take that idiot Congressman who went cruising for dick in the men's room of the Minneapolis airport. Frankly, I think the entire Starr Report was a ribald classic."

\*\*\*

Near the end of 1992, the editors at *Time* magazine named Bill Clinton their "Man of the Year." The magazine suggested that "he might lead Americans to dig out of their deepest problems by reimagining themselves."

Shortly thereafter, the December, "end of the year" edition of Bob Guccione's *Penthouse* appeared for sale across the nation. To the Clinton camp's horror, Bill's former mistress, Gennifer Flowers, was featured on the front cover. Inside, she showed it all to the public. And in a feature story, she revealed the most intimate details ever associated, in the history of the Republic, with a Chief Executive's sexual proclivities and performances.

It all began one morning when Gennifer Flower's agent, Blake Hendrix, called to inform her that Hugh Hefner of *Playboy* magazine might be willing to offer her a million dollars for a nude layout and a "tell-all" feature story—a blatant invasion of the most intimate bedtime details of the President-Elect.

Within days, Hef's competitor, Bob Guccione of *Penthouse*, entered the bidding competition, with the almost too-good-to-be-true suggestion that if she posed for *Penthouse*, he might cut her in on the proceeds of the actual sales of the magazine. The tantalizing potentiality that she might make ten million dollars was dangled before her. She was broke at the time.

She realized that her endorsement of this *exposé* might "leave me fixed for life. I would never have to worry about getting a singing gig—or any other job."

Of course, she found Guccione's offer more seductive than Hef's. Consequently, her agent contacted Hef, learning that he would not be willing to match the lucrative offer from his rival at *Penthouse*.

Art Harris, with "his shaved head and steely, penetrating eyes," showed up at Gennifer's apartment. In time, she came to not trust him when she discovered he was probing into her past life too deeply. As a writer for *Penthouse*, he had already been talking to, or planned to talk with, members of her family, a for-

Gennifer Flowers: Before she was a blonde, before revelations of her affair with Bill Clinton, she was a brunette, as shown in this bosomy publicity photo for her gig as a lounge singer.

mer roommate, and people who either knew her or had interacted with her. Although she feared a "hatchet job," she was reassured by Guccione's commitment to her final approval of the feature story before publication.

For Harris, Gennifer made "hot copy," revealing secrets that had never been aired in public about a U.S. President. Although asserting that he had a small penis, she nonetheless rated him nine on a scale of ten as a lover, mainly because of his skill at cunnilingus.

She alleged that he would perform oral sex on her for fifteen minutes or more until she'd say, "Whoa, boy, come on up here." She also revealed that once, when she was performing fellatio on him, "Bill came in my mouth, the first time that ever happened. He later apologized, claiming, 'Sorry, I thought you wanted me to.'"

She lamented that she had experienced very few orgasms with him. "There were times when he made me get those chills, but I've never had my head blown off. He was a predictable lover who favored the old-fashioned missionary position. No golden showers, no anal sex. I've had better lovers, but he was one of the best overall because of his combination of sweetness. All those caring features put him right up there."

In discussing the anatomy of the President-Elect, she revealed that "even though his penis is on the small side, I never put him down for that. No matter what women say, size does matter. But with Bill, I knew that he'd be aggressive with oral sex."

For her nude photo layout, she flew to Los Angeles to be photographed by Earl Miller. Later, she revealed that he was a true professional and did not come on to her at all.

One of Gennifer's overriding concerns was that her mother would—within her *Penthouse* layout—see "The Precious," their nickname for her vagina. She had made a vow to her mother that she would not display "The Precious," but, according to her contract, it was clearly understood that she would have to expose far more than her breasts.

While posing for Miller, Gennifer told him, "I dare Hillary to bare her butt for any magazine. They don't have a page that broad."

Although Miller's photos made Gennifer—at the age of 42—appear at her most alluring, Guccione wanted her to fly to New York so that he, too, could snap pictures of her. With a swimming pool in the basement, and with Picassos and Renoirs hanging on the walls, she found his brownstone rather spooky, especially the all-black bedroom she'd been assigned upstairs.

When she met the publisher, she found him accessorized with the haircut and clothing of the 1970s, complete with lots of gold chains around his neck. At one point, he suggested that he use his mouth on her nipples to harden them, but she rejected his offer, telling him she could get the same effect just by pinching them, as she'd done for Miller in Los Angeles.

Weeks later, when a copy of *Penthouse* was delivered to her, she reacted in horror at the feature story. Guccione had reneged on the clause in her contract granting her final approval of the photos and text. After reading the article, she discovered that she had been portrayed, in the magazine's words, as a "gold-digging, no-talent, bleached blonde bimbo." She had also violated her promise to her mother. "There it was, 'The Precious,' on ample display."

As suggested by a writer for *The Village Voice* in Manhattan, "All of us got to see what drove the talented tongue of our President into ecstasy."

When Flowers began hustling the taped conversations she had secretly recorded of Bill, she wrote: "My motive for releasing the tapes was not to get rich from the proceeds of the sales, but to put the truth out to the American people and to let them hear Bill in his own words prove that he was willing to manipulate and lie."

In her memoir, she concluded: "I really loved Bill, and I believed he loved me, too. I thought what we had was a real relationship between two passionate, caring people, But I learned otherwise. In the end, he turned out to be nothing more than Cardboard Bill—a flat, two-dimensional piece of hardened paper, empty of all feelings."

When the "Gennifer Flowers" edition of *Penthouse* came out, Hef ordered a hundred copies for the headquarters of *Playboy* so his staff could see it. "I'm glad I didn't get into a bidding war with that Guccione prick," he said. "I also didn't expose Vanessa Williams and make her lose her Miss America crown like Guccione did. I just couldn't pull such a hatchet job on Bill Clinton either. Guccione is a bottom-feeder. We at *Playboy* still have some class."

\*\*\*

Born in the Ozark Mountains, Elizabeth Ward (later, Gracen) grew up to become a world-class beauty, winning, when she was 21, the title of Miss Arkansas in 1981, and a year later, Miss America.

Her acting career included an impressive string of roles in—with some exceptions—relatively minor films and TV shows. Her two claims to notoriety were that she had had a one-night stand with then-Governor Bill Clinton, and that she posed nude for Hugh Hefner for a 1992 issue of *Playboy.*

Her family was so poor that for one of her early competitions in Little Rock, she'd made a gown out of her family's peach-colored tablecloth and had embroidered it with rhinestones.

She hoped that her titles would shoehorn her into an acting career. The same year she won the crown, she married her high school sweetheart, Jon Birmingham, and moved to Manhattan to test her luck as an actress.

A year later, she flew back to Little Rock for a charity event, and it was there that she met Bill, who had just been re-elected governor. She was staying at the Quapaw Tower, and apartment complex where Bill was a frequent visitor because of his sexual trysts with Gennifer Flowers. He offered to give Gracen a lift back to the apartment where she was staying.

In the back of the chauffeur-driven Lincoln, he flirted outrageously with her, but did not come upstairs with her. However, three nights later, he called her, and she invited him to come over, since her husband was still in New York.

What transpired later, she dismissed as "one stupid night of love—and not that memorable—but it changed my life, and not necessarily for the better."

Years would go by before she finally admitted to having had sex with Bill. She did recall that night: "It was rough going, and at one point, he bit down hard on my lip." In that accusation, she was echoing Juanita Broaddrick, who claimed that Bill had severely bitten her lip when he'd raped her. But Gracen clearly admitted that her sex with Bill had been consensual.

Their sex act had taken place in an apartment owned by an unnamed friend of Bill's. After that night, she never saw him again. However, he did call her one night in New York when her husband was at home with her. "I pretended he had the wrong number and put down the phone."

"Even though I never heard from Bill in the years to come, I experienced a reign of terror as *Clintonistas* waged war against me and scared the hell out of me."

When Bill ran for President in 1992, Gracen was "outed" as having been one of his mistresses, which she never was. When forced to speak out at all, she consistently denied the liaison.

"I believed that if I had admitted it, Bill

Somehow, by the time the ex-lover of Bill Clinton made it to the cover of *Playboy*, Elizabeth Gracen had simply stopped being sexy. Informal polls define this as probably the least sexy of any *Playboy* cover in recent memory. According to its critics, the sheer embarassment of the "kiss and tell" profile, and Gracen's efforts to avoid being classified with trashier, more bimbo-ish Arkansas paramours of the president, cast a low-libido pall.

would never have been elected President, not with all those revelations about the Gennifer Flowers scandal."

Before this tight and closeup attention, Gracen had been struggling as an actress, and making television commercials. Suddenly, her career blossomed, and, although it was never proven, there were charges that her boost had come through the influence of Hollywood producer Harry Thomason, one of Bill's closest friends.

"I got an acting job starring in *Sands of Time* in Croatia, of all places," she said. "That was followed by a long-lasting role in Brazil. In other words, I was safely out of the country, and away from reporters."

Back in the States, she landed her biggest break when she was given the sword-wielding role in the long-running TV series, *The Highlander* (1992-1998). *[Gracen would later make her directorial debut in the documentary, The Damn Deal (2014), an intimate portrait of three young drag queens from Arkansas who compete in female impersonator beauty pageants.]*

For years, she continued to deny that she'd had sex with Bill, but in 1997, "the shit hit the fan," as she claimed. She was drawn into the notorious Paula Jones sexual harassment lawsuit against the President. Attempts were made to serve her with a subpoena. This came in the wake of testimony from Gracen's former friends, Judy Ann Stokes, who testified under oath that Gracen had admitted to a sexual tryst with the then governor.

Tipped off in advance, Gracen stayed out of the country for months, showing up in Canada for work. She was even seen in Paris.

With a boyfriend, she flew to the Caribbean island of St. Martin. It was here that her room was ransacked and thoroughly searched. A maid reported two men in suits had entered her room while another man stood guard at the door. They left behind $2,000 in cash and an expensive Rolex watch.

Gracen claimed that she suspected that they were looking for sex tapes similar to the ones that Flowers had sold when she'd secretly recorded her conversations with Bill in Little Rock.

Finally, in 1998, after years of denial, Gracen appeared on NBC, admitting to her one night of love—"If that's what you call it"—with Bill Clinton. During her interview, she apologized to Hillary. "What I did was wrong, and I feel sorry about that," she said. "That's not the way a woman should treat another woman."

In the aftermath of her interview, she claimed that she received more threatening calls from the *Clintonistas*, warning her to keep her mouth shut. She also received notification that the IRS would move in on her and would seize her wages and personal property. Eventually, that nightmare came true.

To conclude and summarize her tawdry, long-ago encounter with Bill, she told a reporter, "I just wish that the producers of *The Highlander,* in which I played the immortal avenger with my beheading sword, would give me a chance to cut off Bill's head."

***

In 2011, a poll was taken of *Playboy* readers to determine who they wanted to fill Hef's velvet bedroom slippers when he passed on. In 1988, he had stepped down as chairman and chief executive, although he was still called in for major decisions.

Both *Vanity Fair* and TV's *60 Minutes* released the results of the reader poll. "That professional train wreck," Charlie Sheen, emerged from the polling as the No. One choice to replace Hef. Trailing by only four points was Bill Clinton, still known as "the Playboy President."

In that poll, Clinton beat out pro golfer Tiger Woods, rocker John Mayer, and the Italian prime minister, Silvio Berlusconi, a wildly controversial womanizer.

***

As the world knows, Hef launched his first issue of *Playboy* with a celebrity centerfold, Marilyn Monroe's nude calendar. In the '50s, he also published photos of other undraped celebrities, especially Jayne Mansfield and Brigitte Bardot. But as he told his editorial staff, "I prefer centerfolds who are young, around nineteen or twenty, and who are unknown, the girl next door."

In the 1980s and '90s, however, he underwent a change of heart. Incredibly, some celebrities, who might have been rejected as "over the hill mamas" based on his previous standards, became centerfolds, and quickly emerged as some of *Playboy's* alltime bestsellers.

In 1983, *Playboy* was experiencing financial difficulties until, in the words of one reporter, "an aging actress came to the aid of the beleaguered company."

For the December issue of that year, Joan Collins, age fifty, disrobed for a pictorial. When pictures of her hit the newsstands, the magazine was grabbed up by eager men across the country. At Buckingham Palace, Prince Philip was said to have ordered his manservant to bring him a copy, discreetly, of course.

A minor film star in the 1950s, Collins appeared set to star in the biggest break of her career when she was offered the lead in *Cleopatra* (re-

491

leased in 1963), but she lost the part to Elizabeth Taylor, who starred in it alongside her "real-life" lover, Richard Burton.

Hef had long been fascinated by Collins and had a standing order that all of her films were to be shown on movie nights at his homes in both Chicago and Los Angeles. His favorites were two softcore porn flicks, *The Stud* (1978), and its sequel, *The Bitch* (1979), based on best-selling novels by her younger sister, Jackie.

Hef had been especially captivated by Collins in 1981 when she became a household word. thanks to her role in the second season of the then-struggling TV soap opera, *Dynasty* (1981-89). As Alexis Carrington, she was the stunningly beautiful ex-wife of tycoon Blake Carrington (John Forsythe). Her regal, endlessly manipulative, presence in *haute couture* with designer hats caused Nielsen ratings to soar. *Dynasty* became as big a hit as its TV rival, *Dallas*. Collins later thanked Sophia Loren for rejecting the role.

Hef read in *Vogue* that, "Joan Collins displays her breasts in *Dynasty* as if bra-cup size was a measure of her profound magnificence."

Jackie, her sister, said, "Joan always lived her life like a man. If she saw a guy she wanted to go to bed with, she went after him, and that was unacceptable behavior back in the good old days."

Collins' list of lovers earned her the derogatory title "The British Open." The list was long and impressive, including, among

In the 1950s, 20th Century Fox hailed Joan Collins as the studio's answer to MGM's Elizabeth Taylor. With her sultry looks, she ended up cast in exotic or seductive roles, her leading men including Paul Newman and Gregory Peck.

Joan Collins' renaissance in 1981 as rich bitch oil queen Alexis in *Dynasty*.

In Hollywood in the 50s, Joan Collins was nicknamed "The British Open" because of her many affairs with some of Hollywood's leading men.

In 1983, she posed for the cover of *Playboy* dressed in a seductive red dress because she still looked fabulous and because it was Christmas.

many other conquests, Warren Beatty, Harry Belafonte, Marlon Brando, Sydney Chaplin, producer George Englund, hotel heir Nicky Hilton, Dennis Hopper, David Janssen, cinema chain heir Arthur Loew, Jr., Ryan O'Neal, Terence Stamp, Robert Wagner, etc., etc.

In spite of her age (or perhaps because of it), she agreed to pose for *Playboy*. "I've got a great body," she told Hef. "Sometimes, it looks terrific. If it's photographed right, it can look absolutely great."

**HAIL BRITANNIA!**

As an actress, Joan Collins could change from a tabloid sexpot to a haughty and vaguely menacing *grande dame*.

In 1987, Queen Elizabeth II "elevated" her to a Dame of the British Empire for her work with charities, worldwide, including the International Foundation for Children With Learning Disabilities.

When presented with her nude photos, crafted (at her insistence) by the most prominent photographer from the most glamorous era of Hollywood, George Edward Hurrell (1904-1992), Hef agreed with her assessment. He ordered them configured, during the peak of Joan's *Dynasty*-related fame, into a 12-page pictorial in *Playboy* to display her assets.

In 2015, Queen Elizabeth made Collins a "Dame" of the British Empire—not for her sexual conquests, and certainly not for her *Playboy* centerfold, but for her charity work.

\*\*\*

Many other celebrity centerfolds followed in the wake of Joan Collins' nude debut.

"A Georgia peach," Kim Basinger, was famously (and disastrously) married (1993-2002) to Alex Baldwin. A successful model in New York in the 1970s, she had gravitated to Hollywood.

Ironically, before posing for Hef, she starred in *Katie, Portrait of a Centerfold* in 1978, in which she played a small-town girl who goes to Hollywood to become an actress, ending up as a centerfold for a popular men's magazine.

In 1981, she posed for a nude pictorial for *Playboy*. But her layout didn't appear until two years later, when she authorized its release to help publicize her role as "The Bond Girl" in *Never Say Never Again* (1983), starring Sean Connery as Master Spy James Bond.

Basinger later credited her winning a star role to her nude layout in *Playboy*. In 1984, she appeared on the screen opposite Robert Red-

In 1983, Sean Connery returned to the screen as the James Bond character in the Warners' release *Never Say Never Again*.

He ended up in the arms of Kim Basinger, the most alluring "Bond Girl" in years. The actress was largely unknown at the time, but her performance as Domino made her a star.

In February of 1983, Hef put her on the cover of *Playboy*.

ford in *The Natural*. The part brought her a Golden Globe nomination as Best Supporting Actress. She went on to win a Best Supporting Oscar for her performance in *L.A. Confidential* (1997).

\*\*\*

The smashing list of centerfold celebs continued with the undraped appearance, in *Playboy's* issue of August 2001, of Belinda Carlisle, a child of Hollywood who gained worldwide fame as the lead singer of the "Go-Gos," one of the most successful female bands of all time, selling more than seven million records around the globe.

Born to a gas jockey in 1958, she was named for her mother's favorite film, *Johnny Belinda* (1948), in which Jane Wyman (Mrs. Ronald Reagan) delivered an Oscar-winning performance.

After the band split up in 1985, Belinda pursued a solo career. In 1986, she married producer Morgan Mason, the son of the distinguished actor James Mason. She later admitted to extensive drug abuse, telling *The Guardian*, "I don't believe I'm not dead." In time, she recovered and discovered Buddhism, and she also wrote her autobiography, *Lips Unsealed*.

Over the years, she became known for her support of many worthwhile causes, including LGBTQ rights. This came in the wake of her son, James Duke Mason, "outing" himself at the age of fourteen.

*** 

To the horror of the Jackson family, La Toya Jackson, sister of Michael Jackson, became a centerfold in the March 1989 issue of *Playboy*. A singer and songwriter on her own, she first gained recognition appearing on the family's TV variety show, *The Jacksons* on CBS beginning in 1976. In time, she made her own recordings, one of her most successful being the hit 1984 single, "Heart Don't Lie."

When she posed topless for *Playboy*, she claimed it was a declaration of her independence from her dominating family and her conservative upbringing in Gary, Indiana. "I wanted to show my mother and father they could no longer dictate my lifestyle," she told Hef. "I wanted them to realize that I was now in charge of my own life."

In November of 1991, she posed once again for *Playboy* to promote her autobiography, *La Toya: Growing Up in the Jackson Family*. In her book she shocked her fans when she charged her father with physical abuse.

La Toya caused even more controversy when she became one of the first celebrities to pose for a *Playboy* video. Released in 1994, it sold 50,000 copies. She later told the press that at first, she had refused to star in the video, but was forced into performing in it because of her domineering husband, Jack Gordon. After his takeover of her career, he promoted a much sexier image of his wife, which led to her being "disfellowshipped" by Jehovah's Witnesses.

As Hef later learned, La Toya fled from Gordon when she learned he was planning for her to star in a porno flick. She escaped from him in

As a "declaration of independence" from her chart-topping family, more celebrity skin and spin was provided by La Toya Jackson as the cover girl and the centerfold within both the U.S. edition of *Playboy* (left), and its spicier Italian counterpart.

*Variety* reported that La Toya "looks far sexier than Michael Jackson, even if (she's) only sucking her finger."

1997 and filed for divorce. She claimed, "I was beaten, abused, controlled, and forced to tell the press horrible things about my brother, Michael, which I did not believe for a moment. Before Michael's death, he forgave me."

\*\*\*

Under Hef's order, *Playboy* celebrity centerfolds continued prominently throughout the 1990s. One of the most stunning centerfolds appeared in the issue of March 1992. The model was "Vickie Smith," who later became notorious after reverting to her birth name of Anna Nicole Smith. She became one of the magazine's most popular models and in 1993, was designated as Playboy of the Year.

It was the same year that Hef invited her to share his bed three times.

As a model and actress, Smith didn't seem to object to seducing octogenarian millionaires. Her second marriage, in 1994, was to 89-year-old J. Howard Marshall, a billionaire who owned sixteen percent of Koch Industries [*America's second largest privately held company*], and whose life had been actively involved as an investor in almost the entire history of the oil industry. He died fourteen months after his marriage, resulting in an estate battle that went all the way to the U.S. Supreme Court.

Like her idol and role model, Marilyn Monroe, Anna Nicole was dead before she turned forty. Her corpse was discovered in a Hollywood, Florida, hotel room, and her death was attributed to an overdose of prescription drugs.

\*\*\*

Nobody ever said fortune-hunting wasn't sexy. *Playboy* got their money's worth when it came to "packaging" Anna Nicole Smith. Here are illustrations of some of the ways her very voluptuous, big-bosomed images were marketed.

Many other centerfolds had lives that were sodden with drug abuse and alcohol. Such was the case of the actress, Drew Barrymore, who had experienced a turbulent childhood She was the daughter of a minor actor, John Drew Barrymore, and the granddaughter of the legendary actor John Barrymore, star of stage and screen. *Playboy* had already run a topless picture of Drew's godmother, Sophia Loren.

Even before her appearance in *Playboy*, Drew was no stranger to being photographed nude. For the July 1992 issue of *Interview*, magazine, she had posed for photographer Bruce Weber, nude, with her fiancé, actor Jamie Walters. The year before, she had released her autobiography, *Little Girl Lost*.

At the age of nineteen, she posed nude for Hef, and he made her a centerfold in his January 1995 issue.

Her godfather, Steven Spielberg, had cast Drew in his *E.T. The Extra-Terrestrial* in 1982. After seeing her centerfold in *Playboy*, he sent her a quilt for her 20th birthday with a note to "Cover Up!"

Drew was daring even on TV. She made an appearance on *The Late Show with David Letterman* in celebration of his birthday. She got up on his desk and bared her breasts to him with her back to the camera.

In an interview in 2003 with *Contact Music*, she said, "I have always considered myself bisexual."

***

Descended from a line of Hollywood superstars noted for their debauchery and fast burnouts, Drew Barrymore seemed to pursue the exhibitionistic examples set by her legendary grandfather.

She followed her breakthrough appearance as an *ingénue* in the teen-friendly science fiction blockbuster, *E.T.* (1982) with layouts, at the age of 19, in both the U.S. (top) and Taiwanese editions of *Playboy*.

Many models were already famous when they posed for centerfolds; others used their exposure in the magazine to launch successful careers in show business.

Jenny McCarthy, sometimes credited as Jenny Wahlberg, was Playmate of the Month for October 1993. When Hef first spotted her, he interpreted her as a "wholesome Catholic girl," and ordered his staff to pay her $20,000 to pose. A year later, in 1994, he selected her from among 10,000 applicants as Playmate of the Year. From there, she went on to become an actress, model, and co-host on the MTV game show, *Singled Out*. In time, she was also designated as one of the co-hosts of the ABC Talk Show, *The View*, which exposed her to millions of viewers, mostly women.

She later wrote about parenting and became an activist promoting research into environmental causes and alternative medical treatments for autism, a disease from which her son suffered.

For her role as Playmate of the Year, she received $100,000. For a while, she also became a host on *Hot Rocks*, a TV show featuring uncensored music videos.

She appeared again in the September 1997 issue of *Playboy*, and the magazine continued, over the years, to use her as a model. As late as 2005, she was on the cover, wearing a leopard-skin version of the company's iconic Bunny suit. She was also featured in a pictorial shot at Elvis Presley's Graceland in the same issue.

Her younger sister, Amy McCarthy, also posed for *Playboy* in 2004, and again in January of 2005.

***

When Nancy Sinatra, the daughter of Frank Sinatra, posed for *Playboy* for its May 1995 issue, she was accused of disgracing him and came under heavy fire from fans of Ol' Blue Eyes. At the time that she was promoting herself—not only in *Playboy* but on various TV shows, too—she was hyping her new album, *One More Time*. Today, she's mostly remembered for her widely known hit single, released in 1966, "These Boots Are Made for Walking."

Born in 1940, Nancy Sinatra was 54 years old when she posed for *Playboy* and was in fabulous physical condi-

Frank Sinatra was particularly nervous about his daughter Nancy Jr., on two occasions—one when she appeared with Elvis Presley in *Speedway* (1968), and again in 1995 when she posed for *Playboy*, opting to wear knee-high boots as a reference to her long-ago hit song.

He phoned Hef, telling him, "As far as Nancy is concerned, you can look—but don't touch, or I'll send the boys after you."

tion. After seeing her pictorial, one writer said, "Ben Franklin would have been proud." *[The statement doesn't make sense unless you know that Franklin had once written about the glory of making love to older women.]*

Across the talk show circuit, Nancy claimed that her father was "proud of the photos." She said that when she told him what Hef was paying her for the spread, he said, "Tell him to double it!"

When (Frank) Sinatra was on Jay Leno's talk show, he claimed that his grandchildren –Nancy Sinatra's two daughters, Angela and Amanda—had approved of their mother posing for *Playboy* before she had agreed to face the camera.

\*\*\*

The beautiful and likable blonde from Texas, Farrah Fawcett, rose to international fame when she posed, in 1976, for an iconic red swimsuit poster. It sold 20 million copies, making it the best-selling pin-up poster in history.

Its success led to her starring role as a private investigator, Jill Monroe, in the first season (1976-77) of the hit TV series, *Charlie's Angels*. By 1996, she was ranked No. 26 on *TV Guide's* "Fifty Greatest TV Stars of All Time."

She had never been opposed to nudity, having appeared topless in the 1988 film *Saturn 3* opposite Kirk Douglas.

Her body was remarkably well-preserved at the age of fifty, when she agreed to pose as cen-

BLONDE AND AMERICAN
THE ULTIMATE INTERNATIONAL COVER GIRL

Farrah Fawcett-Majors, at the end of her often traumatized life, ended up on a lot of *Playboy* covers, worldwide.

The two upper photos are replicas of two of Playboy's U.S. editions. The one on the lower left is for an Australian edition, and the one on the lower right is one of the German editions.

terfold in *Playboy's* issue of December 1995. She returned two years later for an encore session with a *Playboy* photographer.     Hef studied her photographs, calling her "the forever astonishing Farrah."

From 1979 to 1997, Fawcett was romantically linked to Ryan O'Neal. Their relationship produced a son, Redmond James, who would go on to lead a troubled life.

During the courtship of "Farrah & Ryan," *Playboy* editors proposed that Hef should try to persuade the lovers to pose for a nude pictorial. He mulled it over for a while, but finally decided not to pitch the idea to the pair.

Fawcett died of anal cancer in 2009. The magazine, *Men's Health,* listed her as No. 31 on its posting of "The 100 Hottest Women of All Time." The hit song, "Midnight Train to Georgia," was said to have been inspired by Fawcett and Lee Majors.

\*\*\*

A Philadelphia beauty, Kelly Monaco, a former lifeguard, dreamed of a career in modeling. To call attention to herself, she sent a revealing photo of herself to *Playboy.* Eventually, it worked its way up to Hef's bedroom, where he studied it in some detail. "This girl has something."

She was summoned to *Playboy's* headquarters for a photo shoot. It was so successful that it led to her designation as Playmate of the Month in the April 1997 issue. That went over so well that she was later featured in many *Playboy Special Edition* publications.

She parlayed this exposure into a career as an actress and Reality TV personality. She is known for her portrayal of Sam McCall on the hit ABC-TV soap opera, *General Hospital.*

\*\*\*

Before the end of the 90s, Hef did the unthinkable by running a pictorial of a female figure skater, Katharina Witt, from East Germany. Up till then, he had considered athletes he'd seen from the Soviet Union and East Germany

Hailing from East Germany, Katarina Witt was "A Queen on Ice" and one of the world's greatest skaters.

After she agreed to pose for *Playboy*, she changed forever Hef's beliefs about female athletes.

"Amazonian, perhaps lesbians, even men disguised in women's clothing."

Witt had won two Olympic gold medals for East Germany—first in 1984 at Sarajevo, the second in 1988 at Calgary. She was a four-time world champion figure skater (1984, 1985, 1987, and 1998).

Her skating costumes were criticized by some sports fans as being "too theatrical, too sexy." But not for Hef, who was deeply impressed with her appearances on TV.

His agents contacted her and invited her to pose for a *Playboy* pictorial. At the age of 32, she agreed to do it. Much to Hef's surprise, it became one of the alltime bestselling issues of his magazine.

She told Hef, "I don't care for the cute, pretty Sonja Henie Ice Princess image of most figure skaters, and I wanted to change people's perceptions."

\*\*\*

There is no doubt about it: Hef viewed Pamela Anderson as the ultimate sex symbol of the 1990s. She became his Playmate of the Month for the February 1990 issue and went on to become Playmate of the Year. Over an amazing period of 33 years, she would appear on the cover more than a dozen times.

Born in 1967 in the cool summer winds of British Columbia, Pamela in time would head south to Los Angeles to pursue a career as a model

Thanks in large part to Hef's massive exposure of Pamela Anderson in several editions of *Playboy*, Pamela Anderson became the reigning sex symbol of the 1990s.

She has been linked to such notorious figures as Vladimir Putin (left) and Julian Assange. But are all those rumors splashing around really true?

and actress.

She made it clear that she wanted to appear in *Playboy* and subsequently received an invitation to the Los Angeles *Playboy* Mansion.

She revealed in 2014 that as a child, she had suffered much abuse: Molested from ages 6 to 10 by a female babysitter; raped by a 25-year-old man when she was 12; and gang-raped by her then boyfriend and six of his buddies when she was 14.

After her debut and a lot of help from Hef, she was hailed in Hollywood as the biggest blonde bombshell since Marilyn Monroe.

On the British television chat show, *Piers Morgan Life Stories,* she discussed her first visit to the Playboy Mansion. "Everyone was nude in the Grotto. I took it all in. Later, I followed Hef and seven girls to his bedroom. I stood at the foot of the bed watching them until I realized they were watching me. I thought it was time for me to leave."

"There was a lot of craziness going on," she said. "A lot of Bunnies and a lot of Johnson's Baby Oil, Hef's favorite lubricant."

On Morgan's show, she spoke of being pursued by lots of other men, lots and lots of them. "Sylvester Stallone offered to give me a condo and a Porsche if I would become his No. 1 girl. I turned him down…Maybe I shouldn't have."

She confessed that as a teenager, she had dreamed of marrying her favorite singer, the King of Pop, Michael Jackson. In Hollywood, she dated him on occasion, "but nothing happened, so I abandoned that plan." That did not come as a shock to the TV audience.

What did shock them was the suggestion of a possible romance between herself and Vladimir Putin. An animal rights activist, she'd traveled to Moscow, asking him to intervene in saving the seals. She refused to say how far their flirtation went.

After their first *Playboy* shoot, Pamela claimed she underwent breast implant surgery, enhancing her bosom to a bust size of 34D.

After the *Playboy* exposure, she was cast in a role that made her a household name, that of C.J. Parker in TV's *Baywatch,* appearing in it for five seasons (1992-1997).

In February of 1995, after knowing him for only four days, Pamela married Tommy Lee, a drummer for Mötley Crüe. Early in their marriage, they made a private sex tape, which was leaked and went viral, becoming what is perhaps the most-viewed sex tape of all time.

When she posed for her next *Playboy* cover, she told Hef, "My breasts have a career of their own, and I just tag along. It has always been an interesting fascination for me, as they kind of expand on camera."

Throughout her long association with *Playboy,* Anderson made special appearances in the publication's newsstand specials, writing the forward, for example, to the company's coffee table book, *Playboy's Greatest Covers.*

In her final call from Hef, he asked her to pose for the magazine's "last nude cover," which was a 12-page pictorial in the January/February 2016 edition of the magazine. *Playboy* had announced that it was ending its long tradition of featuring nudity, a policy that was later rescinded.

At first Pamela, age 48, had been reluctant to pose for *Playboy.* However, she talked it over with her two sons, who were teenagers, and they urged their Mom to "go for it."

After seeing her layouts, the staff at *Ask Men* wrote, "Hate her or love her, it may take 55 years before a centerfold as popular as Pam Anderson comes along."

"At the last shot, Hef showed up," she said. "I didn't realize it at the time, but he was bidding me farewell. He looked like he was in a lot of pain, and he needed a walker. He was always kind and a gentleman to me, and I never felt exploited."

Pamela's final advice to the *Playboy* reader (something the editors added as an amplification of "just her photos") was something she said she had learned from her aunt: "A girl needs three men in her life: One for sex, one for conversation, another for entertainment."

During the autumn of her long and notorious career, Pamela knew how to keep herself in the limelight. She began a rumored affair with WikiLeaks founder, Julian Assange within the Ecuadorian Embassy in London, into which Assange had fled to escape from extradition based on charges of rape in Sweden. *[In 2017, Sweden dropped the charges.]*

She had been introduced to Assange in 2014 by Vivienne Westwood, the British fashion designer and WikiLeaks acolyte who regularly visited Assange at the Ecuadorian Embassy, and who even dedicated her spring/summer 2017 collection to him. Assange was said to have always had a 'deep crush' on Pamela.

Assange had been holed up in the embassy for six years. Even after Sweden dropped their charges against him, he still believed that if he left the safety of the embassy, he would face charges in Britain over a parole violation. He was also apprehensive that he might be extradited to the United States to face charges for distributing secret (and stolen) government documents.

Pamela made frequent visits to the Ecuadorian Embassy to see Assange, and she and her pneumatic bosom always showed up camera ready. Sometimes she'd be dressed entirely in black from her sky-high heels to her second-skin turtleneck, a black scarf covering her blonde hair.

London tabloids nicknamed Assange and Pamela as "The Odd Couple."

On March 28, 2016, Ecuador announced it was revoking Assange's visitation privileges. Pamela protested the ban to the press. "This is the equivalent of torture. No visitors. No Internet, No link to the outside world. I'm concerned for his health and well-being."

"I've spent more time talking to Julian than to all of my ex-husbands."

*\*\*\**

In 1994, Hef came up with a wicked scheme to strike back at Ronald Reagan for all the pain and financial losses he had suffered at the hands of the Meese Commission during its "porn purges" of the 1980s.

He'd read reports that Reagan and his wife Nancy (the former MGM starlet Nancy Davis) had a rebellious daughter, Patti Davis, and a son, Ron Reagan, Jr., not quite as rebellious.

So as not to be politically associated with her father's politics, Patti had taken her mother's surname.

It was a long shot, but Hef asked his editors if one or two of them would approach Patti and toss out the idea of her posing for a *Playboy* centerfold. She was 41 years old at the time, but from all reports, looked youthful and attractive, with a firm body from frequent workouts.

To his surprise, for the July 1994 issue, Patti agreed to pose for the magazine as a full-frontal nude. The issue would also depict her on its cover.

Patti Davis, the errant daughter of Ronald and Nancy Reagan, shocked more than her parents when she posed, nude, for graphic layouts in *Playboy.*

Even for conservative Reaganites (or their enemies) who might never have looked inside, the cover itself stirred up widespread interest and/or horror with more than a hint of *schadenfreude.* It displayed an African-American man, while fondling her breasts, posing with Patti in a gleefully erotic layout.

Hef—perhaps in an act of revenge against politicians who had persecuted him—fully realized how embarrassing his "exposé" of the First Daughter would be. Friends and foes of Nancy doubted if she'd ever recover.

Hef came up with photo layout idea, which he almost swore Patti would reject. [*To his surprise, she went for it.*]

She would be photographed naked from the waist up, directly facing the camera. A dark-skinned African American male model, standing behind her, would cup each of her breasts in his hands. The headline would read: RONALD REAGAN'S REBELLIOUS DAUGHTER.

"The issue sold like hot cakes," Hef said. "Even female readers rushed to buy it to see how far the Reagan daughter would go. It became one of the most controversial covers I ever published."

Patti went even farther, appearing in a video, "Playboy Celebrity Centerfold," which depicted her cavorting in a lesbian setting outdoors, followed by a masturbation scene.

Reporters hailed her *Playboy* debut as "Patti Making History."

About 17 years later, at the age of 58, Patti Davis showed off her body once again, this time for a nude study in *More* magazine. In an article by Whitney Jefferson, she was quoted as saying: "My kickboxing teacher told me my body was in even better shape than it was when I posed for Hefner's *Playboy*. The night before the shoot, I stood in front of a full-length mirror and agreed he was right: My muscles were leaner, longer, more defined. I felt a sense of victory over the years of abuse I'd subjected my body to, and also over the huge amount of time I'd wasted on addiction. With every workout, I feel as if I'm winning back lost time."

She revealed that at the age of 15, she discovered both "pharmaceutical amphetamines" as well as speed, available as tiny white tablets cooked up in home labs and sold on the street. "The sound of pills was a lullaby in a bottle in the pain of my soul," Patti said. "I went from speed to coke, and by the time I was in my twenties, my muscles were thin and barely visible."

"Finally, I did give up drugs, grabbing on some rope in my heart that I hadn't known was there. A stubborn determination took over, that buried part of me that wanted to survive. I resolved to work my way back to healthy. The self-medicating, the wasted youth. That was behind me now. I succeeded in pulling myself out of a hole to begin living instead of just surviving."

"I knew I would be attacked for posing nude, but I didn't care. I wasn't doing it to spite my parents, as it was reported. I was doing it for me. This was my victory lap. This was standing naked in front of the world when it was a miracle that I was still in this world. I am proof that it isn't easy to die. Since I was a teenager, I was working on dying. Most addicts are."

"There are years of distance between the strong woman I am now, and the wasted girl I once was."

"For this new century, I planned to live the kind of life many playboys did in their twenties and thirties," Hef said. "Many of my contemporary playboys, including a lot of male movie stars past their prime, could be seen hobbling around in such places as Palm Springs or Arizona. Not me!"

"Over a drink these old farts, particularly if they were in show business, would brag about 'the night I fucked Ava Gardner,' or 'the night I fucked Lana Turner.' Inevitably, they will relate at least a one-night stand with Marilyn Monroe, real or imagined."

For Hef, yesterday was dead and gone, the memories of which were growing dimmer as each year passed. He was no longer the pioneering publisher who had launched *Playboy* during a more repressive era. He was no longer the champion of civil rights, or a warrior crossing new frontiers in the Sexual Revolution.

He was more like a Roman Emperor nearing the end of his reign, experiencing Viagra-fueled orgies with a coven of beautiful young women "plucked like lush fruit from the vine" (his assessment).

His former Playmates had grown old and had scattered, unnoticed, across the American landscape, many of them grey-haired and living lives as grandmothers. He said, "Marilyn Monroe was right in her refrain in 'Diamonds Are a Girl's Best Friend,' when she warned, 'We all lose our charms in the end.'"

On one of his last public outings, Hef went with his brother Keith to the home of Elizabeth Taylor, who had visited the Playboy Mansion on many an occasion. Both of them were aging, and he was in a reflective mood.

He sat in her living room surrounded by her friends. Unknown to him, a reporter from *Variety,* Brett McCallum, was among the guests.

Later, to Hef's regret, McCallum submitted a "hatchet piece" to *Variety* for publication. In it, he wrote, "Hugh Hefner, the aging Romeo of yesterday, needs fresh blood like Dracula, preferably girls born in the 1980s, who want to grow up to join the Immoral Majority."

According to Hef, "After my latest marital break-up, it's time for me to enjoy the decades of my labor, to reap the harvest of my endeavors. Girls, girls, girls. Bring on the buxom blondes. No more commitment for me. I'm not husband material—far from it."

"For the first time in my life, I want to do nothing but seek self-fulfillment, to live according to my own desires. Since I will soon be leaving the planet, I want to end my life free from cares and woes. Why face the end carrying a heavy burden? My empire will have to be run by others. Let them take the blows I once suffered."

"For the septuagenarian, group sex is the answer. You can often find stimulation voyeuristically watching others get it on: Man on woman, woman on woman, man on man. All this helps you sustain an erection, that and Viagra. For the octogenarian, the human mouth is a good stimulant, along with only the freshest and most virginal of women. Of course, they should be of legal age. No man wants to get arrested as a pedophile."

"At the dawn of the 21st Century, I have come to feel like a Sultan presiding over his harem of nubile beauties, like those cartoons we used to run in *Playboy*."

"I still need a steady girlfriend. In olden days, it would be known as the 'Sultan's favorite.' In my case, I went through a period where I needed a trio of chief girlfriends, for which I would impose certain rules."

After listening politely to Hef's reflections, Dame Elizabeth signaled her waiter to bring more champagne. "Let's toast Hef," she said. "He gives hope to all of us. Let's keep falling in love until they come to take us to the crematorium."

***

"At this time a young beauty from Oregon entered my life. A 'talent scout' of mine spotted her working as a waitress at a branch of Hooters." Hef invited her to the Playboy Mansion

"The first time I saw Holly Madison, I wanted her and was determined to have her," he confided to Keith. "I found out she was twenty when eighteen might have been more enticing, but twenty was still young enough. I set about to launch myself into a new sexual adventure."

Born in Astoria, Oregon, in 1979, the blonde beauty, Holly Madison, lived for a time in the cold wilderness of Alaska. Returning to her home state when she grew older, she enrolled in Portland State University for two years, studying theater and psychology. Afterward, she transferred to Loyola Marymount University in Los Angeles.

One night, when an associate of Hef's invited her to the Los Angeles Playboy Mansion, she eagerly accepted. "I wondered if I'd meet Gatsby himself, Mr. Hugh Hefner."

It took a bit of time, but Hef did approach her, singling her out for personal attention. According to Madison, "He had a bunch of "horse pills" in a tissue which he held out to me."

"Would you like a Quaalude?" he asked.

"No, thanks," she said. "I don't do drugs."

"That's okay with me," he answered. "Usually I don't approve of drugs, but in the '70s, these pills were called 'thigh openers.'"

After "a night of too much vodka, too much champagne," she remembered stumbling along with seven other girls to Hef's bedroom. Once there, she saw screens showing porn, including *Behind the Green Door* (1972), starring Marilyn Chambers.

As Hef lay flat on his back, the other girls took their turns mounting him. "My turn came," Holly revealed in her memoirs. "It was over before it had really begun. Other girls took over for a quickie."

Awakening in the Mansion the following day with a hangover, she sought Hef out, finding him in his library. At the time, she had no place to stay, and she asked him if she could move into the Mansion.

After thinking about it and looking her over, he said, "You can stay here for a while, and we'll see how it works out."

It took a few weeks, but Hef got around to making her his No. One Girlfriend, providing she followed certain rules of the house. Her main duty was participating in Hef's bizarre bedroom orgies.

"He would watch porn to stimulate himself, smoke pot, and jerk off while the girls around him pretended to be getting off on each other. We would take turns pleasuring Hef, but he always finished off by himself."

"He constantly created drama and infighting by randomly changing his policy of favoring one girl over another. He also demanded that girls be in before a nine o'clock curfew. He told us how he wanted us to dress, preferring over-the-top clothing, sort of trashy outfits including BeDazzled rhinestone *bustiers* or skirts so short there was little point in wearing them."

At the end of every week, Hef called the girls in to give them $1,000 in hundred-dollar bills. "He also paid for plastic sur-

Installed in the *Playboy* Mansion as Hef's No.1 mistress, Holly Madison had good days and bad.

On one particularly bad day, Hef told her, "You look old, hard, and cheap."

She lived in the Playboy Mansion in L.A. from 2003 to 2008.

gery for his girls," Holly said. "Mostly, they were boob jobs, but also nose alterations, even liposuction."

At the frequent parties Hef hosted, he ordered his girls to follow a certain protocol, remaining clustered at his private table. "Dancing was permitted, providing it was done in front of him, and we were allowed brief bathroom breaks," Holly said. "By one in the morning, he always retired and we had to follow him for an orgy. After it was over, all of us had to dress in pink flannel pajamas, always pink."

After several months of living with Hef, as revealed in Holly's memoirs, this 76-year-old man told her he wanted to spend the rest of his life with her. "My rivals had once mocked me, but suddenly were kissing my ass because of my new status as Mistress of the Mansion. They brought me gifts and showered me with compliments about my beauty."

\*\*\*

Other Playmates from that era later spoke or wrote about their time at the Mansion, too. Carla Howe told *The Mirror,* "It was like being with a grandad. Once a nurse was called in when Hef had taken a fall in the Grotto."

Jill Ann Spaulding, in her book *Jill Ann: Upstairs,* said, "When the orgy in his bedroom gets started, his main girlfriend performs oral sex on him, then he has sex with a series of girls with no protection. He just lies there with his Viagra erection. It's a fake erection, and each girl gets on top of him for two minutes while the girls hovering around try to keep him excited, calling out, 'Fuck her, Daddy!'"

"Maybe it was the pot and the alcohol," Holly said, "but drowning myself seemed like the logical way to escape the ridiculous life I was leading."

\*\*\*

Two other blondes entered Hef's life, Kendra Wilkinson, destined to be Girl No. 2, and another, Bridget Marquardt, Girl No. 3.

Born in San Diego in 1985, Kendra was the youngest of what became Hef's famous

*Jill Ann*

*Jill Ann Spaulding*

Former Playboy model, Jill Ann Spaulding, noted for her sexy large bosom, wrote: "My story is about the realization that the Playboy Mansion isn't Barbie's dream house, but a brokerage house where dangerous sex is traded for stardom."

triangle of lovers. In time, she would be far more than Hef's girlfriend, morphing into a TV personality, businesswoman, glamour model, and author.

"Everything just happened after I got my boobs done," she confessed. When her father left home when she was four, she was reared by a single mom. She left home herself during her teens and entered what she called "the dark period of my life."

She was working as a model when she was first invited to the Los Angeles Mansion where Hef was celebrating his 78th birthday in 2004. For the event, she had been hired as one of the "painted girls." (That is, she was nude except for the painted images temporarily adorning her body.) Her job was to parade around and be ogled by men.

"That first night I met all these celebs, including Jack Nicholson, and I was naked. It was weird. As a girl, I wanted to be a marine biologist. Now look at me."

With her voluptuous figure and youthful beauty, she immediately attracted Hef's eye. Within the week, he invited her to move into the Mansion.

She quickly agreed. "It was like, hell, yeah!" she said. "I was living in this small-ass apartment with this ugly-ass bitch. I was praying for anything to get me out of there. When I moved in with Hef, I had just graduated from high school."

Months before, she had developed a drug habit, but "had gone cold turkey and had beaten the odds." The Mansion was like a safe haven for her.

"Hef is the greatest guy in the world," she said. "You always hear guys say they want to be Hugh Hefner. He helped give me a direction, a motivation for life."

"All of a sudden, I found myself waking up in the Playboy Mansion at noon every day, I listen to music, order breakfast, take a shower, brush my teeth, masturbate, and maybe go to the gym for a spin class."

"I realized that having sex with Hef would be part of my duties. It was like a job where you clock in, clock out. It's not like I enjoy hav-

Kendra Wilkinson, in her memoir, *Sliding Into Home*, was one of the stars of *The Girls Next Door* as well as a *Playboy* cover model

In her tell-all, she opens up about life, love, and living with Hugh Hefner: "Looking into Hef's eyes, I knew there was nothing to fear, and Mansion or no Mansion, I was drawn to him in a way that I had never been drawn to a man before."

ing sex with him. After about a minute riding on top of him, I pull away and it's done. Job over! I'm free for the rest of the day."

"I wasn't thinking about how much older Hef was—all the parts worked," she said, "the same way even at his age. At the end of the day, a body is a body."

"I had a boyfriend at the time, name of Zack. Sex with him was the greatest. But Hef made me feel special, loved, and pretty. Isn't that all a girl really wants out of a boyfriend?"

"I knew that moving into the Mansion was a risk, but I also knew I had little to lose. In my gut, I knew it was a good idea, but I worried a bit about what I was getting myself into."

[*Kendra would make these revelations in a memoir,* Sliding Into Home, *published in 2010. Its publisher promoted it with the claim, "Kendra bares all."*]

Steady girl No. 3, Bridget Marquardt, was another blonde beauty, the oldest of the trio, having been born in Oregon back in the "ancient" year of 1973.

Shortly after her birth, her mother moved the family to California where Bridget grew up.

Unlike many Bunnies and Playmates, Bridget had a formal education, receiving a bachelor's in communications from California State University. In 2001, she earned her master's degree at the University of the Pacific.

As she blossomed into the glory of young womanhood, she was praised for her looks and body, and it was suggested that she send a cheesecake photo of herself to *Playboy*, asking how she might become a candidate for Playmate of the Month, knowing that would mean a nude exposure.

In 1998, at the age of 25, she entered *Playboy's* Millennium Playmate search. In the meantime, she supported herself by doing modeling and the occasional acting bit part.

After two unsuccessful tests for *Playboy*, she was nonetheless invited to the Mansion, where she proved to be so popular she became a regular.

In a matter of weeks, Hef not only invited her to move in, but asked her to become a steady girlfriend, joining Kendra and Holly.

Bridget Marquardt became the third model to star on the hit TV show, *The Girls Next Door.*

"Being in *Playboy* was the number one thing for me from a very young age. As soon as I saw those pages, I knew that was what I wanted to be."

"I didn't see it for the nudity, I saw it for, 'Ah, those girls are beautiful.' I hope I'm that beautiful when I grow up."

As Hef's girlfriend, Bridget found him "charismatic and a gentleman who's just a little kid at heart, which makes him really fun. He's also inspirational because of all he's accomplished. He lives the lifestyle he wants to live and doesn't care what people think."

"I told Hef that as a child, I didn't dream of being a Disney Princess. After I saw my father's copy of *Playboy*, I wanted to be featured in the magazine. That was my goal in life."

Bridget never achieved her dream of becoming a Playmate, but she did receive wide exposure on film and in the media. With Holly and Kendra, she was photographed for three cover pictorials in *Playboy:* November 2005, September 2006, and March 2009. She also appeared with Hef and usually with Holly and Kendra in a number of filmed events, including an TV episode of *Curb Your Enthusiasm* in 2005.

In 2009, she made her final appearance in *Playboy* in a nude pictorial with Holly and Kendra, touted as a farewell for *Playboy's* TV series (2005-2010) *The Girls Next Door (aka The Girls of the Playboy Mansion)*.

\*\*\*

It had been in collaboration with the producer Kevin Burns that Hef had devised the idea for a TGV reality series. Originally entitled *The Girls of the Playboy Mansion*, its name was later changed to *The Girls Next Door*, running on *E!* from 2005 until 2010. It starred his three steady girlfriends: Holly Madison, Kendra Wilkinson, and Bridget Marquandt. Hef made frequent appearances on it with Playmates and other celebrities.

In addition to exploring the lives the girls led, the series showcased various events at the Mansion as interpreted by *Playboy*. They included, among others, the Fourth of July, the raucous Midsummer's Night celebration, various Playmate test shoots, wild party nights. Outside the Mansion, the show featured scenes from the Jazz Festival at the Hollywood Bowl, and followed the girls heading for Aspen to ski on its slopes, or visiting New York or Chicago.

The series was an instant hit on *E!*, reach-

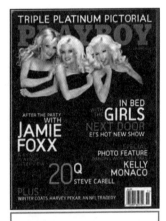

The three platinum blondes from *The Girls Next Door* were featured on this cover: Holly Madison, Kendra Wilkinson, and Bridget Marquardt.

A subhead read: "In Bed with the Girls Next Door."

Cynics complained that a better description of the girls on the cover would be: "In Bed with Hef," a prerequisite that many within *Playboy's* orbit considered necessary for a starring role in the series.

ing 2.16 million viewers by the third season. TV critics called Hef's appearances "grandfatherly."

Each personality within the trio of beauties turned out to be different, although Holly clearly emerges as the dominant mistress. Network executives expected the series to be mainly male, but a survey found the audience was composed of about 70 percent female viewers.

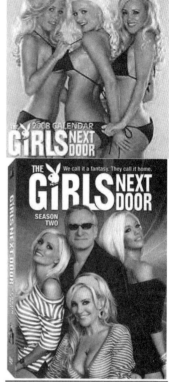

Hef spend his time on camera "holding, hugging, or kissing" his Playmates.

He conceived the character for each girl: Kendra as the fun lover; Bridget as the career girl; and Holly as "the one who cares about me."

The series had its tender moments, as when Bridget, through a stream of tears, claimed that she had auditioned to become a centerfold, but never made it.

Hef's romances with his trio of lovelies had ended by the time Season Six was aired. In the final episode of Season Five, Holly was seen discussing her unhappiness at not being able to get married and have a family with Hef.

Hef stated, "Marriage isn't part of my puzzle. It's not a personal thing. I just haven't had much luck with wedded bliss."

In October of 2008, Holly claimed that she had ended her affair with Hef, but that she, Bridget, and Kendra "were still filming stuff together."

When Hef was asked about the split, he responded, "If Holly says it's over, I guess

Hef's three girlfriends—Holly, Kendra, and Bridget, each of them convivial, bubbly and gorgeous, were the stars of *E!*'s frothy reality TV show, *The Girls Next Door*.

In almost every episode, they share stories of their glamourous lives with their fans, peppering their recollections with anecdotes about their relationship with the Playboy himself.

it's over."

Kendra moved out of the Playboy Mansion in 2009 after meeting her future husband, Hank Baskett, the NFL star.

In January of 2009, the press reported that Bridget had also fled from the Playboy Mansion "to become my own person."

Holly wrote a book about her experiences, entitled *Down the Rabbit Hole*, published in 2015. In the book she revealed that she, Kendra, and Bridget didn't get paid for *The Girls Next Door*. She claimed that Hef argued that the money the trio was paid for posing for *Playboy* constituted their payment for their appearances in the TV show as well. "We got only $25,000 for our shoot."

On looking back at the series, Bridget summed it up: "Hef's life has always been a male fantasy. On *Girls Next Door* and for the first time, my life and the lives of Holly and Kendra, became a fantasy for women."

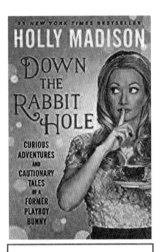

Hef's number one girlfriend, Holly Madison, wrote a tell-all *Down the Rabbit Hole.*

"The girls at the Mansion competed because each of them wanted to be the next centerfold. Hef was a manipulator, and he pitted each girl against another."

\*\*\*

Holly Madison and Kendra Wilkinson were not the only members of Hef's harem to write memoirs about their experiences inside the Playboy Mansion in Los Angeles.

In 2006, Isabella St. James published *Bunny Tales: Behind Closed Doors at the Playboy Mansion,* the story of a "nice Catholic girl" who ended up in Hef's bedroom. She was young, pretty, and blonde, but hardly a dumb blonde, as she had a law degree from Pepperdine University.

She met Hef in 2001, and for two years became one of his "posse of seven succulent beauties and a co-girlfriend of the Father of the Sexual Revolution and the world's most famous hedonist."

He told her that "Quaaludes give a girl a nice buzz and put her in the mood for sex."

She didn't find life at the Mansion all that sanitary. "Hef was used to dirty carpets. Holly Madison, Girlfriend No. 1, had moved into his bedroom with two dogs that were not house-trained. They would do their business right on the carpet. If you visited Hef's bedroom, you'd almost always end up in dog mess."

"The mattresses were disgusting—old, worn, and stained. Each bedroom was mismatched, with random pieces of furniture. It was as if someone had gone to a charity shop and bought the basics for each room."

"Each Friday, we went to Hef's bedroom and waited for him to pick dog poo off the carpet. Then we'd ask for our allowance of a thousand dollars. If Hef had a complaint about one of us, he'd air it then. If we'd committed an infraction, we didn't get our pay. He used the allowance like a weapon."

St. James knew that Hef valued women because depicting them nude had made him rich and famous around the world. "He doesn't really value a woman for all that she is, or all that she can be, or for what she is trying to be. He is not interested in her strength or independence. He just wants girls to look pretty, to sit beside him, and smile. He likes to talk about how *Playboy* gave women freedom, freed them to be sexual, meaning that it made it easier for guys to get laid."

In her book, *Bunny Tales*, Isabella St. James wrote: "When I met Hef, I admired him. I really saw him as an intelligent, accomplished man. And yes, I was attracted to him, not physically, but because he was a brilliant entrepreneur, social icon, and one-of-a-kind individual."

St. James watched a few episodes of *The Girls Next Door*, finding the series "cute and fuzzy." She claimed she could come up with a more exciting *Dynasty*-style plotline. It would go something like this:

"Picture an aging but still handsome magazine tycoon with multiple girlfriends, who is still in love with his ex-wife who lives next door. He has two gorgeous sons waiting to take over his empire from their older sister, who refuses to relinquish control. Imagine the tycoon's girlfriends lusting for his sons since they are the same age and having affairs with the butlers out of sheer boredom. Dramas, love, lust, intrigue."

\*\*\*

Hugh Hefner's sex-crazed life in the 1970s lived again in 2015 when Suzen Fisken published her memoir, *Playboy Mansion Memories from the Sexual Revolution to the Personal Evolution.*

Her saga begins in 1975, when she was a "lusty, busty coed "working her way through college at UCLA. One fateful night, she was invited to attend a party at Hef's Los Angeles Mansion. That night signaled the beginning (her words) "of a five-year wild ride on the front lines of the Sexual Revolution."

"I was a feminist in a sea of old school maleness, having outrageous adventures with millionaires, movie stars, musicians, writers, athletes, Playmates, and princes, with lots of sex, drugs, and jazz."

What makes her memoirs more page-turning and different from any other Playmate memoirs is that she not only named names of celebrities and movie stars she seduced, she detailed these encounters.

Suzen met Hef when he was 46, crediting him as "creating a culture of Mammary Mania."

"Suddenly, this bare-assed icon appeared before me in the Grotto, rubbing Johnson's Baby Oil onto my nude torso." At the time, she found him intriguing when he admitted that his favorite pick-up line was, "Hi, I'm Hugh Hefner."

She later admitted that she had one-on-one sex with the "Grand Fromage," after she'd had dinner with him and his pals. He was dressed in black silk pajamas.

The evening had begun when all of the visitors at the Mansion watched *Casablanca*, Hef for the 50th time. Just as Humphrey Bogart was telling Ingrid Bergman, "We'll always have Paris," he leaned over to her and gave her a passionate kiss.

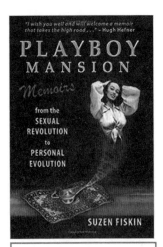

The sex that followed was the last time they would have solo man-woman sex. He told her, "Vanilla boy-girl sex is now *passé*. Group sex is in." On other nights, she joined five or six Playmates in bed with Hef. Sometimes, one of his male friends, perhaps a movie star, would join in the romp.

For a brief time, Suzen dated Hef's oldest son, David, the product of Hef's first marriage. Hef had left home when he was only one year old. Enrolled in a college back East, he visited the Los Angeles Mansion about five or six times a year. He was a photographer, and she posed for him. For the most part, David remained in the background, the son of Hef whom no one knew.

After a month at the Mansion, getting called in for romps in his bed, Suzen concluded that "Hef is just a romantic 18-year-old.

Suzen Fiskin today is an inspirational speaker, feminist, entertainer, and "Happiness Coach and Trainer."

In 1975, she was invited to a party at the Los Angeles Playboy Mansion, and that night marked a roller coaster ride for five years with a man in silk pajamas.

He never quite went beyond that stage."

When she wasn't being summoned to Hef's bed, she found many a celebrity to take his place. Warren Beatty was Suzen's favorite all time playmate, and she described him as "knock-your-panties-off gorgeous with a perfect body and in every way. He was impossibly charming and the sexiest man of all time."

After only one night of sex with him, she found him insatiable, as had his previous mistress, Joan Collins. "I called Warren an erotic Svengali."

Suzen migrated from the arms of Warren into the longer arms of Kareem Abdul-Jabbar, an amazing athlete who still holds the record of scoring the most points for the NBA. An ardent basketball fan, she met the star in 1976 when she found him talking jazz to Mel Tormé, another aficionado.

On her first date with him, Kareem asked her, "How does a black, famous, 7'2" guy fit into this world? Or into any woman?" His answer was provided later that night when she managed to fit her 5'2" body passionately against his frame, defining him afterward as "a great kisser."

Hef's longtime friend, the cartoonist, Shel Silverstein, and Suzen met at the Mansion. He'd been a friend of Hef's and a contributor to *Playboy* since the founding of the magazine. To her, he looked like a "Jewish Cowboy," in his ten-gallon hat and cowboy boots.

"Shel was a man of many emotions," she claimed, "which rose and fell like the waves on the shore." Their relationship, begun that night at the Mansion, endured for many years.

In addition to Beatty, Suzen met another god-like man in the muscular frame of Arnold Schwarzenegger. The

Kareem Abdul-Jabbar was a giant of a man. He dated Suzen Fiskin for more than a year.

According to Fiskin, "We were a study in dark and light, tall and small. He was both gentle and passionate."

Mr. Universe, Arnold Schwarzenegger, shown here in 1974, looked at Suzen with "a glint of the devil before he leaned over and gave me a gentle kiss where the sun doesn't shine."

517

year was 1977 and he'd just filmed *Stay Hungry*. He'd arrived at the Mansion to star in Playboy's *Playmate Party*. His powerful arms were on display as he'd worn a sleeveless shirt, and his muscular legs were also shown off as he appeared in shorty short shorts.

At the age of 29, he was a former Mr. Universe. He got acquainted with Suzen when she showed him how the "sex chair" worked. It was designed for the practice of cunnilingus. They agreed to meet the following night for a date.

She recalled her sexual encounters with him as "springing from the pages of the *Kama Sutra*. "He lifted and positioned me this way and that. I felt weightless," She raved about his Herculean body, undulating muscles, and "every curve, *bulge*, and crevice."

In contrast to Mr. Universe, Suzen also had an affair with Robert Kennedy, Jr., in 1977. *[Born in 1954, and the son of the "Bobby Kennedy," the famous brother of JFK, Robert Kennedy, Jr., is an environmental attorney, author, and activist.]* Peter Lawford introduced her to the young Kennedy as his nephew, claiming he was on spring break from an East Coast college.

She found that he had a "Warren Beatty in-training *savoir-faire*. I was quickly pulled in by his invisible force. I lost myself in his baby blues."

After a romantic moonlit walk on the beach, they retired to a villa in Malibu to make love. Their bout was repeated the next morning before breakfast. But later in the day, she discovered him "shooting up," learning painfully that he was a drug addict.

In 1983, he'd be arrested in Rapid City, South Dakota, for drug possession. He was put on probation for two years.

In time, as she followed his career, she was gratified that he "went from heroin to hero."

Two weeks later, Suzen met Robin Williams one Sunday evening at the Mansion, finding him "boyishly cute." She invited him to sneak away and smoke a joint with her, and he jokingly labeled her "the Cannabis Queen of Shangri-La."

Later, when he undressed, she found him a bit too hairy for her tastes, but she was lured into bed with his sweet, guileless face. "Our first round of lovemaking was like a short-fused fireworks, fast and full of sparks."

Suzen had only a brief fling with Robert Kennedy, Jr., before she discovered he had "a drug problem."

518

She also wrote about some lovers she found "less than fabulous." James Caan had "bunched up my panties when I saw him in *Godfather I* and *II*."

In 1975, she had spotted him dining with Hef, and was told that he was a "regular" at the Mansion. After spending some time alone with him, she arranged a rendezvous with him later at an apartment on Wilshire Boulevard.

"Here I was, alone with a real live movie star."

Suzen found Robin Williams boyishly cute. "He brought out the maternal instinct in me."

The loving couple had several trysts before he married a friend of hers, Sheila Ryan, a blonde beauty who used to hang out at the Mansion. Suzen turned against Caan when she learned of his harsh treatment of her friend.

Kareem had warned Suzen that Wilt Chamberlain "was an asshole with no integrity." She later claimed, "I should have listened to him."

She met Chamberlain at a party at the Mansion, finding the 7'2" basketball star surrounded by blondes. He was wearing white bell bottoms and white cowboy boots.

Suzen found basketball great Wilt Chamberlain "full of himself."

She became one of the 20,000 women he claimed to have bedded.

Later that evening, she managed to speak privately with him, and he invited her for a private rendezvous, which was arranged days later in an apartment. In her own memoirs, she gave him a bad report as a lover, finding him "arrogant and self-centered. Women were just playthings for him."

He must have had a lot of playthings, because in his own memoirs, *A View from Above*, he claimed that he had bedded 20,000 women.

One night, James Caan introduced Suzen to two more movie stars, Robert Duvall and Dustin Hoffman, asserting to them, "This is a nice Jewish girl, fellas,"

Later that night, she slipped away with Hoffman to smoke some joints, and they found a secret hiding spot in the gardens of the Mansion. After love-making, they fell asleep and didn't awaken until morning. He excused himself to make a phone call, promising he'd be back soon.

She waited and waited, finally giving up on him. When she reached the Main House, she saw that he was having breakfast with Caan. As she walked by Hoffman's table, he merely glanced up at her, wordlessly, before resuming a conversation with his fellow movie star.

Before leaving the Mansion, she found Duvall much friendlier, and the two of them arranged a rendezvous in Malibu three days later. She had seen him in *The Godfather Part One* (1972) and *Two* (1974), and later in *Apocalypse Now* (1979) and in other movies, never finding him handsome or sexy, but since he was a star, she agreed to meet with him.

Dustin Hoffman in *Death of a Salesman* in 1985.

"As far as Dustin is concerned, Mrs. Robinson can have him," Suzen said.

She recalled their night snorting cocaine and making love. "We had a grand 'ole time," she said. The next morning, when she got up, he'd left the bedroom. After getting dressed, she went downstairs, finding him in the kitchen. "Good morning," she said.

What happened next came as a complete shock to her. "Why don't you get the fuck out of here, you cunt?"

"I don't understand."

"Let me make it perfectly clear," he shouted. "Get out of here, you fucking cunt! Get out...now!"

Robert Duvall was fine throughout the night.

But in the morning, he ordered Suzen out the door.

Having met Peter Lawford on several occasions at the Playboy Mansion, Suzen called him "the Silver Fox." Like Elizabeth Taylor, she had developed a schoolgirl crush on him when she went to see him in the movies. Now, his career was at twilight. During his marriage (1954-66) to Patricia Kennedy, he had pimped for John F. Kennedy, setting him up for sexual trysts with movies stars who included Marilyn Monroe.

According to Suzen's memoirs, "When I hooked up with Peter, later in life, he'd lost his ability to perform as a man. He was getting his kicks from kinks. He liked to dress up in women's lingerie and tuck his genitals between his legs. He liked to be told what a pretty girl he was."

She went on to claim that one night, he slipped her a Ketamine, a drug sold on the street as a "Green." *[Ketamine, sometimes called a "date-rape drug," is an animal tranquilizer used by veterinarians as an anesthetic. Users have reported experiences they've referred to as a "K-Hole," an "out of body" or "near-death" experience, and often find it difficult to move because of the disassociated, dream-like torpor it creates.]*

Suzen passed out, only remembering waking up briefly when she was being attacked by "two butch women" while Lawford supervised the scene. When she woke up the next morning, "I was sore all over." She never forgave Lawford for that.

Suzen's own invitations to visit the Playboy Mansion began to dwindle, until the time came when she could no longer get inside the gates.

"For me, the time had come to create a new life after *Playboy*."

And so she did.

*** 

What seems to have been the final memoir to come off the press was written by one of Hef's former Playmates and published in 2016, shortly before his death. A blonde beauty—Hef's preferred choice in a woman—Stephanie Heinrich wrote *A Bunny Tells All: Fun and Fame with Hef and the Gang.*

She was a Midwesterner born to working class parents in Cincinnati, a town known for its "Skyline Chili," "Gracter's Ice Cream," and for its barbecue joints.

As she grew up and "blossomed out," she had a dream of auditioning for *Playboy*. "I'd love to be featured in the pages of that magazine, which I'd first seen when I was fourteen, my father's copy, to be envied and admired, to be *somebody*. It seemed impossible, but I would never know unless I tried. That meant heading for Hollywood, where dreams were made or broken."

Stephanie Heinrich was designated as the first "Cybergirl" in a DVD issued by *Playboy* featuring herself and a bevy of other unclothed beauties. In other words, she was among the first in *Playboy's* experimental early days with DVDs.

After a series of complications, the call she'd fantasized about for years came in. *Playboy* agreed to photograph her. She dreamed that night that she'd be following in the footsteps of Marilyn Monroe, Jayne Mansfield, and Anna Nicole Smith.

*Playboy* had launched a new feature, highlighting a different format for alluring photos—a "Cybergirl of the Week," a "Cybergirl of the Month," and eventually, a "Cybergirl of the Year."

Heinrich was told, "You're going to be the Marilyn Monroe of the Internet because you'll be our first Cybergirl. You might become a centerfold for *Playboy*."

She made her first appearance in September 2000 as Cybergirl of the Week. That was followed by her appearance in *Playboy* for the "Girls of Conference USA" issue. After that, an appointment was arranged for her to pose for a photoshoot to see if she were centerfold material. "I was about to go from Cincinnati onto the world stage."

In Los Angeles, she recalled her first meeting with Hef when he walked into the room where she was. She claimed he was surrounded by gorgeous women and was the center of everyone's attention. "He made me stiffen with anticipation." She walked over to him and introduced herself.

"No one would confuse him with Cary Grant," she recalled. "But his chin was strong, and his lips curled into that tight smile of his. His dimples appeared, and his whole face was more attractive than I had expected. I could see why women would love him." That afternoon, she got an invitation to visit the Mansion.

That was followed by other invitations, at which times Hef began to show her more and more attention in spite of all the beauties around him, including "steady" girlfriends. Then one night, he came up to her with the biggest invitation of all: "I want you to move in here."

After she moved into the Mansion, the inevitable happened: She was summoned to Hef's bedroom for sex, finding it was orgy time. He had sex with five to eight girls at a time, and he was 75 years old. It was impressive."

She related that he had this big bathtub, and he liked to watch the girls take bubble baths together. On some nights, the orgy moved to the Grotto.

Her by now familiar tale was one of "love, lust, and redemption," detailing "bedroom frolic with Hef and his buxom live-in girlfriends." Tours of Europe in a private jet broke the routine at the Mansion.

Around the Mansion, Stephanie became part of the coven of young women known as "Hef & His Seven Girlfriends." During the last week of April and the first week of May, 2001, she posed for a centerfold which would be published later that year. "It was the last centerfold to be shot on film, as the world was switching to digital.

Before posing, she was told to shave "down there," and apparently, she shaved off too much. The photographer told her that her vulva would look "too risqué," so a makeup technician was called in to apply fake hair to her pubic region.

As time went by and the months at the Mansion dragged on, Stephanie decided she wanted to get out into the world again and begin life anew. In January of 2002, she met with Hef and told him that she was moving out and gave her reasons why. But because she wanted to remain connected to Hef's empire, he agreed to give her a job at Playboy Promotions.

The day she left was moving day at the Mansion as two of Hef's other girlfriends decided to leave, too. By nightfall, Hef had moved in their replacements.

In the second phase of her life, Stephanie began to date famous celebrities, beginning with Kid Rock. She noted his "John Lennon nose, his ever-present hat, his cool blue eyes, and the way he kept that deliberate scruffy look."

Then Benicio Del Toro walked into her life. "Mister dreamy Latino guy. Never in my life have I been kissed like that. It was magical. He smelled like a guy, very manly, like 'I've-been-working-in-the-yard-all-day' smell."

Van Diesel entered her life in 2003. Her introduction to him led to a sleepover at his residence, where she became acquainted with his "carved marble body. We had a marathon makeout session, For background music, his recording of 'Lean on Me' played."

And so it went, as Stephanie set about to prove that there was life after Hef. Years later, she visited him again at the Mansion, and he told her, "Stephanie, you're welcome back at any time."

"He was still the generous, youthful, man he'd always been. He was young in spirit and usually had more energy than his Playmates."

"I declined his invitation, but *Playboy* will be part of my life forever, and I wouldn't be me without that piece of my life. Okay, one day my kids will grow up and download my nude pictures online—and will know everything. But I'm not ashamed."

***

Hef went into a rage when he was linked to the allegations that surfaced in 2014 against his longtime friend, Bill Cosby. Dozens of women came forward to accuse "America's Father" of drugging them and raping them.

P.J. Masten, a former Bunny, was one of the chief accusers. She claimed she knew at least a dozen former Bunnies who had been attacked by Cosby but were too ashamed to come forward. "Each of them told me they were drugged and raped by Cosby."

During the scandal, some reporters speculated that Hef "had paved the way for Cosby's assault by providing the background for them," a reference to the Playboy Mansion. It was suggested that some of Cosby's attacks had occurred on the premises.

Hef denied all these accusations, saying that Cosby had long been his valued and trusted friend, and he was completely unaware of any assaults.

One reporter said, "If the media had been paying attention to what was really going on at the Playboy Mansion, rather than just attending parties there, hosted by Hef, they might have uncovered many of Cosby's alleged activities."

DAILY NEWS
NEW YORK'S HOMETOWN NEWSPAPER
**Cosby's victims unite in show of strength**

# America's rapist

35 brave women come together to tell their stories, show their faces and speak to the evil of a man we once all loved

MASTEN: PLAYBOY BUNNIES ASSAULTED BY COSBY

Bill Cosby and Hef had begun a friendship that survived the decades. But the lurid charges and unwelcome headlines soured the relationship, and Hef was infuriated that he was blamed unfairly in some circles for his old friend's "deviations."

***

In ailing health, Hef had a dream that his two sons, Marston and Cooper, whom he had conceived during the course of his marriage to Kimberley Conrad, would become his "co-heir apparents" when he stepped down. Christie had resigned as head of Playboy Enterprises on January 30, 2009 to pursue other goals.

It soon became apparent to Hef that whereas Cooper wanted to follow in his father's footsteps, "I don't think Marston is all that intrigued with the idea [of filling in for me in years to come]," Hef said. "Marston has long marched to his own drummer and shows no signs of wanting to become a carbon copy of dear ole Dad."

Cooper had worked for Playboy Enterprises since he was in college. Step by step, he learned the business from the ground up. He also had closely followed the operation's management by his half-sister, Christie.

He exhibited no sibling rivalry, although it might have been obvious that one day he wanted to take her job.

When Scott Flanders stepped in to replace Christie, who'd moved on, Cooper had a bitter argument with him. Flanders had made a decision to eliminate nudity from the magazine, hoping to gain more respectability for *Playboy*. Perhaps in protest, Cooper resigned from Playboy Enterprises for eighteen months.

During his absence, he launched the media startup company, HOP (Hefner Operations and Productions) focused on content and social events for millennials.

After Hef stepped down, Cooper was named chief creative officer at *Playboy* in 2016.

In February of 2017, he announced that nudity would return to *Playboy*, stating "The problem had been the presentation of nude images rather than the nudity itself."

He noted that circulation of the magazine had fallen to 321,315 copies per month, a long way down from its peak of seven million readers decades ago.

Cooper Hefner, Hugh's youngest son, towering over him, becoming the heir apparent to take over his empire.

After Cooper's return, he approved the sale of the Playboy Mansion to 33-year-old Darren Metropoulos, the heir to the Hostess Brands fortune. It sold for $100 million, but, according to the agreement ironed out, Hef could continue to occupy the residence until his death.

Metropoulous had been living next door in the smaller house where Kimberly Conrad, Hef's second wife, had reared their two sons, Marston and Cooper.

With Cooper at the helm, he told the press, "Unlike Dad, I'm not going to wear pajamas to go to work in the office. The only time I'll put on a pair of PJs in public is to attend the annual Midsummer Night's Dream Party."

Darren Metropoulos, heir to the Twinkie (Hostess Brands), Utz (potato chips) and Pabst beer fortune, is the new lord of the Playboy Mansion in Los Angeles.

Playboy Enterprises had become a private company once again in 2011. Hef had arranged a deal, agreeing to buy out the minority stockholders for $6.15 a share. Wall Street hailed the move as "Hefner putting the *Playboy* stock out of its misery."

Playboy stock had plunged 82 percent in value since its peak in 1999 at $43.33 a share. That brief spike had been associated with the Internet mania of that era. Before that, the price of the stock had not made any upward move in two decades.

According to *Forbes* magazine, Playboy earnings rose 39 percent after Cooper's takeover. But that was not based on circulation of the magazine. Looking at the enterprise as a whole, Cooper lamented that *Playboy's* involvement "in lowbrow licensing and some reality TV, like *The Girls Next Door*, was a mistake."

The 25-year-old heir set about to remake and upgrade the *Playboy* image. Outside revenue was the driving force behind the company's success. A pact with the global fragrance company, Coty, brought in $100 million in annual sales. Through a partnership deal with Hangdong United and Bally's, Playboy distributed clothing, footwear, and fashion accessories, with more than a third of its revenue coming from China. Cooper set about to investigate a $25 to $50 million deal that would push *Playboy* into the marketing of lingerie and swimwear.

Playboy Clubs resurfaced in 2017 in New York, London, Hanoi, Bangkok, and several cities in India. The Playboy Jazz Festival at the Hollywood Bowl has been an institution since 1979.

Cooper remembered that when he was growing up, and when he visited his father in the library, he was confronted with a large blow-up of his mother as a nude centerfold. Hef had named Kimberly Conrad as Playmate of the Year in 1989.

He told his Dad, "Every time Marston and I came in to see you, we are confronted with mom's bush. Why can't you put it somewhere else for your viewing pleasure? It's really weird seeing our mother like this. It's like an elephant in the room."

Chris Jones, writing in *Esquire*, said, "Hefner doesn't throw out much. The nude resurfaced in his office. He wears his heartbreak like a teenaged girl."

But as a grown-up man, Cooper was not so offended. In fact, he came up with a novel idea for Mother's Day. His mother was now 54 years old, "but she looks fabulous." He asked her to duplicate her long ago pose for *Playboy*, and, to his surprise, she agreed.

"As my Dad says, once you're a Playmate, you're always a Playmate." The before and after pictures were run in *Playboy's* June 2017 issue.

Love entered Cooper's life when he saw the English actress, Scarlett Byrne, play Pansy Parkinson in the *Harry Potter* series. He wanted to meet her, and an introduction was arranged through Scout Willis, the daughter of Bruce Willis and Demi Moore.

Not only did he meet her, he got her to pose for the March/April 2017 issue of *Playboy*. She told the press, "I saw the shoot as an opportunity to make a statement about equality between the sexes."

In August of 2015, Byrne and Cooper became engaged and are living together at Marina del Rey.

"If Dad could have his Playmates, I'm entitled to at least one," Cooper reportedly said.

***

Ironically, Cooper's older brother, Marston, was born on Hef's birthday. He is said to have "none of his Dad's swagger and the mothlike attraction to the bright lights of Hollywood."

The teenaged boy once told a reporter, "I've been around really hot women all my life, so the average high school girl will just not do it for me."

A reporter once asked him, since he had the name of Hefner, if he ever worried whether people wanted to be friends with him because of his having such a fabled father. He answered, "I can usually weed them out if that's why they want to hang with me."

He admitted that he started reading *Playboy* at a very young age. "I would take old issues and cut out the nudes of Pamela Anderson. I still love the magazine and read it occasionally. Mostly I read *Newsweek* and

The very beautiful Scarlett Byrne moved from a teen-queen role as Pansy Parkinson in three of the *Harry Potter* films to a gig as Playmate of the Year (2015) and emotional links to Cooper Hefner.

"A big thank you to @Playboy, the creative team, and @cooperbhefner for such a unique opportunity. #NakedIsNormal," she wrote.

"A chip of the old block," Hef said when he heard that his youngest son had taken up with Playmate Scarlett Byrne.

*The New Yorker."*

"As for nudity, if I ran *Playboy,* I wouldn't change it so much except I'd make the centerfold cool and more artsy instead of obvious," he said. "I'd make the magazine more multicultural and diverse. Dad is blonde crazy. Actually, I prefer a brunette with blue eyes. I like an intelligent woman I can have a conversation with—not the blonde bimbo type. I also don't like fake boobs. I don't find them attractive."

According to Marston, "As for hanging out at the Mansion, just knowing people are having sex in my house makes me uncomfortable. Growing up, I found my mom a bit of a hard-ass. She had 75 percent custody, and she had to play bad cop to balance my more tolerant Dad. James Caan thought she put a damper on everything at the Mansion. She didn't like one of her boys watching three nude women in the Grotto making out with each other before being joined by a guy with an erection."

"Marston and Cooper grew up around Playmates," their mother Kimberly said, "and the boys more or less take it in stride. It's like working at Krispy Kreme—you don't eat all the doughnuts."

In August of 2010, Marston started dating Clair Sinclair. Born in Los Angeles in 1991, she'd been modeling since the age of 14, taking part in fashion campaigns for Angel Jeans. She'd also starred in episodes of *Playboy TV.*

She told *Maximo TV [a media outlet covering events in Hollywood]* that she and Marston had a "tumultuous relationship."

That relationship exploded into public view when Sinclair charged him with physical assault. He pleaded "no contest" and was sentenced to undergo a 52-week domestic violence program. The judge ordered him to stay away from her.

Sinclair, 20 years old at the time, had been named Playmate of the Year for 2011, but after the sentencing of her lover, she canceled all *Playboy*-related promotions.

Hef had told Fox News that Sinclair's style reminded him of Bettie Page, the popular 1950s pinup model once featured in *Playboy.*

Since his sentencing, Marston has more or less avoided the public eye.

\*\*\*

After the failure of Hef's first marriage to Millie, he'd sworn off marriage for life. He changed

Kimberley Conrad, the mother of Cooper and Marston

his mind when he met Kimberley Conrad—"definitely Playmate material."

Soon he was walking down the aisle once again. From that union had emerged two handsome young boys, Marston and Cooper. That made four in his brood, as he had both David and Christie from his first marriage. "Four kids now call me Papa," he bragged.

After he and Kimberley separated in 1998, they managed to stay friends and often conferred about the rearing of their sons. He'd purchased a large house immediately next door to the Playboy Mansion for $7 million. Kimberley moved into it with their sons, who often visited Hef at the Mansion.

"I love Hef deeply," Kimberly told the press at the time. "But we keep different schedules. I like to go to bed at ten and get up a 6:45 every morning to work out. He likes watching movies until one in the morning, or even later. I found the constant buzz of his life not my scene. Hordes of people came and went. There were almost no peaceful moments."

His enduring friendship with Kimberly came to an end when he sold her house for $18 million, a sizeable profit from the original purchase price. She confronted him, demanding $5 million from the sale. When he refused, she filed a multi-million dollar lawsuit against him.

In an interview with *People*, he claimed that according to their prenup, he did not have to share any profits from the sale of the house, as he had only been obligated to pay her $250,000 annually. Eventually, the warring couple settled out of court, according to terms not disclosed.

The lawsuit embittered Hef and "soured me on marriage forever," he told his brother, Keith. "If you ever hear me talking marriage again, I give you permission to shoot me. There's another thing I have to face. I was born in 1926. It is now 2010, and I've survived a decade into a new century. I never expected to do that. When I had my stroke in 1985, my doctor told me I had only two or three years to live, perhaps not even that. And here I am, still hanging in there."

His firm resolve melted quickly when another beautiful blonde, Crystal Harris, entered his life. He met her in 2008 when she'd arrived at the Mansion for his annual Halloween party. To some degree, she attracted his attention because of her provocative and erotic outfit as Fifi, a French maid.

She'd been born in 1956 in Lake Havasu

Crystal Hefner, looking lovely, as the third Mrs. Hugh Hefner.

City, Arizona, home of the famously reconstructed London Bridge. Her parents were British, and shortly after her birth, they moved back to England, only to return to the U.S. with their daughter seven years later.

As she grew older, she'd been exposed to show business by her late father, Ray Harris, who was both a songwriter and singer. In time, she moved to San Diego to attend the state university there.

She began to model, which led to her first *Playboy* exposure in a feature called "Co-Ed of the Week," and featured on Playboy.com. Here semi-nude shots were published on October 30, 2008, back when she was still billing herself as "Crystal Carter."

In late 2009, Hef got her cast in E's *The Girls Next Door,* appearing with three of his blonde girlfriends, Holly Madison, Kendra Wilkinson, and Bridget Marquardt.

In spite of the six decades that stood between Crystal and himself, Hef in his dotage started dating her—more than dating, really, as she soon evolved into a "sleepover."

Hef certainly became familiar with all of Crystal's charms when she posed for a pictorial to become "Playmate of the Month" for the December 2009 issue of *Playboy.* He had ordered at least a hundred shots taken of her

@hughhefner
Hugh Hefner

Recent events call for a special sticker on the July cover. Look for it on newsstands.
http://twitpic.com/5c44za

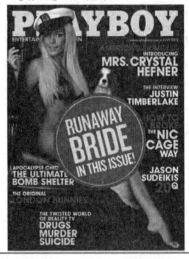

The editorial board at *Playboy* was horrified when Crystal backed out of her wedding plans with Hef. As it was too late to recall the thousands of copies of the July, 2011 issue in which "Mrs. Crystal Hefner" was "formally but informally" introduced to *Playboy* readers as the new Mrs. Hefner, Hef reacted with uncommon grace.

Noting on his Twitter feed the "recent events" associated with the disruption of his wedding plans, he warned readers to look for the "special sticker" on that edition's front cover, an elegantly bemused way of informing his fans that she had bolted.

530

nude charms. Their affair deepened. In an article in *Esquire,* Chris Jones wrote about the hordes of women who still made their way into Hef's bed between marriages. "All the girlfriends, Bunnies, and aspirants, along with the Scandinavian Amazons in St-Tropez, blur into a kind of glamourous mental hurricane. It is the only question that stumps him. 'How many women?' He answers, 'How could I possibly know? Over a thousand, I'm sure. There were chunks in my life when I was married. At those times, I never cheated. But I made up for it when I wasn't married. You've got to have your hand in.'"

As one reader wrote in: "I think Hefner had more than his hand in those gals."

On the night before Christmas in 2010, when his divorce from Kimberley had at long last become final, he proposed marriage to Crystal. "When I gave her a diamond ring, she burst into tears," he said. "This has been the happiest Christmas weekend in my memory."

The July 2011 issue of *Playboy* featured Crystal on its cover, holding a pipe with Hef's smoking jacket slung over her shoulders. The headline read, "America's Princess—Introducing Mrs. Crystal Hefner."

To Hef's dismay, she decided she could not go through with the marriage and, five days before the wedding, on June 14, 2011, she broke it off and fled from the Mansion.

It was too late to stop the magazine which had already been printed. Stickers were applied to the cover with the words "Runaway Bride." Its wording was inspired by the title of the 1999 Julia Roberts film co-starring Richard Gere, her screen lover from the hit movie, *Pretty Woman.*

After being deserted and publicly humiliated by Crystal, Hef, according to his brother, Keith, put on a brave face. "I knew him well enough to know that his heart was broken, but he carried on." Keith noted that he still kept the large portrait of her in the foyer, the work of a former Playmate, Victoria Fuller.

"Do you know what I did for that girl?" he asked Keith. "I introduced her to those 1930s musicals that had starred Fred Astaire and Ginger Rogers. She'd never heard of them."

When a reporter asked him about being stood up at the altar, Hef said, "Ageism is a variation of racism and sexism—and all the other isms."

On his Twitter account, Hef posted this notice: "The wedding is off. Crystal had a change of heart."

***

After dumping Hef, Crystal had no trouble finding another beau. At

Hollywood's fabled Château Marmont, hangout of stars, she was spotted cuddling with Jordan McGraw, Dr. Phil's son. She still wore the engagement ring Hef had given her.

After Crystal escaped from Hef's clutches, things turned a bit nasty. She still used her link to Hef to promote her career. Appearing on the *Howard Stern Show,* she made some disparaging remarks about her sex life with Hef, the host goading her on. She wanted a career of her own and set about pursuing it. In the spring of 2010, she signed a recording contract with Organica Music Group, a division of Universal Music.

She also had aspirations of becoming a fashion designer. She created a line of swimwear with Vanessa Bryce, an Australian. Later, she promoted a line of "intimates, 'athleisure,' and loungewear," co-designed with Rhonda Shear.

Crystal continued to feature Hef and her link to him on her website, RadarOnline.com. She was seen posing with the famous Playboy Logo across her body, while promoting her music career and even her mom, Lee Lovitt, a real estate broker.

She even published a picture of herself cuddling with Hef, and her site maintained that she was planning a summer wedding with him, even though she had called it off.

When she wasn't promoting some product, she listed her interests as "the rain, the seasons, fast cars, good food, volunteering, caring and honest people, the ocean, and animals," of which there were plenty living in the zoo in the gardens of the Playboy Mansion.

Something happened along the way that made Crystal change her mind once again, deciding that she wanted to go through with the marriage to the aging Hef. She showed up at the Playboy Mansion one afternoon, wanting to be reinstated as his bride-to-be.

Some of Hef's friends urged him to reject her. "Why take her back?" one of his pals asked: "She's just using you."

But Keith stood by Hef's decision to take back his runaway bride-to-be. "He's happy now that she's returned. He has a right to be happy."

When Crystal returned to his bed, Hef told his Twitter followers, "I've given Crystal a ring. I love the girl. We are going to be married."

The Playboy Mansion was the setting for Hef's third marriage. Only close friends and family members were invited to the event on New Year's Eve of 2012.

Keith was his best man, and Hef still considered him "the best friend I ever had."

*[Keith Hefner died at the age of 87 on April 8, 2016, one day after Hef's 90th birthday.]*

Crystal spent the next five years in a May-December marriage to Hef. "There were many compromises," Hef said, without going into detail as to what he meant. As each year went by, his health declined, as did his energy.

A year before his death in 2017, Crystal told the press that she had been diagnosed with Lyme disease and a "toxic mold" as well as a "breast implant malfunction."

Hef claimed that she was experiencing "brain fog and chronic fatigue," because of the rupture of her implants and Lyme disease.

Five days after Hef was laid to rest beside the tomb of Marilyn Monroe, Crystal told a reporter from *People* magazine:

*"Hugh Hefner was an American hero. A pioneer. A kind and humble soul who opened up his life and home to the world. I felt how much he loved me. I loved him so much. I am so grateful. He gave me life. He gave me direction. He taught me kindness. I will feel eternally grateful to him to have been by his side, holding his hand and telling him how much I love him. He changed my life, he saved my life. He made me feel loved every single day. He was a beacon to the world, a force unlike anything else. There never has and never will be another Hugh M. Hefner."*

Near the end of his life, proudly alert to the legacies he had crafted, Hef posted this photo of himself, flanked with son Cooper and wife Crystal, on his Twitter feed.

The issue of *Playboy* with Marilyn on the cover that started it all.

In a graveyard, Hef and Marilyn would lie together until their bones turned to dust.

# Epilogue

At the "ripened" age of 91, Hugh Marston Hefner died on September 27, 2017.

His passing made headlines around the world, creating a whirlwind of nostalgia and grief but also provoking venomous assaults on his character and influence.

He had been suffering from a blood infection and a drug-resistant strain of E-coli bacteria.

The four children he left behind, born in this order—Christie, David, Marston, and Cooper—gathered for a memorial dinner. The setting was the Japanese restaurant, Katsuya, in Brentwood. Led by Christie, the oldest, the siblings raised a glass to toast the father who had had such a great influence on all of their lives.

Crystal Harris, the third Mrs. Hugh Hefner, was not there. She told *People* magazine: "I haven't been able to bring myself to write more people back to thank them for their condolences. I am heartbroken. I am still in disbelief."

Hef's body had been driven to its final resting place, that crypt he'd selected in 1992 and for which he'd paid $75,000. His dream had been to be buried next to his long-ago blonde goddess, Marilyn Monroe, who had died mysteriously in 1962.

He credited the nude centerfold of her that he'd run in the first issue of *Playboy* in 1953 as the match that lit the flames of the magazine's phenomenal success.

The black hearse carrying Hef's casket was seen entering the gates of the Westwood Village Memorial Park Cemetery in Los Angeles.

News of his death set off a wave of tributes and vicious attacks on his character, almost equal in measure, every column of praise matched by a denunciation.

The outspoken Linda Stasi of *The New York Daily News* came down hard on the *Playboy* publisher. She denounced him as "living in a world of concubines, a Viagra-fueled fossil in pajamas, who liked Bunnies with massive boobs, but not massive brains. His was a case of the Beauty and the Beast, a modern-day Dracula living in a rotting mansion."

Many of the comments after his death were comical, including one by

Joseph Fusco of the Bronx: "Is it true that Hefner has been reincarnated as a harem eunuch?"

Vin Morabito of Pennsylvania claimed, "In Hef's honor, pipes resembling the ones he was frequently depicted puffing on shall be flown at full staff on only the most erect of poles."

Some social critics, including a writer for the *Baltimore Sun,* had come to view him as "A creepy old guy paddling around his Mansion in slippers, silk pajamas, and a smoking jacket, pathetically cavorting with a new set of bimbos. By now, he's an aging Lothario, a sexualized Peter Pan who refused to grow up."

He was asked, "Are you ever going to grow up?"

"Well, I'm never going to do that," he responded. "Staying forever young is what it's all about. I must hold onto the boy I was so many summers ago. Many of my former Playmates are now grandmothers, or living in retirement communities, but I'm still alive and vital."

Ross Douthat in *The New York Times,* obviously did not believe that one should not speak ill of the dead:

> *"Hef was the grinning pimp of the sexual revolution, with Quaaludes for the ladies and Viagra for himself—a father of smut addictions and eating disorders, of abortions, divorces, and syphilis, a pretentious huckster who published Updike stories no one read while doing fresh procurement for celebrities, a revolutionary whose revolution chiefly benefitted men much like himself."*

In a radically different spin, Norman Lear praised Hefner on Twitter as "a true explorer"; the Rev. Jesse Jackson lauded him for his stand on racial equality; and Larry King labeled him "the giant of free speech."

As the decades rolled on, one aspect of Hef's life never changed: As a young boy growing up a movie addict in Chicago, he fell in love with the platinum blonde goddess Jean Harlow, and her host of imitators, as seen in those Busby Berkeley fantasy films of dancing beauties.

He never wavered from those images and sought them out in modern women in the 1950s, '60s, and '70s, and during the decades that followed.

His final sexual expression occurred with his own blonde goddess, Crystal Harris. She was absent from his bed when the butler arrived with his breakfast tray at noon. Hef confided a deep, dark secret: "My name will forever be associated with sex, but just between you and me, the thrill is gone."

The last film footage taken of Hef was a sad sight, as he seemed to be preparing to be frozen in the carbonite of fame. During the previous two years, he had been suffering from a crippling back infection, and was bedridden for the most part. To get about, he needed a walker. His frame was hunched; his gray hair unkempt, and his body skeletal. He was last seen by his staff wearing a pair of baby blue pajamas.

In 2010, Hef spoke to *The Daily Beast* about his legacy: "I would like to be remembered as someone who contributed to and changed the sexual and social values of my time, and I think my place in that corner of history is fairly secure."

"Big as my boyhood dreams were, they certainly didn't match what came to pass in my life. Back then, how could I have possibly imagined what came to be?"

"I might have created many things, not just *Playboy,* but I feel my most enduring creation is myself."

Chris Jones, writing in *Esquire,* said: "*Playboy* has been on the right side of history—on sex, birth control, civil rights, AIDS, gay marriage, war, social tolerance, personal liberty—while also serving as a vehicle for that history. But it wasn't *Playboy,* really. It wasn't the brand or the rabbit. It was him. It is him and without him, it will be no more."

Hef's final assisted walk was in his self-styled Garden of Eden. For the first days of autumn, a cool breeze was blowing in from the Pacific. "The summer has come and gone," he said, "and I know it will be the last summer I'll spend. The gardens bring back so many memories, not only of my beloved animals, but all those torrid nights in the Grotto."

He turned and looked back at the Playboy Mansion. "Oh, the secrets that stately manse holds. If only it could talk. It was a true pleasure palace, but it's also seen its share of heartbreak and unfulfilled dreams."

"The time is rapidly approaching when I must say farewell to all this, my earthly paradise," he said. "I'll be joining Marilyn Monroe, buried beside her in her crypt. She's been waiting there for me since 1962. We'll spend eternity together—just the two of us."

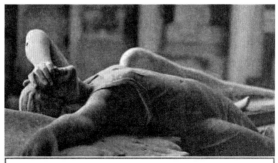

A scene of grief from a late 19th century Italian tomb in Liguria.

Deep in December, the "fires of September" were burning on a low flame. As Hef moved down that dangerous road to the Big 90, he knew he was walking into twilight time for men of his age.

"You can put on my tombstone that I didn't sample all the worlds most beautiful women, only most of them."

# IN MEMORIAM
## REST IN PEACE
# HUGH M. HEFNER
## 1926-2017

# DARWIN PORTER

As an intense nine-year-old, **Darwin Porter** began meeting movie stars, TV personalities, politicians, and singers through his vivacious and attractive mother, Hazel, an eccentric but charismatic Southern girl who had lost her husband in World War II. Migrating from the Depression-ravaged valleys of western North Carolina to Miami Beach during its most ebullient heyday, Hazel became a stylist, wardrobe mistress, and personal assistant to the vaudeville *comedienne* **Sophie Tucker**, the bawdy and irrepressible "Last of the Red Hot Mamas."

Virtually every show-biz celebrity who visited Miami Beach paid a call on "Miss Sophie," and Darwin, as a pre-teen loosely and indulgently supervised by his mother, was regularly dazzled by the likes of **Judy Garland, Dinah Shore,** and **Frank Sinatra.**

It was at Miss Sophie's that he met his first political figure, who was actually an actor at the time. Between marriages, **Ronald Reagan** came to call on Ms. Sophie, who was his favorite singer. He was accompanied by a young blonde starlet, **Marilyn Monroe.**

At the University of Miami, Darwin edited the school newspaper. He first met and interviewed **Eleanor Roosevelt** at the Fontainebleau Hotel on Miami Beach and invited her to spend a day at the university. She accepted, much to his delight.

After graduation, he became the Bureau Chief of *The Miami Herald* in Key West, Florida, where he got to take early morning walks with the former U.S. president **Harry S Truman**, discussing his presidency and the events that had shaped it.

Through Truman, Darwin was introduced and later joined the staff of **Senator George Smathers** of Florida. His best friend was a young senator, **John F. Kennedy.** Through "Gorgeous George," as Smathers was known in the Senate, Darwin got to meet Jack and Jacqueline in Palm Beach. He later wrote two books about them—*The Kennedys, All the Gossip Unfit to Print,* and one of his all-time bestsellers, *Jacqueline Kennedy Onassis—A Life Beyond Her Wildest Dreams.*

For about a decade in New York, Darwin worked in television journalism and advertising with his long-time partner, the journalist, art director, and arts-industry socialite **Stanley Mills Haggart.**

Stanley (as an art director) and Darwin (as a writer and assistant), worked as freelance agents in television. Jointly, they helped produce TV commercials that included testimonials from **Joan Crawford** (then feverishly promoting Pepsi-

Cola); **Ronald Reagan** (General Electric); and **Debbie Reynolds** (Singer sewing machines). Other personalities appearing and delivering televised sales pitches included **Louis Armstrong, Lena Horne,** and **Arlene Dahl,** each of them hawking a commercial product.

Beginning in the early 1960s, Darwin joined forces with the then-fledgling **Arthur Frommer** organization, playing a key role in researching and writing more than 50 titles and defining the style and values that later emerged as the world's leading travel guidebooks, *The Frommer Guides,* with particular emphasis on Europe, New England, and the Caribbean. Between the creation and updating of hundreds of editions of detailed travel guides to England, France, Italy, Spain, Portugal, Austria, Hungary, Germany, Switzerland, the Caribbean, and California, he continued to interview and discuss the triumphs, feuds, and frustrations of celebrities, many by then reclusive, whom he either sought out or encountered randomly as part of his extensive travels. **Ava Gardner, Debbie Reynolds,** and **Lana Turner** were particularly insightful.

It was while living in New York that Darwin became fascinated by the career of a rising real estate mogul changing the skyline of Manhattan. He later, of course, became the "gambling czar" of Atlantic City and a star of reality TV.

Darwin began collecting an astonishing amount of data on Donald Trump, squirreling it away in boxes, hoping one day to write a biography of this charismatic, controversial figure.

Before doing that, he penned more than thirty-five uncensored, unvarnished, and unauthorized biographies on subjects that included **Debbie Reynolds and Carrie Fisher, Donald Trump, Bill and Hillary Clinton, Ronald Reagan and Nancy Davis, Jane Wyman, Jacqueline Kennedy, Jack Kennedy, Lana Turner, Peter O'Toole, James Dean, Marlon Brando, Merv Griffin, Katharine Hepburn, Howard Hughes, Humphrey Bogart, Michael Jackson, Paul Newman, Steve McQueen, Marilyn Monroe, Elizabeth Taylor, Rock Hudson, Frank Sinatra, Vivien Leigh, Laurence Olivier, the notorious porn star Linda Lovelace, Zsa Zsa Gabor and her sisters, Tennessee Williams, Gore Vidal,** and **Truman Capote.**

As a departure from his usual repertoire, Darwin also wrote the controversial *J. Edgar Hoover & Clyde Tolson: Investigating the Sexual Secrets of America's Most Famous Men and Women,* a book about celebrity, voyeurism, political and sexual repression, and blackmail within the highest circles of the U.S. government.

Porter's biographies, over the years, have won thirty first prize or "runner-up to first prize" awards at literary festivals in cities or states which include New England, New York, Los Angeles, Hollywood, San Francisco, Florida, California, and Paris.

Darwin can be heard at regular intervals as a radio and television commentator, "dishing" celebrities, pop culture, politics, and scandal.

A resident of New York City, Darwin is currently at work on a startling new biography of Kirk Douglas: *More Is Never Enough.*

# DANFORTH PRINCE

The co-author of this book, **Danforth Prince** is president and founder of Blood Moon Productions, a publishing venture that's devoted to salvaging, compiling, and marketing the oral histories of America's entertainment industry.

Prince launched his career in journalism in the 1970s at the Paris Bureau of *The New York Times*. In the early '80s, he joined Darwin Porter in developing first editions of many of the titles within *The Frommer Guides*. Together, they reviewed and articulated the travel scenes of more than 50 nations, most of them within Europe and The Caribbean. Authoritative and comprehensive, they became best-selling "travel bibles" for millions of readers.

Prince, in collaboration with Porter, is also the co-author of several award-winning celebrity biographies, each configured as a title within **Blood Moon's Babylon series.** These have included *Hollywood Babylon—It's Back!; Hollywood Babylon Strikes Again; The Kennedys: All the Gossip Unfit to Print; Frank Sinatra, The Boudoir Singer, Elizabeth Taylor: There Is Nothing Like a Dame; Pink Triangle: The Feuds and Private Lives of Tennessee Williams, Gore Vidal, Truman Capote, and Members of their Entourages*; and *Jacqueline Kennedy Onassis: A Life Beyond Her Wildest Dreams.* More recent efforts include *Lana Turner, Hearts and Diamonds Take All; Peter O'-Toole—Hellraiser, Sexual Outlaw, Irish Rebel; Bill & Hillary—So This Is That Thing Called Love; James Dean, Tomorrow Never Comes;* and *Rock Hudson Erotic Fire;* and *Carrie Fisher and Debbie Reynolds, Princess Leia & Unsinkable Tammy in Hell.*

One of his recent projects, co-authored with Darwin Porter, is *Donald Trump, The Man Who Would Be King.* Configured for release directly into the frenzy of the 2016 presidential elections, and winner of at least three literary awards at book festivals in New York, California, and Florida. It's a celebrity exposé of the decades of pre-presidential scandals—personal, political, and dynastic—associated with **Donald Trump** during the rambunctious decades when no one ever thought he'd actually get elected.

Prince is also the co-author of four books on film criticism, three of which won honors at regional bookfests in Los Angeles and San Francisco.

Prince, a graduate of Hamilton College and a native of Easton and Bethlehem, Pennsylvania, is the president and founder of the Georgia Literary Association (1996), and of the Porter and Prince Corporation (1983) which has produced dozens of titles for Simon & Schuster, Prentice Hall, and John Wiley & Sons. In 2011, he was named "Publisher of the Year" by a consortium of literary critics and marketers spearheaded by the J.M. Northern Media Group.

He has electronically documented some of the controversies associated with his stewardship of Blood Moon in at least 50 documentaries, book trailers, public speeches, and TV or radio interviews. Most of these are available on **YouTube.com** and **Facebook** *(keyword: "Danforth Prince")*; on **Twitter** *(#BloodyandLunar)*; or by clicking on **BloodMoonProductions.com**.

He is currently at work researching and writing an upcoming biography on the last remaining male icon of Hollywood's Golden Age, **Kirk Douglas**.

Do you want to meet him up close, personal, and at home? Prince is also an innkeeper, running a historic bed & breakfast in New York City, **Magnolia House** (**www.MagnoliaHouseSaintGeorge.com**). Affiliated with AirBnb, and increasingly sought out by filmmakers as an evocative locale for moviemaking, it lies in the fast-gentrified neighborhood of Saint George, at the northern tip of Staten Island, a district that's historically associated with Henry James, Theodore Dreiser, the Vanderbilts, and key moments in America's colonial history.

Set in a large, elaborately terraced garden, and boasting a history of visits from literary and show-biz stars who have included Tennessee Williams, Gloria Swanson, Jolie Gabor, Ruth Warwick, Greta Keller, Lucille Lortel, and many of the luminaries of Broadway, the inn is within a ten-minute walk to the ferries sailing at 20- to 30-minute intervals to Lower Manhattan.

Publicized as "a reasonably priced celebrity-centric retreat with links to the book trades," and the beneficiary of rave ("superhost") reviews from hundreds of previous clients, **Magnolia House** is loaded with furniture and memorabilia that Prince collected during his decades as a travel journalist for the Frommer Guides.

*Stay with Us! Learn more about "Celebrity-Centric Sleepovers" at Blood Moon's **Magnolia House**, a historic and moderately priced "Airbnb" in New York City.*

For more information about the hospitality that's waiting for you in NYC at the Bed and Breakfast affiliate of Blood Moon Productions, click on

**MagnoliaHouseSaintGeorge.com**

# CARRIE FISHER & DEBBIE REYNOLDS
## PRINCESS LEIA & UNSINKABLE TAMMY IN HELL

It's history's first comprehensive, unauthorized overview of the greatest mother-daughter act in showbiz history, **Debbie Reynolds** ("hard as nails and with more balls than any five guys I've ever known") and her talented, often traumatized daughter, **Carrie Fisher** ("one of the smartest, hippest chicks in Hollywood"). Evolving for decades under the unrelenting glare of public scrutiny, each became a world-class symbol of the social and cinematic tastes that prevailed during their heydays as celebrity icons in Hollywood.

It's a scandalous saga of the ferociously loyal relationship of the *"boop-boop-a-doop"* girl with her inter-galactic STAR WARS daughter, and their iron-willed, "true grit" battles to out-race changing tastes in Hollywood.

Loaded with revelations about "who was doing what to whom" during the final gasps of Golden Age Hollywood, it's an All-American story about the price of glamour, career-related pain, family anguish, romantic betrayals, lingering guilt, and the volcanic shifts that affected a scrappy, mother-daughter team—and everyone else who ever loved the movies.

*"Feeling misunderstood by the younger (female) members of your gene pool? This is the Hollywood exposé every grandmother should give to her granddaughter, a roadmap like Debbie Reynolds might have offered to Billie Lourd."* —**Marnie O'Toole**

*"Hold onto your hats, the "bad boys" of Blood Moon Productions are back. This time, they have an exhaustively-researched and highly readable account of the greatest mother-daughter act in the history of show business:* **Debbie Reynolds and Carrie (Princess Leia) Fisher.** *If celebrity gossip and inside dirt is your secret desire, check it out. This is a fabulous book that we heartily recommend. It will not disappoint. We rate it worthy of four stars."*
—**MAJ Glenn MacDonald**, **U.S. Army Reserve (Retired)**, © **MilitaryCorruption.com**

*"How is a 1950s-era movie star, (TAMMY) supposed to cope with her postmodern, substance-abusing daughter (PRINCESS LEIA), the rebellious, high-octane byproduct of Rock 'n Roll, Free Love, and postwar Hollywood's most scandal-soaked marriage? Read about it here, in Blood Moon's unauthorized double exposé about how Hollywood's toughest (and savviest) mother-daughter team maneuvered their way through shifting definitions of fame, reconciliation, and fortune."*

—**Donna McSorley**

*Another compelling title from Blood Moon's Babylon Series*
*Winner of the coveted "Best Biography" Award from the 2018 New York Book Festival*

### CARRIE FISHER & DEBBIE REYNOLDS,
### UNSINKABLE TAMMY & PRINCESS LEIA IN HELL
#### Darwin Porter & Danforth Prince

*630 pages Softcover with photos. Now online and in bookstores everywhere*
*ISBN 978-1-936003-57-0*

# DONALD TRUMP
## IS *THE MAN WHO WOULD BE KING*

This is the most famous book about our incendiary President you've probably never heard of.

Winner of three respected literary awards, and released three months before the Presidentail elections of 2016, it's an entertainingly packaged, artfully salacious bombshell, a scathingly historic overview of America during its 2016 election cycle, a portrait unlike anything ever published on CANDIDATE DONALD and the climate in which he thrived and massacred his political rivals.

Its volcanic, much-suppressed release during the heat and venom of the Presidential campaign has already been heralded by the *Midwestern Book Review, California Book Watch, the Seattle Gay News*, the staunchly right-wing **WILS-AM radio**, and also by the editors at the most popular Seniors' magazine in Florida, *BOOMER TIMES*, which designated it as their September choice for **BOOK OF THE MONTH.**

**TRUMPOCALYPSE**: *"Donald Trump: The Man Who Would Be King* is recommended reading for all sides, no matter what political stance is being adopted: Republican, Democrat, or other.

"One of its driving forces is its ability to synthesize an unbelievable amount of information into a format and presentation which blends lively irony with outrageous observations, entertaining even as it presents eye-opening information in a format accessible to all.

"Politics dovetail with American obsessions and fascinations with trends, figureheads, drama, and sizzling news stories, but blend well with the observations of sociologists, psychologists, politicians, and others in a wide range of fields who lend their expertise and insights to create a much broader review of the Trump phenomena than a more casual book could provide.

"The result is a 'must read' for any American interested in issues of race, freedom, equality, and justice—and for any non-American who wonders just what is going on behind the scenes in this country's latest election debacle."

**Diane Donovan,** Senior Editor,
California Bookwatch

*DONALD TRUMP, THE MAN WHO WOULD BE KING*
*WINNER OF "BEST BIOGRAPHY" AWARDS FROM BOOK FESTIVALS IN*
*NEW YORK, CALIFORNIA, AND FLORIDA*
by Darwin Porter and Danforth Prince
Softcover, with 822 pages and hundreds of photos. ISBN *978-1-936003-51-8.*

Available now from Amazon.com, Barnes&Noble.com,
and other internet purveyors, worldwide.

# ROCK HUDSON EROTIC FIRE

Another tragic, myth-shattering, & uncensored tale about America's obsession with celebrities, from Blood Moon Productions.

In the dying days of Hollywood's Golden Age, Rock Hudson was the most celebrated phallic symbol and lust object in America. This book describes his rise and fall, and the Entertainment Industry that created him.

Rock Hudson charmed every casting director in Hollywood (and movie-goers throughout America) as the mega-star they most wanted to share PILLOW TALK with. This book describes his rise and fall, and how he handled himself as a closeted but promiscuous bisexual during an age when EVERYBODY tried to throw him onto a casting couch.

Based on dozens of face-to-face interviews with the actor's friends, co-conspirators, and enemies, and researched over a period of a half century, this biography reveals the shame, agonies, and irony of Rock Hudson's complete, never-before-told story.

In 2017, the year of its release, it was designated as winner ("BEST BIOGRAPHY") at two of the Golden State's most prestigious literary competitions, the Northern California and the Southern California Book Festivals.

**Rock Hudson Erotic Fire**

Darwin Porter & Danforth Prince
Another Outrageous Title in Blood Moon's Babylon Series

It was also favorably reviewed by the *Midwestern Book Review, California Book Watch, KNEWS RADIO, the New York Journal of Books,* and the editors at the most popular Seniors' magazine in Florida, *BOOMER TIMES.*

---

### *ROCK HUDSON EROTIC FIRE*

By Darwin Porter & Danforth Prince
Softcover, 624 pages, with dozens of photos, 6" x 9"
ISBN 978-1-936003-55-6

**Available everywhere now, online and in bookstores.**

# PAUL NEWMAN

## THE MAN BEHIND THE BABY BLUES
## HIS SECRET LIFE EXPOSED

Drawn from firsthand interviews with insiders who knew Paul Newman intimately, and compiled over a period of nearly a half-century, this is the world's most honest and most revelatory biography about Hollywood's pre-eminent male sex symbol.

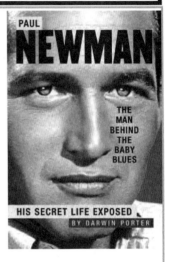

This is a respectful but candid cornucopia of once-concealed information about the sexual and emotional adventures of an affable, impossibly good-looking workaday actor, a former sailor from Shaker Heights, Ohio, who parlayed his ambisexual charm and extraordinary good looks into one of the most successful careers in Hollywood.

Whereas the situations it exposes were widely known within Hollywood's inner circles, they've never before been revealed to the general public.

But now, the full story has been published—the giddy heights and agonizing crashes of a great American star, with revelations and insights never before published in any other biography.

*"Paul Newman had just as many on-location affairs as the rest of us, and he was just as bisexual as I was. But whereas I was always getting caught with my pants down, he managed to do it in the dark with not a paparazzo in sight. He might have bedded Marilyn Monroe or Elizabeth Taylor the night before, but he always managed to show up for breakfast with Joanne Woodward, with those baby blues, looking as innocent as a Botticelli angel. He never fooled me. It takes an alleycat to know another one. Did I ever tell you what really happened between Newman and me? If that doesn't grab you, what about what went on between James Dean and Newman? Let me tell you about this co-called model husband if you want to look behind those famous peepers."*

—**Marlon Brando**

---

*Paul Newman, The Man Behind the Baby Blues,*
*His Secret Life Exposed,* **by Darwin Porter**
Recipient of an Honorable Mention from the New England Book Festival
Hardcover, 520 pages, with dozens of photos.
ISBN 978-0-9786465-1-6        **Available everywhere, online and in bookstores.**

# LANA TURNER

## THE SWEATER GIRL, CELLULOID VENUS, SEX NYMPH TO THE G.I.S WHO WON WORLD WAR II, AND HOLLYWOOD'S OTHER MOST NOTORIOUS BLONDE

### BEAUTIFUL AND BAD, HER FULL STORY HAS NEVER BEEN TOLD.
### UNTIL NOW!

**Lana Turner** was the most scandalous, most copied, and most gossiped-about actress in Hollywood. When her abusive Mafia lover was murdered in her house, every newspaper in the Free World described the murky dramas with something approaching hysteria.

Blood Moon's salacious but empathetic new biography exposes the public and private dramas of the girl who changed the American definition of what it REALLY means to be a blonde.

Here's how **CALIFORNIA BOOKWATCH** and **THE MIDWEST BOOK REVIEW** described the mega-celebrity as revealed in this book:

*"Lana Turner: Hearts and Diamonds Take All* belongs on the shelves of any collection strong in movie star biographies in general and Hollywood evolution in particular, and represents no lightweight production, appearing on the 20th anniversary of Lana Turner's death to provide a weighty survey packed with new information about her life.

"One would think that just about everything to be known about The Sweater Girl would have already appeared in print, but it should be noted that Lana Turner: Hearts and Diamonds Take All offers many new revelations not just about Turner, but about the movie industry in the aftermath of World War II.

"From Lana's introduction of a new brand of covert sexuality in women's movies to her scandalous romances among the stars, her extreme promiscuity, her search for love, and her notorious flings - even her involvement in murder - are all probed in a revealing account of glamour and movie industry relationships that bring Turner and her times to life.

"Some of the greatest scandals in Hollywood history are intricately detailed on these pages, making this much more than another survey of her life and times, and a 'must have' pick for any collection strong in Hollywood history in general, gossip and scandals and the real stories behind them, and Lana Turner's tumultuous career, in particular."

## *Lana Turner, Hearts & Diamonds Take All*
*Winner of the coveted "Best Biography" Award from the San Francisco Book Festival*
By Darwin Porter and Danforth Prince
Softcover, 622 pages, with photos. ISBN 978-1-936003-53-2
Available everywhere, online and in stores.

# LINDA LOVELACE

## INSIDE LINDA LOVELACE'S DEEP THROAT
### Degradation, Porno Chic, and the Rise of Feminism

The most comprehensive biography ever written of an adult entertainment star, her tormented relationship with Hollywood's underbelly, and how she changed forever the world's perceptions about censorship, sexual behavior patterns, and pornography.

**Darwin Porter**, author of some twenty critically acclaimed celebrity exposés of behind-the-scenes intrigue in the entertainment industry, was deeply involved in the Linda Lovelace saga as it unfolded in the 70s, interviewing many of the players, and raising money for the legal defense of the film's co-star, Harry Reems.

In this book, emphasizing her role as an unlikely celebrity interacting with other celebrities, he brings inside information and a never-before-published revelation to almost every page.

*"This book drew me in..How could it not?"*
Coco Papy, *Bookslut*.

The Beach Book Festivals Grand Prize Winner for "Best Summer Reading of 2013"

Runner-Up to "Best Biography of 2013" *The Los Angeles Book Festival*

Another hot and insightful commentary about major and sometimes violently controversial conflicts of the American Century, from Blood Moon Productions.

*Inside Linda Lovelace's Deep Throat,* by Darwin Porter
Softcover, 640 pages, 6"x9" with photos.
ISBN 978-1-936003-33-4

# LOVE TRIANGLE:
# RONALD REAGAN
## JANE WYMAN, & NANCY DAVIS

**HOW MUCH DO YOU REALLY KNOW ABOUT THE REAGANS? THIS BOOKS TELLS EVERYTHING ABOUT THE SHOW-BIZ SCANDALS THEY DESPERATELY WANTED TO FORGET.**

Unique in the history of publishing, this scandalous triple biography focuses on the Hollywood indiscretions of former U.S. president Ronald Reagan and his two wives. A proud and Presidential addition to Blood Moon's Babylon series, it digs deep into what these three young and attractive movie stars were doing decades before two of them took over the Free World.

As reviewed by Diane Donovan, Senior Reviewer at the California Bookwatch section of the Midwest Book Review: *"Love Triangle: Ronald Reagan, Jane Wyman & Nancy Davis may find its way onto many a Republican Reagan fan's reading shelf; but those who expect another Reagan celebration will be surprised: this is lurid Hollywood exposé writing at its best, and outlines the truths surrounding one of the most provocative industry scandals in the world.*

*"There are already so many biographies of the Reagans on the market that one might expect similar mile-markers from this: be prepared for shock and awe; because Love Triangle doesn't take your ordinary approach to biography* and describes a love triangle that eventually bumped a major Hollywood movie star from the possibility of being First Lady and replaced her with a lesser-known Grade B actress (Nancy Davis).

*"From politics and betrayal to romance, infidelity, and sordid affairs, Love Triangle is a steamy, eye-opening story that blows the lid off of the Reagan illusion to raise eyebrows on both sides of the big screen.*

*"Black and white photos liberally pepper an account of the careers of all three and the lasting shock of their stormy relationships in a delightful pursuit especially recommended for any who relish Hollywood gossip."*

In 2015, LOVE TRIANGLE, Blood Moon Productions' overview of the early dramas associated with Ronald Reagan's scandal-soaked career in Hollywood, was designated by the Awards Committee of the **HOLLYWOOD BOOK FESTIVAL** as Runner-Up to Best Biography of the Year.

---

**LOVE TRIANGLE: Ronald Reagan, Jane Wyman, & Nancy Davis**
Darwin Porter & Danforth Prince
Softcover, 6" x 9", with hundreds of photos.   ISBN 978-1-936003-41-9

# PINK TRIANGLE

The Feuds and Private Lives of

## TENNESSEE WILLIAMS, GORE VIDAL, TRUMAN CAPOTE,

& Famous Members of their Entourages

### Darwin Porter & Danforth Prince

This book, the only one of its kind, reveals the backlot intrigues associated with the literary and script-writing *enfants terribles* of America's entertainment community during the mid-20th century.

It exposes their bitchfests, their slugfests, and their relationships with the *glitterati*—Marilyn Monroe, Brando, the Oliviers, the Paleys, U.S. Presidents, a gaggle of other movie stars, millionaires, and international *débauchés*.

This is for anyone who's interested in the formerly concealed scandals of Hollywood and Broadway, and the values and pretentions of both the literary community and the entertainment industry.

*"A banquet... If PINK TRIANGLE had not been written for us, we would have had to research and type it all up for ourselves…Pink Triangle is nearly seven hundred pages of the most entertaining histrionics ever sliced, spiced, heated, and serviced up to the reading public. Everything that Blood Moon has done before pales in comparison.*
*Given the fact that the subjects of the book themselves were nearly delusional on the subject of themselves (to say nothing of each other) it is hard to find fault. Add to this the intertwined jungle that was the relationship among Williams, Capote, and Vidal, of the times they vied for things they loved most—especially attention—and the times they enthralled each other and the world, [Pink Triangle is] the perfect antidote to the Polar Vortex."*
**—Vinton McCabe in the NY JOURNAL OF BOOKS**

*"Full disclosure: I have been a friend and follower of Blood Moon Productions' tomes for years, and always marveled at the amount of information in their books—it's staggering. The index alone to Pink Triangle runs to 21 pages—and the scale of names in it runs like a Who's Who of American social, cultural and political life through much of the 20th century."*
**—Perry Brass in THE HUFFINGTON POST**

*"We Brits are not spared the Porter/Prince silken lash either. PINK TRIANGLE's research is, quite frankly, breathtaking. PINK TRIANGLE will fascinate you for many weeks to come. Once you have made the initial titillating dip, the day will seem dull without it."*
**—Jeffery Tayor in THE SUNDAY EXPRESS (UK)**

*PINK TRIANGLE—The Feuds and Private Lives of Tennessee Williams, Gore Vidal, Truman Capote, and Famous Members of their Entourages*
Darwin Porter & Danforth Prince
Softcover, 700 pages, with photos   ISBN 978-1-936003-37-2   Also Available for E-Readers

# THOSE GLAMOROUS GABORS

## BOMBSHELLS FROM BUDAPEST

Zsa Zsa, Eva, and Magda Gabor transferred their glittery dreams and gold-digging ambitions from the twilight of the Austro-Hungarian Empire to Hollywood. There, more effectively than any army, these Bombshells from Budapest broke hearts, amassed fortunes, lovers, and A-list husbands, and amused millions of *voyeurs* through the medium of television, movies, and the social registers. In this astonishing "triple-play" biography, designated "Best Biography of the Year" by the Hollywood Book Festival, Blood Moon lifts the "mink-and-diamond" curtain on this amazing trio of blood-related sisters, whose complicated intrigues have never been fully explored before.

"**You will never be Ga-bored…this book gives new meaning to the term compelling.** Be warned, *Those Glamorous Gabors* is both an epic and a pip. Not since *Gone With the Wind* have so many characters on the printed page been forced to run for their lives for one reason or another. And Scarlett making a dress out of the curtains is nothing compared to what a Gabor will do when she needs to scrap together an outfit for a movie premiere or late-night outing.

"For those not up to speed, Jolie Tilleman came from a family of jewelers and therefore came by her love for the shiny stones honestly, perhaps genetically. She married Vilmos Gabor somewhere around World War 1 (exact dates, especially birth dates, are always somewhat vague in order to establish plausible deniability later on) and they were soon blessed with three daughters: **Magda**, the oldest, whose hair, sadly, was naturally brown, although it would turn quite red in America; **Zsa Zsa** (born 'Sari') a natural blond who at a very young age exhibited the desire for fame with none of the talents usually associated with achievement, excepting beauty and a natural wit; and **Eva**, the youngest and blondest of the girls, who after seeing Grace Moore perform at the National Theater, decided that she wanted to be an actress and that she would one day move to Hollywood to become a star.

"Given that the Gabor family at that time lived in Budapest, Hungary, at the period of time between the World Wars, that Hollywood dream seemed a distant one indeed. The story—the riches to rags to riches to rags to riches again myth of survival against all odds as the four women, because of their Jewish heritage, flee Europe with only the minks on their backs and what jewels they could smuggle along with them in their *decolletage*, only to have to battle afresh for their places in the vicious Hollywood pecking order—gives new meaning to the term 'compelling.' The reader, as if he were witnessing a particularly gore-drenched traffic accident, is incapable of looking away."

## —New York Review of Books

*Those Glamorous Gabors, Bombshells from Budapest*, by Darwin Porter.
Softcover, 730 pages, with hundreds of photos    ISBN 978-1-936003-35-8

# PETER O'TOOLE

## HELLRAISER, SEXUAL OUTLAW, IRISH REBEL

At the time of its publication early in 2015, this book was widely publicized in the *Daily Mail,* the *New York Daily News,* the *New York Post,* the *Midwest Book Review, The Express (London), The Globe,* the *National Enquirer,* and in equivalent publications worldwide

One of the world's most admired (and brilliant) actors, Peter O'Toole wined and wenched his way through a labyrinth of sexual and interpersonal betrayals, sometimes with disastrous results. Away from the stage and screen, where such films as *Becket* and *Lawrence of Arabia,* made film history, his life was filled with drunken, debauched nights and edgy sexual experimentations, most of which were never openly examined in the press. A hellraiser, he shared wild times with his "best blokes" Richard Burton and Richard Harris. Peter Finch, also his close friend, once invited him to join him in sharing the pleasures of his mistress, Vivien Leigh.

"My father, a bookie, moved us to the Mick community of Leeds," O'Toole once told a reporter. "We were very poor, but I was born an Irishman, which accounts for my gift of gab, my unruly behavior, my passionate devotion to women and the bottle, and my loathing of any authority figure."

Author Robert Sellers described O'Toole's boyhood neighborhood. "Three of his playmates went on to be hanged for murder; one strangled a girl in a lovers' quarrel; one killed a man during a robbery; another cut up a warden in South Africa with a pair of shears. It was a heavy bunch."

Peter O'Toole's hell-raising life story has never been told, until now. Hot and uncensored, from a writing team which, even prior to O'Toole's death in 2013, had been collecting under-the-radar info about him for years, this book has everything you ever wanted to know about how THE LION navigated his way through the boudoirs of the Entertainment Industry IN WINTER, Spring, Summer, and a dissipated Autumn as well.

Blood Moon has ripped away the imperial robe, scepter, and crown usually associated with this quixotic problem child of the British Midlands. Provocatively uncensored, this illusion-shattering overview of Peter O'Toole's hellraising (or at least very naughty) and demented life is unique in the history of publishing.

*PETER O'TOOLE: HELLRAISER, SEXUAL OUTLAW, IRISH REBEL*
**DARWIN PORTER & DANFORTH PRINCE**
**Softcover, with photos. ISBN 978-1-936003-45-7**

# JAMES DEAN

### *Tomorrow Never Comes*

#### *Honoring the 60th Anniversary of his violent and early death*

America's most enduring and legendary symbol of young, enraged rebellion, James Dean continues into the 21st Century to capture the imagination of the world.

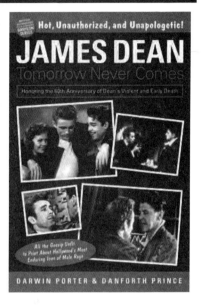

After one of his many flirtations with Death, which caught up with him when he was a celebrity-soaked 24-year-old, he said, "If a man can live after he dies, then maybe he's a great man." Today, bars from Nigeria to Patagonia are named in honor of this international, spectacularly self-destructive movie star icon.

Migrating from the dusty backroads of Indiana to center stage in the most formidable boudoirs of Hollywood, his saga is electrifying.

A strikingly handsome heart-throb, Dean is a study in contrasts: Tough but tender, brutal but remarkably sensitive; he was a reckless hellraiser badass who could revert to a little boy in bed.

A rampant bisexual, he claimed that he didn't want to go through life "with one hand tied behind my back." He demonstrated that during bedroom trysts with Marilyn Monroe, Rock Hudson, Elizabeth Taylor, Paul Newman, Natalie Wood, Shelley Winters, Marlon Brando, Steve McQueen, Ursula Andress, Montgomery Clift, Pier Angeli, Tennessee Williams, Susan Strasberg, Tallulah Bankhead, and FBI director J. Edgar Hoover.

Woolworth heiress Barbara Hutton, one of the richest and most dissipated women of her era, wanted to make him her toy boy.

*Tomorrow Never Comes* is the most penetrating look at James Dean to have   emerged from the wreckage of his Porsche Spyder in 1955.

Before setting out on his last ride, he said, "I feel life too intensely to bear living it."

*Tomorrow Never Comes* presents a damaged but beautiful soul.

## JAMES DEAN—TOMORROW NEVER COMES
### Darwin Porter & Danforth Prince
#### Softcover, with photos. ISBN 978-1-936003-49-5

# JACKO, HIS RISE AND FALL

## The Social and Sexual History of Michael Jackson

Darwin Porter

He rewrote the rules of America's entertainment industry, and he led a life of notoriety. Even his death was the occasion for scandals which continue to this day.

This is the world's most comprehensive historical overview of a pop star's rise, fall, and to some extent, rebirth as an American Icon. Read it for the real story of the circumstances and players who created the icon which the world will forever remember as "the gloved one," Michael Jackson.

"This is the story of Peter Pan gone rotten. Don't stop till you get enough. Darwin Porter's biography of Michael Jackson is dangerously addictive."
— *The Sunday Observer*   (London)

"In this compelling glimpse of Jackson's life, Porter provides what many journalists have failed to produce in their writings about the pop star: A real person behind the headlines."
— *Foreword Magazine*

"I'd have thought that there wasn't one single gossippy rock yet to be overturned in the microscopically scrutinized life of Michael Jackson, but Darwin Porter has proven me wrong. Definitely a page-turner. But don't turn the pages too quickly. Almost every one holds a fascinating revelation."
— *Books to Watch Out For*

This book, a winner of literary awards from both *Foreword Magazine* and the Hollywood Book Festival, was originally published during the lifetime of Michael Jackson. This, the revised, post-mortem edition, with extra analysis and commentary, was released after his death.

Hardcover  600 indexed pages with about a hundred photos

ISBN 978-0-936003-10-5

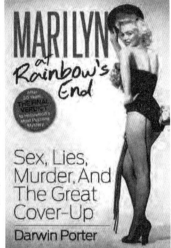

# SCARLETT O'HARA,

## Desperately in Love with Heathcliff,

## Together on the Road to Hell

**Damn You,**
Scarlett O'Hara
The Private Lives of **Vivien Leigh**
and **Laurence Olivier**

by **Darwin Porter** and **Roy Moseley**

Here, for the first time, is a biography that raises the curtain on the secret lives of **Lord Laurence Olivier**, often cited as the finest actor in the history of England, and **Vivien Leigh,** who immortalized herself with her Oscar-winning portrayals of Scarlett O'Hara in *Gone With the Wind,* and as Blanche DuBois in Tennessee Williams' *A Streetcar Named Desire.*

Dashing and "impossibly handsome," Laurence Olivier was pursued by the most dazzling luminaries, male and female, of the movie and theater worlds.

Lord Olivier's beautiful and brilliant but emotionally disturbed wife (Viv to her lovers) led a tumultuous off-the-record life whose paramours ranged from the A-list celebrities to men she selected randomly off the street. But none of the brilliant roles depicted by Lord and Lady Olivier, on stage or on screen, ever matched the power and drama of personal dramas which wavered between Wagnerian opera and Greek tragedy. *Damn You, Scarlett O'Hara* is the definitive and most revelatory portrait ever published of the most talented and tormented actor and actress of the 20th century.

**Darwin Porter** is the principal author of this seminal work.

*"The folks over at TMZ would have had a field day tracking Laurence Olivier and Vivien Leigh with flip cameras in hand.* **Damn You, Scarlett O'Hara** *can be a dazzling read, the prose unmannered and instantly digestible. The authors' ability to pile scandal atop scandal, seduction after seduction, can be impossible to resist."*

—THE WASHINGTON TIMES

# DAMN YOU, SCARLETT O'HARA
## THE PRIVATE LIFES OF LAURENCE OLIVIER AND VIVIEN LEIGH

Darwin Porter and Roy Moseley

Winner of four distinguished literary awards, this is the best biography of Vivien Leigh and Laurence Olivier ever published, with hundreds of insights into the London Theatre, the role of the Oliviers in the politics of World War II, and the passion, fury, and frustration of their lives together as actors in the West End, on Broadway, and in Hollywood.

ISBN 978-1-936003-15-0    Hardcover, 708 pages, with about a hundred photos.

# HUMPHREY BOGART

## THE MAKING OF A LEGEND

### DARWIN PORTER

A "CRADLE-TO-GRAVE" HARDCOVER ABOUT THE RISE TO FAME OF AN
OBSCURE, UNLIKELY, AND FREQUENTLY UNEMPLOYED BROADWAY ACTOR.

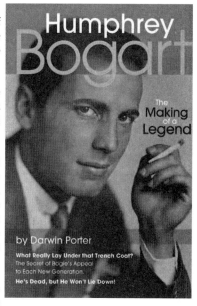

Whereas **Humphrey Bogart** is always at the top of any list of the Entertainment Industry's most famous actors, very little is known about how he clawed his way from Broadway to Hollywood during Prohibition and the Jazz Age.

This pioneering biography begins with Bogart's origins as the child of wealthy (morphine-addicted) parents in New York City, then examines the love affairs, scandals, failures, and breakthroughs that launched him as an American icon.

It includes details about behind-the-scenes dramas associated with three mysterious marriages, and films such as *The Petrified Forest, The Maltese Falcon, High Sierra,* and *Casablanca.* Read all about the debut and formative years of the actor who influenced many generations of filmgoers, laying Bogie's life bare in a style you've come to expect from Darwin Porter. Exposed with all their juicy details is what Bogie never told his fourth wife, Lauren Bacall, herself a screen legend.

Drawn from original interviews with friends and foes who knew a lot about what lay beneath his trenchcoat, this exposé covers Bogart's remarkable life as it helped define movie-making, Hollywood's portrayal of macho, and America's evolving concept of Entertainment itself.

This revelatory book is based on dusty unpublished memoirs, letters, diaries, and often personal interviews from the women—and the men—who adored him.

There are also shocking allegations from colleagues, former friends, and jilted lovers who wanted the screen icon to burn in hell.

All this and more, much more, in Darwin Porter's *exposé* of Bogie's startling secret life.

## WITH STARTLING NEW INFORMATION ABOUT BOGART, THE MOVIES, &
## GOLDEN AGE HOLLYWOOD

542 PAGES, WITH HUNDREDS OF PHOTOS   **ISBN**   978-1-936003-14-3